The Essentials of Academic Writing

The Essentials of Academic Writing

Derek Soles

University of British Columbia

NELSON EDUCATION

NELSON / EDUCATION

The Essentials of Academic Writing, **Canadian Edition**
by Derek Soles

Vice President, Editorial Higher Education:
Anne Williams

Executive Editor:
Laura Macleod

Marketing Manager:
Ann Byford

Developmental Editor:
Roberta Osbourne

Permissions Coordinator:
Sandra Mark

Content Production Manager:
Claire Horsnell

Production Service:
Cenveo Publisher Services

Copy Editor:
Patricia Jones

Proofreader:
Manikandan

Indexer:
BIM Indexing Services

Senior Production Coordinator:
Ferial Suleman

Design Director:
Ken Phipps

Managing Designer:
Franca Amore

Interior Design:
Cathy Mayer

Cover Design:
Carianne Sherriff

Cover Image:
wavebreakmedia/Shutterstock

Compositor:
Cenveo Publisher Services

Printer:
R. R. Donnelley

Library and Archives Canada Cataloguing in Publication

Soles, Derek A. J., 1949–

The essentials of academic writing / Derek Soles.— Canadian ed.

Includes bibliographical references and index.
ISBN 978-0-17-652345-9

1. Academic writing—Handbooks, manuals, etc. 2. English language—Rhetoric. I. Title.

LB2369.S65 2013
808.02   C2012-907358-X

ISBN-13: 978-0-17-652345-9
ISBN-10: 0-17-652345-6

Contents

3 Research Your Topic   36

4 Make a Plan   54

5 Write a Draft   71

6 Revise Your Essay   91

PART TWO Model Academic Essays with Instructional Notes and Commentary 192

PART THREE An Anthology of Academic Writing 337

Alternative Rhetorical Contents

Model Essays Written by Students

Model Essays Classified by Rhetorical Mode

Expository: Examples and Details

Expository: Analysis and Interpretation

Argument

Model Essays Classified by Discipline

Language and Literature

Education

Sociology

Science

Health Sciences

Preface

The purpose of the first Canadian edition of *The Essentials of Academic Writing* is to help college and university students do well in all of their courses that require writing assignments. To accomplish this, the book guides students through the process of completing academic writing assignments successfully and provides many models of good academic writing.

Part One explains the components of the process of successful academic writing, focusing especially on the expository, persuasive, and mixed-genre essays. The steps in the process are presented sequentially—generate ideas, research, compose a thesis, plan, draft, revise, edit, cite sources—but readers are constantly reminded that writing is a recursive, more than a linear, process. To illustrate the process, we track one student writer, Zhen, as she works her way through the stages in composing an essay about the criteria students use or should use when they purchase a backpack. There are two other model student essays in Chapter 8.

Part Two presents five examples of good academic writing, annotated with instructional notes and commentary. The aim of this section of the book is to give students practical insight into the rhetorical strategies experienced writers invoke as they structure, draft, and revise their work to make certain it exemplifies the intelligence, substance, clarity, and energy of good academic work. With the insight into the compositing process this part provides, students will be better able to work through their own writing assignments efficiently and successfully.

Part Three presents eight more models of good academic writing, followed by questions for study and discussion, designed to help students apply what they have learned in Part One and observed in Part Two. The readings are contemporary examples of sound academic writing, drawn from a variety of academic disciplines and documented using different but acceptable formats.

The Essentials of Academic Writing also provides instruction in active reading and critical thinking because successful academic writing depends upon the ability to understand research sources and to assess their validity and reliability.

True to its title, *The Essentials of Academic Writing* is a concise yet thorough guidebook, based upon the simple principle that good writers get good grades.

Acknowledgements

As I was writing and revising this first Canadian edition of *The Essentials of Academic Writing*, I had indispensible help and support from Nelson editors, a group of most astute fellow first-year writing teachers, and my daughter Kate.

From Nelson, I worked closely with Senior Developmental Editor Roberta Osborne, Content Production Manager Claire Horsnell, and Copy Editor Patricia Jones. They are the supportive and insightful collaborators any writer needs, wants, and trusts.

I am grateful to my colleagues who read various versions of the manuscript and offered such practical and intelligent advice.

Dave Buchanan, Grant MacEwan University

Sally Carpentier, Victoria Island University

Scott Duchesne, University of Guelph

Christine Kirchner, Camosun College

Maureen Nicholson, Douglas College

Norma-Jean Nielsen, Canadore College

Harb Sanghara, University of Victoria

Kate Wellburn, Camosun College

Finally, I am grateful to my daughter Kate Soles, M.A., who is responsible for much of the content of Chapter 8 and whose work ethic and incredible eye for detail must come from her mother.

Introduction: The Writing Process

To complete an academic writing assignment successfully, you need to think about your topic, do some research, formulate a plan, compose a thesis, write a draft, and revise and edit your draft. You think about your topic by considering the needs and expectations of your readers, determining your purpose, and freewriting. You research by reading and making notes on books, periodicals, and web sources most relevant to your topic. You construct a preliminary thesis or controlling idea by synthesizing your knowledge and ideas. You plan by jotting down main points in support of your thesis and subordinate points in support of main points. You draft by shaping your plan into complete introductory, body, and concluding paragraphs. You revise by reconsidering the efficacy of the structure, content, and cohesion of your essay or report. And you edit by reviewing, reconsidering, and correcting errors in your grammar, sentence structure, diction, and punctuation.

Writing Is a Recursive Process

In theory, the writing process seems neat, linear, and logical; in practice, it is not. Research into the writing process suggests that good writers do work through each stage in the writing process but in a somewhat random order. They might begin a draft immediately as a form of brainstorming and determine a plan and a direction their research might take based upon what they have written. They might edit while they draft, correcting separate paragraphs, instead of waiting until they have finished a complete rough draft. It is not uncommon for writers to refine, even alter, their thesis, after they have made substantial progress, as they integrate research into a second or third draft and realize the research is taking them in a direction they did not anticipate when they began the assignment. Writing is more a recursive than a linear process.

Zhen, for example, the author of our case study essay, received the prompt for her research paper assignment, asking for an essay about the criteria students use when they purchase a product they have to have, and she immediately began to annotate the assignment sheet, jotting down a rough plan for an essay about buying a good backpack. She drafted a rough plan and a few rough paragraphs before she did any research. She had to change her plan and even her thesis after she learned from her research sources that one of the most important criteria for selecting a backpack was one she had barely considered: preventing back, shoulder, and neck pain or even injury.

Zhen's experience is common. Completing an academic writing assignment is a recursive process, more like running a maze than a marathon.

The Components of the Writing Process

Although writing is recursive, it still makes sense to isolate the skills and practise them sequentially. In hockey practice, players don't just scrimmage—they work on exercises designed to refine their skating, passing, shooting, and team-building skills. *The Essentials of Academic Writing* presents the components of the writing process sequentially; recommends students practise them, not just before but *while* they are working on essays and reports; and reminds students that they will use this knowledge recursively, as they complete their writing assignments.

- **Think about your topic.** As a successful writer, you will take time to reflect upon, to mull over, to consider the subject of your essay. Such reflection is ongoing. It occurs both before and throughout the processes of drafting and revising. It is an essential component of the writing process, fostering as it does an understanding of your purpose in writing and of the needs and expectations of your readers, while helping you formulate a central focus, a controlling idea, a thesis. Several effective methods for thinking systematically about a topic are covered in Chapter 2.

- **Research your topic.** Whenever you are assigned to write an academic essay, you must research your topic. You might have to use print books, available at your college/university library. Most of the journal articles and other sources you might need will be available online. Your research will provide information that can be integrated into an essay to render it well developed and authoritative. You must know how to access information, how to evaluate sources, and how to summarize information contained within these sources. Research strategies are discussed in Chapter 3.

- **Plan your essay.** Planning is an essential component in the process of writing expository, compare/contrast, and persuasive essays. Planning is more than constructing a system of headings and subheadings to use before beginning your draft. It is a continuing process. Those series of points you arrange in a system of headings and subheadings is really only a start. The act of writing stimulates thinking, and, as a result, that preliminary outline likely will change and evolve. Planning is an essential part of the process because it helps establish a structure for the essay. Planning expository, compare/contrast, and persuasive essays is discussed in Chapter 4.

■ **Write a draft.** Planning outlines your essay's beginning, middle, and end; drafting transforms the outline into sentences and paragraphs. The essence of drafting is writing an effective introductory paragraph (or paragraphs for a longer essay), a series of well-developed body paragraphs, and an effective concluding paragraph (or paragraphs for a longer essay). Writing effective introductory, body, and concluding paragraphs is discussed in Chapter 5.

■ **Revise.** Revision is the process of making global changes to a written text, that is, a process of reconsidering, moving, reshaping, and developing whole paragraphs and/or of altering the entire structure of a written work. The revision process is ongoing. You will revise while you draft and while you read and reread a draft. Revision is covered in Chapter 6.

■ **Edit.** Editing is the process of reviewing, changing, and correcting words and sentences within a written text. The editing process includes checking for and correcting errors in grammar, sentence structure, diction, spelling, punctuation, and mechanics. It is, like most components of the writing process, ongoing. It is not something you do only after drafting and revising. You will edit while you draft and as you read and reread a draft. Editing is covered in Chapter 7.

■ **Cite sources.** Academic essays require research (covered in Chapter 3), and research sources have to be properly acknowledged. Professors take seriously the importance of acknowledging and citing any and all sources you use to authenticate and develop your ideas. Three widely used and well-established methods for citing sources thoroughly and accurately are described in Chapter 8.

Reading Academic Writing

Writing is a process best learned by doing, and so the focus of this book is on mastering the components of the writing process. But we can also learn by studying the work of accomplished academic writers, especially if that work is accompanied by notes and annotations that explain what the writer is doing and why he or she is doing it effectively. Part Two of this book is an anthology of five good academic essays with instructional notes and commentary designed to show you how the authors have used the components of the writing process to create an effective finished product. Part Three presents additional academic essays followed by questions for study and discussion designed to further enhance your ability to recognize and consider the elements of effective academic discourse.

There are three examples of exemplary student academic writing in this text. "Selecting a College Backpack" by Zhen Wei is presented as a case study in the components of the process of writing an academic essay. "Saving the Vancouver Island Marmot" by Adam Black serves as our example of an essay cited using the MLA method; "Is Chocolate Good for You?" by Tersa Lyons is a literature review cited using the APA method.

1

The Process of Writing an Academic Essay

CHAPTER 1

What Is Academic Writing?

Academic writing includes a wide variety of texts—articles, essays, reviews, term papers, reports, exams—written by educators contributing to the knowledge in their field and by students fulfilling the requirements of a college or university course.

To be successful at college and university, students need to know

- the types of academic writing assignments they may be required to undertake;
- the discourse conventions of the academic disciplines within which they are working;
- the criteria their instructors and professors will use to evaluate their writing.

The Expository Essay or Term Paper

Perhaps the most common assignment is one that calls upon students to write an essay or term paper, explaining and discussing a topic relevant to the content of a course they are taking. A student taking a modern Canadian history class is busy writing an essay explaining the causes of the conflict in Afghanistan, while her roommate is struggling with her developmental psychology paper on Piaget. Across the hall, a business student is busy at his laptop explaining the reasons for the success of the Absolut vodka marketing campaign, while his roommate, a physical education major, is doing a paper on methods of teaching basketball to Grade Seven girls. Physics majors are writing papers on quantum mechanics, forestry students are explaining the effects of global warming on the growth rates of the Douglas fir, future nurses are explaining the efficacy of a new vaccine for hepatitis, literature students are comparing and contrasting Keats' "To Autumn" with Shelly's "Ode to the West Wind."

These students are writing expository essays, those that present knowledge supported by reliable sources; developed using any combination of examples, details, causes, effects, definitions, comparisons, contrasts, and anecdotes; and written clearly and coherently in standard English.

The Persuasive Essay or Term Paper

Another common assignment calls upon students to take a stand on an issue related to the content of the course and to develop an argument in support of that position. If those students, busy writing expository essays were writing persuasive essays instead, their topics might be

- Should Canada have intervened in the civil war in Afghanistan?
- Are Piaget's theories of language acquisition more accurate than Vygotsky's?
- Was the Absolut Vodka marketing campaign ethical?
- Should Grade Seven basketball teams be co-ed?
- What are the philosophical implications of quantum theory?
- Does global warming affect the growth rate of the Douglas fir?
- Should children under age six be vaccinated against hepatitis?
- Who among the Romantics was the most politically radical poet?

The persuasive or argumentative essay is characterized by a thesis stronger and more distinct than that of the expository essay—the difference between "There are three main reasons why Canada intervened in the civil war in Afghanistan" and "Canada's intervention in the civil war in Afghanistan has damaged Canada's national identity domestically and internationally." An effective persuasive essay makes its case with reference to valid and reliable sources in a calm and rational, not shrill and unreasonable, voice. It acknowledges and refutes the opposing point of view. It might make an emotional appeal but, as a rule, constrains emotion in favour of reason.

The Mixed-Genre Essay or Term Paper

An academic writing assignment will often call for both expository and persuasive content. Indeed, any effective persuasive essay will include exposition. If you argue that Oatmeal Treat is the best cereal on the market, and if one of your points is its nutritional benefits, your nutritional analysis will be expository in the interest of advancing your argument. Similarly, if you discuss three methods of teaching children how to read, you might favour one method and signal your preference, giving a persuasive edge to an otherwise expository essay. Exposition and argument often, if not usually, co-exist in an academic essay or term paper. See the Model Essays Classified by Rhetorical Mode section of the Table of Contents to understand the extent to which the genres of academic writing can overlap.

Other Academic Writing Assignments

The expository, persuasive, and mixed-genre essays/term papers are the standard assignments upon which other genres of academic writing assignments are based. For this reason, they are the main focus of *The Essentials of Academic Writing*. There are other academic writing assignments, which are special, often discipline-specific types of expository/persuasive writing.

The **rhetorical analysis**, requiring the writer to read and respond to a text—a book chapter, for example, or a journal article—is an expository assignment insofar as it requires students to paraphrase the content of the text and a persuasive assignment insofar as it requires students to evaluate the relevance of the content of the text and the style in which it is expressed. It is a common academic writing assignment. A *Literary Analysis* is similar, calling upon students to critique a poem, story, or play, as opposed to a book chapter or article. It is the definitive assignment in a literature class.

A **lab report** is an expository account of a science or a social science experiment, an account which explains and describes the purpose of the experiment, the methods, the subjects, and the equipment the scientists used, the results, and the implications of the study.

An **in-class essay or exam** is an expository and/or persuasive text completed in a limited amount of time. It is usually shorter than a take-home assignment. Support for its points is usually based upon the knowledge of the course content. In-class or exam writing assignments do not usually require research sources.

A **review of previous research** (also known as a **literature review**) is a summary of the research that is relevant to a study the author of the "lit review" is currently undertaking. As such, it is usually a part of the introduction to a larger study, though it may be a self-contained assignment. A social scientist who is conducting a study on the effects of reality television on the social values of middle-school students will include in her study a summary of research already done on this topic. A sociology professor might ask his students to write a review of recent research on the effects of reality television on the values of middle-school students. This is usually an expository assignment, though it will have a persuasive edge if the writer comments on the quality of the studies he or she is reviewing.

A **thesis** or a **dissertation** is very long expository or persuasive research essay or report, the former usually done by students completing a master's degree, the latter done by students completing a Ph.D.

A **narrative** or an **anecdote**, in which a writer tells a story, drawn from personal experience or fictitious, is not, strictly speaking, an example of academic writing, though an expository or persuasive essay might contain an anecdote in support of a thesis or a topic sentence usually to add interest—the human touch—to it. If a writer is developing an argument in support of tougher drunk-driving laws, and if that writer has a friend or a relative who was injured or killed by a drunk driver, the writer might describe the incident and its effect on him or her as a way of intensifying the argument. Personal anecdotes are common and can be effective, especially in persuasive writing.

The Conventions of Academic Discourse

All good academic writing shares some qualities. Its content is trustworthy, supported by reliable research; it presents its topic thoroughly; and it obeys the editing conventions of Standard English. An academic essay or report must also conform to the rules and the conventions of the academic discipline—the subject—for which it is written. The social sciences, the natural sciences, the humanities, technology, and business all have their own subset of discourse conventions which are important for students to know.

Writing for the Social Sciences

The social sciences include anthropology, cultural studies, economics, education, political science, psychology, and sociology. Social scientists conduct empirical research into their particular areas of expertise. An educator, for example, might conduct a study comparing the effectiveness of two methods of improving reading comprehension among economically disadvantaged twelve-year-olds; a psychologist might design and conduct a study to investigate the effect of aging on memory loss. They would write an essay or a research report describing the results of their studies. In "Exposure to Music with Prosocial Lyrics Reduces Aggression," for example, included in the Part Three Anthology, Tobias Greitemeyer reports on several studies he conducted of the effects on listeners of soothing music with upbeat lyrics compared with the effects of more raucous music.

Social scientists generally prefer writing that is concise, to the point, and clearly organized. They usually write in the third person, even though third person does often mean using the somewhat less efficient passive voice (see page 132). Usually, a social scientist will write: "This study was conducted at the University of Toronto," not "I conducted this study at the University of Toronto." Social scientists tend to write using the jargon common in their fields of expertise, reasoning that their readers will be familiar with it. If they are writing for a general, as opposed to a specific, publication, however, or if they are writing a textbook for undergraduates, they will lighten up on their use of jargon or include a glossary of terms. Graphs, charts, and illustrations, which offer an effective visual summary of the results of their research, often appear in the work of social scientists. Their papers often include a system of headings and subheadings in the interest of clarity. They often include an abstract at the beginning of their paper (an abstract is a one-paragraph summary of the nature of the study and its findings). Social scientists usually use the APA (American Psychological Association) method of parenthetical citation to cite their sources.

As an undergraduate social science major, you will be expected to complete a variety of writing assignments. You likely will be asked to write a literature review, which is an essay that summarizes important research on a particular topic. The literature review is a component of research studies, the section in which the authors put their own study in context by reviewing related work done earlier on the subject of their investigation. It is also a separate assignment, a common one in social science courses. One of the student essays in this book, Tersa Lyons' "Is Chocolate Good for You? A Review of Some Online Sources" is an example of a literature review.

You might be asked to write a wide variety of expository essays about the relationship between the individual and society, about different cultures, about the effect of a particular variable on human behaviour, about methods of teaching and learning, about the function and dysfunctions of the human mind, about various political and economic doctrines. "The Consequences of Son Preference and Sex-Selective Abortion in China and Other Asian Countries" by Hesketh, Lu, and Xing in Part Two is an excellent example of an expository social science essay.

You might write a wide variety of persuasive essays in which you argue the advantages of one psychological theory over another, of one social or political or economic system over another, of one learning or teaching style over another. An essay recommending ways in which the unemployment insurance system could be streamlined and made more cost-effective is an example of a persuasive social science/economics essay. Why the new economic policies of the Chinese government will adversely (or positively) affect the Canadian economy; why Freud's concept of the Oedipus complex is flawed; why Asian students outperform other races on measures of mathematical ability; why Marxism has failed (or succeeded) in Cuba—these are other examples of argumentative essay topics that professors in the social sciences often assign. In "The Canadian Human Rights Tribunal on First Nations Child Welfare: Why If Canada Wins, Equality and Justice Lose," Cindy Blackstock presents a thorough and compelling argument in support of her thesis.

The case study is another common social science assignment. The case study is usually an account of how a single individual responds to a particular situation: a teaching style, a psychological survey, a conflict within a group, or some other stressful or significant sequence of events. An education professor, for example, might examine closely the schoolwork, the behaviour, and the social interactions of a single dyslexic child, both to help that child and to develop hypotheses about dyslexia in the hope that this one case study might help in the diagnosis and treatment of other dyslexic children. This text includes a case study of how one student, Zhen, works her way through an academic writing assignment.

Writing for the Sciences

The sciences include astronomy, biology, chemistry, computer science, geography, and physics. Scientists usually value a clear and concise writing style that uses sentences that are typically shorter than sentences humanists and social scientists use. They use the jargon of their fields when they know their readers will be familiar with that jargon but avoid it or provide definitions if they are writing textbooks for undergraduates or essays for general readers. They use the third-person point-of-view and passive voice, writing, for example, "the temperature of the solution was then raised by nine degrees Celsius," as opposed to "I then raised the temperature of the solution by nine degrees Celsius." They make extensive use of charts and graphs. They often use a system of headings and subheadings to improve clarity.

Scientists use a variety of methods to acknowledge secondary sources they have used in their papers or reports, but, in general, they prefer a footnote or endnote system to a parenthetical citation system. The Council of Biology Editors, the American Chemical Society, and the American Institute of Physics all have style manuals which explain the discourse conventions within their disciplines.

Scientists write fewer argumentative essays than do social scientists and humanists, dealing as they do more with fact than opinion. Obviously, there are controversial issues in the world of the sciences, but the natural scientist becomes something of a social scientist when he or she leaves the laboratory to reflect upon the ramifications of scientific experiments and advancements upon society as a whole. The student essay in Chapter 8, pages 163–165, "Saving the Vancouver Island Marmot," is an example of an essay that summarizes and synthesizes scientific research to support a thesis.

If you plan to major in one of the sciences, you will write expository essays about ecosystems; animal physiology and behaviour; the life cycles of plants and animals; the origins and development of the universe; quantum theory and relativity; atoms and molecules; electrolytes, electrolysis, and electrochemical cells; evolution; genetics. The expository essay that explains a process—photosynthesis, chemical and physical reactions, evolution—is especially prevalent in the natural sciences.

One of the most common writing assignments in the sciences is the lab or research report, which presents the results of an experiment. A scientist has a premise or an assumption—in the language of the research report, a hypothesis—he or she wants to test. The lab or research report begins, as all such reports do, with a statement of this hypothesis. The hypothesis typically is followed by a review of other reports (the literature review), which presents the results of a test of the same or similar hypotheses. The hypothesis and the literature review form the introduction to the report. The introduction typically is followed by a clear and detailed description of the methods the scientist used in conducting the experiment and an explanation and description of any materials she used in the course of conducting the experiment. Accuracy and precision are essential in this section of the report; readers (likely other scientists) want to be confident that correct procedure was followed, and they might even want to duplicate the study. The methods section is typically followed by the results section wherein the writer presents the data—which is usually numeric or quantitative—that reveals precisely what the scientist learned in the course of testing the hypothesis. The data is usually summarized with the help of a variety of graphs, charts, and tables. Finally, in the discussion/conclusion section of the report, the writer indicates whether the experiment has validated the hypothesis, discusses the study's implications, and describes what additional research is necessary to continue to explore the validity or lack thereof of the report's hypothesis.

As a science student, you also might be asked to write a literature review or a summary of all of the research published about a particular hypothesis. The literature review is usually organized chronologically—that is, the writer begins his or her review with a summary of the earliest experiment related to the hypothesis and ends with a review of the most recently conducted study. The literature review usually comments, as well, upon the overall implications of the studies considered as a whole. Note that a literature review, usually in a briefer form, is also a part of some laboratory or research reports.

Writing for the Humanities

The humanities include the fine arts, history, languages, literature, philosophy, and religion. Humanists, like all academics, value a clear and concise style of writing, but they tend to value sentence variety more than their counterparts in the social sciences and sciences do. They try, perhaps more than their colleagues in other disciplines, to give some flair and energy to their writing.

Here, for example, is a passage from an article about students' responses to the poetry of Emily Dickinson (Ladin, Jay. "Meeting Her Maker: Emily Dickinson's God." *Cross Currents* 56.3 (Fall 2006): 338–346. Print.):

> I was both delighted by my students' ability to connect Dickinson's work to their personal experience, and startled by the effectiveness of that connection. Rather than oversimplifying the complexities of the text, reading Dickinson through the lens of their religious experience had made my students more effective, subtler readers than they would have been had they adopted the humanist framework I offered them. (Ladin 341)

Compare this with this passage from an article about global warming (Mote, Philip, and Kaser, Georg. "The Shrinking Glaciers of Kiliminjaro: Can Global Warming Be Blamed?" *American Scientist* 95.4 (July–August 2007): 318–325. Print.):

> Melting, sublimation and the warming of ice require energy. Energy in the high-mountain environment comes from a variety of energy fluxes that interact in complex ways. The Sun is the primary energy source, but its direct effect is limited to daytime; other limiting factors are shading and the ability of snow to reflect visible light. Energy can nevertheless reach the glacier through sensible-heat flux ... (Mote and Kaser 321)

The two passages are the same length but the humanist writes two sentences to the scientists' five. This is a common distinction between the humanist and the scientific writing style. Scientists favour simple sentences; humanists, complex. In addition, the humanist adds narration to his expository essay and writes in the first person—"I was…delighted." The scientists use the third person point of view. Instead of writing "Hardy had invited me to join him," for example, they write "Hardy had invited Kaser to join him." The humanist style is academic but less formally so than that of the social or natural scientist.

Humanists use a variety of citation systems. Literature and language scholars usually use the MLA method for parenthetical citation, while historians prefer *Chicago Manual of Style* method footnotes or endnotes.

As a humanities major, you will write a wide variety of expository (or informative) essays in which you will express your knowledge of topics related to works of literature, philosophical systems, historical events and circumstances, painting and sculpture, and tenets of world religions. In "Evil Children in Film and Literature: Notes Toward a Genealogy" in Part Three, for example, Karen Renner surveys the work of several critics and scholars who have studied books and films that feature an evil child or children as main characters and who try to explain the social conditions that have generated our growing fascination with this topic.

The writing you do if you are taking a class in a foreign language will differ from the writing assignments you typically will undertake in other humanities classes. In introductory language classes, the purpose of writing assignments is more to help you learn the language than to present information or to advance an argument. Your professor likely will ask you to write responses to questions based upon fairly simple readings, to compose a simple friendly letter, or perhaps to keep a diary or journal. As you become more fluent in the language, the assignments will become more sophisticated, and, if you major in a foreign language, you eventually will be expected to compose essays in that language that approximate the demands of a writing assignment in any other humanities courses. In some cultures—in Asian and Arabic cultures, for example—the concept and the convention of argument differ from our own, so you will have the additional challenge of composing essays that are not only intelligent, substantive, clear, and energetic, but that are also appropriate within a specific cultural context.

Writing for Business

Business schools offer courses in accounting, finance, human resources, management, and marketing. In business writing, the style is dictated by the genre and the audience. Advertising copy aimed at the general public needs to be clear, lively, and direct. Prospectuses, business letters, and annual reports have to have a fairly formal but still readable style since they are read by both the general public and by specialists in the field. Interoffice memoranda, emails, and text messages can be less formal but must be clear and to the point. A business person may use acronyms and the jargon of his field if he is writing something that will be read only by his peers but should avoid specialized language if he is writing for the general public. In one television commercial, a national car rental company mocks business acronyms, praising its customer for improving ROI (return on investment) through SEO (seasoned equity offerings) all by COB (close of business).

Business majors often begin their program of study believing that their professors won't require much writing from them. In fact, the reverse may be closer to the truth. Business majors do a lot of writing, and businesspeople do even more. Hardly a month passes without a major newspaper somewhere quoting a CEO who is critical of her new employees because they don't possess the communication skills they need to be successful.

Even in a field such as accounting, which we think of as more concerned with numbers than letters, good writing skills are essential. Accountants regularly write reports that explain, summarize, and interpret a company's balance sheet. Clarity and accuracy are obviously crucial to such reports. Accounting firms often ask job applicants to respond in writing to complex questions as part of the interview process. And there is a written component to many of the exams would-be accountants must take to become certified.

If you plan to major in business, you will have to learn how to write a prospectus, an annual report, a marketing report or survey, an interoffice memo, a job description, and various forms of letters. Your professors also likely will ask you to write an expository and/or a persuasive essay to complete the requirements for their courses. Essays about the training and hiring practices of various companies, the management styles of successful business executives, the marketing campaigns for various products, and the ethics of the auto industry, for example, are commonly assigned in business courses. In "Brand and Country-of-Origin Effect on Consumers' Decision to Purchase Luxury Products" in Part Three, for example, Godey et al. explain some consumer values in various countries in the course of offering advice for companies who want to market luxury brand products internationally.

Writing for Technology

Computer scientists, educational technologists, engineers, and others employed in high-tech industries do a tremendous amount of writing in the course of their careers. Senior engineers and high-tech executives often stress the importance of written communication skills to success in their industries. They value clear language, cohesion, concision, logic, structure, good grammar, and correct punctuation in the reports, letters, and proposals they demand from their employees. Written texts produced by computer scientists, engineers, and other technologists typically are replete with charts, tables, graphs, and other visuals. The ability to compose clear and meaningful visual aids is essential to success in technical writing. Writers rely on them to help their readers understand the often very complex information they are trying to convey. For the same reason, technical writing, more than other genres, relies on numbered, point-form, or bulleted information to convey meaning clearly, concisely, and precisely.

Technical writing is often true to its name, in that its content is very discipline specific and hence filled with technical language, difficult for those who are not experts in the field to comprehend. Here, for example, is the abstract from a paper the title of which—"Modeling Turning Processes Parameters for PCD Cutting Tool by Evolutionary Multi-Objective Optimization Techniques Using Micro-Genetic Algorithm"—certainly signals its specialized audience. The paper, by Amaranadh Reddy et al., is in the January 2012 issue of the *International Journal of Advanced Computing*.

In this paper the focus is on describing the Multi-Objective Optimization Problem considering a case from real-world production processes like turning, for non-ferrous metals and abrasive non-metals, which demands high precision tools. The non-linear relationship between the selected parameters from the process and the tool life and material removal rate, which are mutually dependent objectives, needs to be optimized simultaneously. For solving the problem micro-Genetic Algorithm procedures are used, which are characterized as one of the Evolutionary Algorithm conceptual tools.

Clearly the authors of this paper are writing for a highly specialized audience. The paper's system of headings and subheadings and its tables, figures, charts, and graphs seem equally baffling to non-experts, though they no doubt help readers already familiar with the specialized language of the discipline to comprehend the authors' study. Note the use of passive voice—"micro-Genetic Algorithm procedures are used"—instead of the active voice, "We used micro-Genetic Algorithm procedures." Humanists tend to prefer active voice, with its more approachable, less formal style.

If you are a student in computer science, engineering, or another high-tech field, you likely will receive instruction and practice in writing project proposals, project progress reports, user manuals, technical descriptions of machinery or computer hardware, project feasibility studies, and business letters. Technological projects are usually collaborative, so you also likely will learn some strategies for writing collaboratively and productively with one or more colleagues. You also will need to know how to adapt your writing for different audiences since an audience of fellow technologists has very specialized knowledge that a general reader does not have. And you will have to learn how to effectively integrate figures, charts, tables, graphs, and point-form bulleted information into written communication.

Technical reports usually begin with an introduction that explains the problem or the circumstances that generated the need for a report. The introduction also quickly orients readers to the subject of the report and presents its purpose. The introduction usually is followed by the summary, which briefly presents the main results of the report and the recommendations the author is making based upon his findings. The body of the report presents the detailed information, accompanied by the necessary charts, graphs, tables, and figures, which are clearly referenced in the written text of the report's body. Typically, about 75 percent of the report consists of the detailed, well-substantiated, clearly explained information contained within the body. Depending on the report's length, the body might be subdivided into a literature review, analysis, discussion, or other subsections. The conclusion section comes next, wherein the authors present the results of their investigation and analysis. The report ends with recommendations the authors make based upon the conclusions they have reached. In short reports, the conclusions and recommendations are often presented together. In some longer reports, a source list is included, presented as footnotes or in a recognized bibliographical format—technologists use various acceptable methods of citing sources. In addition, longer reports are often preceded by a letter of transmittal from the reports' authors to the reports' commissioners, reminding the commissioners of the circumstances or problems that generated the need for such a report.

How Professors Evaluate Student Writing

Academic writing is always evaluated. When a professor submits an article to a journal in his or her field, a group of peers usually reads the article and decides if it is a well-written and important enough contribution to the field to warrant publication in the journal. When students turn in their essays and reports and term papers, they expect their professor to read the assignment carefully, consider its merits, and assign to it a fair and appropriate grade. If students know ahead of time the criteria their professors will use to evaluate their writing, they have a considerable advantage because they can tailor their essay to fit the criteria.

It is true that different instructors and professors have different notions about what constitutes excellent writing in their field. An English professor might pay more attention to grammar and style than a biology instructor who might favour a comparatively unadorned style, while her colleague in the anthropology department will tend to value creativity more. But there are values that all professors share, and students who are aware of these values will have an advantage over those who don't.

All professors want to see signs of intelligent life in the papers that they grade. In an expository essay, they expect a clear thesis and valid points in support of that thesis based upon solid research and critical thinking. Evidence of critical thinking (see pages 340–341) is even more important in a persuasive essay, as it may lead to an original argument, which, if it is based upon clear thinking and solid research, will certainly impress and please the instructor or professor. Clear, independent thinking is an important goal of a post-secondary education.

Professors also value substance in their students' written work. "Provide an example here"; "develop this point in more detail"; "define this term more accurately"—these are among the most common comments instructors and professors write in the margins of essays as they are grading them. Body paragraphs in academic writing usually have a key point, sometimes expressed in the paragraph as its "topic sentence." Like any reader, professors want to see this key point developed in enough detail so that they understand the point the writer is trying to make.

All professors and instructors value clarity in their students' writing. Clear writing has a beginning, a middle, and an end. Sentences within paragraphs and paragraphs with the essay as a whole are connected together in smooth and logical ways—in other words, there are "transitions" between and among sentences and paragraphs. Essays with good grammar, diction, spelling, and punctuation are clearer than those that contain errors in the use of Standard English.

Finally, professors like to see some evidence that the student is engaged and enthusiastic about and committed to the topic of the paper—they like to see some energy in student writing, some confidence, some forcefulness, some style. Style tends to be a reflection of subject, historians, for example, favouring a lively style, adorned with anecdotes, chemists favouring a more plain and direct style. Professors and instructors don't like perfunctory writing, which conveys the sense that the writer is merely getting a dull task done. They want energy, its level in keeping with the discourse conventions of their discipline.

Intelligence, substance, clarity, energy—ISCE, for short. Most instructors and professors will reward writing strong in each of these categories.

WRITING ASSIGNMENT

Most college and university textbooks represent decent examples of academic writing. Study a recently published textbook written about a subject that interests you. You might use a textbook from a class you are currently taking. Write a paragraph in which you evaluate a chapter or an excerpt from this book based upon the discussion of the elements of good academic writing you have just read. Study the way in which sources are cited in the book. Determine if the citation method is MLA, APA, or something else. Explain how you can tell which citation method the author of the textbook is using.

EXERCISES

Write a paragraph that describes an object that has special significance to you, an object that you treasure: your car, a piece of jewellery, an item of clothing, your smart phone, iPod, tablet, laptop. Then rewrite this paragraph from the perspectives of any two of the following: a marketing major, a sociologist, a chemist, a football coach, a sculptor, a poet.

COLLABORATIVE ACTIVITY

In a small group, share one of the paragraphs you wrote for the exercise above. Then select the one paragraph, from all group members combined, your group will share with the rest of the class. As a group, decide upon the finishing touches that will "perfect" this paragraph before your group leader reads it aloud to the rest of the class.

CHAPTER 2

Getting Started: Consider Topic, Audience, Purpose

In Chapter 1, you learned about the various types of academic writing assignments, the discourse conventions of the various academic disciplines, and the criteria professors use to evaluate student writing. In this chapter, you will learn some methods to generate the content you will need to complete an academic writing assignment successfully. Content also depends upon research, which is discussed in the next chapter. But even before you research, and while you draft, you can use some strategies that will help you generate ideas and some of the content that will help you develop those ideas. To generate content, take some time to

- reflect upon your topic
- consider the needs and expectations of your readers
- establish your purpose
- compose a preliminary thesis

You must, of course, keep the needs and expectations of your readers in mind and continue to refine your purpose while you draft your essay. But if you consider your TAP (topic, audience, and purpose) before you begin to draft, you will generate some ideas you can use to develop your essay, and you will begin to develop the voice and style you want to use to complete the assignment successfully.

Reflect upon Your Topic

If you are like most students, you begin work on an academic essay immediately by annotating the assignment sheet containing the list of topics your professor has given you. You circle the number of the topic that most appeals to you, underline a key phrase or two, and make a few preliminary notes about main points to cover and references to check. Perhaps then you put a question mark beside another topic or two that you could turn to if your first choice doesn't work out. Perhaps in other topics you find information which might provide some insights into the topic you have chosen.

If your teacher wants you to choose your own topic, you likely will undertake a different strategy. You may browse through your lecture notes and textbooks, underlining and highlighting sentences and phrases that interest you, trying to find preliminary connections between and among them, connections that might eventually lead to an interesting and feasible topic.

These are good strategies, good places to begin. The simple process of annotating your assignment sheet or selecting your own topic will centre your assignment, encourage you to come up with some ideas to develop your topic, and help you focus the research you eventually will have to carry out.

Your topic, whether your teacher assigns it or you choose it, likely will contain key words that will help clarify the nature of the assignment. Read the assignment sheet and list of topics carefully. Look for terms such as *describe*, *explain*, *define*, *discuss, compare and contrast*, and *analyze*. To describe, in the context of an academic essay assignment, is to put into words the characteristics of your subject: Describe the architecture of homes designed by Frank Lloyd Wright. To explain usually requires the delineation in words of a process: Explain the process of photosynthesis. To define involves identifying the group to which a concept belongs and then distinguishing it from other members of that group; if you had to define the term *democracy*, you would identify it as a form of government and then illustrate how it differs from other forms. To discuss usually presupposes causes: Discuss the causes of World War I. To compare and contrast requires you to point out the similarities and differences between the two items that are the subject of your essay: Compare and contrast the themes and styles of "Ode to a Nightingale" and "Ode on a Grecian Urn." To analyze is to examine closely one or more of the component parts of a process or an action or an artifact (often a written text), usually as part of the larger process of analyzing the whole: Analyze the business plan for the third quarter of Company X.

Stick to your topic and focus on that key word contained within it. If you are asked to compare and contrast "Ode to a Nightingale" and "Ode on a Grecian Urn," do not discuss the life of John Keats, except insofar as it might be relevant to the main topic. If you are asked to discuss the causes of World War I, do not compare and contrast the peace settlement of World War I with the peace settlement of World War II. Teachers often complain that a recurring problem in student writing is a tendency to drift away from the assigned topic.

● Freewriting

Having considered carefully the wording of your topic, you are ready to do some brainstorming, freewriting, and other creative thinking activities designed to help you come up with information and insights that might eventually be useful in developing the paragraphs in your essay. Freewriting is a form of brainstorming on paper. It is a technique designed to help unblock the creative process by forcing you to write something—anything—about the subject of your assignment. The process is as follows. Using your assignment as a prompt, you write nonstop for a limited period of time, usually about ten minutes. You write whatever comes into your mind without worrying about spelling, grammar, or any other aspects of "correct" writing. No one but you sees your freewriting. After the ten minutes are up, you read your freewriting and extract from it ideas and information that might be useful to you as you write your essay. You can use these ideas as additional prompts and freewrite again and even a third time if you feel the exercise will yield results. (For an example of freewriting done as part of the prewriting process for an academic essay, see on pages 85–88 the freewriting Zhen did when she began working on her essay about backpacks.)

● W5+1H Questions

There are several variations on the freewriting process, other activities designed to do the same thing: to generate ideas. Journalists are taught the W5 and 1H strategy, which is a method of asking and answering *who, what, when, where, why,* and *how* as they are developing and reporting a story. This strategy can be adapted to academic writing as well. When you have selected your topic, make up a list of W5+1H questions about it. Who will be reading this essay? What does he or she want from me? Who are the important people relevant to the topic? Where did important events related to my topic take place? What do I want to accomplish? When did the events relevant to my topic take place? Why did events transpire as they did? Why is this subject important? How did the players react to the events? How is this subject relevant? Some of these questions you will be able to answer, and at least parts of those answers eventually will find their way into your essay. Some questions you will not be able to answer, but by asking them, you at least will begin to focus your research.

● Webbing

Webbing is a similar strategy, one that exploits our ability to generate ideas through free association. In the middle of a piece of paper, write and circle the topic or the concept of the paper that has been assigned to you. Jot down ideas as they occur to you and arrange them randomly around your topic or central concept. Circle each idea and draw lines between and among them and the central concept to illustrate their various relationships to each other. This linking process is especially valuable because it can reveal relationships between ideas that might not otherwise have occurred to you, relationships that might help you see an effective structure for your essay.

Suppose, for example, that you are a business major taking a marketing course. You are assigned to write an essay about how toy manufacturers market dolls, or how you might market them if you were the marketing director of a toy company. Such a topic requires research, of course, but before you begin the research process, you might try to construct a web as a way to provide some focus and impose some structure onto your topic. Write and circle, in the centre of a blank page, the phrase *marketing dolls* and see what connections you can make. (See the following example.)

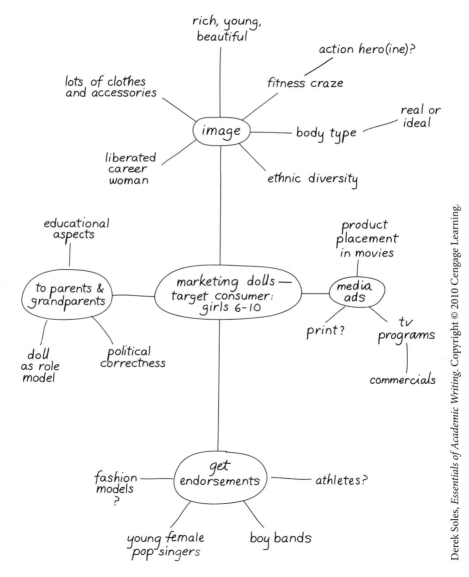

Derek Soles, *Essentials of Academic Writing.* Copyright © 2010 Cengage Learning.

Consider Your Reader

Writing an academic essay is a process of analyzing and synthesizing knowledge, a way of helping us to know and understand our topic in a meaningful, complex, and intense way. Writing is so important a school subject—one of "the three Rs"—because it requires active learning: You learn a lesson thoroughly when you have to express your knowledge of its content in writing.

You don't, however, write academic essays only for yourself. Other less visible but important participants are involved in the process: your readers. You write an essay to inform your readers, to provide them with information you want them to have or that they have requested. Or you write to convince your readers that your position on a debatable issue is valid. It is important that you consider the needs and expectations of your readers before you begin to write and while you draft, revise, and edit. Your readers will influence the content and the style of your text and, on some level, will judge its quality.

● Readers Influence Content

Your primary reader is your instructor/professor. You might share your essay with a classmate, a friend, a tutor in your writing centre, or a family member and get his or her input before you hand your essay in. Your professor might show your essay to a colleague or share it with the rest of the class. After you graduate, you might write for an employer, an employee, or a professional organization to which you belong. Throughout your life, you will write for a variety of readers, and you will have to remember that different readers require different information, even about the same subject. An article about the new Chrysler engine written for an automotive engineer would be quite different from an article on the same subject written for a car salesperson or a potential customer. For now your primary reader is your teacher, and it is his or her needs and expectations you must meet.

Those needs and expectations should be evident from the assignment sheet or from class discussion about the nature of the assignment. If they are not, it is important to find out from your professor what her expectations are. She might want something original, or she might want to know you have a solid understanding of the course content already covered. She might want you to tell her something about the topic she does not already know, or she might want your take on one of the debatable issues discussed in class. Know what your reader wants, try to achieve those expectations while you write, and your work will have a clearer focus.

It will help, as well, to know how long your reader expects your essay to be. Length will determine the level of detail you are expected to provide. An economics professor, for example, could ask for a 1000-word or a 5000-word essay on the law of supply and demand; the length would dictate the level of detail you would include in such an essay. Meet or exceed slightly the required length. If you do not, your ideas likely are not developed in the detail your professor wants.

Finally, clarify any important aspect of the assignment your teacher may not have made clear. Question anything not clear to you: Do you want us to include a plot summary along with our analysis of the story? How many sources do you expect us to cite? Are there sources you particularly recommend? How many words do you want? May we use subtitles? The more you know about what your reader wants, the more successful your writing will be.

● Readers Influence Style

Style identifies the manner in which you present information to your readers. If you are sending a text message to your friend, your writing style will be informal; your sentence structure might be fragmented; you may use slang; you will not be overly concerned about spelling.

The readers of your academic essays, on the other hand, are well-educated women and men working with you in an academic setting. They will expect you to present your information in a mature and relatively formal writing style. You should not be flippant or sarcastic in an academic essay, nor, at the other extreme, should you be pedantic. Try to strike a balance with a style that is smooth and natural but appropriate for a well-educated reader. Consider, for example, this paragraph:

> An outstanding essay, report, or article will also meet the needs and expectations of its readers. Writers for newspapers, magazines, journals, and book publishers have an implied contract with their readers that they will present certain information, at a certain rhetorical level, in a certain style. Student academic writing is usually read and assessed by professors, who expect students to obey the rules of Standard English. They want to see smooth and logical transitions between and among sentences within a paragraph and paragraphs within the essay or report as a whole. They don't want to see errors in sentence grammar, sentence structure, spelling, or punctuation. They want academic voice and academic style. Academic voice is formal and steady, not ostentatious, not flippant, not sarcastic, while academic style is generally clear and concise, specifically aligned with the discourse conventions of the discipline. Scientists, for example, writing for an academic audience, typically use a comparatively simple sentence structure; they will use the language of their discipline, and they will expect their readers to share their knowledge of that language. Humanists will also use the special language—the jargon—of their discipline, but typically they will favour more complex sentence structure.

Note, first, the length of the paragraph. At 198 words, it is longer than the typical paragraph in a letter, email, newspaper, or popular magazine, but not much longer than a typical paragraph in an academic journal. It has nine sentences, with an average length of twenty-two words. The sentence structure is varied: the first sentence is simple; the second, complex; the third, complex; the fourth, simple; the fifth, simple; the sixth, simple; the seventh, complex; the eighth, compound; and the ninth, compound. The voice is clear and formal but not ostentatious. The paragraph is typical of the style of solid academic undergraduate writing.

● Readers Judge Quality

Your friend who receives your text message or tweet will not judge your sentence structure, paragraph structure, spelling, or grammar. He just wants the news, a casual, friendly response to his questions, a diversion.

Those who read your writing in an academic or business setting will judge its quality. Other students might be invited to read and respond to a draft of your essay, to make suggestions about how to make it better. In the future, colleagues and bosses will read your work and, at least indirectly, will judge its quality, especially if it does not give them the information they require.

For now, the primary judge of the quality of your writing is your professor, who will pass ultimate judgment on your work by giving it a grade. You are well advised to try to find out everything you can about the criteria your professor will use to assess your work. If your professor provides you with a list of the criteria, work closely with it as you write and revise your essay. Studies indicate that students who understand the criteria on which their writing will be judged write better essays than students who do not know how their teachers will evaluate their writing. See Chapter 1, pages 17–18, for a concise explanation of the ISCE criteria professors use when they evaluate student writing.

Establish Your Purpose

After you have considered the needs of your reader, consider your purpose in writing this academic essay. We write for many reasons: We write a letter to exchange news with friends; we write a poem to express our feelings; we keep a journal to record daily observations.

Academic writing has usually one of two primary purposes: to provide information that a teacher has requested or to advance an argument about an issue related to the subject you are studying. In other words, academic essays generally are written in either the expository or the persuasive modes, which, of course, often overlap. They were introduced in Chapter 1. Here they are explained in more detail.

● Expository Mode

An expository essay presents complete and accurate information about a specific topic. If you are asked to discuss the causes of the most recent conflict in the Middle East, to explain how to treat a victim of a heart attack, to define post structuralism, to compare and contrast Freudian and Jungian methods of treating obsessive-compulsive disorder, or to explain the rules of basketball, you will write an expository essay. The purpose of an expository essay is to provide your reader with information he or she has requested or can use.

There are several different patterns by which expository academic essays are typically developed. One or any combination of these patterns may be used to structure and develop an expository academic essay. Usually, one pattern will dominate, but others will be present. There may also be some elements of a narrative or persuasive mode within an expository framework.

One common expository mode is the process analysis, which details the parts of a process and their relationships with each other. If your health sciences professor asks you to write an essay about the circulation of the blood through the body or about how the body converts carbohydrates into energy, you will write a process paper. If your physical education professor asks you to write an essay about teaching children how to swim, you will write a process paper.

Another common expository mode is the cause and/or effect essay. Your economics professor, for example, might ask you to write an essay in which you explain the causes of inflation or the effects inflation has on a certain community. Your European history teacher might ask you to explain the causes of the Crimean War or to discuss changes (the effects) to the map of Europe that resulted from the war. Your marketing professor might ask you to write an essay about why an advertising campaign for a fast-food restaurant failed or to write about how the failure affected the management structure and practices of the company. For a major paper, professors often combine the cause and effect modes: What causes inflation, and how does inflation affect an industrialized society? What caused the Crimean War, and how did the war change the map of Europe? Why did the Company X marketing campaign fail, and what effect did the failure have on the company as a whole? "The Effect of Twitter on College Student Engagement and Grades," anthologized in Part Two, is a good example of an effects essay, examining the effects of Twitter on academic performance.

A third expository mode is the compare/contrast essay. Compare and contrast the developmental theories of Jean Piaget and Jerome Bruner; compare and contrast Immanuel Kant's and Johann Goethe's concept of free will; compare and contrast the marketing campaigns of McDonald's and Wendy's. Professors often use compare/contrast assignments because they challenge the analytical ability of their students, who have to juggle and ultimately synthesize similarities and differences between two objects or concepts. The compare/contrast mode demands a fairly sophisticated organizational structure. "The Consequences of Son Preference and Sex-Selective Abortion in China and Other Asian Countries," anthologized in Part Two, compares and contrasts sex-selective abortion practices in several countries.

A fourth expository mode is the analysis/interpretation essay. Analyze and interpret Book I of John Milton's *Paradise Lost*, the foreign policy of Secretary of State Hillary Clinton, the election campaign strategies of the NDP Party in Quebec, Vincent van Gogh's *Starry Night*, Henry VII's role in discrediting Richard III, the advertising campaign of a hybrid car. If you have been a post-secondary student for more than two years you undoubtedly have encountered assignments similar to these. Analysis is the process of dividing your subject of study, your topic, into its component parts. Interpretation is the process of assessing and describing how those parts coalesce into a coherent whole and cause the enterprise you are analyzing to succeed or to break down. To write a successful analysis/interpretation essay, then, you need to define the distinguishing features of the whole, divide the whole into its component parts, analyze the parts, and interpret the relationship of the parts to the whole. "Evil Children in Film and Literature," anthologized in Part Three, is an example of an analysis/interpretation essay.

A fifth expository mode is the problem/solution essay, topics for which are typically framed in the form of questions. Why did Grade Three students from poor families score low on a nationwide math test, and how can educators improve math education for this group? Why is Iran a threat to our national security, and how can we reduce this threat? Why did the Occupy Wall Street Movement turn violent, and how can this violence be curtailed? These essays have two parts: a full explanation of the nature of the problem, followed by an analysis of solutions and their likelihood of success. The student essay in Chapter 8, on "Saving the Vancouver Island Marmot," is a good example of a problem/solution essay. Adam identifies a problem: Once abundant in central and southern Vancouver Island, the marmot has become an endangered species. And he proffers a solution: Fortunately, British Columbia's Ministry of Environment and the general public are aware of the problem and want to implement an aggressive program to save *Marmota vancouverensis* from extinction.

A sixth expository mode is the essay developed by details and examples. Of course, details and examples are important components of all modes of academic discourse, but some academic essays have as their primary developmental system a series of facts, details, and examples. What hockey teams use the neutral-zone trap effectively? What are the most challenging mountains to climb? Who is the leading U.S. sportswear designer? These are examples of topics that require a thesis and details to support the examples. The authors of "Brand and Country-of-Origin Effect on Consumers' Decision to Purchase Luxury Products," anthologized in Part Three, use details and examples extensively in developing their paragraphs.

A knowledge of the modes of the expository essay can help you structure an essay successfully and to stay on topic. But remember that an expository academic essay is often a combination of several expository modes, even though one usually predominates.

● Persuasive Mode

The purpose of a persuasive essay, in part, is to present information to your readers. But its primary purpose is to convince or persuade your readers that your views on a particular controversial topic are valid and legitimate. If you are asked to discuss and describe the sequence of events that led to the legalization of abortion in Canada, you will write an informative essay, but if you are asked if you support or oppose legalized abortion, you will write a persuasive essay. If you are asked to write an essay synthesizing the reasons why Islamic fundamentalists attacked the World Trade Center, you will write an informative essay, but if you are asked to write an essay in support of or in opposition to Canada's military action in Afghanistan as part of a campaign to end terrorism, you will write a persuasive essay. If you are asked to define and to explain the process of poststructuralist criticism, you will write an informative essay, but if you are asked if you believe poststructuralism is a viable method of literary analysis, you will write a persuasive essay.

"The Canadian Human Rights Tribunal on First Nations Child Welfare: Why If Canada Wins, Equality and Justice Lose," anthologized in Part Two, is an example of a persuasive essay. Its thesis is that the federal government needs to fund First Nations children who live on reserves as generously as they do children who do not live on reserves, and the author provides well-sourced evidence in support of her thesis. "The Morality of Fighting in Ice Hockey: Should It Be Banned?" anthologized in Part Two, is another example. The authors gradually martial evidence in support of their thesis, which emerges, as their answer to the title question, near the conclusion of the essay.

● Multi-Genre Mode

Many academic essays are ostensibly expository, but embedded in the exposition is an argument in support of a cause. "Young Adults and Casual Sex: The Relevance of College Drinking Settings," anthologized in Part Three, is a sociological survey based upon students' responses to a series of questionnaires about their participation in social activities where they consumed alcohol and the likelihood that, at such events, they might have sex with someone they have not met before. The main purpose of this study is not to take a stand on the issue it interrogates, but to discover the extent to which there are relationships among engaging in casual sex, drinking, and specific social events. But the authors step out of their role as detached social scientists to consider the implications of the findings of their study on policies university administrators might want to implement. In so doing, they are arguing, however implicitly and logically, for a need to change behaviour.

"The Unwatched Life Is Not Worth Living: The Elevation of the Ordinary in Celebrity Culture," anthologized in Part Two, also contains an implicit argument. The argument is even more pronounced in "Are Contemporary Media Images Which Seem to Display Women as Sexually Empowered Actually Harmful to Women?" in Part Three, though it is also primarily a social science study.

Compose a Preliminary Thesis

The end of the beginning of the writing process is the composition of the thesis statement. The thesis statement is an expression of the central or controlling idea of your entire essay. It is the essence of your academic essay, what would be left if you put your essay into a pot and boiled it down to its most essential component.

Your thesis might be very specific and incorporate the main point you want to make about your topic plus the supporting points. Here is an example of such a thesis statement for an informative essay about taking effective photographs: To take good pictures, a photographer must pay attention to composition, lighting, and point of view. Such a thesis is effective because it provides your reader with a blueprint, a mini-plan of the body of your essay. It suggests to the reader that those three points—composition, lighting, and point of view—will be developed in more detail in subsequent paragraphs.

For a more complex essay, a persuasive essay, for example, a detailed thesis might be difficult to compose and hard to understand. Ariel was writing an explication of John Donne's "The Flea," focusing on the character of the narrator, who, in her view, is somewhere between the playfully flirtatious "typical guy" that some readers see and the sexual predator that some feminist critics recognize. Her point is too complex for a blueprint thesis, so she settled on this:

> While the narrator is cunning, maybe even creepy, in the way he manipulates the argument to get his own way, there is nothing in his flippant tone or language to suggest he will push too hard, if the young woman rejects his advances.

This thesis has a persuasive edge to it, which means the writer will have to acknowledge and refute opposing points and then develop and support her own argument. Here, a general thesis is preferable because a blueprint thesis would have to encompass so much, it would seem unwieldy.

Professors often assign broad topics and expect students to narrow the topic down to a viable thesis. Broad topics are good in that they allow you to compose a thesis of interest to you and to write about whichever aspect of the topic you want to write about. But they do require you to have a strategy for narrowing a topic down to a workable thesis. For such assignments, the invention strategies discussed previously—especially freewriting—work effectively. You can also narrow a topic by thinking about the topic in the context of the rhetorical modes, discussed earlier in this chapter. Does the topic lend itself to a compare/contrast approach? A process analysis? An explanation of causes and/or effects?

Khaliq is a business major taking a course in business ethics. His professor wants a term paper "related to the theme of the course." The course has focused on recent cases of ethical malfeasance in certain corporations and on laws, old and new, that attempt to curtail ethical violations. As Khaliq reviews the content of the course and freewrites about aspects of the course that interest him, he is struck by the number of laws the government has had to pass to regulate business practices. He knows that new laws will probably be needed to regulate Internet businesses, and he considers the Internet and the law as a possible topic. But he knows this is still too broad. As he walks around his campus, he notices that, outside the bookstore, tables are set up and piled with fake Louis Vuitton purses, Burberry scarves, and other faux designer merchandise on sale for a small fraction of the cost of the originals. He is surprised the vendors can sell this merchandise with impunity and wants to find out if what they are doing is legal, and, if it is, if laws need to be developed to prevent the sales of fake goods. Using LexisNexis as his first source, he begins to research the topic. What he finds surprises him. It is illegal for a retailer to sell designer goods that he or she claims are real. But it is not illegal to sell "knockoffs," which are imitations of the real things the vendors admit are imitations. In fact, Khaliq learns that knockoffs do not have an adverse impact on the sales of the original products and may even increase their appeal. His topic becomes "Why Laws against 'Knockoff' Products Will Never Be Passed."

● Placement of the Thesis

The thesis statement is often the final sentence of the introductory paragraph. Here, for example, is the introductory paragraph for an essay called "Prototypes for the Characters in Shakespeare's Sonnets." Note the clear thesis statement that concludes the paragraph:

> William Shakespeare was a master at describing and developing characters who are so complex and intriguing that they have become a part of our shared cultural heritage. Most literate people in the English-speaking world, indeed the whole world, know of Lear, Othello, Falstaff, Hamlet, Macbeth, Romeo and Juliet. Many of Shakespeare's characters

seem so real, in part, because they were based upon historical figures, even if the playwright did take some dramatic license in depicting these people, their motives, and their actions. *Similarly, the people who appear in Shakespeare's famous sequence of 154 sonnets are rendered so authentic that many scholars, encouraged by Shakespeare's tendency to base his characters on real people, have suggested that, taken together, the sonnets tell a story based on the poet's own experiences and that the characters in the sonnets have real-life prototypes.*

The thesis might be expressed in the form of a question, which the rest of the essay will answer. Here is the first paragraph for an essay about gender and pronoun agreement:

There is no doubt that the feminist movement has influenced the English language. Only the most linguistically conservative have problems now addressing a woman, directly or in a letter, as "Ms." Sexist words such as police_man_ and fire_man_ have given way to police officers and firefighters. Restaurants hire servers now, not waiters and waitresses; airlines hire flight attendants, not stewardesses. But one problem with gender-neutral language remains. *How should writers use singular pronouns to refer to a singular gender-neutral noun they use in a sentence?*

The thesis might be spread over two sentences if the essay is long and complex. Many academic essays do not even contain a recognizable single-sentence thesis in their introductions, but the essay's central idea will be implicit, especially when the essay's title helps establish a context for the introduction. The implied thesis often appears in a definition or a "general overview" essay. Here, for example, is the introductory paragraph for Jermaine's essay on political correctness.

Political Correctness (PC) is a value system which attempts to regulate attitudes, behaviour, and speech, especially as they apply to interactions with people who are oppressed because of their race, gender, sexual orientation, or physical appearance. The PC movement insists upon hyper-sensitivity in all social transactions, and adherents will aggressively condemn those who violate PC rules. It is usually associated with the political left and often mocked by the political right, who will, nevertheless, pounce upon anyone on the left who inadvertently violates the tenets of their own politically correct orthodoxy.
    It is difficult to pinpoint exactly when PC began…

Jermaine's paragraph does not contain a single-sentence thesis, which would be along the lines of "In this essay, I will define, explain, and provide a historical overview of the political correctness movement." The sentence would seem superfluous and make cumbersome a paragraph wherein the thesis is implied.

Note, finally, that at this stage of the writing process, your thesis statement is preliminary. As you think more about your topic, do some research, and write a few paragraphs, your central focus might change, and you might return to the beginning of your essay and alter your thesis. Eric, a business major, was writing an essay about the drawbacks of collaborative management. He wanted to make the point that a company is best off with a single strong leader, a person who has the charisma, vision, and work ethic that inspires employees and brings out the best in them. He knew he was going against current conventional wisdom that stressed the value of a collaborative approach—the "there is no 'I' in team" approach. His early attempts at formulating a thesis were heavy-handed, criticizing as they did political correctness, arguing that democracy was fine for a government but counterproductive to business, and suggesting that a benevolent dictatorship was an ideal model for business leadership. His professor pointed out to him that he risked alienating readers, offending them even, if he appeared to question political correctness and support dictatorship in any form. He needed a less threatening, a wittier opening to undercut so controversial a topic. After writing and rejecting several possibilities, he finally settled on the following:

> In today's business climate, collaborative management is held in high esteem, business executives reasoning that teamwork involves all in decision making and fosters a happier and hence more productive work environment. But a camel, the old saying goes, is a horse designed by a committee. When too many people are making decisions, arguing for their own point of view, and, ultimately, being forced to compromise, productivity declines, morale suffers, and decisions are delayed. Although in theory an enlightened and democratic concept, in practice collaborative management is less effective than management by a single person, one who inspires confidence, has some vision, and wins the loyalty of employees.

A Case Study of the Process of Writing an Academic Essay

Getting Started: Consider Topic, Audience, and Purpose

For her first-year writing course, Zhen must complete this assignment.
    English 121
    Essay Assignment
    Popular Products

Select a consumer product that is widely desired and widely used by college/university students. Explain the criteria students use or should use when they decide to purchase this product. To what extent, for example, are brand recognition, cost, size, reputation for quality, design, status important in the decision-making process?

Note that this is not a personal essay about why <u>you</u> decided to purchase the product. You are to research your topic and explain the criteria students use or should use when they make the purchase, though you may use your own experience and decision-making process as an example.

Your essay should be about fifteen hundred words in length.

Use 7 to 10 sources and cite your sources using the MLA method. [See text pages 150–152]

Your essay is due at the beginning of class Monday, June 10.

Your essay will be evaluated based upon the criteria we have discussed in class: the intelligence and substance of its content and the clarity and energy of its style.

On the assignment sheet, Zhen jots down several possible topics: smart phone, iPad, backpack, iPod, PlayStation, designer jeans.

Reasoning that most students will write about technological devices and wanting to do something different, Zhen decides to write about backpacks.

She jots/freewrites about the criteria she used when she purchased her own backpack:

"size—not too big so I look like I am going to fall over backward—

not too small for essentials I need to carry around campus—

laptop, books, notebooks, water bottle, umbrella, wallet"

"cost—I paid just under a hundred dollars for mine—average?

Above, below—have to see if I can find research about

average backpack cost"

"appearance—want something stylish—if that can even apply to
a backpack—not boring black—bright colour"

"features—I like the compartments in my backpack—choose one
with zippered pouches and pockets help keep me organized"

At this point, Zhen thinks she will likely write about the criteria students use when they purchase a backpack. She thinks her title might be along the lines of "How to Choose a Backpack for University" or "How to Choose the Perfect College Backpack," though she is not certain at this point.

She knows her reader—her instructor—expects academic content and a matching tone and style. She does not want to write an essay or an opinion piece that might be published in her college newspaper. She's not texting or emailing her friend or mom to tell them all about the backpack she just bought. She needs a serious discussion of her topic, supported by valid and reliable sources.

She thinks her organizational structure will be based upon the points her freewriting revealed.

She considers mode and thinks she will write a mainly expository essay, though it will likely have persuasive undertones, in that not all backpack users will agree on the most desirable features—and her research might reveal issues in backpack selection she has not considered.

She noodles with a possible thesis: Students make this important decision after considering several factors such as size, cost, and style. She knows this is basic and that her research might expand and refine and maybe even alter her topic and thesis.

WRITING ASSIGNMENT

Write an essay of approximately 500 words in which you describe "the typical reader" of a magazine with which you are familiar. The articles in the magazine, the ads, and the letters to the editor will give you valuable clues about the target audience at which the magazine is aimed. Include in your essay such information as the gender, age, interests, and personality of the typical reader. Note that this assignment calls for an expository essay.

EXERCISES

1. Use the methods discussed in this chapter to generate ideas for an essay on each of the following topics:

   - A person who has had a significant influence on my life
   - Typical characteristics of the dysfunctional family

- The benefits of school uniforms
- A review of a restaurant where you have eaten recently
- An essay about strikes by professional athletes
- An essay about political correctness
- An essay already assigned to you in another course you are taking (make up your own topic if you have not yet been given an assignment)

2. Design an essay topic for each of the six expository modes discussed in this chapter.

COLLABORATIVE ACTIVITY

1. In a small group, select an interesting topic and design a web with this topic at its centre. Make sure your topic is specific and focused, not vague or too broad.
2. Create a thesis based on one of the topics in Exercise 1. In a small group, read your thesis out loud and then discuss ways to make it more focused.

CHAPTER 3

Research Your Topic

In Chapter 2, you learned how important it is to consider the needs of your reader, determine your purpose, and think about your topic before you begin a draft of your essay. By doing this, you will begin to focus your topic and will acquire some ideas and information you might ultimately incorporate into your essay. But you will need more. You will have to find out what other people, especially the experts in the field, have to say about the subject of your essay. An academic essay requires research. Research will provide you with much of the information you will need to develop the ideas you present in your essay. Research also lends that aura of authority to your work, which your readers, especially your professor, will expect.

There are many sources writers can consult to find the information they need. The research source depends, to a certain extent, on the academic discipline for which the research is being conducted. To complete most of the academic essays assigned to you, you will have to read books and journal, magazine, and newspaper articles, in print and online. You might also have to or want to interview people who will have information about the topic of your essay; it would be quite a coup, for example, to interview a poet or a novelist whose work you were explicating. Social scientists often use information from questionnaires they have designed and distributed; psychologists and sociologists observe and analyze the behaviour of individuals and groups and use their "field notes" that become a research source. Having gathered, analyzed, and synthesized your research, you need to incorporate sources into your essay smoothly and cite them appropriately. In this chapter, you will learn how to

- find and use books, including reference books, as sources
- find and use articles from periodicals, including academic journals, magazines, and newspapers
- find and use valid and reliable information from the Web
- incorporate research into your work

- avoid plagiarism
- cite sources (covered thoroughly in Chapter 8)

Books

To find book titles that will provide some of the information you will need to discover and develop the ideas you will present in your essay, check your course syllabus to see if your professor has included a bibliography or a list of further readings relevant to the course material. If he or she has, and if the list includes a title that sounds like it is relevant to your topic, do all you can to find the book and see if it contains relevant information. Study also any bibliographies or lists of further or related readings at the end of textbook chapters or at the end of the textbook itself. Most textbooks contain bibliographies, lists of related readings, or both. You should be able to determine from the titles if these works are likely to contain information that will help you develop the ideas in your essay.

Once you have a list of promising titles, log on to your university library website to determine if your library has the books, what their call numbers are, and if they have been signed out. If a book you want has been signed out, you can usually request it be returned and held for you. The call number is that series of letters and numbers indicating where in the library the book is stored. If, for example, the call number of the book is PE 1471. S65 1997, you find the bookshelf with a label on the end of it indicating that books with a PE call number in the 1400s are located upon this shelf. The information on your computer screen will indicate whether the book is in or has been signed out, and, if it has been signed out, when it is due back. If it is not due back for a long period of time, you can usually put a recall on it and get it sooner. If the book title does not come up on the screen, indicating the library does not have the book, you can sometimes access a copy through interlibrary loan if your library has reciprocal lending privileges with other libraries, as most university libraries do.

If you do not find any specific titles from course outlines or textbook sources, you will have to do a keyword or subject search. Instead of typing authors' names and book titles in the appropriate place on the library's website, try typing in various versions of the subject of your essay. Begin by making your subject search as specific as possible so that you get the most relevant information. Avoid making your search too broad because the number of books you can access is likely to overwhelm you. Keyword searches are a good way of helping you zero in on the specific information you require. They can become quite sophisticated and involve combining words you might not necessarily think of combining. Your university librarian can help, and he or she will be happy to do so. Librarians have access to directories of keywords that can pinpoint information in a way you might not be able to.

Remember, as well, to check reference books such as encyclopedias and biographical and other specialized dictionaries. Such books are useful if you need an overview of your topic.

Periodicals

Periodicals are texts published at regular intervals: daily, weekly, monthly, quarterly, or yearly. They include newspapers, magazines, and academic journals. Some periodicals—mainly newspapers and magazines available at a newsstand— are aimed at the general reader. They are usually published daily, weekly, or monthly. Newsmagazines such as *Time* and *Newsweek,* social-issue magazines such as *Atlantic Monthly* and *Harper's,* and subject specific magazines such as *Psychology Today* and *National Geographic* are some general-audience periodicals you might use while researching an essay. It is possible, though less likely, you would need information from lifestyle magazines such as *Vogue, Cosmopolitan, GQ, Elle,* or *Esquire.*

Many periodicals are for readers with a specific academic interest. They tend to be published quarterly or every other month. Business majors will spend time scanning the pages of the *Harvard Business Review, Journal of Business, Business America, Business and Society, Business Quarterly,* and *Columbia Journal of World Business,* to name a very few of the periodicals in that field. Prospective English teachers will have to familiarize themselves with the *English Journal, Research in the Teaching of English, College Composition and Communication,* and *Teaching English in the Two-Year College.* Physics majors will use the *Journal of Chemical Physics, American Journal of Physics, Journal of Atmospheric and Terrestrial Physics,* and *Trionic Physics* to conduct their research. There are thousands of academic journals, at least one about any topic you can imagine.

Journals are invaluable sources of information for your academic essays. The advantage they have over books is their currency. Because they are published so regularly, the information in them is usually up-to-date.

To find a journal article that will provide you with information you might be able to use in an academic essay, you need to access a search database, such as Google Scholar, JStor, Academic Search Premier, or Wilson Select Plus. By typing key words into the appropriate spaces on these sites, you will be rewarded with a list of articles related to your key word, the journal in which the article is published, and often a link to the entire article which you can then read or, if you think it will an especially valuable research source, print out. These search engines have an invaluable "Advanced Search" option, which allows you to refine your key words or authors' names, limit the nature of your sources to, say, academic journals only, and limit your time range, even to the last few months, if you require the most up-to-date sources.

Web Sources

Through the Internet, you can find the location and availability of the books and periodical articles you need, and, often, especially with articles and increasingly with books, the full text online. You can also find many sources available only online, reference databases such as *Wikipedia*, for example, and, used judiciously, these can provide you with valuable information you might be able to use in your academic writing. You must exercise caution when accessing information online because anyone can publish anything on the Internet. Unfortunately, this includes misinformation and disinformation. Some information on the Internet is biased; some is misleading; some is simply incorrect. You must make certain the website you are using is authoritative.

One clue to a website's trustworthiness is the last three letters of its URL. URLs that end in .gov (for *government*) or .edu (for *education*) are usually trustworthy since their point of origin is typically a university or a government agency. URLs for sites that end in .org (for *organization*) are often biased. The website of the National Rifle Association (www.nra.org) is not a good site on which to look for unbiased information about gun control; the website of Greenpeace (www.greenpeace.org) is not going to give you unbiased information about environmental issues. URLs for sites that end in .com are commercial in nature and often try to sell you something, though there are reputable information sources that end with these letters, for example, *The New York Times* (www.nytimes.com) and *The Wall Street Journal* (www.wsj.com). URLs that end in .htm are usually personal opinion webpages, which are sometimes very biased and unreliable.

A website should not be anonymous; if it is, be somewhat suspicious about its content. Verify that the author is an authority in his or her field before you use the site as a research source. A professor with a Ph.D. affiliated with an accredited university is usually a reliable source of information. The name and address of the university should be included, sometimes in a header or footer. If the site provides any indication that contributions have been *refereed*—that is, screened by an editorial board before being accepted on the site—you can usually be confident the source is valid and reliable. In summary, if you do not have a way of authenticating Internet information, do not use that information in your academic essay.

Ryan is taking a history of music course, and he wants to write his term paper on English madrigal music. His professor spent just one class discussing madrigals, so Ryan's notes are thin. He googles *English madrigal* and at the top of his screen appears the phrase "About 5,040,000 results." Clearly, he has some serious narrowing to do, though he does access the *Wikipedia* information on madrigals, some for YouTube songs, and a couple of potentially useful book titles.

Ryan does a Google Scholar search, checking the "Social Sciences, Arts, and Humanities" box. He narrows his sources down to 15,800. That is obviously still too many, but he scans the first couple of pages and finds some potentially useful articles in such journals as *The Musical Quarterly, Music Review, Music & Letters,* and *Journal of the American Musicological Society.*

Still overwhelmed, Ryan decides to narrow his topic down and write about the music of one prominent English madrigal composer, Thomas Weelkes. A Google search gives Ryan the *Wikipedia* entry on Weelkes; some reference book sources, from *Britannica Online,* for example; and some online performances of some of Weelkes' music. A Google Scholar search gives Ryan leads on potentially good journal articles. Curious about the most recent scholarship on Weelkes' music, Ryan narrows his Google Scholar search down to the past two years, and he gets 58 "hits." He learns that there is a chapter on Weelkes in a recently published book, *A Tudor Miscellany* by D. Trendall and another in a recently published book by M.A. Radice called *Chamber Music: An Essential History.*

Ryan will go to his university library to look for these books and possibly request them through interlibrary loan if his library does not have them. He will also try to access online, and, if they seem especially useful, print out such journal articles as "Thomas Weelkes and the Madrigal," by D.M Arnold, in a 1950 issue of *Music and Letters* and, in a 1972 issue of the same journal "The Two Musical Personalities of Thomas Weelkes," by P. Brett, as well as "Thomas Weelkes: A New Fa-la," by C. Monson from a 1972 issue of *The Musical Times.* If Ryan cannot access them online, he will consult a university librarian who will help him with his research.

Interviews

Research can involve more than words on paper or a computer screen. Interviews can also be excellent sources of information. If you are writing an essay on the benefits and drawbacks of the North American Free Trade Agreement (NAFTA), you might get useful information from participants in a NAFTA conference and the leaders of the protest taking place outside conference headquarters. Interview the author of the novel you are reviewing and you might get insights other critics missed. Interview the local Catholic priest for a perspective on church reform different from the one you are likely to get from articles in *The Globe and Mail.* In some disciplines, especially in the social sciences, interviews are an important source of information.

How do you conduct a successful interview, one that is going to elicit from your subject the kind of information you need? You can take a formal approach and ask your subject specific questions you have prepared in advance.

Alternatively, you can take an informal approach, prepare nothing, and simply engage your subject in a conversation that, you hope, will reveal the information that you need. Or you can choose an in-between approach and conduct a semi-structured interview, one that, although guided by a set of basic questions you need answers to, asks questions in no specific order and encourages responses to evolve into a conversation. The last approach is the most common and generally is considered the most effective.

It is important, if possible, to arrange a specific place where and a time when the interview will take place. Do not expect the interviewees to come to you; instead, meet them at a time and place convenient to them. Tell the interviewees beforehand why you want to interview them and what the questions will be. The meeting will be more relaxed and productive if your subjects know what to expect. Request permission before the interview takes place if you want to record the interview. Avoid engaging your subjects in debate, but don't shy away from tough questions.

Alistair planned to interview one of the leaders of the Occupy Ottawa movement as part of the research he was doing for an essay on the causes and effects of protester violence. He prepared his list of questions and arranged them in order from general to more specific.

- Why have you organized this protest demonstration?
- What do you hope to accomplish?
- Who primarily are you hoping to influence?
- Are you prepared to take forceful action that might disrupt business and inconvenience citizens?
- Do you have any plan to rouse the protestors and encourage violent acts if political leaders ignore your protest?
- Under what circumstances, if any, are you prepared for physical confrontation to get your message heard?

Be polite and solicitous at all times while you conduct your interview, even, especially, if you have reason to be hostile to your subject. Be well prepared. Use the W5+1H heuristic (*who, what, when, where, why*, and *how*) discussed in Chapter 2 to help you generate relevant questions. Assure your interviewees that you will cite the interview appropriately in your essay.

Questionnaires

Researchers, especially social scientists, also acquire information from questionnaires that they distribute, usually to the subjects participating in a study. Questionnaires are a cost-effective method of gathering data, especially now that they are easily distributed via texts and email. It is essential that you define precisely the objectives of the questionnaire before you design and distribute it. Without a clear objective, a questionnaire can contain questions that waste participants' time, complicate the work of the researcher, and compromise the data. Suppose, for example, that a college is considering offering a diploma in technical writing, and the committee proposing the diploma decides to send a questionnaire to potential employers. An objective such as "the purpose of the questionnaire is to determine whether Sundance College should offer a two-year diploma program in technical writing" could result in a cumbersome and unfocused questionnaire that participants are reluctant to complete and return. A clear and specific objective—"the purpose of the questionnaire is to determine whether graduates of a two-year technical writing program at Sundance College could find work within the Tri-City Region"—would generate a shorter and more focused research tool that participants are more likely to respect and respond to.

There are two types of questions a researcher can include on a questionnaire. *Closed format* questions offer participants a choice of answers for each question:

How many technical writers does your company currently employ?

a. none
b. one or two
c. three or four
d. more than four

Open format questions offer participants the chance to provide a brief written response:

Briefly describe the projects your technical writers have participated in during the past twelve months.

With the help of computers and scanners, closed format questions are easy to tabulate and analyze. Open format questions require more time to process but provide richer information for the researchers to use. Most questionnaires use both types, though it is wise to limit open format questions to those that are the most important and relevant to your study. You want as high a response rate as possible, and participants are usually more willing to respond to questionnaires that do not make too many demands on them.

Questions must be clear, succinct, and unambiguous. They should be phrased in such a way as to ensure that all respondents understand the question in the same way. Vague and hypothetical questions rarely elicit useful information. It is better, for example, to ask, "How many technical writers will your company likely be hiring over the next three years?" than to ask, "Do you think all companies need to hire technical writers?" Your questionnaire should include questions that elicit personal information only when such information is crucial to the validity of the results of your study. Responses to these questions should be optional.

For an example of a questionnaire, see the one Zhen designed to acquire information from her classmates on their backpack preferences, page 50.

Incorporating Research

Once you have gathered information from sources—the information that you will use to develop the ideas in your essay—you must decide whether to quote that information just as it appears in the source or to paraphrase it. It is a good strategy to include some direct quotes in a research paper, especially when the quote blends with your own voice and clearly elucidates the point you are making. It is a very poor strategy to use a lot of direct quotes connected together by transitional sentences. This "cut and paste" method yields an essay that is imperfectly organized and dissonant. Too many voices do to an essay what too many cooks do to the broth. It is usually better, then, to paraphrase.

● Direct Quotes

If the information you want to quote directly takes up four lines or fewer in your essay, enclose the quote in quotation marks and integrate it into the text of your essay:

> Nielsen disagrees, insisting that "diplomacy is always worth the risk" and arguing that "a delay of two months does not give a nation without nuclear weapons enough time to acquire them" (35).

If the direct quote is more than four lines, separate it from the rest of the text and do not enclose it in quotation marks, unless the source itself contains them:

> The narrator is typically described as a love-struck adolescent with his first crush on the older sister of his friend. But his anxious intensity suggests that he is more obsessed with Mangan's sister than infatuated with her and his obsession is spiritual in nature:
>
>> Her name sprang to my lips at moments in strange prayers and praises which I myself did not understand. My eyes were often full of tears (I could not tell why) and at times a flood from my heart seemed to pour itself out into my bosom. I thought little of the future. I did not know whether I would speak to her or not or, if I spoke to her, how I could tell her of my confused adoration. But my body was like a harp and her words and gestures were like fingers running upon the wires. (Joyce 62)

● Summarizing

Rather than quote directly, writers of academic papers often summarize or paraphrase a passage from a source. A paraphrase, described on the next page, is a recapitulation of an original passage, expressed in the distinctive voice and style of the essay writer doing the paraphrasing. A summary is simpler. It maintains the style of the original but reduces the original to its essence.

Will is writing a problem/solution essay about rebuilding Haiti, virtually destroyed by natural disasters and corrupt government. Researching the role that humanitarian-minded corporations can play, he reads this paragraph (from Reitman, Janet. "Haiti." *Rolling Stone* (18 Aug. 2011): 60–70. Print.):

> In the absence of government leadership, Digicel has become an influential force in Haiti. The company, which arrived in the country only five years ago, is now its largest taxpayer. It has also built its own infrastructure, outside of the government's purview, constructing roads to and from its various sites and powering its reception towers with generators whose annual diesel costs run into the millions. With more than $400 million invested in Haiti, Digicel is now expanding its brand by building schools, distributing tents, providing cholera-education materials and sponsoring contests to promote Haitian entrepreneurship. Digicel's bright red banners and logos are far more prominent than any other symbol in Haiti—even more, it's often been said, than the Haitian flag. Throughout Port-au-Prince and its refugee camps, Digicel salesmen drawn from the ranks of the homeless operate thriving businesses. (Reitman 70)

In his essay, Will writes:

> One such corporation is Digicel, a cellphone network provider, which has done more for Haiti's economic health than the country's own government. It has provided employment, hiring salespeople who were once homeless. It has build roads and schools. It has distributed tents, provided cholera-education materials, and even sponsored contests to promote Haitian entrepreneurship (Reitman 70). Clothing manufacturing companies have also…

Note that the original contains 138 words, while Will's summary is 31 words. The summary is about a quarter the length of the original, which is about the original-to-summary ratio you want.

● Paraphrasing

Paraphrasing is the process of revising a passage from a written text so that the revised version is written in the manner and style of the paraphraser and not the original author. Writers paraphrase information to make certain that information clearly develops their ideas and to maintain the stylistic integrity—the voice—of their work.

To paraphrase a source effectively, make sure you understand the original completely. Read the original carefully several times; then try to write the paraphrase without consulting the original. In this way, you will be more likely to put the original into your own words and produce a paraphrase that will blend in with your essay clearly and effectively. Then check your paraphrase against the original to make certain you have not altered the meaning of the original. Remember that you want the paraphrased information to blend seamlessly into your own work. Remember too that your paraphrase will often be longer than the original because you might need to establish a context within the paraphrase for your reader. The context often includes the name of the original author, the circumstances under which the author wrote the passage you are paraphrasing, and an explanation, elaboration, or clarification of some of the ideas in the original.

Here is an example of the evolution of an effective paraphrase. Kay was working on an essay about the influence of Bible interpretation on religious reform and wanted to use this information from *Pears Cyclopaedia* (103rd ed.).

> The wholesale vending of indulgences by the papal agents had incensed the people, and when Luther denounced these things he spoke to willing ears. After much controversy, the reformers boldly propounded the principles of the new doctrine and the struggle for religious supremacy grew bitter. They claimed justification (salvation) by faith, and the use as well as the authority of the Scriptures, rejecting the doctrine of transubstantiation, the adoration of the Virgin and Saints, and the headship of the Pope. (J46)

First Kay simply substituted her own words for some of those in the original:

> The selling of absolution from sin by the pope's agents angered the people, and when Luther criticized indulgences the people listened. After much controversy, the reformers touted the principles of the new doctrine and the struggle for religious power grew bitter. Reformers claimed justification (salvation) by faith, and the use as well as the authority of the Bible, rejecting the doctrine of transubstantiation, the worship of the Virgin and Saints, and the supremacy of the Pope.

Kay realized this version did not complement her own writing style and did not support her thesis as strongly as she needed it to. She read the original a few more times then put it aside so her paraphrase would be in her own style and would stress Luther's appeal to the Bible, which is the point most important in defence of her thesis.

> It was not difficult for Luther to undermine the Pope's authority. The people resented the Pope's agents who sold indulgences to the highest bidder. When Luther began to question Papal supremacy, the worship

of the Virgin and the saints, and the doctrine of transubstantiation, the people were predisposed to listen. The struggle grew bitter, but Luther further justified his intransigence by appealing to the authority of the Bible, and, in so doing, won over many converts.

Here are two other original passages followed by effective paraphrases. Study them carefully to get a sense of what you need to do to put someone else's words into your own.

Original

> He that hath wife and children hath given hostages to fortune; for they are impediments to great enterprises, either of virtue or mischief. Certainly the best works and greatest merit for the public have proceeded from the unmarried or childless men: which both in affection and means have endowed the public.
>
> (From "Of Marriage and Single Life" by Francis Bacon)

Paraphrase

Even Francis Bacon, writing some four hundred years ago, denounced the value of family life, advancing the extraordinary argument that family actually inhibits success. A man with a wife and children, wrote Bacon, is less likely to be productive than the single man; indeed, words and deeds that have truly benefited society have come from single or childless men.

Original

> Secondly, the poorer tenants will have something valuable of their own, which by law may be made liable to distress, and help to pay their landlord's rent, their corn and cattle being already seized and money a thing unknown.
>
> (From "A Modest Proposal" by Jonathan Swift)

Paraphrase

Swift's second argument is even more heart-rending. Even the poorest couples, he notes, can have children and will have, therefore, tangible assets which they can sell to pay their rent and other debts. Into this argument Swift injects another attack against the treachery of absentee landlords, attacking their practice of claiming all of the corn and cattle of their tenants without compensation.

Remember that a paraphrase must be cited just as a direct quote from a source is cited. The information does not become yours just because you express it in your own words. You need not acknowledge information about a topic you possessed before you wrote an essay or report about that topic, but you do need to acknowledge all of the information you learned about a topic in the course of writing an essay or report about it.

Plagiarism

If you do not acknowledge all of the sources from which you borrowed information—whether you quoted directly from these sources or paraphrased information—you are likely guilty of the serious academic offence of plagiarism. Plagiarism is the failure on the part of a writer to recognize the work of others. It is the theft of one writer's knowledge or direct written text by another writer, an attempt by one writer to imply to readers that work he has taken from another is actually his own. Because work on such a wide variety of topics is readily available on the Internet, plagiarism has become an increasingly common and serious problem. Fortunately, the Internet is not only a source of the problem but also a source of the solution, since it is as easy for a professor to detect plagiarism through the Internet as it is for a writer to download an essay on the assigned topic. In most schools, plagiarism is punished incrementally: For the first offence, the student fails the assignment; for the second, the course; and for the third, the offending student is at serious risk of being expelled from the college or university.

For a complete definition and discussion of plagiarism, see "Faculty and College Student Beliefs about the Frequency of Student Academic Misconduct" by Hard, Conway, and Moran (*Journal of Higher Education* 7.66, 2006). Here the authors not only define plagiarism, but also identify specific behaviours which constitute plagiarism. You may be guilty of plagiarism if you

- submitted another's material as your own for academic evaluation
- prepared work for another student to submit for academic evaluation
- worked with another student on material to be submitted for academic evaluation when the instructor had not authorized working together
- copied sentences, phrases, paragraphs, tables, figures, or data directly or in slightly modified form from a book, article, or other academic source without using quotation marks or giving proper acknowledgement to the original author or source
- copied information from Internet websites and submitted it as your own work
- bought papers for the purpose of turning them in as your own work

Citing Sources

The extent to which the academic community takes seriously the proper acknowledgement of secondary sources is indicated by the elaborate citation systems it has developed. The Modern Language Association, for example, has a 300-page *MLA Handbook for Writers of Research Papers*, now in its seventh (2009) edition, which explains how to cite sources correctly, if you are writing an essay in the humanities. Similarly, the American Psychological Association publishes a 272-page *Publication Manual of the American Psychological Association*, now in its sixth (2009) edition, which explains how to cite sources correctly if you are writing an essay in the social sciences. The University of Chicago publishes another guide to citing sources, *The Chicago Manual of Style*, now in its sixteenth (2010) edition.

These three methods for citing sources thoroughly and accurately are described in detail in Chapter 8. That chapter also includes two model student essays, one that uses MLA Style and one that uses APA Style.

A Case Study of the Process of Writing an Academic Essay

Researching the Topic

Having reflected upon her topic, the expectations of her reader (her English instructor), and her purpose (basically expository but with a persuasive slant), Zhen is ready to do some research about the criteria students use or should use when they select a backpack.

First, Zhen does a Google search, typing "criteria for purchasing college/university backpack" (without quotation marks, which would return only sources containing that exact phrase) in the search box. She gets millions of hits, but it is easy enough for her to scan the first dozen or so pages and identify the sources that will help her the most. She avoids sources that are clearly irrelevant, commercial sites pushing a specific product, and random blogs. She focuses on sites that seem to be sponsored by reliable consumer agencies, specifically consumersearch. com, bestcovery.com, and universitylanguage.com. She also finds links to several newspaper articles that might prove helpful, though these tend to focus on selecting backpacks for elementary and high-school students. Zhen prints out four articles, listing them now in the prescribed MLA format, so she can simply cut and paste when she is composing her final Works Cited List.

"Backpacks: Full Report: The Best Backpacks for Teens and Adults."
Consumerresearch.com Aug. 2011. n. pag. Web. 22 May 2012.
"Backpacks: Full Report: Top Backpacks for Carrying a Notebook Computer." *Consumerresearch.com* Aug. 2011 n. pag. Web. 22 May 2012.
"Best Backpack for College Students." *Bestcovery.com* n.d. n. pag.
Web. 22 May 2012.
"How to Choose a Backpack for College." *Universitylanguage.com*
13 June 2011. n. pag. Web. 22 May 2012.

Next, Zhen tries a Google Scholar search, using the same keywords she used earlier. However, she restricts her search to the last three years because she wants the most recent information for her essay.

The results of this search surprise her and force her to re-think her approach to her topic. The biggest issue in scholarly backpack research relates to back strain and injury. She had barely considered this point when she began her work, but she realizes that, for an academic essay about backpack selection, this issue will be the most important. Perhaps she will focus on the divide between what students want in a backpack—enough room and lots of pockets and zippers and a cool colour and design—and what they should want—a pack that will not damage their health. Her thesis is likely, now, to be along these lines: College and university students should opt for a backpack that not only looks good, but that also reduces the risk of back and neck injury.

Zhen scans the articles and prints out four that she believes she will cite in her essay:

Heusher, Zachary, David P. Gilkey, Jennifer L. Peel, and Catherine A.
Kennedy. "The Association of Self-Reported Backpack Use and
Backpack Weight with Low Back Pain among College Students."
Journal of Manipulative and Physiological Therapeutics 33.6
(July/August 2010): 432–437. Web. 23 May 2012.
Jayaratne, Kapila, Karen Jacobs, and Dulitha Fernando. "Global
Healthy Backpack Initiatives." *Work: A Journal of Prevention,
Assessment and Rehabilitation* 41 (2012): 5553–5557. Web. 23
May 2012.
Jensen, Daniel B., Jason V. Slack, and Michael Bohne. "What Is the
Average Weight of College Students' Backpacks?" *Proceedings
of the Western Society of Kinesiology and Wellness 55th Annual
Conference*. October 13–15, 2010, Reno, NV. Web. 23 May 2012.

Safikhani, Hassan, Tengku Kamalden, Saidon Bin Amri, and
    Megat Ahmad. "The Effect of Different Backpack Loading
    Systems on Trunk Forward Lean Angle During Walking among
    College Students." *European Journal of Sports and Exercise
    Sciences* 1.1 (2012): 1–5. Web. 23 May 2012.

Zhen does not find, in her college library or on amazon.com, any
books that will help her complete her assignment. Books with "backpack" or "backpacking" in the title are usually about hiking.

Zhen decides she will survey her classmates with a questionnaire
about their own backpack preferences. She asks three questions, leaving
spaces between each question for responses, on the handout she distrib-
utes to her classmates.

- Why did you purchase the backpack you are currently using?
- Why are you satisfied with the choice you made?
- What advice would you give to backpack manufacturers about
  improving their product?

Twenty-seven of the thirty-five students in her class return the questionnaire. The responses tend to confirm Zhen's hunch that size, cost,
look, and features were the main criteria students use when selecting
a backpack. There was more of a focus on durability than Zhen anticipates and a related focus on waterproof fabric, since Zhen's university is
in a rainy city. Three students refer to the importance of back and neck
health. One student is happy with her backpack that has wheels so she
can pull it behind her as well as wear it on her back. One student won-
ders why manufacturers cannot design a backpack that also converts into
a briefcase. A couple of students covet luxury-brand packs. One student
wants a built-in cooler for his beer.

"Criteria for Choosing a College Backpack." Survey. U. Of British
    Columbia. 31 May 2012.

One of the students in Zhen's class tells her he is certain he saw a brief
article in the city newspaper a week or so ago about backpacks and back
health. Zhen searches issues of the paper in her university library and
finds the article easily enough.

Nixdorf, Don. "With All the End-of-Year 'Extras' It's Important to Bal-
    ance Backpack." *Vancouver Sun* 17 May 2012: A12. Print.

Zhen reads her research sources carefully, highlighting sections most
relevant to her essay, making notes in the margins, circling key words.

WRITING ASSIGNMENT

Find some information in popular magazines and on the Internet about one of the following topics. Write an essay of approximately 750 words on the topic you select. (Your instructor might simply want you, at this stage, to gather the information.) Cite correctly the sources you use. See Chapter 8 for more information on citing sources.

- Why _____ is an outstanding (select one) actor, recording artist, talk show host, basketball (or football, hockey, etc.) player, clothing designer, or novelist
- A product I would never buy
- Why soap operas are so popular
- Why mixed martial arts has become such a popular sport

RESEARCH EXERCISES

Select a topic of interest to you. (If you are currently working on an essay for one of your courses, you may use that essay's topic, if your instructor approves.)

1. List five periodicals that are likely to contain information relevant to your topic.
2. Look up your topic in a reference book—in print or online—that includes bibliographies at the end of its entries. Then look up and record the call number of one of the books mentioned in the bibliography. Find the book in the stacks. Read the first chapter of that book and write a brief summary of its contents.
3. Find on the Internet a source of information relevant to your topic. Write a brief summary of its contents.

PARAPHRASING AND SUMMARIZING EXERCISE

Summarize and paraphrase the following passages:

a.

> If we were a people much given to revealing secrets, we might raise monuments and sacrifice to the memories of our poets, but slavery cured us of that weakness. It may be enough, however, to have it said that we survive in exact relationship to the dedication of our poets (include preachers, musicians and blues singers).
>
> (From "Graduation" by Maya Angelou)

b.

> The low cost and lethal convenience of drones—death by remote control—have made them a must-have item for advanced military powers and tin-pot despots alike. The global market for unmanned aerial vehicles is now $6 billion a year, with more than 50 countries moving to acquire

drones. Over the past decade, the military has tested a wide variety of unmanned aircraft—from microdrones that run on tiny batteries to those with 200-foot wingspans, powered by jet fuel or solar energy. The drones used in Iraq and Afghanistan—the Predator and the Reaper—look like large model planes and cost $13 million apiece. A drone the size of a 727, the Global Hawk, was used after the tsunami in Japan and the earthquake in Haiti to provide rescue operations with a bird's eye view of the disasters. One of the largest drones in development today is the SolarEagle, designed by Boeing and DARPA, the experimental research wing of the Defense Department. With a wingspan of more than 400 feet, the SolarEagle will be able to stay in the air for five years at a time, essentially replacing surveillance satellites, which are costly to put into orbit.

(From "The Drone Wars" by Michael Hastings. *Rolling Stone* 26 Apr. 2012: 42–47, 82.)

c.

But every blessing brings its own curse. In this case, many of the wrong word errors appear to be the result of spell-checker suggestions. A student trying to spell "frantic," for example, apparently accepted the spell-checker's suggestion of "fanatic." Wrong word, for sure. In addition, some students seem to be using a thesaurus feature without also using a dictionary to understand the nuances of meaning for various words—"artistic," for example, when "aesthetic" is the appropriate choice. Still other wrong word mistakes seem to result from choosing a word that has a somewhat similar sound: "concur" rather than "conclude" or "analyses" rather than analyzes." Finally, many wrong words seem to come from the simple failure to proofread: writing "begging" for "beginning" is no doubt such a case in point.

(From "Mistakes Are a Fact of Life" by Andrea and Karen Lunsford. *College Composition and Communication* 59.4 (June 2008): 781–806.)

d.

With his commission revoked by the governor of Cuba, Cortés arrived on the mainland as a rebel against both the governor of Cuba and the king of Spain. Much of what he did concerning the great Aztec Empire was an attempt to justify his initial act of insubordination and win back royal support. Cortés burned his ships so that his troops were forced to go with him. Then he founded the city of Vera Cruz, whose town government, which was his own creation, offered him a new commission to proceed inland to Tenochtitlán. He quickly found allies among native groups that for their own reasons wished to see the Aztec Empire destroyed.

(From *Western Civilization: The Continuing Experiment*, by Thomas F. X. Noble et al., Houghton Mifflin, 1999)

COLLABORATIVE ACTIVITY

Working with two or three classmates in a small group, design a questionnaire for a study designed to help solve a problem—parking, traffic, crime, recreation—at your college or university or in the community it serves. Establish a clear objective for the study and identify the group or individuals to whom you would send the questionnaire.

CHAPTER 4

Make a Plan

In this book, planning follows thinking and researching as steps in the writing process, and most writers probably do most of their planning at this point. But planning really begins when you annotate your assignment sheet and choose a topic, and it continues while you write and revise your essay. Always remember that planning an academic essay is an ongoing process, not a single step along the road to the production of a text. You likely will alter your plan as you draft and revise your essay because the drafting and revising processes often stimulate the production of additional ideas and information that you might want to incorporate into your essay. Your plan is made of clay, not granite. You will want to mold it throughout the writing process to change it as you discover new insights into and new information about your topic.

Planning is an important component of the writing process. It is at this point that a writer begins to decide what information needs to be included and establishes the order in which that information can be presented most effectively. I say "begins to decide" because good writers continue to consider content and order as they write; they may add, delete, or reorder information. All of these decisions—what to include, what order to present information in, what to change while drafting is underway—depend upon the writer's commitment to fulfilling her purpose and meeting the needs and expectations of her readers.

Many writers at the planning point in the process produce a point-form summary of the main ideas and supporting ideas they want to include in their essay. Some writers produce a detailed plan in complete sentences divided into any number of headings and subheadings; some writers produce a brief, point-form plan. You can use a system of numbers and letters or simple dashes and indentations to indicate main headings and subheadings.

The discussion in Chapter 2 on reflecting on the purpose for writing points out that academic essays usually are written either in the expository (also known as the informative) or the argumentative (also known as the persuasive) modes, though the two modes often overlap in, for example, a compare/contrast essay. The dominant mode you choose will influence your plan:

- an expository essay
- a compare/contrast essay
- an argumentative essay

Planning an Expository Essay

In Chapter 2, you learned about the various developmental patterns for expository academic essays: process analysis, cause and/or effect, compare/contrast, analysis/interpretation, problem/solution. The outline you develop as a prewriting activity (remember, your outline will evolve as you draft and revise) will depend upon the developmental pattern you choose, which, in turn, will depend upon the way in which your topic is presented. If, for example, the topic on your assignment sheet reads "Explain how and why the Polar Bear became an endangered species and discuss what needs to be done to ensure its survival," your outline will be based upon a problem/solution format: Here is the problem (the Polar Bear is becoming extinct); here are the solutions (end global warming, protect its habitat, do more research; start a fund-raising campaign).

Remember also that an essay might require more than one developmental pattern. If, for example, your topic is the role of complex carbohydrates in a well-balanced diet, you are writing primarily an effects essay: How do complex carbohydrates affect diet and nutrition? But certainly you need to invoke other patterns of development as you compose and revise. Definition is one important aspect of the essay in that you have to define key terms such as *calorie, carbohydrate,* and *fibre.* The details/examples pattern is another important aspect of the essay in that you have to provide *examples* of foods that contain complex carbohydrates and add *details* about the chemical and nutritional content of these foods, before describing how these foods affect human metabolism.

Planning a Compare/Contrast Essay

The compare/contrast essay, in which you are asked to discuss the similarities and differences between two related subjects (two literary works, two economic systems, two political systems, two psychological theories, two marketing strategies) is commonly assigned in college and university courses because it requires students to master two aspects of course content: to analyze each and then to establish some form of synthesis between them. It demands a higher level of thinking than some other expository modes do. There are two ways of organizing a compare/contrast essay: the common traits method or the similarities/differences method.

The **common traits method** is the best method to use if you are writing primarily an informative essay, one in which you want to point out similarities and differences between two entities without suggesting that one is superior to the other. If you are comparing and contrasting two cities, for example, you might isolate common traits of climate, ethnic diversity, and architecture and discuss each trait in the context of the two cities. Mei Ying was comparing and contrasting the talk patterns of men and women. She wanted to compare the reasons why men talk with the reasons why women do; the places women tend to talk with the places men do; and what women talk about with what men do. After reflecting upon her topic and doing some research, Mei Ying developed the following working plan:

Thesis: Men and women communicate in essentially different ways and are often at odds with each other as a result.

I. Why men and women talk

A. Women to build bridges, establish cooperation, negotiate relationships—to form bonds with others.

B. Men not to distance themselves from others but to preserve independence—talk is more competitive—talk to negotiate and maintain status.

II. Where men and women talk

A. Women more communicative at home, on the phone, around the breakfast table

B. Men more silent at home—stereotypically buried behind their laptop at the breakfast table—their silence a source of frustration to wives, as wives' chatter a source of distraction to men—men more communicative in public

III. What men and women talk about

A. Women of internal matters—share secrets, discuss relationships, personal appearance—use personal anecdotes to support an argument

B. Men of external matters—sports—more likely to tell jokes in public—use logic to defend argument and find women's argumentative style inadequate—believe many of the things women talk about unworthy of the energy it takes to utter them

Conclusion: Men complain that women change topic or shift focus before a conversation is finished; women counter that they need to personalize discussion if it is to resonate with them.

Mei Ying's compare/contrast essay offers no judgment about whose conversational style is superior. That is not her purpose. Her purpose is simply to compare and contrast communicative styles along gender lines and to offer a wide range of examples, often in the form of anecdotes, to support her views. For this reason, she uses the common traits approach, as she reflects upon why and where men and women talk and what they talk about.

The **similarities/differences method** is the best one to use if your compare/contrast essay has a persuasive edge to it, that is, if your purpose is to suggest that one of the two items you are comparing and contrasting is superior to the other. Benazir was planning a compare/contrast essay about the whole-language method and the phonics method of teaching reading to young children. She wanted to convey her opinion that the whole-language method is superior. Here is her plan:

Title: Two Methods of Teaching Children to Read
(Preliminary) Thesis: Educators are divided over how to teach children how to read, though the weight of the evidence now favours the whole-language method.

I. Similarities

    A. Both methods have the same aim

    B. Both methods are validated by research

    C. Most teachers use both methods, at some point

II. Differences

    A. The educational theory underlying each method is different

    B. Children enjoy the whole-language method more

    C. Teachers enjoy teaching the whole-language method more

    D. The whole-language method is more authentic

    E. The whole-language method teaches not only reading but also values and attitudes

Conclusion: While both methods of teaching reading are effective, the whole-language method offers additional benefits that the phonics method does not.

Take a moment to compare the two outlines above. Note that the common traits outline contains three main divisions specifying, without value judgment, the main points. The similarities/differences outline, in contrast, has only two main divisions: how the methods are similar and how they are different. Note that under the "Differences" heading, the persuasive edge emerges, as the writer begins to highlight ways in which the whole-language method is superior. The common traits outline has no such argumentative edge.

Planning an Argument

An argumentative academic essay is a written text that makes a claim or asserts a thesis on an issue about which there is disagreement, provides clear evidence in support of the claim or thesis, and summarizes and refutes evidence in opposition to the claim or thesis. Here we use *argument* and *persuasion* as synonymous terms, though some professors draw a distinction between the two, asserting that an argument does not necessarily urge a change in outlook or behaviour while a persuasion does, and that therefore an argument is more dispassionate than a persuasion. The distinction might be valid, but the qualities of effective persuasions and arguments are similar enough that the two modes can be considered together. The ultimate purpose of a persuasive/argumentative essay is to convince readers that your opinion on an issue is thoughtful and reasonable and therefore valid.

Arguing convincingly and persuasively is an art that requires careful planning and a good knowledge of various argumentative strategies. An argument is more complex than an exposition. Both arguments and expositions assert a thesis and present details, facts, anecdotes, statistics, causes, effects, comparisons, contrasts, and examples in a series of paragraphs in support of that thesis. Both cite authoritative sources to support and develop a thesis. But an argument has a different purpose. While the expository academic essay informs and teaches, the argument attempts to convince readers of the validity of one side of an issue and—equally important—the invalidity of the other side; in its persuasive incarnation, it may urge readers to change their own minds, even commit themselves to a course of action. To present a convincing case, an argumentative academic essay takes shape in a way an exposition does not.

To support an expository thesis, for example, you have to present all important and relevant information. When you write an argument, you must not be deceptive, but you can be selective in the information you present to strengthen your case, stressing those points that strongly support your thesis and downplaying those that do not. Brenda was writing an essay expressing her opposition to the Canadian seal hunt. In the course of her research, she discovered how important the hunt is as a food source for the Inuit, and she learned that an overpopulation of seals might threaten the fishing industry. She did not ignore this information, but she tried to downplay its significance, pointing out that exceptions might be made for certain groups under certain circumstances and that the damage to the fishing industry is speculative.

In addition, argumentative essays often include an emotional appeal, rarely part of an exposition. You can sway an audience by appealing to its emotions. In the anti-seal hunt essay she was writing, for example, Brenda included heart-rending descriptions of the inhumane ways seal pups are killed and sometimes left to bleed to death. There is a fine balance here, of course. Emotional appeals must be measured. If you are too dramatic and too sentimental, your chances of alienating your readers become greater than your chances of winning them over.

Finally, an argument includes an acknowledgement and refutation of the opposing point of view, which an exposition does not. You might think that you weaken your argument if you openly admit that there is another side to your case, but in fact you strengthen it. If you do not admit it openly, your readers will still know that there is. They will conclude that you are afraid to raise those issues that weaken your argument; you will lose credibility; and the strength of your case will diminish. This strategy of acknowledging the opposition also strengthens the voice of your essay. You appear fair, honest, and trustworthy, and you (and therefore your argument) are more likely to be taken seriously. And remember that you are acknowledging the opposition in order to refute it, so you are supporting, not undermining, your thesis.

Dwight wanted to present an argument defending Black Liberation Theology against charges that it is a racist and divisive movement within the Christian church, against charges that it is, in fact, anti-Christian. He talked about the success that BLT churches have had recruiting new members at a time when attendance rates at most Christian churches are declining precipitously. He described the many successful programs BLT churches sponsored to feed the homeless, raise scholarship money so minority students could attend college and university, and build affordable housing. He pointed out that BLT churches preached against sexual promiscuity and praised the sanctity of the family, both important Christian values. He did not shy away from criticisms that the rhetoric coming from the pulpits of BLT churches was often incendiary and anti-white, nor did he deny that such rhetoric is a part of the culture of Black Liberation Theology churches. Instead, he made the elegant argument that the pastors were using a tried-and-true rhetorical strategy—hyperbole—less to provoke white rage or even prove their arguments than to underscore their passion for reform. He further refuted the opposing position by making the clever case that the Black Liberation Theology sermon is a form of theatre, a one-act-play, which the parishioners recognize and accept as creative non-fiction. Dwight made a strong case for his thesis and buttressed it further by acknowledging and refuting the opposing point of view.

A strong argument, then, requires not only solid facts, evidence, statistics, examples, and details but also a strategy for planning and for presenting such information in a way that maximizes its credibility. Some leading philosophers and scholars have developed sophisticated systems of presenting the kind of evidence writers need to develop and support an argument. Some basic knowledge of these systems will help you gather the information you need to argue effectively and to plan a strategy for presenting the information clearly and will suggest methods of conveying that information convincingly.

● Aristotle: Logos, Ethos, Pathos

Aristotle believed that an effective arguer uses logic and reason to support and advance his case, conveys an impression of trustworthiness and sincerity to win his audience's respect and attention, and appeals to his audience's feelings and emotions to draw them in on a personal level to support the position he is advancing. Logos, ethos, pathos—these are the three foundations of an effective Aristotelian or classical argument.

Logos

To Aristotle, an effective argument is a logical argument. A logical argument presents evidence, refutes opposing viewpoints, and avoids logical fallacies. A logical argument incorporates statistics, facts, and quotes from experts to convince readers of the veracity of the writer's thesis. It also anticipates and avoids errors in logic, which undermine the evidence the writer is presenting. **Logical fallacies**—that is, errors in logic—usually present overly simple arguments in support of complex problems or insufficient evidence in support of a point.

Hasty Generalization

Suppose, for example, you are a new student in the College of Education, and you have gone to your first two classes. The professors in both classes are not exactly lively and inspiring. You email your friend, telling him that education professors are all dull. You have a flaw in logic here, usually known as the **hasty generalization**. You have drawn a conclusion, made a general statement, based on insufficient evidence. You cannot generalize based on a sample size of two.

Post Hoc Ergo Propter Hoc

An editorial in a national newspaper argues for a ban on violent video games such as Grand Theft Auto because a fifteen-year-old boy hijacked a car and threatened the driver with a handgun right after playing the game. The game might have been one factor, but usually a complex set of experiences, behaviours, and personality traits causes serious crime. You cannot argue that the game *caused* the crime. This logical fallacy is called **post hoc ergo propter hoc**, which in Latin means "after this, therefore because of this." You can argue that one event or action contributed or may have contributed to another, but avoid claiming that one event or action caused another.

False Analogy

Suppose you argue that all exams should be open-book because, in the real world, doctors, lawyers, business people, and others must consult books in order to do their work effectively, and one of the purposes of a post-secondary education is to prepare students for the real world. This is a **false analogy**. College or university prepares students for the real world, but *it* is not the real world. A test measures knowledge more than it measures the ability to perform a certain task. To equate surgery, say, to a written exam is to make an inaccurate comparison, to draw a false analogy.

Ad hominem

You oppose a Member of Parliament's proposal to increase the level of government-funded health care to First Nations children because that MP is

First Nations and an NDP MP. This is a common logical fallacy known as **ad hominem**, which is Latin for "against the man." Instead of dealing with the argument, you preempt any discussion by basically saying, "I cannot listen to anyone who does not share my social and political values." You indeed may decide you don't like the argument the MP is making, but it is your job to poke holes in the argument, not to engage in a personal attack.

Straw Man

A similar logical fallacy is known as the **straw man**. Suppose, for example, you are making the case for your belief that the spirits of dead people can continue to communicate with the living. As part of your argument, you claim that people who don't share your views are atheists. It is likely true that atheists have problems believing in a spiritual existence after death, but not true that only atheists disagree with you. Nor is it relevant. It is an attempt to run away from opponents by pretending they are insubstantial people—straw men. An effective argument does not deflect or avoid opponents but acknowledges and confronts them.

Either/Or Fallacy

The military dictator of a third-world country defends his management style by arguing that denying a few freedoms is better than anarchy. This is an example of the **either/or fallacy**, which suggests that there are only two solutions to a problem and that it is better to choose the lesser of the two evils. Obviously, there are several systems of government that fall between the extremes of dictatorship and anarchy.

Slippery Slope

You argue against drilling for oil in environmentally sensitive areas of Canada, claiming that next mining companies will demand mining rights, then hydroelectric companies will insist on building dams, and soon the Canadian wilderness will be destroyed. This is the **slippery slope** fallacy. Rather like the post hoc fallacy, it illogically implies a series of inevitable and drastic consequences that result from an action or policy. Unless you have evidence that mining engineers are preparing to petition the government the moment oil companies get permission to drill, avoid this "where will it all end?" strategy.

Note that a logical fallacy is not necessarily factually incorrect, and that a claim that is logically fallacious is not one that should automatically be eliminated from your argument. An addiction to video games might, indeed, influence behaviour. A First Nations Member of Parliament will likely be sympathetic to First Nations causes. But exercise caution if you are making a point that is developed only with an argument that might be logically inconsistent or unsupported. In other words, the potential fallacy can be evaded with supporting information: "In his own written statement, Eric admitted that his addiction to Grand Theft Auto influenced his decision to turn fantasy into reality…."

Ethos

Aristotle also believed that an effective argument is an ethical argument. An ethical argument is calm, firm, but rational, and conveys a sense of respect for the readers' intelligence and for the opposing point of view; an unethical argument is loud and obnoxious, angry, shrill, flippant, even abusive, and it usually alienates more than it impresses readers. When you raise your voice, the old saying goes, you have lost the argument. The essence of an ethical argument is its voice; an effective arguer speaks or writes in the voice of a wise and reasonable—an ethical—person.

Note, for example, the voice or tone of Cindy Blackstock's essay, "The Canadian Human Rights Tribunal on First Nations Child Welfare: Why If Canada Wins, Equality and Justice Lose" in Part Two. Blackstock is clearly passionate about her cause and her passion comes through, but she carefully, rationally, and calmly presents her case, referencing scholarly articles, court decisions, and personal experience in support of her thesis. Her essay, especially the "I Am a Witness" sub-section, also illustrates how a restrained appeal to pathos can bolster an argument.

Pathos

Finally, an effective argument evokes some emotion from its readers. Describe the harsh beauty of the Alaskan wilderness and the wildlife threatened by oil exploration, and you help sway your readers to your point of view. Tell the touching story of a lonely widow comforted by a medium who put her in touch with the spirit of her departed husband, and you win your readers' sympathy and, hence, their attention. In classical argument, pathos, as long as it is measured, is an appropriate and effective rhetorical strategy.

For example, in his essay in Chapter 8 about saving the Vancouver Island marmot, Adam Black describes the physical appearance of the marmot, using an emotional appeal as an argument in support of its survival. "The Vancouver Island marmot," Adam writes, "is blessed with great looks, covered as it is in rich chocolate-brown fur broken with patches of white. People tend to react to posters and television images of the marmot the same way they do when an adorable puppy scratches at their feet." Such emotional appeals are common in papers about endangered species. The text is often accompanied by photographs. A photo of a baby polar bear, tentatively jumping off an ice flow into arctic water or of a baby panda playing with its siblings tug at the heart strings and strengthen the author's thesis.

● Toulmin: Claim, Support, Warrant

A modern rhetorician, Stephen Toulmin, asserts that a sound argument consists of three parts: the claim, the support, and the warrant. The claim is synonymous with the thesis; it is the argument's controlling idea, its main point. Toulmin's system has three types of claim. The claim can be expressed as a fact, for example:

> Professional hockey players are more prone to concussions than any other professional athletes are.
>
> Iran's nuclear program is a direct threat to Israel and an indirect threat to peace throughout the Middle East.

Note that these are claims of fact; they need to be proved. The claim may be expressed as a value judgment:

> *The Descendants,* not *The Artist,* should have won the Academy Award for best picture of 2011.
>
> Iran, under the Shah, was a more prosperous and democratic country than it is today.

Or the claim may be a statement of public policy:

> The Liberal Party should select a woman to challenge Saskatchewan's current premier.
>
> Canada should adopt a more isolationist policy in its relationships with other nations.

The **support** (or, as it is also known, the grounds) consists of the facts, details, statistics, comparisons, contrasts, causes, effects, emotional appeals, and refutations of opposing arguments that the writer marshals and presents in support of the claim. To support the claim that hockey players are more prone to concussions than other athletes are, the writer needs to provide examples, compare and contrast with other sports the nature of the body contact in hockey, consider the impact of ice over grass or AstroTurf, discuss the uniforms and protective equipment athletes wear, or compile some medical evidence on sports injuries—concussions especially—and individual sports. To provide grounds for the claim that *The Descendants* should have won the Academy Award for best picture, the writer needs to compare its merits with those of other nominated films, especially *The Artist,* which beat it. She might try to convince readers that *The Descendants* is a complex film about family values and relationships, its serious tone lightened with humour, while *The Artist* for all of its cleverness is gimmicky and superficial. To provide grounds for the claim that Canada should return to an isolationist foreign policy, the writer needs to lay out the foreign policy as it currently is, point out its weaknesses, discuss the advantages gained from isolationism under previous administrations, and speculate on the advantages present day Canada would realize if it were less interventionist. In the Toulmin system, as in classical arguments, the support is the main focus of the essay's body paragraphs.

The **warrant** is an assumption underlying the claim: Head injuries are a concern for professional athletes; Iran is building a nuclear bomb; the Academy Award should reward the best among those who compete for it; nations should be prosperous and democratic; women have been unfairly underrepresented in races for high political office; current Canadian foreign policy is flawed. Toulmin believed that an effective argument obviously defends its claim, but it might also have to defend its warrant. The decision depends upon the warrant's level of general acceptability. The warrant that states that certain professional athletes are at risk for head injuries is undeniable and does not need defending. The warrant that implies an Academy Award recognizes the best is shaky, in that some readers might see it as an award for the most popular or as a victory for a film studio's marketing campaign. The writer making this claim needs to include in her essay some defence of the warrant that underlies it. The warrant that states that women have been unfairly underrepresented in races for high political office likely needs to be defended as well.

The defence of the warrant is what distinguishes Toulmin's system from the others. Such a defence can cap an already strong argument and strengthen one that is in need of extra ammunition.

● Rogerian Argument

Carl Rogers was a contemporary of Toulmin, but he advocated a different argumentative strategy. Both Toulmin and Aristotle believed that a solid argument addresses the opponent's point of view by showing respect for it, making a fair presentation of its points, and then following it by a firm and direct refutation. Respect and recognition of the opposition is one part of both the Toulmin and the classical argument. But it is the essence of Rogerian argument. By background a humanistic psychologist, Rogers believed that "empathetic listening" is the key to effective argument. Before a writer presents a thesis, before he presents evidence in support of his thesis, he must take the time to illustrate the extent to which he understands and respects the opposing position. Empathy builds mutual understanding and respect and motivates readers to consider opinions contrary to their own.

A Rogerian argument, then, typically begins by establishing common ground, by indicating the values, beliefs, attitudes, and ideals—insofar as they relate to the issue that forms the subject of the essay—that the writer shares with readers. Next, the writer presents her position objectively, in a way that suggests it is a widely shared view, threatening to no one, and worthy of some consideration. And, unlike the classical and Toulmin arguments, which typically begin with a thesis, the Rogerian argument typically ends with the thesis. The Rogerian thesis usually implies that the writer has made considerable concessions to the opposition, while expressing hope that the opposition will return the courtesy and consider the writer's point of view.

Keith was crushed when his baseball team lost the seventh game of the world series because of what was, in his opinion, a wrong call by the home plate umpire, who gave a batter a walk on a ball four that the replay, aided by computer technology, showed to be a third strike. His thesis for his persuasive essay assignment was "Computers are far more accurate than human sight and should replace the home plate umpire for calling balls and strikes in baseball." Keith knew a change as dramatic as the one he proposed would rock the baseball establishment and outrage the many fans who would argue that home plate umpires have called baseball pitches since the middle of the nineteenth century and that errors are a part of the game and that bad calls, in the long run, benefit and penalize teams equally. He therefore selected the Rogerian method to make his argument. He assured readers of his love of and respect for the history of the game. He talked about his own experience as a player good enough to earn a sports scholarship to a Kansas university. He has friends who are baseball umpires. He admitted that there are studies that suggest that the accuracy rate of baseball umpires is about 80 percent. In Rogerian argument fashion, Keith tried to anticipate and mollify the virulent opposition he knew his arguments would face. He then calmly advanced his own argument, noting that the increased speed and curvature of pitches in the modern game make it more difficult for umpires to see them; that other sports are using technology more often to make important calls; that as a catcher himself he is more aware than others of umpire fallibility. In the end, again in true Rogerian fashion, he does not recommend a sudden and dramatic change in the way the game is officiated. He recommends his solution be tried for one season or in a minor league, that the results be assessed, and that a decision be rendered thereafter.

Audience and Purpose in Argument

You have, then, at least three strategies to draw upon as you plan your argumentative academic essay. Which one should you choose? The answer depends, as it usually does in academic writing, on your audience and purpose. Your professor might specify the form she wants your argument to take. If she does not, however, consider your purpose, the implications of your thesis, and your commitment to it. If you feel strongly about an issue and know you are directing your argument to a neutral audience, you probably should use a classical strategy as you plan your work. If you want to convince your readers, for example, that America's borders should be more open, that it should be easier for Mexican citizens to immigrate to the United States, you need to advance a logical argument expressed in the voice of a reasonable but authoritative person. And you want to include the appeal to pathos that the classical mode recommends. Stories about Mexicans living in poverty and dying in their attempts to cross the border illegally bolster your argument.

If you need to convince your readers that your warrant is valid, choose the Toulmin system. If, for example, you want to convince your readers that, even though Spanish is widely used now in business and social interaction, the United States should make English its official language, your warrant is that a country runs more efficiently and its citizenry are happier and more productive when there is only one official language. Since there are several liberal democratic countries, such as Canada, with more than one official language, this warrant is challengeable, and you should discuss ways bilingual countries are disadvantaged by their language policies.

If you know you have a hostile and defensive audience, one that needs to be won over before it will listen, go with the Rogerian method. If, for example, you want to make the case that Canada should abolish its allegiance to the monarchy, you are in for a fight, and you will have to assure your readers of your patriotism and your respect for the nation's history as you make your case.

Of course, you can also use any combination of the three systems, taking the most useful strategy from each one as you plan and draft your argument.

Walt saw the 2011 film *Anonymous* and was intrigued by the possibility that Edward de Vere, 17th Earl of Oxford, and not William Shakespeare was the author of the plays and poems attributed to Shakespeare. Doing more research, he became convinced there was something to the theory and chose to write his argument essay on this topic. Knowing how hostile some readers, likely including his instructor, would be, he took a page from Carl Roger's book and included (See Part E of his outline, below)an expression of empathy and understanding for those readers who think it is sacrilege to cast any doubts upon Shakespeare's reputation.

Title: Alias William Shakespeare: The Case for the de Vere Authorship
Thesis: Significant evidence exists indicating that Edward de Vere is the real author of the great plays and poems attributed to William Shakespeare.

A. The author had a classical education and an insider's knowledge of the court
   1. Shakespeare's background and education
   2. de Vere's background and education

B. de Vere artifacts
   1. The de Vere Bible contains annotated and underlined passages found in the plays
   2. The de Vere coat of arms an English lion shaking a broken spear

C. Characters in the plays
  1. Hamlet, Falstaff, Lear, and Prospero have experiences strikingly similar to some of de Vere's own
  2. Polonious as Lord Burghley
  3. Helena as Anne Cecil

D. Sonnets
  1. The story the sonnets tell mirrors de Vere's own life
  2. The characters in the sonnets resemble people he knew

E. Refute opposition
  1. De Vere hid his authorship because it was unseemly for aristocrats to be too involved in the theatre
  2. The dating of the plays is uncertain so the fact that de Vere died in 1604 does not prove he did not write plays allegedly written after his death

Conclusion: The case for de Vere is strong and will grow stronger as more about de Vere's life is discovered.

Note the comprehensiveness of this outline. Walt offers four points in support of his thesis. Then he acknowledges and refutes opposing viewpoints in a way that provides him with a fifth point in support of his thesis. Note how direct and unequivocal the thesis is: The author leaves his readers without any doubts about the position his essay will defend. The conclusion promises even more evidence in support as more details about de Vere's life are uncovered.

Planning is an important part of writing a sound academic essay. Do not, however, get locked into a formal, carefully structured plan early in your process of writing your essay—a plan should be fluid and flexible. Early in the writing process, you might feel the need to design a careful, formal plan for your essay. But allow your plan to change as you write your essay. Writing is, among many things, a process of discovery, and you might discover a more effective way of organizing and presenting your thoughts and ideas as you work through successive drafts of your essay. You might have a fresh insight or discover a good research source that contains information that will strengthen your paper. Be willing to alter your plan as you work. If your professor wants you to hand in a plan or outline of your essay with the essay itself, compose that final version of your outline later rather than earlier in the process.

Keep in mind, also, the extent to which the rhetorical mode you are writing in will shape and determine your structure. There are at least two ways to shape a compare/contrast essay and at least three ways to build an effective argument. Choose the structure that will most effectively engage your readers and help you realize your purpose.

A Case Study of the Process of Writing an Academic Essay

Making a Plan

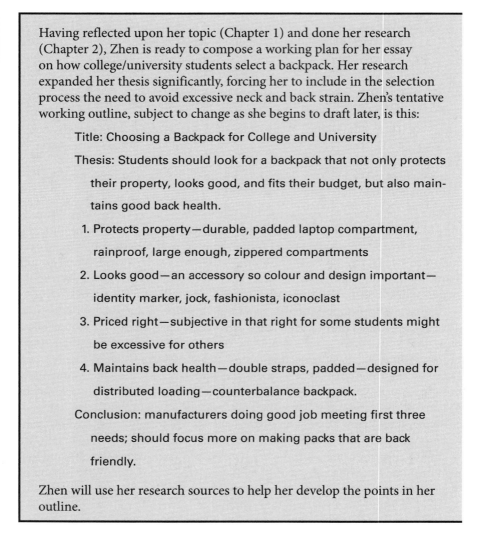

Having reflected upon her topic (Chapter 1) and done her research (Chapter 2), Zhen is ready to compose a working plan for her essay on how college/university students select a backpack. Her research expanded her thesis significantly, forcing her to include in the selection process the need to avoid excessive neck and back strain. Zhen's tentative working outline, subject to change as she begins to draft later, is this:

Title: Choosing a Backpack for College and University

Thesis: Students should look for a backpack that not only protects their property, looks good, and fits their budget, but also maintains good back health.

1. Protects property—durable, padded laptop compartment, rainproof, large enough, zippered compartments

2. Looks good—an accessory so colour and design important—identity marker, jock, fashionista, iconoclast

3. Priced right—subjective in that right for some students might be excessive for others

4. Maintains back health—double straps, padded—designed for distributed loading—counterbalance backpack.

Conclusion: manufacturers doing good job meeting first three needs; should focus more on making packs that are back friendly.

Zhen will use her research sources to help her develop the points in her outline.

WRITING ASSIGNMENT

Select one of the following topics on a current social issue or a different issue of interest to you if that topic is not included on the list. Make sure your topic, if you select your own, is not too broad. Note that this assignment calls for a persuasive/argumentative essay.

Find and read carefully two books, two print articles, and two online articles about the topic you have selected. Write an essay of approximately 1000 words on this topic. Cite correctly at least four of the six sources you have consulted. (At this stage, your instructor might ask only for the plan or outline for this assignment.) See Chapter 8 for information on citing sources correctly.

Submit the plan of your essay along with your finished product. Remember that you likely will begin with a tentative plan but compose the final plan of your essay only after you have finished writing.

- Why _____ has become an endangered species and what we need to do to save it
- Oil companies should or should not drill for oil in the wilderness of Alaska
- School vouchers are or are not a good idea
- Gay/lesbian couples should or should not enjoy all of the same rights heterosexual couples enjoy
- Hate crimes should or should not be punished any more severely than crimes motivated by homophobia or racism
- The tactics of some environmental groups are counterproductive
- We would all be healthier if we didn't eat meat
- The lyrics of some popular songs need to be censored by the government
- Mothers with children under five should not work outside of the home
- English should (should not) be, by law, the official language of the United States

EXERCISES

1. In a magazine you enjoy reading, find an example of an informative essay that you think is well written. Compose a plan from which the author might have worked. Identify the thesis, the points the author makes to support or develop the thesis, and the points the author uses to develop each main idea.
2. In a magazine you enjoy reading, find an example of an argumentative essay that you think is well written. Determine the argumentative method—classical, Toulmin, Rogerian, or a combination—that the writer uses. Write a two-paragraph assessment of the effectiveness of the argument.
3. Freewrite for ten to fifteen minutes on one of the topics listed in the writing assignment above. Then turn the product of your freewriting into a preliminary outline for an essay.

COLLABORATIVE ACTIVITY

Design an essay topic related to your major or to the discipline you are considering majoring in. Share your topic with others in a small group of two or three. Together develop a preliminary plan for each topic you and your group members have selected.

CHAPTER 5

Write a Draft

In theory, writing the "rough draft" of an essay is a fairly simple process of fleshing out the plan. In reality, it is not simple at all, because writers often modify the plan of the essay as they draft. They also edit and revise *while*, not just *after*, they draft. But drafting does have a primary focus, and that focus is the paragraph. By all means, alter your outline and edit and revise as you draft, but focus your attention at this point on the writing process involved in composing

- a clear and specific opening
- complete body paragraphs
- explicit conclusions

Write a Clear and Specific Opening

First impressions are important in academic writing. You want to write an introductory paragraph (or paragraphs, if your assignment is a major research paper) that will engage your readers' interest and encourage them to continue reading. You must also clearly establish the topic of your paper in your opening paragraph or paragraphs so that the context of your thesis is clear. Finally, you must present the thesis, which often will appear at the end of your introductory paragraph, though it may be implied instead of stated explicitly in a single sentence. Let's look at five examples of introductions to academic essays and judge, discuss, and analyze the effectiveness of these paragraphs based on the three criteria mentioned above:

- Does it engage the readers' interest?
- Does it clearly establish the topic?
- Does it present the thesis?

● Sample Introductory Paragraphs

Sample Introductory Paragraph 1: Aisha

Drones have become the most powerful weapon in the American military arsenal. Used sparingly in 2003, during the invasion of Iraq, drones are used now to gather intelligence, drop bombs on hostile enemy targets and patrol the Mexican border. They are technological marvels, which allow an air force to subdue a terrified enemy, without risk to the "pilots" who can control a drone from anywhere. But they are far from infallible, and they have been responsible already for the death of many civilians and other innocent victims. They kill by remote control, absolving their operators, some of whom compare the experience to playing a video game (Hastings 41), from any pang of guilt or remorse human pilots might feel.

Analysis

Aisha is pleased enough with the opening paragraph of her essay, expressing her ambivalent views about the American military's use of drones. It's an interesting topic, and she feels her thesis engages her readers' interest, but she feels her paragraph might be bland, given the explosive nature of her topic. She recalls a line from a Yeats' poem she had to read in high school—"A terrible beauty is born"—and she is struck by how applicable it is to the use of drones. She also feels her paragraph could use some more dramatic details. She revises as follows:

Drones, highly sophisticated unmanned aircraft, have become the most widely used weapon in the American military arsenal, which now deploys about 19,000 of them (Hastings 42). Used sparingly in 2003, during the invasion of Iraq, drones are used now to gather intelligence, drop bombs on hostile enemy targets, and patrol the Mexican border. They are a terrible beauty, sleek and off-white, but spooky with that single cold pulsing eye where a pilot in a cockpit used to sit. They are technological marvels that allow an air force to subdue a terrified enemy without risk to the "pilots," who control a drone, cocooned in the safety of a military base. But they are far from infallible, and they have already killed innocent civilians. They kill by remote control, absolving their operators, some of whom have admitted the process is like playing a video game (Hastings 41), from the pang of guilt and remorse which might restrain the excesses of a human pilot.

Sample Introductory Paragraph 2: Maureen

No composer influenced Mozart's work more than the music of Johann Sebastian Bach. Around 1782, living in Vienna, Mozart, then twenty-five, first heard Bach's music. Immediately he began to blend Bach's style and technique with his own. The result was the birth of a new musical style, which has come to be known as Viennese classical.

Analysis

Introductory paragraph 2 should engage the interest of most readers since the music of Mozart and Bach has such universal appeal. Maureen has also established a clear context for her topic. But what exactly is the essay's thesis? Will she now describe in detail the nature of the influence, tell her readers about the Viennese classical style, or do some combination of both? The paragraph has potential, but it seems somewhat anemic. Another sentence at the end is required to clearly establish the essay's thesis and to provide the reader with a sense of the direction the essay will be taking. Compare the following with the original:

> No music influenced Mozart's work more than the music of Johann Sebastian Bach. Around 1782, living in Vienna, Mozart, then twenty-five, first heard Bach's music. Immediately he began to blend Bach's style and technique with his own. The result was the birth of a new musical style, which has come to be known as Viennese classical. It is characterized by complex melodies and harmonies, which, paradoxically, create a lighter and more joyous impression, evident especially in the sonatas and four-movement symphonies Mozart composed in the latter part of his career.

Sample Introductory Paragraph 3: Alan

> The stars in our sky, revealing themselves to us on a clear dark night, appear randomly scattered. There are large gaps where few stars appear and occasional clusters of many stars grouped together. It is as if some divine presence has filled his two hands with many-pointed sparkling rocks and thrown them into the night sky where they have stuck. In fact, astronomers, some of whom worked 5000 years ago, have imposed a pattern on our random collection of stars. At first the patterns were based on a form of celestial connect-the-dots, as ancient astronomers drew imaginary lines connecting stars together and concluded that they resembled mythological figures: Leo, Taurus, Orion. These astronomers lived in the northern hemisphere so they could not map the stars in the southern sky. They missed, as well, distant stars, glowing faintly, even those in their own hemisphere. Then in 1928, the International Astronomical Union established a more sophisticated system, dividing the sky into eighty-eight regions with clearly defined, though invisible, boundaries, much like the boundaries that exist between countries. These eighty-eight celestial counties are called constellations.

Analysis

Alan's introductory paragraph captures the readers' interest in its first few sentences, which are well written and interesting, especially the third sentence with its effective use of metaphor. But soon the paragraph begins to drift. It introduces information that might be better placed within the body of the essay about stars in the southern hemisphere and distant stars. This is a common flaw among student introductory paragraphs: They sometimes contain information that really belongs later in the essay. Moreover, the paragraph seems almost like a complete essay in itself and does not contain an exact thesis. The last sentence suggests that the rest of the essay will elaborate on the definition and description of constellations, but this is a guess on the reader's part. An essay's introduction needs to be clear and explicit. Some of the information in this paragraph should be saved for the essay's body. The following revised paragraph is more focused:

> The stars in our sky, as they reveal themselves to us on a clear dark night, appear randomly scattered. There are large gaps where few stars appear and occasional clusters of many stars grouped together. It is as if some divine presence has filled his two hands with many-pointed sparkling rocks and thrown them into the night sky where they have stuck. In fact, astronomers, some of whom worked 5000 years ago, have imposed a pattern on our random collection of stars. We have, today, a highly sophisticated map of eighty-eight celestial counties called constellations.

Sample Introductory Paragraph 4: Tana

> At the time he wrote "Ode to a Nightingale," in the spring of 1819, Keats had been diagnosed with tuberculosis and knew he had not long to live. This news came soon after Keats, who had trained as a physician, had cared for his brother Tom, as he died slowly and painfully of the same fatal illness. In "Ode to a Nightingale," Keats gives voice to his despair. In the poem, he describes his anguish and his suffering; he expresses his desire to escape from his world of pain and sorrow with the help of the nightingale's beautiful song; and he describes the initial success but ultimate failure of his attempt to escape his reality.

Analysis

Introductory paragraph 4 begins with an anecdote, a story, which is an effective way to engage readers' interest. It clearly indicates that the essay will be about Keats's poem "Ode to a Nightingale." The paragraph ends with a strong thesis that cues the reader to what will follow in the body of the essay. The thesis is complex; it is a long sentence, about fifty words. Tana might have gone with a more general thesis: In "Ode to a Nightingale," Keats explains how he might try to cope with the despair with which life has surrounded him. A more general thesis, however, might make the introductory paragraph seem rather short and would not provide readers with that sense of direction the longer thesis does.

Sample Introductory Paragraph 5: Letty

For twenty centuries, the life of Jesus has been shrouded in mystery. Only one main source documents his birth, though it does so in the most vivid detail. This source skips his childhood and picks up his story only in the last few of the approximately thirty years he lived. It documents his death with the same intensity with which it documents his birth. This source is, of course, the New Testament. The New Testament is gospel (literally) to some, but most biblical historians read, or have read, it skeptically, questioning its historical accuracy. In the last forty years, however, new archaeological discoveries have shed new light on Jesus' life. These new discoveries have, for the most part, confirmed, sometimes dramatically, the New Testament account of the life of Christ. Three discoveries in particular suggest that the New Testament authors were much more historians than novelists.

Analysis

Introductory paragraph 5 is a good start for an academic essay. Letty engages readers by clearly presenting an interesting topic. Her paragraph also establishes the necessary historical context for the topic and presents a clear thesis in the last sentence so readers know what to expect from the rest of the essay.

Write Complete Body Paragraphs

● Compose a Topic Sentence

Your introduction will be followed by any number of body paragraphs (depending on the nature of the assignment and the number of words your professor expects) that will elucidate your thesis. Each body paragraph in your essay should include a topic sentence, which presents the subject of the paragraph. The topic sentence is to the paragraph what the thesis is to the essay as a whole: Just as the other paragraphs within an essay support the thesis, the other sentences within a paragraph support and illuminate the topic sentence.

Where in the body paragraph should you place the topic sentence? It is often, of course, the first sentence. If the first sentence is transitional—that is, if it refers back to the content of the previous paragraph—the topic sentence might be the second one. If the supporting sentences build up to the topic sentence, the topic sentence can also work well at the end of the paragraph, providing a climax. The topic sentence, like a thesis statement, can be inferred from and often is implied by its supporting sentences, though many professors prefer the clarity that an explicit topic sentence provides to its paragraph.

● Develop Your Topic Sentence

A typical paragraph in the body of an academic essay must be developed in enough detail to satisfy the needs and expectations of its readers. In a long essay, you might have a short paragraph to signal a transition from one main idea to the next; however, most paragraphs in the body of an academic essay will consist of at least four sentences: the topic sentence and at least three others in support of the topic.

One of the most common faults in undergraduate academic essays is an inadequately developed topic sentence, which creates an underdeveloped paragraph. Compare, for example, these two paragraphs:

> It was a vexing celestial mystery. Through a telescope it looked like an ordinary, if faint, star. But it emitted far more ultraviolet radiation and more radio signals than astronomers had observed coming from ordinary stars. It was, indeed, something new and different, a quasar.
>
> It was a vexing celestial mystery. Through a telescope it looked like an ordinary, if faint, star. But in its wake were red spectral lines of hydrogen, indicating it was hurtling away from the earth at a supernatural speed astronomers estimated at 30,000 miles per second. And it emitted far more ultraviolet radiation and more radio signals than astronomers had observed coming from ordinary stars. It was, indeed, something new and different. It was not a star but a quasi-star, a quasi-stellar radio source—a quasar.

The paragraphs share an implied topic sentence: Astronomers did not distinguish stars from quasars until they studied differences between them. The first paragraph provides only two points of comparison: the amount of ultraviolet radiation and the intensity of the radio signals. These two alone do not develop the topic sentence adequately. The second paragraph is more effective because it provides a third point of comparison: the quasar's movement indicated by its red tail of hydrogen. The second paragraph also provides a longer concluding sentence that establishes a clearer context for the comparison and a better explanation for the name astronomers decided to use for quasars.

Once you have a strong topic sentence, make certain your body paragraphs are well developed by providing details and examples to support and illuminate your topic sentence. Define key words your readers might not understand. Use comparisons and contrasts, descriptions, or any one of the other methods for developing paragraphs discussed in Chapter 2. Relate an anecdote to elucidate your topic sentence if the anecdote is relevant and useful. Do not leave your body paragraphs underdeveloped.

● Maintain Paragraph Unity

Body paragraphs must have unity, which means that all of the sentences within the paragraph must develop, explain, add detail to, or otherwise relate to and elucidate the topic sentence. A body paragraph is typically about one subject specified within the topic sentence. All of the other sentences within a body paragraph must relate to the topic sentence. As you revise, check that all of the sentences in your body paragraphs relate to the topic sentence. Compare, for example, these two paragraphs:

> In quantum mechanics the distinction between a wave and a particle is blurred. Physicists have proved that entities such as electrons, which would normally be classified as particles, can behave like waves under certain conditions. Similarly, entities we classify as waves—light being the most obvious example—can manifest the behaviour of a particle. Electrons must produce the diffraction of a wave if they are to pass through the narrow slits of atoms. Light must act like a particle if it is to be absorbed by electrons in solids. It is not the composition of the entity itself but the process that entity has to complete that determines its particulate or wavelike nature.
>
> In quantum mechanics the distinction between a wave and a particle is blurred. Physicists have proved that entities such as electrons, which would normally be classified as particles, can behave like waves under certain conditions. Similarly, entities we classify as waves—light being the most obvious example—can manifest the behaviour of a particle. Classical or Newtonian physics does not account for quantum mechanics or for relativity developed earlier by Einstein. Relativity describes the physics of very massive and fast entities, while quantum mechanics, which emerged in the 1920s, deals with the physics of microscopic objects. Electrons must produce the diffraction of a wave if they are to pass through the narrow slits of atoms. Light must act like a particle if it is to be absorbed by electrons in solids. It is not the composition of the entity itself that determines its particulate or wavelike nature but the mission the entity has to accomplish.

These paragraphs share the same topic sentence, the first. But note how in the second version, the author drifts away from the topic sentence in the middle of the paragraph when he starts talking about Newtonian physics and relativity. That information belongs somewhere else in the essay, not in a paragraph defining quantum mechanics.

You violate the important principle of paragraph unity if sentences in a body paragraph drift away from the topic. Often these are strong sentences that do not relate to the paragraph's topic but do somehow relate to the essay's thesis and therefore can be effectively used in a different body paragraph. Edit out sentences that destroy paragraph unity or, if possible, integrate them into other more relevant paragraphs.

● Sample Body Paragraphs

Here are five examples of body paragraphs, each followed by an analysis of their strengths and weaknesses.

Sample Body Paragraph 1: Frieda

> But today, intelligence and integrity are not enough. We also expect our politicians, in this age of multimedia, to be charismatic. The word *charisma* is from the Greek word meaning "gift of grace," and, as the "grace" aspect of the definition suggests, the word originally had religious connotations. It maintains some of these connotations, as evident in "charismatic" evangelical sects, who worship Christ as the personification of charisma. But its meaning has softened over the years. We do not expect our presidents and prime ministers to be godly, but we do want them to exude a self-confidence and a serenity that, in turn, calms us, the people they govern. We expect them to have a vision for the nation they can articulate clearly and persuasively. Charismatic leaders are always inspiring speakers. We expect them to light up a room when they enter it, to command the attention of others by virtue of their physical presence alone.

Analysis

Frieda's body paragraph 1 is well done. It has a topic sentence, the second: "We also expect our politicians, in this age of multimedia, to be charismatic." The first sentence is transitional; it refers back to other traits of good politicians discussed in earlier body paragraphs. The topic sentence is well developed in supporting sentences. Frieda might have included a few specific examples, though this is a definition paragraph. All of the supporting sentences relate to the topic sentence, giving the paragraph unity.

Sample Body Paragraph 2: David

> Even more baffling is the support for the death penalty, proclaimed by members of the Christian right. Christians follow the teaching and emulate the actions of Jesus. One of the most famous New Testament stories reveals Jesus as an abolitionist. A group of new Christians brought before Jesus a woman who was convicted of adultery, then a capital crime in the Holy Land. Before they stoned the woman to death, they sought advice from their spiritual leader. As John tells the story (8: 3–11), Jesus "lifted himself up and said unto them, 'He that is

without sin among you, let him cast the first stone.'" One by one, the would-be executioners dropped their stones. The woman was freed, with Jesus' stern admonition that she "sin no more." As the personification of the compassion and forgiveness that define Christianity, Jesus opposed the death penalty, and so must, therefore, any who profess to follow the Christian faith.

Analysis

Body paragraph 2 is from a persuasive essay in opposition to capital punishment. Its topic sentence, which is not stated but is implicit, is that one argument against the death penalty is that it is anti-Christian. This paragraph is a good example of the use of an anecdote or story to develop a topic sentence, though perhaps David could have established the context for the story more clearly. He might have provided more details about the nature of the woman's "crime" and about the nature of capital punishment at that time.

Sample Body Paragraph 3: Ralph

The real level of social responsibility that corporations need to exercise lies somewhere between the ravings of the Marxists for state control and the "greed-is-good" mentality of the one per-centers. Certainly, corporations set up shop in third-world countries where they can pay workers a fraction of what they would have to pay Canadian workers and thereby increase their treasured profit margin. Yet the governments of these countries are reluctant to nationalize such companies partly because a poor wage by first-world standards is often a fair wage by other standards and partly because the governments know they lack the expertise to manage the companies effectively. Comparatively low wages and the spectre of the presence of foreign capitalism on their sovereign soil are preferable to absolute poverty and the threat of political revolution. On the other hand, there are companies that employ children who should be going to school and whom the companies do pay poorly, even by the standards of the countries where they work. Child labour is unconscionable, anathema to developed countries for the past one hundred years. Recently, certain celebrities have been publicly scolded and ridiculed for advertising and even allowing their own names to be placed on clothing made by children who live barely above the poverty level. There are other products besides clothing, which businesses manufacture in third-world countries to take advantage of low wages. Nor is there any excuse for substandard working conditions. Adequate pay will not buy loyalty if third-world workers are subject to lead poisoning, work in factories without sufficient sanitation, and long hours without breaks.

Analysis

In body paragraph 3, Ralph has two, maybe three, body paragraphs crammed into one. The paragraph touches on Marxism, capitalism, nationalism, child labour, and working conditions. The first sentence sounds like a topic sentence for a compare/contrast paragraph, but Ralph abandons his topic sentence to touch on celebrities and other manufactured products. The paragraph lacks unity. It needs to be divided into two or three paragraphs, each with its own well-developed topic sentence. Besides the first, there are two other topic sentences in this paragraph:

> Child labour is, of course, unconscionable under any circumstances, and governments even in the poorest countries must take measures to curtail the exploitation of children.
>
> Celebrities must also take responsibility for the circumstances under which clothing that bears their names is manufactured.

If Ralph chooses to write just one paragraph, he needs to edit out the material that doesn't fit.

Sample Body Paragraph 4: Akira

> Why does Norma Jean decide to leave Leroy? She decides to leave partly because Leroy annoys her. She admits she was happier when he was driving his truck and was away from home much of the time. Because of his injury, he is always at home now, underfoot, smoking marijuana, and dreaming of building a log cabin, in which Norma Jean has little interest. But the real cause of her discontent, the real reason she leaves, has to do with her newfound identity. Norma Jean has grown up. She is a different person from the eighteen-year-old girl who had to get married because she was pregnant. She is working, attending college classes, and even thinking about standing up, at last, to her overbearing mother. Leroy, annoyed, asks his wife if all of this is some "women's lib thing." His retort is meant to be sarcastic, but it contains more truth than he realizes or cares to admit.

Analysis

Body paragraph 4 is from Akira's essay analyzing Bobbie Ann Mason's story, "Shiloh." It is a good example of a body paragraph that uses a question as its topic sentence and then uses the other sentences to answer the question. It is also an example of how a body paragraph can build up to a key point. Minor answers to the topic-sentence question are presented early in the paragraph, and then the middle sentence begins, "But the real cause ..." This is an effective way of highlighting the key information a body paragraph contains.

Sample Body Paragraph 5: Roberta

The clitellum, a whitish band near the worm's anterior end, forms four to six weeks after birth. It contains both male and female reproductive organs. To mate, two worms join together at the clitellum, their heads pointing in opposite directions. Each worm passes sperm to the other; each stores the sperm in tiny sacs, which evolve into cocoons, tinier than a grain of rice. As the worms back out of the cocoons, they leave behind both eggs and sperm, which unite to form the worm embryo within the cocoon. Anywhere from one to five worm embryos will be in each of the two cocoons. In two to three weeks, the cocoons break open and the new-borns emerge. They are nearly transparent and less than an inch long.

Analysis

Body paragraph 5 is from Roberta's essay about the life cycle of the common earthworm. Its implied topic sentence is "here is the process worms go through when they mate and reproduce." It describes the process clearly and illustrates good use of detail, as the writer includes such information as the size of the cocoon and the size of the newborn worms.

Write an Explicit Conclusion

A good academic essay needs a clear and strong conclusion. In an essay of fewer than 1000 words, the conclusion will usually be a single paragraph. In a longer essay or report, the conclusion will be longer in proportion to the length of the essay. A 100-page essay or report might have a 10-page conclusion.

Whatever its length, an effective conclusion must establish a sense of *closure*. The tone and the content of a concluding paragraph or paragraphs must indicate that the essay's purpose has been fulfilled. Readers will recognize such an ending when they read it and feel that nothing else needs to be said about the essay's thesis. A concluding paragraph or paragraphs might also *summarize* the content of the essay's body and will often *reaffirm* the thesis. But, above all, the conclusion must give readers the sense that the writer has fulfilled her obligations: She has said what she had promised she would say.

Let's look at five examples of concluding paragraphs from academic essays and analyze their effectiveness based upon the criteria for good conclusions discussed above.

● Sample Concluding Paragraphs

Sample Concluding Paragraph 1: Daniela

In summary, there is no independent scientific evidence to support any claim by any cosmetics company that one of their "miracle creams" performs anything close to miracles. Studies that cosmetic companies refer to in their advertisements are clearly suspect, conducted as they were by dermatologists employed by those same companies and undertaken without the controls that scientific studies must have to be considered valid. Why do millions of women believe the companies' claims? They believe because they want to think they can recapture their youthful beauty. The billion dollar U.S. cosmetics industry is a monument to the triumph of vanity and fantasy over science.

Analysis

Daniela's concluding paragraph's introductory phrase, *in summary*, suggests that this is the concluding paragraph of the essay since summaries are generally included at the end. Some professors are not enthusiastic about concluding paragraphs that begin with *in summary* or *in conclusion*, viewing them as limited and unimaginative. Often such phrases are redundant since the context makes clear that a summary is being presented and since paragraphs placed at the end of the essay are obviously "in-conclusion" paragraphs. The sample paragraph's first sentence also reiterates the essay's thesis, something concluding paragraphs often do. The second sentence reminds readers of key points in the body of the essay, while the third sentence is a question, which is answered in the final two sentences. The question is answered unequivocally and with a blunt tone that indicates the essay is finished.

Sample Concluding Paragraph 2: Edie

Eventually, though, Keats would resolve the anguish and torment that comes through so powerfully in "Ode to a Nightingale." He would resign himself to the reality of his illness and accept the fact that his illness meant his life would be so very brief. He would come to learn that the truth cannot be ignored, but that, even though the truth does hurt, it does not have to diminish the beauty of life. As he would learn and write in his next poem, "Ode on a Grecian Urn," "Beauty is truth, truth beauty."

Analysis

Edie's concluding paragraph ends an essay that explains the meaning of Keats's poem "Ode to a Nightingale." It concludes the discussion of the poem and then relates the poem to the next one Keats would write. This technique of hinting at a future concern is common in concluding paragraphs and is used effectively here. The paragraph also ends with a quotation, another common and effective strategy in a concluding paragraph.

Sample Concluding Paragraph 3: Jan

With networks, writers can revise and edit work collaboratively much more efficiently than they could passing hard copy around a room. With spell checks, writers can correct a word in a fraction of the time it takes to look a word up in an old-fashioned paper dictionary. With grammar checks, writers are cued to correct incomplete or rambling sentences. But computers can't think for themselves or develop a weak idea or make style more graceful. The computer makes writing, as it makes so many of the tasks of life, easier, but it needs the guidance of a human mind to make writing more interesting and intelligent.

Analysis

Concluding paragraph 3 is from Jan's essay about the benefits and drawbacks of composing on a computer. It provides a good summary of the points presented in the essay, the points that support computer-based writing and those that express the computer's limitations. In fact, the paragraph is really only summary, though the thesis is implicitly restated, and the last sentence, while still part of the summary, does communicate that sense of closure important in concluding paragraphs.

Sample Concluding Paragraph 4: Jake

The U.S. government should not pressure the Honduran government to shut down its sweatshops, nor should it use sanctions to coerce the Hondurans into enacting child labour laws that would prevent children from working in them. A poor wage is better than no wage. Food, shelter, and clothing trump education in the hierarchy of human needs. But the analysis presented here certainly suggests that the governments of countries whose citizens consume the goods produced in third-world countries could pressure these countries to improve working conditions without provoking the governments of underdeveloped countries into threats of closing down the factories altogether. Citizens of first-world countries can continue to exercise their rights to enrich celebrity designers by paying top dollar for clothes made by poor twelve-year-olds, earning a dollar a day.

Analysis

Concluding paragraph 4, from Jake's essay about the problem of U.S. clothing manufacturers using underpaid child labour in third-world countries to make their garments, appears to summarize the body of the essay and restate the thesis. Unfortunately, the thesis is ambiguous. The first part of the paragraph suggests that we are benefiting the economy of Honduras by sending its citizens work, even if the workers are young and underpaid by our standards. But the end of the paragraph suggests that we are exploiting third world children. Moreover, the first part of the paragraph suggests that the essay focuses on one country, but, by the end of the paragraph, it seems as if the essay focuses on underdeveloped countries in general. Academic writing should never be ambiguous. A concluding paragraph especially must reflect specifically the content of the essay it is meant to bring to closure. Jake revised his paragraph as follows:

> As the analysis presented here suggests, the governments of affluent nations and their citizens need to apply gentle pressure on those countries that exploit child labour. No one benefits if poor countries, in response to the threat of sanctions or to other draconian measures, close down clothing factories that provide work for their people. Gentle pressure would include incentives for leaving children in school and for improving the working conditions of the adults—mainly young women—who work in the factories. Given the profit cheap labour helps them realize, U.S. garment manufacturers and their celebrity spokespeople can well afford to support educational initiatives and better conditions for the many workers in underdeveloped countries who enrich them.

Sample Concluding Paragraph 5: Tim

> By about 1770, the popularity of the rococo style was fading, even in cities such as Prague, Munich, Dresden, and Vienna, where it had flourished. Trendsetters were beginning to look upon the asymmetrical ornamentation, which was a hallmark of the rococo style, as more ungainly and unbalanced than light-hearted and whimsical. Inevitably, rococo would give way to the symmetry of the neoclassical style, which would dominate European architecture until the end of the century.

Analysis

Concluding paragraph 5, from Tim's brief essay tracing the history of rococo architecture, ends appropriately by mentioning the year around which the rococo period began to fade. In an essay organized chronologically, such an ending is appropriate and effective. You might also notice that even though the essay is not about the neoclassical style, which superseded rococo, the paragraph does mention the transition. This technique of ending an essay by hinting at a future trend or development is common and, as long as the essay topic lends itself to the technique, effective.

There is an old adage in writing instruction: Tell them what you're going to tell them, then tell them, and then tell them what you've told them. The adage trivializes the complex process of writing, but it is worth remembering while you plan and draft your essay because it reinforces the importance of structure and the function of introductory, body, and concluding paragraphs.

A Case Study of the Process of Writing an Academic Essay

Drafting, Revising, and Editing

Writing is a recursive process. The pre-writing activities of reflecting on a topic, researching, composing a thesis, and making a plan are somewhat sequential though certainly subject to change as the writing process evolves. Drafting, revising, and editing are important components of the process, but they are even less sequential; writers revise and edit while they draft.

Having reflected upon her topic (Chapter 1), done some research (Chapter 2), and developed a working plan (Chapter 3), Zhen is ready to write a draft. She does not write a draft and then revise it and then edit it. She edits and revises while she drafts, and then she prints out a copy of the draft and studies it carefully, annotating and striking out as necessary, and looking for ways to improve her final product.

Here is a part of the working draft of Zhen's essay, annotated with her handwritten comments. It is a "working" draft more than a first or rough draft because Zhen has already done a substantial amount of revising and editing. It is "working" in the sense that it is the draft Zhen will print out to read and annotate by hand. Writers often annotate a print copy before making final changes, believing that they might process print differently from hypertext and that this new perspective might lead to insights and changes they might not otherwise have considered.

Choosing a College Backpack

When they finish high school and prepare to attend college, students usually shop for a backpack. They will likely do more walking at college than they did at high school *carry heavier books. They* and ~~they~~ will want a pack that is large enough to carry *smart phone* a laptop, heavy text books, notebooks and other school *no locker* supplies, lunch and maybe a water bottle and workout clothes. They won't want to break their budget, but they will want a backpack that is commodious enough, looks good and is durable enough to protect valuable property. ~~Stereotypically believing they are invulnerable~~, Students tend not to focus on or even think about back and neck

A good ergonomic design....important consideration

~~health, but this is an important criterion students should~~ consider when they are making their choice. ~~Perhaps the most important criterion is the one most frequently over-looked.~~

Research suggests that students want a backpack that is strong and durable enough to protect their property, expensive laptops and other tech devices, especially

How to Choose

("Survey"; "Top"). Nylon and other synthetic fabrics are lightweight and generally more durable than canvas.

luxury

Leather is expensive and used for ~~lusxury~~ products. Many backpacks come with a padded compartment, designed especially for protecting a laptop, and this feature is

trade-off here

highly valued by college students. There is a trade off here because padding adds weight. ~~In climates where~~ On campuses where snow and rain are common, students will want a pack that is waterproof.

Size and space are other important criteria. A large backpack will have a capacity of about 2400 cubic inches;

for Teens and Adults

a small one, 1200 ("Best"). College textbooks can be

, much

humongous larger than the ones students used in high school, and a student who has three classes in one day will need a large pack. As more textbooks become available for e-readers, there may be a trend towards smaller packs. Women generally opt for ~~for~~ the smaller packs, some of which are designed especially for their smaller frames ("Best"). There may be a trend to smaller backpacks, as more and more textbooks are downloaded to e-readers.

Include sentence - zippered/ unzippered pockets

The look of a backpack is also important, to some students. Jocks might favour Nike and Reebok products. Fashionistas like a pack that prominently displays the LaCoste alligator or the Ralph Lauren polo pony or the Tommy Hilfiger flag. Those who are into conspicuous consumption and who want others to know it might spend many hundreds of dollars ~~[or even more]~~ on a Louis Vuitton or Marc Jacobs or Coach or

Juicy? Roots?

Gucci product made of exquisite leather though not neces-

sarily more durable than far less expensive backpacks
~~[are made]~~. There are many good quality packs made by
reputable manufactuers *manufacturers* who charge less than a hundred
dollars for a backpack eqwuiped *equipped* with all the pockets,
compartments and other bells, *and* whistles that students want. *flags and*
JanSport products are moderately priced at between thirty *environmentalists*
and a hundred dollars and regularly top best-backpack lists
("Best").

Students don't often identify ~~among their criteria~~ the
maintenance of good back health among their criteria for
selecting a backpack. In a recent (2012) survey only two
of twenty-seven students even hinted at the importance
of the relationship between a backpack and their spinal
chord. But there is research that suggests that pain likely *for back and neck*
associated with backpack use is on the rise (Heuscher et al.
432). It is important for students to have a few guidelines
for selecting safe and healthy backpacks.

One-strap messenger bags are less healthy than two- *too brief*
strap bags (Jayaratne 5554) ~~not good~~ for back health if
they contain more than a few light notebooks. They can
bend the spine out of alignment, in a way that walking
exacerbates. Backpacks that are loaded unevenly, so the *Alison quote/*
weight in them is improperly distributed, have a similar *sources*
effect. Nor is it safe to wear a backpack too low down on
the back. *more specific here*
Some chiropractors recommend (Nixdorf A12) ~~insist~~
a back friendly backpack will not weigh more than about
15% of body weight. This is a somewhat contentious
number because there are studies that make no correlation ~~no correlation~~ between back health, body weight, and
backpack weight (Heuscher ~~et al~~ *et al* 432). This is likely because
physical fitness is more important, *than...* ~~A backpack should be~~ *make two*
~~able to be worn close to the body and~~ A healthy backpack *paragraphs?*
is one that can be worn close to the body, {tight} at about
shoulder-blade level. Waist and chest straps that help to
mimimize *minimize* forward lean when walking to compensate

for the weight and positioning. This forward lean places strain on the back. It is also important to have a pack that makes it easy to distribute weight evenly when it is being loaded (Nixdorf A12). Backpacks with three compartments, decreasing in size—the largest closest to the back—are popular and their design helps to ensure optimal weight distribution.

The counterbalance backpack might be the best choice of all. The counterbalance backpack basically drapes over the shoulders and has space at both its front and back. In addition to its better weight ~~weight~~ distribution, it allows access for items ~~that~~ such as keys and wallets and smart phones you might like to access without putting your pack down. Unfortunately, they are not yet widely available. Perhaps they are unpopular among students because they make them look like they are wearing a life jacket and they wrinkle shirts, sweaters. They are scarce not only on college and university campuses but also in stores. Apparently there is not much of a market for them. This might change if and when back health becomes more of a criterion for consumers interested in buying. Their look may not ~~may also not~~ be appealing.

Safikhani study here?

add space

Concluding paragraph -- quality danger but reiterate ergonomic design

WRITING ASSIGNMENTS

1. Read an article that interests you from a recently published academic journal. Closely examine a section consisting of about five paragraphs of the body of the paper. Based upon the characteristics of effective body paragraphs discussed in this chapter, write a 300-word analysis of this passage.
2. Select one of the following topics and write an introductory paragraph and a concluding paragraph that would work well for that topic. (You may select two topics, one for an introductory paragraph and another for a concluding paragraph, if you prefer.)

   - the responsibility of professional athletes as role models
   - classic novels made into movies
   - compare and contrast hamburgers from two different fast-food chains
   - television's best sitcom

EXERCISES

1. Write an opening paragraph for an essay about the characteristics of effective opening paragraphs for an academic essay.
2. Analyze the opening paragraph of an academic essay you have already written, turned in, and have had graded and returned to you. Write a one-paragraph evaluation of the quality of your opening based upon the criteria and the examples discussed in this chapter.
3. In an academic journal or a collection of academic essays related to your major or to a subject you are interested in, find an example of an effective opening. In one paragraph, explain why you think this opening is effective.
4. In an academic journal or a collection of academic essays related to your major or to a subject you are interested in, find an example of an ineffective opening. In one paragraph, explain why you think this opening is ineffective.
5. Correct the violations in paragraph unity contained within the following passage. You may divide the passage into two paragraphs if you wish. You may add to, but not delete from, the information contained within the passage.

> *The Castle of Otranto,* by Horace Walpole, is another example of a novel of the "mystery and terror school." *The Castle of Otranto* is a Gothic novel. Horace Walpole was born in 1717 and died in 1797. He was a novelist and also something of an art critic and historian. A renaissance man, Walpole was a member of the British Parliament from 1741 to 1767. He followed in his father's footsteps. His father, Robert, was twice prime minister of Great Britain. The main character is Manfred, the Prince of Otranto, who decides to marry Isabella, the daughter of the Marquis of Vincenza, after Otranto's son, who was betrothed to Isabella, dies under mysterious circumstances. Isabella wants no part of Manfred and runs off, her escape aided by the Peasant Theodore. A series of supernatural events follows, culminating in the collapse of the castle. Theodore is declared heir and marries Isabella. The Gothic novel is characterized by horror, terror, the supernatural, murder, and violence. Gothic novels are often set in gloomy, isolated castles. Horace Walpole even built his own imitation Gothic castle in Twickenham.

6. Select one of the following thesis statements. Compose three topic sentences, one for each of three body paragraphs for an essay that would have the thesis you selected. Develop one of the topic sentences into a complete body paragraph.

   - Some professional athletes are not very good role models.
   - Classic novels do not necessarily translate into good movies.
   - The quality of the hamburgers varies widely from one fast-food restaurant to the next.
   - Some television sitcoms have a lot of situation but not much comedy.

7. Compose a concluding paragraph that ends with an effective and relevant quotation.
8. Compose a concluding paragraph that ends by hinting at a future concern related to the essay's topic. See sample concluding paragraphs 2 and 5 on pages 82 and 84 respectively for examples.
9. Compose a concluding paragraph that includes a relevant question.

COLLABORATIVE ACTIVITY

In small groups, discuss one or several readings from the anthology of readings in Part Two or Three. Discuss the effectiveness of the opening, body, and concluding paragraphs in these articles. Use the criteria for good opening, body, and concluding paragraphs described in this chapter.

CHAPTER 6

Revise Your Essay

Revision is the process of altering, improving, and clarifying the overall structure of a written text and of reviewing the content of a text to make certain it satisfies the needs and expectations of readers. It is distinct from editing, discussed in the next chapter, which is the process of altering and improving a text, primarily at the sentence level. When writers revise their work, they make certain the essay or report has a sound overall structure, they confirm that the content of the essay or report meets the needs and expectations of their readers, and they double check for the presence of cohesive ties between sentences and paragraphs. During the revising stage of the process, writers also check and reconsider the style in which their paper is written, checking to make sure their sentence structure is varied and that the voice or tone—that attitude to the topic writers convey to their readers—is effective and appropriate. When revising a draft of an academic writing assignment, review it for

- structure
- content
- cohesive ties
- style

Structure

In Chapter 4, you learned how to plan and structure an academic essay or report. Specifically, you learned various strategies for organizing an argument and for planning various kinds of expository or informative essays. Expository essays, remember, present information to readers. An expository essay, for example, might describe a process, explain the causes of an important event or natural phenomenon, recount how an important event or natural phenomenon influenced or affected society, present details and examples to illustrate an idea, compare and contrast related entities, or define a complex term or procedure. Often an expository essay will combine any number of these developmental patterns to support its main idea. A persuasive/argumentative essay might also describe a process, present details and examples, give causes and effects, make comparisons and contrasts, or supply definitions to inform readers, but the persuasive essay bears the additional burden of trying to convince readers that the writer's opinion on a controversial issue is valid. For this reason, an important component of the argument is an acknowledgement and refutation of the opposing point of view.

As you revise your work, keep in mind its developmental patterns and the rhetorical expectations those patterns provoke in the minds of readers. If you are writing a compare/contrast essay, for example, check to make sure the essay you are working on is organized using either the common traits or the similarities/differences organizational structure, usually the best choices for comparing and contrasting. If you are presenting an argument, make sure, first, that you have included all of the components of an effective argument: ample evidence in support of your thesis and, if necessary, your warrant; and acknowledgement of, respect for, and refutation of opposing arguments. Make sure, as well, that you have presented these elements in an order that maximizes your chances of winning your readers over to your side. That order is somewhat arbitrary and will depend upon the nature of your argument and upon your readers' level of hostility, skepticism, and cynicism. Proponents of classical argument, remember, recommend you begin with a thesis followed by support, while Rogerians suggest you present evidence leading up to a thesis.

Readers want and expect a clear and logical progression of arguments and ideas. They expect the writer to lead them along competently without getting them lost. A sound structure, based upon clear points in support of a thesis and upon ideas and details that clearly elucidate those points in support of the thesis, helps readers understand a writer's work. Remember that you likely will not establish that structure in its entirety before you draft your essay but will discover an effective structure as you write and revise.

Content

Revise your essay for content. Make sure you have provided enough information in the form of details, examples, comparisons, contrasts, causes, effects, definitions, and anecdotes to fulfill the expectations of your readers. This requires some empathy on your part, an ability to put yourself in your readers' shoes. Don't assume your readers know what you know. You live with a writing assignment for some time, you have researched your topic, and you know a lot about it. Certain points of information might seem obvious to you because you have read about them in several different sources. But this does not mean your readers share your knowledge. Certainly, it is possible to go on too long, but it is generally better to err on the side of providing more information rather than less.

You might have to do additional critical thinking, freewriting, and research as you revise your essay. We tend to conceptualize critical thinking and research as prewriting activities, but to do so limits our chances of success as writers. Good writers often consult new sources during the revising stage in order to generate additional needed content for their essays.

Remember that the single most frequent marginal comment professors make on their students' papers does not concern grammar or spelling or sentence structure. It is some kind of request for additional information, some kind of complaint that the student has not provided enough information to solidify the point or the argument he or she is trying to advance. Remember also that it is generally a good idea to meet or slightly exceed the word limit your professor has requested. Quality is more important than quantity, but the quantity must be such that your readers understand and appreciate the information you are presenting or the argument you are advancing.

Cohesive Ties

A cohesive tie is a word or a phrase that connects a sentence or a paragraph to the sentence or the paragraph that precedes or follows it. Cohesive ties help readers follow the writer's train of thought. They signal the nature of the relationships between and among sentences and paragraphs, and, in so doing, help make writing clear. Cohesive ties include transitional words and phrases, key words that are repeated throughout a paragraph, synonyms that are substitutes for key words, and pronouns that refer to key words. In other words, you can establish cohesion in your writing through transition, repetition, and substitution.

● Transition

A transitional word or phrase defines the nature of the relationship between and among sentences and paragraphs. Transitional words and phrases such as *furthermore*, *in addition*, and *also* suggest that the sentence containing this word or phrase will add something to a previous sentence, something that will provide further related information. Similarly, transitional words or phrases such as *another*, *a second*, and *a third* suggest that a new point will be made. Transitional expressions such as *consequently* or *therefore* suggest a cause/effect relationship between two sentences or paragraphs. Transitional words such as *but* and *however* signal a contradiction or a contrast between a sentence and the one that follows. Notice the use of transitional expressions (which appear in boldface) in this passage:

The human spinal column is an intricate and complex structure. **As a result**, the human back, the lower back especially, is susceptible to trouble. **Indeed**, back problems are one of the most common reasons for a visit to the doctor.

One such problem is simple back strain, which typically follows the exercise of muscles that are not used to so much attention. **For example**, back muscles are often put to work for which they are not ready—shovelling that first snow fall of the year, **for instance**—and, **consequently**, feel uncommon stress, which leads to mild but still painful inflammation.

Another more serious problem is the so-called slipped disk. **Now** the disks between each vertebra in the human back are attached to ligaments and cannot, literally, slip. They can, **however**, prolapse, which means that a portion of the disk may protrude through the fibres of the ligaments....

Examine carefully the transitional words and phrases used in the passage above and note how they improve clarity by establishing the relationship between and among the sentences and between paragraphs. Read the passage without its transitional words and you will notice the extent to which transitional words and phrases aid clarity.

● Repetition

You can also establish cohesion by repeating a key word or by repeating a particular sentence pattern. Here is a paragraph that repeats a key word to help keep the reader on track:

The **Sabbath** is a Jewish day of rest and worship. After they were sent into exile, Jews proclaimed their identity, in part by insisting upon the holiness of their **Sabbath** day. Jesus supported the **Sabbath** in principle, but was vexed by the number of rules needed to keep the **Sabbath** holy. He refused to honour the **Sabbath** as a day of rest and, as a result, was condemned by the Pharisees.

Here is a paragraph that repeats a sentence pattern to help establish a sense of coherence:

Unfortunately, all forms of government are imperfect. Left-wing governments are strong on social justice but weak on economic prosperity. Right-wing governments are strong on economic prosperity but weak on social justice. In good economic times, left-wing governments should assume power so that wealth is equitably distributed. In bad economic times, right-wing governments should assume power to work their magic on the economy. Under such a shared system, economic prosperity will lead to social justice.

Notice how the structure of the third sentence in the preceding paragraph mirrors the structure of the sentence that precedes it. Similarly, the fourth sentence mirrors the structure of the third. This creates a sense of balance within the paragraph that helps create the sense that the paragraph sticks together, that it is cohesive.

● Substitution

As you learned earlier in this chapter, coherence can be established in a paragraph by repeating a key word. You do not want to repeat a key word too many times in the course of a single paragraph, of course, because such repetition can make your paragraph appear boring and unimaginative. But what you can and should do is substitute the key word with a synonym or pronoun that refers back to the key word. Note the use of substitution for the key word *tourist* to maintain the coherence in the following paragraph:

> Tourists are instantly recognizable by their physical appearance. **They** are usually dressed in baggy shorts and souvenir T-shirts, and **they** usually come armed with camcorders under their arms or hoisted onto their shoulders. These **visitors** also have a way of walking that distinguishes them from the locals. **They** meander quite aimlessly, stopping at every other intersection to gaze up at the street signs or to point their smart phones at buildings, the architectural significance of which usually eludes their hosts. Tourists also tend to have happily vacant facial expressions, in contrast to the grim determination set in the expression of the locals. Still, the locals welcome these **alien invaders** who can be counted on to boost the local economy.

Style

Academic writing should be clear and straightforward, but there is no reason why it should be dull. An interesting subject makes an interesting essay, but that interest is diminished if the information is conveyed in a dull writing style. A dull writing style is characterized mainly by a series of short, choppy sentences joined together, if at all, by conjunctions such as *and*. A short, simple sentence does not make a dull style. Indeed, a short, simple sentence can be used effectively, especially to emphasize a particular point. What you want to avoid in your writing is a series of short, choppy sentences, which make your writing sound as if it were written by a ten-year-old or by a less than competent journalist.

The key to avoiding a passage of dull sentences is to read your essay out loud while you are revising it. If you have written a passage consisting of too many short, dull sentences, you will be able to hear the problem (as will your readers), and you can make the necessary revisions to make your style more pleasing. In a variety of ways, you can vary your sentence structure and thereby improve your writing style. Three common and effective methods are these:

- Use subordination to combine a series of short, choppy sentences together.
- Establish parallelism within a sentence.
- Vary the order of words and phrases in a sentence.

● Subordination

You can combine a series of three or four short, choppy sentences into two or even one more interesting and sophisticated sentence by changing some of the sentences into clauses or phrases and adding those clauses or phrases on to one complete sentence. This process is called **subordination**. The writer takes one sentence and changes it into a **phrase** or a **clause** and attaches the phrase or clause to a complete sentence. The phrase or clause thereby becomes "subordinate" to the main clause, the complete sentence. Let's look at an example. Consider this passage:

> The word *discreet* is an adjective. It means prudent or modest. Here is a sentence that uses the word *discreet* correctly: He was too discreet to reveal her age. The word *discrete* is also an adjective. But spelled this way it means separate or distinct. Here is an example: We are officially part of their department, but we operate as a discrete entity.

This is an informative paragraph, but its pedestrian style has a somnolent effect on the reader and detracts from the interesting information the paragraph contains. A more interesting version of the same paragraph might read like this:

> The word *discreet* is an adjective, which means prudent or modest, as in this sentence: He was too discreet to reveal her age. The word *discrete* is also an adjective, but, spelled this way, it means separate or distinct, as in this sentence: We are officially part of their department, but we operate as a discrete entity.

This version has a rhythm and flow that signals a more mature writing style and makes the paragraph more authoritative. What accounts for the improvement in the style of this paragraph? The second sentence has been subordinated into a clause, the third sentence has been subordinated into a phrase, and both have been attached (with a comma) to the first sentence. The same process has been repeated with the fourth, fifth, and sixth sentences.

Let's look at one more example. Here is a paragraph written in an uninspired style, consisting, as it does, of a succession of short, choppy sentences:

William Penn was an English Quaker. His father was a prominent admiral. The British government gave Penn a large tract of land in the new colony of America. They gave him the land in recognition of his father's naval career. Penn decided to establish a Quaker colony in America. In 1681, Penn and his cousin, William Markham, went to America. They were accompanied by a group of hearty Quaker colonists. They made their way to the junction of the Schuylkill and Delaware Rivers. Here they founded a City of Brotherly Love. This city eventually became Philadelphia. It became the capital of the state named after William Penn.

Here is the same paragraph revised to improve its sentence variety:

William Penn was an English Quaker, the son of a prominent admiral. The British government gave Penn a large tract of land in the new colony of America, in recognition of his father's naval career. Penn decided to establish a Quaker colony in America. In 1681, Penn and his cousin, William Markham, journeyed to America, accompanied by a group of hearty Quaker colonists. They made their way to the junction of the Schuylkill and Delaware Rivers, where they founded a City of Brotherly Love. This city eventually became Philadelphia, the capital of the state named after William Penn.

The first version of the paragraph is not incorrect, but an adult reader likely would find it sophomoric and dull. The revised version is more readable because, through subordination, the choppy sentence structure has been replaced with sentences that have a better sense of rhythm and flow.

● Parallelism

As a term in written composition, **parallelism** describes a sentence within which words, phrases, or clauses complement each other and create a sense of rhythm and balance within the sentence. Effective parallelism can create a graceful and striking sentence. Note the use of parallel structure in this excerpt from Winston Churchill's speech to the House of Commons on October 8, 1940. He was speaking about Great Britain's participation in World War II:

Death and sorrow will be the companions of our journey; hardship our garment; constancy and valour our only shield. We must be united, we must be undaunted, we must be inflexible.

Without parallelism, the passage loses much of its strength:

Death and sorrow will be the companions of our journey. We will also experience much hardship which we will have to endure. We will have

> to shield ourselves with constancy and valour. We must be united. We
> cannot let our enemy frighten us. We must be inflexible.

This version is grammatically correct, but it lacks the passion, concision, and emphasis of the original because Churchill's effective use of parallelism is replaced by short, rather dull sentences.

Here is another example, this time from President John F. Kennedy's inaugural address made on January 20, 1961:

> Let the word go forth from this time and place, to friend and foe alike,
> that the torch has been passed to a new generation of Americans, born
> in this century, tempered by war, disciplined by a hard and bitter peace,
> proud of our ancient heritage, and unwilling to witness or permit the
> slow undoing of those human rights to which this nation has always
> been committed, and to which we are committed today at home and
> around the world.
>
> Let every nation know, whether it wishes us well or ill, that we shall
> pay any price, bear any burden, meet any hardship, support any friend,
> oppose any foe, in order to assure the survival and the success of
> liberty.

Without the parallel structure Kennedy uses so effectively, this passage loses that stirring tone that complements the author's forthright message:

> Let the word go forth from this time and place, to friend and foe alike,
> that the torch has been passed to a new generation of Americans. These
> Americans were born in this century, and they have been tempered by
> war. In addition, they have been disciplined by a hard and bitter peace.
> They are proud of our ancient heritage and unwilling to witness or
> permit the slow undoing of those human rights to which this nation
> has always been committed. We will remain committed to these rights
> today at home and around the world.
>
> Let every nation know, whether it wishes us well or ill, that we shall
> pay any price to assure the survival and the success of liberty. Further-
> more, we will bear any burden and meet any hardship in the interest of
> the same cause. Finally, we will support any friend, oppose any foe, in
> order to assure the survival and the success of liberty.

The use of parallel structure can improve a writing style by making it at once more concise and more dramatic.

● Order

Most English sentences are structured so that a subject is followed by a verb:

> Their debate was typical. The NDP candidate promised to increase
> public spending on education and health care, to win the votes of the

soccer moms. The Conservative promised to lower taxes, to win the votes of the business community.

You can make your writing style and hence your message more interesting if, on occasion, you don't begin the sentence with the standard "subject followed by a verb" pattern.

> Their debate was typical. To win the votes of the soccer moms, the NDP candidate promised to increase public spending on education and health care. To win the votes of the business community, the Conservative promised to lower taxes.

Such sentences begin with a phrase and so withhold their main points (contained in the independent clause) until the end. The technique is effective because, being at the end, the main clause is stressed. Sentences that delay their main clause are called **periodic sentences**.

The order of words in an English sentence is alterable to a considerable degree. Consider the following sentences:

> The tenants refused to pay one more penny of rent until the landlord repaired the plumbing.
>
> Until the landlord repaired the plumbing, the tenants refused to pay one more penny of rent.
>
> One more penny of rent the tenants refused to pay, until the landlord repaired the plumbing.
>
> The tenants refused to pay, until the landlord repaired the plumbing, one more penny of rent.

Which sentence is the most effective? It depends upon form and shape of the other sentences around it, on the writer's purpose and audience, and on the extent to which the writer wants to emphasize certain information within the sentence. The word order in the third version seems especially unique and emphatic.

If you notice when you are revising your work that the vast majority of your sentences follow the typical subject–verb pattern, consider experimenting with the word order of some of your sentences. There is no "right" way to determine which version of a sentence is the best. It does help to read your work out loud while you revise it. You will be able to hear the rhythm and flow of your sentences and alter them in order to display them to their best advantage.

● Academic Voice

Written discourse reflects the personality and the attitude of the writer, or at least the personality and the attitude the writer chooses to assume for a given assignment. This personality and attitude is known as the writer's **voice** or **tone**.

Writers must assume a voice that complements the purpose of their work, the audience for whom it is intended, and the genre in which it is written. A movie reviewer might choose to use a sardonic voice if she is panning a film. Valedictorians typically assume a solemn, rather formal voice. Your latest text to a friend probably includes slang, inside jokes, and incomplete sentences, establishing a casual, informal, familiar voice.

Our concern here, of course, is with revising your essay to make sure it is written in **academic voice**, which is the persona writers assume when writing an essay for a professor or an article for a professional journal. A good student academic voice is formal and authoritative but never too lofty or grandiose. Academic voice is clear and concise. For her first-year writing course, Pauline wrote an essay on avoiding gender biased language. Read this paragraph from Pauline's essay, paying particular attention to her voice:

> Another controversial way of avoiding the discord caused by the repetition of both the masculine and feminine pronoun is to use only the feminine form—A student at this university will have *her* library privileges suspended if *she* accumulates more than three overdue fines. There are several arguments in support of this usage. The first is that it does solve the problem of the discordant repetition caused by the use of both pronouns. A second argument is that for hundreds of years writers have used the male form exclusively, and now it is time to even things out. Feminists have fought for more than thirty years for linguistic democracy and it's time their struggle was rewarded. A new millennium is a perfect occasion for progress. A more compelling argument is based upon current usage: the exclusive use of the feminine pronoun has been creeping into the published prose of some professional writers for about a decade and is therefore becoming accepted, if not yet standard, usage (Macher, 2010). Even President Clinton, in his 1998 State of the Union Address, endorsed at least the partial use of the feminine pronoun, when he read this sentence: "If you know a child from a poor family, tell her not to give up—she can go to college." When a President sanctions such a construction by using it in a State of the Union Address, its acceptance is endorsed, if not guaranteed.

Note that the tone—the voice—of the passage is calm and measured, even though the writer is making a controversial suggestion. It is written, of course, in Standard English, so the grammar, sentence structure, spelling, and punctuation are correct. The diction and vocabulary are neither too casual nor too grandiose or pompous. There is no slang, which is completely out of place in academic writing. The writer comes across as a thoughtful and intelligent person, and her readers will be inclined to trust the accuracy of the information she gives them and to consider her argument seriously.

Which point of view to use with the academic voice is a topic of some debate. Some of your professors will *not* want you to use the first-person pronouns (*I* or *we*) in your essays; others might object to the use of the second person (*you*). They will insist upon an objective point of view, devoid of any personal pronouns. In social science studies, for example, the authors will generally not write "We received responses from 329 of the 452 school counsellors to whom we sent questionnaires," preferring instead the more detached passive voice, "Responses were received from 329 of the 452 school counsellors to whom questionnaires were sent."

On the other hand, there are some academic journals even in the social sciences that have no problem with first-person point-of-view. It is left to the discretion of the author. Quist et al. use it in "Integrating Social Knowledge and Physical Cues When Judging the Attractiveness of Potential Mates," published in the *Journal of Experimental Social Psychology* and included in Part Two: "We found that women reported...." But Greitemeyer, who published "Exposure to Music with Prosocial Lyrics Reduces Aggression" in the same journal, carefully avoids first-person, writing; for example, "it was addressed whether the effects of music exposure on aggressive behaviour...," instead of "I addressed...."

Point of view depends upon audience and purpose. If you want to establish a sense of familiarity with your readers or to convey a personal touch, the *I* point of view is acceptable. If you are directly instructing your readers, the *you* point of view is effective. If you want to maintain distance from your readers, use an objective point of view.

Academic voice does not require the use of **ostentatious language**, that is, words and phrases that are used not because they are the most appropriate but because they are the most complex and obscure. Writers who use ostentatious language are merely trying to impress their readers with their extensive and sophisticated vocabulary. But readers usually suspect the truth: that the writer has consulted his thesaurus one too many times. Usually a plain and simple style, one that is not pedestrian or dry but clear and straightforward, is most effective in academic writing.

Peer Review

One effective way to revise your essay is to have a classmate look over your draft and suggest constructively critical ways of improving it. So valuable is this exercise, in fact, that your teacher likely will free up some class time for peer review of drafts, usually done in small groups of three or four. In a peer review session, each writer typically reads his or her essay aloud while other members of the group follow along with their own copy of the draft. When the reading is complete, each group member presents opinions about the strengths and weaknesses of the essay. The writer listens carefully to these opinions, without hostility and in the collegial spirit a good peer conferencing session fosters, and considers making some of the revisions that group members suggest.

To be most effective, peer review of drafts should not be comprehensive; that is, reviewers should not attempt to comment on every aspect of the writing process as it relates to the particular assignment the group is considering. Peer review is most effective when its scope is limited to two or three aspects of the writing process, usually those aspects the instructor wants to stress at the time the peer review is occurring. Peer review is also most effective when that focus is on the global or broad aspects of writing: Are the paragraphs well developed? Does each paragraph relate to the essay's thesis? Is the essay's structure coherent?

But whatever the focus of the peer review session is, it is always a good idea to work with a checklist or a rubric of some kind. A checklist that tries to account for all of the components of good writing would be several pages long and impractical for peer review. An effective checklist isolates certain components of good writing. If, for example, your teacher wants to focus on cultivating an effective style for an academic essay and organizes peer review sessions for this purpose, she might distribute a rubric like this:

WEEK EIGHT PEER REVIEW: CULTIVATING AN EFFECTIVE WRITING STYLE

This week we read each other's drafts and focus on the effectiveness of each writer's style. Consider especially these questions:

- Does the writer avoid any prolonged use of short, choppy sentences?
- Is there a sense of rhythm and flow in the writer's essay?
- Is the tone (the voice) of the essay in sync with its audience and purpose?
- Is there variety in the writer's sentence structure?

Remember, this is one possible rubric for one aspect of good writing. There are many other ways a peer review session could be structured. If your teacher wanted to work on paragraph development, sentence grammar, or effective openings, the rubric would be tailored to meet these needs. The key point is that effective peer review sessions do have a specific purpose and structure.

We learned at the beginning of this chapter the difference between revising and editing: Revising changes overall structure and paragraph content; editing changes words and sentences. Many student writers are obsessed with editing—with getting words spelled correctly, commas in the right places, and sentence fragments healed—somewhat at the expense of revising. Students often arrive at college or university believing that good writing is correct writing. They are half right. Good writing certainly follows the conventions of editing, and, in the next chapter, those conventions will be presented in detail. But good writing is more than correct writing. Good writing has a robust form; it is interesting and informative, complete and comprehensive. Make changes—revisions—to the structure, the coherence, and the content of your essays until you are satisfied that your readers will be able to follow your train of thought and will understand what it is you want to tell them.

A Case Study of the Process of Writing an Academic Essay

Final Copy

Zhen Wei

English 161

June 10, 2012

Choosing a College Backpack

When they finish high school and prepare to attend college, students usually shop for a backpack. They will likely do more walking at college than they did at high school and carry heavier books. They are less likely to have a locker in the building where they will take most of their classes. They will want a backpack that is large enough to accommodate a laptop, heavy text books, notebooks and other school supplies, lunch, a smart phone, and possibly an MP3 player, a water bottle, and workout clothes. They won't want to break their budget, but they will want a backpack that is commodious enough, looks good and is durable enough to protect valuable property. Students don't usually worry about back, neck, and shoulder strain when they are purchasing a backpack, but there are health risks associated with poorly designed and incorrectly loaded packs. A good ergonomic design is not usually listed among the criteria students select when they are purchasing a backpack, but it is an important consideration.

Research suggests that students look, first, for a backpack that is strong and durable enough to protect their property: expensive laptops and other technological devices, especially ("Survey"; "Top"; "How to Choose"). Nylon and other synthetic fabrics are lightweight and generally more durable than canvas. Leather is durable and looks good, but it is less commonly chosen because it is more expensive. Many backpacks come with a padded compartment designed especially for protecting a laptop, and this feature is highly valued by college students ("Best"). There is a trade-off here because padding does add some extra weight. On campuses where snow and rain are common, students want a pack that is waterproof ("Survey").

Size and space allocation are other important criteria. A large backpack will have a capacity of about 2400 cubic inches or 39 litres; a small one, 1200 inches or 20 litres ("Best for Teens and Adults"). College textbooks can be humongous, much larger than the ones students used in high school, and a student who has three classes in one day will need a large pack. The most highly rated backpacks have a capacity of more than two thousand cubic inches, though women often opt for smaller packs. As more textbooks become available on e-readers, there may be a trend towards smaller packs. Students love multiple compartments to help keep them well organized, unzipped pockets for items they want easy access to, and zippered for property they want to protect.

The look of a backpack is also important to many students, who consider it an accessory. Backpacks come in dozens of colours and patterns, though the more subdued solid colours seem more popular. Backpacks are often identity markers. Fashionistas like a pack that prominently displays the logo of their favourite designer: the Lacoste alligator, Ralph Lauren polo pony, Tommy Hilfiger flag, Juicy Couture puppies, the Roots beaver. Jocks often opt for products made by companies such as Nike and Reebok, which specialize in athletic gear and do manufacture popular backpacks. Patriots love a pack which displays their national flag. Environmentalists might prefer a pack made of hemp. Students who ride a bike or walk home at night often opt for a pack that has reflective stripes. Those who are into conspicuous consumption and who want others to know it might spend many hundreds of dollars or even more on a Louis Vuitton or Marc Jacobs or Coach or Gucci product finely crafted out of exquisite leather.

Students don't often identify the maintenance of good back health among their criteria for selecting a backpack. In a recent (2012) survey, only two of twenty-seven students even hinted at the importance of a good relationship between a backpack and their spinal cord. But there is research that suggests that pain likely associated with backpack use is on the rise (Heuscher et al. 432; Jayaratne, Jacobs, and Fernando 5555; Jensen, Slack, and Bohne). It is important for students to include in their criteria for selecting a backpack a few that will help maintain a healthy back and neck.

One-strap messenger bags are less healthy than two-strap packs. "I tried to play it cool," Alison writes, "by using a messenger bag when I was a freshman, but after some serious shoulder and back pain, I finally caved and joined the backpack-carrying masses on my campus— and never regretted it" ("How to Choose" 1). There is research to vali-date the wisdom of Alison's decision (Jayaratne, Jacobs, and Fernando 5554). Messenger bags are not good for back health if they contain more than a few light notebooks. They misalign the spine. Walking exacer-bates the misalignment and the result can be back pain, even, in the worst case, a herniated disk. Similar problems can occur if a backpack is loaded unevenly, so the weight is improperly distributed to one side of the body. Nor is it healthy to wear a backpack too low down on the back; it is healthiest when worn between the shoulder blades. One study concluded that "a load placement with the centre of gravity at the 12 spinal segment resulted in the least postural deviation" (in Heuscher et al. 435).

Professional agencies such as the International Chiropractor Pedi-atric Association and the American Occupational Therapy Association recommend that backpacks, when fully loaded, do not weigh more than about 15 percent of the user's body weight (Jayaratne, Jacobs, and Fernando 5554; Nixdorf A12). This is a somewhat contentious number because there are studies that find no correlation between back health, body weight, and backpack weight (Heuscher et al. 432). It is likely that physical fitness level is more important than body weight and that the physically fit can comfortably use backpacks that weigh more. Still, the American Occupational Therapy Association recommends a loaded backpack weight below 15 percent of body weight, and they sponsor a "Pack It Light, Wear It Right" campaign to get this message out. And the Heuscher et al. study did find "a 25 percent increase in the odds of annual self-reported low back pain for each 4-kg increase in the estimated backpack weight" (434).

Adjustable shoulder straps are highly recommended and are a feature of most backpacks designed for college and university students. Chest and waist straps, a common feature of hikers' backpacks but less common in packs designed for students, help secure a backpack in its optimal position, which means that which minimizes forward lean while walking (Safikhani et al. 4) This forward lean places strain on the back. For the same reason, it is important to have a pack that makes it easy to distribute weight evenly when it is being loaded (Nixdorf A12). Backpacks with three compartments, decreasing in size—the largest closest to the back—are popular, and their design helps to ensure optimal weight distribution.

Those with a history of back issues or who believe they might be susceptible should seriously consider a counterbalance backpack. Recommended by some experts (Safikhani et al. 4-5), the counterbalance backpack basically drapes over the shoulders and has compartments at both its front and back. It allows for optimal distribution of weight and hence it minimizes forward lean. Concluding their study, Safikhani et al. note:

> According to the finding of this study the counterbalance backpack allows [a] person to [maintain his or her] upright position, by shifting the gravity of the load forward…. When considering the kinematics and ergonomics of load carriage, the counterbalance backpack has significant benefits. (5)

Of course, the counterbalance pack also allows easier access for items such as keys and wallets and cellphones the user might like to get at without putting their pack down. Unfortunately, they are not yet widely available. Perhaps they are unpopular among students because they make them look like they are wearing a life jacket and because they hide and wrinkle cool shirts, blouses, and sweaters. They are hard to find in stores and are seen more often on hiking trails than on campuses. This might change if the trend towards increased incidences of back strain continues.

It is not as if the health hazard, for young adults, is so threatening that drastic measures need to be taken. There may be too many reports of back problems among college students, but there is no epidemic. Moreover, by the time they reach college age, most students have stopped growing so the spinal cord is developed and strain will less likely turn into a more serious condition than it might in children who have not reached their full height. (Nixdorf A12). College and university students will continue to look for backpacks that will carry and protect all their stuff, look cool, proclaim to the world who they are, and fit their budget. But still the possibility of missing the dance because of a strained back caused by an improperly designed or loaded backpack should be real enough to convince students to add practical ergonomic design to their list of criteria for purchasing a backpack.

Works Cited

"Backpacks: Full Report: The Best Backpacks for Teens and Adults." *Consumerresearch.com* Aug. 2011. n. pag. Web. 22 May 2012.

"Backpacks: Full Report: Top Backpacks for Carrying a Notebook Computer." *Consumerresearch.com* Aug. 2011. n. pag. Web. 22 May 2012.

"Best Backpack for College Students." *Bestcovery.com* n.d. n. pag. Web. 22 May 2012.

"Criteria for Choosing a College Backpack." Survey. U of British Columbia. 31 May 2012.

Heusher, Zachary, Gilkey, David P., Peel, Jennifer L., and Kennedy, Catherine A. "The Association of Self-Reported Backpack Use and Backpack Weight with Low Back Pain among College Students." *Journal of Manipulative and Physiological Therapeutics* 33.6 (July/August 2010): 432–437. Web. 23 May 2012.

"How to Choose a Backpack for College." *Universitylanguage.com* 13 June 2011. n. pag. Web. 22 May 2012.

Jayaratne, Kapila, Jacobs, Karen, and Fernando, Dulitha. "Global Healthy Backpack Initiatives." *Work: A Journal of Prevention, Assessment and Rehabilitation* 41 (2012): 5553–5557. Web. 23 May 2012.

Jensen, Daniel B., Slack, Jason V., and Bohne, Michael. "What Is the Average Weight of College Students' Backpacks?" *Proceedings of the Western Society of Kinesiology and Wellness 55th Annual Conference*. October 13–15, 2010, Reno, NV. Web. 23 May 2012.

Safikhani, Hassan, Kamalden, Tengku, Amri, Saidon Bin, and Ahmad, Megat. "The Effect of Different Backpack Loading Systems on Trunk Forward Lean Angle during Walking among College Students." *European Journal of Sports and Exercise Sciences* 1.1 (2012): 1–5. Web. 23 May 2012.

WRITING ASSIGNMENT

Read an article in an academic journal on a topic of interest to you. Study carefully four sequential paragraphs in the body of the article. Identify the topic sentence of each paragraph. (Remember that the topic sentence might be implied rather than stated explicitly.) Study carefully the author's methods of establishing cohesion within each paragraph and among the four paragraphs.

Write one paragraph in which you describe the methods the writer uses to develop his or her body paragraphs adequately. In another paragraph, describe the author's use of transition, repetition, and substitution as cohesive ties within each paragraph and among the three paragraphs. See the commentary that accompanies the essays in Part Two for examples.

EXERCISES

1. Revise each of the following paragraphs to improve their style. Do not alter the meaning of the paragraphs by adding anything to them or taking anything from them. You may rearrange the order and structure of sentences in ways you think most effective.

Archimedes was a Greek mathematician. He discovered that the weight of the fluid that was displaced when an object was put in fluid could be used to measure the mass of that object. There is a legend associated with this discovery. Archimedes was in his bath one day. He watched the water rise as he settled into his bath. He shouted "Eureka" and danced into the Athens streets wearing only his towel.

Chad is a landlocked country in north-central Africa. Chad is slightly smaller than the state of Alaska. Libya is north of Chad. The Sudan is east of Chad. The Central African Empire is south of Chad. Cameroon is also south of Chad. Nigeria is southwest of Chad. Niger is west of Chad. Lake Chad is the largest body of water in Chad. It is in the west. It spills into neighbouring Niger and Nigeria. In the north is a desert. It is part of the Sahara Desert.

Mercury is the planet nearest the sun. It is named after the Roman messenger to the gods. Mercury was famous for his speed as a runner. It is an appropriate name for the planet. Mercury whizzes around the sun. It travels at the speed of thirty miles per second. It completes one circuit in 88 days. But it rotates slowly on its axis. It takes fifty-nine days for Mercury to make a single rotation. It spins at the rate of about six miles per hour. The Earth spins at the rate of about a thousand miles per hour.

In Egyptian mythology Ra is the God of the Sun. He is the supreme god in Egyptian mythology. He was the son of Nut. Nut is the goddess of the heavens. Egyptian pharaohs claimed to be descended from Ra. Ra is sometimes represented as a lion. Ra is sometimes represented as a cat. Ra is sometimes represented as a falcon.

When Canada was founded, the average human life span was thirty-five years. By 1900, the average life span had increased to forty-seven years. Today, the average Canadian lives to be seventy-six years old. An elderly Canadian is defined as one over the age of sixty-five. In 1900, one in twenty-five Canadians were over the age of sixty-five. Today, one in eight Canadians is over the age of sixty-five. The explosion in the growth of the number of elderly Canadians has significant social and political ramifications.

The land that now makes up the state of Wyoming was purchased in 1803. It was a part of the Louisiana Purchase. Great Britain bought land from France in the Louisiana Purchase. In 1846, the United States obtained Wyoming from the British. The takeover was one of the conditions of the Oregon Treaty.

2. Revise the following paragraphs to improve their unity and coherence. Add words and combine sentences together as needed to create a more readable paragraph.

Achilles fought at the Trojan War. He had magnificent armour. He was killed. An arrow pierced his heel. His heel was the only vulnerable part of his body. His mother, Thetis, knew the war would endanger Achilles' life. She dipped him, when he was a baby, into the River Styx to protect him from injury. She held him by the heel, which did not get covered in water. Odysseus and Ajax fought over Achilles' armour. Odysseus and Ajax were both fearsome warriors. Odysseus killed Ajax. Years later, Odysseus had occasion to visit the land of the dead. Ajax refused to talk to him.

In September 1970, Salvador Allende was elected president of Chile. He was the first politician of a noncommunist country to run as a Marxist-Leninist and be elected in a free vote. He normalized relations with Cuba. He normalized relations with the People's Republic of China. He nationalized American companies. The military despised his policies. Augusto Pinochet was the Army Chief of Staff. In September 1973, he led a junta against Allende and seized power.

For years, astronomers did not know much about the planet Mercury. It is, in our solar system, the planet closest to the sun. The most powerful telescopes could not get a good view of Mercury. There was too much glare from the sun to see Mercury clearly. In the mid 1970s, NASA launched *Mariner 10*. It sent photographs of Mercury back to astronomers on Earth. The photos revealed a mountainous planet. It has cliffs 2 kilometres high and 1500 kilometres long. It contains a crater almost 1300 kilometres in diameter. Its surface is covered by a crust of light silicate rock. It is rich in iron.

COLLABORATIVE ACTIVITY

Exchange the draft of an essay with another student. Make suggestions on ways your partner might revise his or her essay to improve it. Resist the urge, for now, to correct errors in sentence grammar, sentence structure, punctuation, and spelling. Focus on improving the structure, the content, and the cohesion of your partner's paper.

CHAPTER 7

Edit Your Essay

Editing is the process of correcting and improving the sentences and words within a written text. It is a multifaceted aspect of the composing process that includes checking for good grammar, effective sentence structure, proper punctuation, and clear diction. It is an ongoing process, a task a writer works on while she writes and revises her essay.

Editing can be one of the most taxing aspects of the writing process. Some grammar and punctuation rules are complex; others are arbitrary; and there are hundreds of them. There are editing conventions some professors insist their students adhere to, and they penalize students who violate those conventions. Other professors, when grading, flag but forgive a *who* that should be a *whom*, an *I* that should be a *me*, or a comma that should be a semicolon.

What is the most effective way to edit a written text? Experienced writers often read their work out loud and base their editing decisions on "what sounds right." This is not a bad strategy, especially for those who, by virtue of their social and cultural background, have had extended exposure to the rules of Standard English. These rules—the patterns of Standard English—become fixed in our minds, and when a convention is violated, we literally hear it: "Me and my brother are coming home for Christmas." "I didn't do too good on my last biology exam." The more reading and writing you do and the more indelibly these language patterns acceptable within the academic community become fixed in your mind, the fewer errors you will make.

Some editing conventions, however, still deceive that sense of "what sounds right." Spoken English is less formal than written English, and sometimes a rendition common in spoken English is transferred to a written text even though the spoken version is grammatically incorrect. It might sound fine to say and hence to write, "My mother can't wait for my brother and I to come home for Thanksgiving," but the *I* is grammatically incorrect and should be changed to *me*—"She can't wait for *me* to come home."

This chapter will focus on those editing errors that college student writers make most frequently in their written work. We know what these are thanks to the work of Andrea Lunsford, Robert Connors, and Karen Lunsford. In 1988, Robert Connors and Andrea Lunsford published a paper called "Frequency of Formal Errors in Current College Writing" (*College Composition and Communication*, 39.4, pp. 395–409) and, in 2008, Andrea Lunsford and her niece Karen Lunsford updated the study in a paper called "Mistakes Are a Fact of Life." (*College Composition and Communication*, 59.4, pp. 781–806).

This chapter provides a concise but comprehensive account of editing conventions, focusing on instruction in those editing conventions that most frequently vex student writers. It discusses those rules you most need to know, as they apply to

- grammar
- sentence structure
- punctuation
- diction

Edit for Grammar

Grammar is the study of the order, the function, and the form of words in sentences and of the rules that govern this order, function, and form. Professors take the rules of English grammar seriously; they do not like to see grammatical errors in the essays that they grade, and they are likely to penalize an essay that contains grammatical errors. Grammar and spelling errors diminish the impact of your essay. Readers are not likely to take your ideas seriously if your paper contains grammatical errors. When you revise and edit your academic essays, check your grammar. In particular, check to make certain that

- your verbs agree with their subjects
- your pronouns clearly refer to the correct nouns
- the case of your pronouns is correct
- your verb tense is correct

● Subject–Verb Agreement

Singular subjects take singular verbs—A poet *paints* with words. Plural subjects take plural verbs—Poets *paint* with words. Usually, subject–verb agreement is that simple. You will write some sentences, however, that will require a moment's thought before you choose the correct verb form.

When Words Intervene Between the Subject and the Verb

If words come between the subject and the verb, be careful not to agree the verb with one of those words. In the sentence "One of my books is out of print," *one* is the subject, which is why the singular verb *is* is used. Compare the following two sentences:

> My books <u>are</u> out of print.
>
> One of my books <u>is</u> out of print.

When the Verb Precedes the Subject

You might write a sentence in which the verb precedes its subject. In this sentence, for example, the verb *are* comes well before the subject *philosophers*:

> There <u>are</u> many more important nineteenth-century philosophers whose work we did not study.

The verb must be the plural *are*, not the singular *is*, because the subject *philosophers* is plural.

When the Subject Is an Indefinite Pronoun

An indefinite pronoun is one that replaces an indefinite or inexact noun. Some examples of indefinite pronouns are *another, anybody, anyone, anything, each, either, every, everybody, everyone, everything, neither, nobody, no one, nothing, somebody, someone, something*. Indefinite pronouns usually require the singular form of the verb:

> Neither of my professors <u>is</u> available on Fridays.

Note that *neither*, not *professors*, is the subject with which the verb *is* must agree.

The indefinite pronouns *both* and *many* are always plural:

> Both of my professors <u>are</u> available on Fridays.

The indefinite pronouns *all, any, more, most, none*, and *some* can take either singular or plural verbs; the choice depends upon the context:

> All of the money <u>is</u> missing, but all of the employees <u>are</u> safe.

When the Noun Following the Verb Is Different in Number from the Subject

Be careful when you have a singular subject followed by a verb followed by a plural noun, as in this sentence:

> The worst part about writing an academic essay <u>is</u> all the grammar rules you need to know.

Because the noun *rules* is plural, you might be tempted to use the plural verb *are* instead of the correct verb *is*, but remember it is the subject the verb must agree with. If you have a plural subject followed by a singular noun, the same condition applies:

The rules of English grammar <u>are</u> a problem for many students.

Do not use the singular noun *is* because it is followed by a singular noun *problem*. The plural verb *are* is required because the subject *rules* is plural.

Collective Noun as Subject

A collective noun is one that identifies a group: *family, team, orchestra, class, audience.* Usually, a collective noun takes a singular verb:

The press <u>is</u> not welcome.

If the collective noun is not acting as a unit but rather is having its individual members emphasized, use the plural form of the verb, as in this sentence:

The press <u>are</u> arguing about who will get the interview.

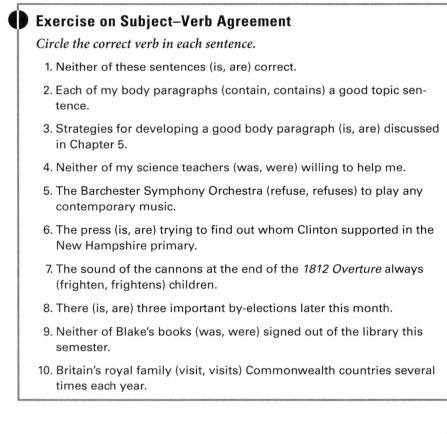

Exercise on Subject–Verb Agreement

Circle the correct verb in each sentence.

1. Neither of these sentences (is, are) correct.

2. Each of my body paragraphs (contain, contains) a good topic sentence.

3. Strategies for developing a good body paragraph (is, are) discussed in Chapter 5.

4. Neither of my science teachers (was, were) willing to help me.

5. The Barchester Symphony Orchestra (refuse, refuses) to play any contemporary music.

6. The press (is, are) trying to find out whom Clinton supported in the New Hampshire primary.

7. The sound of the cannons at the end of the *1812 Overture* always (frighten, frightens) children.

8. There (is, are) three important by-elections later this month.

9. Neither of Blake's books (was, were) signed out of the library this semester.

10. Britain's royal family (visit, visits) Commonwealth countries several times each year.

● Pronoun Reference

Pronouns replace nouns. The noun the pronoun replaces is called the antecedent of that pronoun. There are three pronoun–antecedent pitfalls to avoid.

First, make certain your pronouns agree in number with their antecedents.
In other words, if the antecedent is singular, the pronoun should be singular.
Consider these three sentences:

> The <u>manager</u> of a Burger World franchise cannot employ members of
> <u>their</u> immediate family.

> The <u>manager</u> of a Burger World franchise cannot employ members of
> <u>his or her</u> immediate family.

> <u>Managers</u> of Burger World franchises cannot employ members of
> <u>their</u> immediate families.

The first sentence is grammatically incorrect because *manager* is a singular noun
and *their* is a plural pronoun. *Manager* is the antecedent of *their*. They don't
agree in number. The second sentence is correct because *their* has been changed
to the singular pronouns *his or her*. The third sentence is correct because *manager* has been changed to *managers* to match the plural *their*.

Here is another example. Again, the first sentence is incorrect because the
noun is singular and the pronoun that replaces it later in the sentence is plural:

> If a <u>soldier</u> is given a command <u>they</u> believe is inappropriate, <u>they</u>
> can ask for the command to be issued in writing.

> If a <u>soldier</u> is given a command <u>he or she</u> believes is inappropriate,
> <u>he or she</u> can ask for the command to be issued in writing.

> If <u>soldiers</u> are given commands <u>they</u> believe are inappropriate, <u>they</u>
> can ask for the commands to be issued in writing.

Some writers and readers will find the repetition of "he or she" in the second
version of the sentence jarring; it disrupts the flow of the sentence. Using only
one of these pronouns is not grammatically incorrect, but your readers might
object to the exclusion, especially of the feminine pronoun.

Remember from the above discussion of subject–verb agreement that
indefinite pronouns such as *anyone, everyone, nobody,* or *somebody* are usually singular. Strictly speaking, this means that if a pronoun has an indefinite
pronoun as its antecedent, that pronoun should be singular. However, the use
of the plural pronoun in conjunction with an indefinite pronoun is becoming
widespread. Strictly speaking, the first of the following sentences is grammatically correct and the second is not, but most readers either will not recognize the
error in the second sentence or will not worry enough about it to hold it against
the writer. Most readers are not going to lose confidence in the work of a writer
who uses the plural pronoun *they* when its antecedent is the singular indefinite

pronoun *everyone*. If you are writing an academic essay, however, either check with your instructor to see if he or she (not they) will accept the plural or play it safe and use the singular.

> Anyone interested in applying for this job should send his or her resumé to the personnel manager.

> Anyone interested in applying for this job should send their resumé to the personnel manager.

Similarly, the grammar police would insist that this sentence is ungrammatical:

> Everyone complains about the taxes they have to pay, but no one is willing to cut those social programs that benefit them.

They would insist that the sentence be changed to something like this:

> Everyone complains about the taxes he or she has to pay, but no one is willing to cut those social programs that benefit him or her.

The second pronoun reference pitfall to avoid is the pronoun that seems to refer to more than one antecedent. Consider, for example, this sentence:

> The president hoped to meet the prime minister in Madrid, but, fearing an assassination attempt, he did not show up.

The pronoun *he* could refer to either the president or the prime minister. You would have to revise this sentence to clarify the identity of *he*—change the *he* to either *president* or *prime minister* to correct the ambiguity.

Finally, edit sentences that contain a pronoun that does not appear to have any antecedent at all. Consider this sentence:

> There was a vigorous debate in the House, but Members of Parliament knew the Senate would not agree to it.

The pronoun *it* has no apparent antecedent. Be specific by changing *it* to *the bill*, *the resolution*, or *the amendment*—whatever the pronoun is supposed to refer to—and the sentence becomes clear.

When you revise your essays, check all of your pronouns to make certain their antecedents are never ambiguous.

Exercise on Pronoun Reference

Correct the pronoun reference errors in these sentences.

1. He used the calculator to complete the form, and then he gave it to his roommate.

2. After Rendell and Fisher debated the issues on television, his approval ratings went up three percentage points.

3. Diana is overweight and Melissa is not, so she got the part.

4. Each candidate will have ten minutes to explain their platform.

5. Not every student at Juan de Fuca College will finish their degree in four years.

6. The ceremony was held at the tomb of the Unknown Soldier, who sacrificed their life to preserve the freedom of their countrymen.

7. A runner who trains five days a week, twice a day, will reach their top level of fitness within two months.

8. The city decided to renovate the stadium rather than build a new one because they did not want to raise taxes.

9. As soon as the young girl walked away from her mother and boarded the plane, she began to cry.

● Pronoun Case

There are three types or three cases of pronouns: subjective, objective, and possessive. English-language pronouns divide as follows into their three cases:

Subjective	Objective	Possessive
I	me	my, mine
you	you	your(s)
he	him	his
she	her	her(s)
we	us	our(s)
they	them	their(s)
who	whom	whose
it	it	its

Derek Soles.

The rules for correct pronoun use are straightforward. Pronouns in the subjective case are used as subjects of verbs:

He was born in 1795.

Pronouns in the objective case are used as objects of verbs:

He met her at a flea market.

or as objects of prepositions:

He knew she was the girl for him.

Pronouns in the possessive case are used to show possession:

He liked <u>her</u> long blond hair, and she liked <u>his</u> red suspenders.

The rules are straightforward, but applying these rules sometimes requires concentration. There are four pronoun pitfalls to avoid.

Noun–Pronoun Combinations

Be careful when you use a noun and a pronoun together; it is easy to make an error. You are unlikely to make an error if the noun–pronoun combination is acting as a subject, as in this sentence:

Dr. Johnson and <u>I</u> met for tea at the Strand.

But remember that you must use the objective case if the pronoun is the object of a verb, even if it is in combination with a noun:

The staff at the Strand expected Dr. Johnson and <u>me</u> to come for tea every Thursday afternoon.

Similarly, you must use the objective case of the pronoun if the pronoun is the object of a preposition, even if the pronoun is used in combination with a noun:

The staff at the Strand wanted to know who was coming with Dr. Johnson and <u>me</u>.

If this use of the objective case of the pronoun sounds wrong to you, eliminate the noun and you will know immediately that the objective case must be right:

They are expecting <u>me</u>.

They want to know who is coming with <u>me</u>.

Pronouns in a Comparison

When you use a pronoun in a comparison, complete the comparison (in your mind if not in the text) and you will select the correct pronoun. If you write, "She reads poetry more often than me," you are saying, "She reads poetry more than me does," when you obviously mean more than I do. In fact, if you write, "She reads poetry more often than me," you are saying, "She reads poetry more often than she reads me." The grammatically correct form is to write, "She reads poetry more often than I." Imagine the omitted word is included at the end of the sentence, and it will be easier for you to pick the correct pronoun: "She reads poetry more often than I [do]."

Pronouns in comparisons can, indeed, cause confusion. Be careful. If you write, "My mother likes mushrooms more than me," you are saying your mother likes mushrooms more than she likes you. If you mean to say she likes mushrooms more than you like mushrooms, change the *me* to *I*: "My mother likes mushrooms more than I [do]."

Who and Whom

Who is the subjective case of the pronoun, and *whom* is the objective case. *Who*, then, is used as a subject of a verb:

> I know <u>who is coming</u> with you.

Who is the subject of the verb *is coming*. *Whom* is used as the object of a verb:

> Dr. Johnson did not know <u>whom he could trust</u>.

Whom is the object of the verb *could trust*. That verb already has a subject, *he*, so the subjective pronoun *who* cannot be used.

Whom is also used as the object of a preposition:

> I think you know that journalist <u>with whom</u> Dr. Johnson is speaking.

Is it also correct to write the following sentence?

> I think you know that journalist <u>whom</u> Dr. Johnson is speaking <u>with</u>.

To do so puts the preposition at the end of the sentence. Many academics think the rule about never ending a sentence with a preposition is archaic and do not penalize essays that contain such sentences. Some academics, however, still think that ending a sentence with a preposition is a solecism, and they may penalize such a sentence.

Whom used as the object of a verb causes more problems than *whom* used as the object of a preposition. Remember that if the clause needs a subject, *who* is correct; if the clause needs an object, *whom* is correct. Compare these two sentences, both of which are grammatically correct:

> We all know whom you believe.

> We all know who you believe is telling the truth.

Do you see the difference between them? In the first sentence, *whom* is correct because it is the object of the verb *believe*. In the second sentence, *who* is correct because it is the subject of the verb *is telling*.

It's and Its

Its is a possessive pronoun, and *it's* is a contraction for "it is." These two words are often confused because we indicate possession by adding an apostrophe, and therefore, we might reason that *it's* indicates possessive. It does not. It is only a contraction for "it is." Never use *it's* as the possessive form of the pronoun *it*. Memorize this sentence so you have a reminder of the difference:

> <u>It's</u> a good movie, though I didn't like <u>its</u> ending.

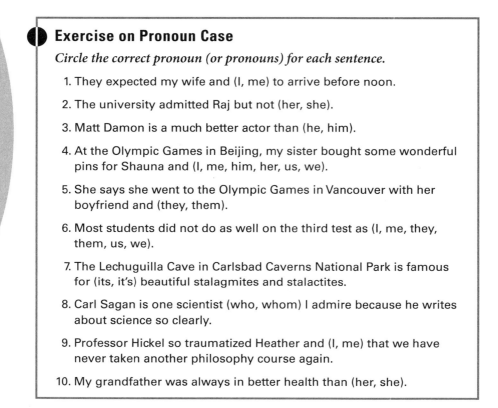

Exercise on Pronoun Case

Circle the correct pronoun (or pronouns) for each sentence.

1. They expected my wife and (I, me) to arrive before noon.

2. The university admitted Raj but not (her, she).

3. Matt Damon is a much better actor than (he, him).

4. At the Olympic Games in Beijing, my sister bought some wonderful pins for Shauna and (I, me, him, her, us, we).

5. She says she went to the Olympic Games in Vancouver with her boyfriend and (they, them).

6. Most students did not do as well on the third test as (I, me, they, them, us, we).

7. The Lechuguilla Cave in Carlsbad Caverns National Park is famous for (its, it's) beautiful stalagmites and stalactites.

8. Carl Sagan is one scientist (who, whom) I admire because he writes about science so clearly.

9. Professor Hickel so traumatized Heather and (I, me) that we have never taken another philosophy course again.

10. My grandfather was always in better health than (her, she).

Verb Tense and Mood

Verbs express action, and verb forms or tenses change to indicate if that action is taking place in the present, has taken place in the past, or will take place in the future. It is essential that the verb tenses you choose clearly indicate when the action that the verb expresses occurred. Choosing the correct verb is usually quite straightforward because we rely upon "what sounds right" and upon the logical relationships between actions and their subjects:

> (Was, Were) he alive today, Alexander Graham Bell (would be amazed, is amazed, was amazed) to see how his invention, the telephone, (evolves, has evolved).

We don't need to rely upon sophisticated rules of grammar to select the correct verbs for this sentence:

> Were he alive today, Alexander Graham Bell would be amazed to see how his invention, the telephone, has evolved.

But there are times when verb choice is not a simple matter of "what sounds right." To make certain you edit your writing correctly, you need to learn a few verb tense and mood rules that often cause errors. Be especially careful with the following:

- past tense of irregular verbs
- perfect verb forms
- subjunctive mood

Past Tense of Irregular Verbs

Verbs typically add the suffix-*ed* to indicate past tense:

> She attend<u>ed</u> York University.

An auxiliary or helping verb establishes the precise tense of the main verb that follows it (*was* hidden; *will* stay). When an auxiliary or helping verb precedes the past tense, the form of the past tense (called the past participle when preceded by an auxiliary verb) remains the same:

> She <u>has attended</u> York University for the past three years.

Irregular verbs, however, indicate tense by changing a vowel:

> I <u>gave</u> you my phone number already, and I will not give it to you again.

Complicating matters even further, irregular verbs often have a third form that must be used when such verbs are preceded by an auxiliary, or helping, verb. In other words, the past participle form of an irregular verb might be different from its past tense form:

> I <u>have given</u> you my phone number already. I <u>gave</u> it to you yesterday after class.

> It <u>breaks</u> my heart to know he <u>broke</u> your heart because my heart <u>has been broken</u> before.

> I see him every day. I <u>saw</u> him just yesterday. <u>I have seen</u> too much of him.

Be careful with irregular verbs. Make sure you use the correct past tense and past participle forms of irregular verbs. If you are not sure if the verb you are using has an irregular past and past participle form, simply look the verb up in the dictionary. In the *Canadian Oxford Dictionary*, for example, the entry for the verb *freeze* is followed immediately by its past tense and past participle forms—*froze* and *frozen*.

Perfect Verb Forms

Sentences with more than one verb often require more than one verb tense:

> She <u>knows</u> she <u>saw</u> him last Tuesday.

> I <u>know</u> you <u>will win</u>.

As is the case with single-verb sentences, time and logic dictate tense, and therefore you usually will not make a tense error:

> I <u>know</u> [now, in the present] you <u>will win</u> [at some point in the future].

But be careful using the perfect form of the verb, which is the form preceded by the auxiliary verbs *has, had,* or *have.* Consider these two sentences:

> She <u>has seen</u> *Gone with the Wind* twenty-seven times.

> She <u>saw</u> *Gone with the Wind* twenty-seven times.

A subtle difference in meaning exists between the two sentences. The first sentence, which uses the perfect form of the verb (*has seen*), implies that she might see the film again. The second sentence, which uses the simple past (*saw*), suggests she will not. The perfect verb form indicates such subtle differences in meaning.

Similarly, there is a subtle, but important difference between these two sentences:

> She was certain she <u>saw</u> him in the audience.

> She was certain she <u>had seen</u> him in the audience.

The second sentence implies another related *past* action: He denied he was there, but she was certain she had seen him in the audience. There may be another action associated with the first sentence as well, but not another past action: He denies he was there, but she was certain she saw him in the audience.

Finally, consider the difference in meaning between these two sentences:

> She will attend college next fall if she <u>earns</u> enough money.

> She will attend college next fall if she <u>has earned</u> enough money.

The first sentence suggests that the earning will take place at a specific time: She will attend college next fall if she earns enough money this summer. The second sentence does not suggest a specific time when the earning will take place: She will attend college next fall if she has earned enough money by then.

When you are revising your academic essays, check your verbs, especially your perfect-tense verbs, to make certain they express your meaning precisely.

Subjunctive Mood

In addition to conveying tense, verbs convey mood. Verb mood describes the attitude a sentence is conveying. A sentence like "Shut the door!" or "Get out of my way!" is expressing an imperative attitude and is said to be in the imperative mood. Note that the subject (*you*) is understood, not stated explicitly.

The subjunctive mood is used to express a condition contrary to fact, a conjecture, a wish, a recommendation, a demand, or an indirect request. In its present tense, the subjunctive mood is formed by using the uninflected or infinitive form of the verb. You normally would write, for example:

> She <u>sees</u> a psychiatrist once a month.

But if that sentence is preceded by a demand, its tense changes to indicate subjunctive mood:

> Her doctor insisted she <u>see</u> a psychiatrist every month.

In its past tense, the subjunctive mood usually requires the *were* form of the verb *to be*:

> If she <u>were</u> the prime minister, she would raise taxes.

However, some professors do not penalize the use of *was* in such sentences. The rule prescribing the use of *were* to indicate the subjunctive mood is less absolute than it once was.

If a verb is not in the imperative or the subjunctive mood, it is in the indicative mood. The vast majority of verbs in any given text are in the indicative mood.

◗ Exercise on Verb Tense and Mood

Correct errors in verb tense and mood in the following sentences

1. If I was a rich man, I would donate money to my alma mater.

2. Scientists discovered that certain microorganisms has survived, even after they were frozen for five years.

3. In March 1999, two adventurers finally succeeded in sailing a hot air balloon around the world on a journey that takes them twenty days.

4. By the third day of the journey, they realized they have not brought enough drinking water with them.

5. The Mountie insisted that she drives the rest of the way home.

6. The flag of Luxembourg, like the French flag, is composing of a red, a white, and a blue stripe, but on the Luxembourg flag the stripes are horizontal, while on the French flag they are vertical.

7. Since he had chose not to attend, he could hardly criticize her performance.

8. It was only six o'clock, but it was already obvious they had drank too much.

9. I let her finish the candy bar because I already brushed my teeth.

10. It is not likely Martha would have married him if he was a lawyer.

Edit for Sentence Structure

A sentence is a unit of communication that describes at least one act (in the verb) and one agent (the subject) undertaking that action: "Alice is working." Usually, sentences also include phrases and clauses that develop the subject and the verb: "Alice is working on her French essay, which is due tomorrow morning." Because sentences contain a variety of words, phrases, and clauses, sentence structure can become complex and susceptible to error. Before you hand your essays to your professors, check the structure of each sentence. You likely will lose a mark if a sentence in your essay is incomplete, awkward, improperly punctuated, or ambiguous. Watch especially for those common errors in sentence structure that often weaken student writing:

- sentence fragments
- run-on sentences
- misplaced or dangling modifiers
- faulty parallelism
- wordiness

● Sentence Fragments

A sentence fragment is an incomplete sentence masquerading as a complete one. A sentence must contain a subject and a verb. It is a fragment if one of these elements is missing, as in the following example:

> Alice is busy tonight. Working on her French essay.

"Working on her French essay" is not a sentence because it does not contain a subject. To correct this sentence fragment, attach it to the preceding sentence and replace the period with a comma:

> Alice is busy tonight, working on her French essay.

A word group can contain a subject and a verb but still be a fragment:

> Alice will be working on her French essay all night. Because it is due in her first class tomorrow morning.

The second word group does contain a subject and a verb but is not a complete sentence. It is a sentence fragment because it begins with the word *because*, which is one of those words that introduce subordinate or dependent clauses. A subordinate or dependent clause does contain a subject and a verb but cannot stand alone; it "depends" upon, it is "subordinate" to, a main clause (which is synonymous to a complete sentence). Therefore, the subordinate clause should be a part of the sentence:

> Alice will be working on her French essay all night because it is due in her first class tomorrow morning.

It is also acceptable to put the subordinate clause at the beginning of the sentence, though minor alterations should be made to it:

> Because her French essay is due in her first class tomorrow morning, Alice will be working on it all night.

Other words that introduce subordinate or dependent clauses include *after*, *before*, *if*, *since*, *that*, *when*, *which*, *while*, *who*, and *whose*. Learn these words and check to make sure that they appear within a sentence and do not begin a fragment when you use them in your essays. Note that if the preceding sentence had been punctuated like this, it would be a sentence fragment error:

> Learn these words and check to make sure that they appear within a sentence and do not begin a fragment. When you use them in your essays.

Let's look at one more example. The second sentence in the following pair is also a fragment:

> Alice is working on her French essay tonight. The last paper that she needs to hand in to complete the course requirements.

To correct this fragment, make it a complete sentence:

> Alice is working on her French essay tonight. This is the last paper that she needs to hand in to complete the course requirements.

Or attach it to the main clause:

> Tonight Alice is working on her French essay, which is the last paper that she needs to hand in to complete the course requirements.

Note that the word introducing the dependent clause, the word *that*, could be left out because its presence in the sentence is implicit.

Professional writers occasionally use a fragment deliberately, usually for emphasis:

> The prime minister refused to attend the king's funeral. What an insult! To the king's nation as well as to our own.

The last two word groups are fragments but acceptable because they are used deliberately, for emphasis. When writing an academic essay, however, play it safe and avoid fragments altogether.

Exercise on Sentence Fragments

Rewrite the following passages to correct any sentence fragments they contain.

1. The Berlin Wall was built at the end of World War II. Dividing the eastern part of Berlin into a communist sector and the western part of the city into a capitalist sector.

2. Americans were at first puzzled and then annoyed. When the Toronto Blue Jays won the World Series.

3. After World War II, the demand for public education increased dramatically. Mainly as a result of the baby boom.

4. People suffering from hypothermia need blankets and warm, non-alcoholic liquids. Or else they could become unconscious.

5. More Canadians will be travelling abroad this summer than they did last summer. Mainly because of the rise in the value of the loonie.

6. The hawk and the eagle are both diurnal birds of prey, but the eagle is more common on the West Coast. Where there is an abundance of the small animals that eagles use as their food supply.

7. The hare has longer ears and legs than the rabbit, so hares can outrun their predators. Instead of burrowing into the ground as rabbits must.

● Run-On Sentences

A run-on sentence consists of two complete sentences incorrectly joined together, either by a comma (an error called a comma splice) or without any punctuation at all (an error called a fused sentence). It is certainly acceptable to join two sentences together to make one, but the merger must be done correctly.

Two complete sentences cannot be separated from each other merely by a comma. (Note that if the comma is missing, this error is referred to as a fused sentence.) Here is a clear example of two separate sentences joined together, incorrectly, by a comma:

> Alice is working on her French essay tonight, she can't come to the game.

There are several ways to correct this type of run-on sentence. You may replace the comma with a period or, if the two sentences are related, with a semicolon. A comma is not considered a strong enough pause to separate two sentences, but a semicolon is. You may place a coordinate conjunction (*and*, *but*, *or*) after the comma:

> Alice is working on her French essay tonight, and she can't come to the game.

You may change one of the sentences into a dependent (subordinate) clause:

> Since Alice is working on her French essay tonight, she can't come to the game.

If both subjects refer to the same person, you may add a coordinate conjunction and eliminate the second subject. Note that if you eliminate the second subject, you also dispense with the comma:

> Alice is working on her French essay tonight and can't come to the game.

Note also that this solution is not always a possibility, as the following sentence illustrates:

> Alice is working on her French essay tonight, it is due first period tomorrow.

You would need to correct this run-on sentence using one of the other methods. You could change the comma to a period or a semicolon. Or you could reduce one of the sentences to a subordinate clause:

> Alice is working on her French essay tonight because it is due first period tomorrow.

> Tonight Alice is working on her French essay, which is due first period tomorrow.

Here is one more example. The first sentence is a run-on because it uses only a comma to separate two complete sentences. The sentences below it illustrate ways of correcting the run-on.

> Another common error in sentence structure is the run-on sentence, a run-on sentence consists of two complete sentences joined together by a comma.

> Another common error in sentence structure is the run-on sentence. A run-on sentence consists of two complete sentences joined together by a comma.

> Another common error in sentence structure is the run-on sentence; a run-on sentence consists of two complete sentences joined together by a comma.

> Another common error in sentence structure is the run-on sentence, which consists of two complete sentences joined together by a comma.

> Another common error in sentence structure is the run-on sentence, consisting of two complete sentences joined together by a comma.

Note especially the last method of correction. The second sentence is reduced not to a subordinate clause, as the sentence above it is, but to a phrase introduced by the participle *consisting*. This is another effective method of correcting a run-on sentence.

Exercise on Run-On Sentences

Rewrite the following passages to correct any run-on sentence errors they contain.

1. The aardvark is a nocturnal mammal about 1.5 metres long, it feeds on termites and ants.

2. Cats have excellent vision, they can see as well at night as they can during the day.

3. Leonard Cohen was an influential songwriter, especially during the 1960s, his songs were recorded by artists in several different countries.

4. A contract is an agreement between two people to allow for the exchange of goods and services, one person provides a product or a service, the other person pays for it.

5. Newgate Prison was destroyed in the Great Fire of 1666, it was not rebuilt until 1778, it was destroyed by fire again during the Gordon Riots of 1780.

6. Creon thought Polynices was a traitor and refused to grant him a state funeral, however Polynices's sister Antigone defied Creon and buried her brother with full military honours.

Misplaced and Dangling Modifiers

Modifiers are words and phrases that describe, clarify, and refine subjects and verbs and other key elements (usually other nouns and verbs) within sentences. You must be careful to place your modifiers within your sentences so that they clearly modify what you intend them to modify.

A misplaced modifier is a word or group of words that describes a word in a sentence other than the word it is supposed to describe. In this sentence, "I was able to find two books and several articles in the library that will be useful to me," the phrase "that will be useful to me" is misplaced because it modifies "library" but is meant to modify "two books and several articles." If the sentence is revised to read, "I was able to find two books and several articles that will be useful to me in the library," we still have a misplaced modifier, in this case the phrase "in the library," implying as it does that the books and articles will be useful to me in the library but not necessarily anywhere else. If the phrase "in the library" is placed at the beginning of the sentence, the error is corrected:

> In the library, I was able to find two books and several articles that will be useful to me.

Similarly, if the same phrase is placed after the infinitive *to find*, the error is corrected:

> I was able to find, in the library, two books and several articles that will be useful to me.

Consider a second example:

> The future of the Earth relies almost entirely on the sun, a massive ball of flaming gas 330,000 times as large as the Earth, which is slowly running out of energy.

The last clause modifies *Earth*, but the writer intends it to modify *sun*. A misplaced modifier often indicates that the sentence containing it is too long, and sometimes the best way to correct a misplaced modifier is to compose two shorter sentences:

> The sun is a massive ball of flaming gas 330,000 times as large as the Earth. The future of the Earth relies almost entirely on the sun, which is slowly running out of energy.

A dangling modifier is a word or a group of words that is supposed to modify a word in a sentence but that "dangles" because that needed word is missing from the sentence. In this sentence, for example, "When writing an essay, the rules for good writing should be kept in mind," the phrase "When writing an essay" dangles at the beginning, in search of a word it can modify. But there is no such word in the sentence. In fact, it sounds as if "the rules" are writing the essay. The sentence needs to be revised to give "When writing an essay" a word it will clearly modify. Here are two possibilities:

> When writing an essay, writers should keep in mind the rules for good writing.

> When you are writing an essay, you should keep the rules for good writing in mind.

Here is another example:

> Looking at present trends in carbon dioxide levels in the air, predictions can be made that levels will drop to 140 parts per million in 500 million years.

Predictions cannot look at present trends. Astronomers can, though. Therefore, the sentence should be revised to read:

> Looking at present trends in carbon dioxide levels in the air, astronomers can predict that levels will drop to 140 parts per million in 500 million years.

Misplaced and dangling modifiers make sentences ambiguous. When you are revising your essay, check the placement of your modifiers to make sure they do not make any of your sentences awkward or unclear.

Exercise on Misplaced and Dangling Modifiers

Rewrite the following sentences to correct misplaced and dangling modifiers.

1. After waiting for over an hour, the concert finally began.

2. To survive a winter in Winnipeg, warm clothing and patience are essential.

3. The candidate gave the same speech opposing the bill in every town in the county.

4. I gave my old copy of the text to my friend with all of the exercises completed.

5. I thought I might be fired after I refused to pour coffee for the truckers in their own thermoses.

6. Professor Higgins collected all of the assignments about the civil war on Friday.

7. Passengers may not take a suitcase onto a plane that won't fit into the overhead compartment.

8. The bicycle we found at the dump that is missing its handle bars can easily be repaired.

9. While trying to sneak into the house past curfew, a vase crashed to the floor.

10. An old man accompanied my wife whom I had never seen before.

11. Hiking along the West Coast Trail, it is not uncommon to spot a cougar.

Faulty Parallelism

Faulty parallelism is an error in sentence structure that occurs when words or phrases that should be syntactically equal within a sentence are not. Faulty parallelism adversely affects the balance of a sentence. "He managed to make the team even though he is short, awkward, and weight is a problem for him" lacks parallelism because the phrase "weight is a problem for him" does not balance the adjectives *short* and *awkward*. The sentence comes parallel when the phrase is changed to the adjective *overweight*.

He managed to make the team even though he is short, awkward, and overweight.

Here is another example of faulty parallelism:

The company will either go bankrupt or there was a leveraged buyout possibility that could save it.

"Go bankrupt" does not balance "there was"; "be saved" is a much better match. The following revision establishes a parallel structure and makes the sentence more fluent:

The company will either go bankrupt or be saved by a leveraged buyout.

Exercise on Parallelism

Rewrite the following sentences to improve their parallel structure.

1. While he was secretary general of the United Nations, Dag Hammarskjold worked tirelessly for peace in the Middle East and the Congo, and the Nobel Prize for peace was awarded to him in 1962.

2. Alan is planning to attend the local junior college, Chris is going to the state university, while the decision Jenny has made is to go to work in her mother's business.

3. By the end of the movie, the main character has become quite unstable, losing his identity and, ultimately, he commits suicide.

4. Sports psychologists feel that some athletes take steroids not so much because they crave victory but it is from having low self-esteem.

5. Hydrogen is the lightest of all the elements, but it can be explosive when mixed with air, and bomb making has been one of its uses.

Wordiness

The structure of some sentences appears shaky because the writer has used more words than necessary to express the ideas the sentence contains. Here is an example of a wordy sentence:

This essay will explore several different theories that have been developed by paleontologists for attempting to explain why dinosaurs reached the point of becoming extinct.

Read the sentence out loud and you will hear the wordiness. The first half is not too bad; the second half is a wordy disaster, especially "reached the point of becoming extinct," which could be reduced simply to "became extinct." The sentence is improved when revised as follows:

> This essay will explore several theories paleontologists have developed to explain why dinosaurs became extinct.

Some teacher will find "This essay will explore" unnecessary on the grounds that it is already implied. They might favour a more concise version of the sentence:

> Paleontologists have developed several theories to explain why dinosaurs became extinct.

Wordiness is a matter of degree, to a certain extent. You want your sentences to be concise but complete.

Here is another example of a wordy sentence:

> In 1916, the disease of polio reached epidemic proportions when 27,363 cases of polio were reported by health care workers in America and more than 7000 people died of polio as a result in the worst outbreak of polio in the history of the country.

Again, read the sentence out loud, and the need to edit for concision is apparent. "The disease of" is unnecessary; it is not necessary to repeat "polio" three times; "as a result" is implied. The sentence could be half as long and say the same thing more eloquently:

> In 1916, American health care workers reported 27,363 cases of polio and over 7000 deaths in the country's worst polio epidemic.

One of the enemies of concision in both of the above wordy sentences is passive voice. Passive voice is a form of a verb that adds part of the verb *to be* to a past participle: *was thrown, is forbidden, am disappointed, have been developed, were reported*. Passive voice tends to be wordy. "The ball was thrown by my brother" is wordier than "My brother threw the ball." Passive voice is not wrong; indeed, it is useful if the subject of the sentence is indeterminate: "Smoking is forbidden in this building." But passive voice is wordy when a word that should be the sentence's subject is stuck somewhere else, usually as the object in a prepositional phrase. There is nothing wrong with "Three of the goals were scored by defencemen," but it is less concise than writing, "Defencemen scored three of the goals."

Exercise on Wordiness

Rewrite each sentence to make it more clear and concise.

1. Acid rain is rain that contains too much acid, especially too much acidity, which is found in the nitric acid and the sulphuric acid, which are components of acid rain.

2. Psychotherapy is not a single method of treating mental illness but a term that encompasses many other types of therapies for treating mental illness using a variety of methods.

3. A black hole is a star that has such a strong gravitational force that nothing can escape its gravitational pull, including light, which is why a black hole cannot be seen and its existence is speculated upon.

4. Hundreds of tourists from all over the world enjoying the innovative architecture, the excellent art gallery, and the variety of shops account for the crowds along Robson Street in the Canadian city of Vancouver.

5. Astronomers can study the outer layers of the sun and its corona when the light from the sun is obscured by the moon during an eclipse when the sun is not too bright to study, and they are eager to do so.

6. Dixieland jazz originated in the city of New Orleans in the early 1900s and became popular later on when famous people such as F. Scott Fitzgerald, whose glamorous friends and fictional characters danced to it, embraced it.

7. Thunder follows lightening because thunder is caused by the intense vibrations in the air, which are the by-products of the heat generated by the lightening that then cools rapidly and causes the explosive noise common to thunder.

Edit for Punctuation

Another important aspect of the editing process is the punctuation check. Sentences need to be properly punctuated if they are to be clear and readable. An unpunctuated sentence reads like a puzzle that must be solved before its meaning can be grasped. The sentence "If you can come before it gets too dark" is confusing; it reads, in fact, like a sentence fragment. But the meaning becomes clear when a comma is placed after *can*: "If you can, come before it gets too dark."

When you are revising your writing, check to make sure it is punctuated correctly. Check your use of punctuation marks in the following locations:

- at the end of sentences
- within sentences
- within words

● Punctuation at the End of Sentences

At the end of most declarative, informative sentences, you use a period. You may use an exclamation point for extra emphasis, but, in an academic essay, do so sparingly. A question mark, of course, comes at the end of a question.

It is acceptable to use a semicolon at the end of a sentence, if the next sentence continues on the same topic:

> American Motors manufactures fewer than half a million passenger cars a year; Ford Motors manufactures well over a million.

> The Canadian economy faltered in the spring of 2010; lately it has shown signs of a recovery.

A period would be acceptable between these sentences, but the semicolon does emphasize the relationship between them. A comma would not be acceptable. A comma cannot come between two complete sentences unless the comma is followed by a coordinate conjunction.

It is acceptable to use a colon at the end of a sentence if the next sentence explains or clarifies a topic mentioned in the preceding sentence:

> He realized, with great sorrow, that there was no other choice: He would have to fight his own brother.

> In the course of the lecture, he explained to us that the city's name derives from the native language: *hono* means "bay" and *lulu* means "sheltered."

A period would be acceptable between these sentences, but the colon does stress the fact that the second sentence embellishes the first. Note that when a complete sentence follows a colon, the first word may be capitalized. (The first word following a semicolon is not capitalized, unless it is a proper noun.)

● Punctuation Within Sentences

Seven punctuation marks can occur within sentences: commas, semicolons, colons, quotation marks, dashes, parentheses, and ellipses. (Remember that semicolons and colons are also used at the ends of sentences. See the examples in the preceding section.)

Commas

Four main rules govern the use of commas in academic writing.

1. A comma comes before a coordinate conjunction in a compound sentence:

> The topic sentence should contain the main idea of the paragraph, and the other sentences should develop the main idea.

(Note that this rule is also covered in the "Run-On Sentences" section of this chapter.)

2. Commas separate a nonrestrictive word, phrase, or clause from the rest of the sentence. A nonrestrictive element is one that is not essential to the meaning of the sentence. It is the opposite of a restricted element, which is essential to the meaning of the sentence. Consider carefully these two sentences:

> Sheehy's *Guide to Reference Books,* which should be at the reference desk of your library, lists sources that you will find useful.

> All of the books that I need to research my essay have been signed out of the library.

Note that the clause "which should be at the reference desk of your library" is separated from the rest of the sentence by commas. Commas are used because the clause is nonrestrictive, that is, not essential to the meaning of the sentence. The word *which* is used also because the clause is nonrestrictive. To test whether a clause is nonrestrictive, eliminate the clause and see if the sentence still makes sense, which in this case it does:

> Sheehy's *Guide to Reference Books* lists sources that you will find useful.

Now note the clause "that I need to research my essay" in the second sentence. This clause is not separated from the rest of the sentence by commas. It is a restrictive clause; that is, it is essential to the meaning of the sentence. The word *that* is used also because the clause is restrictive. To test whether a clause is restrictive, eliminate the clause and see if the sentence still makes sense, which in this case it does not:

> All of the books have been signed out of the library.

If you can eliminate a word, phrase, or clause from a sentence without the sentence losing its meaning, then that word, phrase, or clause is nonrestrictive and should be separated from the rest of the sentence by commas.

Consider this sentence:

> Windsor Castle was damaged by a serious fire.

This sentence is short, simple, and self-contained. Any clauses or phrases added to this sentence would be nonrestrictive and therefore separated from the rest of the sentence by commas. Note carefully the commas in this sentence:

> In 1992, Windsor Castle, the queen's house on the banks of the Thames, was damaged by a serious fire.

Transitional and parenthetical words and phrases are almost always nonrestrictive and, therefore, are set off from the rest of the sentence by commas. Note carefully the placement of commas in these sentences. They separate transitional and parenthetical words and phrases from the rest of the sentence:

> There is, however, no reason why a new policy cannot be implemented immediately.

> Finally, we are considering the implementation of a new policy that should reduce the rate of recidivism.

> On the other hand, the current policy has reduced the crime rate in some sections of the city.

> That, too, remains to be decided.

There is an exception to the rule that states that restrictive words, phrases, or clauses are not set off from the rest of the sentence with commas: Even a restrictive word phrase or clause usually is followed by a comma if that restrictive element begins the sentence. Compare these two sentences:

> Their starting point guard will not be able to play unless her Achilles tendon is better.

> Unless her Achilles tendon is better, their starting point guard will not be able to play.

3. Use a comma between coordinate, but not cumulative, adjectives. Coordinate adjectives modify the same noun. In the phrase "a bright, colourful skirt," both adjectives modify the noun *skirt* and are separated from each other by a comma. A cumulative adjective qualifies the adjective that follows it; the second adjective modifies the noun. In the phrase "a black leather skirt," the adjective *black* qualifies the adjective "leather" which then modifies the noun "skirt." These are cumulative adjectives and are not separated from each other by commas. An often-used test to determine if adjectives are coordinate or cumulative is to see if the word *and* can be placed between the adjectives. If it can, the adjectives are coordinate and need a comma between them: "a bright and colourful skirt." If *and* sounds awkward placed between the adjectives, a comma is not required: "She wore a black [not *and*] leather skirt."

4. Use commas to separate words, phrases, or clauses in a series. Note the use of the commas in this sentence:

> In this chapter, we are learning the uses of the period, the comma, the semicolon, the colon, and the dash.

Commas separate the series of punctuation marks mentioned in the sentence. Note that there is a comma between the words *colon* and *dash*. This comma is optional. Note, as well, the comma after the introductory phrase "In this chapter." It is a nonrestrictive phrase and is therefore set off from the rest of the sentence by the comma.

Semicolons

There are two uses for the semicolon in academic writing.

1. Use a semicolon to separate two complete but related sentences:

On one side of the street were protesters who wanted the child returned to his father in Cuba; on the other side were protesters who insisted the child be allowed to stay in the country.

The schools in the senator's district all have access to the Internet; inner-city schools do not have even basic computer equipment.

2. Use a semicolon to separate phrases or clauses in a series when there are commas within those phrases or clauses:

You want your essay to be well organized; you want your sentences within your paragraphs and your paragraphs within the essay to be logically connected, in other words, to cohere; you want your diction to be accurate and appropriate; you want to avoid errors in grammar, spelling, and punctuation; and you want your prose to be concise.

Colons

Earlier in this chapter, you learned that a colon could come between two sentences if the second sentence explained or clarified the first, for example, "He adhered to the golden rule: Do unto others as you would have others do unto you."

A colon also precedes a word or a phrase that explains or clarifies a sentence:

Calgary is a long way away: 296 kilometres, to be exact.

Given his personality, he chose an appropriate pseudonym: Joe Average.

Note that the clarifying words or phrases often take the form of a list:

She claimed there were just three qualities she was looking for in a husband: ambition, compassion, and a good sense of humour.

Quotation Marks

In academic writing, quotation marks serve two functions.

1. Quotation marks indicate that you are quoting someone else's spoken or written words.

"I write slowly," Mullen told one interviewer. "It can take me months to complete a single sonnet."

In her preface to *Satan's Rainbow*, Mullen responds to criticism that her work is obscure, arguing that her ambiguous syntax is a "deliberate strategy to free readers to interpret my work in ways that mean the most to them."

Note that if a written quote is more than about three lines in length, it is set off from the rest of the text and does not contain quotation marks (unless the source being quoted also contains them).

Note also that, on occasion, you might need to use quotation marks in a context in which other quotation marks already occur. When this happens, revert to single quotation marks to indicate the quote within the quote:

> In her analysis of Keats's sonnet, Foster notes that "the repetition of the adverb 'still' is typical of Keats's style."

2. Quotation marks enclose minor titles. Titles of short stories and poems, for example, are placed within quotation marks:

> My favourite sonnet is "Bright Star" by Keats.

Dashes

In academic writing, the dash is used mainly to enclose a nonrestrictive word group that contains commas:

> She eats something from each food group—protein, dairy, fruits and vegetables, and grains—at every meal.

A dash is also used to signal an abrupt change or shift in thought, but a sentence that contains such a shift is rare in academic writing:

> Students can also pay for a database search—if they want to waste their time and money.

Parentheses

Parentheses enclose information of borderline importance to a sentence, in other words, information that a writer decides to include but does not consider vitally important:

> The first volume (in a twelve-volume series) should be published before the end of the month.

Ellipses

The ellipsis mark (a succession of three periods: ...) is an important punctuation mark in academic writing, used to indicate that unneeded words have been omitted. The ellipsis comes in handy if you are quoting from a secondary source and want to keep the quote concise and relevant by omitting unnecessary words:

> "Computer viruses are more annoying than harmful, and most hackers cannot do anywhere near the damage ... they claim they can."

Use four dots if a period is included in the information you omit or if the remaining material reaches a natural ending point to the sentence:

> Kafka writes poignantly of Gregor's isolation: "Gregor now stationed himself immediately before the living room door, determined to persuade any hesitating visitor to come in...."

● Punctuation Within Words

There are two punctuation marks that can occur within a word: the apostrophe and the hyphen.

Apostrophes

Apostrophes are used in nouns to indicate ownership. Study carefully the following sentences:

> The professor claimed he had misplaced his student's essay.
>
> The professor claimed he had misplaced his students' essays.
>
> For that assignment, the men's essays were not as well written as the women's.

In the first sentence, the apostrophe comes before the *s* because the noun *student* is singular. There is only one student. In the second sentence, the apostrophe comes after the *s* because the noun *students* is plural. The rule, then, is put an apostrophe before the *s* to indicate singular possession and after the *s* to indicate plural possession.

What about the third sentence? Men and women are plural: Why does the apostrophe come before the *s*? It comes before the *s* because *men* and *women* are nouns that form their plural not by adding an *s* but by changing a vowel: *Man* becomes *men*; *woman* becomes *women*. The apostrophe comes before the *s* in nouns that form their plural by changing a vowel. We write *children's toys*, never *childrens' toys*.

If a noun ends in the letter *s*, you may put the apostrophe after the *s* and not add another *s* even if the noun is singular:

> I enjoy reading Keats' poetry.
>
> I enjoy reading Keats's poetry.

Choose the version that sounds the best to you.

Apostrophes are also used in contractions such as *don't*, *isn't*, and *weren't*. But note carefully the difference between *it's* and *its*. *It's* is a contraction for "it is." *Its* is a possessive pronoun and never needs an apostrophe because it is already in possessive case. Memorize this sentence to avoid confusing the two:

> It's missing one of its pages.

Finally, note the placement of the apostrophe in these sentences:

> We are having dinner at Mary and Tom's house.
>
> I wrecked my brother-in-law's car.

Hyphens

Hyphens are used within compound words such as *mother-in-law*, *forty-one*, *one-third*, and *run-on*. Hyphens also are used to join two or more words that modify a noun they precede:

> She wore five-inch heels.

Exercise on Punctuation

Punctuate the following sentences correctly.

1. We planned to serve key lime pie but my brother is allergic to citrus fruit.

2. Oscar will be fighting an inexperienced opponent and experts are predicting an early knockout.

3. Your essay should be double spaced and should have one and a half inch margins on both sides of the page.

4. My uncle who played basketball in college taught me how to dribble behind my back.

5. She decided to retire early, she could not handle the stress any longer.

6. Both a coordinate conjunction and a conjunctive adverb link sentences together, a conjunctive adverb is preceded by a semicolon.

7. The schools in the senators district now have access to the Internet, however inner-city schools are still waiting to get basic computer equipment.

8. Ellis did not hand in two of his assignments, therefore he did not get a passing grade in his sociology course.

9. Tia Maria Drambuie Benedictine and Curacao are among the most popular liqueurs and are sold throughout the world.

10. The tern is a slender gull like bird and with it's long pointed wings and a deeply notched tail it flies with grace energy and strength.

11. The silver that is mined in Ontario is considered superior to the silver mined in Colorado.

12. The upper limit of the biosphere the part of earth where life can exist is about 9000 metres above sea level the lower limit is approximately 3000 metres beneath the surface of the ocean.

13. A portion of the play the third scene of the final act to be precise was excluded to meet a two hour time limit.

14. The anteaters tongue is covered with sticky saliva that allows it to trap ants termites and other insects on which it feeds.

15. Daves new interest is cybernetics the science that among other things compares brain functions to the function of machines especially computers.

16. France lost Alsace and Lorraine to Germany in 1871 after a war in which the Germans who were better prepared than the French won nearly every battle.

17. The greyhound wolfhound and deerhound hunt by sight the blood-hound foxhound and beagle hunt by scent.

18. Diabetics lack insulin which controls the supply of sugar from the blood to the muscles however with proper insulin injections diabetics can live a normal life.

19. Film adaptations of novels are usually disappointing but the film version of Kinsellas *Field of Dreams* is better than the book.

20. Since the beginning of the century the Nobel Prize has been awarded to men and women for outstanding contributions to the following fields physics chemistry medicine literature peace and economics.

21. As T.S. Eliot writes in Little Gidding one of the poems from his book *Four Quartets* What we call the beginning is often the end. And to make an end is to make a beginning.

22. Originally the word *tycoon* from the Japanese *taikun* referred to the commander in chief of the Japanese army but now its used often in a derogatory sense to describe a powerful influential businessperson.

23. The plane will make a ninety minute stop in St. Louis where you are free to disembark for thirty minutes a twenty minute stop in Minneapolis where you may not disembark and a ninety minute stop in Chicago where you may disembark for twenty minutes.

Edit for Diction

The word may be the smallest unit of written communication, but it is no less important than the sentence or the paragraph. "The difference between the right word and the nearly right word," Mark Twain once said, "is the difference between lightning and a lightning bug." When you are editing your writing, you want to check to make certain that the words you have used show respect for your readers and a commitment to your purpose. Check, especially, to make sure your words are appropriate to the context of your essay and convey the meaning you wish to convey as clearly and precisely as possible.

● Context

The words you choose must be appropriate to the context in which you use them. Academic writing is relatively formal, so the connotation of your words as well as the denotation must be accurate. The denotation of a word is the word's literal, dictionary definition. The connotation refers to the intellectual or emotional associations a word carries with it. Words can have identical denotations. A 6-foot-tall, 130-pound man can be described as *skinny* or *slender*, but he likely would prefer *slender* because the connotations of that word are more positive.

Slang words usually have connotations too informal for academic writing. In this sentence, some verbs would be acceptable in academic writing, and others would not:

> The senator was too (drunk, inebriated, intoxicated, blitzed, bombed, tipsy, trashed, pissed to the gills, wasted, looped, polluted) to debate the bill.

The use of jargon also depends upon context. Jargon is language specific to a certain social or professional group. Lawyers, stockbrokers, doctors, professional sports fans, computer programmers, forest rangers, civil servants, and musicians can all speak and write in a language they understand but outsiders do not. Readers can usually identify the social or professional group using the jargon but not the meaning of all of the words and phrases they use. We can figure out, for example, that the writers of these sentences are a car buff, a basketball fan, and a fashion writer respectively, but we will have a harder time determining what exactly they are talking about.

> It has side rocker panels, flared wheel wells, and an inline 6-cylinder, 2.5-litre, 168-horsepower engine.

> They may have won the cup, but they relied so heavily on the neutral zone trap that the finals were hardly exciting.

> By cutting on the bias, she accentuated the drape on the handkerchief hems she will show in next spring's collection.

The use of jargon is not necessarily an error. Its appropriateness depends upon the writer's knowledge of her audience. If the writer knows her readers will understand the jargon because they are members of the apposite subculture, she may use that subculture's jargon. But if her readers are not a part of that subculture, the writer must avoid its jargon and use layman's language. Otherwise, she runs the risk that her readers will not fully understand the text; they may even resent the writer who is making them feel like outsiders.

● Meaning

The meaning of words is hardly absolute. Words have nuances and shades of meaning. Good writers edit their work to make certain they have used words that most accurately convey their intended meaning.

As a rule, choose the specific and concrete word over the vague and abstract one. Concrete and specific words add important shades of meaning to the sentences in which they appear. If a beautiful young woman or a handsome young man is sitting on a park bench reading a *book*, we know less about them and see them less clearly than we would if we are told they are reading *Advanced Calculus, The Collected Poems of Emily Dickinson, The Unauthorized Biography of Britney Spears*, or *Das Kapital*. Give a title to the vague and abstract *book* and the writing becomes more vivid.

For example, compare these two sentences:

> Eric was at the bus stop when a car sped past him, hit the puddle, and splashed water over his new suit.

> Eric was at the bus stop when a Mercedes sped past him, hit the puddle, and splashed water over his new suit.

Only one word has been changed: *car* has become *Mercedes*. But the effect of the change is considerable. The reader now sees more vividly what the writer is trying to describe. And Eric's anger has an additional cause. A Mercedes driver suggests wealth, which in turn suggests an indifference to poor people waiting for buses. The Mercedes adds insult to the injury. The Mercedes makes a relatively neutral sentence considerably more meaningful.

Your meaning will also be enhanced if you use euphemisms sparingly. A euphemism is a word or a phrase that, at best, is deliberately obscure and, at worst, is deliberately deceptive. There are two reasons for using a euphemism.

First, euphemisms are sometimes used to avoid being too blunt or offensive. A teacher might like to write on a report card: "Arthur is loud and obnoxious. He annoys me and the other children. We can't get any work done when he is around, so I often have to kick him out of class." But, unwilling to risk the ire of parents and principals, she more likely will resort to euphemism: "We appreciate Arthur's exuberant personality, though it does interfere sometimes with class work. I encourage Arthur to work independently, which he seems to enjoy."

But second, sometimes euphemisms are used to deflect the truth, to deliberately mislead readers. Management cannot let the plant close, so an accident becomes a "reportable occurrence," which sounds much less threatening. The military can't admit it erred, so civilians killed in the bombing raids are referred to as "collateral damage," which sounds like an unfortunate but inevitable and harmless byproduct of war. The government "initiates revenue enhancement programs" so we don't quite realize our taxes are going to go up. This type of euphemism, unlike the type discussed earlier, does not avoid offending readers. It obfuscates and misleads and should, therefore, be avoided.

Academic essays must be written in Standard English, in that form of our language used by and expected from those who work in business, government, educational institutions, and other social organizations. In Standard English, words are spelled correctly, commas are in the right places, sentences are complete, verbs agree with their subjects, modifiers don't dangle, pronouns are in the correct case, and verbs use the correct tense. If you edit your essays carefully so that they conform to the rules of Standard English, your work will be clear and forceful and you will meet the expectations of your readers.

WRITING ASSIGNMENTS

1. Identify a grammatical error that has given you some trouble in the past. (You might look through your old essays to see where your instructors thought you needed some help.) In an essay of 500 to 750 words, describe this error and discuss strategies writers can use to detect, avoid, and correct it.
2. In an essay of approximately 500 words, compare and contrast the use of the colon and the semicolon.
3. Select a popular magazine that specializes in covering a particular field: sports, fashion, entertainment, computers, interior design, geography, travel, or current affairs. Find several examples of jargon used in an issue of that magazine. Write a brief (200- to 300-word) analysis of the use of jargon, focusing on how it both defines and panders to the magazine's target audience.

EXERCISES

1. Compose a sentence fragment followed by three sentences illustrating three different ways of correcting the fragment.
2. Compose a run-on sentence followed by three sentences illustrating three different ways of correcting the run-on sentence.
3. Compose a sentence rendered comical because it contains a misplaced modifier. Write a corrected version of the sentence as well.
4. Compose five sentences, each of which contains an example of one of the diction errors covered in this chapter:
   - inappropriate connotation
   - jargon
   - vague/abstract language
   - euphemism
   - ostentatious language

   Then write a revised version of each sentence in which you correct the diction errors.

COLLABORATIVE ACTIVITY

In a small group, edit the following text.

Camelot was the most famous castle in the medeeval legends of King Arthur. Where he reigned over Britain before the Saxon conquest. Camelot was the home of the Knights of the Round Table. A group of brilliant statemen and chivalrous warriers. It was from Camelot that a group of these knights set off on a quest for the Holy Grail, the Holy Grail is the cup from which Jesus and his disciples drunk at the Last Supper. It is impossible to determine precisely where Camelot Castle was located. Sir Thomas Malory sets his epic poem Le Morte D'arthur in Winchester while Wales is where the favoured location is for Geoffrey of Monmouth in his History of the Kings of Britain but he can't know for sure where the exact location of the castle is. The best guess are probably in Somerset near Cadbury Castle or it may have been the castle which was excavated in the 1960's and determined to be built during the Iron Age which looks over the Vale of Avalon. Which is close to a river called Cam. According to one of Henry VIIIs historians local people referred to Cadbury Castle as "Camalat," they believed it to be the home of King Arthur. But their are many versions of the legend. There has come to be a sprititual aura around the legend of King Arthur. Followers believe that Camelot was a Utopia. In the USA that period of time when John Kennedy was President is sometimes referred to as Camelot. King Arthur will return some day to rule it again.

CHAPTER 8

Acknowledge Your Sources

By Kate Soles and Derek Soles

To write a complete and successful academic essay, you need to acquire information from a variety of sources including books, articles in journals and magazines, and the Internet. In Chapter 3, you learned how to research the information you might need to include in an essay or report. It is essential that you acknowledge these sources accurately and completely. If you do not, implying instead that the work from which you are borrowing information is your own, you are guilty of plagiarism.

Plagiarism is a form of literary misconduct resulting from a writer's failure to acknowledge sources he or she has used, creating instead the impression that the information the writer has presented is his or her own work, when it is really the work of someone else. In its most blatant form, plagiarism is the use of whole passages of text taken from a source and inserted, without acknowledgment, into another's work. But plagiarism is not limited to word-for-word copying. It includes, as well, the failure to acknowledge information taken from another source even if you paraphrase that information. Information that is paraphrased or summarized (see Chapter 3) also must be acknowledged. Plagiarism is considered to be a serious offence in the academic community.

In academic writing, sources usually must be cited twice, once, in shorthand form within parentheses within the text of the essay and again in a source list at the end of the essay. As a rule, "common knowledge" does not have to be sourced, even if this knowledge was not common to you when you began your essay. When he began his essay for his European History class about the invasion of the Spanish Armada, Basel, who was raised in Afghanistan, did not know that Elizabeth I was Queen of England when the Armada sailed in 1588, but a fact such as this would fall into the "common knowledge" realm. But when he wrote, "The Spanish fleet consisted of about 130 ships carrying about 8000 sailors," he had to cite his source. If you are not certain if information you are using is common knowledge or not, it is better to include a citation.

Citing sources accurately and correctly is challenging but important. There are many types of sources—books, journals, newspapers, the Internet, television— and each type has its own citation format. This format is prescribed and must be adhered to precisely. Commas, dates, volume numbers, parentheses all have to be accurate and placed correctly within the citation. Moreover, there is not a single method agreed upon by all members of the academic community for citing sources. If you are taking a biology, a history, and a psychology course, you might have to use different citation methods in each course. Rules that govern the location of the date of publication, the use of capital letters, the use of italics or underlining, and indentation differ from one method to the next. Some methods require footnotes for in-text citations, some require endnotes, and some require parenthetical cita- tion. Citing sources is the albatross of the academic life. A student's life would be so much easier if we could all agree upon one method. Unfortunately, this is not likely to happen. Biologists, anthropologists, psychologists, historians, and other scholars tend to think their method is the best and would be reluctant to change.

There are a variety of methods that academics use to acknowledge the sources from which they have borrowed information that they use in their work. Three of the most common methods are explained in this chapter. Most professors will accept one of these three methods; they will usually indicate on the assignment sheet which method they want you to use. The three most common methods, explained here, are the

- **MLA method**, developed and prescribed by the Modern Language Association;
- **APA method**, developed and prescribed by the American Psychological Association;
- *Chicago Manual of Style* **(CMS) method**, developed and prescribed by the University of Chicago.

MLA Method of Parenthetical Citation

The Modern Language Association is a professional organization composed pri- marily of professors of English and other languages. Your English and foreign language teachers will want you to acknowledge your sources using the MLA method. Some of your other professors probably will accept this method as well. Others will not. Many of those others will ask you to use the APA or the CMS method of citing sources; these methods are explained later in this chapter.

The manuals for writers who use the MLA method are the seventh edition of the *MLA Handbook for Writers of Research Papers* (New York: MLA, 2009) and the third edition of the *MLA Style Manual and Guide to Scholarly Publishing* (New York: MLA, 2008). The information that follows is based upon these books. The MLA method requires two citations for each secondary source. The first is a brief citation enclosed within parentheses within the text of the essay. The second is a complete citation organized alphabetically by the authors' last names in a Works Cited list at the end of the essay.

● Parenthetical Citations Within the Text of the Essay

Direct quotations taken from a secondary source must be acknowledged with a parenthetical citation. To indicate a direct quote from a secondary source, place quotation marks around the words you are quoting and then put the author's last name and the page number from the secondary source on which the information can be found. Short direct quotes are integrated into the text of the essay and placed between quotation marks "so a short direct quote properly acknowledged would look like this" (Author 34). Note the quotation marks around our imagined quote from a secondary source and note that there is not a comma between the author's last name (*Author* in our example) and the page number.

If the author's name is already mentioned in the text, only the page number is placed in parentheses: As Author notes, "only the page number is required" (34).

Long quotes are indented and blocked off from the text of the essay. The distinction between short quotes and long ones is somewhat arbitrary, but quotes of more than about three lines should be set off from the rest of the essay in the manner illustrated here:

> Note that the quotation marks have been eliminated. The indentation indicates that the material is quoted directly from a secondary source. Quotation marks are used only if the original uses quotation marks. Note also that after a short quote comes the parenthetical citation followed by a period. In the long, indented quote the period precedes the parenthetical citation. (Author 39)

In addition to direct quotes, you must cite other information taken from a secondary source. The general rule is that if you possessed the information before you began the essay, you do not need to cite it, but if you acquired the information in the course of writing the essay, you do need to cite it. Again, put in parentheses the author's last name and the page number on which the information can be found. You need to include the page number even if you have paraphrased the information.

If you have used two or more works by the same author, you need to provide a short-hand version of the title of the source to distinguish it from other titles by the same author (Author, *Short* 34). Note the use of the comma after the author's name but not between the title and the page number. If the author's name is mentioned, his or her name is not included in the citation: As Author has shown, "citing sources can be frustrating" (*Short* 34).

If your source is written by four or more people, you need only name the first author followed by the Latin words *et al.* (meaning "and others") and, of course, the page number (First et al. 145). Note the period after "al." Again, note that no commas are used. *Et al.* is also used in place of all but the first author's name if you mention the author's name in the text of the essay: Smith et al. have conducted research that suggests that "students enjoy writing academic essays" (145).

If your source is written by a corporate author, treat the corporate author as you would a single author: According to government sources, ten-year-olds watch an average of four hours of television per day (Royal Commission on Elementary Education 234).

If the author of your source is anonymous, name the title or a shortened version in the parenthetical citation. Italicize a book title; put quotation marks around an article title. If you use a shortened version, include the first word in the title since it will be alphabetized by title in the Works Cited list. If, for example, the title of your source is "Rating the Quality of the Undergraduate Programs of British Universities," your citation could be as short as the word "Rating" ("Rating" 86).

If you quote from a novel, follow the procedure for a single author. You may also include the chapter number to help your readers find the passage in a different edition of the novel from the one you used. If you include the chapter number, put a semicolon between the page number and the chapter number (Austen 79; ch. 6). Usually you do not have to include the author's name because the context of your discussion will make clear who the author is.

If you quote from a poem, give the line numbers you are quoting instead of the page number on which the quote appears (Wordsworth 34–40). Provide a shortened version of the title if you quote from more than one poem by the same author and if the context has not made clear the author and the title (Wordsworth, "Tintern" 34–40). Note the punctuation.

If you quote from a Shakespearean play or from another play in verse, list the act, scene, and line numbers, separated by periods (4.2.9–11).

If you quote from the Bible, list the chapter and the verse or verses, separated by a period. Include an abbreviated title of the book, if the context does not make it clear (Lev. 12.2–4).

If you quote from a work from an anthology, remember it is the author's name and not the name of the anthology editor that appears in parentheses.

If you quote from an indirect source—a source quoted in one of your sources—include the abbreviation for "quoted in" in your parenthetical citation: Smith notes that "indirect sources must be cited appropriately" (qtd. in Robins 257). Note carefully the way the citation is punctuated.

If you got the same information from more than one source or if you want to underscore the authority of a point by citing more than one source, do so by separating the sources from each other with semicolons: Experts agree that the semicolon can be used between sources (Wilson 34; Martens 68; Pelies 124).

If your source has no page numbers (as many electronic sources do not), you may omit the page numbers or include the paragraph number if the paragraphs are numbered (as they sometimes are in electronic sources): If necessary, "you should cite the paragraph number in place of the page number" (Smith, par. 12). Note the way this citation is punctuated.

● Works Cited List

The in-text parenthetical citations provide readers with minimal information about the sources from which the writer borrowed information or quoted directly. Readers require the complete bibliographical information about the sources in case they want to learn more about the subject of the essay they are reading. This complete information is provided in the Works Cited list at the end of the essay.

The Works Cited list contains only those sources actually cited within the essay. For most academic essays, this is all that is required. Some professors, however, might want you to include in your source list not only the sources you actually cite but also sources you read but did not cite specifically within your essay. This list—of all sources you checked whether or not you cited them in your essay—is called Works Consulted. Most academic essays conclude with a Works Cited list.

Here is an example of a Works Cited list. Study it carefully. Included on this Works Cited list are examples of nearly all of the kinds of sources—books, periodicals, electronic—that you might use to gather the research that you need. As you study this list, note the following:

- The title "Works Cited" is centred and appears in roman type. Do not use italics, boldface, or large lettering. Note that one line is left between the title and the first entry.
- The Works Cited list is arranged alphabetically by the author's last name. If the author of the source is anonymous, the source is placed in the list alphabetically by its title. The sources are not numbered.
- The list uses hanging indentation. The first line of each source is not indented but all subsequent lines are.
- Book, journal, newspaper, and magazine titles are italicized, but article titles are placed in quotation marks.
- Page numbers are included for articles in journals, newspapers, and magazines and for articles or essays included in an edited anthology or collection of essays.
- Citation of print sources end with the word "Print", preceded and followed by a period.

- There is a number between the title of a journal and its year of publication. This number refers to the volume number. For example, the article by Pratt in the Works Cited list below is from the journal *Profession,* volume number 91. Some journal article citations, such as the one below by Pickett, have two numbers, separated by a period. The second number refers to the issue number. There is an important distinction here. Some journals are continuously paginated, which means that they are paginated by year and not by issue. If, for example, the first issue for the year 2011 of the journal *Quantum Mechanics Quarterly* began on page 1 and ended on page 159, the next issue for the year 2011 would begin on page 160. Citations for journals that are continuously paginated (for a full year) include only the volume number. But some journals are paginated by issue—each issue begins on page 1. Citations for journals paginated by issue require the volume number followed by a period followed by the issue number.

- Citations for online sources include both the date the source appeared online and the date the user of the source accessed the source. The second date is essential because the author of the source could go online and change the content of his article after the researcher has cited the earlier version.

Works Cited

Armstrong, Isobel. Personal interview. 5 Feb. 2012.

Ballenger, Bruce. *Beyond Note Cards: Rethinking the Freshman Research Paper.* Portsmouth, NH: Boynton Cook, 1999. Print.

Bartholomae, David. "Inventing the University." *When a Writer Can't Write: Studies in Writer's Block and Other Composing Possibilities.* Ed. Mike Rose. New York: Guilford, 1985. 134–65. Print.

Basney, Lionel. "Teacher: Eleven Notes." *The American Scholar* 71 (Winter 2002): 80–96. Web. 3 Mar. 2012.

Council of College Teachers. *Initiation into the Academy.* Chicago: CCT Press, 1998. Print.

Daniels, Christine. "The Decline of English Grammar." *Haverford Daily Times* 9 Feb. 2011: B2+. Print.

Collier, Lorna. "Effective Vocabulary Instruction." *Council Chronicle* Mar. 2007. n. pag. Web. 25 Oct. 2007.

George, Alice. "Reading Scores on the Rise at Last." *Clarion* Feb. 1999: 18–22. Print.

Haynes, Cynthia. "Inside the Teaching Machine: Actual Feminism and (Virtual) Pedagogy." *Computers, Writing, Rhetoric, and Literature* 2.1 (1996): n. pag. Web. 8 Feb. 2007.

Leslie, Peter M. "Education Policy." *Canadian Encyclopedia*. 1988. Print.

Levine, George. "The Two Nations." *Pedagogy* 1 (Winter 2001): 10. Print.

Lindemann, Erika. *A Rhetoric for Writing Teachers*. 3rd ed. New York: Oxford UP, 1995. Print.

Mansfield, Harvey C. "Grade Inflation: It's Time to Face the Facts." *The Chronicle Review* 6 Apr. 2001. n. pag. Web. 4 Apr. 2012.

McCallum, Andrew. *Creativity and Learning in Secondary English: Teaching for a Creative Classroom*. New York: Routledge, 2012. Print.

Moulthrop, Stuart. "You Say You Want a Revolution? Hypertext and the Laws of Media." *Postmodern Culture* 1.3 (1991). Web. 12 July 2006.

Oxford Essential World Atlas. New York: Oxford UP, 1996. Print.

Pratt, Mary Louise. "Arts of the Contact Zone." *Profession* 91 (1991): 33–40. Print.

Rapkin, Angela A. "The Uses of Logic in the College Freshman English Classroom." *Activities to Promote Critical Thinking: Classroom Practices in Teaching English*. Urbana: NCTE, 1986. 130–35. CD-ROM. *ERIC*. SilverPlatter. 1995.

Schiwy, Marlene A. "Saturating Language with Love." *Wise Women: Reflections of Teachers at Midlife.* Ed. Margaret Morganroth Gullette. New York: Routledge, 2000. 28–41. Print.

Smith, Charles. Foreword. *A Sourcebook for Writing Teachers*. By Catherine Nobine. Santa Monica: Lantern Press, 1999. viii–xiii. Print.

Stevens, David. *A Guided Reader for Secondary English: Pedagogy and Practice.* New York: Routledge, 2012. Print.

● Sample MLA Works Cited Entries

Here are examples of MLA Works Cited entries for the kinds of print and electronic sources you will likely reference in your academic essays. The examples are based upon the *MLA Handbook for Writers of Research Papers*, seventh edition, and the *MLA Style Manual and Guide to Scholarly Publishing, third edition*. For additional examples, consult these manuals. You should be able to find them in both your university library and bookstore.

In accordance with the *MLA Handbook*, the examples below are divided into four sections: web publications, nonperiodical print publications, periodical print publications, and additional common sources.

Web Publications

Citations for web publications need not only the date the source was published but also the date you accessed the information. This is because the source could be altered after you have accessed it. Note that MLA no longer requires a URL for web publications.

A journal article accessed online

Note the differences between web and print citations: If you have accessed the journal article online, the word "Web" replaces the word "Print" and the date of access is also included.

> Heusher, Zachary, David P. Gilkey, Jennifer L. Peel, and Catherine A. Kennedy. "The Association of Self-Reported Backpack Use and Backpack Weight with Low Back Pain among College Students." *Journal of Manipulative and Physiological Therapeutics* 33.6 (July/August 2010): 432–437. Web. 23 May 2012.
>
> Jayaratne, Kapila, Karen Jacobs, and Dulitha Fernando. "Global Healthy Backpack Initiatives." *Work: A Journal of Prevention, Assessment and Rehabilitation* 41 (2012): 5553–5557. Web. 23 May 2012.
>
> Safikhani, Hassan, Tengku Kamalden, Saidon Bin Amri, and Megat Ahmad. "The Effect of Different Backpack Loading Systems on Trunk Forward Lean Angle During Walking among College Students." *European Journal of Sports and Exercise Sciences* 1.1 (2012): 1–5. Web. 23 May 2012.

An entire Internet site

If you wish to cite an entire online information database or homepage, follow the models below.

> Salda, Michael N., ed. *The Cinderella Project*. Vers. 1.1. De Grummond. Dec. 1997. Web. 21 June 2012.
>
> *Children's Lit. Research Collection*, U of Southern Mississippi. May 2003. Web. 21 June 2012.
>
> LEARN@PZ. *Project Zero*. Homepage. Harvard Graduate School of Education. Jan. 2010. Web. 10 May 2012.
>
> Marshall, Barry. *English 2354*. Course homepage. Sept. 2010–Apr. 2011. Dept. of English, Cutter University. Web. 30 Nov. 2011.
>
> Rexroth, Samantha. Homepage. 12 Apr. 2007. Web. 28 Aug. 2011.
>
> Willett, Perry, ed., *Victorian Women Writers Project*. Indiana U. May 2000. Web. 22 Oct. 2011.

An online book

> Austen, Jane. *Pride and Prejudice*. Ed. Henry Churchyard. 1996. *Jane Austen Information Page*. Web. 6 June 2012.
>
> Keats, John. "Ode on a Grecian Urn." *Poetical Works*. 1884. *Project Bartleby*. Ed. Steven van Leeuwen. May 1998. Columbia U. Web. 8 May 2012.

An online government publication

Canadian Bureau of Citizenship and Immigration Services. *Welcome to the New Office of Citizenship*. By Eduardo Aguirre, Jr. 17 Sept. 2003. Web. 1 Oct. 2011.

An article in an online journal

Harvey, Peter. "Avoiding Unintended Harm to the Environment and the Buddhist Ethic of Intention." *Journal of Buddhist Ethics* 14 (2007): n. pag. Web. 20 May 2011.

Haynes, Cynthia. "Inside the Teaching Machine: Actual Feminism and (Virtual) Pedagogy." *Computers, Writing, Rhetoric, and Literature* 2.1 (1996): n. pag. Web. 27 Mar. 2012.

Shane, Aaron. "The Decline of the American Middle Class." *American Economic Review* 98.2 (Apr. 2006): 412–31. Web. 7 Sept. 2011.

An article in an online magazine

Snell, Marilyn. "Jamaica Kincaid Hates Happy Endings." *Mother Jones* Sept.–Oct. 1997. Web. 15 Jan. 2010.

Morgan, Fiona. "Banning the Bullies." *Salon.com* 15 Mar. 2010. Web. 23 Jan. 2011.

An article in a newspaper

Leonnig, Carol D. "Redskins Can Keep Trademark and Logo." *Washington Post* 1 Oct. 2003. Web. 17 July 2011.

Conrad, Peter. "The A to Z of Britney." *The Observer* 17 Feb. 2002. Web. 14 Feb. 2012.

If the article is from a newswire such as Associated Press, the entry begins with the title of the article since no author is referenced. Whenever the article's author is not stated, begin with and alphabetize by title.

An editorial

"Unfriendly Friendly Fire." Editorial. *The Calgary Herald* 3 May 2010. Web. 2 Aug. 2011.

A review

Ebert, Roger. Rev. of *Hugo*, dir. Martin Scorsese. *Chicago Sun-Times Online* 26 Sept. 2011. Web. 8 Oct. 2011.

An article from an online service

Langhamer, Claire. "Love and Courtship in Mid-Twentieth-Century England." *Historical Journal* 50.1 (2007): 173–96. *ProQuest*. Web. 27 May 2009.

An online encyclopedia
Dull, Jack L. "Wu-ti." *Encyclopedia Britannica Online.* Encyclopedia Britannica, 2011. Web. 30 Oct. 2011.

"Buddhism." *Wikipedia.* Wikimedia Foundation, 26 July 2010. Web. 20 July 2011.

Twitter
Murray, Steve (Sportcast). "Predicting England 1 nil over Italy—better strikers." 24 June 2012, 10:40 a.m. Tweet.

Nonperiodical Print Publications

A book by one author
Gladwell, Malcolm. *Outliers: The Story of Success.* Boston: Little, Brown, 2008. Print.

If the book has gone into a second or later edition, place the edition number between the title and the place of publication:

White, Edward M. *Teaching and Assessing Writing.* 2nd ed. San Francisco and London: Jossey-Bass, 1994. Print.

An anthology, a compilation, or an edited book
Jacobus, Lee A., ed. *Literature: An Introduction to Critical Reading.* Compact ed. Upper Saddle River, NJ: Pearson Education, 2002. Print.

Taylor, Kate, ed. *Going Hungry.* New York: Random House, 2008. Print.

See below for citation of separate articles from a collection of essays and of literary works from a literature anthology.

Two or more books by the same author
Shields, Carol. *Jane Austen: A Life.* New York: Penguin, 2005. Print.

——. *The Stone Diaries.* Toronto: Vintage Can., 1993. Print.

Note that three hyphens replace the author's name for the second citation and that the alphabetization is by book title.

A book by two or three authors
Blake, Raymond, and Jeffrey Kenshen. *Narrating a Nation: Canadian History Post-Confederation.* Toronto: McGraw, 2010. Print.

Dopp, Jamie, Luke Bradley, and Richard Harrison. *Now Is the Winter: Thinking About Hockey.* Toronto: Wolsak and Wynn, 2009. Print.

A book by more than three authors
If you use a source by three or more authors, you do not have to list all of the authors' names. You need only list the first author's name followed by the Latin abbreviation *et al.*, meaning "and others."

Patterson, Edward J., et al. *Lighting in Miloz Milozovic's Theatrical Productions.* Cambridge: Harvard UP, 1999. Print.

A book by a corporate author

Modern Language Association of America. *MLA Handbook for Writers of Research Papers.* 7th ed. New York: MLA, 2009. Print.

A work in an anthology

Bricen, Robert. "Leather and Lace." *Fashion in the Sixties.* Ed. Luke M. Walker. Vancouver: Ricards, 2010. 134–56. Print.

Note that if you use more than one essay from one anthology, you should cite the entire anthology the way you would an edited book:

Walker, Luke M., ed. *Fashion in the Sixties.* Vancouver: Ricards, 2010. Print.

Then you need only cite the essays by name, article title, editor's last name, and page numbers, for example:

Bricen, Robert. "Leather and Lace." Walker 134–56.
Waller, Kate. "Hippie Threads." Walker 46–59.

A literary work in an anthology

McKay, Don. "Slow Spring on Vancouver Island." *Field Marks: The Poetry of Don McKay.* Ed. Méira Cook. Waterloo, ON: Wilfrid Laurier University Press, 2008. Print.

A work originally published elsewhere and reprinted in an anthology

Flower, Linda. "Cognition, Context, and Theory Building." *College Composition and Communication* 40 (1989): 282–311. Rpt. in *Cross Talk in Comp Theory: A Reader.* Ed. Victor Villanueva, Jr. Urbana, IL: National Council of Teachers of English, 1997. 701–33. Print.

An article in an encyclopedia or other reference book

Cronin, Blaise. "The ARIST DATA Set." *The Annual Review of Information Science & Technology.* Vol. 37. New Jersey: Information Today Inc., 2002. Print.
Leslie, Peter M. "Education Policy." *Canadian Encyclopedia.* 1988. Print.

If the article is anonymous, alphabetize the article by its title:

"Mandarin." *The Encyclopedia Americana.* 2005 ed. Print.

An introduction, a preface, a foreword, or an afterword

Ivins, Molly. Introduction. *Pipe Dreams: Greed, Ego, and the Death of Enron.* By Robert Bryce. New York: PublicAffairs, 2002. xv–xvii. Print.
Skelton, David. Foreword. *Stay, Breathe with Me: Stories of Courage, Healing, and Love.* By Helen Allison. Burns Lake: Cairndow, 2010. x–xiv. Print.

Cross-references

If you need to cite more than one work from an anthology of literary works or a collection of related essays, you need not provide the full bibliographical information for the entire book with each citation. You should provide the full bibliographical information just once, as you do for an edited book. Suppose, for example, that you need to cite three articles from *The Brooklyn Reader*. You need only to cite the entire book once:

> Sexton, Andrea Wyatt, and Alice Leccese Powers, eds. *The Brooklyn Reader: Thirty Writers Celebrate America's Favorite Borough.* New York: Harmony, 1994. Print.

The citations for the articles or essays you have used from the book may be shortened, as follows:

> McCullers, Carson. "Brooklyn Is My Neighborhood." Sexton and Powers 143–47.
> Walcott, Derek. "A Letter from Brooklyn." Sexton and Powers 264–65.

A book by an anonymous author

> *The Chicago Manual of Style.* 16th ed. Chicago: U of Chicago P, 2003. Print.

This book is alphabetized in the Works Cited list by its title, in this case, under *C*.

An edition

Sometimes books, especially those written years ago, are prepared for publication by someone other than the author. Such books have an editor as well as an author, and the editor's name must be included in the citation:

> Chaucer, Geoffrey. *The Canterbury Tales: Nine Tales and the General Prologue.* Eds. V. A. Kolve and Glending Olson. New York: Norton, 1989. Print.

A book translated from a foreign language

> De Romilly, Jacqueline. *Great Sophists in Periclean Athens.* Trans. Janet Lloyd. Oxford: Clarendon Press, 1992. Print.

A book published in a second or subsequent edition

> Feuer, Jane. *The Hollywood Musical.* 2nd ed. Bloomington: Indiana UP, 1993. Print.

If the title page indicates that the book is a revised edition, use the abbreviation *Rev. ed.* after the title. If the title page indicates that the book is an abridged edition, use the abbreviation *Abr. ed.* after the title.

A multivolume work

> Raine, Kathleen. *Blake and Tradition.* Vol. 1. Princeton: Princeton UP, 1968. Print.

If you use all volumes, the work cited entry appears as follows:

Lauter, Paul, et al., eds. *The Heath Anthology of American Literature.*
5th ed. 5 vols. Lexington, MA: Heath, 2009. Print.

Montgomery, Lucy Maud. *The Selected Journals of L.M. Montgomery.*
Eds. Mary Rubio and Elizabeth Waterston. 5 vols. Toronto: Oxford
UP, 1985–2004. Print.

A book in a series

Anderson, Danny, and Jill S. Kuknheim, eds. *Cultural Studies in the
Curriculum: Teaching Latin America.* New York: MLA, 2003. Print.
Teaching Languages, Literatures and Cultures.

The book referenced above is part of a series of books. The series is entitled
"Teaching Languages, Literatures and Cultures." Note that the series title is
not italicized. The number of the book in the series is also included. The word
"Print" comes before the series title.

A republished book

Simpson, Elizabeth. *The Perfection of Hope: A Soul Transformed
Through Critical Illness.* 1998. Toronto: Macfarlane Walter & Ross,
1999. Print.

The book cited above came out in hard cover in 1998; a paperback version was
then published in 1999.

A pamphlet

Welcome to Victoria. Victoria: Victoria Visitors Information Bureau,
2011. Print.

A government publication

United States Department of Health and Human Services. *National
Evaluation of Welfare-to-Work Strategies: Do Mandatory Welfare-
to-Work Programs Affect the Well-Being of Children?* Washington:
GPO, 2000. Print.

The Province of British Columbia. *Vehicle Safety and Inspections Standards Legislation Manual.* Victoria: Crown Printers, 2012. Print.

Conference proceedings

Young, Trevor, ed. *Proceedings of the Pacific Northwest Regional
Conference on Whole Language Pedagogy.* 9–12 April 1999, Seattle.
Tacoma: Howson UP, 2000. Print.

A single paper presented at a conference is cited as follows:

Carson, Heather. "The Romance of Marianne Moore." *McGill University
Graduate Conference on Language and Literature.* 8–10 March 2008.
Montreal: McGill University, 2008. Print.

A book without stated publication information or pagination
Some publishers do not provide adequate bibliographical information for the books they publish. They might not list the date of publication, the place of publication, or even number the pages. If you use a source without all the necessary bibliographical information, cite as much as you can and use the following abbreviations to indicate omissions:

n.p. for no place of publication or for no publisher
n.d. for no date
n. pag. for no pagination

Use brackets if you have provided bibliographical information the publisher has not provided but of which you have knowledge.

> Malachi, Zvi, ed. *Proceedings of the International Conference on Literary and Linguistic Computing.* [Tel Aviv]: [Fac. of Humanities, Tel Aviv U], n.d. Print.

A dissertation

> Estrada, Mariko. "Effects of Anxiety on Children's Working Memory." Diss. U of Toronto, 2009. Print.

If the dissertation is published, italicize the title as opposed to enclosing it within quotation marks. If it is published by University Microfilms International, add, after the date of publication, "Ann Arbor:" and the acronym "UMI," followed by the date of microfilm publication, followed by the order number.

> Wechsler, Joyce. *Emily Dickinson and Nature's Spiritual Awakening.* Diss. University of Rochester, 2002. Ann Arbor: UMI, 2003. ATT 3023542. Print.

Periodical Print Publications

An article in an academic journal continuously paginated

Continuously paginated means that the pages in the journal are numbered by the year as opposed to by each issue. For example, suppose a journal is published four times a year. The first issue would begin on page 1. Suppose it ended on page 236. The second issue of the year would then begin on page 237. Suppose it ended on page 400. The third issue of the year would begin on page 401. Suppose it ended on page 589. The fourth and final issue of the year would begin on page 590. The first issue published the following year would begin again on page 1.

> Chivers, Sally. "Ordinary People: Reading the TransCanadian Terry Fox." *Canadian Literature* 202 (2009): 80–94. Print.
> Russell, David R. "Romantics on Writing: Liberal Culture and the Abolition of Composition Courses." *Rhetoric Review* 6 (1988): 132–48. Print.

> Webb, Colleen. "A Complete Classification of Darwinian Extinction in Ecological Interactions." *The American Naturalist* 161 (2003): 181–205. Print.

An article in an academic journal paginated by issue

The only difference in citation between an article in a journal continuously paginated and one in a journal paginated by issue is the inclusion of the issue number in a citation of a paginated-by-issue journal article. Note that a period comes between the volume number and the issue number.

> Williams, Linda. "Of Kisses and Ellipses: The Long Adolescence of American Movies." *Critical Inquiry* 32.2 (2006): 288–340. Print.

An abstract in an abstracts journal

> Ferguson, Tamara J., and Susan L. Crowley. "Gender Differences in the Organization of Guilt and Shame." *Sex Roles* 37 (1997): 19–44. *Psychological Abstracts* 85 (1998): item 4265. Print.

A newspaper article

> Carey, Benedict. "H.M., Whose Loss of Memory Made Him Unforgettable, Dies." *New York Times* 5 Dec. 2008: A6+. Print.

The letter *A* refers to the section number. The number *6* refers to the page number in section A. Use a plus sign to indicate that the article continues later on in the same section.

Note the following also:

- If the city where the newspaper is published is not included in the name of the newspaper, add the name of the city in square brackets, after the name of the paper. You do not have to add the name of the city to nationally published papers such as *USA Today* and *The Globe and Mail.*
- If an edition is named on the masthead (natl. ed.; late ed.), include this information after the date.
- Abbreviate all months except May, June, and July.

> Knox, Jack. "Former NHLer Geoff Courtnall's New Path Leads to Boston Marathon." *Times Colonist* [Victoria] 10 Apr. 2012: B4. Print.
>
> Trachtenberg, Jeffrey A. "What's in a Movie Soundtrack? Catchy Tunes and Big Business." *The Wall Street Journal* 1 Apr. 1994, eastern ed.: B1. Print.

An editorial

If you cite an editorial, place the word "Editorial" between the title of the article and the name of the paper.

> "A Victory Won with Dignity." Editorial. *Globe and Mail* 5 Nov. 2008: A20. Print.

A letter to the editor
> Smythe, Mary Lou. Letter. *Canadian Living.* 3 Apr. 2010: 8. Print.

A review

If a review is anonymous, begin the citation with "Rev. of" but alphabetize by title. Include the title of the review, if there is a title, after the author's name.

> Rev. of *Romeo and Juliet,* by William Shakespeare. Mission Viejo Playhouse, Mission Viejo, CA. *Mission Viejo Gazette* 14 Mar. 2009: 8. Print.
> Basilieres, Michel. "Diderot Derivative." Rev. of *Beatrice and Virgil,* by Yann Martel. *Literary Review of Canada* 18.5 (2010): 19. Print.
> Updike, John. "No Brakes." Rev. of *Sinclair Lewis: Rebel from Main Street*, by Richard Lingeman. *New Yorker* 4 Feb. 2002: 77–80. Print.

An article in a monthly or bimonthly magazine
> Albom, Mitch. "The Courage of Detroit." *Sports Illustrated* 22 Sep. 2009: 45–47. Print.
> Dittrich, Luke. "The Brain That Changed Everything." *Esquire* Oct. 2010: 67–70. Print.
> Kaylin, Lucy. "Johnny in Paradise." *GQ* Aug. 2003: 92–96, 157–58. Print.

An article in a weekly magazine
> Kidder, Tracy. "The Good Doctor." *New Yorker* 10 July 2000: 40–57. Print.

If the article is anonymous, alphabetize it by title, ignoring articles (*a, an, the*).

Citing Additional Common Sources

A television or radio program
> "Gardens of Babylon." *Ancient Discoveries.* History Channel. 14 Oct. 2008. Television.
> "Qatar." *The Singular Tourist.* Narr. Heather Jenks. Writ. Heather Jenks. ATV. Edmonton. 27 Jan. 2000. Television.
> Keillor, Garrison. *A Prairie Home Companion.* Perf. Ledward Ka'apana and Owana Salazar. Minnesota Public Radio. 18 Oct. 2002. Radio.
> "Catherine." *Veep.* Perf. Julia Louis-Dreyfus. 21 June 2012. Television.

A sound recording

You may list first the name of the conductor, the composer, or the performer. Your choice will depend upon the person you are emphasizing in your paper.

> Adele (Adele Adkins). "Someone Like You." *21.* Columbia Records, 2011. CD.
> Boublil, Alain, and Claude-Michel Schonberg. *Miss Saigon.* Perf. Lea Salonga, Claire Moore, and Jonathan Pryce. Cond. Martin Koch. Geffen, 1989. CD.

McFerrin, Bobby. "Kalimba Suite." *Beyond Words*. Blue Note, 2002. CD.

A film or video recording

There is some leeway in the information you include for citing a film or a DVD. Start with the title and include the name of the director, the distributor, and the year of release. You may add the names of the star or stars, the writer or writers, and/or the producer if you wish to highlight their contributions.

Away from Her. Dir. Sarah Polley. Mongrel Media, 2006. DVD.

If you are citing the contribution of a particular individual, put that person's name first:

Polley, Sarah, dir. *Away from Her*. Mongrel Media, 2006. DVD.

A live performance of a play

Two Pianos Four Hands. By Ted Dykstra and Richard Greenblatt. Dir. Richard Greenblatt. The Belfry Theatre, Victoria, B.C. 13 Apr. 2011. Performance.

A musical score or libretto

Mozart, Wolfgang Amadeus. *The Marriage of Figaro*. 1786. New York: Dorchester, 2002. Print.

An interview

Jiwani, Almas. Interview by Peter Mansbridge. *Mansbridge One on One*. CBC News Network, Toronto. 12 Mar. 2011. Television.

If you conducted the interview, begin with the interviewee's name, followed by the medium (personal interview, telephone interview, email interview), followed by the date (day, month—abbreviated if necessary—and year).

An advertisement

Tiffany & Co. Advertisement. *Vanity Fair* Jan. 2003: 10–11. Print.

A lecture, a speech, an address, or a reading

McCallum, Megan. "The Sonnets of Sir Philip Sidney." English 421. University of British Columbia. 1 Apr. 2012. Lecture.

Information taken from a CD-ROM

"Olympic Games." *Encarta 1996*. 1996 ed. Redmond, WA: Microsoft, 1996. CD-ROM.

"The Price Is Right." *Time* 20 Jan. 1992: 38. *Time Man of the Year*. Washington, DC: Compact Publishing, 1993. CD-ROM.

Student Essay: Examples of MLA Citation and Works Cited

Adam Black   Black 1

Professor Giamatti

English 101

30 April 2012

Saving the Vancouver Island Marmot

A member of the Sciuridae family, which includes squirrels, the Vancouver Island marmot is a furry brown and white mammal. Adults compare in size to a large house cat, weighing about six kilograms. Once
abundant in central and southern Vancouver Island, the marmot has
been an endangered species for the past twenty years. In the 1990s, the
death rate of Vancouver Island marmots exceeded the birth rate, so the
species was in serious danger of becoming extinct. The logging industry
destroyed much of the marmot's natural habitat; abundant wolves, cougars, and golden eagles preyed upon scarce Vancouver Island marmots;
and disease and cold weather took a toll. By the mid-1990s, there were
fewer than forty Vancouver Island marmots in existence (Keeley 2).
Fortunately, British Columbia's Ministry of Environment, the logging
industry, and the general public became aware of the dangers to this
species and began to support an aggressive program to save *Marmota
vancouverensis* from extinction.

This program combines funding from government, the general public,
and the logging industry to breed marmots in captivity and then rein-
troduce them into their native habitat. Zoos and conservation centres in
Calgary, Langley, Toronto, and Mount Washington on Vancouver Island
have been breeding marmots in captivity since they became endangered.
They hope they can raise enough animals and then refamiliarize them
with their native habitat, where they will thrive. Success has been slow
but steady. By 2004, the marmot population was about 130; by 2007, it
stood at 255 (Shea B1) and in 2009, researchers counted nearly 300 marmots. Most of the animals remain in captivity, but eighty-five have been
released into the wild, and forty-two have survived (Aaltonen 2182).

However, significant barriers remain to the survival of the Vancouver
Island marmot. One major challenge is predation; the marmot is a food

source for wolves, cougars, and golden eagles, all of which live and hunt on Vancouver Island. According to Shea, predators accounted for the vast majority of known marmot deaths, over 80 percent (B2). The deer population, the main food source for marmot predators, has declined on the island, and the wolf and cougar populations have increased (Shea B3), making marmots more vulnerable than ever. Biologists now find themselves in the awkward position of having to recommend that some species—wolves, cougars, and maybe even eagles—be culled to save another (Markels 7).

Another challenge is funding. Breeding the marmots in captivity and implanting radio transmitters in them so biologists can track their progress in the wild costs millions of dollars. At the present time, the Marmot Recovery Foundation is adequately, if not generously, funded. The provincial and federal governments provide funding, assisted by grants from forest companies Wyerhaeuser and TimberWest and donations from the public. But it will likely cost another fifteen million dollars to achieve the dream of reestablishing a viable marmot population that can survive indefinitely in the wild (Hume B4). There is no guarantee that the governments will continue the funding, especially given public pressures to increase money allotted to health care and education. Nor is it certain that the forest companies will continue to provide funds to atone for their clear-cutting practices, which contributed to the decline in the marmot population.

A third problem is one that might be termed "Darwinian." Some politicians and even biologists argue that species extinction is part of the normal course of natural selection and survival of the fittest. Many species, they note, have become extinct and humankind is no worse off as a result. Perhaps we should not tamper with Mother Nature. Sometimes one species dies off so others have a better chance to survive and thrive. Maybe we should simply let nature take its course, the argument goes, and let the marmots die off in the wild, if that is their evolutionary destiny.

Will *Marmota vancouverensis* survive? There is reason to be optimistic. The Vancouver Island marmot is blessed with great looks, covered as it is in rich chocolate brown fur broken with patches of white. People tend to react to posters and television images of the marmot in the same way they do when an adorable puppy scratches at their

feet. Thus, there is considerable public support for the marmot's survival. The most ardent advocates have organized an adopt-a-marmot
program, which urges members of the public to donate ten dollars a
month to the cause. This program raises almost half a million dollars a
year (Hume B4). It is likely, as well, that the government and the logging
industry will continue to provide funding.

Another cause for optimism is the work being done at the captive
breeding sites. Biologists and veterinarians are learning more about the
nutritional requirements of marmots so they can maximize the health
of those reared in captivity. They are studying mating behaviour so
as to establish conditions within which mating is most likely to occur.
And they are learning more about the genetic makeup of the marmot
to determine, among other things, if it is best to breed one genetically
advantaged male with several females. At the present time, marmots
are breeding more successfully in the captivity than they are in the wild.

Text continues

Works Cited

Aaltonen, Kristen, et al. "Reintroducing Endangered Vancouver Island
 Marmots: Survival and Cause-specific Mortality Rates of Captive-
 born Versus Wild-born Individuals." *Biological Conservation* 142
 (2009): 2181–2190. Print.

Hume, Mark. "Toronto Zoos Awarded for Work Saving Endangered
 Marmots." *Globe and Mail* 22 Sept. 2011: B4. Web. 1 Apr.
 2012.

Keeley, T., et al. "The Reproductive Endocrinology and Behavior of Vancouver Island Marmot (*Marmota vancouverenis*)." *Zoo Biology* 29
 (2011): 1–16. Print.

Markels, Alex. "Last Stand." *Audubon* May 2004. Web. 1 Apr. 2012.

Shea, Courtenay. "Inside Toronto's Hidden Zoo." *The Globe and Mail*
 11 Nov. 2011: B1–3. Web. 1 Apr. 2012.

APA Method of Parenthetical Citation

Many of your professors will expect you to cite your sources using the APA method, developed and sanctioned by the American Psychological Association. The information in this chapter about using the APA method is based on the sixth edition (2010) of the *Publication Manual of the American Psychological Association.*

Like the MLA system, the APA method has two components to it: parenthetical citations within the text of the essay and a References list at the end of the essay. Note, however, that there are significant differences in the format of the two systems. Be careful you do not get the two systems confused.

● Parenthetical Citations Within the Text of the Essay

Direct quotations from a secondary source must be acknowledged with a parenthetical citation. To indicate a direct quote from a secondary source, place quotation marks around the information you are quoting and then put the author's last name, the year the work was published, and the page number from the secondary source on which the information can be found. Short direct quotes are integrated into the text of the essay and placed between quotation marks, "so a short direct quote properly acknowledged would look like this" (Author, 2012, p. 34). Note that there are quotation marks around our imagined quote from a secondary source and that there are commas between the author's last name and the year of publication and between the year of publication and the page number. The word *page* is abbreviated as "p." Note how this parenthetical citation differs from an MLA citation.

Longer quotes (40 words or more) should be blocked off from the text of the essay. They should be indented about half an inch from the left margin.

> Note that the quotation marks have been eliminated. The indentation indicates that the material is quoted directly from a secondary source. Note also that after a short quote comes the parenthetical citation followed by a period. In the long, indented quote, the period precedes the parenthetical citation. (Author, 2011, p. 39)

In addition to direct quotes, you must cite other information taken from a secondary source. The general rule is that if you possessed the information before you began the essay you do not need to cite it, but if you acquired the information in the course of writing the essay, you do need to cite it. Again, put in parentheses the author's last name, the year of publication, and the page number on which the information is found. You are encouraged to include the page number even if you have paraphrased the information.

If the author's name is already mentioned in the text, the date follows the author's name and the page number follows the quote or the borrowed information: As Author (2011) noted, "the date follows the author's name and the page number follows the quote or borrowed information" (p. 34).

If your source is written by two authors, include both names in the parenthetical citation. Separate the two names with an ampersand (Author & Author, 2011, p. 57).

If your source is written by three, four, or five people, you need only cite all of the authors the first time you cite the source (Author, Author, & Author, 2011, p. 751). Thereafter, you may use only the name of the first author followed by the Latin words *et al.* (meaning "and others") and, of course, the year of publication, and the page number (First Author et al., 2012, p. 145). Note the period after *al.* If a source you use is written by six or more authors, you provide only the last name of the first author followed by *et al.*, even in the first parenthetical citation.

If your source is written by a corporate author, treat the corporate author as you would a single author: According to government sources, 10-year-olds watch an average of four hours of television per day (Royal Commission on Elementary Education, 2011, p. 234). You may shorten a corporate author's name, if it is lengthy: spell it out in full in the first citation, but add the abbreviation in square brackets—and use the abbreviated form in subsequent citations.

If the author of your source has chosen to remain anonymous, use "Anonymous" in your in-text citation in place of the author name, followed by the date, and punctuate it in the usual manner. In the reference list, the source will be alphabetized under the word "Anonymous." If the source has no author listed, alphabetize it by its title in the references list, and use the first few words of the title, either in double quotes or in italics, depending on its format, in the in-text citation.

● References List at the End of the Essay

The APA References list, like the Works Cited list in MLA, contains all of the references you have cited in your essay.

Features of the APA References list include the following:

- The list is arranged alphabetically by the authors' last name. If the source is anonymous, it is placed in the list alphabetically under "Anonymous."
- Authors' first names are not used; only their initials are. (In the MLA method, first names are used.)
- Words in the titles of articles contained within books or journals are not capitalized, except for the first word, the first word in a subtitle, and proper nouns.
- Book titles are capitalized the same way article titles are, but book titles are placed in italics, while article titles are not.

- Words in journal titles are capitalized, and journal titles are placed in italics.
- Electronic sources include the online address, unless a digital object identifier (DOI) is provided.
- If the source has more than one author, the authors' names are separated from each other with commas, except for the name of the last author, which is separated from the others with a comma and an ampersand: &.
- The volume number is placed after the title of the journal. For example, the article by Borrayo in the References list below is from the journal *Substance Use & Misuse,* volume 42. Note that the volume number is placed in italics. Some journal article citations, such as the one below by Flegal, Carroll, Ogden, and Johnson, have two numbers, the second enclosed within parentheses. The second number refers to the issue number. There is an important distinction here. Some journals are continuously paginated, which means that they are paginated by year and not by issue. If, for example, the first issue for the year 2011 of the journal *Quantum Mechanics Quarterly* began on page 1 and ended on page 160, the next issue for the year 2011 would begin on page 161. Citations for journals that are continuously paginated (for a full year) include only the volume number. But some journals are paginated by issue—each issue begins on page 1. Citations for journals paginated by issue require the volume number followed by the issue number in parentheses.

References

Assembly of First Nations, First Nations Information Governance Committee. (2007). *First nations regional longitudinal health survey 2002–2003: Results for adults, youth and children living in first nation communities.* Ottawa, Canada: Assembly of First Nations.

Bobzien, R. (2010). *No excuses!: The war on obesity.* Bloomington, IN: Authorhouse.

Borrayo, E. (2007). Using a community readiness model to help overcome breast health disparities among U.S. Latinas. *Substance Use & Misuse, 42,* 603–619.

Flegal, K. M., Carroll, M. D., Ogden, C. L., & Johnson, C. L. (2002). Prevalence and trends in obesity among U.S. adults, 1999–2000. *Journal of the American Medical Association, 288*(14), 1723–1727.

Lee, T., & Oliver, J. E. (2002). *Public opinion and the politics of America's obesity epidemic.* Retrieved from ksgnotes1.harvard.edu /Research/wpaper.nsf/rpw/RWP02-017/$File/rwp02_017_lee.pdf

National Restaurant Association. (2003, November 9). *Industry at a glance.* Retrieved from http://www.restaurant.org/research /ind_glance.cfm

Schlosser, E. (2001, April 7). The bitter truth about fast food. *The Guardian*, p.13.

Schlosser, E. (2002). *Fast food nation: The dark side of the all-American meal.* New York, NY: Perennial.

Sample APA Reference List Entries

Here are examples of APA References entries for the kinds of print and electronic sources you will likely reference in your academic essays. For additional examples, consult the *Publication Manual of the American Psychological Association.*

In accordance with the APA *Publication Manual,* the examples below are divided into nine sections: periodicals; books, brochures, and book chapters; technical and research reports; proceedings of meetings and symposia; doctoral dissertations and master's theses; unpublished work and publications of limited circulation; reviews; audiovisual media; and electronic media.

Periodicals

An article in an academic journal continuously paginated

Morrow, R. L., Garland, E. J., Wright, J. M., Maclure, M., Taylor, S., & Dormuth, C. R. (2012). Influence of relative age on diagnosis and treatment of attention-deficit/hyperactivity disorder in children. *Canadian Medical Association Journal, 184,* 755–762.

An article in an academic journal paginated by issue

Karran, T. (2009). Academic freedom in Europe: Reviewing Unesco's Recommendation. *British Journal of Educational Studies, 57*(2), 191–215.

A newspaper article, no author

Market and roadside bombs leave 16 dead. (2011, April 12). *The Vancouver Sun*, p. B3.

A magazine article

Smith, K. (2011, June). Pearly whites. *Today's Parent,* 40–47.

Books, Brochures, and Book Chapters

A book by one author

Guiliano, M. (2005). *French women don't get fat.* New York, NY: Knopf.

Rosenthal, R. (1991). *Meta-analytic procedures for social research.* Newbury Park, CA: Sage. (Original work published 1984)

Rosenthal's book is cited as a republished edition here. If the book is a second or subsequent edition, that information must also be included in parentheses, after the title.

Williams, J. D. (2003). *Preparing to teach writing* (3rd ed.). Mahway, NJ: Erlbaum.

An edited book
Kalaidjian, W., Roof, J., & Watt, S. (Eds.). (2004). *Understanding literature: An introduction to reading and writing.* Boston, MA: Houghton Mifflin.

Two or more works by the same author published the same year
Bornstein, R. F. (1993a). *The dependent personality.* New York, NY: Guilford.
Bornstein, R. F. (1993b). Parental representations and psychopathology: A critical review of the empirical literature. In J. Masling & R. Bornstein (Eds.), *Psychoanalytic perspectives on psychopathology* (pp. 1–41). Washington, DC: American Psychological Association.

A book by a corporate author
Canadian Psychological Association. (2010). *Canadian code of ethics for psychologists* (5th ed.). Ottawa, Canada: Author.

An article in an edited book
Bradburn, N. M. (1983). Response effects. In P. H. Rossi, J. D. Wright, & A. B. Anderson (Eds.), *Handbook of survey research* (pp. 289–328). New York, NY: Academic Press.
Gilbert, H. (2009). Contemporary Aboriginal theater. In C. Howells & E. M. Kröller (Eds.), *The Cambridge history of Canadian literature* (pp. 518–535). Cambridge, England: Cambridge University Press.

An unauthored article in an encyclopedia or other reference book
Neanderthal man. (1994). In C. Cook (Ed.), *Pears cyclopaedia* (Vol. 103, pp. F55–F56). London, England: Pelham.

An authored article in an encyclopedia or other reference book
Applebaum, E. L. (1998). Ear diseases and hearing disorders. In *The new encyclopaedia Britannica* (Vol. 26, pp. 216–220). Chicago, IL: Encyclopaedia Britannica.

A book translated from a foreign language
Rousseau, J. (1979). *Émile, or On education* (A. Bloom, Trans.). New York, NY: Basic Books. (Original work published 1762)

A multivolume work
Baker, R. S., & Sexton, J. (Eds.). (1998–2002). *Aldous Huxley: Complete essays* (Vols. 1–5). Chicago, IL: Ivan Dee.

A government publication

National Institutes of Health. (2003). *Child care linked to assertive, noncompliant and aggressive behaviors: Vast majority of children within normal range.* Bethesda, MD: Author.

Technical and Research Reports

A report available from the Government Printing Office with government institute as author

Labor Department, Bureau of International Labor Affairs. (2003). *Foreign Labor Trends: Switzerland, 2003* (Publication No. FLT 03-10). Washington, DC: Government Printing Office.

An ERIC (Educational Resources Information Center) document

Soles, D. (2001). *Sharing scoring guides.* Retrieved from ERIC database. (ED450379)

Proceedings of Meetings and Symposia

A paper presented at a conference

Blair, H., & Sanford, K. (1999, April). *Single-sex classrooms: A place for transformation of policy and practice.* Paper presented at the annual meeting of the American Education Research Association, Montreal, Canada.

A paper presented at a symposium

Wheeler, D. (1991). Creating culturally specific AIDS interventions: An example of the ethnographic approach to program evaluation. In K. J. Jaros & G. C. St. Denis (Eds.), *Proceedings of the 1991 Public Health Social Work Institute* (pp. 36–54). Pittsburgh, PA: University of Pittsburgh.

Doctoral Dissertations and Master's Theses

A doctoral dissertation abstracted in Dissertation Abstracts International

Willard, S. (2003). *Relationship of emotional intelligence and adherence to combination antiretroviral medications by individuals living with HIV disease* (Doctoral dissertation). Retrieved from Dissertation Abstracts International. (Accession No. 3087159)

An unpublished master's thesis

Soles, K. (2009). *Skepticism, illusion and rigorous observation: Marianne Moore's poetic pursuit of hope* (Unpublished master's thesis). University of Victoria, Victoria, Canada.

Unpublished Work and Publications of Limited Circulation

An unpublished manuscript never submitted for publication

> Eisner, F. N., & Bartleby, A. E. (2002). *The effect of profiling miscues on the police investigation of the Washington serial sniper case.* Unpublished manuscript.

Note: If the authors are affiliated with a university, put a comma after *manuscript* followed by the name of the department, the name of the university, and its location.

A publication of limited circulation

> *Dragon benefits.* (2002). Available from Human Resources, Drexel University, 3141 Chestnut Street, Philadelphia, PA, 19103.

Reviews

A review of a book

> Latterell, C. G. (2003). A guide to composition pedagogies [Review of the book *A guide to composition pedagogies*, by G. Tate, A. Rupiper, & K. Schick]. *College Composition and Communication, 54,* 502–505.

A film review

> Groen, R. (2012, March 20). *The hunger games*: A modern allegory and a rare treat [Review of the film *The hunger games*, produced by Lionsgate and Color Force, 2012]. *The Globe and Mail,* p. R1.

Audiovisual Media

A television or radio program

> McKeon, R. (Writer), Guerriero, L., & Softly, P. (Producers/Directors). (2012). The wreck of the *Costa Concordia* [Television series episode]. In J. Williamson (Executive producer), *The fifth estate.* Toronto, Canada: CBC.

A record, tape cassette, or CD

> Mozart, W. A. (1786). Overture to *Le nozze di Figaro* [Conducted by C. M. Giulini]. On *Le nozze di Figaro* [CD]. London, England: EMI Classics. (1990)

Note that the first name listed is that of the song's composer. The first date listed (1786) is the date of composition; use copyright date if applicable. The last date (1990) is the recording date.

Electronic Media

An online book

> Blossom, J. (2009). *Content nation: Surviving and thriving as social media technology changes our lives and our future.* Retrieved from http://www.wiley.com

An article in an online journal or magazine
> Bloom, P. (2010, May). Moral life of babies. *The New York Times Magazine*. Retrieved from http://www.newyorktimes.com

An electronic copy of a journal article retrieved from database such as ProQuest or Academic Search Premier
> Cyboran, S. F., & Goldsmith, C. (2012). Making the case: New study shows it does, indeed, pay to become a healthy enterprise. *Benefits Quarterly, 28*(1), 26–37. Retrieved from http://www.sibson.com

A document available on university program or department website
> Wilcox, S. (2002). *Prints and drawings*. Retrieved from http://www.yale.edu/ycba/collections/index.htm

A government report
> Canadian Citizenship and Immigration Services. (2003). *Visa waiver program*. Retrieved from http://www.immigration.gov.ca/graphics/shared/lawenfor/bmgmt/insptct.vwpp.htm

A report from a private organization
> Bombardier. (2010). *Turning obstacles into opportunity: Bombardier annual report year ended January 31, 2010*. Retrieved from http://www2.bombardier.com

An online reference book
> Etzkowitz, H., & Dzisah, J. (2009). University–industry relationships. In J. B. Callicott & R. Froderman (Eds.), *Encyclopedia of environmental ethics and philosophy* (Vol. 2, pp. 344–346). Retrieved from http://www.gale.cengage.com/

A daily newspaper article
> All four pillars needed to combat drug scourge. (2004, May 15). *The Vancouver Sun*. Retrieved from http://www.thevancouversun.com

For additional examples of citing online sources, see the References list in Tersa's essay which follows.

Twitter
> Harper, S. [Stephen]. (2012, March 14). Launched the Vimy Foundation Pin Campaign to raise awareness of the Battle of Vimy Ridge. Lest we forget. http://ow.ly/9F9KK [Tweet]. Retrieved from http://twitter.com/#!/pmharper

Student Essay: Examples of APA Citation and References

Abstract

Recent studies suggest that, contrary to popular belief, chocolate can be a part of a healthy and nutritious diet. This literature review examines five articles that discuss the health benefits of chocolate. One article questions the results of the studies that claim chocolate contains beneficial minerals and antioxidants and does not recommend chocolate consumption. The other four support the health benefits of chocolate, under the condition that chocolate supplements but does not replace more nutritious fruits and vegetables.

Is Chocolate Good for You?

A Review of Some Online Sources

Chocolate is certainly one of North America's favourite indulgences but we often feel guilty about consuming it due to chocolate's bad reputation. Most view chocolate as an unhealthy food, high in calories, high in fat, high in sugar, and too tasty to have any nutritional value. The purpose of this paper is to examine the validity of this assumption by reviewing some of the literature available online about the nutritional benefits or lack thereof of chocolate.

McShea, Leissle, and Smith (2009) asserted that "moderate consumption of chocolate can actually be good for you" (para. 4). Chocolate does contain unhealthy saturated fat, but only in the form of stearic acid, which does not raise cholesterol. Furthermore, stearic acid may thin blood just as aspirin does, reducing the risk of clogged arteries. In fact, chocolate might actually lower cholesterol because, like olive oil, it contains monounsaturated fat, in the form of oleic acid. Chocolate is also a source of protein, a typical bar containing three or four grams. It contains antioxidants in the form of flavonoids, which might reduce the risk of cancer and other age-related chronic diseases. Chocolate contains the minerals copper, magnesium, and calcium. Finally, contrary to popular belief, chocolate does not cause tooth decay because it contains tannins, which help prevent cavities.

Nurk et al. (2009) corroborated this position, confirming that chocolate contains "polyphenols, the same anti-oxidants that are found in red wine and green tea" and that they "help reduce the formation of plaque in the arteries" (p. 122). They also agreed that the flavonoids in chocolate "decrease platelet stickiness, which reduces blood clotting and, therefore, the chance of having a heart attack" (p. 123). Perhaps most interestingly, the researchers found that a higher intake of flavonoid-rich chocolate correlates with better cognitive test performance, hinting that chocolate may be a true health food. The researchers did, however, point out that "dark chocolate, with at least 70 percent cocoa, is the healthy treat" (p. 124), whereas milk chocolate is considerably less beneficial. And they cautioned against

CHOCOLATE: LITERATURE REVIEW   4

substituting dark chocolate for fresh fruits and vegetables, whose content of antioxidants, fiber, vitamins, and minerals are superior.

In "Chocolate and prevention of cardiovascular disease: A systematic review," Eric Ding, Susan Hutfless, and Xin Ding of Harvard's School of Public Health and Saket Girotra of the Medical College of Wisconsin (2006) reviewed 136 articles on "experimental, observational, and clinical studies of relations between cocoa, cacao, chocolate, stearic acid, flavonoids ... and the risk of cardiovascular disease" (Abstract). The results of their review indicated that "cocoa and chocolate may exert beneficial effects on cardiovascular risk" (Abstract). Their review confirmed the connections between the flavonoids in chocolate and heart health. They were less enthusiastic about stearic acid, agreeing that it did not raise cholesterol but expressed concerns about the methodological limitations of the studies on stearic acid they reviewed. They suggested, as well, that most of the studies on the health benefits of chocolate looked at short-term effects and therefore recommended more studies of the long-term effects of chocolate consumption.

"Chocolate: Food of the gods" (2005), from the *Yale-New Haven Nutrition Advisor,* also confirmed the health benefits of chocolate. The author explained why stearic acid does not raise LDL cholesterol, even though it is a saturated fat, noting that "stearic acid is converted in the liver to oleic acid, a heart-healthy monounsaturated fat" (p. 1). The author cited a 1997 study which suggests chocolate is healthier than butter, which does raise LDL cholesterol. The author also cited a study by Waterhouse that confirms the presence in chocolate of phenols, which help prevent the buildup of plaque in the arteries. Dark chocolate, which contains more cocoa butter, is especially rich in phenols. Chocolate is a rich source of magnesium and phosphorous and has a fraction of the amount of caffeine as coffee. This author added a cautionary note, claiming that "in some people, chocolate has been associated with kidney stones, headaches, acne, allergies, dental cavities and premenstrual syndrome" (p. 2) and warned against substituting chocolate for fruits and vegetables.

Text continues

CHOCOLATE: LITERATURE REVIEW   5

References

Chocolate: Food of the gods. (2005, March). *The Yale-New Haven Nutri-tion Advisor.* Retrieved from http://www.ynhh.org/online/nutrition/advisor/chocolate.html

Ding, E. L., Hutfless, S. M., Ding, X., & Girotra, S. (2006). Chocolate and prevention of cardiovascular disease: A systematic review. *Nutrition & Metabolism, 3*(2). Abstract retrieved from http://www.nutritionandmetabolism.com

McShea, A., Leissle, K., & Smith, M. (2009, November). The essence of chocolate: A rich, dark, and well-kept secret. *Nutrition, 25*(11). Retrieved from http://www.nutritionjrnl.com

Nurk, E., Refsum, H., Drevon, C. A., Tell, G. S., Nygaard, H. A., Engedal, K., & Smith, A. D. (2009). Intake of flavinoid-rich wine, tea and choco-late by elderly men and women is associated with better cognitive test performance. *The Journal of Nutrition, 139*, 120–7. Retrieved from http://www.jn.nutrition.org

Rimbach, G., Egert, S., & Pascual-Teresa, S. (2010). *Chocolate: (Un)healthy source of polyphenols?* Retrieved from http://www.worldcocoafoundation.org/scientific-research/research-library/documents/Rimbach2010.pdf

Chicago Manual of Style Method of Citing Sources

If you are using the MLA or the APA method of citing sources, discussed earlier in this chapter, you will acknowledge your sources first in parentheses and again, at the end of the essay, in a Works Cited (MLA) or a References (APA) list.

But some of your teachers might want you to cite your sources within the text of your essay, using footnotes or endnotes instead of parentheses. If they do, you will need to learn and use the *Chicago Manual of Style* method. The CMS method does offer now an in-text citation option, but there are still professors—especially in history, some of the other humanities, and business—who require their students to use footnotes or endnotes, so we include an explanation of this system in this book. The method is explained in full in the sixteenth edition of *The Chicago Manual of Style*, published in 2010 by the University of Chicago Press.

● Footnotes/Endnotes

After you have quoted directly from or paraphrased information from a source, place a number in superscript (that is, above the line) after the quoted or paraphrased information. If you want to add additional information that you don't want in the text of your essay, you may place that information in a footnote or endnote as well. The note numbers are repeated either at the bottom of the page or on a separate page at the end of the essay, and each number is followed by the complete bibliographical information, including page numbers. Notes at the bottom of the page are footnotes; those at the end of the paper are endnotes; either method is acceptable. If you use endnotes, place them on a separate page at the end of the essay but before the Bibliography. Use "Notes" as your heading, centred at the top of the page.

Here is an example of a CMS endnote citation:

> This alarming trend continues. In the 2010 election, only 36.4 percent of Canadian citizens eligible to vote actually voted.[1] Such voter apathy, argues Columbian Plains University's Edgar Holman, "indicates a serious disengagement with the political process."[2]

Note that the number follows the punctuation mark, and that there is no space between the punctuation mark and the number. The information in the footnotes or endnotes for the sources cited above is formatted as follows:

> 1. Carl Risterson, "Voter Patterns in Canadian National Elections, 1960–2012," *Aegis Quarterly* 2 (2012): 21–54.
>
> 2. Edgar Holman, *What America Cares About* (Pittsburgh: Plains Press, 2007), 45.

Note that the first line of the endnote or footnote is indented three spaces. The article title is in quotation marks, and the journal title and book title are italicized.

If you use the same source again, you do not have to provide all of the information again in your footnote or endnote. Use the author's last name, followed by a comma, followed by the relevant page number:

> 5. Risterson, 26.

Note that you do not use an abbreviation (*p.*) for page number.

If you use two different works by the same author, and cite one or both of them again in a footnote or endnote, use a shortened version of the title for the second citation:

> 8. Risterson, *America,* 51.

Note that the Latin abbreviations *ibid.*, *op. cit.*, and *loc. cit.* are not often used now in the CMS method.

Here is an example of a brief endnotes page with sources cited using the CMS method. Remember that this page would come after the essay but before the Bibliography. As you browse through this list, note the following:

- The first line is indented.
- The authors' names are not reversed and are given in full. (In the Bibliography, the author's last name does come first because the Bibliography is organized alphabetically.)
- Book titles are italicized and article titles are in quotation marks.
- Page numbers refer to the precise location of the source. (In the Bibliography, the range of page numbers is provided.)
- The format of the second Toron citation indicates the same source is used again.
- The date of access of the Internet citation (Remington) follows the url.

Endnotes

1. Kit Dobson, *Transnational Canadas: Anglo-Canadian Literature and Globalization* (Waterloo: Wilfrid Laurier University Press, 2009), 9.
2. Aileen Kelly, "Dostoevski and the Divided Conscience," *Slavic Review* 47 (Summer 1988): 250.
3. Health Canada, *Eating Well with Canada's Food Guide: A Resource for Educators and Communicators* (Ottawa: Health Canada, 2007), 35.
4. Al Purdy, "On the Flood Plain" in *An Anthology of Canadian Literature in English*, 2nd ed., eds. Donna Bennett and Russell Brown (Toronto: Oxford University Press, 2010), 582.
5. Alison Toron, "The Model Prisoner: Reading Confinement in *Alias Grace*," *Canadian Literature* 208 (2011): 23.
6. Toron, 25.
7. Nicholas B. Mayer, "Catalyzing Prufrock," *Journal of Modern Literature* 34, no. 3 (2011): 188, http://muse.jhu.edu/journals/journal_of_modern_literature/v034/34.3.mayer.html.
8. Elton L. Remington, "The Role of DNA Evidence in the Release of Felons Incarcerated in American State Prisons," *Criminal Justice Quarterly of Hawaii* 34 (2001), http://www.uhawaii.cjqh-34.edu/rem.uh (accessed January 28, 2012).

● Source List at the End of the Essay

At the end of the essay, provide a complete source list alphabetized by the author's last name or by title if there is no author. The source list is usually referred to as a Bibliography. Note that, because all of the bibliographical information is included in the footnotes or endnotes, some journals do not ask their authors to include a Bibliography. This is especially true when the essay concludes with a list of Endnotes.

Citations in the Bibliography are similar to those in complete footnotes, but there are important differences to note. You use the author's first name first in a footnote but his or her last name first in your Bibliography, which, remember, is alphabetized. You use paragraph indentation in footnotes or endnotes and hanging indentation in bibliographical entries. You place parentheses around the place of publication, the name of the publisher, and the date of publication in a footnote or endnote but not in a bibliographical citation. And you include the page number in the footnote or endnote but not in the bibliographical citation.

Here is the same endnote page that was shown above set out as it would look as a Bibliography.

As you study this Bibliography, note the following:

- The bibliography is arranged alphabetically, not numerically.
- Page numbers for books are not included.
- The full range of page numbers for articles from books and journals is included.
- Most of the information within parentheses in endnote citations is not enclosed within parentheses in bibliography citations.

Bibliography

Dobson, Kit. *Transnational Canadas: Anglo-Canadian Literature and Globalization.* Waterloo: Wilfrid Laurier Univeristy Press, 2009.

Health Canada. *Eating Well with Canada's Food Guide: A Resource for Educators and Communicators.* Ottawa: Health Canada, 2007.

Kelly, Aileen. "Dostoevski and the Divided Conscience." *Slavic Review* 47 (Summer 1988): 239–60.

Mayer, Nicholas B. "Catalyzing Prufrock." *Journal of Modern Literature* 34, no. 3 (2011): 188, http://muse.jhu.edu/journals/journal_of_modern_literature/v034/34.3.mayer.html.

Purdy, Al. "On the Flood Plain." In *An Anthology of Canadian Literature in English.* 2nd ed. Edited by Donna Bennett and Russell Brown, 582–84. Toronto: Oxford University Press, 2010.

Remington, Elton L. "The Role of DNA Evidence in the Release of Felons Incarcerated in American State Prisons." *Criminal Justice Quarterly of Hawaii* 34 (2001). http://www.uhawaii.cjqh-34.edu/rem.uh (accessed January 28, 2012).

Toron, Alison. "The Model Prisoner: Reading Confinement in Alias Grace." *Canadian Literature* 208 (2011): 12–28.

● Sample CMS Bibliography Entries

In all of the following examples, the footnote or endnote entry comes first, followed by the bibliographical entry for the same source.

Books

A book by one author

1. Richard Gwyn, *John A.: The Man Who Made Us* (Toronto: Random House Canada, 2007), 242.

   Gwyn, Richard. *John A.: The Man Who Made Us.* Toronto: Random House Canada, 2007.

If the book has gone into a second or later edition, place the edition number between the title and the place of publication:

2. Edward M. White, *Teaching and Assessing Writing,* 2nd ed. (San Francisco and London: Jossey-Bass, 1994), 46–47.

   White, Edward, M. *Teaching and Assessing Writing.* 2nd ed. San Francisco and London: Jossey-Bass, 1994.

An anthology, a compilation, or an edited book

3. Phillip Lopate, ed., *The Art of the Personal Essay: An Anthology from the Classical Era to the Present* (New York: Anchor-Doubleday, 1994), 89.

   Lopate, Phillip, ed. *The Art of the Personal Essay: An Anthology from the Classical Era to the Present.* New York: Anchor-Doubleday, 1994.

4. Wolfgang Martin, Maria Gomez, and Edward Johns, eds., *The Effects of Gender on Child Development in Custody Cases* (Oxford: Oxford University Press, 1996), 34.

   Martin, Wolfgang, Maria Gomez, and Edward Johns, eds. *The Effects of Gender on Child Development in Custody Cases.* Oxford: Oxford University Press, 1996.

See below for citation of separate articles from a collection of essays and of literary works from a literature anthology.

Two or more books by the same author

5. R. J. Waller, *The Bridges of Madison County* (New York: Warner, 1992), 39.

6. R. J. Waller, *Slow Waltz in Cedar Bend* (New York: Warner, 1993), 48.

7. Waller, *Bridges*, 76.

8. Waller, *Waltz*, 19.

   Waller, R. J. *The Bridges of Madison County.* New York: Warner, 1992.

   ——. *Slow Waltz in Cedar Bend.* New York: Warner, 1993.

Note that three hyphens replace the author's name for the second citation. Note that the alphabetization is by book title (the "The" in *The Bridges of Madison County* does not count).

A book by two or three authors

> 9. William A. Covino and David R. Jolliffe, *Rhetoric: Concepts, Definitions, Boundaries* (Boston: Allyn and Bacon, 1995), 90.
>
> Covino, William A. and David A. Jolliffe. *Rhetoric: Concepts, Definitions, Boundaries*. Boston: Allyn and Bacon, 1995.

A book by more than three authors

If you use a source by three or more authors, you do not have to list all of the authors' names in a footnote or endnote. You need only list the first author's name followed by *and others* or the equivalent Latin abbreviation, which is *et al.* (You may list all authors if you prefer.) In the Bibliography, however, typically all author names are used.

> 10. John L. Smith and others, *Moving to Las Vegas*, 3rd ed. (East Brunswick, Australia: Barricade Books, 2002), 23.
>
> Smith, John L., Patricia Smith, Theresa A. Mataga, and Lloyd W. Mixdorf. *Moving to Las Vegas*, 3rd ed. East Brunswick, Australia: Barricade Books, 2002.

A book by a corporate author

> 11. Guelph Historical Society, *Guelph: Perspectives on a Century of Change, 1900–2000* (Guelph: Guelph Historical Society), 24.
>
> Guelph Historical Society. *Guelph: Perspectives on a Century of Change, 1900–2000*. Guelph: Guelph Historical Society.

A work in an anthology

> 12. Katherine Govier, "Home for Good," in *The Penguin Anthology of Stories by Canadian Women,* ed. Denise Chong (Toronto: Penguin, 1998), 310.
>
> Govier, Katherine, "Home for Good," in *The Penguin Anthology of Stories by Canadian Women,* edited by Denise Chong, 307–17. Toronto: Penguin, 1998.

An article in an encyclopedia or other reference book

> 13. *Encyclopaedia Britannica,* 15th ed., s.v. "Laos."

Note that the page number and volume number are not included; they are not necessary because encyclopedia entries are alphabetized. The entry in the encyclopedia ("Laos" in the example above) comes at the end preceded by the abbreviation *s.v.*, which is Latin for *sub verbo* or "under the word." You do not have to list well-known reference books in your bibliography.

A book by an anonymous author

14. *The Chicago Manual of Style*. 16th ed. (Chicago: University of Chicago Press, 2010), 88.

> *The Chicago Manual of Style*. 16th ed. Chicago: University of Chicago Press, 2010.

This book would be alphabetized in the Bibliography list by its title.

A book translated from a foreign language

See the subsection on page 181 entitled "An Anthology, a Compilation, or an Edited Book." Use the same format for a translation, except insert the abbreviation *trans.* in place of *ed.*

A book published in a second or subsequent edition

15. Jane Feuer, *The Hollywood Musical*, 2nd ed. (Bloomington: Indiana University Press, 1993), 145–47.

> Feuer, Jane. *The Hollywood Musical*. 2nd ed. Bloomington: Indiana University Press, 1993.

If the title page indicates that the book is a revised edition, use the abbreviation *Rev. ed.* after the title. If the title page indicates that the book is an abridged edition, use the abbreviation *Abr. ed.* after the title.

A multivolume work

16. Kathleen Raine, *Blake and Tradition* (Princeton, NJ: Princeton University Press, 1968), 1:321.

> Raine, Kathleen, *Blake and Tradition*. Vol. 1. Princeton, NJ: Princeton University Press, 1968.

If you use all volumes, the work cited entry would be:

> Lauter, Paul, ed. *The Heath Anthology of American Literature*. 4th ed. 2 vols. Boston: Houghton Mifflin, 2002.

A government publication

17. Ministry of Education of British Columbia, *The 2011 B.C. Science Assessment: General Report*. (Victoria, B.C.: Queen's Printer, 2011).

> Ministry of Education of British Columbia. *The 2011 B.C. Science Assessment: General Report*. Victoria: Queen's Printer, 2011.

A dissertation

18. Melvin Kinison, "The Influence of Augustan Poets on the Poetry of Samuel Taylor Coleridge" (Ph.D. diss., Howson University, 2006), 29.

> Kinison, Melvin. "The Influence of Augustan Poets on the Poetry of Samuel Taylor Coleridge." Ph.D. diss. Howson University, 2006.

If the dissertation is published, then italicize the title as opposed to enclosing it within quotation marks. If it is published commercially in a microform edition, treat the publication details much like you those of a book, adding the fiche, frame, and row if available.

Articles

An article in an academic journal continuously paginated

Continuously paginated means that the pages in the journal are numbered by the year as opposed to by each issue.

> 1. Barbara A. Spellman and Simone Schnall, "Embodied Rationality," *Queen's Law Journal* 35, no. 1 (2009): 119.
>
> Spellman, Barbara A. and Simone Schnall. "Embodied Rationality." *Queen's Law Journal* 35, no. 1 (2009): 117–64.

An article in an academic journal paginated by issue

> 2. Andrea A. Lunsford, "Toward a Mestiza Rhetoric: Gloria Anzaldua on Composition and Postcoloniality," *Journal of Advanced Composition* 18, no. 1 (1998): 22.
>
> Lunsford, Andrea A. "Toward a Mestiza Rhetoric: Gloria Anzaldua on Composition and Postcoloniality." *Journal of Advanced Composition* 18, no. 1 (1998): 1–27.

A newspaper article

> 3. Brian MacLeod, "Media Must Explain Why Truth Matters," *Niagara Falls Review,* November 24, 2010, sec. A.
>
> MacLeod, Brian. "Media Must Explain Why Truth Matters." *Niagara Falls Review,* November 24, 2010, sec. A.

A review

> 4. Bernard Lewis, review of *Autumn of Fury: The Assassination of Anwar Sadat*, by Mohamed Heikal, The New York Review of Books, May 31, 1984, 26.
>
> Lewis, Bernard. *Review of Autumn of Fury: The Assassination of Anwar Sadat*, by Mohamed Heikal. The New York Review of Books, May 31, 1984, 25–27.

If the review is anonymous, begin the footnote or endnote citation with "Unsigned review of." In the Bibliography, the name of the newspaper or journal stands in for the author and is therefore used to alphabetize the entry.

An article in a magazine

> 5. Alice George, "Reading Scores on the Rise at Last," *Clarion,* February 1999, 19.
>
> > George, Alice. "Reading Scores on the Rise at Last." *Clarion,* February 1999, 18–22.

Note that if you are citing a source from a weekly magazine, you would include the day of the month also.

Electronic Sources

An information service

> 1. Derek Soles, "Gender Equity and the State of the Union," ERIC Clearinghouse on Reading, English, and Communication, 1999. ERIC Document Number 430 227.
>
> > Soles, Derek. "Gender Equity and the State of the Union." ERIC Clearinghouse on Reading, English, and Communication, 1999. ERIC Document Number 430 227.

An online database

> 2. John Keats, "Bright Star," *Literature Online*, http://lion.chadwyck .co.uk/.
>
> > Keats, John. "Bright Star." *Literature Online.* http://lion.chadwyck .co.uk/.

A listserv

> 3. Allen Renter, "Investing in High-Tech Stocks," posting to WI electronic bulletin board, March 5, 2002, http://WI@investop.com.
>
> > Renter, Allen. "Investing in High-Tech Stocks." Posting to WI electronic bulletin board. March 5, 2002. http://WI@investop .com.

An article in an online journal or magazine

> 4. Cynthia Haynes, "Inside the Teaching Machine: Actual Feminism and (Virtual) Pedagogy," *Computers, Writing, Rhetoric, and Literature* 2, no. 1 (1996), http://www.en.utexas.edu/~cwrl/v2n1/haynes/index.html.
>
> > Haynes, Cynthia. "Inside the Teaching Machine: Actual Feminism and (Virtual) Pedagogy." *Computers, Writing, Rhetoric, and Literature* 2, no. 1 (1996). http://www.en.utexas.edu/~cwrl/v2n1/ haynes/index.html.

5. Katharine Mieszkowski, "A Deluge Waiting to Happen," *Salon*, July 3, 2008, http://www.salon.com/news/feature/2008/07/03/floods/index.html.

Mieszkowski, Katharine, "A Deluge Waiting to Happen." *Salon*, July 3, 2008. http://www.salon.com/news/feature/2008/07/03/floods/index.html.

An article from a website

6. George P. Landow, "Victorian and Victorianism," Victorian Web, last modified August 2, 2009, http://victorianweb.org/vn/victor4.html.

Landow, George P. "Victorian and Victorianism." Victorian Web, last modified August 2, 2009. http://victorianweb.org/vn/victor4.html.

Audio-Visual Sources

A film or video recording

1. *Hamlet*, by William Shakespeare, dir. Kenneth Branagh (1996; Burbank, CA: Warner Bros.), videocassette.

Hamlet. By William Shakespeare. Directed by Kenneth Branagh. Burbank, CA: Warner Bros, 1996. Videocassette.

Student Essay: CMS Citation

Here is an excerpt from Zhen's essay "Choosing a College Backpack," with sources acknowledged using the CMS method.

One-strap messenger bags are less healthy than two-strap packs. "I tried to play it cool," Alison writes, "by using a messenger bag when I was a freshman, but after some serious shoulder and back pain, I finally caved and joined the backpack-carrying masses on my campus—and never regretted it."[1] There is research to validate the wisdom of Alison's decision.[2] Messenger bags are not good for back health if they contain more than a few light notebooks. They misalign the spine. Walking exacerbates the misalignment and the result can be back pain, even, in the worst case, a herniated disk. Similar problems can occur if a backpack is loaded unevenly, so the weight is improperly distributed to one side of the body. Nor is it healthy to wear a backpack too low down on the back; it is healthiest when worn between the shoulder blades. One study concluded that "a load placement with the centre of gravity at the 12 spinal segment resulted in the least postural deviation."[3]

1. "How to Choose a Backpack for College," *Universitylanguage.com*, 13 June 2011, accessed 22 May 2012, http://www.university language.com/blog/13/backpack-for-college.
2. Jayaratne, Kapila, Jacobs, Karen, and Fernando, Dulitha, "Global Healthy Backpack Initiatives," *Work: A Journal of Prevention, Assessment and Rehabilitation* 41 (2012): 5553–5557, accessed 23 May 2012, http://www.iospress.nl/journal/work.
3. Heusher, Zachary, Gilkey, David P., Peel, Jennifer L., and Kennedy, Catherine A, "The Association of Self-Reported Backpack Use and Backpack Weight with Low Back Pain among College Students," *Journal of Manipulative and Physiological Therapeutics* 33.6 (July/ August 2010): 432–437, accessed 23 May 2012, http://www.ncbi.nlm .nih.gov/pubmed/20732580.

Bibliography

"How to Choose a Backpack for College." *Universitylanguage.com*. 13 June 2011. Accessed 22 May 2012. http://www.universitylanguage .com/blog/13/backpack-for-college.

Heusher, Zachary, Gilkey, David P., Peel, Jennifer L., and Kennedy, Catherine A. "The Association of Sefl-Reported Backpack Use and Backpack Weight with Low Back Pain among College Students." *Journal of Manipulative and Physiological Therapeutics* 33.6 (July/ August 2010): 432–437. Accessed 23 May 2012, http://www.ncbi.nlm .nih.gov/pubmed/20732580.

Jayaratne, Kapila, Jacobs, Karen, and Fernando, Dulitha. "Global Healthy Backpack Initiatives." *Work: A Journal of Prevention, Assessment and Rehabilitation* 41 (2012): 5553–5557. Accessed 23 May 2012, http://www.ncbi.nlm.nih.gov/pubmed/20732580.

Acknowledging sources is something of a cross students have to bear because there are so many different citation systems and the rules that govern the systems are so exacting. Internet sites, with their long URLs and sometimes questionable content, have exacerbated the challenge. But the effort is worthwhile because sources carelessly acknowledged or, worse, not acknowledged at all cause problems ranging from lower grades to failing grades, even suspension. On the other hand, sources properly acknowledged add depth and authority to academic writing, qualities essential to winning the respect and attention of your readers.

WRITING ASSIGNMENTS

1. In an essay of approximately 500 words, define the term *plagiarism*, provide an example, and discuss the procedures writers must follow to avoid a plagiarism charge.
2. In an essay of approximately 1000 words, compare and contrast any two of the three citation methods covered in this chapter.

EXERCISES

1. Correct any errors you spot in the following examples of MLA Works Cited entries. (This is not a topical list, so you need not put the entries in alphabetical order.)

   Lori Lansens, *The Girls.* Vintage Canada: Toronto, 2006.

   S. I. Hayakawa, *Language in Thought and Action.* Fourth edition. New York: Harcourt, 1978.

   Trans. Stuart Gilbert. Camus, Albert. *The Stranger.* New York: Random House, 1946.

   Art Young and Toby Fulwiler, eds. *Writing Across the Disciplines: Research into Practice.* Odell, Lee. Foreword. Upper Montclair, NJ: Boyton, 1986.

   Letter to the *Toronto Star* by Andrew S. Eliot. 20 September 2011: C3.

   Different Places, Different Voices. Eds. Janet H. Momsen and Vivian Kinnaird. London: Routledge: 1993. 211–226. Fairbairn-Dunlop, Peggy. "Women and Agriculture in Western Samoa."

   Bai, Matt. "Ventura's First Round." *Newsweek* 1999: 30–32. 15 Feb.

   Chan, Evans. "Postmodernism and Hong Kong Cinema." <u>Postmodern Culture Volume 10 Issue 3 year 2000.</u> Project Muse website without page numbers. Read it Jan 30, 2007.

   Telesford, Frank. "From Each According to His Means." *Synprax* 4.1 (2000). January 2000. www.isotrop.cityscape.edu/pmc/text-only/issue.200/4.1telesford. txt. Internet 10 May 2000.

   "Industrial Revolution." Redmond: Microsoft, 1994. *Concise Columbia Encyclopedia. Microsoft Bookshelf.* 1994 addition. CD-ROM.

2. Correct any errors you detect in the following entries from an APA References list. (This is not a topical list, so you need not put the entries in alphabetical order.)

   Brunner, C. and David Bennett. Technology and gender: Differences in masculine and feminine views. *NASSP Bulletin, 81*(592), 46–51. 1997.

Kubler-Ross, E. (1969). "On Death and Dying." New York: Macmillan.

Arthur Dedecker. Clinton and Obama Debate in Philadelphia. Germantown Daily News, April 19, 2008. Online version at http://www.germantowndailynews/clintonandobamadebate/04/19/08/ppr.htm

Mele, A. (1997). Real self-deception. ***Behavioural and Brain Sciences,*** *20,* 91–136. 1997, pp. 91–136.

Fowles, D. "Electrodermal activity and antisocial behaviour: Empirical findings and theoretical issues." In J. C. Roy, W. Boucsein, D. Fowles, & J. Gruzelier (Eds.), Progress in electrodermal research (pp. 223–237). London: Plenum, 1993.

Castellow, W., Chia, R., and Kenneth Wuensch: <u>Paper presented at the meeting of the American Psychological Association, Atlanta, GA.</u> *Physical attractiveness, sex, and cultural differences in juridic decisions.* (1988, August).

Schneider, D. J. (1973). Implicit personality theory: A review. Psychological Bulletin, 79, 294–309.

Kongshem, L. (1997, January). [1998, March 10]. Censorware: How well does Internet filtering software protect students? *Electronic School* [Online]. Available: http://www/electronic-school.com/0198fl.html

Feherty, David (2001, August). Get weird with your wedge. *"Golf Magazine,"* 43, pages 135–140.

Berton, I. (2001, September 24). An ounce of prevention. [Editorial.] *Meryton Gazette*, p. A11.

Schulman, R. (Ed.). (1998). *The Einstein papers project* [Online]. Boston University. Available: http://albert.bu.edu [1998, March 10].

3. Correct any errors you spot in the following examples of *Chicago Manual of Style* footnote and bibliography entries. (This is not a topical list, so you need not put the entries in alphabetical or numerical order.)

1. Welty, Eudora. [*One Writer's Beginnings]* (Cambridge: Harvard University Press, 1984), page 44.

Kelly, Alfred H., Winfred A. Harbison, and Herman Belz. (Norton, 1983). *"The American Constitution: Its Origins and Development."* New York: W. W. Norton, 1983.

1. Milan Kundera, *The Unbearable Lightness of Being,* translated into English by Michael Henry Heim in 1999. (New York: HarperPerennial Library, 1999), 73.

1. Edward, Wyatt; "A High School Without a Home,*"* *The New York Times*, 3 December 1999, sec. B1.

Marc Norman and Stoppard, Tom. *Shakespeare in Love* (New York: Miramax Films/Universal Pictures, 1999), videocassette.

Riordan, William L. *Plunkitt of Tammany Hall*. Edited by Terence J. McDonald. Published in 1994 in Boston by Bedford Books

Darnton, Robert. "The Pursuit of Happiness." *Wilson Quarterly* volume 19, number 4 1995 42–52.

McGann, Jerome J. *"Dante Gabriel Rossetti: A Brief Biography."* *The Complete Writings and Pictures of Dante Gabriel Rossetti: A Hypermedia Research Archive*. 19 March 1997. Available at http://jefferson.village.virginia.edu/rossetti/dgrbio.html [cited from the Internet on 23 March 1997].

1. Elinor Harrison, *The Music of the Night*, second edition Birmingham: Phonemart, 2002

Kidson, Peter. "Architecture and City Planning." In *The Legacy of Greece*, M. I. Finley, New York: Oxford University Press, 1981 pages 376 to 400.

COLLABORATIVE ACTIVITY

Devote one of your peer response sessions to examining only each other's citations of sources in an essay you are currently working on or have recently completed. Check citations within the essay, and check the format of the source list at the end of the essay.

2

Model Academic Essays

with Instructional Notes and Commentary

I f you are to succeed as a college or university student, you need to learn the components of the process of writing an academic essay: reflect upon your topic, research your topic, compose a thesis, plan, draft, revise, and edit. This information is covered in Part One of the text.

Another part of the process of learning to write effective academic essays is to read and reflect upon well-written examples of academic writing. We learn best by doing, but we also learn by studying the techniques of those who have already mastered the skill we are trying to learn and by reflecting upon and trying to imitate their techniques.

The aim of this section is to provide you with examples of well-written and informative academic essays, glossed with instructional notes and commentary that will help you understand the process the writers went through to create effective texts and the various methods they used to make their work readable. This, in turn, will help you to use the same techniques yourself as you plan, draft, revise, and edit your own work.

PART TWO

This article was published in the *Journal of Experimental Social Psychology,* volume 48, 2012, pages 770–773.

The title seems cumbersome, but it clearly describes the article topic. The editors of ———— a women's lifestyle magazine might use the research presented here in an article on what women find attractive in men. How might the title change if such an article appeared in a popular magazine?

Note that this study was conducted in the UK, and the authors use the British convention of using single quotation marks where we in North America would use double quotation marks.

Abstract   Like most articles in social science journal, this one begins with an ———— Abstract, summarizing the article's content. Abstracts are useful when you are researching a topic, in that they help you determine how relevant the article's content will be for the project you are working on.

Integrating Social Knowledge and Physical Cues When Judging the Attractiveness of Potential Mates[†]

Michelle C. Quist [a], Lisa M. DeBruine [a], Anthony C. Little [b], Benedict C. Jones [a] *

[a] School of Psychology, University of Aberdeen, UK
[b] School of Natural Sciences, University of Stirling, Stirling, UK

ARTICLE INFO

Article history:
Received 1 September 2011
Revised 9 November 2011
Available online 31 December 2011

KEYWORDS:

Face perception
Facial attractiveness
Sexual dimorphism
Mate choice
Sexual strategy

ABSTRACT

Although many women find masculine men physically attractive, the perception that such men are prone to infidelity may limit their appeal as romantic partners. To explore this issue, we first investigated the interplay between the effects of men's face shape (masculinity versus femininity) and social knowledge of men's behavior in previous romantic relationships (faithful versus unfaithful) on women's judgments of men's attractiveness. Analyses suggested that the extent to which women rated masculine men to be more attractive than feminine men was significantly greater when judging men labeled as faithful than when judging men labeled as unfaithful. In a second experiment, we obtained similar results when the women in our study were instructed to imagine they were on a date with each of the men and that, while on the date, they observed him either flirting or not flirting with another woman. These interactions suggest that social knowledge about men's behavior in romantic relationships can offset one of the costs that women associate with choosing a masculine mate, increasing the appeal of masculine men. More fundamentally, these findings suggest integration of social knowledge and information from facial cues in women's attractiveness judgments.

[†] Reprinted from *Journal of Experimental Social Psychology*, volume 48, 2012, Michelle C. Quist, Lisa M. DeBruine, Anthony C. Little, and Benedict C. Jones, "Integrating Social Knowledge and Physical Cues When Judging the Attractiveness of Potential Mates," pages 770–773. Copyright 2012, with permission from Elsevier.

* Corresponding author at: Face Research Laboratory, School of Psychology, University of Aberdeen, UK. *E-mail address:* ben.jones@abdn.ac.uk (B.C. Jones).

Introduction   The authors review some previous research on the social benefits of ————|
physically attractive faces. fMRI stands for functional magnetic resonance imaging, and it is a way of measuring brain activity in response to stimuli , in this case photographs of human faces. Because their work is published in an academic social science journal, the authors assume their readers will know about fMRI.

Paragraph 2   In the second paragraph of the Introduction, the authors explain how ————|
their experiment builds upon yet is different from previous research. Note the use of numbers to specify these differences. Numbered or bulleted points are common in social science papers.

Paragraph 3   The third paragraph of the Introduction continues to lead readers ————|
towards the questions their own studies will attempt to answer. They will examine not just physical attractiveness but the effect of social knowledge about fidelity on perceptions of attractiveness. Note in the parenthetical citations how careful the authors are to include all studies relevant to the point they are making—the first citation references three studies.

INTRODUCTION

Most studies of facial attractiveness have focused on the effects of physical characteristics that are relatively invariant (e.g., effects of symmetry, averageness, and sexual dimorphism, Rhodes, 2006). However, several behavioral and neurobiological studies recently reported interactions between effects of invariant facial characteristics and others' attitudes and intentions signaled by implicit cues, such as gaze direction and emotional expressions (reviewed in Main, DeBruine, Little, & Jones, 2010). fMRI experiments suggest the reward value of physically attractive faces is greater when they appear to demonstrate positive social interest in the viewer (e.g., make eye contact or smile, Kampe, Frith, Dolan, & Frith, 2001; O'Doherty et al., 2003). Similarly, participants report stronger attraction to physically attractive faces, relative to less physically attractive faces, when they are smiling at the participant than when they are shown with averted gaze or more negative expressions (Conway, Jones, DeBruine, Little, Hay, et al., 2008; Jones, DeBruine, Little, Conway, & Feinberg, 2006; Main et al., 2010). These enhanced preferences for physically attractive individuals who appear willing to reciprocate investment of social effort may function to promote efficient allocation of social effort (i.e., allocate more social effort to attractive individuals who appear willing to reciprocate, Jones et al., 2006).

Although previous studies have shown that more explicit social knowledge about an individual (e.g., knowledge that they are trustworthy) can influence attraction (e.g., Barclay, 2010), it is not known whether (1) people integrate this social knowledge with information from physical characteristics in faces when judging others' attractiveness, (2) such knowledge and stereotypic information from facial cues have independent, non-interacting effects on attraction, or (3) one type of information overrides the other. Integrating these types of information may be particularly important for women's attraction to masculine versus feminine men, however.

Masculine characteristics in men are associated with many attributes that women consider attractive (e.g., good long-term health and physical strength, Fink, Neave, & Seydel, 2007; Rhodes, Chan, Zebrowitz, & Simmons, 2003; Thornhill & Gangestad, 2006), but are also associated with anti-social personality traits that women find unattractive in long-term partners (e.g., a tendency to infidelity, Hughes, Dispenza, & Gallup, 2004). Thus, attraction to masculine versus feminine men may reflect how women resolve this trade-off between the costs and benefits of choosing a masculine mate (Gangestad & Simpson, 2000). Because the correlations between these attributes and masculine characteristics in men can be rather weak (Rhodes, 2006), however, integrating information from physical cues in men's faces with knowledge about their typical behavior in romantic relationships could help women

Paragraph 4   In the final paragraph of the Introduction, the authors present their
hypotheses. The first is that women are more attracted to masculine than feminine
male faces and even more attracted to men who are both attractive and faithful.
The second is similar but the context is social rather than simply observational: the
participants are to imagine they are on a date with the men whose images they are
observing.

Experiment 1   Note the system of sub-titles, common in reports of a social science
experiment.

Methods: Participants   What is most interesting here is that this was an online
study, a comparatively recent trend in social science research. The authors are
careful to assure readers that online studies such as the ones they are conducting
have been validated. N stands for the number of people—in this case 144 young
women—who participated in the study.

Methods: Stimuli   The authors explain how they selected and manipulated the
pictures of male faces to feminize or masculinise them. In Figure 1, they present
an example of one face (of the 28 they used in the study) that has been subtly
manipulated.

maximize the potential benefits of their mate choices. For example, masculine men are perceived to be particularly prone to infidelity, which may detract from their attractiveness (Kruger, 2006). That a man has been faithful to his previous romantic partners may, therefore, have a greater positive effect on the attractiveness of masculine than feminine men.

Here, we investigated the effects of social knowledge on women's attrac- 4 tiveness judgments of masculinized versus feminized versions of men's faces. We assessed women's ratings of masculinized versus feminized images of men's faces when judging men labeled as having been either faithful or unfaithful to their previous romantic partners, hypothesizing that women would report stronger attraction to masculine versus feminine men when judging 'faithful' than 'unfaithful' men. Such results would suggest that women integrate social knowledge and information from physical cues when assessing men's attractiveness. If both social knowledge and stereotypic perceptions from facial appearance affect attractiveness independently, however, we would expect only main effects of both factors. If social knowledge overrides stereotypic perceptions, we would expect only a main effect of social knowledge. In a second experiment, we tested for evidence of an interaction between the effects of social knowledge and masculinized versus feminized shape cues when women were instructed to imagine they were on a date with each of the men depicted and that, while on the date, they observed him either flirting or not flirting with another woman.

EXPERIMENT 1
Methods
Participants

Heterosexual women (N = 144, mean age = 22.80 years, SD = 4.93 years) 5 were recruited for an online study of attractiveness by following links from various social bookmarking sites (e.g., stumbleupon). Previous studies have demonstrated that online and laboratory studies of attractiveness judgments produce very similar patterns of results (Conway, Jones, DeBruine, & Little, 2008; Fraccaro et al., 2010).

Stimuli

Following previous studies (DeBruine, Jones, Crawford, Welling, & Little, 6 2010; Perrett et al., 1998), we used prototype-based image transformations to manipulate 2D shape in digital face images (Fig. 1). 50% of the linear shape differences between symmetrized male and female prototypes were added to or subtracted from face images of 28 young White adult men (Mean age = 23.9 years, SD = 3.53 years).

Methods: Procedure   The authors explain how the 28 faces were divided into
4 groups of 7, so they could test their hypothesis.

Paragraph 8   Note, in the second Procedure paragraph, how careful the authors are
to assure readers of the measures they have taken to construct the study in such a
way that the results will be valid.

Fig. 1. Examples of masculinized (left) and feminized (right) male face images used in our experiments.

These images were taken under standardized lighting conditions, with neutral expressions, and against a constant background, and were purchased from an online image database (www.3d.sk). This process creates masculinized and feminized versions of the images that differ in sexual dimorphism of 2D shape and that are matched in other regards (e.g., identity, skin color and texture, Tiddeman, Perrett, & Burt, 2001).

Procedure

Participants were told that they would be asked to rate men's faces for attractiveness. However, they were also told that, when rating the men's attractiveness, we would like them to imagine that these are men that they don't know, but who are members of the same social club as some of their friends. Some of the men have a reputation for being unfaithful to their girlfriends and are labeled 'unfaithful' (i.e., a text box under the face image will contain the text 'unfaithful'). The other men have a reputation for being faithful to their girlfriends and are labeled 'faithful' (i.e., a text box under the face image will contain the text 'faithful'). 7

Each participant was then presented 28 male face images (each a different individual), in a fully randomized order, and was instructed to rate each man's attractiveness using a 1 (very unattractive) to 7 (very attractive) scale. Seven of the men were presented as masculinized and labeled 'faithful', seven were presented as feminized and labeled 'faithful', seven were presented as masculinized and labeled 'unfaithful', and seven were presented as feminized and labeled 'unfaithful'. The unmanipulated versions of the faces in each of the four groups of seven men possessed equivalent rated masculinity (based on masculinity ratings of the unmanipulated faces that were made by 100 women in an initial pilot study). Which of the four groups were presented to an individual woman as masculinized or feminized and faithful or unfaithful was fully counterbalanced 8

Results   The Results are presented clearly and are carefully supported with the statistical analyses the authors used. Do any of the results surprise you? Note the reference to Figure 2, which presents a visual summary of the results of the first experiment.

across participants. Inter-rater agreement for attractiveness ratings was very high in each condition (all Cronbach's alphas > 0.82).

Results

Stimuli, rather than participants, served as our unit of analysis. Thus, for each 9 face presented, we calculated (separately) the average attractiveness rating in each of the four conditions. None of these scores differed significantly from a normal distribution (all Kolmogorov–Smirnov $Z < 0.81$, all $p > 0.51$).

A repeated-measures ANOVA with the factors *facial characteristic* 10 (masculinized, feminized) and *social knowledge* (unfaithful, faithful) revealed significant main effects of *facial characteristic* ($F(1,27) = 7.88$, $p < 0.001$, partial eta$^2 = 0.23$) and *social knowledge* ($F(1,27) = 114.8$, $p < 0.001$, partial eta$^2 = 0.81$). Masculinized versions ($M = 2.60$, SEM = 0.12) were rated as more attractive than feminized versions ($M = 2.38$, SEM = 0.12) and men were rated as more attractive when labeled 'faithful' ($M = 2.66$, SEM = 0.12) than when labeled 'unfaithful' ($M = 2.32$, SEM = 0.11). However, these effects were qualified by a significant interaction between *facial characteristic* and *social knowledge* ($F(1,27) = 4.80$, $p = 0.037$, partial eta$^2 = 0.15$, Fig. 2).

Masculine versions were rated as more attractive than feminine versions in 11 the faithful condition ($t(27) = 3.23$, $p < 0.001$). Masculine versions also tended to be rated as more attractive than feminine versions in the unfaithful condition, but this difference was not significant ($t(27) = 1.99$, $p = 0.057$). Men were rated as more attractive in the faithful than the unfaithful conditions for both masculinized ($t(27) = 8.25$, $p < 0.001$) and feminized ($t(27) = 7.66$, $p < 0.001$) versions. The interaction reported above indicates that the effect of masculinity was significantly greater in the faithful than unfaithful condition and the effect of fidelity was significantly greater for masculinized than feminized versions.

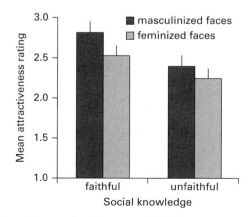

Fig. 2. The significant interaction between *facial characteristic* and *social knowledge* in Experiment 1.

Experiment 2: Methods   The authors describe the similarities and differences between their two experiments, highlighting here how conditions in the second experiment differed from those in the first.

Results   The Results of Experiment 2 are similar to those in Experiment 1. Note that in both experiments, masculine faces were rated more attractive, even when behaviour was inappropriate, though a masculine face coupled with appropriate behaviour was rated highest.

EXPERIMENT 2

Methods

Methods were identical to those in Experiment 1, except that participants were 12 138 women (Mean age = 22.38 years, SD = 4.30 years) who had not taken part in Experiment 1. Instructions were also slightly different from Experiment 1. Participants were told to imagine they were on a date with each of the men and that, while on the date, they saw another woman flirting with him. In some cases, the men flirted back. These men were labeled 'did flirt'. In other cases the men did not flirt back. These men were labeled 'did not flirt'. Inter-rater agreement for attractiveness ratings was very high in each condition (all Cronbach's alphas > 0.80) and none of these sets of scores differed significantly from a normal distribution (all Kolmogorov–Smirnov Z < 1.14, all p > 0.15).

Results

A repeated-measures ANOVA with the factors *facial characteristic* (masculinized, 13 feminized) and *social knowledge* (did not flirt, flirted) revealed significant main effects of *facial characteristic* ($F(1,27) = 11.2$, $p < 0.001$, partial eta^2 = 0.29) and *social knowledge* ($F(1,27) = 36.3$, $p < 0.001$, partial eta^2 = 0.57). Masculinized versions (M = 2.66, SEM = 0.12) were rated as more attractive than feminized versions (M = 2.34, SEM = 0.13) and men were rated as more attractive when labeled 'did not flirt' (M = 2.62, SEM = 0.12) than when labeled 'flirted' (M = 2.39, SEM = 0.13). The interaction was significant ($F(1,27) = 4.75$, $p = 0.038$, partial eta^2 = 0.15, Fig. 3). Masculine versions were rated as more attractive than feminine versions in both the 'did not flirt' ($t(27) = 4.69$, $p < 0.001$) and 'flirted' ($t(27) = 2.16$, $p = 0.040$) conditions. Men were rated as more attractive in the 'did not flirt' than the 'flirted' conditions for both the masculinized ($t(27) = 5.62$, $p < 0.001$) and feminized ($t(27) = 3.46$, $p = 0.002$) versions.

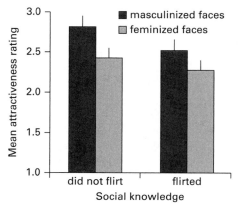

Fig. 3. The significant interaction between *facial characteristic* and *social knowledge* in Experiment 2.

Discussion   The authors summarize the results of their experiments, highlighting what they found about the effect of social knowledge on perception of
attractiveness.

Paragraph 15   In the second paragraph, they begin to place their study in the context
of others on related topics. They note their study expands knowledge in this field by
suggesting the influence of social knowledge.

Paragraph 16   In the third paragraph, they consider another explanation as to
why faithful masculine men are judged especially attractive: they challenge the
stereotype. What three reasons do they provide to reject this possibility?

DISCUSSION

The extent to which women reported stronger attraction to masculine over 14 feminine men was significantly greater when judging men with a reputation for being faithful than when judging men with a reputation for being unfaithful (Experiment 1) and when judging men who did not flirt with another woman on a hypothetical date than when judging men who did flirt (Experiment 2). These interactions suggest that women integrate information from physical cues in men's faces with social knowledge about those men's behavior and complement those observed between the effects of physical and social cues in faces in previous research (e.g., Jones et al., 2006; Main et al., 2010).

Trade-off theories of attractiveness judgments propose that the strength 15 of women's attraction to masculine men reflects, at least in part, how they resolve the trade-off between the costs (e.g., tendency to infidelity, Hughes et al., 2004) and benefits (e.g., good long-term health and physical strength, Fink et al., 2007; Rhodes et al., 2003; Thornhill & Gangestad, 2006) that would be associated with choosing a masculine mate (Gangestad & Simpson, 2000). To date, however, most evidence for this proposal has come from studies demonstrating that individual differences in women's circumstances that affect the nature of this trade-off shape women's judgments of men's attractiveness in predictable ways. For example, women's interest in pursuing short-term, uncommitted relationships (e.g., Provost, Troje, & Quinsey, 2008), women's own attractiveness (Little, Burt, Penton-Voak, & Perrett, 2001; Vukovic et al., 2010), and regional differences in health- and violence-related factors (Brooks et al., 2011; DeBruine et al., 2010, 2011; DeBruine, Jones, Little, Crawford, & Welling, 2011; see also Penton-Voak et al., 2004) are correlated with the strength of women's reported attraction to masculine men. Here, we present a different kind of evidence for trade-off theories of attraction; knowledge about men's behavior appears to reduce the perceived costs of preferring those specific masculine mates and increase women's reported attraction to masculine men. Langlois et al. (2000) has previously suggested that stereotypes associated with facial appearance influence attitudes towards individuals even when other information is available for people to base their judgments on. Our findings extend this claim by suggesting that social knowledge might also modulate the effects of facial appearance on social perception.

An alternative explanation for our findings is that masculine men dis- 16 playing masculine-atypical behaviors, such as fidelity, are judged as especially attractive because stereotype violation makes individuals more distinctive and/ or memorable. We suggest that this explanation is unlikely for three reasons. First, if our results were simply due to stereotype violation, one would expect that masculine men would be rated more attractive when paired with feminine behaviors, but that feminine men would be rated more attractive when paired with masculine behaviors. However, in both experiments, presenting incompatible behavioral information increased the appeal of masculine, but not feminine, men, suggesting that stereotype violation alone cannot explain our results. Second, stereotype violation increases the cognitive resources required to process individuals (Macrae et al., 1994), which *decreases* their attractiveness (Rhodes, 2006). Indeed, distinctiveness is *negatively* correlated with facial attractiveness (Rhodes, 2006). Third, while women's memory for events involving men displaying masculine characteristics is enhanced, this enhancement does not alter subsequent masculinity preferences (Allan et al., in press; Smith et al., in press). Together, these findings suggest that our findings are unlikely to reflect effects of stereotype violation alone.

An unresolved issue is whether effects similar to those we observed would 17 also occur in more naturalistic (i.e., real) social settings. On this point, we note that the extent to which partnered women rate masculinized versions of men's faces as more attractive than feminized versions predicts the masculinity of their romantic partners, linking attractiveness ratings of face images to actual partner choice (Burriss, Welling, and Puts, 2011; DeBruine et al., 2006). Other recent work suggests that social information gleaned during speed dates influences attractiveness judgments in ways that are strikingly similar to the effects of social knowledge acquired indirectly in laboratory experiments (e.g., Place et al., 2010). These findings suggest the effects we observed may well generalize to choices during actual interactions. Nonetheless, we suggest that studies using richer, more natural social contexts to explore interactions between the effects of perceptions of men's fidelity and masculinity are a potentially important direction for future research. A challenge for such work would be to design practical experiments that decouple the natural correlation between physical masculinity and sexual behavior in men, whereby women are more likely to perceive masculine men as unfaithful (Kruger, 2006) and fidelity and masculinity are positively correlated among men (Hughes et al., 2004). Without decoupling these traits, perceived fidelity and masculinity would be confounded and interactions could come about simply because of systematic differences in the way in which women perceive the fidelity of relatively feminine and masculine men, irrespective of the men's actual (i.e., observed) behavior.

We found that women reported significantly stronger attraction to mas- 18 culine men over feminine men when judging men who show cues of high commitment than when judging men who show cues of low commitment. These results suggest that women integrate social knowledge about behavior and information from physical facial cues when assessing men's attractiveness. Mating effort is a finite resource and the need to allocate it in an efficient manner is likely to influence attractiveness judgments and mate preferences (e.g., Conway, Jones, DeBruine, & Little, 2008; Jones et al., 2006). Integrating explicit social knowledge and information from physical cues in men's faces may function to promote efficient allocation of this effort by, in this case, encouraging attraction to men with an optimal balance of health/strength and faithfulness/commitment. More fundamentally, our study presents new evidence for trade-off theories of attraction and highlights the integrative processes that may underpin judgments of facial attractiveness.

REFERENCES

Allan, K., Jones, B. C., DeBruine, L. M. & Smith, D. (in press). Evidence of adaptation for mate choice within human females' long-term memory. *Evolution and Human Behavior.*

Barclay, P. (2010). Altruism as a courtship display: Some effects of third-party generosity on audience perceptions. *British Journal of Psychology, 101,* 123–135.

Brooks, R., Scott, I. M., Maklakov, A. A., Kasumovic, M. M., Clark, A. P., & Penton-Voak, I. S. (2011). National income inequality predicts women's preferences for masculinized faces better than health does. *Proceedings of the Royal Society of London B, 278,* 810–812.

Burriss, R. P., Welling, L. L. M., & Puts, D. A. (2011). Mate-preference drives mate-choice: Men's self-rated masculinity predicts their female partner's preference for masculinity. *Personality and Individual Differences, 51,* 1023–1027.

Conway, C. A., Jones, B. C., DeBruine, L. M., & Little, A. C. (2008). Evidence for adaptive design in human gaze preference. *Proceedings of the Royal Society of London B, 275,* 63–69.

Conway, C. A., Jones, B. C., DeBruine, L. M., Little, A. C., Hay, J., Welling, L. L. M., Perrett, D. I., & Feinberg, D. R. (2008). Integrating physical and social cues when forming face preferences: Differences among low and high anxiety individuals. *Social Neuroscience, 3,* 89–95.

DeBruine, L. M., Jones, B. C., Crawford, J. R., Welling, L. L. M., & Little, A. C. (2010). The health of a nation predicts their mate preferences: Cross-cultural variation in women's preferences for masculinized male faces. *Proceedings of the Royal Society of London B, 277,* 2405–2410.

DeBruine, L. M., Jones, B. C., Little, A. C., Boothroyd, L. G., Perrett, D. I., Penton-Voak, I. S., Cooper, P. A., Penke, L., Feinberg, D. R., & Tiddeman, B. P. (2006). Correlated preferences for facial masculinity and ideal or actual partner's masculinity. *Proceedings of the Royal Society of London B, 273,* 1355–1360.

DeBruine, L. M., Jones, B. C., Little, A. C., Crawford, J. R., & Welling, L. L. M. (2011). Further evidence for regional variation in women's masculinity preferences. *Proceedings of the Royal Society of London B, 278,* 813–814.

Fink, B., Neave, N., & Seydel, H. (2007). Male facial appearance signals physical strength to women. *American Journal of Human Biology, 19,* 82–87.

Fraccaro, P. J., Feinberg, D. R., DeBruine, L. M., Little, A. C., Watkins, C. D., & Jones, B. C. (2010). Correlated male preferences for femininity in female faces and voices. *Evolutionary Psychology, 8,* 447–461.

Gangestad, S. W., & Simpson, J. A. (2000). The evolution of human mating: Trade-offs and strategic pluralism. *The Behavioral and Brain Sciences, 23,* 573–644.

Hughes, S. M., Dispenza, F., & Gallup, G. G. (2004). Ratings of voice attractiveness predict sexual behavior and body configuration. *Evolution and Human Behavior, 25,* 295–304.

Jones, B. C., DeBruine, L. M., Little, A. C., Conway, C. A., & Feinberg, D. R. (2006). Integrating gaze direction and expression in preferences for attractive faces. *Psychological Science, 17,* 588–591.

Kampe, K. K., Frith, C. D., Dolan, R. J., & Frith, U. (2001). Reward value of attractiveness and gaze. *Nature, 413,* 589.

Kruger, D. J. (2006). Male facial masculinity influences attributions of personality and reproductive strategy. *Personal Relationships, 13,* 451–463.

Langlois, J. H., Kalakanis, L., Rubenstein, A. J., Larson, A., Hallam, M., & Smoot, M. (2000). Maxims or myths of beauty? A meta-analytic and theoretical review. *Psychological Bulletin, 126*, 390–423.

Little, A. C., Burt, D. M., Penton-Voak, I. S., & Perrett, D. I. (2001). Self-perceived attractiveness influences human female preferences for sexual dimorphism and symmetry in male faces. *Proceedings of the Royal Society of London B, 268*, 39–44.

Macrae, N., Milne, A. B., & Bodenhausen, G. V. (1994). Stereotypes as energy-saving devices: A peek inside the cognitive toolbox. *Journal of Personality and Social Psychology, 66*, 37–47.

Main, J. C., DeBruine, L. M., Little, A. C., & Jones, B. C. (2010). Interactions among the effects of head orientation, emotional expression and physical attractiveness on face preferences. *Perception, 39*, 62–71.

O'Doherty, J., Winston, J., Critchley, H., Perrett, D., Burt, D. M., & Dolan, R. J. (2003). Beauty in a smile: The role of medial orbitofrontal cortex in facial attractiveness. *Neuropsychologia, 41*, 147–155.

Penton-Voak, I. S., Jacobson, A., & Trivers, R. (2004). Populational differences in attractiveness judgements of male and female faces: Comparing British and Jamaican samples. *Evolution and Human Behavior, 25*, 355–370.

Perrett, D. I., Lee, K. J., Penton-Voak, I. S., Rowland, D. R., Yoshikawa, S., Burt, D. M., et al. (1998). Effects of sexual dimorphism on facial attractiveness. *Nature, 394*, 884–887.

Place, S. S., Todd, P. M., Penke, L., & Asendorpf, J. B. (2010). Humans show mate copying after observing real mate choices. *Evolution and Human Behavior, 31*, 320–325.

Provost, M. P., Troje, N. F., & Quinsey, V. L. (2008). Short-term mating strategies and attraction to masculinity in point-light walkers. *Evolution and Human Behavior, 29*, 65–69.

Rhodes, G. (2006). The evolutionary psychology of facial beauty. *Annual Review of Psychology, 57*, 199–226.

Rhodes, G., Chan, J., Zebrowitz, L. A., & Simmons, L. W. (2003). Does sexual dimorphism in human faces signal health? *Proceedings of the Royal Society of London B, 270*, S93–S95.

Smith, D., Jones, B. C., Feinberg, D. R., & Allan, K. (in press). A modulatory effect of male voice pitch on long-term memory in women: Evidence of adaptation for mate choice. *Memory & Cognition.*

Thornhill, R., & Gangestad, S. W. (2006). Facial sexual dimorphism, developmental stability, and susceptibility to disease in men and women. *Evolution and Human Behaviour, 27*, 131–14.

Tiddeman, B. P., Perrett, D. I., & Burt, D. M. (2001). Prototyping and transforming facial textures for perception research. *IEEE Computer Graphics and Applications, Research, 21*, 42–50.

Vukovic, J., Jones, B. C., DeBruine, L. M., Feinberg, D. R., Smith, F. G., Little, A. C., Welling, L. L. M., & Main, J. C. (2010). Women's own voice pitch predicts their preferences for masculinity in men's voices. *Behavioral Ecology, 21*, 767–772.

This article was published in the September 6, 2011, issue of the *Canadian Medical Association Journal*, pages 1374–1377.

This is a social science essay about the consequences of sex-selective abortions in some Asian countries, a practice that has resulted in a gender imbalance in societies where male children are favoured over female. It is expository to the extent that some of the consequences have been established; it is persuasive to the extent that the authors speculate on issues that might arise in the future. It is also a good example of a problem/solution essay.

Thesis and Introduction: Paragraphs 1–6   The thesis of this article, implicit in both the title and the introduction, is that the preference for sons over daughters in Chinese and other Asian country families has serious social consequences now that ultrasound technology can facilitate sex-selective abortion. This is a combination expository/ persuasive essay: the excess number of males is a fact, but the consequences of this fact are somewhat open to the speculation in which the authors engage.

In the introduction, the authors must indicate that families in China and other Asian countries do prefer sons to daughters, and they must show that this preference leads to aborting significantly more female than male foetuses.

Paragraph 1   The first paragraph offers reasons why in certain countries sons are valued more highly than daughters.

Note the numbers in superscript in this and other paragraphs throughout the essay. The *Canadian Medical Association Journal* acknowledges sources using a system developed by the International Committee of Medical Journal Editors, known as the Vancouver System because it was first developed at a conference there in 1978.

Paragraph 2   The second paragraph comments on the discrimination against girls, sometimes with serious consequences, that preference for boys has caused. The transitional word "But" at the beginning of the second sentence alerts readers to the social and cultural changes that ultrasound technology have caused and are continuing to cause. The consequences are "very serious and unprecedented sex-ratio imbalances." To this point, the authors may have implied but have not stated if these serious consequences are negative.

Paragraph 3   The third paragraph presents a key definition: Sex Ratio at Birth or SRB. In academic writing, it is always important to define key terms.

This paragraph also provides the first example of a country—South Korea— where the SRB has risen significantly.

The Consequences of Son Preference and Sex-Selective Abortion in China and Other Asian Countries*

Therese Hesketh MD PhD,[†] Li Lu MD PhD, Zhu Wei Xing MD MPH

Parents' preference for sons is common in countries in East Asia through 1
South Asia, to the Middle East and North Africa. Sons are preferred because they have a higher wage- earning capacity (especially in agrarian economies), they continue the family line and they usually take responsibility for care of parents in illness and old age.[1] There are also specific local reasons for son preference: in India, the expense of the dowry; and in South Korea and China, deep-rooted Confucian values and patriarchal family systems.[2]

For centuries, son preference has led to postnatal discrimination against 2
girls; this has resulted in practices ranging from infanticide to neglect of health care and nutrition, often ending in premature mortality.[3] But in the 1980s, ultrasound technology started to become available for diagnostic purposes in many Asian countries, and the opportunity to use the new technology for sex selection was soon exploited. In countries where there is a combination of son preference, a small-family culture, and easy access to sex-selective technologies, very serious and unprecedented sex-ratio imbalances have emerged. These imbalances are already affecting the reproductive age groups in a number of countries, most notably China, South Korea, and parts of India.[1,3,4]

The sex ratio at birth (SRB) is defined as the number of boys born to 3
every 100 girls and is remarkably consistent in human populations at around 105 male births to every 100 female births. South Korea was the first country to report a very high SRB, because the widespread uptake of sex-selective technology in South Korea preceded that of other Asian countries.[4] The SRB started to rise in South Korea in the mid-1980s, and by 1992 the SRB was reported to be as high as 125 in some cities.

---

† **Correspondence to:** Dr. Therese Hesketh, t.hesketh@ich.ucl.ac.uk

Paragraph 4   Here the authors move from South Korea to China. Note the first sentence, which makes the transition from the previous paragraph effectively. Note also the details, the statistics, facts, and figures in this paragraph. Note the reference to Figure 1. Tables, charts, and figures are important accessories to academic writing, used especially widely in science, social science, business, and technology essays and articles.

China soon followed. Here, the situation is complicated by the one- 4
child policy, which has undoubtedly contributed to the steady increase in
the reported SRB from 106 in 1979, to 111 in 1990, 117 in 2001 and 121 in
2005.[5] Because of China's huge population, these ratios translate into very
large numbers of excess males. In 2005 it was estimated that 1.1 million excess
males were born across the country, and that the number of males under the
age of 20 years exceeded the number of females by around 32 million.[5] These
overall figures conceal wide variations across the country. Figure 1 shows
these variations at the regional level: the SRB is over 130 in a strip of provinces
from Henan in the north to Hainan in the south, and it is close to normal
in the large, sparsely populated provinces of Xinjiang, Inner Mongolia, and
Tibet. High reported SRBs can result from female infanticide and underreg-
istration of female births. However, in China, there is now clear evidence that
sex-selective abortion accounts for the overwhelming number of "missing
women."[2,3,5]

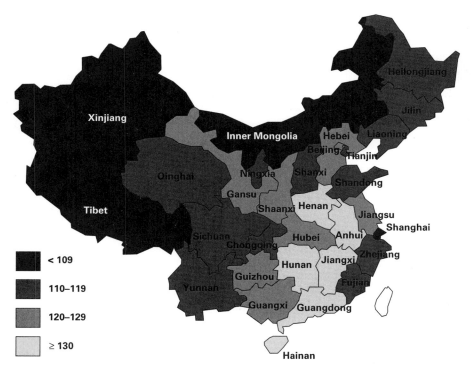

**Fig. 1. Sex ratios in the one-to-five age group in Mainland China in 2005.
Adapted by permission from *BMJ* Publishing Group Ltd. Zhu WX, Li L,
Hesketh T. China's excess males, sex selective abortion and one child policy:
analysis of data from 2005 national intercensus survey. *BMJ* 2009;338:b1211.[5]**

Paragraph 5   In the fifth paragraph, the authors move to India. Note again the clear
and effective transition, underscored by the use of the transitional word "also."
Note, also, the use of the passive voice, in the phrase "It is found...." Some
writing teachers prefer the more concise active voice, "We find," but some disciplines prefer the passive to avoid the use of first person. See also page 132.

Paragraph 6   The sixth paragraph introduces a new point: SRB increases
dramatically when the first child is a girl and even more dramatically if the first
two children are daughters. Note again how studies support the information the
authors are providing.

Consequences of High Sex Ratios, Paragraphs 7–10   The sub-title signals the
full development of the essay's thesis. The authors will identify four consequences of
the gender imbalance, three negative and one positive.

Paragraph 7   The seventh paragraph reaffirms the dramatic increase in the number
of males of marriage age and admits the consequences are "still largely speculative."
The paragraph goes on to discuss one of the consequences of societies with many
more young men that women: men with low socioeconomic status may find it especially difficult to find a wife. The authors again include facts and figures, supported
by research, referenced with numbered endnotes.

In India there are also marked regional differences in SRB. Incompleteness [5] of birth registration makes the SRB difficult to calculate accurately, but using the closely related ratio of boys to girls under the age of six years, it is found that there are distinct regional differences across the country. Several states in the north and west such as Punjab, Delhi, and Gujarat have sex ratios as high as 125, but in the south and east, several states such as Kerala and Andhra Pradesh have sex ratios of around 105.[3]

A consistent pattern in all three countries is the marked trend related to [6] birth order and the influence of the sex of the preceding child. If the first child is a girl, couples will often use sex-selective abortion to ensure a boy in the second pregnancy, especially in areas where low fertility is the norm. A large study in India showed that for second births with one preceding girl the SRB is 132, and for third births with two previous girls it is 139, whereas sex ratios are normal where the previous child was a boy.[6] In China this effect is even more dramatic, especially in areas where the rural population are allowed a second child only after the birth of a girl, as is the case in some central provinces. The SRB across the country for first-order births is 108, for second-order births it is 143 and for the (albeit rare) third-order births it is 157.[5]

Key Points

- In China, son preference and sex-selective abortion have led to 32 million excess males under the age of 20 years.
- Men for whom marriage is unavailable are assumed to be psychologically vulnerable and may be prone to aggression and violence.
- Policy-makers are addressing some causes of the high sex ratio at birth, but more could be done.
- It will be several decades before the sex ratio at birth in countries like India and China is within normal limits.

CONSEQUENCES OF HIGH SEX RATIOS

Prenatal determination of sex became accessible only in the mid-1980s, and [7] later than that in rural areas; therefore, the large cohorts of surplus young men have only now started to reach reproductive age. Because of this, the consequences of this male surplus in the reproductive age group are still largely speculative. However, there is no disputing that over the next 20 years in large parts of China and India there will be a 10 to 20 percent excess of young men. These men will be unable to marry, in societies where marriage is regarded as virtually universal, and where social status and acceptance depend, in large part, on being married and creating a new family.[7] When there is a shortage of women in the marriage market, women have the opportunity to "marry up," inevitably leaving the least desirable men with no marriage prospects.[8] The

Paragraph 8 Another potential consequence: low self-esteem and increased susceptibility to a range of psychological difficulties. These, in turn, may lead to sexual frustration, manifesting itself in aggression and violence. The worst case scenario is that these men will become an outcast culture which could threaten the stability and security of some Asian communities.

The authors are careful to admit the evidence for such serious consequences is circumstantial. Available evidence suggests low self-esteem and psychological vulnerability as genuine problems, while violence and aggression are potential problems. Academic writing is usually measured and reasoned, not sensational.

Paragraph 9 Another potential consequence: an expansion of the sex industry.

Again, the authors admit that they have no concrete evidence of this. There has been a rise in the number of sex workers in China, but factors other than the surplus of young men may explain this rise.

Paragraph 10 This paragraph comes as something of a surprise, noting as it does that there may be positive consequences to the sex ratio imbalance. Note the paragraph's topic sentence, which signals the discussion of positive consequences. Then the consequences are listed: the female infant mortality rate will decrease; population growth will be curtailed; and women will be more valued in societies that have historically privileged males. Ultimately, the problem of sex-selective abortion may be self-correcting. Numbers—first, second, third—are used to transition from one point to the next. Such a careful organizational structure is characteristic of good academic writing.

result is that most of these men who are unable to marry are poor, uneducated peasants. In China these men are referred to as "guang gun," meaning "bare branches," signifying their inability to bear fruit. In China, 94 percent of all unmarried people aged 28–49 are male, and 97 percent of them have not completed high school.[9]

A number of assumptions have been made about the effects of the male surplus on these men who are unable to marry. First, it has been assumed that the lack of opportunity to fulfill traditional expectations of marrying and having children will result in low self-esteem and increased susceptibility to a range of psychologic difficulties.[9] It has also been assumed that a combination of psychologic vulnerability and sexual frustration may lead to aggression and violence in these men.[10] There is good empirical support for this prediction: crosscultural evidence shows that the overwhelming majority of violent crime is perpetrated by young, unmarried, low-status males.[11] In China and parts of India the sheer numbers of unmated men are a further cause for concern. Because they may lack a stake in the existing social order, it is feared that they will become bound together in an outcast culture, turning to antisocial behaviour and organized crime, thereby threatening societal stability and security.[9] But as yet there is limited evidence for these hypotheses. Our own ongoing research in this area in China suggests that most of these men do indeed have low self-esteem, are inclined to depression, and tend to be withdrawn. But there is no evidence that they are prone to aggression or violence, nor are reports of crime and disorder any higher in areas where there are known to be excess men. This may be because there is not yet a large enough critical mass of unmated men to have an impact, or because the assumptions about male aggression do not apply in this context. 8

It is also thought that large numbers of excess men will lead to an expansion of the sex industry. The sex industry has expanded in India and China in the last decade.[12,13] However, the part played by a high sex ratio in this expansion is impossible to isolate; there is no evidence that numbers of sex workers are greater in areas with high sex ratios. The recent rise in numbers of sex workers in China has been attributed more to increased socioeconomic inequality, greater mobility and a relaxation in sexual attitudes than an increase in the sex ratio.[14] 9

There may also be positive aspects of this easy access to sex selection. First, access to prenatal sex determination probably results in an increase in the proportion of wanted births, leading to less discrimination against girls and lower female mortality.[15] India, South Korea, and China have all reported reductions in differential mortality in the last decade.[3,16] Second, it has been argued that an imbalance in the sex ratio could be a means to help to reduce growth in the population.[17] Third, as numbers of women in society fall, they become more highly valued and their social status increases.[18] Not only will 10

The point about increased respect for women is especially interesting. Feminists fought hard for abortion rights, only to see abortion used to discriminate against female infants in some countries. But the resulting shortage of women will increase their social status, in a sense a feminist victory. Here is a point you might consider in whole-class or small group discussions.

The Policy Response, Paragraphs 11– 16 This section of the body of the essay presents a thorough account of policy changes that have been made, and those that still need to be made, in order to assuage the problems sex-selective abortions have created.

Paragraph 11 The authors introduce this section of their essay, noting that the misguided policy may force governments to take corrective measures. They will have to outlaw sex selective abortions and reconsider their society's preference for sons

Paragraph 12 The authors note that the first solution is already in play: laws forbidding fetal sex determination and sex-selective abortion exist in Asian countries. But, except in South Korea, enforcement is perfunctory. And if abortion is legal, it is not easy to prove a woman's reason for opting for one. Note the careful use of statistics.

this benefit the women's self-esteem, mental health and well-being, but the improved status of women should result in reduced son preference, with fewer sex-selective abortions and an ultimate rebalancing of the sex ratio.[1]

THE POLICY RESPONSE

Nothing can realistically be done to reduce the current excess of young males, 11 but much can be done to reduce sex selection now, which will benefit the next generation. Realization of the potentially disastrous effects of this distortion in the sex ratio has led governments to take action. There are two obvious policy approaches: to outlaw sex selection and to address the underlying problem of son preference.

There are already laws forbidding fetal sex determination and sex-selective 12 abortion in China, India, and South Korea. But only in South Korea has the law been strongly enforced. As early as 1991, physicians in Seoul had their licences suspended for performing sex determination, with a resulting fall in the SRB from 117 to 113 in the following year.[4] In South Korea this enforcement, along with public awareness campaigns, contributed to a reduction in the SRB from a high of 118 in 1990 to 109 in 2004.[19] The fact that in China and India sex-selective abortion is still carried out with impunity, by medical personnel, usually qualified doctors, in hospitals and clinics, not in backstreet establishments, makes the failure of government to enforce the law all the more surprising. However, although sex-selective abortion is illegal, abortion itself is readily available, especially in China, and it is often difficult to prove that an abortion has been carried out on sex-selective, as opposed to family-planning, grounds.

China's successful Care for Girls publicity campaign, which includes billboards, focuses on the value of female children and the problems facing the over-abundance of young men.

Paragraph 13   While taking measures against sex-selective abortions is realistic, changing values, as the authors admit here, will be more challenging. In this paragraph, the authors focus on China, where the government is taking measures to convince citizens of the need for gender equity. Note the examples the authors use in support of their topic sentence.

Paragraph 14   This paragraph provides further examples of the push in China for gender equity. They note the progress that is being made.

Paragraph 15   Still, the authors argue that the one-child policy is the root of the problem. They explain the ways in which the policy is already being adjusted in China. The rule changes indicate the high degree of government involvement in regulating family size, an intrusion that would be difficult to imagine in Canada. Here is another issue to consider in whole-class or small-group discussion.

To successfully address the underlying issue of son preference is hugely 13 challenging and requires a multifaceted approach. In China, large public awareness campaigns, including poster and media campaigns, have focused on gender equity and the advantages of having female children. Recognition that intense intervention would be necessary to change these centuries-long traditions led to the Care for Girls campaign, instigated in 2003 by China's National Population and Family Planning Commission. This campaign is a comprehensive program of measures, initially conducted in 24 counties in 24 provinces, which aims to improve perceptions of the value of girls and emphasizes the problems facing young men in finding brides. In addition, there has been provision of a pension for parents of daughters in rural areas. The results have been encouraging: in 2007, a survey showed that the campaign had improved women's own perceived status and that stated son preference had declined. In one of the participating counties in Shanxi province, the SRB reduced from 135 in 2003 to 118 in 2006.[20]

Evidence from areas outside Asia strongly supports the notion that higher 14 status for women leads to less-traditional gender attitudes and lower levels of son preference.[21] The Chinese government has already made important moves toward gender equity in terms of social and economic rights. In 1992, the Law on the Protection of Rights and Interests of Women ensured equal legal rights for women in politics, culture, education, work, some property rights, and marriage.[22] These measures, together with socioeconomic improvements and modernization, have led to improvements in women's status, which is gradually influencing traditional gender attitudes.[19]

But the sex ratio is persistently very high, so other policy options should 15 be considered. The first relates to relaxation of the one-child policy. There has been gradual relaxation over the past decade. In large urban centres, if a husband and wife were both only children, two children are permitted. Starting in late 2011, this exception will apply if either spouse was an only child, if they reside in one of five large eastern provinces, which will massively increase the number of couples who will be allowed two children. In itself, this will probably have only a small effect on the sex ratio, because the high sex ratio is a greater problem in rural areas. But this signals a considerable relaxation in the previously strictly applied one-child rule in urban areas. In rural areas, a similar relaxation, especially to allow a third child after two girls, could lead to a substantial reduction in the sex ratio. The greatest contribution to the high sex ratio is in second-order births in rural areas. Evidence from studies that have explored preferred family size suggests that fears of a resulting rural population explosion would be unfounded, because a small minority of couples claim to want more than two children.[23]

The second policy option addresses the underlying problem of the value of [16] female children. Women in rural China still marry into their husband's family and cannot inherit family land, so daughters are often perceived as having "no value" to parents. In urban areas these traditions of inheritance have broken down and gender discrimination has decreased. It has been argued that changes in these laws in rural China could fundamentally influence attitudes about the value of women, which could lead, in turn, to a decrease in the sex ratio.[2]

THE FUTURE

Despite the grim outlook for the generation of males entering their reproduc- [17] tive years over the next two decades, there are encouraging signs. In South Korea the sex ratio has already declined markedly, and China and India are both reporting incipient declines. In China, the SRB for 2008 was reported as 119, down from a peak of 121, and 14 provinces with high sex ratios are beginning to show a downward trend. India is now reported to have an SRB of about 113, down from a peak of about 116.[19]

However, these incipient declines will not filter through to the repro- [18] ductive age group for another two decades, and the SRBs in these countries remain high. It is likely to be several decades before the SRB in countries like India and China are within normal limits.

COMPETING INTERESTS:

Therese Hesketh declares that her institution has received grants or has grants pending from the Department for International Development, the Economic and Social Research Council, and Wellcome Trust. None declared by Li Lu or Wei Xing. This article has been peer reviewed.

REFERENCES

1.   Hesketh T, Zhu WX. Abnormal sex ratios in human populations: causes and consequences. *Proc Natl Acad Sci U S A* 2006;103:13271–5.
2.   Das Gupta M, Jiang L, Xie Z, et al. Why is son preference so persistent in East and South Asia? A cross-country study of China, India and the Republic of Korea. *J Dev Stud* 2003;40:153–87.
3.   Sen A. Missing women revisited. *BMJ* 2003;327:1297–8.
4.   Park CB, Cho NH. Consequences of son preference in a low fertility society: imbalance of the sex ratio at birth in Korea. *Popul Dev Rev* 1995;21:59–84.
5.   Zhu WX, Li L, Hesketh T. China's excess males, sex selective abortion and one child policy: analysis of data from 2005 national intercensus survey. *BMJ* 2009;338:b121.
6.   Jha P, Kumar R, Vasa P, et al. Low male-to-female sex ratio of children born in India: national survey of 1.1 million households. *Lancet* 2006;367:211–8.
7.   Buss DM, Schmitt DP. Sexual strategies theory: an evolutionary perspective on human mating. *Psychol Rev* 1993;100:204–32.
8.   Zeng Y, Tu P, Gu B, et al. Causes and implications of the recent increase in the reported sex ratio at birth in China. *Popul Dev Rev* 1993;19:283–302.
9.   Hudson V, Den Boer A. A surplus of men, a deficit of peace. *Int Secur* 2002;26:5–38.

10. Barber N. The sex ratio as a predictor of cross-national variation in violent crime. *Cross-Cultural Res* 2000;34:264–82.

11. Messner SF, Sampson RJ. The sex ratio, family disruption and rates of violent crime: the paradox of demographic structure. *Soc Forces* 1991;69:693–713.

12. Dandona R, Dandona L, Kumar GA, et al. Demography and sex work characteristics of female sex workers in India. *BMC Int Health Hum Rights* 2006;6:5.

13. Tucker JD, Henderson GE, Wang TF, et al. Surplus men, sex work and the spread of HIV in China. AIDS 2005;19:539–47.

14. Hesketh T, Zhang J, Dong JQ. HIV knowledge and risk behaviour of female sex workers in Yunnan Province, China. *AIDS Care* 2005;17:958–66.

15. Goodkind D. On substituting sex ratio strategies in east Asia: Does prenatal sex selection reduce postnatal discrimination? *Popul Dev Rev* 1996;22:111–25.

16. Klasen S, Wink C. A turning point in gender bias in mortality? An update on the number of missing women. *Popul Dev Rev* 2002;28:285–312.

17. Arnold F. The effect of son preference on fertility and family planning: empirical evidence. *Popul Bull UN* 1987;23:44–55.

18. South SJ, Trent K. Sex ratios and women's roles: a cross-national analysis. *Am J Sociol* 1988;93:1096–115.

19. Das Gupta M, Chung W, Li S. Evidence for an incipient decline in numbers of girls in China and India. *Popul Dev Rev* 2009;35:401–16.

20. Li SZ, Yan SH. A special study on "care for girls" campaign [article in Chinese]. *Population and Family Planning* 2008;10:23–4.

21. Bolezendahl C, Myers D. Feminist attitudes and support for gender equality: opinion change in women and men, 1974–1998. *Soc Forces* 2004;83:759–90.

22. All-China Women's Federation. Laws and regulations. Available: www.women.org.cn/english/english/laws/02.htm (accessed 2011 Feb. 16).

23. Ding QJ, Hesketh T. Family size, fertility preferences, and sex ratio in China in the era of the one child family policy: results from national family planning and reproductive health survey. *BMJ* 2006;333:371–3.

AFFILIATIONS:

From the UCL Centre for International Health and Development (Hesketh), London, UK; the School of Public Health (Lu), Zhejiang University, and the College of Law and Political Science (Xing), Zhejiang Normal University, Zhejiang, China

CONTRIBUTORS:

All authors contributed to the content of the article. Therese Hesketh drafted the article, which Li Lu and Zhu Wei Xing revised. All authors approved the final version submitted for publication.

This article was published in the *Journal of Computer Assisted Learning*, volume 27, issue 2, 2011, pages 119–132.

This is an article in educational technology as the title and the place of publication   ⎯⎯⎯
indicate. Note the clear and precise title, typical for social science and education
studies. The format of this report is typical for those published in social science academic journals. Note that this journal uses the Harvard Citation Style to acknowledge sources, a system similar to the APA method.

Abstract   The editors of most journals in technology, education, the sciences, and   ⎯⎯⎯
the social sciences want authors to begin with an abstract, which summarizes the
purpose of the study, the methods used to collect the data, and the results. Abstracts
are invaluable, as they will help you determine if this is a study you want to read
in detail and use as one of the sources for your writing assignments. Note that the
Abstract takes up about half a page of a twelve-page study.

Introduction   The main purpose of the Introduction is to establish a context for the   ⎯⎯⎯
study undertaken by the authors.

The Effect of Twitter on College Student Engagement and Grades*

R. Junco,[†] G. Heiberger[‡] & E. Loken[§]

[†]*Lock Haven University, Lock Haven, PA 17745, USA*
[‡]*South Dakota State University, Brookings, SD 57007, USA*
[§]*The Pennsylvania State University, University Park, PA 16802, USA*

ABSTRACT

Despite the widespread use of social media by students and its increased use by instructors, very little empirical evidence is available concerning the impact of social media use on student learning and engagement. This paper describes our semester-long experimental study to determine if using Twitter—the micro-blogging and social networking platform most amenable to ongoing, public dialogue—for educationally relevant purposes can impact college student engagement and grades. A total of 125 students taking a first year seminar course for pre-health professional majors participated in this study (70 in the experimental group and 55 in the control group). With the experimental group, Twitter was used for various types of academic and co-curricular discussions. Engagement was quantified by using a 19-item scale based on the National Survey of Student Engagement. To assess differences in engagement and grades, we used mixed effects analysis of variance (ANOVA) models, with class sections nested within treatment groups. We also conducted content analyses of samples of Twitter exchanges. The ANOVA results showed that the experimental group had a significantly greater increase in engagement than the control group, as well as higher semester grade point averages. Analyses of Twitter communications showed that students and faculty were both highly engaged in the learning process in ways that transcended traditional classroom activities. This study provides experimental evidence that Twitter can be used as an educational tool to help engage students and to mobilize faculty into a more active and participatory role.

KEYWORDS

cooperative/collaborative learning, learning communities, media in education, post-secondary education, social media, teaching/learning strategies.

INTRODUCTION
Social media in higher education

Social media are a collection of Internet websites, services, and practices that support collaboration, community building, participation, and sharing. These technologies have attracted the interest of higher education faculty 1

* Accepted: 25 August 2010. Correspondence: Reynol Junco, 104 Russell Hall, Lock Haven University, Lock Haven, PA 17745, USA. Email: rey.junco@gmail.com
Credit: R. Junco, G. Heiberger, and E. Loken, "The Effect of Twitter on College Student Engagement and Grades," *Journal of Computer Assisted Learning*, Vol. 27, issue 2, 2011, pages 119–132. Copyright © 2011 by John Wiley & Sons, Inc.

Social Media in Higher Education   The first sub-section in the introduction defines the key term "social media" and begins a discussion of the application of social media to higher education, supporting the discussion with a review of some previous research. The "literature review" is an important component of a research study.

Note the parenthetical citations. The *Journal of Computer Assisted Learning* uses the Harvard system, which is very similar to the APA system, but, in the Harvard system, there is no comma between the author's name and the date.

The authors discuss social networking in general terms before they zero in on Twitter, the use of which is the main subject of their study.

Note the care the authors take acknowledging the sources included in their literature review.

members looking for ways to engage and motivate their students to be more active learners (Hughes 2009). There has been interest in integrating various social media tools (such as blogs, microblogs, video-sharing sites, and social networking) into the learning process (Grosseck & Holotescu 2009; Rankin 2009; Ebner et al. 2010; Schroeder et al. 2010), especially by faculty members with a disposition towards the use of newer technology in education (Crook 2008).

A major category of social media activity is social networking. Social 2 networking websites, such as Facebook, Myspace, and Twitter, have become an integral part of U.S. college students' lives (Junco & Mastrodicasa 2007; New Media Consortium 2007; Cotton 2008). The Higher Education Research Institute (HERI 2007) reported that 94% of first year college students use social networking websites, and data from a survey by Mastrodicasa and Kepic (2005) showed that 85% of students at a large research university had accounts on Facebook, the most popular social networking site. These data are congruent with more recent statistics on social networking website use and reinforce the fact that social networking is an important part of college students' lives (Jones & Fox 2009; Matney & Borland 2009).

While Facebook has been the most popular social networking site for 3 American college students to date, educators have been more willing to try to integrate Twitter as part of the learning process (Grosseck & Holotescu 2009; Rankin 2009; Ebner et al. 2010; Schroeder et al. 2010). Twitter is more amenable to an ongoing, public dialogue than Facebook because Twitter is primarily a microblogging platform (Ebner et al. 2010). Indeed, some have described Twitter as a blog that is restricted to 140 characters per post but that also includes the functionality of social networking (McFedries 2007).

Student engagement

In 1984, Alexander Astin proposed a developmental theory for college stu- 4 dents that focused on the concept of involvement, which he later renamed engagement. Astin defined engagement as 'the amount of physical and psychological energy that the student devotes to the academic experience' (Astin 1984, p. 297). Today, engagement is conceptualized as the time and effort students invest in educational activities that are empirically linked to desired college outcomes (Kuh 2009). Engagement encompasses various factors, including investment in the academic experience of college, interactions with faculty, involvement in co-curricular activities, and interaction with peers (Pascarella & Terenzini 2005; Kuh 2009). Kuh (2009) emphasizes two major facets: in-class (or academic) engagement and out-of-class engagement in educationally relevant (or co-curricular) activities, both of which are important to student success.

Social Media and Student Engagement   Having identified the connection between learning and engagement, the authors must now speculate on a correlation between social media and engagement. There is some evidence to suggest technology increases engagement and some evidence to suggest that social media, especially, correlates with increased engagement.

The authors are especially careful to summarize the two studies which found relationships between time spent on social media and student engagement, since these are most relevant to their own study. Read this paragraph carefully—the last paragraph of this sub-section—as a good lit review model.

Chickering and Gamson (1987) proposed seven principles for good 5 practice in undergraduate education, all of which are related to student engagement. They are: (1) student/faculty contact; (2) cooperation among students; (3) active learning; (4) prompt feedback; (5) emphasizing time on task; (6) communicating high expectations; and (7) respecting diversity. Later, Chickering and Ehrmann (1996) gave examples of how technology can be used to help implement the seven principles. Kuh (2009) reported that institutions of higher education can directly influence engagement by implementing these seven principles.

Since 1984, the construct of engagement has been extensively researched. 6 As Kuh (2009) states: 'student engagement and its historical antecedents… are supported by decades of research showing positive associations with a range of desired outcomes of college' (p. 698).

We know that academic and co-curricular engagement are powerful 7 forces in both student psychosocial development and academic success. Improvement in grades and persistence has been noted across a variety of populations, including minority students, first generation students, and students who are not adequately prepared for college academic work with increased engagement (Pascarella & Terenzini 2005; Kuh et al. 2008). Institutions can create programmes that help increase student engagement, and thereby increase the chances that students will reach the desired outcomes of a college education (Kuh 2009).

Social media and student engagement

While there is little research focusing on the relationship between social 8 media and student engagement in higher education, a number of studies have found relationships between technology use and engagement. For instance, King and Robinson (2009) found that college students who used electronic voting systems reported they were more likely to answer questions in their math course. Annetta et al. (2009) observed that students who played an educational game designed to teach genetics concepts were more engaged in their work than a control group. In a study using data from the National Survey of Student Engagement (NSSE), Chen et al. (2010) found significant correlations between the use of educational technology and student engagement. While these studies have been important contributions to the research on technology engagement, they have been limited by either their measurement of engagement (single variables) or their scope (cross-sectional).

Two recent studies have focused specifically on social media and engage- 9 ment and have found relationships between time spent on social media and student engagement as described by Astin (1984), and measured through single survey items. Heiberger and Harper (2008) conducted a study of 377 undergraduate students at a Midwestern institution, while the HERI (HERI

Purpose of the Study and Research Questions   Having reviewed previous research relevant to their own study, the authors conclude their Introduction with a clear statement of their own purpose for undertaking the study. They note the need to go beyond the cross-sectional and correlational studies previously undertaken. They note the need, especially, to consider the effect of Twitter on learning. They note the importance of determining the effect of Twitter not only on student engagement but also on student grades.

Using statistical analyses, the authors will measure the difference in performance between two groups of students, a "control group" which did not use Twitter and an "experimental group," which did. This is a classic *quantitative*, social science experiment, in that mathematical analyses—statistics—will be used to determine the results of the study.

But the authors also announce their intention to include a *qualitative* analysis of some of the student tweets, which means they will do a more subjective assessment of the linguistic content of the tweets, not to "measure" but to analyse more subjectively the level of student engagement.

Note that the Introduction concludes with the two questions—the first about engagement, the second about grades—the study is designed to answer. This is a typical and effective rhetorical strategy for an educational study.

Methods   Who is participating in the study? What tasks did the subjects have to undertake? How was their performance measured? Are the methods for measurement reliable? What statistical procedures were used to assess performance? These are the questions that the authors of educational studies typically address in the Methods section of their reports.

2007) used the Your First College Year survey to collect data from over 31 000 students at 114 colleges and universities. Both the Heiberger and Harper (2008) and HERI (2007) studies found a positive correlation between social networking website use and college student engagement. For instance, a higher percentage of high users of social networking websites participated in and spent more time in campus organizations than low users. Additionally, more of the high users reported that they interacted daily (in the real world) with close friends and felt strong connections to them (HERI 2007).

Purpose of the study and research questions

Although some research has been conducted on the effects of social media on student engagement (HERI 2007; Heiberger & Harper 2008), studies up to this point have been cross-sectional and correlational in nature, and therefore it has been difficult to make causal inferences. More specifically, no studies have examined the effect of using Twitter as part of an educational intervention on student engagement. Therefore, the current study serves to extend previous research by using an experimental design to examine the causal link between educationally relevant social media use and student engagement in a sample of American university students. Because of the strong links between engagement and student success (Pascarella & Terenzini 2005; Kuh 2009), this study will also examine student grades as an outcome variable. Additionally, we will conduct a qualitative analysis of tweets to provide examples of how students engaged via Twitter. The research questions examined were: 10

- What effect does encouraging the use of Twitter for educationally relevant purposes have on student engagement?
- What effect does encouraging the use of Twitter for educationally relevant purposes have on semester grades?

METHODS

Sample

Seven sections of a one-credit first-year seminar course for pre-health professional majors (students planning to apply to dental, chiropractic, medical, physical therapy, etc. schools) were used for the study. Four of the sections were randomly assigned to the experimental group and three to the control group. The experimental group used Twitter as part of the class while the control group did not (complete procedures described next). None of the students used Twitter before participating in this study. Both groups used Ning (http:// www.ning.com; a service that allows users to create their own social networking site) instead of a learning management system as a regular part of the course. Students were asked to participate in the study by taking a 11

Sample   The authors identify the participants in the study. The participants are
divided into two groups. The "control" group receives regular instruction; the
"experimental" group receives the specialized instruction, the efficacy of which the
researchers are investigating. In this study, there are more students in the experimental group, but the difference should not skew the sophisticated statistical procedures that will be used to compare performance.

Participants in both groups took a pre-test survey to assess their level of engagement as university students. The participants are profiled carefully, as they must be
in a study of this nature. Readers learn about the age, gender, and race of the participants. Readers also learn about the duration of the study and about reason why a
few students dropped out.

Twitter Procedure   This study was conducted before Twitter was as ubiquitous as
it is today, so the experimental group needed some training in the use of Twitter,
described in the first paragraph of this section.

The authors go on to explain the Twitter-related activities the students had to
engage in during the course.

pre- and post-test (the survey containing the engagement instrument). Although participation was voluntary, participants could enter to win drawings of cash deposits to their university flex accounts throughout the semester. The drawings were announced via Twitter for the experimental group and via Ning for the control group.

Of the 132 students in the seven sections, 125 took the pre-test survey 12 for an overall 95% participation rate. In the experimental group, 70 out of 74 (95%) students participated while 55 out of 58 (95%) participated in the control group. There was no significant difference between groups in participation rate. Sixty per cent of those who took the pre-test were female and 40% were male. The mean age of our sample was 18.2, with a standard deviation of 0.445. The age of our participants ranged from 17 to 20, although over 98% were between 18 and 19 years old. Twenty-eight per cent of the sample reported that neither parent had a college degree. In terms of race and ethnicity, our sample was overwhelmingly Caucasian, with 91% of students listing that as their race. Additionally, 6% of our sample was Latino, 3% Native American and 1% Asian American. We had no African Americans in our sample. The race and ethnic breakdown of our sample was similar to that of the overall university population, with the exception of a slight overrepresentation of Latinos and a slight underrepresentation of Asian Americans in our sample.

The study ran for 14 weeks. During those 14 weeks, there were seven 13 dropouts from the study, five (7%) from the experimental group and two (4%) from the control group. We followed up with the seven students who dropped out of the study. Five of the students dropped the class with the most frequent reason being change of major, while two reported they were transferring to universities closer to home. Final sample sizes were 65 students in the experimental group and 53 in the control group. The final sample was 92% Caucasian, 5% Latino and 3% Native American.

Twitter procedure

During the second week of the semester, the sections in the experimental 14 group received an hour-long training on how to use Twitter. This training was supplemented by question-and-answer periods over the next few class meetings. Students were taught the basics of Twitter [how to sign up for an account, how to send tweets (Twitter messages), how to use hashtags (clickable keywords within tweets) and @ replies (replies to other users)], and were shown how to enable privacy settings. All students were asked to send an introductory tweet during the training session. Students from experimental group sections were asked to follow a single Twitter account created for this study as well as follow each other so that they could interact across sections. Right after the Twitter training sessions, both the experimental and control groups were sent links to the online engagement instrument. The posttest instrument was sent during the last week of the study.

The Twitter class account was administered by two of the authors. 15 Based on previous research on engagement (Chickering & Ehrmann 1996; Pascarella & Terenzini 2005; Kuh 2009), engagement in social media (HERI 2007; Heiberger & Harper 2008), and case studies of Twitter use, we used Twitter for the following educationally relevant activities:

- Continuity for class discussions: Because the first-year seminar met only once a week for an hour, Twitter was used to continue conversations begun in class. For instance, students were asked to discuss the role of altruism in the helping professions.

- Giving students a low-stress way to ask questions: Oftentimes, first-year and/or introverted students are less comfortable asking questions in class. The dynamics of Twitter allow students to feel more comfortable asking questions given the psychological barriers inherent in online communication (Kruger et al. 2005).

- Book discussion: All first-year students read the same book as part of their first-year reading programme. The book, *Mountains Beyond Mountains* (Kidder 2004), focuses on Dr Paul Farmer's medical relief work in Haiti and was used to stimulate discussion about altruism and the helping professions.

- Class reminders: As students all took a similar sequence of courses, we were able to remind them of due dates for assignments and dates for exams in multiple classes via one Twitter feed.

- Campus event reminders: At the beginning of the semester, we used SocialOomph (formerly TweetLater) to schedule tweet reminders for the entire semester. These reminders included campus events, speakers, concerts and volunteer opportunities.

- Providing academic and personal support: We regularly posted information about academic enrichment opportunities on campus (for instance, the location and hours for the tutoring centre), both periodically and in response to student requests for help. Additionally, we provided encouragement and support when students reported things such as feeling 'stressed out' or being worried about exams.

- Helping students connect with each other and with instructors: The 'cohort effect' or the intentional creation of learning communities is an important concept in ensuring student persistence (Keup 2005–2006). Additionally, student/faculty interaction is an NSSE factor shown to be related to student success (Kuh 2002).

- Organizing service learning projects: As part of this course, students needed to participate in a service learning volunteer opportunity. Students used the Twitter feed to coordinate volunteer times with each other.
- Organizing study groups: With only a little encouragement from the authors via the Twitter feed, students organized study groups for two of their more difficult courses, Chemistry and Biology.
- Optional assignments: Students had the option of completing two assignments via Twitter. The two assignments were:

  1. Attend an upper-class student panel and tweet two questions they had for panelists.
  2. Tweet reactions to their shadowing experience (where they shadowed a healthcare professional in the community for a day).

- Required assignments: Students in all experimental group sections had four required Twitter assignments during the final 4 weeks of the semester. They were:

  1. Students were required to post two tweets and two replies to other students, discussing how reading *Mountains Beyond Mountains* has changed their ideas about people who are less fortunate than they are.
  2. Students were asked to watch a video of the Hurst family's medical volunteer work at the Pine Ridge Indian Reservation, read an online article about the Hursts, read the article *100 People: A World Portrait*, and discuss their reactions by posting two tweets and tweeting two responses to other students' reactions.
  3. Students were asked to react to the statement that what Paul Farmer was doing in *Mountains Beyond Mountains* was only a band-aid for the problem by posting two tweets and sending two tweet responses to other students' posts.
  4. Students were asked to discuss their service project in the context of their future career. They were also asked to compare and contrast their experience to that of Paul Farmer and to use examples from their assigned readings.

By the end of the semester, we had sent 301 tweets via the Twitter account. 16 Of those 301, 89 were replies (@ replies) to students while 18 were retweets (forwarding tweets from another user). Our goal was to select activities that were reflective of all of Chickering and Gamson's (1987) and Chickering and Ehrmann's (1996) seven principles for good practice in higher education and to maximize active learning. The control group was provided all of the same information that was posted to the Twitter group; however, this information was posted through the comment wall of the Ning social network. Our analyses of the Ning activity show that the control group engaged with faculty in

Instrument and Measures   The authors explain in more detail the instruments
they used to measure levels of student engagement.

They tailored the instrument to suit the needs of their study. Here, the second
paragraph of this sub-section, the authors refer to an Appendix, additional information at the end of their study, in this case a copy of the engagement scale, not
published as part of the journal article. Due to space concerns, journals often omit
study appendices. Note the detailed explanation of how the engagement scale the
authors used was coded.

Remember that grades as well as level of engagement is a variable the authors
will examine. In the last paragraph of this section, they note that they received permission from students to access their academic records. It is important to the study
that there is not discrepancy between the grade point averages of the two groups, a
discrepancy which might call into question the results of the study.

Engagement Instrument Reliability and Validity   Note the extent to which this
section of the article presupposes an audience that is familiar with statistical procedures. Many readers of the *Journal of Computer Assisted Learning* will understand
the type of statistical testing the authors explain here to validate the results of their
study. But readers who are less familiar with statistical procedures are only slightly
disadvantaged here. The key point is that the authors included a sub-section to give
readers confidence in the importance and validity of their study.

all of the educationally relevant activities listed previously, with the exception of forming study groups.

Instrument and measures

The NSSE is an established instrument that was developed to measure [17] engagement in educationally relevant activities and the desired outcomes of college (Pascarella & Terenzini 2005; Kuh 2009). The NSSE exhibits acceptable psychometric properties (see Kuh 2002) and items focusing on good practices in undergraduate education consistently predict development during the first year of college based on multiple objective measures (Pascarella *et al.* 2009). Items from the larger NSSE have been used to develop shorter scales to measure engagement in educationally relevant practices and engagement in online courses (Kuh et al. 2008; Chen et al. 2010).

We selected 19 items from the NSSE to use in our engagement scale [18] (Appendix S1). The 19-item engagement scale was administered as part of a survey that also included demographic items, items inquiring about student's technology use, and items that were included for forthcoming analyses. Engagement scale items 1–14 were coded using a four-point Likert scale ranging from 'Very often' to 'Never'. For our analyses, 'Never' was coded as 1, 'Sometimes' as 2, 'Often' as 3, and 'Very often' as 4. Question 15–17 were presented as a seven-point Likert scale and were coded with responses 1 or 2 as '1', responses 3 or 4 as '2', responses 5 or 6 as '3', and response 7 as '4'. Responses for question 18 were coded 1 for 'Very little', 2 for 'Some', 3 for 'Quite a bit', and 4 for 'Very much'. Lastly, responses for question 19 were coded 1 for 'Poor', 2 for 'Fair', 3 for 'Good', and 4 for 'Excellent'. Given the instrument's demonstrated reliability (discussed next), an aggregate engagement score was created using the sum of the individual items. The minimum score possible on the instrument was 19 and the maximum was 76.

Students gave the researchers permission to access their academic record to [19] obtain their semester grade point averages (GPAs), as well as their high school GPAs to examine the differences in grades between the experimental and control group. Grades were measured on a 4.0 scale ranging from 0 for 'F' to 4.0 for 'A'.

Engagement instrument reliability and validity

Reliability analyses found that the data from both administrations of the [20] survey were internally consistent. Cronbach's α for the pre-test administration was 0.75, and for the post-test administration it was 0.81. Our instrument's reliability was similar to the α of 0.82 reported by Kuh *et al.* (2008) and the α of 0.85 reported by Hytten (2010) using a different 19-item scale from the NSSE. Also, our instrument's reliability was similar to the α of 0.85 obtained by examining the data on the 22 college activity items (Kuh 2002). Our Cronbach's α of 0.75 and 0.81 indicate that the items measure a single latent construct, which in this case is engagement.

Statistics   Here the authors continue to explain how statistical analyses were used to ——————|
measure differences in performance between the two groups and they specify which
statistical software package they used in measuring their data.

Results   ——————|

Twitter Usage   This sub-section confirms that experimental-group students   ——————|
used Twitter extensively, while control-group students did not use it at all. This is
essential information to include in the study because the results might be skewed
if Twitter use was low or if control-group students also used it. The authors refer
readers to a visual aid, Figure 1, which charts the use of Twitter throughout the
semester. Such visuals are common features of education studies.

Because the engagement instrument was created for this study, no validity [21] data existed on this grouping of 19 items. However, the NSSE has a long history supported by research, of being used as a measure of college student engagement. Additionally, we collected some evidence for the construct validity of the instrument by correlating the total score on the engagement scale to the number of hours students reported that they spent in a typical week participating in co-curricular activities (such as involvement in campus organizations, campus publications, student government, fraternity or sorority, intercollegiate or intramural sports, etc.) on campus. Because, theoretically, students who are more engaged in general spend more time in co-curricular activities, one way to show evidence of construct validity of the engagement instrument would be if the scores on the engagement instrument correlated with the amount of time students spent in co-curricular activities. Indeed, we found that scores on the engagement instrument, both at the pre-test and the post-test, correlated significantly with the hours per week students reported spending in co-curricular activities (Pearson's $r = 0.26$, $P = 0.005$ at the pre-test, and Pearson's $r = 0.33$, $P = 0.001$ at the post-test). Although the correlations were significant, the correlation coefficients were modest, indicating that our instrument measures more than just co-curricular engagement—a finding supported by the theoretical background of our instrument as an omnibus measure of student engagement.

Statistics

To assess differences in engagement and grades, we used mixed effects analysis of [22] variance (ANOVA) models, with class sections nested within treatment groups. In order to assess changes between the pre- and post-test measurement of engagement, we used difference scores as the dependent variable. To calculate difference scores we subtracted the total pre-test score on the engagement instrument from the total post-test score. Using difference scores is equivalent to a repeated measures design with two time points (Bonate 2000). We used PASW (spss; IBM Corporation, Somers, NY, USA) Statistics Version 17.0 for all analyses.

RESULTS

Twitter usage

We collected data on the percentage of students sending tweets and the [23] number of tweets sent by using the Twitter Application Programming Interface. As can be seen in Fig. 1, students participated in Twitter throughout the semester. The spike in Twitter activity at week 12 was because of the start of the required Twitter assignments. The average number of student tweets sent over the entire study was 48.20, with a standard deviation of 52.87 and a median of 30. No students in the control group reported using Twitter during the study period.

Research Question 1   The authors repeat the question then provide the answer, an
effective way of reminding readers of the purpose and results of the study. With its
reference to statistical procedures, this sub-section acknowledges the expertise of
the readers of the journal, but any intelligent reader will pick up on the main point:
experimental-group students were more engaged in the course than control-group
students. The authors reference another visual, Table 1, the left half of which summarizes the scores which illustrate the dramatic extent to which experimental-
group students were more engaged.

Research Question 2   Again, the authors repeat the question and provide the
answer. Again, they refer to Table 1, this time to the right half of the table, which
summarizes the GPAs of students in each of the seven sections of the course (four
sections in the experimental group and three in the control group) and which illustrates the higher average GPA of experimental-group students. The difference of .51
may not seem that high but is "statistically significant." The authors are careful to
point out that they assessed student high-school GPAs to make certain there were
no significant differences between the groups prior to the study. The "N" on the far
right of the Table stands for the number of students in each group.

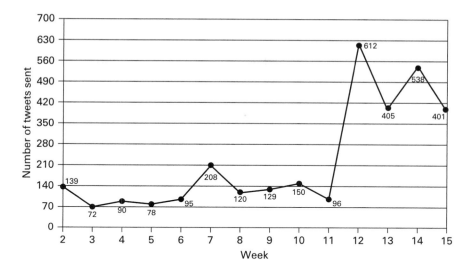

Fig. 1. Number of tweets sent each week of the semester. Note: Twitter use began on the second week.

Research question 1

Question 1: What effect does encouraging the use of Twitter for educationally 24 *relevant purposes have on student engagement?*

To examine the effect of Twitter on student engagement, we used a mixed effects ANOVA model, with sections nested within treatment groups. The dependent variable was the difference score between the post-test administration of the engagement instrument and the pre-test administration. Table 1 shows the descriptive data for engagement score difference by group and nested sections. The experimental group had significantly higher difference scores, with $F(1, 4.9) = 12.12$, $P = 0.018$. We also conducted a mixed effects ANOVA model with pre-test engagement scores as the dependent variable and found that there were no pre-existing differences in engagement by group and nested sections [$F(1, 4.9) = 2.80$, $P = 0.156$].

Research question 2

Question 2: What effect does encouraging the use of Twitter for educationally 25 *relevant purposes have on grades?*

For these analyses, we also used a mixed effects ANOVA model, with sections nested within treatment groups. The dependent variable was overall first semester GPA. Table 1 shows the descriptive data for GPA by group and nested sections. The semester GPAs of the experimental group were significantly higher than those of the control group with, $F(1, 4.9) = 8.01$, $P = 0.037$.

Analysis of Twitter Activity   Having illustrated, through a *quantitative* analysis of the data, the positive effects of Twitter on engagement and grades, the authors now turn to a *qualitative* analysis of the data. A qualitative analysis would examine the content of the tweets to assess the levels of student engagement. Given the high numbers (65 students sending an average of 48 tweets), the authors chose to limit their analysis to some of the Twitter discussion of three key aspects of the course.

Book Discussion   The authors include the Twitter exchanges of selected students as they tweeted about one of the course reading assignments. Their analysis of the content of these tweets notes the high level of student engagement and the willingness of all students, especially those who might be shy in a classroom setting, to share their views electronically.

TABLE 1

Means, standard deviations, and sample sizes by treatment group and nested sections for engagement difference scores and semester grade point averages (GPAs).

Group	Section	Engagement score difference Mean	SD	Semester GPA Mean	SD	N
Experimental	1	4.94	4.92	2.48	0.91	16
	2	6.93	7.77	3.05	0.82	15
	3	5.20	5.99	2.66	0.83	15
	4	3.79	7.70	2.94	0.81	19
	Overall	5.12[1]	6.69	2.79[2]	0.85	65
Control	1	1.79	7.37	2.36	1.18	14
	2	3.11	8.48	2.09	1.08	20
	3	1.84	7.38	2.41	1.03	19
	Overall	2.29[1]	7.67	2.28[2]	1.08	53

[1]Experimental group had significantly higher difference scores on engagement ($P < 0.05$).
[2]Experimental group had significantly higher semester GPAs ($P < 0.05$).

We also conducted a mixed effects ANOVA model with high school GPA as the dependent variable and found no pre-existing differences between groups [$F(1, 4.9) = 1.24, P = 0.316$].

Analysis of Twitter activity

While an exhaustive review of the qualitative data generated during this study 26 is impractical given the scope of this paper, we selected three examples to illustrate student engagement. An examination of the content of the tweets suggests that students engaged with faculty and each other in a vibrant and connected virtual learning community.

Book discussion

Students were required to participate in discussing the *Mountains Beyond* 27 *Mountains* book (Kidder 2004). The following is a sample of a conversation that is representative of the type of academic engagement we observed during book discussions.

Faculty:	How has reading MBM changed your ideas about responsibility or obligations toward people who are poorer than you are?
Student01:	@Faculty Reading mbm has made me less self centered. I realized alot of ppl need help and you can help them by doing simple things:)
Student02:	@Faculty It made me realize how selfless I need to be, just like how Farmer put his dedication toward helping others before his own needs.
Student03:	I've realized that helping the less fortunate is a social and moral responsibility that nobody is exempt from to help make the world better.
Student04:	@Faculty it helped me to see that one person really can make a difference if the effort is put forth
Student02:	@Student03 I definitely agree. It's not up to just one person. Farmer had lots of others help him, like the MacArthur Foundation.
Student02:	@Student04 Do you think that just one person can make a difference, or that one person inspires many people to help make a difference?
Student04:	@Student02 i think in a way its the same thing because that one person inspiring others is still making it all happen by involving others
Student02:	@Student04 That's a good point. Farmer made a difference in people's lives while inspiring others, like us, at the same time!
Student05:	Simply volunteering throughout the community like at the Harvest Table is a small step towards bettering the world.
Student06:	This book showed how selfish people are and makes me want to learn to be more selfless so I can serve those in need for the rest of my life
Student07:	@Faculty I enjoying volunteering, and look forward to doing more in the future. Its an awesome feeling!
Student06:	@Student07 Volunteering really is great in the fact that it is doing good for someone else and by doing so you actually feel good!
Student08:	@Faculty I believe that it has showed me how my life is a blessing and others should realize it do, we are privileged kids in every way
Student09:	@Student08 we don't realize how good we have it until we actually see how the other half lives … and its a rude awakening.

Paragraph 29   In the final paragraph of this sub-sub-section, the authors claim ————
that the use of Twitter helped forge interpersonal relationships. They provide two
examples in support of this paragraph's topic sentence.

Upper Class Panel   Here the authors include sample tweets for an optional course ————
assignment. Students attended a panel discussion of students further advanced in
the health care programs they were interested in and, via Twitter, asked questions of
the panellists. The authors' qualitative analysis of the questions confirms the high
level of experimental-group engagement. Note the extent to which the paragraph
develops, using details and examples, the topic sentence, the first sentence of the
final paragraph in this sub-sub-section.

Using Twitter produced a more rich discussion of student's relationship 28
to themes covered in the book than would have been possible during the
limited class time. Twitter allowed us to extend conversations in ways that
would not have been practical during the hour-long class sessions. The first-
year seminar was only 1 h each week, and while it would take students some
time to 'warm up' to talk about personally impactful themes from the book,
they did this readily via the electronic format. Students were also surprisingly
comfortable with candid expressions of their feelings and their shortcomings
as evidenced by this sample of tweets. They also engaged in a great deal more
cross-communication about the book than first-year students typically do
during class sessions.

Some students who were engaged in academic discussions via Twitter also 29
forged interpersonal relationships. While they discussed the reading, students
made connections when realizing they had shared values and interests. For
instance, the conversation between Student02 and Student04 led them to
realize that they have a mutual friend and a shared extra-curricular interest.
While these connections may have happened eventually in class, they happened quickly over Twitter as traditional classroom discussion boundaries did
not exist (i.e. 'don't talk about personal things during academic discussions').
Indeed, one of the striking effects of having students communicate on Twitter
is how they built strong relationships across diverse groups—something that
rarely happens with first-year students at this institution. One particularly
noteworthy example was an extroverted student who is a popular athlete who
became good friends with a more introverted student who is interested in
comic books—a connection that may have never happened in the real world.

Upper class panel

One of the optional assignments was for students to attend a panel of upper- 30
class pre-health professional students and to tweet questions they had for the
panelists. Students in both groups had the option to submit a short paper with
their questions in lieu of tweeting or posting them on Ning. The following are
example tweets from this thread.

Faculty:	Class canceled next week (10/21). Instead you are req'd to attend the upper-class student panel on Wed. (21st) at 12pm in SNP 103
Faculty:	3 min paper option for the 21st is to tweet questions you have for upper-class pre-health professional students. Due 12pm 10/21.
Student01:	@Faculty I have a psych class at noon. How am I supposed to attend?

Study Groups   Here the authors analyze tweets related to experimental-group
students' desire to form study groups. Their analysis suggests that the use of Twitter
encouraged the formation of groups and facilitated exchanges among students.

Faculty:	@Student01 If you can't attend because of scheduling conflict, please complete 3 min paper about last class.
Student02:	@Faculty Why are you training to become a health professional? is what I would ask them, could I go to the discussion. Alas, Bio lab.
Student03:	@Faculty My question is, How many of you are planning to go into radiology and why?
Student04:	@Faculty My question is – What made you decide the specific career in the health field you want to pursue?
Student05:	@Faculty My question is: How many Medical schools did you apply to and how did you choose which ones to apply to?
Student06:	What is the hardest part of the application process for PT school and do you have any advice on how to make it easier?
Student07:	Where is SNP? My question is. How many of you have changed your majors and how many times?
Student08:	@Faculty What inspires you to complete all the schooling for your profession? How do you manage your time so you are not always stressed?

An examination of these tweets reveals some of the ways that students were 31 engaging via Twitter. First, a review of the number of questions proposed (over 75) and the number of students involved in the discussion (55) shows that students took advantage of having Twitter as a forum to ask questions. Indeed, student use of Twitter generated more and different types of questions than would have been generated in typical class discussions on the same topic. For instance, the statement and question by Student01 was uncharacteristically candid for a first-year student and lends support to the idea that Twitter helped students feel more comfortable asking questions they may not be comfortable with asking in class. Second, the questions proposed by students reflected many of the typical issues faced by first-year pre-health professional students—i.e. 'am I on the right track?', 'what do I need to do to get into graduate school?', 'what should I look forward to as I progress in the major?' Third, much in the same way that professionals can attend conferences virtually via Twitter, students were able to ask questions of the panel, even though they had scheduling conflicts and were not able to attend (as evidenced by Student02's response).

Study groups

Pre-health professional students take a similar sequence of courses which 32 includes introductory Biology and Chemistry courses. We used Twitter to encourage students to arrange study groups for their more difficult courses, Chemistry and Biology. The following tweets are examples of a discussion about study groups that arose after students were tweeting about being anxious about their upcoming Chemistry exam.

Faculty:	Anyone interested in forming a study group?
Student01:	@Faculty for what class
Student02:	@Faculty For what class?
Student03:	@Faculty study group for what?
Student04:	for?
Faculty:	Student01 @Student02 @Student03 @Student04 What class would you like to form a study group for? Chem?
Student05:	Both Chemistry and Biology would be nice OK how about a Chem and Bio study group? Who is in?
Student06:	Anyone that wants to have a study group for Bio or Chem. Let me know and I'm in!
Faculty:	@Student01 @Student02 @Student03 @Student04 Both @Student05 and @Student06 suggest both Chem and Bio. What is a good time for you to meet?
Faculty:	How about a study group for Chem tonight starting at 7pm 2nd floor of the library – at the blue couches. Who will be there? Please RSVP
Student05:	I'm planning on coming to the study group
Student06:	Sounds good
Student01:	I'm in
Faculty:	So it looks like @Student05 @Student06 and @Student01 will be at the study group. Any others planning to attend?
Student07:	Count me in
Student03:	I'll be there

A review of these tweets shows that it took little effort on the part of the faculty member to help students create and attend a study group. Interestingly, after the first meeting of five students, they continued to set up study groups (without faculty intervention) that saw increased attendance as the semester progressed. Two issues are particularly noteworthy about student engagement in creating a study group: First, it was relatively easy to help students create a study group on short notice. Within hours, students went from chatting about their concerns about an upcoming exam to holding a study group

Discussion   The Discussion section of an educational study report reviews the findings, considers their implications, and addresses the limitations of the study.

Research Question 1   The first sub-division of this section reiterates the positive effect of Twitter on student engagement in the course.

Research Question 2   The second sub-division of this section reiterates the positive effect of Twitter on improving students' grades.

Analysis of Twitter Activity   The third sub-division of this section reiterates the positive effect, based upon a qualitative analysis, of Twitter on student engagement. Note that qualitative analysis could not be used to measure the effect of Twitter on grades.

meeting in the library. Second, the public nature of Twitter helped students be more comfortable asking each other for help. In our experience, pre-health professional students at this institution rarely develop study groups in their first semester. Their eagerness to form study groups could be partly because of the fact that their anxieties about the exam were being expressed in a public forum and therefore, they discovered that others felt the same way. When students made such a discovery, it may have been easier to then realize that they could benefit from studying with others in the same situation.

DISCUSSION

Research question 1

Question 1: What effect does encouraging the use of Twitter for educationally 34
relevant purposes have on student engagement?

The analyses of difference scores show that there was a greater increase in engagement scores for the experimental group than the control group. From this we can conclude that using Twitter in educationally relevant ways had a positive effect on student engagement as measured by our instrument. Because we conducted analyses on difference scores, we took into account pre-existing differences in engagement level.

Research question 2

Question 2: What effect does encouraging the use of Twitter for educationally 35
relevant purposes have on grades?

Our analyses show that encouraging the use of Twitter for educationally relevant purposes has a positive effect on grades. We found no pre-existing differences between the groups on high school GPA, indicating that the groups were equivalent in terms of academic ability.

Analysis of Twitter activity

The examination of tweet content shows that students were motivated and 36 engaged with each other. In ways that rarely happen with pre-health professional first-year students at this institution, students were actively engaged in thoughtful and personally meaningful conversation about themes addressed in the *Mountains Beyond Mountains* book. These conversations extended over hours and sometimes days as students would log off Twitter, then back on to find a response to a previous statement and continue the conversation. An examination of tweets about the upper-class student panel showed that students were engaged in asking questions of their peers about academic milestones they expected to need help with.

Our examination of the tweets related to setting up study groups for 37 Chemistry and Biology showed that a group of students were enthusiastic

Implications   The authors return to seven principles of good practice in under-graduate education, and they show how the use of Twitter can help teachers achieve each of them. Note the use of the seven bullet points, one for each principle. The authors provide an example or two to illustrate how the use of Twitter facilitated the application of each principle.

about collaborative learning through study groups. With our encouragement and help, these students set up their first study group for Chemistry. After the first meeting, students independently organized additional study groups. Study group participation grew throughout the semester and expanded beyond Chemistry to other courses.

Implications

Our results suggest that Twitter can be used to engage students in ways that [38] are important for their academic and psychosocial development. We were able to leverage Twitter to support Chickering and Gamson's (1987) seven principles for good practice in undergraduate education:

- We improved contact between students and faculty (principle 1) by providing an avenue for contact congruent with their digital lifestyles.
- The use of our Twitter protocol also encouraged cooperation among students (principle 2)—students used Twitter to ask each other questions, not only about the material in the first-year seminar course, but also about material in other courses. Students also collaborated on their service learning projects via the Twitter feed, provided emotional support to each other, and created and scheduled real-world study groups via Twitter.
- The Twitter assignments promoted active learning (principle 3) by helping students relate the course material to their own experiences both inside and outside of the classroom.
- Twitter allowed us to provide prompt feedback (principle 4) to students, not only for their assignments, but also for a wide variety of questions and issues they faced. For example, a few students tweeted about having trouble viewing an online video that was required for the course, and within 10 min we provided feedback as to how they could solve the problem.
- One of the great benefits of using Twitter in this way with our first-year experience courses was that we were able to maximize time on task (principle 5). The course only met for an hour each week; however, thanks to the Twitter stream, we were able to continue discussion and build a strong learning community among students.
- We used Twitter to communicate high expectations (principle 6) in student's academic work, service learning projects, and out-of-class activities.
- Lastly, using Twitter showed a respect for diversity (principle 7) because, in addition to discussing diversity issues via the Twitter feed, we encouraged students who otherwise may not be active participants in class to participate online.

Paragraph 39   In the first paragraph following the bullet points, the authors expand
upon their analysis of the results, noting that, by virtue of its interactive nature,
Twitter urges faculty into a more active role in student engagement. They compare
Ning unfavourably with Twitter because Ning does not urge such engagement.

Paragraph 40   The next paragraph continues on the same theme: in a Twitter
classroom, faculty engage with students more frequently and more meaningfully.
The example is interesting in that it is in the form of a personal anecdote, a
comparatively rare but effective method for paragraph development in an
educational study.

Paragraph 41   The final paragraph of this sub-section contains another, more
dramatic anecdote to illustrate how Twitter fostered engagement between and
among students, even if the nature of the engagement was not related to the content
of the course.

Even though our results were positive, it is important to note that these results may not be solely attributable to the technology. While Twitter facilitated communication, engagement, and the democratization of roles and relationships in ways that may not have happened in the real world, the introduction of Twitter into the learning process mobilized faculty into a more active role with students that was different than when using Ning. Students in both the Twitter and the Ning groups received the same information and performed the same activities; however, Twitter lent itself more to a conversation between students and faculty. While Ning announcements took the form of static bulletin board postings, Twitter announcements were met with active responses by students which were met by even more interaction by faculty. Indeed, 30% of tweets from the faculty account were responses to students, whereby less than 1% of posts on Ning were responses to students—students on Ning did not ask as many questions or engage faculty in the same way as they did on Twitter. 39

The use of Twitter also demanded that two of the faculty members involved in this study regularly monitor and participate in the Twitter feed. This helped increase students' sense of connection with faculty and the institution, one facet of engagement. It also helped increase student's academic engagement. The frequency and intensity of faculty queries about both academic and co-curricular issues was much more than what is typically experienced by first-year students. Students in the Twitter group had the benefit of almost- always-on support for academic, co-curricular, and personal issues. For instance, when a student tweeted 'Procrastinators unite! … Tomorrow. It's a bad habit I developed in high school thats hard to break,' we immediately asked 'what helps your procrastination?' which led to a conversation with the student about what motivates her. Later in the conversation, we discover that the student has trouble 'clearing [her] head' and we provide links to resources to learn diaphragmatic breathing (which helps in anxiety reduction). Responses by faculty members generated even more tweets from students. This positive feedback loop of interaction kept the Twitter feed very busy (as can be seen in Table 1) and highly interactive. 40

In addition to engendering motivation to engage students on the part of the faculty, the use of Twitter created a culture of engagement between students. As was reported in the results, students interacted with each other a great deal around academic and co-curricular issues, which led to deepening of their interpersonal connections. It was common to see students support one another when someone would tweet about their stress or workload. One striking example was when a student tweeted about wanting to harm himself. Quickly, another student tweeted 'are you ok? Not that I know you or anything but your status sounds not so good.' They engaged in a conversation that helped the original tweeter feel like he did not want to hurt himself until a faculty member could intervene and have a face-to-face meeting with him. 41

Limitations   Research studies in education and the social sciences must carefully designed and executed, the subjects representative, the methods for gathering and analyzing data precise and accurate. Such studies will make valuable contributions to the knowledge in their field. No study can be perfect, however, and responsible researchers will usually acknowledge the limitations of their work, the purpose of this sub-section. The authors acknowledge four limitations.

Paragraph 42   In the first paragraph, the authors note that their subjects do not represent American college students, as a whole, because of the lack of ethnic diversity. Moreover, because they are students planning to pursue similar majors, their aptitude for technology might be different from other students planning different majors. The authors urge their study be replicated, using different student populations. This recommendation is common in such studies.

Paragraph 43   The authors go on to admit that the instrument used to measure engagement was imperfect. They specify ways in which measurement might have been less than perfect. They urge future research, using more accurate engagement measures.

Paragraph 44   The authors go on to admit that their own enthusiasm for the technology might have influenced the results. They wanted the experimental group to do well, and so they might have been more than usually involved and had a stake in student success. They note that this is a variable difficult to measure, though those who undertake similar studies in the future should try to do so.

Limitations

There are a number of limitations to the current study. The first and most important limitation is that the study was conducted on a narrow sample of the overall student population at an institution that is not necessarily representative (with respect to racial, ethnic, and income factors) of all institutions in the United States, let alone internationally. Furthermore, students who choose to be pre-health professional majors are a specific population unto themselves, with characteristics that may not match the characteristics of most students in higher education. It will be important to replicate this study with more diverse samples in terms of race, ethnicity, income, and academic majors and settings. It will also be important to specifically determine whether using Twitter can help engage students who are historically less engaged to begin with, such as those who may not be adequately prepared for college, those from minority backgrounds, and those who are first-generation students (Kuh 2009). 42

Another limitation is the engagement instrument. It is important to note that we measured the construct of engagement through self-report and not actual student engagement. The engagement instrument appeared to measure engagement adequately, and we found a correlation with scores on the instrument and time spent in campus activities. However, we would like to further investigate evidence of the instrument's relationship to actual indices of engagement. Moreover, the real-world implications of a difference of almost three points in engagement scale score means are unclear. Further research should be conducted to see if the engagement instrument correlates with indices such as observed participation in class discussion, campus activities, and interactions with students and faculty. Additionally, future research should measure indices of actual engagement (such as observation of classroom behaviour) as dependent variables to attempt to determine the best way to measure engagement. 43

One further limitation was the fact that we are unable to tease out how much of the variance in increased student engagement and improved grades is as a result of Twitter and how much is because of a possible orientation of faculty to be more engaged. Crook (2008) notes that the integration of social media depends on 'considerable creative involvement from teachers' (p. 35) and that adoption of these technologies may be more reflective of a disposition that is adopted by these faculty. In this sense, it is important to focus more on a 'Web 2.0 mentality' than on the technology (Crook 2008). In other words, the increases in engagement and grades may be able to be explained more by an overarching attitude about teaching and learning than about the technology itself. The disposition described by Crook (2008) may very well be related to an increased faculty interest and ability to engage students. While 44

there is no way to tease out this variance, future studies may want to examine possible dispositional variables that may lead to educationally relevant adoption of technology.

A final limitation was the structure of the study. We had a modest sample 45 size and because the study was structured across just seven sections as the units of randomization, the design was somewhat limited. In this case, the limited number of sections required us to run conservative statistical tests using section as a nested, random effect, and thus had few degrees of freedom for error. Future research should try to randomize across more classes and include a larger sample.

CONCLUSION

This study provides the first piece of controlled experimental evidence that 46 using Twitter in educationally relevant ways can increase student engagement and improve grades, and thus, that social media can be used as an educational tool to help students reach desired college outcomes. We provided evidence to suggest that students and faculty were both highly engaged in the learning process through communication and connections on Twitter. As there is continuing growth in the use of social media by college students and faculty, it is hoped that this study will motivate further controlled studies of Twitter and other social media to evaluate how emerging technologies can be best used in educational settings and to tease out the variance between the effects of the actual technology and of the 'Web 2.0 mentality.'

ROLE OF THE FUNDING SOURCE

Funding for this research was provided by the Midwest Consortium for 47 Service-Learning in Higher Education and the Corporation for National and Community Service. The study sponsors did not play any role in the study design; in the collection, analysis, and interpretation of data; in the writing of this report; or in the decision to submit this paper for publication.

REFERENCES

Annetta L.A., Minogue J., Holmes S.Y. & Cheng M.T. (2009) Investigating the impact of video games on high school students' engagement and learning about genetics. *Computers & Education* **53**, 74–85.

Astin A. (1984) Student involvement: a developmental theory for higher education. *Journal of College Student Personnel* **25**, 297–308.

Bonate P.L. (2000) *Analysis of Pretest-Posttest Designs.* CRC Press, Boca Raton, FL.

Chen P.S.D., Lambert A.D. & Guidry K.R. (2010) Engaging online learners: the impact of web-based learning technology on college student engagement. *Computers & Education* **54**, 1222–1232. forthcoming.

Chickering A.W. & Ehrmann S.C. (1996) Implementing the seven principles: technology as a lever. *AAHE Bulletin* **October**, 3–6.

Chickering A.W. & Gamson Z.F. (1987) Seven principles for good practice in undergraduate education. *AAHE Bulletin* **March**, 3–7.

Cotten S.R. (2008) Students' technology use and the impacts on well-being. In *Using Emerging Technologies to Enhance Student Engagement. New Directions for Student Services Issue #124* (eds R. Junco & D.M. Timm), pp. 55–70. Jossey-Bass, San Francisco, CA.

Crook C. (2008) *Web 2.0 technologies for learning: The current landscape – opportunities, challenges, and tensions.* Becta Research Reports. Becta, Coventry. Available at: http://research. becta.org.uk/upload-dir/downloads/ page_documents/research/web2_technologies_learning. pdf (last accessed 7 January 2010).

Ebner M., Lienhardt C., Rohs M. & Meyer I. (2010) Microblogs in higher education – a chance to facilitate informal and process-oriented learning. *Computers & Education* **55**, 92–100. forthcoming.

Grosseck G. & Holotescu C. (2009) *Can we use Twitter for educational activities?* Proceedings of the 4th International Scientific Conference: eLearning and Software for Education, Bucharest, Romania. Available at: http://adlunap.ro/eLSE_publications/papers/2008/ 015.-697.1.Grosseck%20 Gabriela-Can%20we%20use.pdf (last accessed 12 January 2010).

Heiberger G. & Harper R. (2008) Have you Facebooked Astin lately? Using technology to increase student involvement. In *Using Emerging Technologies to Enhance Student Engagement. New Directions for Student Services Issue #124* (eds R. Junco & D.M. Timm), pp. 19–35. Jossey-Bass, San Francisco, CA.

Higher Education Research Institute (2007) *College freshmen and online social networking sites.* Available at: http://www.gseis.ucla.edu/heri/PDFs/pubs/briefs/brief-091107-SocialNetworking.pdf (last accessed 7 March 2010).

Hughes A. (2009) *Higher education in a Web 2.0 world. JISC Report.* Available at: http://www.jisc. ac.uk/media/ documents/publications/heweb20rptv1.pdf (last accessed 7 January 2010).

Hytten K.J. (2010) *Facebook's contribution to educationally purposeful activities and college student engagement.* Unpublished PhD Thesis, The University of Vermont, Burlington.

Jones S. & Fox S. (2009) *Generations online in 2009.* Data memo. Pew Internet and American Life Project, Washington, DC. Available at: http://www.pewinternet.org/~/ media//Files/ Reports/2009/PIP_Generations_2009.pdf (last accessed 7 March 2010).

Junco R. & Mastrodicasa J. (2007) *Connecting to the Net. Generation: What Higher Education Professionals Need to Know about Today's Students.* NASPA, Washington, DC.

Keup J.R. (2005–2006) The impact of curricular interventions on intended second year re-enrollment. *Journal of College Student Retention* **7**, 61–89.

Kidder T. (2004) *Mountains beyond Mountains: The Quest of Dr. Paul Farmer, A Man Who Would Cure the World.* Random House, New York, NY.

King S.O. & Robinson C.L. (2009) 'Pretty lights' and Maths! Increasing student engagement and enhancing learning through the use of electronic voting systems. *Computers & Education* **53**, 189–199.

Kruger J., Epley N., Parker J. & Ng Z.-W. (2005) Egocentrism over e-email: can we communicate as well as we think? *Journal of Personality and Social Psychology.* **89**, 925–936.

Kuh G.D. (2002) *The National Survey of Student Engagement: Conceptual Framework and Overview of Psychometric Properties.* Center for Postsecondary Research, Indiana University, Bloomington. Available at: http://nsse.iub.edu/pdf/psychometric_framework_2002.pdf (last accessed 25 February 2010).

Kuh G.D. (2009) What student affairs professionals need to know about student engagement. *Journal of College Student Development* **50**, 683–706.

Kuh G.D., Cruce T.M., Shoup R., Kinzie J. & Gonyea R.M. (2008) Unmasking the effects of student engagement on first-year college grades and persistence. *Journal of Higher Education* **79**, 540–563.

Mastrodicasa J.M. & Kepic G. (2005) *Parents gone wild*. Paper presented at the National Meeting of the National Academic Advising Association, Las Vegas, NV.

Matney M. & Borland K. (2009) *Facebook, blogs, tweets: How staff and units can use social networking to enhance student learning*. Presentation at the annual meeting of the National Association for Student Personnel Administrators, Seattle, WA.

McFedries P. (2007) *All A-Twitter. ieee spectrum*. Available at: http://spectrum.ieee.org/computing/software/all- atwitter (last accessed 7 July 2010).

New Media Consortium (2007) *The Horizon Report*. Available at: http://www.nmc.org/pdf/2007_Horizon_Report. pdf (last accessed 7 March 2010).

Pascarella E.T. & Terenzini P.T. (2005) *How College Affects Students: A Third Decade of Research*. Jossey-Bass, San Francisco, CA.

Pascarella E.T., Seifert T.A. & Blaich C. (2009) *Validation of the NSSE Benchmarks and Deep Approaches to Learning against Liberal Arts Outcomes*. University of Iowa Center for Research on Undergraduate Education, Iowa City.

Rankin M. (2009) *Some general comments on the 'Twitter experiment.'* Web post by Monica Rankin. Available at: http://www.utdallas.edu/~mrankin/usweb/twitter conclusions.htm (last accessed 7 January 2010).

Schroeder A., Minocha S. & Schneider C. (2010) The strengths, weaknesses, opportunities, and threats of using social software in higher and further education teaching and learning. *Journal of Computer Assisted Learning* **26**, 159–174. forthcoming.

SUPPORTING INFORMATION

Additional Supporting Information may be found in the online version of this article:

APPENDIX S1.

Engagement instrument.

Please note: Wiley-Blackwell are not responsible for the content or functionality of any supporting materials supplied by the authors. Any queries (other than missing material) should be directed to the corresponding author for the article.

This article was published in the *Publication of the Modern Language Association,* volume 126, issue 4, 2011, pages 1061–1069.

This is a persuasive essay, in which the author argues that the Internet and reality television have changed celebrity culture.

Note that there is no abstract because the *PMLA* is a humanities journal. It follows the MLA citation method.

Paragraph 1   The first paragraph illustrates the extent to which articles in humanities journals can differ from those in social science journals. The article begins with a personal anecdote, a common feature of humanities articles but less common in social science journals. Note also the self-mocking voice of the author, which would seem out of place in a social science, science, or technology journal.

Paragraph 2   Here the author begins to move toward his thesis. Returning to a study of celebrity culture after an absence of several years, he is struck by the impact of the Internet, which has expanded coverage of the lifestyles of the famous and also brought instant, temporary, accidental fame to others. This is a good example of a paragraph developed by the use of examples. Note the metaphor with which the paragraph concludes—a rhetorical flourish that might seem out of place in a science or technology journal.

Paragraph 3   Here is the author's thesis paragraph, wherein he states the purpose of his essay. The tone changes, becomes more serious, as the author begins to explain his controlling idea. Note that at the end of the paragraph he frames his thesis as two questions the rest of the article will answer. This can be an effective rhetorical strategy. Note the citation at the end of the paragraph. The name of the source is in the sentence, so only the page number is in parenthesis. Note also that superscript numbers refer <u>not</u> to citations but to additional information the author wishes to add; the numbers in the text direct readers to corresponding numbers at the foot of the page or, as in this article, the end of the essay.

The Unwatched Life Is Not Worth Living: The Elevation of the Ordinary in Celebrity Culture[†]

Joshua Gamson*

When my first daughter was born a few years ago, I entered a celebrity news   1
blackout, a somewhat discomfiting condition for a sociologist of celebrity. When she entered preschool, though, I resubscribed to *Us Weekly* and
devoured its morsels like a starving man at McDonald's: Kim Kardashian and
her then-boyfriend ate at Chipotle on their first date! Ashton Kutcher was
mad about his neighbor's noisy construction! Lindsay Lohan is back in rehab!
I felt less disconnected from others, comforted by the familiar company, a
little dirtier and a little lighter.

I meandered through online celebrity culture, too, where things were   2
not quite as familiar, visiting mean Internet gossip sites like *Gawker* and
PerezHilton.com and listening to remixes of Christian Bale's foul-mouthed
rant at a cameraman. I also watched an array of *YouTube* celebrities, most of
whom had been adopted by fans for some quirk they'd exhibited intentionally or just by living their lives: Tay Zonday, a tiny PhD candidate with a giant
singing voice; the jumbo Yosemite dweller whose awed response to a double
rainbow was viewed over twenty million times; and Antoine Dodson, whose
interview clip from a local news show ("hide your kids, hide your wife, hide
your husband, cause they raping everybody out here") was a *YouTube* sensation, leading to remixes on iTunes, a T-shirt line, a ringtone, and Halloween
costumes. Via *Twitter*, I could receive a barrage of 140-character tidbits from
celebrities, such as info about Tina Fey's lunch (Caramello bar), Demi Moore's
adoption rumor (false), and her daughter Rumer's highway experience ("Two
words: Trafic sucks"). If returning to celebrity culture was a bit like coming
home—I'd written a book on the subject, *Claims to Fame*, back in the 1990s—
that home also seemed to have been significantly remodeled.

This essay maps that perplexing architecture, considering how and with   3
what significance twenty-first-century American celebrity culture builds on
and departs from earlier forms.[1] In particular, I highlight what is arguably the
most prominent development in American celebrity culture over the past two
decades: the decisive turn toward the ordinary. As opposed to earlier periods,

---

[†] Reprinted by permission of copyright owner, the Modern Language Association of
America from "The Unwatched Life Is Not Worth Living: The Elevation of the Ordinary in
Celebrity Culture," *PMLA* 126.4 (2011) : 1061–1069. Print.

* JOSHUA GAMSON, professor of sociology at the University of San Francisco, is the
author of *Claims to Fame: Celebrity in Contemporary America* (U of California P, 1994),
Freaks Talk Back: Tabloid Talk Shows and Sexual Nonconformity (U of Chicago P, 1998),
and *The Fabulous Sylvester: The Legend, the Music, the Seventies in San Francisco*
(Picador–H. Holt, 2005). A recent Guggenheim fellow, he is working on a book about
unconventional family creation.

Paragraph 4   Now look at the much longer citation at the end of the first sentence
of this paragraph. The Works Cited list includes two sources by Gamson, so the
parenthetical citation must include a short-form of the title to distinguish between
the two sources. Note also that the point cited is general in nature, hence entire
chapters as opposed to page numbers are referenced. For the same reason, a
second source is cited, following the semicolon. See the Works Cited for the full
bibliographical information on these two sources.

The author proceeds to refine his thesis and provide additional context. Note
the first person point-of-view ("I document..."), more common in humanities
essays. Note, also, the phrase "I argue," wherein the author announces the main
genre—persuasive—of his article.

This is the last paragraph of the introduction, which seems long but is in
proportion to the length of the essay as a whole.

Paragraph 5   This is the first paragraph of the first section of the essay, entitled
"Twentieth-Century Celebrity Culture: Ordinariness as a Persistent Theme."
Sub-titles within articles are not always used for humanities essays. Sometimes
journal editors add them to stress the essay's organizational structure and hence
improve its clarity.

Note the style here. The author is now using the more specialized vocabulary of
the experts in his field of cultural studies.

This is a cause/effect paragraph. The author discusses the role of the producers
of celebrity culture, then, in the sentence that begins "Consumers..." shifts his focus
to effects of the consumption of celebrity gossip. What are the three ways in which
consumers use celebrity stories?

when American celebrities were a class of people perceived as extraordinary and treated to extraordinary lives—a "powerless elite," as Francesco Alberoni once called them—celebrity culture is increasingly populated by unexceptional people who have become famous and by stars who have been made ordinary. What are the roots and contours of this cultural transformation? What are we to make of the triumph of the ordinary celebrity, of what Graeme Turner has called the "demotic turn" in celebrity culture (82)?

The tension between the extraordinary and the ordinary in American   4 celebrity culture—and, relatedly, between merit and manufacture, authenticity and fakery—is not new (Gamson, *Claims*, chs. 1–2; Braudy). Yet the emergence of reality TV and of the Internet, especially Web 2.0 phenomena, has pushed ordinariness into the cultural forefront. In what follows, I document the propulsion of ordinary folks into stardom, the focus on the ordinary lives of famous people, and the rise of new celebrity types. Although it is tempting to interpret these developments as uniformly democratizing, I argue that they are met also with pullbacks toward the centralized celebrity industry and may even reinforce the rarity and value of the "extraordinary" celebrity. In the end, the significance of the ordinary in celebrity culture is found not so much in what it reveals about how fame is differently produced as in its harmony with the increased expectation, and everyday experience, of being watched.

TWENTIETH-CENTURY CELEBRITY CULTURE: ORDINARINESS AS A PERSISTENT THEME

The analytic categories with which celebrity is best apprehended remain useful   5 even in the midst of change: celebrity culture is at once a commodity system, an industry, a set of stories, and a participatory culture. The commodity at stake is embodied attention; the value of the celebrity inheres in his or her capacity to attract and mobilize attention, which is then typically attached to other products (a television show, a magazine cover, a record album) or sold for cash directly to people making those other products. In its most conventional form, celebrity in the United States emerges from, and is managed by, a tightly controlled, wellresourced industry, linked institutions centered mostly in Los Angeles and New York. From those centers, often in a conflict-ridden negotiation between publicists and journalists (Gamson, *Claims*, chs. 3–5), the stories of celebrity arise: not just about famous people but about fame as well, about the machinery of publicity, about what is and isn't admirable, about distinguishing the real from the fake, the private self from the publicly presented one. Consumers of celebrity culture then do all sorts of things with these stories, often giving them new meanings. Some make use of celebrity stories to fantasize a different life, to construct their identities, or to

Paragraph 6   Here the author begins to zero in on one of the main points of his article: how people who have done nothing extraordinary might become celebrities. The author references three experts in the field of celebrity studies. But note that he is not referring to studies in the same sense a social scientist might, studies which include a hypothesis, subjects, methods, statistical analysis. The experts here are more thinkers and philosophers than social scientists. Can you think of an even more recent example of the kind of "ordinary celebrity" the author is writing about?

Paragraph 7   Here is a model compare/contrast paragraph. Note how the use of transitional expressions—"in one," "in the other"—maintain the unity of the paragraph.

model themselves on people they admire or envy; others use them as fodder for connecting socially with one another, by gossiping with impunity about the behavior and relationships of these commonly held figures; still others use the stories to have conversations in which they attempt to distinguish the real person from the massproduced commodity (Gamson, Claims, chs. 6–8; Turner, pt. 3).

Within this cultural system, which remains very much intact, ordinari-   6
ness has a long, complex, and vexed history. Some critics have argued that celebrity by definition disconnects exceptionality from fame; in what is perhaps the foundational text of "celebrity studies," Daniel Boorstin argues that celebrities are "human pseudoevents," people who are "wellknown for their wellknownness" (67), as opposed to heroes, who were famous for doing great things. As Leo Braudy has amply demonstrated, fame never simply resulted from heroic action; yet one need only look as far as Paris Hilton, or her foremother Zsa Zsa Gabor, to see that the modern celebrity system has the wherewithal, incentives, and tendency to value visibility in and of itself. To do its work, the celebrity industry certainly doesn't *need* its celebrities to be extraordinary. What the celebrity industry does require of its humans is that they live, whether glamorously or not, for the camera. As Neal Gabler suggests, what distinguishes celebrities—most of whom are actually known for something they've done—is narrative: a celebrity stars in his or her own "life movie" and provides entertainment by "the very process of living" (5). In this system, there has long been plenty of room for ordinariness to flourish.

Indeed, the story lines of American celebrity culture have been built on a   7
set of tensions in which ordinariness plays a crucial role. American culture, at least as an ideological environment, is often hostile toward anything resembling aristocracy, which conflicts with egalitarian beliefs. The presence of a celebrity class has thus presented a bit of a problem. Contemporary celebrity has been composed of two major, often competing narratives about the relation between celebrity status and merit. In one, people become famous because of achievement, merit, talent, or special internal qualities, earning admiration and attention; they are cream at the top of a meritocracy. In the other, people become famous because they have been made so, artificially produced for mass consumption by a team of investors, publicists, makeup artists, magazine publishers, and the like; they are factory products. In the first, they are successful because they are extraordinary, unlike us, and more powerful than we are; in the second, they are ordinary people, just like us, only luckier, prettier, and better marketed. In the first, their elevated social status is justified; in the second, arbitrary. In the first, they are to be revered or vicariously consumed; in the second, to be disdained or consumed as objects of identiication.[2]

These two stories have coexisted, sometimes uncomfortably, for quite a   8
while. In the days of the Hollywood studio system, where celebrity production was tightly controlled, it was possible to build and maintain images of extraordinariness (deCordova). After its demise, beginning with antitrust actions in the late 1940s, celebrity production became dispersed among a greater number of interested parties and the control of images and stories more conflict-ridden. Celebrity production also became more visible, heightening the suspicion that celebrity status was artificially produced and undeserved. Here displays of ordinariness quickly took a central place, offering up the "real" self behind the "manufactured" celebrity image, with images of famous people's "everyday lives" as the means to approximate that realness (Gamson, *Claims*, chs. 1–2).

The most common narrative strategy— "come see what they're really   9
like"—invites identification with celebrities. The suggestion that celebrities are ordinary folks offers, in place of cynicism, the fantasy of intimacy with the famous (Dyer; Schickel). Thus, for instance, one often encounters photos that demonstrate simultaneously celebrities' extraordinary glamour and awesome beauty on the red carpet and their just-like-us, unglamorous trips to the grocery store or a restaurant. Gossip columns and tabloids, also widespread since the beginning of modern, twentieth-century celebrity culture and exploding in the 1970s, propose to puncture the public image of celebrities with the often sordid or ugly "truths" of their private lives, their ordinary human foibles, their feet of clay. The supermarket magazine racks declare that, like everyone else, celebrities look plain or blemished without makeup, lie about their sexuality, get fat, betray lovers, go into wild rages; despite their publicists' protestations, they are ordinary mortals. In these ways, as celebrity has become suspect as fabricated and false, the ordinary life has been made to stand in for the real and true. Admiration and resentment, honor and suspicion, egalitarian and hierarchical impulses have thus been precariously held together.

REALITY TV: THE CELEBRATION OF THE ORDINARY

In 1968 Andy Warhol quipped that "in the future, everyone will be world-   10
famous for fifteen minutes." When that line became tired, he changed it to "In fifteen minutes, everybody will be famous" (Warhol and Colacello 48). Hyperbole was Warhol's trademark, but he wasn't exactly wrong. If ordinariness has been a persistent part of American celebrity discourse for at least a century—in part because it connotes the democratic openness of Warhol's predictions—it seems to have overwhelmed that discourse in the last twenty-five years. Several forces, most notably new television programming strategies and new Web technologies, have pushed the ordinary to the forefront.

So-called reality TV developed in the late 1980s in response to changing 11
economic conditions in Hollywood characterized, among other things, "by
the rising costs of network program production, competition for advertising revenue among more distributors," and "greater debt incurred by the
networks" (Collins 96; see also Raphael). Reality programming had several
advantages: it was quicker and cheaper to produce than scripted programming, since it needed neither writers nor actors, and it bypassed union constraints and agents' fees, since it used nonunion "actors." As Turner describes
it, reality TV producers take control of the "economy of celebrity by turning
it into an outcome of a programming strategy" (53). They take "civilians,"
often with no special abilities or achievements, and, by filming them, make
celebrities "out of nothing, bypassing what we might think of as the conventional conditions of entry (specialized training, or a history of performance,
for instance)." Given the vast and unending oversupply of ordinary people
seeking visibility and reality TV contestants' status as commodities owned by
the production company, these "dispensable celebrities" are cheap and easily
replaced (Collins 89). Ordinariness, because of its benefits to producers, is an
essential programming strategy.

The making of celebrities out of ordinary folks is not just one of reality TV's 12
chief consequences but also one of its main story lines (Holmes). Consider
the main subgenres of reality programming. On reality talent competitions
like *American Idol, So You Think You Can Dance,* and *America's Next Top
Model,* the central narrative is in some ways old-school: ostensibly, the shows
are a means of finding deserving stars and watching as they earn the right to
fame. At the same time, the shows' interest comes from observing the process
by which ordinary people become celebrities, how they are explicitly transformed, commodified, and marketed—what Tom Mole calls "hypertrophic
celebrity" culture, in which fascination is directed at the mechanics of celebrity production. On *American Idol,* for example, contestants talk openly about
how they intend to position themselves within "the industry," and their movement from obscurity to celebrity is dramatized, complete with screaming fans,
makeovers, and, not incidentally, weekly roles in Ford ads.

Other reality subgenres dramatize the ordinary becoming celebrated 13
more obliquely but just as powerfully. On reality games like *Survivor, The
Apprentice,* or *The Bachelor,* allegedly real people are given unusual tasks, and
their manipulations and stamina are dramatized; on reality "docusoaps" such
as *The Real World, Teen Mom,* or the various *Real Housewives* franchises, previously unfamous people are followed around, their interactions, relationships,
and especially conflicts presented as melodramatic documentary (Collins
90). In each the story is not just the game or the interpersonal dramas but also
the "celebrification" (Rojek 186–87), visible in external coverage promoted

by the shows' producers, as well as within the shows' discursive environment. (Indeed, many of the "real housewives" have been shown marketing themselves over the course of a season, launching books, music careers, or skincare lines on the basis of their new found notoriety.) In Nick Couldry's terms, reality TV works by persistently, even ritualistically, telling the story of how ordinary people move from the periphery to the cultural center, becoming "media people" (85).

Another subgenre, dubbed "celebreality" by VH1, one of its main pur- 14 veyors, makes ordinariness central in a different manner: reviving fading fame through the display of the ordinary lives of (mostly has-been) celebrities, on shows like *Celebrity Fit Club*, *Dancing with the Stars*, and *Celebrity Survivor* or programs built around figures like Scott Baio, Danny Bonaduce, Bobby Brown, and Tori Spelling. Filming ordinary lives (including moments of celebrity flatulence and bowel movements, discussion of sexual positions, and unusual uses of Preparation H) is here the means of celebrity rehabilitation. To regain their fame, these celebrities purportedly show that they are real people, free of the artifice of the star system they are working so hard to reenter.

To a degree, then, reality TV—financially driven, industrially produced, 15 centrally controlled—has transformed celebrity culture by opening up unprecedented space for ordinary people to become celebrities. Perhaps more significant, it has accentuated the story of how a nobody becomes a somebody, pushing forward the rhetorical fantasy of democratized celebrity. Shows like *America's Got Talent* present celebrity as an elected status, in which "America" (as the audience is constantly addressed) votes on which ordinary person is most deserving of stardom. On shows like *The Real World*, celebrity appears as an equal-opportunity status that could land on anyone; on *Celebrity Rehab*, celebrity offers no protection from the quotidian struggles of body and psyche. For reality TV, ordinariness becomes a credential for stardom, not its antithesis; the means of getting attention, not something that must be hidden.

INTERNET CELEBRITY: ANTICELEBRITIES, DO-IT-YOURSELFERS, AND MICROCELEBRITIES

The Internet, especially Web 2.0 phenomena such as *YouTube*, *Myspace*, and 16 *Facebook*— collaborative, participatory sites "where users are increasingly involved in *creating* web content as well as *consuming* it" (Beer and Burrows)—has rapidly changed the dynamics of celebrity culture. In many ways, the Internet has simply extended the reach of the existing entertainment industry, which uses it as another marketing outlet, and expanded the business of gossip, since "rumors of bad behavior among celebrities likely travel faster online than any other kind of hearsay" (Grazian 203; see also Burns). But

Paragraph 17   The author notes that in some cases the Internet introduces a talent who goes on to succeed as a television star or recording artist. But there remains a distinctive Internet celebrity culture, wherein fame is fleeting and based upon a quirky talent or unusual behaviour.

Paragraph 18   This is an extension of the previous paragraph, offering numerous examples. Note the topic sentence with which the paragraph begins and the examples in support of the topic sentence.

beyond the uses of new Web technologies for more of the familiar celebrity marketing and gossip, the Web has also generated a sort of bottom-up, do-it-yourself celebrity production process that is partly autonomous from its predecessors (Turner 54), since the "digital tools of self-publicity are increasingly available to ordinary people" (Bennett and Holmes 76). In the established Hollywood-based celebrity system, one has to navigate the tight gatekeeping structure, already tipped toward the young, beautiful, or talented; find, create, or wait for a break; get an agent, a job, a recording contract, and perhaps a publicist. The Internet drastically widens the pool of potential celebrities by lowering the entry barriers—a computer and a bit of moxie, and you've got a shot—and bypassing the tightly controlled publicity system and the tightly controlling middle people of Hollywood. In this arena, the fans are extremely active in the creation of celebrity: "viral" celebrity grows primarily through links forwarded from one person to another, reaction videos and blog postings, tagging, and so on (Sorgatz). Thus, many of the stories being generated, about celebrities and celebrity, are written outside the Hollywood star system.

Often this different celebrity environment means simply that the Internet 17 is a launching pad for performers who manage to build an audience online that they then use to break into the off-line entertainment world—the teen megastar Justin Bieber comes to mind here—becoming like more conventionally derived celebrities. Yet the Internet has also given rise to a distinctive celebrity culture, in which the audience celebrates its own star-making power: online celebrity is driven by the energy of "Hey, you guys, let's make somebody famous!"

The kinds of celebrities generated on the Internet tend to be quite different from the old image of the Hollywood star, yet in ways that once again 18 promote the ordinary over the exceptional. One dominant type of Internet celebrity is the anticelebrity, a collective in-joke, in which the most unlikely candidate becomes the most celebrated, circulated star. These celebrities tend to be ordinary people—exhibiting no special talents or admirable qualities, offering no claims to greatness, and operating out of their living rooms—aside from a quirk that marks them as amateurs or outsiders. For instance, one of the earliest Web celebrities was a thirty-seven-year-old Turkish accordionist-journalist named Mahir Cagri, whose Web page became a sensation in 1999 (Gamson, "Web"). The site featured photos of the mustachioed Cagri in a teeny bathing suit, playing Ping-Pong, and with his accordion. It offered a welcome of "I Kiss You!!!!!" and frank proclamations such as "I like sex," some of which were apparently added by a Turkish hacker. Within months of his posting, his page views in the millions, Cagri was brought on a stateside tour, appeared on major talk shows, was profiled in *Time*, and was listed as one of

Paragraph 19   Note the clear transition" "A second dominant...." This paragraph provides two examples of unlikely stars who acquired fame by being outrageous. Note the metaphor: "an end run around the Hollywood gate keeping system." The X-rated language here may seem inappropriate in academic writing, but it is used to illustrate the argument the author is advancing.

Paragraph 20   Again note the transition, as this paragraph begins: "A final variety...." Earlier in the essay, Andy Warhol's famous dictum on fifteen minutes of fame is referenced, and here it is cleverly twisted into "famous to fifteen people," linking this section of the article with the earlier one. The author defines the key term "microcelebrity" and provides an example of how one microcelebrity achieved wider fame.
Note the Tanz citation as an example of citing a source within another source.

Forbes's one hundred most influential people in the entertainment industry. Since then, this logic of the anticelebrity has driven much of Internet celebrity. For instance, Chris Crocker's video blog about Britney Spears ("Leave Britney alone!" he rants tearfully) has been viewed more than 36 million times, received over 550,000 comments, and generated extensive media coverage and numerous parodies. Countless other examples emerge daily: the sexy philologist, the guy who started the "free hugs" movement, performers of unusual dances and weird lipsyncs, histrionic superfans, dancing babies. Until being pushed aside by Bieber and Lady Gaga, *YouTube*'s most viewed video was *Charlie Bit My Finger*, a family video of a young boy sticking his finger in his brother's mouth, which made both boys "unlikely international stars" (Moore).

A second dominant character in Internet celebrity is the self-made, do-it-yourself celebrity, who has pursued fame outside, despite, and sometimes in opposition to the established celebrity system. These stars tend to offer claims of extraordinariness, but their stories routinely assert that in the digital age anyone can game the system, create and brand an identity, and become a star. Tila Tequila, who went from *Myspace* popularity to reality TV stardom, is a prime example. She looks like a pinup, and indeed that is one of her many identities, but she got there by doing an end run around the Hollywood gatekeeping system. She is the queen of self-branding, having successfully created and marketed herself without industry support (Trebay).[3] Similarly, Jefree Star, an androgynous, openly gay former club kid, makeup artist, model, and performer, became one of the biggest stars of *Myspace*, blogging and declaiming online and generating thousands of comments on each new posted photo; he is now a successful club music artist, among other things (Immediato). Star describes himself as "half super bitch and half mega cunt," " brazenly sexual and openly subversive," and the "consummate fame-sucking whore." He also notes his cultural significance: "He carries the torch as a self made celebrity," Star says, referring to himself in the celebrity third person. "Some celebrities are manufactured by the system. Others beat the system and manufacture themselves." For sale on his merchandise Web site are T-shirts that say, "Fuck me, I'm a celebrity." [19]

A final variety of Internet celebrity, a close relative of the self-made star, is the microcelebrity, famous to a small community of fans who participate directly in producing the celebrity (Sent 25; Marwick and boyd). Some of what makes this fame micro is its scope; a new cliché suggests that soon we will all be famous to fifteen people (Momus). Another factor is the way the fame is generated: through the interactive dissemination of information about one's everyday life (Chaudhry; Thompson). This type of celebrity is made possible by online publishing and social-networking sites: anyone can blog about his [20]

Paragraph 21   This paragraph provides a conclusion to this section of the article.
Note the punctuation of the first sentence, a good example of the use of the semicolon to separate parallel phrases having internal commas. (See pages 136–137).

This paragraph clearly connects this section of the article to the article's main
thesis.

Paragraph 22   This is the first paragraph of the final section of the article, entitled
"Conclusion: Democratized Fame and Self-Surveillance."

Here the author reaffirms his thesis about the democratization of fame,
stressing the point about the power of the audience to create celebrity, not just
consume the products packaged by agents and publicists.

Paragraph 23   The previous paragraph opened with the phrase "On the one hand,"
so, as we would expect, this paragraph begins with the phrase "On the other hand,"
the counterpart to the common transitional phrase pairing.

or her everyday life to a potentially large audience, design a public profile with words and images, and instantaneously send "clever observations and ripostes targeted at dozens of adoring fans/friends," as one journalist and microcelebrity put it (Sorgatz). Self-publicity has become technologically easy, and the revelation of the ordinary self in everyday activity becomes a mechanism of attention getting—nothing else is needed. As one such star, the New York City self-promoter Julia Allison, put it, "In the past, I would have had to go through a reporter or a PR rep. Now we are all our own publicists. And we all have to learn the tricks" (qtd. in Tanz). Allison is now a "media personality," a "professional talking head" who has "made over 350 on-air appearances in the past year alone" ("Bio").

Internet celebrity culture has, then, made it easy for ordinary people to build an audience, bypassing the traditional celebrity industry; elevated the role of fans or audiences, turning them into powerful producers of celebrities, hyperaware of their star-making capacity; and moved to the forefront new celebrity characters and narratives that seem to defy the traditional celebrity system. Although the seeds were planted long ago, Web and reality-based culture have helped bring to fruition a significant trend in American celebrity: a rapid increase in the spectacle of ordinary people becoming celebrities and of celebrities being shown as entirely ordinary and a resurgence of the rhetorical claim that celebrity is available to anyone, no matter how unexceptional—in short, the lionization of the ordinary. 21

CONCLUSION: DEMOCRATIZED FAME
AND SELF-SURVEILLANCE

On the one hand, one can see in these developments a further democratization of celebrity. Access to celebrity appears to have opened up radically, as ordinary people are pursued for entertainment and as publicity technologies not in control of Hollywood gatekeepers have become relatively easy and inexpensive to access. Celebrity cultivation has been at least partially decentralized, so that it is in the hands of many rather than a few. Through the Internet in particular, the power of audiences to create celebrity, not simply consume it, appears to have dramatically increased (Jenkins). Alternative visions of celebrity are thriving, many of them more egalitarian than their predecessors. Some are anti-industrial; some evade the commodification of celebrity; others celebrate the empowered self-commodifier; still others assert that ordinary lives can be, at least for a bit, worthy of attention. 22

On the other hand, it is easy to overestimate these changes. Even if much celebrity creation now takes place outside the entertainment centers of Los Angeles and New York, the control center of celebrity culture has hardly shifted. The interests of those with the capital to give celebrity its value remain 23

The "other hand" is that the locus of celebrity has shifted, but it has not relocated. Indeed, the author illustrates the extent to which traditional fame culture has co-opted and poached upon those who have achieved fame through reality television and the Internet.

Paragraph 24 What are the implications of the author's thesis? There seems to be, as this paragraph suggests, a widespread desire in contemporary society to live our lives publicly, to reveal private and intimate details about ourselves in order to get noticed. Is the author correct, and, if so, why have we become so keen on self-promotion? The final sentence of this paragraph is worth considering in whole-class or small-group discussion.

Paragraph 25 The author concludes with provocative speculations about the true function of *Facebook* and *YouTube*. Are they as popular as they are because we want to connect with others or because they offer the opportunity for self-aggrandizement? Note the final "take" on Andy Warhol's famous "fifteen minutes of fame" observation.

primary. Web celebrity, for instance, still has nowhere near the social and commercial value of a good old-fashioned television appearance or studio contract. Internet users may be flexing their muscles at the moment of discovery, but cyberstars tend to try to convert their online celebrity into conventional Hollywood-ish currency. Moreover, the established entertainment industry has been quick to absorb celebrities whose fame is generated outside its quarters. In fact, the Internet takes much of the guesswork out of discovery, reducing risks and costs for major entertainment companies, since aspirants do the initial development and marketing. At the discursive level, too, the existing celebrity system is adept at absorbing these changes. The emergence of a vast layer of semiknown people whose celebrity has a "rapid rate of decay" can be mobilized to reinforce the value and distinction of those at the top of the celebrity hierarchy (Kurzman, Anderson, Key, Lee, Moloney, Silver, and Van Ryn 354). It is probably not coincidental that the elevation of ordinary celebrity has coincided with the popularizing of the notion of A-list and D-list celebrities (interestingly, one rarely hears mention of the B and C grades). The crowd of ordinaries—D-listers, wannabes, microcelebrities, YouTube and reality stars—often take their place as evidence that merited celebrity is rare, extraordinary, and justifiably more heavily rewarded (Palmer).

There are pulls and counterpulls at work, toward and away from a more 24 egalitarian, popularly controlled celebrity system. Rather than being evidence of a democratized celebrity system, perhaps the ascent of the ordinary is significant for the everyday understandings of publicness that it both encourages and crystallizes. The ordinary turn in celebrity culture is ultimately part of a heightened consciousness of everyday life as a public performance—an increased expectation that we are being watched, a growing willingness to offer up private parts of the self to watchers known and unknown, and a hovering sense that perhaps the unwatched life is invalid or insufficient.

Many of us, with or without celebrity status, seem to be learning to do 25 what Mark Andrejevic has called "the work of being watched," induced by heightened surveillance. Expecting, as Couldry describes it, "*any* everyday activity legitimately to be put under surveillance and monitored for a huge unknown audience" (91), we are "auto-spies" who see ourselves through the constant "gaze of the other" (Andrejevic, "Visceral Literacy" 339). On *Facebook* and elsewhere, we design self-flattering profiles, post status updates, upload photos of ourselves and get tagged in others' uploads, labor to choose the right "25 random things about me," which are, of course, not random at all. Video cameras are marketed with a one-touch-upload-to-*YouTube* function. It is not so much that everyone gets fifteen minutes of fame or that anyone can be a star but that everyone already is a star: we ordinary people are growing accustomed to not just watching but also being constantly watched.

NOTES

1. Although fame has a cultural history reaching back many centuries (Braudy), the celebrity culture to which I refer is by definition contemporary, a phenomenon dependent on media industries capable of producing and disseminating images on a mass scale.

2. In a similar vein, Chris Rojek distinguishes between "achieved celebrity," which recognizes rare skills or talents (16), and "attributed celebrity," which arises from the work of "cultural intermediaries" (18).

3. Lisa Nakamura notes the racial meanings carried by Tequila's "'user generated' as well as self-made" construction of her own celebrity, which is "racialized as diasporic and polysexual" (1680).

WORKS CITED

Alberoni, Francesco. "The Powerless 'Elite': Theory and Sociological Research on the Phenomenon of the Stars." *Sociology of Mass Communications: Selected Readings.* Ed. Denis McQuail. Harmondsworth: Penguin, 1972. 75–98. Print.

Andrejevic, Mark. *Reality TV: The Work of Being Watched.* Lanham: Rowman, 2004. Print.

———. "Visceral Literacy: Reality TV, Savvy Viewers, and Auto-spies." *Reality TV: Remaking Television Culture.* 2nd ed. Eds. Susan Murray and Laurie Ouellette. New York: New York UP, 2009: 321–42. Print.

Beer, David, and Roger Burrows. "Sociology and, of and in Web 2.0." *Sociological Research Online* 12.5 (2007): n. pag. Web. 11 Jan. 2011.

Bennett, James, and Su Holmes. "The 'Place' of Television in Celebrity Studies." *Celebrity Studies* 1.1 (2010): 65–80. Print.

"Bio." *Julia Allison.* N.p., n.d. Web. 11 Jan. 2011.

Boorstin, Daniel J. *The Image; or, What Happened to the American Dream.* New York: Atheneum, 1962. Print.

Braudy, Leo. *The Frenzy of Renown: Fame and Its History.* New York: Oxford UP, 1986. Print.

Burns, Kelli S. *Celeb 2.0: How Social Media Foster Our Fascination with Popular Culture.* Santa Barbara: Praeger, 2009. Print.

Chaudhry, Lakshmi. "Mirror, Mirror on the Web." *Nation* 29 Jan. 2007: 19–22. Print.

Collins, Sue. "Making the Most out of 15 Minutes: Reality TV's Dispensable Celebrity." *Television and New Media* 9.2 (2008): 87–110. Print.

Couldry, Nick. "Teaching Us to Fake It: The Ritualized Norms of Television's 'Reality' Games." *Reality TV: Remaking Television Culture.* 2nd ed. Eds. Susan Murray and Laurie Ouellette. New York: New York UP, 2009: 82–99. Print.

deCordova, Richard. *Picture Personalities: The Emergence of the Star System in America.* Urbana: U of Illinois P, 1990. Print.

Dyer, Richard. *Stars.* London: British Film Inst., Educ. Advisory Service, 1979. Print.

Gabler, Neal. *Toward a New Definition of Celebrity.* Los Angeles: Norman Lear Center, U of Southern California Annenberg School of Communication, 2001. Print.

Gamson, Joshua. *Claims to Fame: Celebrity in Contemporary America.* Berkeley: U of California P, 1994. Print.

———. "The Web of Celebrity." *American Prospect* 11 Sept. 2000: 40–41. Print.

Grazian, David. *Mix It Up: Popular Culture, Mass Media, and Society.* New York: Norton, 2010. Print.

Holmes, Su. "It's a Jungle Out here! Playing the Game of Fame in Celebrity Reality TV." *Framing Celebrity: New Directions in Celebrity Culture.* Ed. Holmes and Sean Redmond. London: Routledge, 2006. 45–66. Print.

Immediato, Linda. "Jeffree Star, the Fairest One of All." *LA Weekly* 9 May 2007. Web. 11 Jan. 2011.

Jenkins, Henry. *Convergence Culture: Where Old and New Media Collide.* New York: New York UP, 2006. Print.

Kurzman, Charles, Chelise Anderson, Clinton Key, Youn Ok Lee, Mairead Moloney, Alexis Silver, and Maria W. Van Ryn. "Celebrity Status." *Sociological Theory* 25.4 (2007): 347–67. Print.

Marwick, Alice E., and danah boyd. "I Tweet Honestly, I Tweet Passionately: Twitter Users, Context Collapse, and the Imagined Audience." *New Media and Society* 13.1 (2010): 114–33. Print.

Mole, Tom. "Hypertrophic Celebrity." *M/C Journal* 7.5 (2004): n. pag. Web. 11 Jan. 2011.

Momus. "Pop Stars? Nein Danke!" Momus: Becoming a Unit. Momus, n.d. Web. 11 Jan. 2011.

Moore, Matthew. "Finger-Biting Brothers Become *YouTube* Hit." *The Telegraph.* Telegraph Media Group, 5 Dec. 2008. Web. 20 Nov. 2009.

Murray, Susan, and Laurie Ouellette, eds. *Reality TV: Remaking Television Culture.* 2nd ed. New York: New York UP, 2009. Print.

Nakamura, Lisa. "Cyberrace." *PMLA* 123.5 (2008): 1673–82. Print.

Palmer, Gareth. "The Undead: Life on the D-List." *Westminster Papers in Communication and Culture* 2.2 (2005): 37–53. Print.

Raphael, Chad. "The Political Economic Origins of RealiTV." *Reality TV: Remaking Television Culture.* 2nd ed. Eds. Susan Murray and Laurie Ouellette. New York: New York UP, 2009: 123–40. Print.

Rojek, Chris. *Celebrity.* London: Reaktion, 2001. Print.

Schickel, Richard. *Intimate Strangers: The Culture of Celebrity.* Garden City: Doubleday, 1985. Print.

Senft, Theresa M. *Camgirls: Celebrity and Community in the Age of Social Networks.* New York: Lang, 2008. Print.

Sorgatz, Rex. "The Microfame Game and the New Rules of Internet Celebrity." *New York Magazine.* New York Media, 17 June 2008. Web. 11 Jan. 2011.

Star, Jeffree. "It's Jeffree, Bitch! on *Myspace*." *Myspace.* n.d. Web. 11 Jan. 2011.

Tanz, Jason. "Internet Famous: Julia Allison and the Secrets of Self-Promotion." *Wired.* Condé Nast Digital, 15 July 2008. Web. 11 Jan. 2011.

Thompson, Clive. "The Age of Microcelebrity: Why Everyone's a Little Brad Pitt." *Wired* 27 Nov. 2007: n. pag. Web. 11 Jan. 2011.

Trebay, Guy. "She's Famous (and So Can You)." *New York Times.* 28 Oct. 2007. Web. 12 Aug. 2011.

Turner, Graeme. *Understanding Celebrity.* London: SAGE, 2004. Print.

Warhol, Andy, and Bob Colacello. *Andy Warhol's Exposures.* New York: Grosset, 1979. Print.

This article was published in *Children and Youth Services Review,* Volume 33, 2011, pages 187–194.

Abstract   The Abstract indicates that this is a persuasive essay. It is clear, especially when we take the title into consideration, that the author hopes the Canadian Human Rights Tribunal will find in favour of the First Nations organizations who are trying to convince the government to increase welfare funding for First Nations children on reserves.

The Canadian Human Rights Tribunal on First Nations Child Welfare: Why If Canada Wins, Equality and Justice Lose[†]

Cindy Blackstock*

ARTICLE INFO

Article history:
Received 10 July 2010
Received in revised form 4 September 2010
Accepted 7 September 2010
Available online

KEYWORDS:

First Nations
Indigenous
Human rights
Child welfare
Funding

ABSTRACT

Repeated reports indicate that First Nations children on reserve receive less child welfare funding than other children in Canada despite the fact that First Nations children have higher child welfare needs. After the Government of Canada failed to implement two joint solutions to address the inequality, First Nations organizations in Canada filed a human rights complaint alleging that the Government of Canada is discriminating against First Nations children on the basis of race and national ethnic origin. This historic case is now before the Canadian Human Rights Tribunal and marks the first time that Canada has been held to account before a legal body for its current treatment of First Nations children and their families. This opinion article presents the facts leading up to the filing of the human rights case, the grass roots advocacy and legal processes after the complaint was filed, and the implications for: First Nations children, individuals from minority groups, and the moral fabric of the country if the Government of Canada wins the case.

[†] Reprinted from *Children and Youth Services Review*, 33(1), 2011, Cindy Blackstock, "The Canadian Human Rights Tribunal on First Nations Child Welfare: Why If Canada Wins, Equality and Justice Lose," pages 187–194. Copyright 2011, with permission from Elsevier.
* Correspondence to: Cindy Blackstock, *First Nations Child and Family Caring Society of Canada, 302 251 Bank Street, Ottawa, ON K2P 1X3, Canada.* Tel.: + 1 613 230 5885, + 1 613 853 8440; fax: + 1 613 230 3080. *E-mail address*: cblackst@fncaringsociety.com.

Introduction   The author begins with a quote from her own diary, an unusual
strategy in an academic essay, though effective in this case in that the diary excerpt
closely parallels the article's thesis.

The author provides some background information, citing several sources in
support of her point that First Nations children are over-represented in welfare
care compared to other Canadian children. Note that the writer is the author or
co-author of several of these sources. This might seem to call her information into
question, but Ms. Blackstock is the leading authority on First Nations child welfare.

1. INTRODUCTION

It is a morning when history will be made for Aboriginal children but very   1
few Canadians will notice. These are the times when the conscience of a
nation is defined — in small corners away from large press galleries who are
too often seduced by the issues of the time instead of the moral struggles
of the time. At stake is whether Canada is able to under fund government
services for any group of people on a discriminatory ground — in this case
race. The government wants off the equality hook arguing that funding
is not a service so governments cannot be held accountable under the
Canadian Human Rights Act even if they fund unequally on a discriminatory ground. What if they win?

Blackstock (2009a)

On February 26, 2007, the Assembly of First Nations [AFN], a political   2
organization representing all First Nations in Canada, and the First Nations
Child and Family Caring Society of Canada [the Caring Society], a national
non-profit organization providing services to First Nations[1] child welfare
organizations, took the historic step of holding Canada accountable before
the Canadian Human Rights Commission for its current treatment of over
160,000 First Nations children resident on reserve. The complaint alleges that
the Government of Canada discriminates against First Nations children on
reserves[2] by providing them with less government child welfare funding, and
therefore benefit, than other children in Canada (First Nations Child and
Family Caring Society of Canada, 2009).

There are more First Nations children in child welfare care today than   3
ever before and the over-representation of First Nations is unrelenting and
staggering (Blackstock, 2003; Assembly of First Nations, 2007). Overall, the
estimated 27,000 First Nations children in child welfare care account for 30 to
40% of all children in child welfare care even though they represent less than
5% of the child population (Blackstock & Trocmé, 2005). Neglect, driven by
structural risks such as poverty, poor housing, and substance misuse linked
to colonialism (Blackstock & Trocmé), account for a substantial proportion
of the over-representation (Blackstock & Trocmé, 2005; Blackstock, 2008).
Culturally-based and equitable programs targeted to poverty, poor housing,
and substance misuse are needed to deal with this and other problems experienced by First Nations children and their families. Unfortunately, there is
pervasive evidence that First Nations receive inequitable resources to prevent

---

1. First Nations are the Indigenous peoples in Canada who are not Inuit or Métis. First
Nations are also referred to as status and non-status Indians.
2. Reserves are Crown lands set aside for the use of Indians pursuant to the Indian Act
(1985).

Paragraph 4   The author offers a blueprint for her article, presenting the three main ———
points she will develop. Note that the case against the government was pending at
the time Blackstock wrote the article. You might want to search online to find out if
the case has since been heard and what the Tribunal's decision is.

Colonialism: The Birthplace of First Nations Child Welfare   The author begins ———
each sub-section of her article with a relevant quotation.
      Here the author provides necessary background information. Note how
carefully, in the first paragraph, she defines key terms and explains the provisions in
Canada's Indian Act.

and respond to maltreatment as compared to other Canadians (McDonald & Ladd, 2000; Clarke, 2007; Auditor General of Canada, 2008; Standing Committee on Public Accounts, 2009).

This article presents the facts leading up to the filing of the human rights 4
case, the process after the complaint was filed, and the implications for First Nations children, individuals from minority groups, and the moral fabric of the country if the Government of Canada wins the case.

1.1. Colonialism: the birthplace of First Nations child welfare

A confidential 1966 departmental report [Department of Indian and 5
Northern Affairs, Canada] estimated that 75 percent of the children in the schools [residential schools] were from homes which, by reason of over-crowding and parental neglect or indifference are considered unfit for school children.

Royal Commission on Aboriginal Peoples (1996), Chapter 10, p.13

Canada is a federalist country composed of a national government, ten pro- 6
vincial governments, three territorial governments, and Aboriginal[3] govern-ments. Canada is also one of the few countries in the world that continue to apply a race-based piece of legislation known as the Indian Act (1985). The Indian Act (1985) is the oldest piece of federal legislation in the country with the first rendition dating back to the time of confederation. Amongst other powers, the Indian Act (1985) gives the federal government responsibility for the definition and maintenance of Indians and lands reserved for Indians (Sinclair, Bala, Lilles, & Blackstock, 2004). What this means in practice is that the Government of Canada determines which Indigenous peoples are recognized for the purposes of treaty making and treaty benefit. Those who meet certain blood quantum criteria designed by the federal government are recognized as eligible treaty holders and are therefore called "status Indians." Those who fall short of government blood quantum requirements are called "non-status Indians" for which Canada recognizes no land rights or treaty obligations. If Canada holds onto its current blood quantum method of clas-sifying status versus non-status Indians, demographers predict that there will be no status Indians in 200 years effectively absolving Canada from any land obligations (Clatworthy, 2005). The Indian Act (1985) also defines the struc-ture of First Nations governments, wills and estates, commercial enterprise, land and resource use, and the establishment of reserve boundaries. Basically, reserves are Crown lands set aside for the use of Indians, which means that First Nations peoples can live on reserves, but the Crown actually owns the

---

3. Aboriginal means persons who are First Nations (also known as Indians), Métis and Inuit.

Paragraph 7   She discusses the 1996 Royal Commission on Aboriginal Peoples and ——————|
the failure of the government to implement its recommendations.

Historical context continues with a description of the residential schools where
so many Aboriginal children were sent. Even as the schools closed down, the
number of children requiring welfare services increased.

Historical context continues into the 1970s, when First Nations leaders began
running child welfare agencies on reserves. The author is critical of the government
which places restrictions on these agencies and does not understand the needs of
the children they serve.

This sub-section ends on an upbeat note, detailing some success, albeit limited,
in keeping First Nations children in their communities.

land and strictly governs the use thereof. The various provisions of the Indian Act yield little opportunity for First Nations to generate revenue linked to land ownership or resource extraction contributing to widespread poverty amongst First Nations community members (National Council on Welfare, 2008).

A Royal Commission on Aboriginal Peoples [RCAP] was conducted 7 in 1996 to direct Canada away from the Indian Act — fourteen years later most of the recommendations remain unimplemented. There is no sign that the Canadian government is interested in leaving the definition of who is Indigenous in Canada to a matter of self-identity, as Australia and New Zealand did decades ago, and there has been little progress in resolving outstanding land and resource disputes (Blackstock, 2008).

The Indian Act (1985) also plays a significant role in the safety and well- 8 being of First Nations children and families. Beginning in the 1870s the government of Canada began forcibly removing First Nations children aged 5–15 years old from their families and placing them in residential schools with a goal of assimilating them under the guise of Christian education objectives (Milloy, 1999). At the height of their operations in the 1940s approximately 8900 children attended the schools (Milloy, 1999). Although the schools began closing in the 1950s, the last federally run school did not close until 1996 (Department of Indian and Northern Affairs Canada, 2003) and many children were placed in the schools as child welfare placements (Milloy, 1999). One study suggests that by the 1960s, child welfare placements accounted for over 80% of residential school admissions in Saskatchewan (Caldwell, 1967). The harms to the Aboriginal children who attended residential schools included extremely high rates of death due to preventable causes of disease (Bryce, 1922), abuse, and negligence, as well as prolific cultural and linguistic erosion (Royal Commission on Aboriginal Peoples, 1996; Milloy, 1999; Blackstock, 2003). In fact the harms were so egregious that in 2008, the Prime Minister of Canada issued a public apology for residential schools and launched a truth and reconciliation commission (Harper, 2008).

An amendment to the Indian Act in the 1950s allowed provincial/ territo- 9 rial child welfare and education statutes to apply on reserve (Sinclair et al., 2004), however, the federal government was expected to fund these services on reserves. The provinces began delivering child welfare services in the mid 1950s, but social workers who had little or no knowledge about colonization and residential schools often mistook symptoms of systemic discrimination as parental failure (Royal Commission on Aboriginal Peoples, 1996; Union of BC Indian Chiefs, 2002; Blackstock, 2003). As a result, First Nations children were removed in large numbers and placed in residential schools (Caldwell, 1967) or with non-Aboriginal families, often permanently (Royal Commission on Aboriginal Peoples, 1996). Johnston (1983), a researcher for the Canadian Council on Social Development, termed this period of mass removals the "60s scoop." Today, many social workers in Canada understand that the "60s scoop" was poorly thought out and resulted in harm to Aboriginal families (Union of BC Indian Chiefs, 2002), but the reality is that the proportion of First Nations children in child welfare has reached record levels eclipsing both the "60s scoop" and residential schools (Blackstock, 2003).

In an effort to stem the tide of removals, First Nations mobilized and began 10 establishing their own child welfare agencies in the 1970s. These agencies are located on reserve and are funded by the federal government (McKenzie & Flette, 2003). Although First Nations agencies are expected to deliver cultur- ally-based child welfare services comparable to what other children in similar circumstances receive (Department of Indian and Northern Affairs Canada, 2005), their ability to do so is substantially restricted. The agencies must wear the straightjackets of provincial legislation and federal government funding regimes that are often not culturally appropriate and are rarely grounded in research evidence relevant to First Nations (Blackstock, 2003). It would be reasonable for provincial and federal governments to impose child wel- fare policy and practice on First Nations child welfare agencies if they could muster evidence of the efficacy of their solutions, but in the vast majority of circumstances they have not. This wholesale imposition of provincial and federal child welfare systems creates an untenable situation that stifles innovation in a system that desperately needs it.

Despite all odds, First Nations agencies have created some space for 11 culturally-based practices and emerging evidence suggests that they are having a positive impact in keeping First Nations children safely in their com- munities and in developing award winning programs responsive to the needs of First Nations children (Blackstock, 2003; Loxley et al., 2005). First Nations, however, understand that much more needs to be done and are actively chal- lenging the legislative and funding barriers that block progress including the inequitable level of federal child welfare funding on reserves (Assembly of First Nations, 2007).

1.2. Inequality as a risk factor for First Nations children

Circumstances are dire. Inadequate resources may force individual agencies 12 (First Nations child and family service agencies) to close down if their man- dates are withdrawn, or not extended, by the provinces. This would result in provinces taking over responsibility for child welfare, likely at a higher cost to Indian and Northern Affairs Canada (INAC)… in addition to escalating costs for INAC, culturally appropriate services would be compromised. This would be contrary to the United Nations Convention on the Rights of the

Paragraph 14   The author explains the reasons for the over-representation of First Nations children in child welfare. Note that the author reaffirms one of her main arguments: problems created by inadequate funding from the federal government.

Paragraph 15   Note the author's use of well-documented facts, figures, and statistics—essential in academic writing—in support of her argument.

   She continues, illustrating the extent to which the government underfunds education. What is her strongest argument in support of her position that the government should increase education funding for First Nations students?

Child which guarantees specific rights for children including the right to non-discrimination and the preservation of families and indigenous culture.

Department of Indian Affairs and Northern Development, n.d., pp. 1, 6

The confluence between provisions in the Indian Act giving the federal gov- 13 ernment responsibility for Indians and lands reserved for Indians and the provincial government's assertion of child welfare laws creates a jurisdictional quagmire that further erodes the safety and well-being of First Nations children. Provincial/territorial child welfare laws apply on and off reserve but the provinces/territories expect the federal government to fund the service for on-reserve children. If the federal government allocates funds at lower levels than other children receive through the province, the province/territory typically does not top up the funding levels resulting in a two-tiered child welfare system where First Nations children get less (Auditor General of Canada, 2008; First Nations Child and Family Caring Society of Canada, 2009).

First Nations children are being placed in out of home care at 6–8 times the 14 rate of other children (Auditor General of Canada, 2008; Standing Committee on Public Accounts, 2009). Research suggests that the over-representation of First Nations children in child welfare care cannot be accounted for by differences in substantiated child sexual, physical or emotional abuse reports between First Nations and other children (Blackstock, Trocmé, & Bennett, 2004; Trocmé, Knoke, & Blackstock, 2004; Trocmé et al., 2006). It is neglect that fuels the over-representation of First Nations children in child welfare and this form of maltreatment is highly associated with poverty (Blackstock et al., 2004; Trocmé et al., 2004; Blackstock & Trocmé, 2005; Trocmé et al., 2006). The good news is that these factors can be mediated by services. However, federal child welfare funding on reserves is inequitable and is particularly lacking with respect to the funding of services especially designed to keep First Nations children safely in their homes known as "least disruptive measures" (Assembly of First Nations, 2007; Blackstock, 2008).

The inequalities in First Nations child welfare funding on reserves are long- 15 standing and well documented (Royal Commission on Aboriginal Peoples, 1996; McDonald & Ladd, 2000; Loxley et al., 2005; Amnesty International, 2006; Assembly of First Nations, 2007; Auditor General of Canada, 2008; Standing Committee on Public Accounts, 2009) as are the tragic consequences of First Nations children going into child welfare care due, in part, to inequitable services (Kimmelman, 1985; McDonald & Ladd, 2000; Blackstock & Trocmé, 2005; Amnesty International, 2006; Clarke, 2007; Auditor General of Canada, 2008; National Council on Welfare, 2008; Blackstock, 2008; Martin & Blackstock, 2009; Standing Committee on Public Accounts, 2009). Estimates are that First Nations children on reserves receive 22% less per capita in child welfare funding than other children (McDonald & Ladd, 2000) and the funding shortfall is particularly acute with regard to services intended to keep children safely at home (Loxley et al., 2005; Auditor General of Canada, 2008; Standing Committee on Public Accounts, 2009).

This inequity is further amplified for First Nations children by shortfalls [16] in education funding, housing, and publicly funded voluntary sector supports (RCAP, 1996; Assembly of First Nations, 2007; Blackstock, 2007; 2008; National Council on Welfare, 2008; Loppie-Reading & Wien, 2009). For example, the federal government shortchanges First Nations elementary and secondary school funding even though only one in four First Nations children finishes high school. Estimates are that federal funding for elementary schools on reserves falls short by 40%, and the problem is even worse in secondary schools where the federal government spends 70% less on First Nations students than they do for other children (Matthew, 2000). The shortfall in publicly funded voluntary sector is even more acute. Whereas Canadians receive approximately 67 billion dollars in publicly funded services, which translates into $2400 per person delivered through voluntary sector organizations each year (Canadian Council on Social Development, 2003), many First Nations receive no publicly funded voluntary sector supports such as food banks, non-profit parenting support programs, domestic violence programs, and social housing (Nadjiwan & Blackstock, 2003).

First Nations worked with the Canadian government to develop two [17] research based solutions to the child welfare inequality over a ten year period, the federal government did not implement them (McDonald & Ladd, 2000; Loxley et al., 2005) and the number of First Nations children entering child welfare care continued to grow (Blackstock, 2007; Auditor General of Canada, 2008). The federal government and the Assembly of First Nations commissioned McDonald and Ladd (2000) to author the first report known as *the Joint National Policy Review on First Nations Child and Family Services* [NPR]. McDonald and Ladd (2000) found that federal child welfare funding on reserves fell 22% below what was provided to children off reserves funded by the provinces. They also found that an acute shortfall in services intended to keep children safely at home known as "least disruptive measures" contributed to the number of First Nations children entering child welfare care increasing by a staggering 71% between 1995 and 2001. The McDonald and Ladd (2000) report set out 17 recommendations for improvements to First Nations child welfare funding on reserves but the federal government failed to implement them in a timely fashion. By 2004, the federal government viewed the McDonald and Ladd (2000) report as dated and, along with the Assembly of First Nations, commissioned a second report to document a research based and detailed funding formula and policies for First Nations child welfare on reserves. This solution, known as the Wen:de solution (Blackstock, Prakash,

Paragraph 18   The final paragraph of this sub-section is dramatic and effective. Having carefully made her case in previous paragraphs, the author describes the action that agencies which support First Nations causes were forced to take: under the authority of the Canadian Human Rights Act, they would formally charge the federal government with racial discrimination. The author effectively persuades her audience to read on to discover how the case will proceed.

The Canadian Human Rights Complaint   Note the appeal to emotion in the introductory quote, especially in the words of First Nations leader Phil Fontaine. Emotional appeals, as long as they are measured, can be effective components of an argument.

The agencies bringing the complaint against the federal government for underfunding First Nations children will file their complaint under the Canadian Human Rights Act. It is important, therefore, that the author explain the mandate of the Canadian Human Rights Commission under the Canadian Human Rights Act, as she does here.

Loxley, & Wien, 2005; Loxley et al., 2005), was developed by over 20 leading researchers representing disciplines as diverse as economics, child welfare, community development, law and sociology. The Wen:de solution suggested that, at minimum, the federal government should provide an additional 109 million per annum nationally (excluding the Province of Ontario and the Territories) using a funding formula and policies structured in specific ways to achieve a basic level of culturally-based equity in child welfare services on reserves. After the Wen:de solution was released in 2005, the federal government publicly acknowledged the links between the funding inadequacies and the growing number of First Nations children in care, (Department of Indian Affairs and Northern Development Canada, 2006; Prentice, 2007) but was not disposed to fix the problem despite running a 22 billion dollar surplus budget in 2005 and more recently spending billions to stimulate the economy.

First Nations were confronted with a choice: continue to work with gov- 18 ernment and hope they redress the inequality voluntarily or consider legal options. After ten years of negotiations that failed to achieve results, it was apparent that voluntary strategies aimed at convincing Canada to provide equitable and culturally-based child welfare services to First Nations children were unlikely to succeed. An independent body would be needed to force the Canadian government into providing equitable funding for child welfare on reserves. After exploring all options, the decision was made that the First Nations Child and Family Caring Society of Canada and the Assembly of First Nations would file a historic complaint pursuant to the Canadian Human Rights Act [CHRA], (R.S. 1985, c. H-6) alleging that the Canadian government was racially discriminating against First Nations on reserves by providing a lesser level of child welfare funding and benefit. For the first time ever, Canada would be held accountable for its current and systemically discriminatory treatment of First Nations children (First Nations Child and Family Caring Society of Canada, 2009).

1.3. The Canadian human rights complaint

A national organization representing Native Canadians, the Assembly   19
of First Nations, filed a complaint with the Canadian Human Rights
Commission over what the group says is a lack of financing for child welfare
programs that has put thousands of indigenous children at risk. "It is really
sad we have been pushed to do this," said Phil Fontaine the group's leader.

Mason (2007)

The Canadian Human Rights Act (1985) authorizes the Canadian Human 20 Rights Commission [Commission] to receive, assess, and adjudicate human rights complaints (Canadian Human Rights Tribunal, n.d.). The Commission

Paragraph 21   The author notes some irony in the timing of the complaint. A delegation from the Canadian government was at the United Nations arguing that Canada would not support the UN Declaration on the Rights of Aboriginal People because its Human Rights Act already provided such protection. Here the author effectively anticipates and invalidates an objection to her own argument. This is a strategy she employs effectively throughout her argument. To anticipate and confront an opposing point of view is an effective rhetorical strategy. See pages 57–65.

Paragraph 23   The author begins to summarize Commissions process as it adjudicated the complaint against the federal government. The First Nations organizations bringing the complaint won an initial victory when the Commission accepted the complaint and recommended it proceed to the tribunal.

has the authority to make these determinations on its own or refer the matter to the Canadian Human Rights Tribunal [Tribunal] for a full hearing. Should the Commission or Tribunal find that a human rights violation has occurred, they have the power to order a remedy which is enforceable in Federal Court (Canadian Human Rights Act, 1985). The First Nations Child and Family Caring Society (the Caring Society) and the Assembly of First Nations (AFN) chose the human rights complaint over other legal options as the Canadian Human Rights Act (1985) includes the power to order specific relief for the discrimination.

At the time the complaint was filed, the Government of Canada joined 21 with four other countries, including Australia, New Zealand, and the United States, to oppose the United Nations Declaration on the Rights of Indigenous Peoples [Declaration] (Strahl, 2008). In an apparent effort to deflect attention away from Canada's degradation of its historic leadership as an international champion for human rights, the Canadian government sent a delegation to the United Nations to issue a statement that specifically mentioned the human rights protections afforded to Aboriginal peoples under the Canadian Human Rights Act (Strahl, 2008). Filing the human rights case on behalf of First Nations children provided a unique and powerful test of Canada's commitment to First Nations human rights specifically and the Canadian Human Rights Act more broadly.

The United Nations General Assembly adopted the UN Declaration on 22 the Rights of Indigenous Peoples in September of 2007. The vote was 143 Nation States in favor, 11 abstained and 4, including Canada, voted against (UN News Centre, 2007). Subsequent to the vote, Australia and New Zealand are now supporting the Declaration leaving only Canada and the USA as officially opposed. These results suggest that world opinion is running against the Canadian Government's views on the rights of Indigenous peoples.

The first step of the Commission's process is to offer mediation to the com- 23 plainants (AFN and the Caring Society) and the respondent (Government of Canada). The Caring Society and AFN agreed whilst the Canadian government refused. The Commission then ordered an assessment of the complaint to determine whether or not the Commission would formally accept the case and, if so, to recommend a process to resolve the complaint. The assessment phase would last over a year, with the Government of Canada refusing mediation a second time, repeatedly raising technical objections, questioning the authority of the Commission to hear the complaint and even alleging procedural unfairness. In the end, the Commission's assessment report accepted the complaint and recommended that a full tribunal be held on the merits of the case. The Commission's assessment report also recommended that the Canadian Human Rights Commission appoint its own legal counsel to represent the public interests at the tribunal as the implications for human rights were so significant. What this means in practical terms is that the Canadian Human Rights Commission becomes a legal actor in all future legal proceedings.

When the assessment report, including all of its recommendations, 24 was formally accepted by the Canadian Human Rights Commissioners in September of 2008 and the tribunal was ordered to proceed, the Canadian government appealed the decision to Federal Court in an effort to overturn the Commission's decision and dismiss the case on the basis of two arguments related to the jurisdiction of the Canadian Human Rights Act (CHRA) (Abel, 2009; Attorney General of Canada v. the First Nations Child, Family Caring Society of Canada, the Assembly of First Nations, the Canadian Human Rights Commission, the Chiefs of Ontario, & Amnesty International Canada, 2009). The first argument deals with whether federal government funding falls within the scope of the CHRA and the second issue relates to whether or not there is a comparator group for First Nations children served by child welfare on reserve. The Canadian Human Rights Act (1985) has jurisdiction over cases alleging discrimination associated with a good, accommodation, or service. The federal government argues that their funding is not a good or an accommodation, nor is it a service, and thus the child welfare complaint falls outside of the jurisdiction of the CHRA. The funding is not a service argument basically suggests that even when a funder (in this case the Canadian government) knowingly provides a lesser level of funding for a statutory government services (such as child welfare) to any group on a discriminatory ground, they cannot be held accountable under the CHRA (Abel, 2009). This argument, if successful, sets a foundation for Canadian governments to discriminate with impunity so long as that discrimination is related to providing lesser levels of funding on a discriminatory ground rather than the direct purchase of fewer services. Clearly this could have broad and destructive consequences for a wide array of minority groups in Canada.

In the comparator argument, the federal government argues that the 25 Canadian Human Rights Act (1985) requires the complainants to substantiate their discrimination claim by identifying a comparator group to First Nations children on reserve receiving child welfare services funded by the federal government (First Nations Child et al., 2010). The federal government wants to limit any comparator group analysis to First Nations children on reserve implying that: 1) it funds all First Nations children on reserves equally and thus there is no discrimination and 2) funding for non-Aboriginal child welfare is outside of the federal government's mandate and thus any comparisons to provincial child welfare funding for other children is irrelevant (First Nations Child et al., 2010).

The evidence quickly points to substantial weaknesses in Canada's com- 26 parator group arguments. For example, numerous reports suggest that the federal government provides very different levels of funding, and thus benefit, to First Nations children across Canada and these differences are unrelated to variations in child welfare need, context or statute (Auditor General of Canada, 2008; Standing Committee on Public Accounts, 2009). This means that even if Canada is successful in narrowing the comparator group to First Nations children on reserve, there is substantial independent evidence that the federal government's child and family services program results in the differential treatment of First Nations children in ways that are unrelated to legitimate service factors.

Canada's second legal argument rejecting a comparison to non-Aboriginal 27 child welfare services funded by the provinces is also highly suspect. Canada specifically invokes a provincially funded comparator group in the following statement of program goals and objectives taken from its *National Program Manual for First Nations Child and Family Services* (Department of Indian and Northern Affairs Canada, 2005) "[T]he child and family services offered by FNCFS on reserves are to be culturally relevant and comparable, but not necessarily identical, to those offered by the reference province or territory to residents living off reserve in similar circumstances." (p. 6).

The complainants argue that a comparator group is not required to prove 28 a discrimination claim and, even if it was required, there are a number of relevant comparator groups (First Nations Child et al., 2010). For example, child welfare is governed by child welfare laws that apply to all children in a given jurisdiction meaning it is legitimate to compare the benefit of First Nations children on reserves to other children. This is reinforced by the federal government's program manual (Department of Indian and Northern Affairs Canada, 2005) and the Canadian Charter of Rights and Freedoms which guarantees all residents of Canada equal benefit under the law meaning all children subject to a given statute should receive equal benefit.

More recently, the federal government has advanced the argument that 29 their funding is equitable. This statement has been made in the Federal Court record and reiterated by counsel representing Canada in federal court on September 14, 2009, but the Government of Canada has provided no reliable independent evidence to support its equity assertion (Canadian Human Rights Tribunal, 2009).

Overall, Canada's arguments prioritize legal technicalities over the central 30 question of whether or not First Nations children are receiving a lesser child welfare benefit because of federal government policies and practices. Canada's pattern of behavior seems out of step with its international human rights obligations to prioritize the safety and well-being and non-discrimination of children as set out in the Convention on the Rights of the Child and the Declaration on the Rights of Indigenous Peoples.

Paragraph 32   But note the first sentence of the last paragraph of this sub-section, especially the use of the word "ravages." Does the author overstate her case here or has she made the case that would justify the use of this comparatively strong language?

   This sub-section ends with a discussion of the government's unwillingness to televise or otherwise make public the proceedings. What arguments did the government advance in favour of their position?

Justice for Children in a Democracy Is Expensive   Again the author anticipates and confronts a possible counter-argument about the ethics and logic of an agency funded by the federal government suing the federal government for inadequate funding. She admits that the Assembly of First Nations is government funded but explains that the Caring Society no longer receives government funding.

Canada's third and fourth periodic report to the United Nations 31 Committee on the Rights of the Child filed in November of 2009 comments on First Nations child welfare, but is silent on the fact that the government is facing a human rights tribunal on the issue. It seems that Canada is not particularly inclined to be transparent with the international community when it comes to respecting the rights of First Nations children (Canada, 2009).

This is consistent with Canada's apparent strategy of trying to keep the 32 discrimination against First Nations children under wraps so they can continue the ravages of this policy unabated. While First Nations have insisted on a public process, Canada has argued against having its witnesses cross examined in public (First Nations Child et al., 2010) and has opposed an application by the Aboriginal Peoples Television Network (APTN) to broadcast the tribunal. In its legal arguments, Canada says it opposed a public cross examination of its witness, a senior bureaucrat, because the presence of the public might distract her from her answers (First Nations Child et al., 2010) and opposed the broadcasting of the tribunal as it claims unnamed witnesses for the Government would be concerned that their testimony may erode relationships with First Nations (First Nations Child et al., 2010). First Nations expressed no such concerns and lobbied strongly for the inclusion of the public in all phases of the hearing and in particular emphasized the importance of respecting the right of children to participate in matters affecting them as set out in the United Nations Convention on the Rights of the Child (First Nations Child et al., 2010). On May 28, 2010, the Tribunal Chair ruled in favor of Canada and the APTN has filed an appeal in Federal Court (Aboriginal Peoples Television Network et al., and Canadian Human Rights Commission, Attorney General of Canada (representing the Minister of the Department of Indian Affairs and Northern Development Canada), First Nations Child and Family Caring Society of Canada, Assembly of First Nations, Chiefs of Ontario and Amnesty International, 2010.) The Caring Society will support APTN's appeal and will again rely on the importance of oral history in Aboriginal cultures and the rights afforded to children under the United Nations Convention on the Rights of the Child to participate in matters affecting them.

1.4. Justice for children in a democracy is expensive

"It's a unique case," he said. "I just hope people will do something with this 33 story once they've heard it. I think it will be impossible not to. It's such a compelling case."

Irwin Elman, Ontario Child Advocate quoted by Monsebraaten (2009)

Paragraph 35 Note the author's sudden use of first person—"in my view"—in the second paragraph of this sub-section. Why do you think the author makes this shift here?

Note the appeal to emotion throughout this sub-section. Is this an effective rhetorical strategy here?

Democracy is expensive and so is justice for the children, especially when the 34 subject of the complaint is a national government. The reality is that the Government of Canada can, and does, draw upon unlimited legal and financial resources funded by the taxpayer and the Canadian Government can draw from the taxpayer to fund cases even when the interests of government differ with interests of many Canadians. In the past, the Caring Society received federal government funding. Now the organization receives no funding from the Canadian government even though it has won numerous awards of excellence and is the only national organization working specifically for Aboriginal children and families. The Caring Society has four staff and works out of a low cost office complex where they do their own janitorial work to keep down costs. The Assembly of First Nations is a larger organization, but it is almost entirely government funded, leaving it with little to no resources for legal challenges involving government. A program to subsidize public interest human rights cases, such as the child welfare tribunal, was eliminated by the federal government several years ago, meaning that funds for the case must be raised privately. This reality has imposed two financial hardships on the Caring Society. The organization must raise funds to keep the organization going and simultaneously raise funds to pay for the legal fees for the case. The receipt of the Atkinson Social Economic Justice Fellowship and donations from other foundations, individuals as well as revenue from contract work has helped sustain the Caring Society. Legal fees for the Caring Society have surpassed $150,000 and have been funded by community donations, fund raisers and Caring society independent revenue. The legal costs were also partially alleviated thanks to pro-bono legal counsel on the Federal Court matters, the Canadian Human Rights Commission taking the lead role in presenting evidence at the Tribunal, and many other legal volunteers and champions.

Any organization taking on a government needs to be prepared for the 35 financial hardships related to fighting with a financial Goliath but it should not stop organizations from fulfilling their mission statements and standing up against systemic human rights violations sourced in government policy — even if taking this step means risking the organization. The reality is that the federal government funds a substantial portion of the non-profit sector in Canada and this can have the effect of muting activities that are not in concert with government interests. In my view, the Canadian government relies on NGO's not speaking freely about wayward government policy in order to maintain operational funds for the organization and this is largely a successful strategy. Advocacy is used broadly amongst Canadian NGOs but in many cases it translates into the most modest, and often ineffective, activities such as writing letters to government. There are very few cases where NGOs have launched peaceful non-voluntary challenges with the capacity to force government into changing its policy.

Despite all odds, the Caring society has survived the complete loss of fed- 36
eral government funding and can speak freely about issues of concerns to
its constituents without moderation. This freedom serves to bolster public
confidence as the organization demonstrates its willingness to "bite the hand
that feeds it." Memberships in the Caring Society, for example, have increased
over 400% since the human rights complaint was filed and communities have
mobilized to host fund raisers and awareness campaigns.

No matter what the financial hardships, the Caring Society made a moral 37
decision to put its mission before its organizational interests. It was, and is,
willing to risk the organization in order to achieve culturally-based equity for
children.

The decision about how much an organization or human rights champion 38
is prepared to risk and the moral framework that frames operations are critical
decision points for any organization challenging institutions or systems as
powerful as the federal government because there is nothing more threatening
to federal politicians and policy makers than a group that operates in moral
ways and has nothing to lose. When the "nothing to lose" organization is
willing to reach beyond politicians and bureaucrats to the caring public then
a social movement begins to take root.

1.5. I am a witness campaign

I attended the hearings in the morning on both days. My overall percep- 39
tion is that Canada has no platform to stand on and there were contradic-
tions. I noticed Canada was just dragging out the topic. I'm left assuming
that Canada has no justification for trying to get out of its responsibilities.
I want to say that when I first started the process of "being a witness," I
only learned one side of the story… the First Nations' children's side. After
witnessing both days of the Tribunal hearings, I realize that there is NO
OTHER SIDE OF THE STORY. Shannara Nafe, Elizabeth Wyn Wood
Student reflection on her attendance at the Tribunal hearings on June 2, 3,
2010 on Canada's motion to dismiss the case

(Nafe, 2010)

Reconciliation means not saying sorry twice (Blackstock, 2008). A year after 40
the Prime Minister apologized for the wrongs done to Aboriginal children
during the residential school era (Harper, 2008), it is important to measure
the sincerity of the apology against how the Canadian government is treating
First Nations children today (First Nations Child and Family Caring Society
of Canada, 2009). A public education and engagement movement called the
"I am a witness campaign" was launched to educate and engage the public
by inviting individuals and organizations to follow the tribunal. Being a witness means the person or organization commits to following the tribunal

either in person or via the media/internet/social networking sites so that they can hear all the facts and make up their own mind about whether or not the Government of Canada is treating First Nations children fairly. The idea of engaging people in a process where they self-educate and make up their own minds versus asking people to support our position in the Tribunal outright respects the facility and dignity of each witness whilst also providing a framework for sustainable change in public opinion. If people learn on their own about the rights violation they are much more likely to act on that knowledge than having it spoon fed to them. There is no charge to being a witness and people of all ages can sign up. This ensures the active engagement of all Canadians, particularly children and young people, and those of low economic means who are much more likely to come into contact with the child welfare system (Blackstock & Trocmé, 2005). The campaign is promoted using social networking sites, a website, and personal presentations and appeals. Over 6000 individuals and organizations registered as witnesses in its first 10 months of operation (First Nations Child and Family Caring Society of Canada, 2009) making the Canadian Human Rights Tribunal on First Nations child welfare the most formally watched court case on children's rights in Canadian history.

The underlying strategy of the "I am a witness" campaign is rooted in a fundamental belief in the value of democracy in correcting government policies that are contrary to the public good. The hope is that growing public awareness will put increased levels of public pressure on the Canadian Government to treat First Nations children equitably. The efficacy of engaging Canadians in policy changes affecting First Nations children has been demonstrated by the passage of Jordan's Principle, a child first principle to resolving inter-governmental jurisdictional disputes regarding the access of public services by First Nations children (Blackstock (2009b)). First Nations children are routinely denied public services available to other children as the federal and provincial governments cannot agree on who should pay for services on reserve. Jordan's Principle is named after Jordan River Anderson, a First Nations child, who tragically spent two years unnecessarily in hospital while governments argued over payment for his home care. If he was non- Aboriginal the province would have picked up the cost and the child would have gone home when doctors determined he was medically able to do so. Jordan's Principle says that when a government service is available to other children and a jurisdictional dispute erupts over services for a First Nations child, the government of first contact pays for the service and then resolves the billing issue later. Jordan's Principle passed unanimously through the Canadian House of Commons on December 12, 2007 due, in part, to the large number of people and organizations who had formally registered their support on a web-based joint declaration of support (Blackstock (2009b)).

The democratic assumptions and strategies invoked in the "I am a witness"   42
campaign are very similar to those used for Jordan's Principle, and clearly the
organizers are hoping for a similar success. There is every reason to believe
that the new campaign will be as successful as Jordan's Principle since it provides a medium for public education and immediate, cost free engagement
that results in meaningful impact.

1.6. The tribunal begins…will Canada turn the page on racial discrimination?

> At a time when federal leaders are meeting a few blocks away to discuss   43
> what issues matter the most to Canadians – this case calls them back to
> the conscience of the Nation. Great governments, and great leaders, are
> not measured by interests and issues. They are measured by whether they
> stand on guard for the values that define our country the most – equality,
> freedom, justice, and an unwavering commitment to human rights. In this
> case, the federal government has relied on a series of legal technicalities
> to question the jurisdiction of the tribunal to hear the case. They might be
> successful. And if they are what happens to the First Nations children who
> are denied equitable treatment by another Canadian government? And
> what happens to our Canada if vulnerable children can be denied equitable
> government services simply because of their race or other discriminatory
> grounds?
>
> Blackstock (2009c)

On September 14, 2009 the historic Canadian Human Rights Tribunal on First   44
Nations child welfare began. An opening statement was made by the First
Nations Child and Family Caring Society (Blackstock (2009c)) and motions
were argued regarding whether or not Amnesty International Canada and the
Chiefs of Ontario should be granted interested party status in the proceedings.
The Caring Society, The Assembly of First Nations (AFN), and the Canadian
Human Rights Commission (the Commission) supported both applications
for interested party status and were keen to proceed with a witness testimony
in November of 2009. The Government of Canada vigorously opposed either
group being granted interested party status and they requested an adjourn-
ment of the proceedings until January 2010. The decision by the Tribunal was
to grant interested party status to both Amnesty International and the Chiefs
of Ontario and to begin evidentiary hearings on the facts in November of
2009 (First Nations Child and Family Caring Society of Canada, 2009).

There was a change of course in November of 2009, when a newly   45
appointed Tribunal chair, Shirish Chotalia, vacated the dates of the hearing
on the merits for reasons that are still not clearly understood by the Caring
Society. The Canadian Government then brought a motion to the Canadian
Human Rights Tribunal to dismiss the tribunal on the legal loophole arguing
funding is not a service (Attorney General of Canada v. the First Nations

Child, Family Caring Society of Canada, the Assembly of First Nations, the Canadian Human Rights Commission, the Chiefs of Ontario, & Amnesty International Canada, 2009) after they tried, and failed, to get the Federal Court to derail the tribunal on substantially the same arguments (Attorney General of Canada v. the First Nations Child and Family Caring Society of Canada and the Assembly of First Nations, November 24, 2009). The Canadian Government appealed the Federal Court decision and lost again (Attorney General of Canada v. the First Nations Child et al., 2009) so the motion to dismiss at the tribunal, heard on June 2nd and 3rd, 2010, was Canada's best option to avoid a hearing on the merits. The Tribunal Chair is expected to release her decision on Canada's motion to dismiss in 2010.

2. CONCLUSION

> I felt ashamed by the lack of action on the part of the Federal Government   46
> and its focus on legal loopholes at the expense of the human dimension.
> They chose to dismiss the complaint rather than to address the real issue —
> the severe mistreatment of vulnerable First Nations children and families on
> reserves. I came to realize that the dynamics of what transpired in those two
> days is a microcosm of what has been going on in this country for centuries.
> Gillian McCloskey, Associate Executive Director, Ontario Association of
> Social Workers reflection on her attendance at the Tribunal hearings on
> June 2, 3, 2010 on Canada's motion to dismiss the case.
>
> (McCloskey, 2010, pp. 1–2)

Canada's decision to prioritize its jurisdictional arguments before the inter-   47
ests of vulnerable children coupled with its efforts to avoid a hearing on the merits and keep the hearing out of the public eye raise important questions about its motivation. Amongst the various explanations for Canada's decision making and conduct, the fact that Canada appears to have a very weak case on the merits may be playing a role. Not only is the government facing an impressive list of expert witnesses and reports being put forward by the First Nations Child and Family Caring Society of Canada and the Assembly of First Nations, but they are also faced with having to explain why a host of provincial governments (Auditor General of Canada, 2008) and Canada's own documents and reports (Department of Indian Affairs and Northern Development Canada, 2006) confirm the inequality. Canada has also reported problems securing expert and lay witnesses to testify on its behalf. In fact, it is proposing only one expert witness from an accounting firm contracted to produce a report to refute the testimony of the five independent expert witnesses supporting the First Nations case. In addition, Canada has been unable to identify even one social work expert who is willing to testify on their behalf.

Canada may also be concerned that, if the Tribunal finds that federal 48 funding is a service and has resulted in discrimination it would set an important, and expensive, precedent of equality in government services for children on reserves. It is, of course, unconscionable, if not illegal, for a country to use racial discrimination against children to reduce government costs or to rely on government funding shortfalls as a justification for failing to remedy it.

No matter what Canada's motivations for wanting to derail a hearing on 49 the merits, it is clear that its various tactics have the effect of delaying the proceedings, and the remedy to the inequality, for tens of thousands of vulnerable children and their families.

The efficacy of Canada's legal tactics in the Canadian Human Rights 50 Tribunal and federal court actions will be determined over time, but all Canadians should hope they are not successful. If the Canadian government wins this case on the service or comparator issue, they effectively immunize themselves from ever being held accountable for discriminatory funding practices for public services. This will substantially erode the democratic and equality principles that define the country. Moreover, another generation of First Nations children will grow up being discriminated against by the Canadian government in ways that directly imperil their safety and well-being. If First Nations children win, then the Canadian government will not be above its own human rights laws and for the first time in history, First Nations children will be treated equally — at least in this one program area.

The Canadian Government is faced with a choice that will test the moral 51 fabric of the nation. Does it choose to continue to perpetrate racial discrimination against First Nations children or not? No matter what their choice, the role of the international social work community is to make the Canadian Government famous. Discrimination prospers in darkness and silence and wilts with light and voice.

REFERENCES

Abel, L. (2009, June, 22). Interview with Cindy Blackstock, First Nations Child and Family Caring Society of Canada: Interview about a human rights case against the feds launched by the Caring Society. Narrator, Lisa Abel, CHUO radio.

Aboriginal Peoples Television Network and Canadian Human Rights Commission, Attorney General of Canada (representing the Minister of the Department of Indian Affairs and Northern Development Canada), First Nations Child and Family Caring Society of Canada, Assembly of First Nations, Chiefs of Ontario and Amnesty International, (2010). Federal Court of Canada: Notice of Application; Court File No. T-1008-10.

Amnesty International (2006). *It is a matter of rights: Improving the protection of economic, social and cultural rights in Canada.* Ottawa: Amnesty International Canada.

Assembly of First Nations (2007). Leadership action plan on First Nations child welfare. Ottawa: Assembly of First Nations.

Assembly of First Nations (2007). Reclaiming our nationhood; Strengthening our heritage: Report to the Royal Commission on Aboriginal Peoples. Ottawa: Assembly of First Nations.

Attorney General of Canada v. the First Nations Child and Family Caring Society of Canada and the Assembly of First Nations (November 24, 2009). Federal Court of Canada Order: Docket T-1753-08.

Attorney General of Canada v. the First Nations Child and Family Caring Society of Canada and the Assembly of First Nations (March 30, 2010). Federal Court of Canada: Order and reasons for Order: Docket T-1753-08; Citation: 2010 FC 243.

Attorney General of Canada v. the First Nations Child and Family Caring Society of Canada, the Assembly of First Nations, the Canadian Human Rights Commission, the Chiefs of Ontario and Amnesty International Canada (December 21, 2009). Notice of motion of the respondent for an order to dismiss the complaint. Filed with the Canadian Human Rights Tribunal on December 21, 2009.

Attorney General of Canada v. the First Nations Child and Family Caring Society of Canada, the Assembly of First Nations, the Canadian Human Rights Commission, the Chiefs of Ontario, and Amnesty International Canada (September 28, 2009). Statement of particulars of the respondent, the Attorney General of Canada, in response to the amended statement of particulars of the Commission. Filed with the Canadian Human Rights Tribunal on September 28, 2009.

Auditor General of Canada (2008). First Nations child and family services program—Indian and Northern Affairs Canada. 2008 May: Report of the Auditor General of Canada. Retrieved October 4, 2009, from http://www.oag-bvg.gc.ca/internet/ English/aud_ch_ oag_200805_04_e_30700. tml#hd3a.

Blackstock, C. (2003). First Nations child and family services: Restoring peace and harmony in First Nations communities. In K. Kufeldt & B. McKenzie (Eds.), *Child welfare: Connecting research policy and practice* (pp. 331–342). Waterloo, ON: Wilfred Laurier University Press.

Blackstock, C. (2007). Residential schools: Did they really close or just morph into child welfare? *Indigenous Law Journal, 6*(1), 71–78.

Blackstock, C. (2008). *Reconciliation means not saying sorry twice: Lessons from child welfare. From truth to reconciliation: Transforming the legacy of residential schools.* Ottawa: Aboriginal Healing Foundation.

Blackstock, C. (2009a). Canadian Human Rights Tribunal diary. Unpublished document. Ottawa: First Nations Child and Family Caring Society of Canada.

Blackstock, C. (2009b). Jordan's Principle: How one boy inspired a world of change. *Canadian supplement to the state of the world's children, 2009: Aboriginal children's health — leaving no child behind* (pp. 46–52). Toronto: UNICEF.

Blackstock, C. (2009c). Opening statement by Cindy Blackstock, PhD, executive director First Nations Child and Family Caring Society of Canada at the Canadian Human RightsTribunal on First Nations child welfare. Retrieved October 4, 2009, at http://fnwitness.ca/docs/ Opening_Statement_by_Cindy_Blackstock.pdf.

Blackstock, C., Prakash, T., Loxley, J., & Wien, F. (2005). *Wen:de – We are coming to the light of day.* Ottawa: First Nations Child and Family Caring Society of Canada.

Blackstock, C., & Trocmé, N. (2005). Community based child welfare for Aboriginal children. In Michael Ungar (Ed.), *Handbook for working with children and youth: Pathways to resilience across cultures and contexts* (pp. 105–120). Thousand Oaks: Sage Publications.

Blackstock, C., Trocmé, N., & Bennett, M. (2004). Child welfare response to Aboriginal and Caucasian children in Canada: A comparative analysis. *Violence Against Women, 10*(8), 901–916.

Bryce, P. H. (1922). *The story of a national crime: An appeal for justice to the Indians of Canada.* Ottawa: James, Hope & Sons.

Caldwell, G. (1967). *Indian residential schools: A research study of the child care programs of nine residential schools in Saskatchewan.* Ottawa: The Canadian Welfare Council.

Canada (2009). *Convention on the Rights of the Child: Third and fourth reports of Canada covering January 1998–December 2007.* Retrieved December 6, 2009, at http://rightsofchildren.ca/wp-content/uploads/canadas-third-and-fourth-report-on-crc.pdf.

Canadian Council on Social Development (2003). *Funding matters: The impact of Canada's new funding regime on non-profit and voluntary sector organizations.* Ottawa: Canadian Council on Social Development.

Canadian Human Rights Act (R.S., 1985, c. H-6). Retrieved October 3, 2009, at http://laws.justice.gc.ca/en/h-6/index.html.

Canadian Human Rights Tribunal (n.d.). *What happens next? A guide to the tribunal process.* Ottawa: Canadian Human Rights Tribunal.

Canadian Human Rights Tribunal (2009). *Recording of proceedings First Nations Child and Family Caring Society of Canada and the Assembly of First Nations versus Attorney General of Canada (representing the Minister of Indian Affairs): September 14, 2009.* Ottawa: Canadian Human Rights Tribunal.

Clarke, S. (2007). Ending discrimination and protecting equality: A challenge to the INAC funding formula of First Nations child and family service agencies. *Indigenous Law Journal, 6*(1).

Clatworthy, S. (2005). *Indian registration, membership, and population change in First Nations communities.* Department of Indian Affairs and Northern Development Canada: Strategic Research and Analysis Directorate.

Department of Indian Affairs and Northern Development (n.d.). First Nations Child and Family Services (FNCFS) Q's and A's. Retrieved on July 10, 2010, from http://www. fnwitness.ca/docs/INAC-Access-to-Info-Q&A.pdf.

Department of Indian and Northern Affairs Canada (2003). *Backgrounder: The residential school system.* Ottawa: Indian and Northern Affairs Canada. Retrieved October 8, 2009, at http://www.ainc-inac.gc.ca/ai/rqpi/nwz/2008/20080425a_is-eng.asp.

Department of Indian and Northern Affairs Canada (2005). *First Nations child and family services national program manual.* Ottawa: Indian and Northern Affairs Canada.

Department of Indian Affairs and Northern Development Canada (2006). *First Nations child and family services.* Retrieved January 10, 2009, at http://www.ainc-inac.gc.ca/ai/mr/is/fncfseng.asp.

First Nations Child and Family Caring Society of Canada (2009). *I am a witness.* Retrieved October 4, 2009, at http://www.fnwitness.ca.

First Nations Child and Family Caring Society of Canada, Assembly of First Nations and the Canadian Human Rights Commission v. the Attorney General of Canada (February 24, 2010). Submission of the First Nations Child and Family Caring Society of Canada for cross-examination of affidavits to be open to the public. Filed with the Canadian Human Rights Tribunal on February 24, 2010.

First Nations Child and Family Caring Society of Canada and Assembly of First Nations and Canadian Human Rights Commission and Attorney General of Canada and Chiefs of Ontario and Amnesty International Canada (May 14, 2010). Submissions of the First Nations Child and Family Caring Society of Canada (respondent's motion to dismiss). Filed with the Canadian Human Rights Tribunal on May 14, 2010.

First Nations Child and Family Caring Society of Canada and Assembly of First Nations and Canadian Human Rights Commission and Attorney General of Canada and Chiefs of Ontario and Amnesty International Canada (May 21, 2010). Reply of the Attorney General of Canada (respondent's motion for an order to dismiss the complaint). Filed with the Canadian Human Rights Tribunal on May 21, 2010.

First Nations Child and Family Caring Society of Canada and Assembly of First Nations and Canadian Human Rights Commission and Attorney General of Canada and Chiefs of Ontario and Amnesty International (May 28, 2010). Ruling Canadian Human Rights Tribunal, Member Shirish P. Chotalia. Ottawa: Canadian Human Rights Tribunal.

Harper, S. (2008). Statement of apology on behalf of Canadians for the Indian residential school system. Retrieved September 28, 2009, at http://www.ainc-inac.gc.ca/ai/rqpi/apo/index-eng.asp.

Indian Act (R.S., 1985, c. I-5). Retrieved October 4, 2009, at http://laws.justice.gc.ca/en/I-5/.

Johnston, P. (1983). *Native children and the child welfare system*. Ottawa: Canadian Council on Social Development.

Kimmelman, E. (1985). *No quiet place: Manitoba review on Indian and Métis adoptions and placements*. Winnipeg: Manitoba Ministry of Community Services.

Loppie-Reading, C., & Wien, F. (2009). *Health inequalities and social determinants of Aboriginal peoples' health*. Prince George: National Collaborating Centre for Aboriginal Health.

Loxley, J., De Riviere, L., Prakash, T., Blackstock, C., Wien, F., & Thomas Prokop, S. (2005). *Wen:de: The journey continues*. Ottawa: First Nations Child and Family Caring Society of Canada.

Martin, P., & Blackstock, C. (2009). Shortage of funds; surplus of suffering. Op.Ed. *Toronto Star*, November 23, 2009.

Mason, C. (2007). World briefing — Americas: Native Canadians file rights complaint over child welfare. *The New York Times*. Retrieved December 2009, at http://query.nytimes.com/gst/fullpage.html?res=9505E4DE113EF937A15751C0A9619C8B63.

Matthew, M. (2000). *The cost of quality First Nations education*. West Vancouver: First Nations Education Steering Committee.

McCloskey, G. (2010). Social worker's reflections on being a witness at the Canadian Human Rights Tribunal hearing, June 2, 3, 2010, on the under-funding of child welfare services for First Nations children on reserves. Retrieved July 10, 2010, from http:// www.oasw.org/en/membersite/pdfs/WitnessArticle-GMcCloskey-June2010.pdf.

McDonald, R., & Ladd, P. (2000). *Joint national policy review of First Nations child and family services joint national policy review*. Ottawa, ON: Assembly of First Nations.

McKenzie, B., & Flette, E. (2003). Community building through block funding in Aboriginal child and family services. In Kathleen Kufeldt & Brad McKenzie (Eds.), *Child welfare: Connecting research policy and practice* (pp. 343–354). Waterloo: Wilfred Laurier University Press.

Milloy, J. (1999). *A national crime: The Canadian government and the residential school system-1879 to 1986*. Winnipeg: University of Manitoba Press.

Monsebraaten, L. (2009). Native children flooding into children's aid societies. *Toronto Star*, November 22, 2009 (pp. 1).

Nadjiwan, S., & Blackstock, C. (2003). *Caring across the boundaries*. Ottawa: First Nations Child and Family Caring Society of Canada.

Nafe, S. (2010). Witness reflections. Retrieved July 10, 2010, from http://www.fnwitness.ca/witness-reflections.php.

National Council on Welfare (2008). *First Nations, Métis and Inuit children and youth: Time to act*. Ottawa: National Council on Welfare.

Prentice, J. (2007). The Alberta partnership on child welfare on-reserve. Retrieved March 16, 2009, from http://www.ainc-inac.gc.ca/ai/mr/spch/2007/apcw-apr2707-eng.asp.

Royal Commission on Aboriginal Peoples (1996). *Report of the Royal Commission on Aboriginal Peoples*. Ottawa, ON: Indian and Northern Affairs Canada.

Sinclair, M., Bala, N., Lilles, H., & Blackstock, C. (2004). Aboriginal child welfare. In N. Bala, M. Kim, Zaph J. Williams, R. Vogl, & J. Hornick (Eds.), *Canadian child welfare law: Children, families, and the state*, 2nd ed. Toronto: Thompson Educational Publishing.

Strahl, C. (2008). Speaking notes for the Honorable Chuck Strahl, PC, MP, Minister of Indian Affairs and Northern Development and Interlocutor for Métis and Non-Status Indians. Retrieved October 3, 2009, at http://www.ainc-inac.gc.ca/ai/mr/spch/2008/may0108-eng.asp.

Standing Committee on Public Accounts (2009). Chapter 4: First Nations child and family services program – Indian and Northern Affairs Canada of the May 2008 report of the Auditor General: Report of the Standing Committee on Public Accounts. Retrieved March 24, 2009, from http://www.fncaringsociety.com/docs/402_PACP_Rpt07-e.pdf.

Trocmé, N., Knoke, D., & Blackstock, C. (2004). Pathways to the overrepresentation of Aboriginal children in Canada's child welfare system. *The Social Service Review, 78*(4), 577–601.

Trocmé, N., MacLaurin, B., Fallon, B., Knoke, D., Pitman, L., & McCormack, M. (2006). *Mesnnmimk Wasatek: Catching a drop of light: Understanding the over-representation of First Nations children in Canada's child welfare system: An analysis of the Canadian incidence study of reported child abuse and neglect (CIS-2003)*. Ottawa: First Nations Child and Family Caring Society of Canada.

Union of BC Indian Chiefs (2002). *Calling forth our future: Options for the exercise of indigenous peoples authority in child welfare*. Vancouver: Union of BC Indian Chiefs.

UN News Centre (2007). United Nations adopts the Declaration on the Rights of Indigenous Peoples. Retrieved October 19, 2009, at http://www.un.org/apps/news/ story.asp?NewsID=23 794&Cr=indigenous&Cr1.

3

An Anthology of
Academic Writing

Eight additional examples of good academic writing are presented in Part Three of this book. Collectively, they illustrate that academic writing is a diverse and extensive genre. The style, diction, jargon, and citation method vary from one essay to the next. But as diverse and extensive as the academic genre is, good essays still share several basic characteristics. They are *informative:* The authors present interesting ideas and present them in enough *detail* so that readers can understand the information and arguments the author is presenting. They are *clear.* The specialized language of the discipline within which the writer is writing might send general readers to the dictionary a few more times than they would like, but once readers have those definitions, they can read the text quite easily. And good essays have *energy.* Varied sentence structure provides rhythm and flow to maintain readers' attention and interest.

Following each reading is a set of questions for study and discussion, designed to help you understand why the essay is a good example of the kind of writing your professors value. Your professors will not expect you to produce comparable work, of course, but to do your best to approach in content and style the sophistication exemplified by these models.

Reading Actively and Critically

To read academic writing in a way that will help you learn to write academic essays, and in order to discuss articulately and respond in writing to academic discourse, you need to develop some active and critical reading skills. Critical reading is considerably more demanding than the casual reading you do while you relax with your favourite magazine or a popular novel. It demands more attention and concentration. You read your magazines and bestsellers first for pleasure and second for intellectual stimulation; academic writing you read first for intellectual stimulation and second for pleasure. It is wise to cultivate a strategy for reading academic writing, a strategy for reading critically.

Begin by reflecting on what you already know about the topic of the book or article. Reading experts talk about the benefits of activating prior knowledge as a prereading strategy. What they mean is that if you take some time before you read to reflect on what you already know about the topic, you will enhance your understanding. Many experts in reading comprehension support the notion of *schema theory,* which asserts that the human mind is a schema, composed of a highly intricate series of elaborately connected bites of information. The schema is constantly being reconstituted and reorganized as we accept and process new bites of information. If we activate the appropriate schema by reflecting on the topic before we begin to read a difficult text, our understanding of that text will be enhanced.

Suppose, for example, you are taking a geology course and have to read a paper about how gold deposits form beneath the Earth's surface. Before you read, reflect on what you already know about gold, the other minerals within which gold might be embedded, and the formation of other metals and minerals beneath the Earth's surface. By activating your "gold" schema, your "mining" schema, and your "geology" schema, you prime your mind for the new information it is about to receive, meaning it will receive it more efficiently. When you start reading complicated material—for example, descriptions about how magma heats ground water and forces that water into the Earth's surface, where it then triggers intricate chemical processes that produce gold, or explanations about how gold-bearing solutions are expelled from magma as it cools—you will better understand the author's meaning and intentions.

Next browse through the book or article, trying to get the general drift and overall structure of the discussion. This should give you a good, if preliminary, understanding of the article's main ideas. If you are reading the article as part of the research you are doing for a paper, this skim-through will also help you decide whether the article is worth a detailed study or whether it will give you the kind of information you need to make your own assignment stronger. Some journal articles include a synopsis or an abstract right below the title—these will really help you understand the essence of the article before you begin to read it in detail. If you are reading a book, pay special attention, at this stage, to its table of contents; read the table of contents carefully and you will get a good sense of whether the book will be useful to you.

You are ready now for a detailed, active, and critical reading. This is a hand–eye activity, because to read actively and critically means to highlight important passages, annotate the margins of the text (if the book is yours and not borrowed from the library or your teacher), or take notes summarizing and paraphrasing key points. If you take notes, it is a good idea to put the book or article aside after you have studied it and then paraphrase and condense those notes. The knowledge really becomes your own if you reconstitute it in this way, though, of course, you still must acknowledge the source with a citation.

If you know you will need the information contained within this book or article for an academic essay you are working on, and if you already have at least a rough draft of your essay, read the book or the article as you revise your essay. Alternate your attention between your draft and the source, revising your draft in the context of what you are reading. This is an efficient, time-saving strategy. You must read closely and critically to understand how this knowledge can be integrated into your essay, and you must accommodate your essay to this new knowledge and information. In other words, you read and revise almost simultaneously, thereby abridging the demanding process of composing a research paper.

You need, as well, a strategy to evaluate the authority of the text you are reading. If the book or article is on your reading list or was, in some other way, recommended by your professor, and if the work is written by a reputable author and published by a reputable firm or in a reputable journal, you can be confident that the information is authoritative (though you still want to read it with a critical eye). If you found the book or article in the library or downloaded it from the Internet, it is especially important that you activate some critical reading strategies as you read. An effective way of reading critically is to read slowly and deliberately, pausing at appropriate places to consider and take notes on these questions:

- What is the thesis, and does the thesis address a relevant and important issue?
- Does the author offer ample support for the thesis, and is the support on topic—does it elucidate the thesis?
- Are the thesis and the support the author offers logical? (See pages 60–61 for information on logical fallacies.)
- Does the author cite sources, and are these sources valid and reliable?
- Is the voice, the tone, of the essay strong and confident? Does the author convey the sense that he is committed to the topic and sure of his position?

If you can give positive answers to these questions, you can be confident that the information contained within the book or article is authoritative, and you can use this information as your own academic essay takes shape.

Try to use these active and critical reading strategies as you read the essays that follow. And consider the questions that follow each essay; discuss the questions with classmates or compose a written response for your journal. It's true that academic articles are not usually followed by questions designed to help you understand the content of the article. But by responding to the questions at the end of the articles anthologized here, you will further develop your active and critical reading skills and will begin to acquire an understanding of what is important in academic writing, an understanding that will carry over as you read independently.

Critical Thinking

It is also important, as and after you read, to think critically about the information the author has presented, especially if the author is presenting an argument. Critical thinking is the ability to process, evaluate, analyze, and synthesize information with an open, reflective, curious, and inquisitive mind. It presupposes a willingness to refine and even alter belief and behaviour in the wake of the critical thinking process. It is suspicious of zealotry. You can cultivate your critical thinking skills by keeping in mind these questions, as you read or listen:

- Is the source of this information biased?
- Do logical fallacies embedded in the information call its accuracy into question?
- Is the information fairly presented and adequately supported?

If the source of the information is a neo-Nazi or conspiracy-theory or anarchist book or website, it is inherently biased, false, and misleading and not worth the valuable research time or critical thinking energy you might expend on it. Bias is not synonymous with lying, however. The website of a political party will select information which supports its point of view and calls into question the views of competing political parties. The information might be accurate, but limited. Similarly, a cable news channel or news magazine might favour one political/socio-economic point of view. Critical thinkers do not necessarily disregard information from such sources, but they might calibrate their confidence in the accuracy of the information, based upon possible bias.

A logical fallacy is a product of a flaw in the reasoning process. A fallacy is not a lie. It is a proposition in need of deeper or more relevant support. An *ad hominem* logical fallacy, for example, asserts that a point of view cannot be refuted because the track record of the person supporting it is questionable: He voted for Harper—of course he will oppose higher taxes on the rich. There may be a correlation between support for a politician and support for a particular social or economic value, but an argument in favour of higher taxes on the rich may be based primarily upon economics and not merely on the political affiliations of those making the argument. A knowledge of logical fallacies and an ability to detect them are powerful adjuncts to effective critical thinking. Logical fallacies are defined and discussed on pages 60–61.

An effective argument does not shy away from opposition. It confronts and refutes it. If a source you are using ignores the opposing point of view, your critical thinking antennae will alert you to ask why. Similarly, it is important but not enough that the source you are reading is written by and published in a valid and reliable source. The sources the authors use in support of their positions must also be valid and reliable. This is a main reason why complete and accurate source lists are so important in academic writing. They will tell readers that the authors are offering solid support for their views and ideas.

The art of critical thinking is not easy to acquire because there is some authority inherent in the written word, that authority increasing as the status of the source, its authors, and its place of publication increase. Authority should not be ignored, but it should be examined for possible bias, flawed logic, and selective support.

This article was published in *Psychology of Women's Quarterly*, volume 35, issue 1, 2011, pages 38–45.

Are Contemporary Media Images Which Seem to Display Women as Sexually Empowered Actually Harmful to Women?[†]

Emma Halliwell[1,*], Helen Malson[1], and Irmgard Tischner[2]

[1]*Centre for Appearance Research, University of the West of England, UK*
[2]*Institute of Health and Society, University of Worcester, UK*

ABSTRACT

There has been a shift in the depiction of women in advertising from objectifying representations of women as passive sex objects to agentic sexual representations where the women appear powerful and in control (Gill, 2007a, 2008), and there is substantial evidence that these representations have a negative impact on women's body image. However, to our knowledge, this study is the first experimental research that aims to compare passively objectifying and more recent sexually agentic representations. British undergraduate women ($N = 122$) participated in an experiment in which they were randomly assigned to view sexually passive, sexually agentic, or control print advertisements. Exposure to both types of representations of women, compared to viewing control images, was associated with increased weight dissatisfaction. The sexually agentic representations were singularly associated with increased state self-objectification. Media exposure research tends to focus on the models (e.g., their thinness) shown in advertising and pay little attention to the framing of the image. Our results highlight the powerful impact different framings can have on women's body image concerns as well as suggest that recent shifts in advertising may be particularly problematic because contemporary images increased both weight concern and self- objectification. Therefore, these images may have a more powerful impact on psychological well-being and disordered eating behaviors than traditional images.

KEYWORDS

body image, physical attractiveness, body weight, mass media, advertising, empowerment

---

[†] Emma Halliwell, Helen Malson, and Irmgard Tischner, "Are Contemporary Media Images Which Seem to Display Women as Sexually Empowered Actually Harmful to Women?" in *Psychology of Women's Quarterly*, volume 35, issue 1, 2011, pages 38–45. Copyright © 2011. Reprinted by permission of SAGE Publications.

[*] **Corresponding Author:** Emma Halliwell, Centre for Appearance Research, Department of Psychology, University of the West of England, Frenchay, Coldharbour Lane, Bristol, BS16 9QY Email: emma.halliwell@uwe.ac.uk

We investigate the impact of contemporary advertising images on aspects of young British women's body evaluations. Drawing on Objectification Theory (Fredrickson & Roberts, 1997) and recent critiques of advertising (Gill, 2007a, 2008), we explore experimentally whether recent changes in the framing of women depicted in advertising images have an impact on women's immediate self-evaluations and on their reactions to the advertisements. Typically, experimental research in this field compares exposure to ultra-thin models with exposure to control images that do not display models or, in a few cases, to average size models. The focus to date has been on the model's body weight, with little attention being given to the slogans framing the images of women. To our knowledge, ours is the first study to compare the impact of these different framings of the thin ideal on women. [1]

A substantial body of research has examined associations between media representations of female beauty and women's body image concerns and self-esteem. Correlational studies consistently demonstrate a positive relationship between exposure to appearance-focused media and body dissatisfaction (e.g., Harrison, 2001; Tiggemann & Pickering, 1996). In addition, there is some longitudinal evidence that exposure to body-focused media leads to increased body dissatisfaction among vulnerable girls and women (Stice, Spangler, & Agras, 2001). Experimental studies generally report that exposure to ultrathin bodies idealized in the media leads to body dissatisfaction, weight dissatisfaction, and negative affect among many women (e.g., Grabe, Ward, & Hyde, 2008; Groesz, Levine, & Murnen, 2002) across countries such as Australia, Canada, Great Britain, and the United States (Grabe et al., 2008). There is also some evidence that exposure to these images has a direct impact on women's food restriction (e.g., Krahe & Krause, 2010; Mills, Polivy, Herman, & Tiggemann, 2002). Negative media exposure effects can be explained by the extent to which women make self-evaluative social comparisons with media models (Tiggemann & Polivy, 2010). [2]

Images of artificial and sexualized female beauty are implicated in Objectification Theory as causing women to internalize an observer's perspective about themselves and their appearance (Fredrickson & Roberts, 1997). Consistent with this reasoning, Aubrey (2006) found that trait self-objectification was related to exposure to sexually objectifying TV shows. Fredrickson and Roberts (1997) argued that repeated exposure to direct and indirect pressures to match cultural beauty ideals leads women to internalize the motives for their efforts to improve their appearance as freely chosen, or even natural. As Spitzack (1990) argued, when the desire to be beautiful is constructed as a personal choice, rather than an externally imposed prescription, women are more willing to strive for an idealized appearance. Research investigating the causes and consequences of self-objectification [3] has explored individual differences in women's self-reported levels of trait self-objectification and also the impact of situational factors on levels of state self-objectification experienced at a specific moment (Moradi & Huang, 2008). Temporary fluctuations in self-objectification are referred to as state self-objectification and are the focus of our article.

Research investigating individual differences in trait self-objectification 4 indicate that the internalization of an observer's view of the self is associated with a host of negative states including disordered eating (Calogero, Davis, & Thompson, 2005; Greenleaf, 2005; Muehlenkamp & Saris-Baglama, 2002; Tiggemann & Kuring, 2004; Tiggemann & Slater, 2001; Tylka & Hill, 2004) and depression (Tiggemann & Kuring, 2004; Muehlenkamp & Saris-Baglama, 2002; Muehlenkamp, Swanson, & Brausch, 2005). Temporary fluctuations in state self-objectification have been explored by placing participants in situations which heighten self-objectification such as standing in front of a mirror wearing revealing clothes (Fredrickson, Roberts, Noll, Quinn, & Twenge, 1998) or anticipating interacting with a male stranger (Calogero, 2004). Harper and Tiggemann (2008) found that viewing advertisements featuring ultrathin models leads to increased state self-objectification, compared to viewing control images.

Based on her analysis of media images, Gill (2007a, 2008) discusses a 5 recent change in how women are represented in advertising wherein representations of women as fairly passive sexual objects are increasingly replaced by representations of women as active subjects (Goldman, 1992). As such, advertisers increasingly frame images of women as liberated and in control. However, the mode through which women's control is displayed in this new breed of advertising is in "the commodification of their appearance" (Gill, 2007a, p. 89). In part, this approach can be seen as a response by advertisers to feminist criticisms of the depiction of women as passive objects of male desire (Gill, 2007a; Goldman, 1992) such that more "post-feminist" advertisements now represent women as actively sexually agentic. This analysis is consistent with Levy's (2005) critique of shifts in contemporary culture whereby women are now encouraged to display their liberation and empowerment through their own sexualization. She argues that the emergence of "raunch culture" is not commonly understood as signaling the failure of feminism, but instead as a result of the achievements made through feminism. This rationalization of raunch culture argues that women are now liberated enough to take pleasure in presenting themselves as sex objects, for example through reading porn or taking lap dancing classes. There is evidence that these changes have an impact on women's behavior. Research shows that viewing sexually objectifying depictions of women in the media is positively related to young women's likely participation in self-sexualizing behaviors (such as taking part in a wet t-shirt competition or attending pole dancing classes) and their acceptance of such behaviors in other women (Nowatzki & Morry, 2009).

Gill (2007a) describes three contemporary "postfeminist" constructions 6 of women that emphasize this female sexual empowerment: exposure of the young, heterosexually desirable "midriff" (mid-torso); the vengeful woman set on punishing her partner or ex-partner for his transgressions; and the "hot lesbian" displayed entwined with another beautiful woman. The most dominant of these, the "midriff," portrays "a young, attractive, heterosexual woman who knowingly and deliberately plays with her sexual power and is always 'up for it' (that is, sex)" (p. 41). These midriff images are objectified images in that they typically focus on ultrathin, White, young female bodies, yet in contrast to traditional passive images, they emphasize women's presumed empowerment and sexual confidence. These images represent, therefore, "a shift from objectification to sexual subjectification" (p. 41). Rather than women being displayed as objects of male desire, in the new representations women are portrayed as actively choosing to display themselves sexually in order to demonstrate their independence and liberation (Gill, 2007a). The four key characteristics of midriff images are that they focus not just on women's bodies but also on their sexual agency, autonomy, and empowerment. Often this framing is achieved through the use of humorous and ironic slogans. Young women read these images in complex ways and, to some extent, they are viewed as entertaining, but at the same time, these models' power is understood as being limited to their sexual appeal (Malson, Halliwell, Tischner, & Rudolfsdottir, in press). This paradox is consistent with feminist analyses of postfeminist cultures (e.g., Amy-Chinn, 2006), illustrating that these images cannot be viewed "as wholly 'good' or wholly 'bad'" (Malson et al., in press).

The sexually agentic framing of woman apparently challenges the equa- 7 tion of femininity with passivity (e.g., Jordanova, 1989) and the denial of female sexual desire (Fine, 1988) in earlier advertising. Gill (2008) notes that it is possible to interpret this change in media representations of women positively because it acknowledges women's sexual desire. Furthermore, Gill argues that their humor and irony may make these images more appealing to women. However, it is still women's sexual attractiveness that is central to the image. This new representation, despite its connotations of empowerment, must conform to all the same constraints and efforts of constructing beauty as traditional images wherein the woman's value remains solely physical.

Theoretically then, both representations of women as passive sexual objects 8 and as agentic sexual subjects are depictions of self-objectification because they prioritize women's appearance over any other characteristic. Indeed, the sexually agentic framing of women may actually amplify state self-objectification. Gill (2007a, 2008) argues that contemporary depictions of women as sexually agentic, although responding to feminist critiques about the objectification of women, are nevertheless more pernicious than passively objectifying depictions. In many contemporary representations, women appear to actively court the male gaze and yet, at the same time, they also appear to have internalized the perspective of this male gaze as their own. This internalization is central to understandings of self-objectification. In this sense, such contemporary representations may be more powerful in leading women to internalize an outsiders' (masculinist) viewpoint and thus to engage in state self-objectification. However, these contemporary depictions of women (as agentically rather than passively sexual) may also be more difficult to challenge, particularly because the new figures of sexual agency appear to offer empowerment and a welcome shift away from passive representations (Gill, 2008). It is important, then, to investigate women's evaluation of these images as well as the impact they have on women's body image and self-objectification.

Our study, therefore, extends previous literature because it is the first 9 known study to examine how the framing of advertising images to emphasize women's presumed sexual empowerment or passivity impacts women's reactions, specifically, state self-objectification and weight dissatisfaction. We included state weight dissatisfaction because it focuses specifically on women's evaluation of their weight rather than their appearance more generally and has been shown to be particularly affected by media exposure (Halliwell & Dittmar, 2008).

In our study, the passively objectifying representations of women were 10 operationalized through the presentation of images of women in their underwear framed by slogans emphasizing their physical appearance. In contrast, the sexually agentic representations were operationalized by framing these same images with slogans emphasizing the woman's control, empowerment, and sexual self-confidence. Our first hypothesis is that, because the characteristics of idealized beauty do not differ between the images, women will report higher levels of weight dissatisfaction after viewing images of ultrathin models, regardless of framing than after viewing control images (not featuring women). In contrast, the additional emphasis on sexual empowerment in agentic images may well have a stronger impact than passive representations on women's levels of self-objectification because such portrayals increase striving for an idealized appearance (Spitzack, 1990). Hence, our second hypothesis is that state self-objectification will be higher after exposure to the sexually agentic framing compared to the objectifying framing or control images. Finally, we will examine women's evaluation of each of these advertising images. Due to the apparent empowerment represented in the sexually agentic framing, our third hypothesis is that the sexually agentic framing will be rated more positively than the passively objectifying framing.

METHOD

Participants

Female psychology students ($N = 122$) in the United Kingdom were recruited 11 to take part in a study on "Attitudes to Advertising" in return for course credits. Their mean age was 19.98 years ($SD = 3.83$, range 18–40), and their mean body mass index (BMI: weight in kg/height in m^2) was 22.18 ($SD = 3.93$, range 14.20–41.87). Most women (114; 95%) identified as White, 4 as Black, and 2 as mixed race; 115 (96%) identified as heterosexual and 5 as bisexual, with 2 participants missing information on each measure. Women were randomly assigned to condition: 41 women to the sexually agentic condition, 38 to the passively objectifying condition, and 43 to the control condition. There was no difference in the age, $F(2, 119) = 0.31$, $p = .73$, or BMI, $F(2, 114) = 0.31$, $p = .72$, of women assigned to each condition.

Materials and Measures

Advertising images. For the sexually agentic condition, we used five advertise- 12 ments identified for, and discussed in, Gill's (2007b) review of advertisements published between 1994 and 2001. All the female models in these images were White. For the objectifying condition, we used the same images, but we changed the slogans so that they focused on the model's appearance by shifting the frame from sexually agentic to passively objectifying. The first advertisement was for a push-up bra. It displayed a woman holding a ribbon on the bra she is wearing with the accompanying slogan "I pull the strings." In the objectifying condition, this slogan was changed to "For a beautiful figure." The second advertisement displayed a woman wearing a bra with the slogan "New hair, new look, new bra. And if he doesn't like it, new boyfriend" (sexually agentic) or "When it feels great, it looks great" (objectifying). The third advertisement for slimming tights showed the torso and legs of a woman wearing fishnet stocking stating "While you don't necessarily dress for men, it doesn't hurt on occasion to see one drool like the pathetic dog that he is" (sexually agentic) or "Sex appeal and support for a longer, thinner look" (objectifying). The fourth advertisement showed a woman in her underwear reclined in the hay, with the slogan "Who said a woman can't get pleasure from something soft" (sexually agentic) or "To look as good as you feel" (objectifying). The final advertisement featured a woman in a bra with "I can't cook, who cares?" across her cleavage in the sexually agentic condition and no slogan in the objectifying condition.

In the control condition women viewed five product-only advertisements 13 selected from women's magazines. The first advertisement was for hand cream with the slogan "Discover the secret of Shea Butter," the second was for body cream with the slogan "Indulge your senses," the third was for make-up foundation with the slogan "The new foundation from Chanel: A source of youth and light," and the fourth was for a watch and was accompanied by the brand name but no slogan. The final advertisement was for chewing gum: it featured an image of whitening toothpaste and a toothbrush with the slogan "There is an easier way to keep your teeth white."

State self-objectification. State self-objectification was measured by 14 adapting Noll and Fredrickson's (1998) well-validated individual difference measure of trait self-objectification, the Self-Objectification Questionnaire (SOQ), to provide a state measure of women's view of their bodies. Participants indicated the extent to which they viewed their bodies in appearance-based (objectified terms) or competence-based (non-objectified) terms. The questionnaire consisted of 10 items, 5 of which were appearance-related (weight, sex appeal, physical attractiveness, firm/sculpted muscles, and measurements) and 5 which were competence-related (physical coordination, strength, energy level, health, and physical fitness). Participants were asked to rank how important they rated each attribute *right now* from 0 *(least impact)* to 9 *(greatest impact).* Final scores were obtained by summing separately the ranks for appearance-based and competence-based items, and then subtracting the sum of competence ranks from the sum of appearance ranks. The possible range of scores was –25 to 25, with higher positive scores indicating greater emphasis on physical appearance and thus higher state self-objectification.

Weight dissatisfaction. The state version of the Self-Discrepancy Index ([SDI] 15 Dittmar, Beattie, & Friese, 1996; Halliwell & Dittmar, 2006) was employed as a measure of weight dissatisfaction. The measure asks participants to describe five aspects of themselves that they would ideally like to change *right now* by filling in the blanks for five sentences of the format "I___ but I would like___." They then rate each self-discrepancy statement in terms of magnitude, ranging from 1 (a *little different)* to 6 *(extremely different),* and psychological salience, ranging from 1 (a *little important)* to 6 *(extremely important).* This procedure enables us to measure unobtrusively the extent to which respondents are thinking about self-discrepancies specifically related to weight and body size. The SDI has been validated in previous research (e.g., Halliwell & Dittmar, 2006).

The self-statements were coded as weight-related if they explicitly referred to 16 weight or body size, as opposed to other aspects of the self. For example, the statement "I *am chubby* but I would like *to be slimmer"* was coded as weight-related, but the statement "I *am quiet* but I would like *to be more outgoing"* was coded as unrelated to weight. Two of the authors independently coded the data, and there was 100% agreement between the coders. For the weight-related statements, the magnitude and salience ratings were multiplied and then summed for each individual, giving a single score that ranged from 0 to 180, with higher scores indicating greater state weight dissatisfaction. For example, if a weight-related discrepancy received a difference rating of 6, indicating that it was extremely different, and an importance rating of 4, indicating that it was quite important, the score for that statement would be 24. This product was added to the other weight-related difference × importance products listed by the participant to give a total weight- dissatisfaction score. Previous research has found state weight-dissatisfaction scores in the range of 3.4–15.8 depending on exposure condition and internalization of the thin ideal (Dittmar, Halliwell, & Stirling, 2009). There is a danger of introducing demand characteristics in experimental research examining exposure effects, particularly when the body dissatisfaction measure is not disguised (Mills et al., 2002). Therefore, our unobtrusive measure of weight dissatisfaction is well suited to this type of investigation.

Advertising evaluation. Women were asked to give two ratings of their 17 impression of the advertisement and two ratings of their impression of the brand, ranging from 1 *(very unfavourable)* to 6 *(very favourable)* and 1 *(very negative)* to 6 *(very positive)*. They also rated how much they liked the advertisement from 1 *(not at all)* to 6 *(very much)* and how effective the advertisement was from 1 *(not at all)* to 6 *(very effective)*. In total, they gave six ratings for each advertisement. Because we were interested in comparing women's responses to the different framing slogans, we calculated an overall advertising evaluation score for each condition. Cronbach's αs were .89 for the sexually agentic advertisements, .80 for the objectifying advertisements, and .82 for the control advertisements.

Procedure

To reduce demand characteristics, we were careful to present an appropriate 18 advertising effectiveness cover story. Participants were told that the study investigated women's attitudes toward advertising and that they would be asked to rate a number of advertisements. They were also told that because current mood and thoughts about oneself are known to influence preferences for advertising, they would be asked a few additional questions about how they were feeling when they took part in the study. Women were randomly assigned to one of the three conditions using a computer-generated randomization table and were given a pack containing the corresponding advertisements and advertising rating scales. This pack was followed by the state weight dissatisfaction measure, by the state self-objectification measure, and finally by demographic questions (age, height, weight, ethnicity, sexual orientation, and relationship status). At the end of the experiment, in order to check that the women had believed the cover story, they were asked to state the purpose of the study in their own words. All of the women were naive to the actual aims of the research and were not aware of the focus on body image or self-objectification. The participants were thanked and given a written debrief reminding them of their right to withdraw now that they knew the true aims of the study and including details about how to contact the researchers.

TABLE 1

Mean Scores for Weight Dissatisfaction and State Self-Objectification for Each Experimental Condition.

Condition	Weight Dissatisfaction		State Self-Objectification	
	M	SD	M	SD
Sexually agentic	13.76$_b$	14.07	12.00$_b$	10.11
Objectifying	16.08$_b$	18.48	5.82$_a$	11.38
Control	5.42$_a$	8.51	1.61$_a$	10.74

Note. Means in the same column that do not share subscripts differ at $p < .05$ in the post hoc Tukey comparison.

RESULTS

The mean scores for weight dissatisfaction and state self-objectification for women in each condition are reported in Table 1. Weight dissatisfaction and self-objectification were positively correlated, $r(118) = .26$, $p = .01$.

We conducted a one-way analysis of variance (ANOVA) to test our first hypothesis that weight dissatisfaction would be higher after viewing advertisements in both conditions featuring thin models than in the control condition. There was a statistically significant effect for condition, $F(2,119) = 6.55$, $p = .01$, partial $\eta^2 = .10$. A post hoc Tukey analysis revealed that weight dissatisfaction was significantly higher after viewing both sexually agentic images $(p = .02)$ and objectifying images $(p = .01)$ than in the control condition. Moreover, there was no significant difference between levels of weight dissatisfaction in the two model conditions $(p = .75)$.

The second hypothesis was that state self-objectification would be higher after viewing the sexually agentic framing than after the objectifying framing or the control images. Again, an ANOVA revealed a significant main effect for condition, $F(2,115) = 9.42$, $p < .001$, partial $\eta^2 = .14$. Consistent with our hypothesis, state self-objectification was significantly higher in the sexually agentic condition than in both the control condition $(p < .001$ and the objectifiying condition $(p = .03)$. Furthermore, there was no significant difference between state self-objectification in the objectifying and control conditions $(p = .20)$.

Our third hypothesis was that women would rate the sexually agentic advertisements more favorably than the objectifying advertisements. Because the control images were qualitatively different from the images featuring thin idealized models, we ran the analysis only with the two model conditions. There was no significant difference in the overall ratings given in the objectifying condition *(M* = 3.58, *SD* = .64) and the sexually agentic condition *(M* = 3.69, *SD* = .84), *t*(77) = .69, *p* = .49.

DISCUSSION

The present study investigated the impact of framing idealized images of 23 women as passive sexual objects or as agentic sexual subjects on women's weight dissatisfaction and state self-objectification. Both kinds of representation were associated with increases in women's weight dissatisfaction compared to viewing control images. This finding is consistent with the vast majority of previous research demonstrating negative media exposure effects on body image, based on the assumption that women make evaluative social comparisons with media models (Halliwell & Dittmar, 2005). In addition, we found that the framing of the images was important in terms of their impact on state self-objectification. Viewing contemporary representations of women framed as agentic sexual subjects was associated with higher state self-objectification than viewing control images as well as passive, objectifying representations of women. This finding is consistent with Gill's (2007a, p. 90) proposal that contemporary representations of women encourage an internalized "self-policing narcissistic gaze."

Taken together, these two results suggest that contemporary depictions 24 of women as active sexual subjects may be even more damaging than previous representations because they continue to increase weight dissatisfaction among women and in addition lead to more state self-objectification than passive representations. There was no significant difference between the effectiveness ratings given to the objectifying and sexually agentic advertisements, contrary to Gill's (2007a) suggestion that women find the new representations more appealing.

In the current study, the sexually agentic exposure condition was associ- 25 ated with increased state self-objectification. Although both sets of images display objectifying representations of women, the slogans framing the sexually agentic images refer to women's sexual appeal and to their sexual power in relationship with men. In contrast, the passively objectifying slogans refer to women's appearance and the importance of looking good in general. Fredrickson and Roberts (1997) argue that the sexualized nature of images of women is central to the process of self-objectification. In addition, research suggests that appearance concerns vary across situations and are considered particularly important in intimate relationships (Cash, 2002). Therefore, emphasizing sexual relationships may be a particularly powerful way to elicit state self-objectification.

Our findings are not fully consistent with those of Harper and Tiggemann 26 (2008), because exposure to the passively objectifying framings of women in our study did not lead to increased state self-objectification compared to the control condition. The reasons for this inconsistency are unclear. Harper and Tiggemann used examples of advertising from women's magazines, but they do not provide information about the framing of the images, and it may well be that they included sexually agentic representations in their sample. However, there were also differences in the way that self-objectification was assessed in these studies. One notable difference is that Harper and Tiggemann used an idiographic method, so participants reported any aspect of themselves which was salient, whereas we used the SOQ, which is nomothetic and requires ratings of particular body attributes. In fact, in this respect, Harper and Tiggemann's measure is similar to our measure of weight dissatisfaction, and it is important to note that the findings of the two studies are consistent on these idiographic measures.

The advertising effectiveness cover story was convincing because none of 27 the women guessed our focus on the impact of media representations on body image and self- objectification. Furthermore, the unobtrusive assessment of weight dissatisfaction is a methodological strength of our study. However, our study assessed only short-term exposure effects in a relatively small sample. There is evidence that exposure effects are compounded over longer periods; for example, Stice, Spangler, and Agras (2001) found that subscription to a teenage fashion magazine led to increased body image concerns among vulnerable girls. Furthermore, negative reactions to thin media models in an exposure experiment predicted body dissatisfaction and drive for thinness 2 years later (Hargreaves & Tiggemann, 2003). Therefore, we would expect that exposure to agentic images also has a cumulative effect on women's self-objectification and weight dissatisfaction.

It would have been informative to, and future research should, include 28 an additional condition where advertisements featuring nonsexualized framings of women are used. This addition would allow us to disentangle further the impact of viewing thin idealized models per se from the impact of viewing these models framed as sexualized in various ways. Indeed the substantial evidence that media exposure leads to negative body evaluation (e.g., Grabe et al., 2008) points to the powerful impact of viewing any images of idealized beauty. The current study focused on sexual empowerment. There are, of course, alternative representations of empowerment (e.g., Zerbe-Enns, 2004) that have not been examined here. Clearly, advertising communicates multiple messages about the construction of femininity and women's reading of and responses to these messages will be equally complex. The value of the current research is in demonstrating that agentic, sexualized framings of idealized beauty may be more damaging than passive representations.

The current study attempted to isolate and change the framing of the image while keeping all other aspects of the model images identical. This approach has some clear strengths because we can be confident in attributing differences in women's self-objectification to the differences in the slogan framing between conditions. However, the approach also lacks some ecological validity because many aspects of an image also indicate agency and power. Future research should compare the impact of passive and agentic images currently in circulation. [29]

A further limitation is that the sample consisted of young, primarily White, and heterosexual women so that it is unclear whether the exposure effects demonstrated here would extend to a more diverse sample, particularly considering that dominant representations of beauty display young and White bodies. There is evidence that the nature of women's body image concerns are related to ethnicity, for example African American women report less body dissatisfaction and less frequent comparisons with media images than European American women (Jefferson & Stake, 2009). However, body image problems and eating disorders are increasingly evident among girls and women of all ethnicities and socioeconomic backgrounds (Gordon, 2001), and this pervasiveness is frequently understood in terms of a globalization of beauty ideals (Bordo, 2009). Furthermore, exposure to media featuring Black models and actresses is associated with Black adolescent girls' endorsement of the importance of appearance (Gordon, 2008). The effects on girls and women of diverse ethnic and cultural backgrounds of exposure to these ideals remains unclear, and further research on more diverse samples of participants is plainly required. [30]

Despite these limitations, our study is informative because it indicates that agentic, sexualized representations of women in the media are associated with equivalent levels of weight dissatisfaction as passive, objectifying images and are more strongly associated with self-objectification. The empowerment displayed in contemporary images remains rooted in women's appearance and their conformity to cultural ideals of beauty and sexuality. Therefore, the sexual agency implied in these images represents a form of pseudo empowerment and does not, in fact, have an empowering impact on young women; rather it seems to be more damaging than passively objectifying representations. In sum, what on the face of it appears to be a positive step forward toward empowering women consumers of sexualized advertising actually appears to be a step backward. [31]

DECLARATION OF CONFLICTING INTERESTS

The author(s) declared no potential conflicts of interests with respect to the authorship and/or publication of this article.

FUNDING

The author(s) received no financial support for the research and/or authorship of this article.

REFERENCES

Amy-Chinn, D. (2006). This is just for me(n): How the regulation of postfeminist lingerie advertising perpetuates women as object. *Journal of Consumer Culture, 6,* 155–175.

Aubrey, J. S. (2006). Effects of sexually objectifying media on self-objectification and body surveillance in undergraduates: Results of a 2-year panel study. *Journal of Communication, 56,* 366–386.

Bordo, S. (2009). Not just 'a White girl's thing': The changing face of food and body image problems. In H. Malson & M. Burns (Eds.), *Critical feminist approaches to eating dis/orders* (pp. 46–59). London, UK: Psychology Press.

Calogero, R. M. (2004). A test of objectification theory: The effect of the male gaze on appearance concerns in college women. *Psychology of Women Quarterly, 28,* 16–21.

Calogero, R. M., Davis, W. N., & Thompson, J. K. (2005). The role of self-objectification in the experience of women with eating disorders. *Sex Roles, 52,* 43–50.

Cash, T. F. (2002). Cognitive-behavioral perspectives on body image. In T. F. Cash & T. Pruzinsky (Eds.), *Body image: A handbook of theory, research, and clinical practice* (pp. 38–46). New York, NY: Guilford Press.

Dittmar, H., Beattie, J., & Friese, S. (1996). Objects, decision considerations and self-image in men's and women's impulse purchases. *Acta-Psychologica, 93,* 187–206.

Dittmar, H., Halliwell, E., & Stirling, E. (2009). Understanding the impact of thin media models on women's body-focused affect: The roles of thin-ideal internalization and weight-related self-discrepancy activation in experimental exposure effects. *Journal of Social and Clinical Psychology, 28,* 43–72.

Fine, M. (1988). Sexuality, schooling and adolescent females: The missing discourse of desire. *Harvard Educational Review, 58,* 29–53.

Fredrickson, B. L., & Roberts, T. A. (1997). Objectification theory: Towards understanding women's lived experiences and mental health risks. *Psychology of Women Quarterly, 21,* 173–206.

Fredrickson, B. L., Roberts, T. A., Noll, S. M., Quinn, D. M., & Twenge, J. M. (1998). That swimsuit becomes you: Sex differences in self-objectification, restrained eating, and math performance. *Journal of Personality and Social Psychology, 75,* 269–284.

Gill, R. (2007a). *Gender and the media.* Cambridge, UK: Polity Press.

Gill, R. (2007b, June). *Supersexualize me! Advertising and the midriffs.* Paper presented at the Critical Sexology Seminar Series, Embodying Femininity. South Bank University, UK.

Gill, R. (2008). Empowerment/sexism: Figuring female sexual agency in contemporary advertising. *Feminism and Psychology, 18,* 35–60.

Goldman, R. (1992). *Reading ads socially.* London, UK, and New York, NY: Routledge.

Gordon, M. K. (2008). Media contributions to African American girls' focus on beauty and appearance: Exploring the consequences of sexual objectification. *Psychology of Women Quarterly, 32,* 254–256.

Gordon, R. (2001). Eating disorders east and west: A culture-bound syndrome unbound. In M. Nasser, M. Katzman, & R. Gordon, (Eds.), *Eating disorders and cultures in transition* (pp. 1–21). London, UK, and New York, NY: Bruner-Routledge.

Grabe, S., Ward, L. M., & Hyde, J. S. (2008). The role of the media in body image concerns among women: A meta-analysis of experimental and correlational studies. *Psychological Bulletin, 134,* 460–476.

Greenleaf, C. (2005). Self-objectification among physically active women. *Sex Roles, 52,* 51–62.

Groesz, L. M., Levine, M. P., & Murnen, S. K. (2002). The effect of experimental presentation of thin media images on body dissatisfaction: A meta-analytic review. *International Journal of Eating Disorders, 31,* 1–16.

Halliwell, E., & Dittmar, H. (2005). The role of self-improvement and self-evaluation motives in social comparisons with idealised female bodies in the media. *Body Image, 2,* 249–261.

Halliwell, E., & Dittmar, H. (2006). Associations between appearance-related self-discrepancies and young women's and men's affect, body image, and emotional eating: A comparison of fixed-item and respondent-generated self-discrepancy measures. *Personality and Social Psychology Bulletin, 32,* 447–458.

Halliwell, E., & Dittmar, H. (2008). Does size matter? The impact of ultra-thin models on women's body image and on advertising effectiveness. In H. Dittmar (Ed.), *Consumer culture, identity and wellbeing: The search for the 'good life' and the 'body perfect'* (pp. 121–146). London, UK: Psychology Press.

Hargreaves, D., & Tiggemann, M. (2003). Longer-term implications of responsiveness to thin-ideal television: Support for a cumulative hypothesis of body image disturbance. *European Eating Disorder Review, 11,* 465–477.

Harper, B., & Tiggemann, M. (2008). The effect of thin ideal media images on women's self-objectification, mood and body image. *Sex Roles, 58,* 649–657.

Harrison, K. (2001). Ourselves, our bodies: Thin-ideal media, self-discrepancies, and eating disorder symptomatology in adolescents. *Journal of Social and Clinical Psychology, 20,* 289–323.

Jefferson, D. L., & Stake, J. E. (2009). Appearance self-attitudes of African American and European American women: Media comparisons and internalizations of beauty ideals. *Psychology of Women Quarterly, 33,* 396–409.

Jordanova, L. (1989). *Sexual visions: Images of gender in science and medicine between the eighteenth and twentieth centuries.* London, UK: Harvester Wheatsheaf.

Krahé, B., & Krause, C. (2010). Presenting thin media models affects womens' choice of diet or normal snacks. *Psychology of Women Quarterly, 34,* 349–355.

Levy, A. (2005). *Female chauvinist pigs: Women and the rise of raunch culture.* New York, NY: Free Press.

Malson, H., Halliwell, E., Tischner, I., & Rúdólfsdóttir, A. (in press). Post-feminist advertising laid bare: Young women's talk about the sexually agentic woman of 'midriff' advertising. *Feminism and Psychology.*

Mills, J. S., Polivy, J., Herman, P., & Tiggemann, M. (2002). Effects of exposure to thin media images: Evidence of self-enhancement among restrained eaters. *Personality and Social Psychology Bulletin, 28,* 1687–1699.

Moradi, B., & Huang, Y. (2008). Objectification theory and psychology of women: A decade of advances and future directions. *Psychology of Women Quarterly, 32,* 377–398.

Muehlenkamp, J. J., & Saris-Baglama, R. N. (2002). Self-objectification and its psychological outcomes for college women. *Psychology of Women Quarterly, 26,* 371–379.

Muehlenkamp, J. J., Swanson, J. D., & Brausch, A. M. (2005). Self-objectification, risk taking, and self-harm in college women. *Psychology of Women Quarterly, 29,* 24–32.

Noll, S. M., & Fredrickson, B. L. (1998). A mediational model linking self-objectification, body shame, and disordered eating. *Psychology of Women Quarterly, 22,* 623–636.

Nowatzki, J., & Morry, M. M. (2009). Women's intentions regarding, and acceptance of, self-sexualizing behaviour. *Psychology of Women Quarterly, 33,* 95–107.

Spitzack, C. (1990). *Confessing excess: Women and the politics of body reduction.* Albany, NY: State University of New York Press.

Stice, E., Spangler, D., & Agras, W. S. (2001). Exposure to media-portrayed thin-ideal images adversely affects vulnerable girls: A longitudinal experiment. *Journal of Social and Clinical Psychology, 20,* 270–288.

Tiggemann, M., & Kuring, J. K. (2004). The role of body objectification in disordered eating and depressed mood. *British Journal of Clinical Psychology, 43,* 299–311.

Tiggemann, M., & Pickering, A. S. (1996). Role of television in adolescent women's body dissatisfaction and drive for thinness. *International Journal of Eating Disorders, 20,* 199–203.

Tiggemann, M., & Polivy, J. (2010). Upward and downward: Social comparison processing of thin idealized media images. *Psychology of Women Quarterly, 34,* 356–364.

Tiggemann, M., & Slater, A. A. (2001). Test of objectification theory in former dancers and non-dancers. *Psychology of Women Quarterly, 25,* 57–64.

Tylka, T. L., & Hill, M. S. (2004). Objectification theory as it relates to disordered eating among college women. *Sex Roles, 51,* 719–730.

Zerbe-Enns, C. (2004). *Feminist theories and feminist psychotherapies: Origins, themes and diversities* (2nd ed.). New York, NY: Routledge.

QUESTIONS

1. What is the purpose of this study? What are the three hypotheses the authors test?
2. How do the hypotheses differ from those of similar previous studies?
3. Summarize the demographic of the study's participants.
4. The authors altered the captions for sexually agentic advertisements to make them more passive. What do you think of the changes they made?
5. What, do the authors admit, are the limitations of this study?
6. To what extent do the results of the study validate the authors' hypotheses?
7. The participants in this study were young women. If the participants were young men and the advertisements they viewed were altered accordingly, do you think the results of the study would be any different?
8. If this article were re-written for a women's lifestyle magazine for which the demographic is young women ages late teens to late twenties and interested in fashion, relationships, and celebrity gossip, what changes would the author have to make?
9. Answer "no" to the question posed in the article title and defend your answer.
10. Define/explain these terms: raunch culture, self-policing, ecological validity, sexually agentic.

This article was published in the *Journal of Business Research*, volume 65, issue 10, October 2012, pages 1461–1470.

Brand and Country-of-Origin Effect on Consumers' Decision to Purchase Luxury Products*

Bruno Godey [a,†], Daniele Pederzoli [a,1] Gaetano Aiello [b,2], Raffaele Donvito [c,3]
Priscilla Chan [d,4] Hyunjoo Oh [e,5], Rahul Singh [f,6] Irina I. Skorobogatykh [g,7]
Junji Tsuchiya [h,8], Bart Weitz [i,9]

[a] Rouen Business School
[b] Università di Firenze
[c] Università di Firenze
[d] Manchester Metropolitan University
[e] David F. Miller Center for Retailing Education & Research
[f] Birla Institute of Management Technology
[g] Plekhanov Russian University of Economics
[h] Waseda University
[i] David F. Miller Center for Retailing Education & Research

ARTICLE INFO

Article history:
Received 1 March 2011
Received in revised form 1 June 2011
Accepted 1 August 2011
Keywords:
Country of origin
Luxury
International
Cross-cultural analysis
Consumer behavior

* The authors thank Ulrike Mayrhofer, IAE Lyon, and Ewan Ormiston, RBS, for their comments on an earlier draft, which were very helpful in revising this paper. The authors alone are responsible for all limitations and errors that may relate to the study and the paper.

† **Corresponding Author:** *Rouen Business School, Boulevard André Siegfried, BP 215, 76825 Mont-Saint-Aignan Cedex, France,* Tel.: +33 2 32 82 58 24. *E-mail address:* bruno.godey@rouenbs.fr (B. Godey), dpd@rouenbs.fr (D. Pederzoli), gaetano.aiello@unifi.it (G. Aiello), raffaele.donvito@unifi.it (R. Donvito), p.chan@mmu.ac.uk (P. Chan), hyunjoo.oh@cba.ufl.edu (H. Oh), rahul.singh@bimtech.ac.in (R. Singh), iskorobogatykh@yahoo.com (I.I. Skorobogatykh), junji.tsuchiya@waseda.jp (J. Tsuchiya), bart.weitz@cba.ufl.edu (B. Weitz).

ABSTRACT

This research aims to update the factors influencing consumer purchase of luxury goods and, more specifically, to consider the combined effect of brand and country of origin (CoO) on the purchasing decision. This article extends an exploratory phase constructed from qualitative data previously gathered on this topic. The study includes administering a questionnaire online in seven countries (China, France, India, Italy, Japan, Russia, and the USA) to a total sample of 1102 respondents. The richness of this research relates to the possibility of an intercultural analysis of the results from seven countries. These results concern the differences in the relative importance of components of the consumer decision-making process in respect of the purchase of luxury and non-luxury goods; the relative importance of CoO for consumers making purchasing decisions relating to luxury goods; and the variation in consumers' decision-making criteria depending on the maturity of the luxury market. This research allows the authors to confirm, develop, and generalize results previously obtained in the exploratory phase of their work. They are interesting in terms of management recommendations for a company that wishes to expand internationally in a geographic area covered by the study, since the research found significant differences. The results of the research contribute also to the theoretical controversy concerning the importance of CoO in the consumer decision-making process.

1 *Rouen Business School, Boulevard André Siegfried, BP 215, 76825 Mont-Saint-Aignan Cedex, France,* Tel.: +33 2 32825785, E-mail address: dpd@rouenbs.fr

2 *Dipartimento di Scienze Aziendali, Università di Firenze, Edificio D6, Terzo piano, Stanza n.60, Via delle Pandette 9, 50127 Firenze, Italy,* Tel.: +39 055 4374726. *E-mail address:* gaetano.aiello@unifi.it (G. Aiello)

3 *Dipartimento di Scienze Aziendali, Università di Firenze, Edificio D6, Terzo piano, Stanza n. 3.36, Via delle Pandette 9, 50127 Firenze, Italy,* Tel.: +39 055 4374679. *E-mail address:* raffaele.donvito@unifi.it

4 *Department of Clothing Design and Technology, Hollings Faculty Manchester Metropolitan University, Old Hall Lane, Manchester M14 6HR, United Kingdom* Tel.: +44161 2472778. *E-mail address:* p.chan@mmu.ac.uk

5 *David F. Miller Center for Retailing Education & Research, 302 Bryan Hall, Warrington College of Business Administration, University of Florida, Gainesville, FL 32611, USA* Tel.: + 1 352 2733291. *E-mail address:* hyunjoo.oh@cba.ufl.edu

6 *Birla Institute of Management Technology, 5, Knowledge Park-II Greater Noida, National Capital Region, UP 201 306, India. E-mail address:* rahul.singh@bimtech.ac.in

7 *Plekhanov Russian University of Economics, Stremyanny per. 36, 117997, Moscow, Russia. E-mail address:* iskorobogatykh@yahoo.com

8 *Waseda University, 1-104 Totsukamachi, Shinjuku-ku, Tokyo 169-8050, Japan. E-mail address:* junji.tsuchiya@waseda.jp (J. Tsuchiya)

9 *David F. Miller Center for Retailing Education & Research, 200 Bryan Hall, P.O. Box 117153, University of Florida, Gainesville, FL 32611, USA. E-mail address:* bart.weitz@cba.ufl.edu

1. INTRODUCTION AND OBJECTIVES

The effect of country of origin (CoO) on consumers' perceptions and pur-   1
chasing intentions is a common theme in marketing research (Bloemer, Brijs,
& Kasper, 2009; Usunier, 2006). This research aims to update the factors influencing consumer purchase of luxury goods. The study focuses on this sector
as the internationalization of business is inseparable from its economic development in recent years. In this context, brands (especially Italian and French)
conventionally use the argument of CoO in their international communication strategies.

Research in consumer behavior takes two theoretical directions to explain   2
the consumption of luxury goods. Such research initially drew on the work
of social psychology to focus almost exclusively on socially oriented motivations (Dittmar, 1994; Eagly & Chaiken, 1993). Theoretical explanations based
on a personally oriented vision complement this trend (Vigneron & Johnson,
1999, 2004; Wong & Ahuvia, 1998). Regardless of the perspective used, prior
research in the field of luxury shows the particular importance that brands
play as vectors of strategies that consumers use in their decision-making processes (Dubois, Czellar, & Laurent, 2005; Kapferer, 1997, 1998; Vigneron &
Johnson, 1999, 2004).

Following the difficulties experienced in 2008–2009 and despite fore-   3
casts in return-to-growth in 2010–2011 (for example, Bain et al., 2011), businesses need to make smart strategic choices in international marketing. This
research is part of the managerial perspective of improving understanding
of the cultural differences in perception and purchasing behavior relating to
luxury brands.

The study focuses specifically on the configural effects of brand and CoO   4
on the purchasing decisions of consumers. However, the study includes additional elements, such as design, price, and guarantee, which can influence the
purchasing decisions of consumers. The choice of these variables depends on
the definition of what a luxury brand is. Researchers generally agree about
the lack of substantial definitions of luxury, that is to say, definitions based on
general intrinsic characteristics of products and techniques employed, or on
techno-economic characteristics of the industry (Bomsel, 1995). However, a
certain consensus is emerging about the major characteristics that the consumer of luxury brands desires. The common denominators are beauty, rarity,
quality, and price, and also an inspirational brand endorsing the product. In
this context, brands compete on the basis of their ability to evoke exclusivity,
brand identity, brand awareness, and perceived quality for the consumer
(Phau & Prendergast, 2000).

This article complements an exploratory phase, conducted from qualita-   5
tive data gathered previously on this subject (Aiello et al., 2009). The wealth

of results relates to the intercultural nature of the analysis, based on a questionnaire administered in seven countries (China, France, India, Italy, Japan, Russia, and the USA), with a total sample of 1102 respondents.

After describing the conceptual framework and methodology for the 6 study, this paper presents the results. The study firstly characterizes the specificities of the luxury market in terms of decision making, and secondly identifies important elements in this decision. At each stage, the methods chosen allow comparison of the results obtained in the different countries represented in the sample.

2. LITERATURE REVIEW

The motivation to acquire luxury brands traditionally derives from the notion of 7 conspicuous purchase. This idea tends still to be more or less the strategic foundation for the management of luxury brands (Corneo & Jeanne, 1997; Dittmar, 1994; O'Cass & Frost, 2002; Vigneron & Johnson, 1999, 2004). From this perspective, which has its origins in sociology and social psychology via the theory of impression management, consumers strongly orient their behavior towards the creation of a favorable social image that they can build through their purchases (Eagly & Chaiken, 1993). They then use brands as vectors to implement two distinct consumption strategies. On one hand, brands are the visible symbols of consumer tastes (i.e., social salience); on the other hand, brands are icons representing certain social groups and thus helping consumers to strengthen their membership of these groups (i.e., social identification).

A number of researchers enrich the traditional vision of luxury consump- 8 tion (Tsai, 2005; Vigneron & Johnson, 1999, 2004; Wiedmann, Hennigs, & Siebels, 2009; Wong & Ahuvia, 1998). In this revised paradigm, two types of luxury consumption orientation (social and personal) exist in the management of luxury brands. Wong and Ahuvia (1998) were the first to show that personal orientation towards luxury brands was more important for some consumers than others. When these consumers choose a luxury brand, utilitarian, emotional, and symbolic dimensions usually underlie their personal orientation.

This research fits within this theoretical perspective, taking into account the 9 particular role played by the brand in the consumer's decision-making process. However, if research traditionally recognizes the brand as a central driver of the consumer's decision, this study observes that companies also link brand to CoO to develop their international marketing strategies. This topic has not, as far as the authors are aware, been the subject of specific research in the luxury sector.

Since Dichter's (1962) reference to the significance of the "made-in" dimen- 10 sion, research on CoO effects has become one of the major domains within the scientific literature on international marketing and consumer behavior (Bloemer et al., 2009; Usunier, 2006). In fact, large numbers of studies exist on consumers' beliefs and buying behavior with respect to the CoO of a product or service.

However, CoO is also one of the most controversial research fields, and many studies reach opposite conclusions (Bhaskaran & Sukumaran, 2007; Pereira et al., 2005; Verlegh & Steenkamp, 1999). Some (e.g., Agrawal & Kamakura, 1999; Ahmed & d'Astous, 2008; d'Astous & Ahmed, 1999; Laroche et al., 2002) conclude that CoO has a significant influence on the choice of a product or service, while others (e.g., Ettenson et al., 1988; Liefeld, 1993, 2004; Lim & Darley, 1997; Lim et al., 1994) conclude that the influence of CoO is very weak.

Despite the efforts of researchers to validate and relate the numerous 11 approaches to CoO, recent reviews still deplore the lack of conceptual, methodological, and theoretical transparency (Bloemer et al., 2009; Laroche et al., 2005; Papadopoulos & Heslop, 2003; Usunier, 2006; Verlegh & Steenkamp, 1999).

2.1. Country-of-origin effect on consumer perceptions and purchasing behaviors

Previous researchers working on the effects of CoO take two complementary 12 directions. On one hand, they consider the composition of product-country images (Agrawal & Kamakura, 1999; Roth & Diamantopoulos, 2009; Roth & Romeo, 1992; Usunier & Cestre, 2007). On the other hand, they have an interest in how consumers use CoO as an evaluation of product quality (Bloemer et al., 2009; Veale & Quester, 2009; Verlegh et al., 2005). This article is part of this second perspective, and examines the influence of CoO on perceptions and purchasing intentions of consumers in the field of luxury goods.

According to Bilkey and Nes (1982), one of the most popular approaches 13 towards the use of CoO-cues is the cognitive approach, which sees a product as a cluster of cues. This approach usually distinguishes between product-intrinsic cues (such as taste, design, material, and performance) and product-extrinsic cues (such as price, brand name, store reputation, warranty, and CoO).

Research has shown that consumers generally rely more on intrinsic 14 attributes when forming their opinions. However, in certain circumstances, consumers prefer extrinsic attributes, finding them more credible and reliable than their own assessment (Srinivasan et al., 2004). The use of extrinsic attributes can also relate to situational factors, especially when status or self-image affects the purchase of a product (Piron, 2000; Quester & Smart, 1998).

The CoO impacts consumer perceptions and behaviors through the image 15 of the product's CoO. The image is the representation, reputation, or stereotype of a specific country, which consumers associate with the products (Nagashima, 1970, 1977). According to Roth and Romeo (1992), a country's image arises from a series of dimensions that qualify a nation in terms of its production profile. Such dimensions include innovative approach (superior, cutting-edge technology); design (style, elegance, balance); prestige (exclusiveness, status of the national brands); and workmanship (reliability, durability, quality of national manufacturers). Usunier (1993, 2006) provides a more comprehensive definition of the country image as a multidimensional construct influenced by cognitive components, affective components, and stereotypes. The strong associations between the country image and product quality in relation to product/ brand evaluations (Kotler & Gertner, 2002) necessitate the identification of how global consumers perceive the redefined concept of CoO. They perceive the CoO as the country of design (CoD), and as the country of manufacture/ assembly (CoM/A). The use of different products in different countries causes contradictory findings in previous studies of the effect of the CoO on consumer perceptions and purchasing behaviors.

Two explanations exist for the conflicting results observed in previous 16 research on the impact of CoO. On one hand, the use of different types of products from different sources may result in opposite conclusions on the effect of origin on consumers' perceptions and purchasing behaviors (Veale & Quester, 2009; Verlegh & Steenkamp, 1999). On the other hand, previous work (Agrawal & Kamakura, 1999; Peterson & Jolibert, 1995; Verlegh & Steenkamp, 1999) shows the impact of CoO on the process of consumer decision making to be relatively low in studies combining several factors. One of the most important criticisms of research concerning CoO is that the latter has a real impact on product evaluation in the (unrealistic) event of other information not varying. This research therefore includes, in addition to CoO, other variables involved in how consumers assess and choose luxury goods.

2.2. Brand functions and brand relational dimension

The current crisis is encouraging companies to look more deeply into the 17 links between consumers and luxury brands. Consumers buy luxury products for two main reasons: for their own pleasure, and as a symbol of success. Kapferer (2009) bases the future of luxury brands on the search for balance between these two motivations, by geographical area. In addition, consumers often buy luxury products to give as gifts. Yet whatever the reason for the purchase, the brand remains the main vehicle for connecting with the consumer.

A brand may influence customers' perceptions and attitudes in several 18 ways. Analysis of the dominant components of this influence is possible through the investigation of two complementary key issues: the functional dimension and the relational dimension. The functional brand derives from the commonly accepted view that the brand usually represents the memory of a firm, which encompasses all the investments, research activities, and process technologies or innovations that the firm carries out over time

(Rego et al., 2009). Nevertheless, customers may use brands as a vehicle or mode of expression of attitudes, individualism, and needs (Keegan et al., 1992). According to Keller (2008), brands can simplify choices, be synonymous with a particular level of quality, reduce risk, and generate trust.

The development of the concept of brand equity results in a significant 19 evolution of the brand concept itself. The model of brand equity proposed by Keller (1993) is dominant, providing the link between its two dimensions: brand awareness and image. A set of associations (Keller, 2008; Keller & Lehmann, 2006) characterizes the image of a brand in the consumer's mind. In this perspective, the brand's meaning derives from functional elements of performance or more abstract elements related to the imaginary (Keller, 1993, 2001). Brand performance links to its intrinsic properties and to how consumers perceive the fit between the brand and their functional needs (features, quality of product, services related to the brand, style and design, price). Brand meaning also involves extrinsic properties and how the brand meets the psychological or social needs of consumers (user profiles, situation, personality and values, heritage and experiences).

The examination of specific functions that the brand performs further 20 illuminates the analysis of brand influence over consumers' perceptions, and purchasing decisions. Kapferer and Thoenig (1989), in addition to Lambin (1991), classify a series of utility functions attributable to the brand. These functions can be useful both for customers (placement, guarantee, personalization, practicality, pleasure functions), and for manufacturers (protection, positioning, capitalization). According to Keller (2008) the structure of the brand centers on three fundamental components: the identity component (signs of recognition); the perceptual component (cognitive associations and perceptions) (Peter & Olson, 1987); and the trust component (confirmation of expectations).

The *brand relational dimension*, meanwhile, derives from the continua- 21 tion of work on brand equity and on the process of creating abstract associations, with current research aiming to consider the brand as a symbolic entity with which the consumer maintains an interpersonal relationship (Aaker, 1997; Fournier, 1998). Thus, some researchers extend and enrich work on possessions (Belk, 1988; Kleine et al., 1995; Wallendorf & Arnould, 1988) to apply them to the brand.

From this perspective, consumers search for emotional elements, which 22 sometimes have their anchor in socio-cultural trends towards which they feel a sense of belonging (Fournier, 1998). Customers search for emotional elements when they are tangible, and objective elements play a secondary role. Therefore, firms attempt to create a symbolic universe, surrounding their products as a way to reinforce consumers' brand loyalty.

2.3. The interaction between CoO and brand: effects on consumer behavior

Scholars also direct their attention towards the phenomenon of how brand 23 and CoO interact, specifically in relation to individuals' perceptions and purchasing intentions (Haubl, 1996; Haubl & Elrod, 1999). These interactions may exist at different levels: assimilation of the two concepts, joint effects, or influence of CoO on the brand equity.

As noted earlier, the brand is a variable that works as a summary in for- 24 mulating purchasing intentions (see also Erickson et al., 1984). Sometimes, brand names substitute CoO because of their association with specific countries (Bhaskaran & Sukumaran, 2007); in fact consumers often infer the CoO from the brand name (Terpstra & Han, 1988). According to Haubl (1996), purchasing intentions in relation to luxury products are likely to flow from both brand and CoO; customers consider both the brand's attributes and the place of manufacture or place of assembly in their purchasing decisions (Ahmed & d'Astous, 1996; Tse & Gorn, 1993). Many important brands with good reputations link to countries with high CoO images.

Aaker (1991) and Keller (1993) both highlight that CoO could affect the 25 brand equity by generating secondary associations for the brand, and even a foreign-sounding name is able to affect the brand equity (Leclerc et al., 1994). Positive brand images can reduce if the CoD or CoM/A has a negative image (Johansson & Nebenzahl, 1986), while a very strong brand could decrease the relevance of CoO (Papadopoulos & Heslop, 1993). This finding reveals that information on the manufacturer's country does not significantly affect the evaluation of branded products when this information is congruent with the brand origin. However, when the CoM/A has a weaker image than the country of the brand origin, this information produces a significant negative effect on product evaluation: an effect that tends to be more severe for low-equity than high-equity brands (Koubaa, 2008). Some researchers (Norjaya Mohd et al., 2007) investigate the relationships between CoO image and brand equity for electrical appliances; they discover that CoO has a significant impact on brand dimensions and specifically on brand loyalty.

Haubl and Elrod (1999) note that perceptions of a product are more 26 favorable when brand and country of production are coherent. Some research likewise points out that the effect of the interaction between brand image and CoO image varies in direction and intensity depending on the perceptual consonance of these two aspects. Since this perceived place of origin is little short of a demographic variable and contributes to shaping the brand personality (Thakor & Kohli, 1996), brand and CoO must display intrinsic coherence.

Analysis of CoO and brand interactions is of particular importance for 27 global brands, often represented by products with a different CoD and CoM/A.

An important step therefore is to explore whether and to what extent customers consider the brand name as a completely autonomous factor, a factor exerting a certain influence, or even an estimator of the CoO. According to Pecotich and Ward (2007), a brand gradually takes on the function of a summarizing construct in the eyes of customers as they grow increasingly familiar with the brand. The greater the familiarity, the less the customer will consider other extrinsic information such as the price or CoO. Again, according to Pecotich and Ward (2007), a familiar brand is actually able to increase the perception of the CoO with which consumers associate the brand, and even to neutralize the negative effect often linked to developing countries.

Finally, Pappu et al. (2005, 2007), stating CoO to be an important variable 28 that can affect the equity of a brand, assert that marketing managers operating in an international context must identify the sources of brand equity, and understand the importance of incorporating CoO into their brand-equity measurement.

3. RESEARCH QUESTION, HYPOTHESIS, AND METHOD

Our research centers on understanding the factors that influence the deci- 29 sion to purchase luxury goods. Specifically, the study examines the relative influence of brand and CoO on the purchasing decision. This focus informs three hypotheses. The first important step is to specify the research context when attempting to identify luxury goods in a purchasing decision. The first hypothesis (H1) is therefore: differences occur in the relative importance of components of the consumer decision-making process in respect to the purchase of luxury and non-luxury goods. Since CoO is a variable used in the communication strategies of international companies, an interesting question is whether CoO is indeed a motivator of consumer choice. The second hypothesis (H2) is then: CoO is relatively important for consumers making purchasing decisions on luxury goods. Finally, this research intends to make specific recommendations for international marketing strategists, hence the third hypothesis (H3): consumers' decision-making criteria vary depending on the maturity of the luxury market, that is between countries where luxury is traditionally present (France, Italy, Japan, USA) and those where luxury is still a relative newcomer (China, India, Russia).

This research involves interviewing customers from the seven countries 30 of the research team. The study includes a sample of around 150 people for each country (see Table 1A); the structure of the sample respects the age and gender distribution of the total population of the country. The sample comprises 50.7% women and 49.3% men, and the research team defines the following age categories: aged under 20 years, from 20 to 29, from 30 to 39, from 40 to 49, from 50 to 59, and 60 and over.

TABLE 1A
Geographical origins of the respondents.

Country	Respondents	
China	170	
France	157	
India	166	
Italy	142	
Japan	149	
Russia	152	
USA	166	
Total	1102	

The results of the questionnaire, defined with the agreement of all the national research groups, were gathered via internet. The final questionnaire was in English, being the common working language for the research team. 31

Students from the different universities and business schools involved administered the questionnaire; their task was to find respondents in line with the age and gender quotas mentioned above and to help respondents fill in the questionnaire, explaining the questions or translating into the national language if needed. This assistance was fundamental, to avoid the limits of having only respondents fluent in English and familiar with the use of online surveys. The students' role was also to ensure that respondents chose brands belonging to the sphere of fashion. The questions asked respondents to express their opinions and evaluations on a five-point Likert scale, with the minimum value being 1 and the maximum value 5. Data collection took place from June to October 2008, according to the availability of students in the different countries. 32

The age distribution of the total sample shows that the age category from 20 to 29 years contains the largest proportion of respondents, with the next two categories (30 to 39 years, and 40 to 49 years) showing similar percentages (see Table 1b). 33

4. RESULTS AND DISCUSSION

In examining the purchasing decisions of consumers, this study uses the following criteria: brand, CoO, CoD, CoM/A, price, warranty, design, and advertising. This section presents the results of the research, structured by hypothesis area. 34

TABLE 1B
Age of the respondents.

Country	Mean	Standard deviation
China	39.8	12.8
France	47.9	17.2
India	34.5	11.8
Italy	40.4	12.4
Japan	41.1	14.3
Russia	38.7	13.0
USA	38.2	13.4
Total	40.0	14.1

Age	Distribution (total sample)
<20	0.5%
20–29	33.2%
30–39	22.4%
40–49	25.7%
50–59	8.9%
≥60	9.3%
Total	100.0%

4.1. Characterization of the specificities of the decision to purchase luxury goods (H1: differences occur in the relative importance of components of the consumer decision-making process in respect to the purchase of luxury and non-luxury goods)

The study attempts to characterize the specifics of the decision to purchase products from the luxury sector as opposed to non-luxury goods (see Table 2a).

Factors driving consumer choice are very different from one product category to another. The results in Table 2a indicate that the brand plays a more important role than CoO for both product categories. A more detailed examination of the findings reveals that the most important factor affecting customers' decision to purchase non-luxury goods is price ($\bar{x} = 4.07$), followed by design ($\bar{x} = 3.62$), guarantee ($\bar{x} = 3.37$), and brand ($\bar{x} = 3.11$). CoO appears only in sixth place ($\bar{x} = 2.99$), with CoM/A playing a slightly more important role ($\bar{x} = 3.03$).

Results for luxury goods show a marked disparity, with the most important element affecting consumers' purchasing decision being design ($\bar{x} = 4.33$), closely followed by brand ($\bar{x} = 4.26$). Guarantee is in third place

TABLE 2A
Comparison of factors influencing the purchasing decision: luxury versus non-luxury goods.

| Rank | Luxury goods | | Non-luxury goods | |
:---:	Criterion	Mean	Criterion	Mean
1	Design	4.33	Price	4.07
2	**Brand**	**4.26**	Design	3.62
3	Guarantee	3.99	Guarantee	3.37
4	Price	3.91	**Brand**	**3.11**
5	**CoO**	**3.68**	CoM/A	3.03
6	CoM/A	3.59	**CoO**	**2.99**
7	CoD	3.56	Advertising	2.90
8	Advertising	3.28	CoD	2.80

($\bar{x}$ = 3.99), followed by price ($\bar{x}$ = 3.91). CoO appears in fifth position only ($\bar{x}$ = 3.68), with a very similar score for CoD and CoM/A. However, the two criteria of particular interest to this study—brand and CoO (shown in bold in Table 2a)—seem to matter more to consumers when purchasing luxury goods.

After observing the criteria for selecting luxury and non-luxury products 39 in the two categories individually, the study uses a paired-samples t-test to compare these. This test compares the mean of two variables for one group, calculating the difference in values between the two variables for each observation and testing whether the mean differs from 0. As expected, the criteria that govern the choices of consumers differ significantly depending on whether the products are luxury ones, regardless of the country observed. Brand, CoD, design, and CoO seem to be the elements of choice that best characterize the world of luxury goods compared to that of non-luxury goods (see Table 2b).

Going on to clarify whether differences exist between countries, the study 40 then looks at the differences between these criteria by each area of consumption, using a variance analysis (one-way ANOVA). This method allows the use of a univariate analysis of variance on a quantitative dependent variable by one factor (independent variable). The research uses analysis of variance to test the hypothesis of equality of means (see Table 2c).

TABLE 2B
Comparison of factors influencing the purchasing decision (paired-samples t-test).

Pairs	Items (luxury versus non-luxury)	Mean	Std. deviation	Std.error mean	95% confidence interval of the difference Lower	95% confidence interval of the difference Upper	T	df.	Sig. (2-tailed)
Pair 1	Brand	1.16	1.43	.044	1.08	1.25	26.47	1058	.000
Pair 2	CoO	.69	1.32	.041	.61	.77	16.80	1052	.000
Pair 3	CoD	.75	1.27	.039	.67	.82	18.97	1046	.000
Pair 4	CoM/A	.56	1.27	.039	.49	.64	14.33	1042	.000
Pair 5	Price	-.15	1.33	.041	-.23	-.07	-3.64	1061	.000
Pair 6	Guarantee	.63	1.34	.041	.55	.71	15.39	1055	.000
Pair 7	Design	.72	1.32	.040	.64	.80	17.79	1059	.000
Pair 8	Advertising	.36	1.40	.043	.28	.44	8.36	1056	.000

TABLE 2C
Comparison of factors influencing the purchasing decision (ANOVA).

		Sum of Square	Df.	Mean Squares	F	Sig.
Gap brand	Between groups	91.87	6	15.31	7.77	.000
	Within groups	2072.87	1052	1.97		
	Total	2164.74	1058			
Gap CoO	Between groups	56.49	6	9.42	5.51	.000
	Within groups	1788.47	1046	1.71		
	Total	1844.95	1052			
Gap CoD	Between groups	58.98	6	9.83	6.27	.000
	Within groups	1629.94	1040	1.57		
	Total	1688.91	1046			
Gap CoM/A	Between groups	28.84	6	4.81	3.01	.006
	Within groups	1653.67	1036	1.60		
	Total	1682.51	1042			
Gap price	Between groups	84.05	6	14.01	8.21	.000
	Within groups	1800.45	1055	1.71		
	Total	1884.49	1061			
Gap guarantee	Between groups	63.53	6	10.59	6.11	.000
	Within groups	1817.91	1049	1.73		
	Total	1881.44	1055			
Gap design	Between groups	36.94	6	6.16	3.60	.002
	Within groups	1800.84	1053	1.71		
	Total	1837.78	1059			
Gap advertising	Between groups	63.47	6	10.58	5.55	.000
	Within groups	1999.91	1050	1.91		
	Total	2063.39	1056			

The differences appear to be significant at the 5% level and for all gap vari- 41
ables. The Fisher's F-test provides the opportunity to test the equality of two
variances by the ratio of two variances and to verify that this ratio does not
exceed a certain theoretical value. This test shows that the greatest differences
exist for the variables of price, brand, and CoD.

The study goes on to determine those countries for which perceptions 42
differ significantly, using Scheffe post-hoc tests. For the four variables that
best characterize luxury (brand, CoD, design, and CoO), these tests show that
the seven countries have significantly differentiated perceptions of luxury.
Thus, Chinese consumers seem to have a clearer vision of a luxury product,
forming their perception using all the criteria studied except design. In contrast, Indian consumers perceive the least difference between the two worlds
of consumption, characterizing luxury goods almost exclusively from the
price variable. The third developing country, Russia, appears in the average
scores, showing levels of assessment of items very close to those of most developed countries. As for the developed countries, their evaluations are close to
each other on all criteria. However, Italian consumers appear to attach little
importance to the price, while Japanese consumers pay little regard to CoO,
in their differentiated assessment of both categories of product.

To determine whether characteristic groups of countries exist, the study 43
employs a classification tree procedure, which classifies cases into groups
of countries. The research selects each gap variable as a dependent variable
and each country as an independent variable, and uses Exhaustive CHAID
(CHi-squared Automatic Interaction Detection) as the growing method. This
method is a modification of CHAID, and examines all possible splits for each
predictor. The work focuses on whether the differentiations in the perceptions of the world of luxury were common to groups of developed and developing countries. The results are less clear-cut than expected, demonstrating
the richness and complexity of multicultural studies and therefore the need to
go beyond conventional wisdom.

An examination of brand (the first element of differentiation for luxury) 44
and CoO (the fourth element)—on which this article focuses—reveals that
the classification is into three stable groups with similar perceptions between
China and Italy; France, Russia, and the USA; and Japan and India (see Fig. 1).

4.2. Decision criteria for purchasing luxury goods (H2: CoO is relatively important for consumers making purchasing decisions on luxury goods)

Having characterized what differentiates consumers' purchasing decisions in 45
the luxury market, this study now looks specifically at the criteria that govern
these decisions (see Table 3a).

Gap Brand	Gap CoO	Gap CoD	Gap CoM/A	Gap Price	Gap Guarantee	Gap Design	Gap Advertising
F = 7,770; Sig. = 0,000	F = 5,506; Sig. = 0,000	F = 6,272; Sig. = 0,000	F = 3,102; Sig. = 0,000	F = 8,208; Sig. = 0,000	F = 6,110; Sig. = 0,000	F = 3,600; Sig. = 0,000	F = 5,554 ; Sig. = 0,000
1,69 China							
1,42 Italy							
1,24 France							
1,16 Total							
1,12 Russia							
1,10 USA	1,08 China	1,06 Italy			1,00 China	0,94 USA	
		1,04 Italy				0,89 Italy	
	0,90 Italy		0,87 China		0,82 USA	0,81 France	0,83 China
0,88 Japan		0,79 Russia	0,74 Italy		0,72 Italy	0,74 China	
0,75 India	0,72 Russia	0,74 Total			0,66 France	0,72 Total	
	0,69 Total	0,72 Japan				0,69 Russia	
	0,66 USA	0,72 France	0,56 Total		0,63 Total	0,68 Japan	0,49 Italy
	0,62 France	0,58 USA	0,55 Russia				0,40 France
	0,52 India		0,52 USA		0,55 Japan		0,39 USA
			0,47 France		0,51 Russia		0,36 Total
			0,45 India			0,34 India	0,24 India
	0,31 Japan	0,34 India	0,35 Japan	0,28 China			0,19 Japan
				0,11 India	0,18 India		
				−0,05 Japan			0,01 Russia
				−0,12 USA			
				−0,15 Total			
				−0,29 Russia			
				−0,44 France			
				−0,59 Italy			

⌐ ⌐ ⌐ ⌐ ⌐ ⌐ ⌐ Groups of countries from the classification tree procedure

Fig. 1. Comparison of factors influencing the purchasing decision: luxury versus non-luxury goods (mean and classification tree procedure).

On average across all countries, the most valued criteria in the decision to [46] purchase luxury products are design, brand, and guarantee, with the CoO of luxury goods appearing in fifth position only.

On the basis of this sample, the research uses a principal components [47] factor analysis (PCA) with Varimax rotation, in an attempt to identify underlying variables to explain the origin of correlations within all the observed variables. As a preliminary, tests assess the suitability of the data sample for factor analysis. To conduct a factor analysis, the Kaiser–Meyer–Olkin (KMO) measure of sampling adequacy must be greater than 0.5. This measure varies between 0 and 1, with values closer to 1 being better; a value of 0.6 is a suggested minimum. The Bartlett's test of sphericity tests the null hypothesis that the correlation matrix is an identity matrix; the Bartlett's test must be significant. For this analysis, the study verifies the two conditions (KMO = 0.762 and Bartlett test x^2 (28) = 2004, $P < 0.001$) and also tests the internal reliability of this measure. Cronbach's alpha ($\alpha = 0.715$) shows good internal consistency of the measure. Tables 3b, 3c, and 3d present the decision criteria for purchasing luxury goods.

TABLE 3A
Decision criteria for purchasing luxury goods (descriptive statistics).

Country		Brand	CoO	CoD	CoM/A	Price	Guarantee	Design	Advertising
China	Mean	4.26	3.90	3.76	3.86	4.17	3.96	4.31	3.59
	N	152	156	157	155	157	156	157	156
	Std. dev.	.83	.92	.94	.97	.85	.96	.78	.98
France	Mean	4.44	3.46	3.25	3.31	3.60	4.03	4.10	3.18
	N	153	153	152	151	153	153	153	153
	Std. dev.	.78	1.27	1.26	1.20	1.17	1.08	1.04	1.23
India	Mean	4.08	3.49	3.46	3.53	3.91	3.74	4.04	3.73
	N	166	166	162	164	165	164	165	164
	Std. dev.	.87	1.06	1.08	1.08	.96	1.04	1.18	1.12
Italy	Mean	4.38	3.99	3.83	3.72	3.53	4.31	4.36	3.21
	N	141	141	141	141	141	141	141	141
	Std. dev.	1.08	1.19	1.16	1.16	1.26	.91	.99	1.34
Japan	Mean	3.97	3.68	3.64	3.78	4.32	3.99	4.41	3.18
	N	146	145	145	144	146	146	145	146
	Std. dev.	1.14	1.19	1.22	1.14	.86	1.14	.86	1.25
Russia	Mean	4.39	4.09	3.92	3.83	3.78	4.14	4.56	2.90
	N	152	152	151	151	152	152	151	151
	Std. dev.	.97	1.02	1.07	1.07	1.15	1.06	.77	1.34
USA	Mean	4.32	3.15	3.05	3.12	4.06	3.82	4.54	3.09
	N	158	151	152	149	158	158	158	158
	Std. dev.	1.03	1.33	1.32	1.30	1.15	1.35	.75	1.31
Total	Mean	4.26	3.68	3.56	3.59	3.91	3.99	4.33	3.28
	N	1068	1064	1060	1055	1072	1070	1070	1069
	Std. dev.	.97	1.18	1.19	1.16	1.09	1.09	.95	1.26

TABLE 3B
Decision criteria for purchasing luxury goods (KMO and Bartlett's tests).

KMO measure of sampling adequacy		.76
Bartlett's test of sphericity	Approx. chi-square	2004.96
	df.	28
	Sig.	.000

TABLE 3C
Decision criteria for purchasing luxury goods (total variance explained).

		Initial eigenvalues			Rotation sums of squared loadings[a]	
Factor	Total	% of variance	Cumulative %	Total	% of variance	Cumulative %
1	2.89	36.07	36.07	2.35	29.42	29.42
2	1.31	16.33	52.40	1.65	20.65	50.07
3	1.02	12.75	65.15	1.21	15.09	65.15
4	.85	10.57	75.73			
5	.67	8.41	84.14			
6	.61	7.66	91.80			
7	.34	4.29	96.09			
8	.31	3.91	100.00			

Extraction method: principal components analysis.
[a] The values in this panel of the table represent the distribution of the variance after the Varimax rotation. Varimax rotation tries to maximize the variance of each factor, so the table redistributes the total amount of variance accounted for over the three extracted factors.

Three factors explain the 65.15% variance. The first factor (with an eigenvalue of 2353 and accounting for 29.42% of the variance) comprises the CoO, CoD, and CoM/A. This result is entirely consistent with the literature, since the factor includes the CoO with both internal components (CoD and CoM/A). The second factor (with an eigenvalue of 1652 and accounting for 20.65% of the variance) includes design, brand, and advertising, and brings together the components of brand equity. Advertising and design in this case are vectors of reputation and image. The third factor (with an eigenvalue of 1207 and accounting for 15.09% of the variance) includes the price and guarantee. These two items may relate to consumers' motivation to reduce risk. The item guarantee directly measures—and the high price (standing for perceived quality) indirectly measures—this benefit for the consumer.

TABLE 3D

Decision criteria for purchasing luxury goods (rotated factor matrix[a]).

	Factor		
	1	*2*	*3*
CoO	.87		
CoM/A	.86		
CoD	.84		
Design		.73	
Brand		.69	
Advertising		.61	
Price			.91
Guarantee			.54

Extraction method: principal components analysis.
Rotation method: Varimax with Kaiser normalization.
[a] The rotation converges in 5 iterations. This table contains the rotated factor loadings, which are the correlations between the variable and the factor. Because these are correlations, possible values range from 1 to +1. Using the option that tells SPSS not to print any of the correlations that are 0.5 or less makes the output easier to read by removing the clutter of low correlations (which are probably not meaningful anyway).

4.3. Comparison of decision criteria for purchasing luxury goods in different countries (H3: consumers' decision-making criteria vary depending on the maturity of the luxury market)

As for the gap analysis above, the study then performs a one-way analysis of variance and Scheffe post-hoc tests (see Table 3e).

For all variables, the seven countries show significant differences (F from 4.645 for guarantee to 12.908 for CoO for $P < 0.05$). If the three main criteria for choosing a luxury product (design, brand, and guarantee) have universal value in all countries, CoO does not; on the contrary, major differences exist.

If the Scheffe post-hoc tests allow updating of significant differences between countries, classification trees fail to identify stable groups of countries. Instead, each choice variable requires separate analysis. However, some general trends emerge from the results. For the three main factors of choice (design, brand, and guarantee), India is in the final or penultimate position. China is also in the lower part of the group, although relatively close to the mean, while Russia, on the other hand, is in the upper range. Marked differences therefore exist between the three developing countries in the study regarding the criteria for purchasing luxury products.

TABLE 3E
Decision criteria for purchasing luxury goods (ANOVA).

		Sum of squares	df.	Mean square	F	Sig.
Brand	Between groups	27.89	6	4.65	5.03	.000
	Within groups	979.65	1061	923		
	Total	1007.54	1067			
CoO	Between groups	101.52	6	16.92	12.91	.000
	Within groups	1385.61	1057	1.31		
	Total	1487.13	1063			
CoD	Between groups	92.85	6	15.47	11.63	.000
	Within groups	1400.87	1053	1.33		
	Total	1493.72	1059			
CoM/A	Between groups	72.98	6	12.16	9.43	.000
	Within groups	1351.76	1048	1.29		
	Total	1424.74	1054			
Price	Between groups	75.11	6	12.52	11.00	.000
	Within groups	1211.83	1065	1.14		
	Total	1286.93	1071			
Guarantee	Between groups	32.93	6	5.49	4.65	.000
	Within groups	1256.03	1063	1.18		
	Total	1288.95	1069			
Design	Between groups	38.99	6	6.49	7.50	.000
	Within groups	920.53	1063	.87		
	Total	959.51	1069			
Advertising	Between groups	78.56	6	13.09	8.68	.000
	Within groups	1602.58	1062	1.51		
	Total	1681.14	1068			

Consumers in developed countries show greatly differentiated behaviors. 52 Thus, Japanese consumers, who are rather average on six of eight criteria, differ in highly valuing price and attaching relatively less significance to brand than consumers from other countries. Consumers from the USA appear to pay great attention to design and very little to the various components of CoO. However, they value guarantees less than consumers in other countries. Italian consumers attach roughly the same level of importance to brand ($\bar{x} = 4.38$), design ($\bar{x} = 4.36$), and security ($\bar{x} = 4.31$). For this last variable, they are also ahead of other nations. For French consumers, brand takes a preeminent place but design is relatively unimportant and they rarely take into account CoO and its components (see Fig. 2).

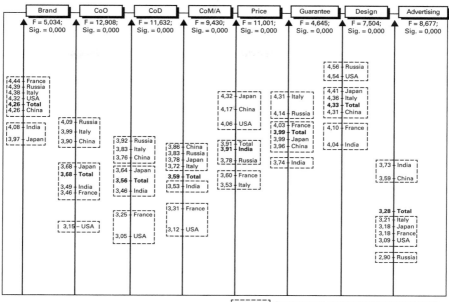

Fig. 2. Decision criteria for purchasing luxury goods (mean and classification tree procedure).

5. CONCLUSIONS, LIMITATIONS, AND FUTURE RESEARCH

The authors intuitively assumed significant differences to exist between 53 homogenous groups of countries according to their level of maturity in the market for luxury goods. However, the situation appears to be more complex and therefore to require a finer distinction between countries. In particular, for countries in the sample where the luxury market is still developing (China, India, and Russia), and so which have a strategic goal to encourage the purchase of luxury goods, consumer behavior is strikingly different from one country to another.

Firstly, this research clearly distinguishes those elements that best charac- 54 terize the luxury sector to consumers. In terms of managerial recommendations, this result is interesting for companies wishing to enter this market, showing them which strategic elements they should rely on to differentiate rapidly. The study identifies four main elements: brand, CoD, design, and CoO. However, refinement of these recommendations is necessary depending on the target location, since the value of the criteria differ significantly between the countries in the sample.

Secondly, the study examines the criteria governing the decision to pur- 55 chase luxury goods. The criteria that companies should emphasize are design, brand, and guarantee. Here again, differences exist between countries. CoO, which does not generally form part of the elements valued by consumers of luxury goods, displays the largest difference between countries. However, consumers in all countries widely recognize brand as a criterion of choice in the purchase of luxury goods.

From a managerial point of view, a more precise analysis of the results 56 is interesting. The research forms two groups of countries according to the maturity level of the luxury market. The study analyzes the results of each developed country relative to the group mean, showing that for French consumers, the predominant elements in decision making are brand, design, and guarantee. However, while brand and guarantee score above the mean for developed countries, design does not. CoO, whether considered overall or in its variations, plays a minor role, receiving a score below the mean for developed countries. Consumers from the USA are very close to the French in the relatively small weighting they give to CoO. Guarantee is also a less-valued criterion compared to the mean of developed countries. In contrast, the criteria of design, brand, and price receive rankings above the mean for developed countries. Italian consumers attach great importance to guarantee and brand. Of all developed countries studied, Italy considers CoO and its variations most, with a score well above the mean of other developed countries on these criteria. In contrast, price appears to be less important as a decision criterion than in other developed countries. Finally, Japanese consumers attach particular importance to price in making purchasing decisions. They also take into account in a very significant way design and CoO, even if the results on these criteria are closer to the mean of developed countries. In contrast, the Japanese are the only consumers in developed countries to attach little importance to brand.

As for how specific developing countries compare to the group means, 57 Chinese consumers attach particular importance to price but also to CoO and its variations. They are, however, only just in the group mean for design, brand, and guarantee. Consumers in Russia attach more specific significance to design and CoO dimensions than those in the other two countries in the group. In addition, evaluation of brand and guarantee is very close to that of developed countries. Finally, Indian consumers do not seem to have a very familiar image of luxury goods. They give scores below the group mean and the mean of the total sample for all factors except advertising. Even if brand and design factors generally score more highly than others, Indian consumers attach importance to the factor furthest removed from the product itself.

From the academic point of view, this research makes a contribution to 58 previous studies concerning CoO and branding through a multicultural analysis that takes into account seven countries and more than 1000 customers. The results provide a number of responses to the controversy surrounding the importance of CoO in the decision-making process of consumers (Bloemer et al., 2009; Laroche et al., 2005; Papadopoulos & Heslop, 2003; Usunier, 2006). In the specific case of luxury goods, the study highlights that the impact of CoO is weaker than that of brand.

Some other interesting results emerge from the research, especially concerning the possibility of identifying potential country groups based on the analysis variables. The respondents seem to grasp fully the globalization of markets and—especially—of the value chain, from conception and design to the manufacture of a product.

Further research is necessary; of particular interest would be a comparison between the perceptions and purchasing decisions of consumers in each country during the introduction of luxury brands. Other avenues of future research could interest both researchers in the area of luxury brands and others wishing to learn more about the perception of CoO in a multicultural context. Finally, while this research demonstrates the central role of brand, a complementary study could deepen the analysis of consumers' lasting emotional ties with luxury brands through the concept of brand attachment, using structural equation modeling.

REFERENCES

Aaker DA. *Managing brand equity.* New York: The Free Press; 1991.

Aaker JL. Dimensions of brand personality. *Journal of Marketing Research* 1997;34(August):347–57.

Agrawal J, Kamakura WA. Country of origin: a competitive advantage. *International Journal of Research in Marketing* 1999;16(4):255–67.

Ahmed SA, d'Astous A. Antecedents, moderators and dimensions of country-of-origin evaluations. *International Marketing Review* 2008;25(1):75–106.

Ahmed SA, d'Astous A. Country-of-origin and brand effects: a multi-dimensional and multi-attribute study. *Journal of International Consumer Marketing* 1996;9(2):93–115.

Aiello G, Chan P, Donvito R, Godey B, Pederzoli D, Hennigs N, et al. An international perspective on luxury brand and country of origin effect. *Journal of Brand Management* 2009;16(5–6):323–37.

Bain, et al. Bain & Company predicts eight percent growth in global luxury goods sales in May. http://www.bain.com/about/press/press-releases/bain-predicts-eight-percent-growth-in-global-luxury-goods-sales-in-2011aspx.

Belk RW. Possessions and the extended self. *The Journal of Consumer Research* 1988;15(2):139–68.

Bhaskaran S, Sukumaran N. National culture, business culture and management practices: consequential relationships? *Cross-Cultural Management* 2007;14(1):54–67.

Bilkey WJ, Nes E. Country-of-origin effects on product evaluations. *Journal of International Business Studies* 1982;13 (Spring/Summer):89–99.

Bloemer J, Brijs K, Kasper H. The CoO-ELM model: a theoretical framework for the cognitive processes underlying country of origin-effects. *European Journal of Marketing* 2009;43(1–2):62–89.

Bomsel O. L'industrie du luxe ou comment associer objets et représentations (Luxury industry or how to combine objects and their representations). [July–August] *Annales des Mines – Réalités Industrielles;* 1995. p. 14–20. [in French].

Corneo G, Jeanne O. Conspicuous consumption, snobbism and conformism. *Journal of Public Economics* 1997;66:55–71.

d'Astous A, Ahmed SA. The importance of country images in the formation of consumer product perceptions. *International Marketing Review* 1999;16(2–3):108–26.

Dichter E. The world customer. *Harvard Business Review* 1962;40(July–August):113–22.

Dittmar H. Material possessions as stereotypes: material images of different socioeconomic groups. *Journal of Economic Psychology* 1994;15:561–85.

Dubois B, Czellar S, Laurent G. Consumer segments based on attitudes toward luxury: empirical evidence from twenty countries. *Marketing Letters* 2005;16(2):115–28.

Eagly AH, Chaiken S. *The psychology of attitudes.* New York: Harcourt Brace Jovanovich; 1993.

Erickson GM, Johansson JK, Chao P. Image variables in multi-attribute product evaluations: country-of-origin effects. *The Journal of Consumer Research* 1984;11 (September):694–9.

Ettenson R, Wagner J, Gaeth G. Evaluating the effect of country of origin and the "Made in the USA" campaign: a conjoint approach. *Journal of Retailing* 1988;64(1):10–1.

Fournier S. Consumers and their brands: developing relationship theory in consumer research. *The Journal of Consumer Research* 1998;24 (March):343–73.

Haubl G. A cross-national investigation of the effects of country of origin and brand name on the evaluation of a new car. *International Marketing Review* 1996;13(5):76–97.

Haubl G, Elrod T. The impact of congruity between brand name and country of production on consumers' product quality judgements. *International Journal of Research in Marketing* 1999;16(3):199–215.

Johansson JK, Nebenzahl ID. Multinational production: effect on brand value. *Journal of International Business Studies* 1986;17:101–26.

Kapferer JN. Managing luxury brands. *Journal of Brand Management* 1997;4(4):251–60.

Kapferer JN. Why are we seduced by luxury brands? *Journal of Brand Management* 1998;6(1):44–9.

Kapferer JN. The specificity of luxury management: turning marketing upside down. *Journal of Brand Management* 2009;16(5/6):311–22.

Kapferer JN, Thoenig JC. *La Marque: moteur de la compétitivité des entreprises et de la croissance de l'économie* (Brand: driver of business competitiveness and economic growth). Paris: McGraw-Hill; 1989 [in French].

Keegan W, Moriarty S, Duncan T. *Marketing.* Englewood Cliffs: Prentice Hall; 1992.

Keller KL. Conceptualizing, measuring, managing customer-based brand equity. *The Journal of Marketing* 1993;57(1):1–22.

Keller KL. Building customer-based brand equity: a blueprint for creating strong brands. *Marketing Management* 2001;10(July/August):15–9.

Keller KL. *Strategic brand management.* 3rd ed. Upper Saddle River: Prentice Hall; 2008.

Keller KL, Lehmann DR. Brands and branding: research findings and future priorities. *Marketing Science* 2006;25(6):740–59.

Kleine SS, Kleine RE, Allen CT. How is a possession "me" or "not me"? Characterizing types and an antecedent of material possession attachment. *The Journal of Consumer Research* 1995;22(3):327–43.

Kotler P, Gertner D. Country as brand, product and, beyond: a place marketing and brand management perspective. *Journal of Brand Management* 2002;9(4):249–61.

Koubaa Y. Country of origin, brand image perception, and brand image structure. *Asia Pacific Journal of Marketing and Logistics* 2008;20(2):139–55.

Lambin JJ. *Marketing.* 1st ed. Milano: McGraw-Hill; 1991.

Laroche M, Tomiuk MA, Bergeron J, Barbaro-Forleo G. Cultural differences in environmental knowledge, attitudes, and behaviours of Canadian consumers. *Canadian Journal of Administrative Sciences* 2002;19(3):267–83.

Laroche M, Papadopoulos N, Heslop LA, Mourali M. The influence of country image structure on consumer evaluations of foreign products. *International Marketing Review* 2005;22(1):96–115.

Leclerc F, Schmitt BH, Dube L. Foreign branding and its effects on product perceptions and attitudes. *Journal of Marketing Research* 1994;31(2):263–70.

Liefeld JP. Experiments on country-of-origin effects: review and meta-analysis of effect size. In: Papadopoulos N, Heslop LA, editors. *Product-country images: importance and role in international marketing.* New York NY: International Business Press; 1993. p. 117–56.

Liefeld JP. Consumer knowledge and use of country-of-origin information at the point of purchase. *Journal of Consumer Behaviour* 2004;4(2):85–96.

Lim JS, Darley WK. An assessment of demand artefacts in country-of-origin studies using three alternative approaches. *International Marketing Review* 1997;14(4–5):201–18.

Lim JS, Darley WK, Summers JO. An assessment of country of origin effects under alternative presentation formats. *Journal of the Academy of Marketing Science* 1994;22(3):274–83.

Nagashima A. A comparison of Japanese and US attitudes toward foreign products. *The Journal of Marketing* 1970;34(1):68–74.

Nagashima A. A comparative 'made-in' product image survey among Japanese businessmen. *The Journal of Marketing* 1977;41(3):95–100.

Norjaya Mohd Y, Mohd Nasser N, Osman M. Does image of country-of-origin matter to brand equity. *The Journal of Product and Brand Management* 2007;16(1):38–48.

O'Cass A, Frost H. Status brands: examining the effects of non-product brand associations on status and conspicuous consumption. *The Journal of Product and Brand Management* 2002;11:67–88.

Papadopoulos N, Heslop LA. *Product–country images: impact and role in international marketing.* New York, NY: International Business Press; 1993.

Papadopoulos N, Heslop LA. Country equity and product–country images: state-of-the-art in research and implications. In: Jain SC, editor. *Handbook of research in international marketing.* Northhampton, MA: Edward Elgar Publishing; 2003. p. 402–33.

Pappu R, Quester PG, Cooksey RW. Consumer-based brand equity: improving the measurement – empirical evidence. *The Journal of Product and Brand Management* 2005;14(2–3):143–54.

Pappu R, Quester PG, Cooksey RW. Country image and consumer-based brand equity: relationships and implications for international marketing. *Journal of International Business Studies* 2007;38:726–45.

Pecotich A, Ward S. Global branding, country of origin and expertise. An experimental evaluation. *International Marketing Review* 2007;24(3):271–96.

Pereira A, Hsu CC, Kundu SK. Country-of-origin image: measurement and cross-national testing. *Journal of Business Research* 2005;58:103–6.

Peter P, Olson J. *Consumer behaviour. Marketing strategy perspectives.* Richard Irwin, Inc.; 1987.

Peterson RA, Jolibert AJP. A meta-analysis of country-of-origin effects. *Journal of International Business Studies* 1995;26(4):883–99.

Phau I, Prendergast G. Consuming luxury brands: the relevance of the "rarity principle." *Journal of Brand Management* 2000;8:122–38.

Piron F. Consumers' perceptions of the country-of-origin effect on purchasing intention of inconspicuous products. *Journal of Consumer Marketing* 2000;17(4):308–21.

Quester PG, Smart J. The influence of consumption situation and product involvement over consumers' use of product attribute. *Journal of Consumer Marketing* 1998;15(3):220–38.

Rego LL, Billett MT, Morgan NA. Consumer-based brand equity and firm risk. *The Journal of Marketing* 2009;73(November):47–60.

Roth KP, Diamantopoulos A. Advancing the country image construct. *Journal of Business Research* 2009;62:726–40.

Roth MS, Romeo GB. Matching product category and country image perceptions: a framework for managing country of origin effects. *Journal of International Business Studies* 1992;23(3):477–97. [Winter].

Srinivasan N, Jain SC, Sikand K. An experimental study of two dimensions of country-of-origin (manufacturing country and branding country) using intrinsic and extrinsic cues. *International Business Review* 2004;13:65–82.

Terpstra V, Han CM. Country-of-origin effects for uni-national and bi-national products. *Journal of International Business Studies* 1988;19(2):235–55.

Thakor MV, Kohli CS. Brand origin: conceptualisation and review. *Journal of Consumer Marketing* 1996;13(3):27–43. [Summer].

Tsai S. Impact of personal orientation on luxury-brand purchase value. *International Journal of Market Research* 2005;47:429–54.

Tse DK, Gorn GJ. An experiment on the salience of country-of-origin in the era of global brands. *Journal of International Marketing* 1993;1(1):57–76.

Usunier J-C. *Marketing across cultures.* Hemel Hempstead: Prentice Hall; 1993.

Usunier J-C. Relevance in business research: the case of country-of-origin research in marketing. *European Management Review* 2006;3:60–73.

Usunier J-C, Cestre G. Product ethnicity: revisiting the match between products and countries. *Journal of International Marketing* 2007;15(3):32–72.

Veale R, Quester P. Do consumer expectations match experience? Predicting the influence of price and country of origin on perceptions of product quality. *International Business Review* 2009;18:134–44.

Verlegh PWJ, Steenkamp JBEM. A review and meta-analysis of country-of-origin research. *Journal of Economic Psychology* 1999;20:521–46.

Verlegh PWJ, Steenkamp JBEM, Meulenberg MTG. Country-of-origin effects in consumer processing of advertising claims. *International Journal of Research in Marketing* 2005;22:127–39.

Vigneron F, Johnson LW. A review and a conceptual framework of prestige-seeking consumer behaviour. *Academy of Marketing Science Review* 1999;3(1).

Vigneron F, Johnson LW. Measuring perceptions of brand luxury. *Journal of Brand Management* 2004;11(6):484–506.

Wallendorf M, Arnould EJ. "My favorite things." A cross-cultural inquiry into object attachment, possessiveness, and social linkage. *The Journal of Consumer Research* 1988;14(4):531–47.

Wiedmann KP, Hennigs N, Siebels A. Value-based segmentation of luxury consumption behavior. *Psychology and Marketing* 2009;26(7):625–51.

Wong NY, Ahuvia AC. Personal taste and family face: luxury consumption in Confucian and Western societies. *Psychology and Marketing* 1998;15:423–32.

QUESTIONS

1. What are the objectives of this study?
2. What, according to social-psychology theory, is the appeal of luxury brand merchandise?
3. How, according to the authors, does their study differ from previous similar studies?
4. Upon what criteria is a country's "production profile" based?
5. Why do consumers buy luxury products?
6. Express in your own words the hypotheses of this study.

7. Summarize the characteristics of the participants in the study.
8. Whom does this study benefit? Why?
9. Why do the authors provide such a detailed account of the statistical analyses they used to interpret the results of their study?
10. Select any three of the countries surveyed in this study and write a summary of the criteria consumers from each country use in purchasing luxury brands.
11. What further related studies do the authors recommend be undertaken?
12. The authors do not mention specific luxury brands. Why is this so, and do you think it is a limitation of the article?
13. Do the results of this study surprise you? If you have or were to purchase a luxury consumer product, are the criteria identified in this study the same ones you would apply?

This article was published in the *Journal of Experimental Psychology*, volume 48, 2001, pages 28–36.

Exposure to Music with Prosocial Lyrics Reduces Aggression: First Evidence and Test of the Underlying Mechanism[†]

Tobias Greitemeyer[*]

University of Innsbruck, Austria

ARTICLE INFO

Article history:
Received 25 November 2009
Revised 27 July 2010
Available online 14 August 2010
Keywords:
Aggression Music
Media effects

ABSTRACT

Previous research has predominantly focused on negative effects of music exposure by demonstrating that listening to antisocial music increases aggression and aggression-related variables. The present research tests the idea that listening to prosocial (relative to neutral) music decreases aggressive outcomes. In fact, five studies revealed that prosocial music exposure decreased aggressive cognition, affect, and behavior. Mediational analyses showed that the effect of music condition on aggressive behavior was accounted for by differences in aggressive affect. Implications of these results for the predictive validity of the general learning model (Buckley & Anderson, 2006) for the effects of media exposure on social tendencies are discussed.

Previous research has predominantly focused on negative effects of media 1
exposure on social tendencies. For instance, playing antisocial (relative to
neutral) video games has been shown to have serious consequences, such as
criminal actions (Anderson & Dill, 2000) or physical violence (Gentile, Lynch,
Linder, & Walsh, 2004). Likewise, listening to aggressive (relative to neutral)
music increases aggressive cognition, affect (Anderson, Carnagey, & Eubanks,

---

[†] Reprinted from *Journal of Experimental Social Psychology*, 47(1), January 2011. Tobias Greitemeyer, "Exposure to Music with Prosocial Lyrics Reduces Aggression: First Evidence and Test of the Underlying Mechanism," pages 28–36. Copyright 2011, with permission from Elsevier.
[*] *E-mail address*: Tobias.Greitemeyer@uibk.ac.at.

2003), and behavior (Fischer & Greitemeyer, 2006). Recently, however, it has been argued that the effects of media exposure depend to a large extent on the content of the media (Buckley & Anderson, 2006): whereas media with antisocial content should increase antisocial outcomes and decrease prosocial outcomes, media with prosocial content is assumed to increase prosocial outcomes and to decrease antisocial outcomes. In fact, there has been some initial research showing that helping behavior is promoted by exposure to prosocial video games (Gentile et al., 2009; Greitemeyer & Osswald, 2010) and prosocial music (Greitemeyer, 2009a,b). In contrast, it is less known whether aggressive behavior is indeed decreased by exposure to prosocial media.

Thus, the present research examines the idea that exposure to prosocial 2 (relative to neutral) media is associated with aggression and aggression-related variables. Concretely, the hypothesis was tested that listening to prosocial music decreases aggressive cognition, affect, and behavior. Moreover, it was addressed whether the effects of music exposure on aggressive behavior (if there are any) would be mediated by aggressive cognition and/or aggressive affect. It is important to note that aggressive behavior is not simply the mirror image of helping behavior. For example, people can be both high in aggressive (e.g., toward their foes) and helpful (e.g., toward their friends) behaviors. Likewise, some variables do not have opposite but parallel effects on pro- and antisocial behavior. For instance, negative (relative to neutral) mood states have been shown to increase both helping (Cialdini, Baumann, & Kenrick, 1981) and aggression (Berkowitz, 1989). Thus, it is not clear from the beginning whether media effects on pro- and antisocial outcomes are reciprocally related. If listening to prosocial music indeed decreases aggressive outcomes, this would further strengthen the notion that media exposure does not inevitably harm but may also benefit social relations.

THEORETICAL PERSPECTIVE: THE GENERAL LEARNING MODEL

To explain the effects of media exposure on action, one can refer to the 3 general learning model (GLM) proposed by Buckley and Anderson (2006). According to the GLM, person (such as sex and trait aggression) and situation variables (such as media exposure) (sometimes interactively) may affect a person's internal state, consisting of cognition, affect, and arousal. This internal state in turn influences how events are perceived and interpreted. Finally, this decision process shapes a person's behavior in a social encounter.

Most relevant to the present research, the GLM suggests that depending 4 on the content of the media exposed, either negative or positive effects of media exposure on social behavior are to be expected: whereas exposure to antisocial media should increase antisocial and decrease prosocial outcomes, exposure to prosocial media is assumed to decrease antisocial and to increase prosocial outcomes. There have been accumulative investigations into the effects of exposure to antisocial media. In contrast, evidence regarding prosocial media effects is very limited. In particular, little is known about whether and why exposure to prosocial media decreases aggression. These issues were addressed in the present series of studies.

EFFECTS OF EXPOSURE TO ANTISOCIAL MEDIA

Correlational evidence suggests that exposure to antisocial music is related 5 to a wide range of undesirable phenomena. For instance, a preference for rap and heavy metal music has been shown to be associated with psychoticism (North, Desborough, & Skarstein, 2005), tolerance of racial and sexual discrimination (Gan, Zillman, & Mitrook, 1997), vandalism and drug use (Arnett, 1991, 1992), and violence and aggression (Rubin, West, & Mitchell, 2001) in young adults. Providing causal evidence, Anderson et al. (2003) found that listening to violent (relative to neutral) music increased aggression-related cognition and affect. Subsequently, Fischer and Greitemeyer (2006) showed that participants who had listened to violent music were more likely to behave aggressively than participants who had listened to neutral music. Moreover, by matching artists and genre in the experimental and the control condition and by controlling for measured arousal, Anderson et al. (2003) and Fischer and Greitemeyer (2006) made sure that the effects of violent songs on aggression and aggression-related variables were not due to the specific arousal properties of the songs used.

Likewise, the effects of violent video games on aggressive thoughts, feel- 6 ings, and behavior are well-documented. Meta-analytic evidence (Anderson et al., 2010) suggests that exposure to violent video games causes an increase in aggression and aggression-related variables. Moreover, long-term changes as a result of repeated encounters with violent video games have been demonstrated in a recent longitudinal study (Anderson, Gentile, & Buckley, 2007). These authors found that children who had played more violent video games early in a school year became more aggressive later in the school year (even after controlling for Time 1 aggressive tendencies).

EFFECTS OF EXPOSURE TO PROSOCIAL MEDIA

Whereas there has been abundant evidence documenting the effects of expo- 7 sure to antisocial media, research into the effects of exposure to prosocial media has been relatively sparse. There is evidence that television with prosocial content promotes prosocial behavior (Hearold, 1986; Mares & Woodard, 2005). Greitemeyer (2009a,b) tested the hypothesis that exposure to prosocial (relative to neutral) music increases prosocial tendencies. Participants were exposed to songs, which were either prosocial or neutral in content. Afterwards, prosocial cognition, affect, and behavior were measured. As expected, listening to prosocial music increased the accessibility of prosocial thoughts, led to more empathy, and fostered helping behavior. Likewise, playing prosocial video games increases prosocial cognitions and behavior (Gentile et al., 2009; Greitemeyer & Osswald, 2010). Finally, Greitemeyer and Osswald (2009) examined the effects of exposure to prosocial video games on aggressive cognitions. Two studies revealed that playing a prosocial (relative to a neutral) video game decreased the hostile expectation bias and the accessibility of antisocial thoughts.

Although these results are encouraging, research into the effects of proso- 8 cial media is still rather in its infancy. In particular, more research into the effects of exposure to prosocial media on aggression and aggression-related variables is needed. Perhaps most pressing is whether and why prosocial media exposure decreases aggressive behavior. According to the GLM, the effects of media exposure on behavior may operate through the activation of cognition related to behavior. In fact, there is some evidence that cognitive variables mediate the effects of media exposure on behavior. Anderson and Dill (2000) found that playing a violent (relative to a neutral) video game led to a greater accessibility of aggression-related thoughts, which then increased aggressive responses. Likewise, Greitemeyer and Osswald (2010) showed that participants who had played a prosocial (relative to a neutral) video game listed more prosocial thoughts, which then led to prosocial behavior. Thus, because exposure to prosocial video games appears to reduce aggressive cognitions (Greitemeyer & Osswald, 2009), there are good reasons to assume that prosocial media exposure decreases aggressive behavior.

However, the GLM proposes two other main routes (affect and arousal) by 9 which media exposure may instigate behavior. In fact, it appears that the effect of prosocial (relative to neutral) music on prosocial behavior is mediated by prosocial affect (Greitemeyer, 2009b): Listening to prosocial music increased empathy, which in turn promoted helping. Thus, it may well be that any effects of prosocial music on aggression work through the affective route of the GLM. Because both prosocial and neutral media can affect arousal, the arousal route is arguably scientifically less interesting than the other two routes. Nevertheless, it is important to measure and to control for the effects of arousal on aggression. In sum, it was anticipated that exposure to prosocial (relative to neutral) music would decrease aggressive cognition, affect, and behavior (while controlling for arousal). In addition, the effect of prosocial music on aggressive behavior should be mediated by one or both of aggressive cognition and affect.

THE PRESENT RESEARCH

The present research had two main aims. First, it addressed whether expo- 10 sure to prosocial (relative to neutral) music would decrease aggression and aggression-related variables. Second, it aimed to clarify the causal mechanisms by which exposure to prosocial music decreases aggressive behavior. To these ends, five studies were carried out. In all studies, participants were exposed to either prosocial or neutral music. Because measurement of the possible mediators may influence subsequent measures of aggressive behavior (e.g., Lindsay & Anderson, 2000), in Studies 1–4, the possible mediators and aggressive behavior were assessed in different studies. Studies 1–3 tested the effects of exposure to prosocial (relative to neutral) music on aggressive cognition and affect. Study 4 addressed the effects of prosocial music exposure on aggressive behavior. Finally, Study 5 aimed to provide an initial test of why exposure to prosocial music decreases aggressive behavior by examining whether aggressive cognition and/or aggressive affect mediates the effect of music exposure on aggressive behavior. Taken together, this series of studies aims to clarify whether and why exposure to music with prosocial lyrics reduces aggression. By so doing, it provides the first comprehensive test of the predictive validity of the GLM for the effects of prosocial media exposure on antisocial outcomes.

STUDY 1

Anderson et al. (2003) examined the effects of exposure to antisocial (relative to neutral) music on the accessibility of antisocial thoughts. They found that participants who were exposed to antisocial songs were more likely to generate aggressive word completions than participants who were exposed to neutral songs. Likewise, it was expected that listening to prosocial (relative to neutral) music would decrease the accessibility of antisocial thoughts in that participants who were exposed to prosocial songs are assumed to be less likely to generate aggressive word completions than participants who were exposed to neutral songs. 11

Method

Participants and design

Participants were 59 students (25 women and 34 men) of the Ludwig-Maximilians University in Munich, Germany, who were randomly assigned to one of the two music conditions (prosocial vs. neutral). There were 26 participants (14 women and 12 men) in the prosocial condition and 33 participants (11 women and 22 men) in the neutral condition. Participants were tested in small groups of three to four people. 12

Procedure and materials

At the outset, participants were welcomed by the experimenter and learned that they would participate in a marketing survey on music preferences. To 13 this end, they would listen to four songs. To make sure that participants listened to the lyrics, they were told that they would evaluate the songs toward the end of the study. Participants in the prosocial condition were exposed to: "Heal the world" (Michael Jackson), "Ein bißchen Frieden" (Nicole), "We are the world" (Liveaid), and "Help" (Beatles). Participants in the neutral condition were exposed to: "On the line" (Michael Jackson), "Spiel um deine Seele" (Peter Maffay), "An Englishman in New York" (Sting), and "Octopus's garden" (Beatles). Greitemeyer (2009b) employed these songs and found that the lyrics of the prosocial songs were perceived as being more prosocial than the lyrics of the neutral songs. In addition, liking and perceived aggressive content of the prosocial and the neutral songs were relatively similar. Finally, by matching genre in the prosocial and the neutral condition and by controlling for measured arousal and mood, he made sure that any effects of listening to the songs are unlikely to be due to specific arousal and mood properties of the songs used.

Then, participants learned that a short delay was necessary before they 14 could evaluate these songs. To bridge this time gap, they would respond to a filler task (which, in fact, constituted the main dependent measure, namely, a word completion task to assess aggressive thought accessibility). Participants received a list of 11 word fragments (e.g., Anderson et al., 2003). Their task was to fill in the missing letters to form a word. For instance, "schla___" can become the aggressive word "schlagen" ("to hit") or the neutral word "schlafen" ("to sleep"). Accessibility of aggressive thoughts was the proportion of word completions that were aggressive. In determining whether a word completion was antisocial or not, we used the coding scheme developed by Anderson and his colleagues.

Finally, participants answered demographic questions and were thanked 15 and probed for suspicion. None of the participants indicated any suspicion of a relationship between listening to the songs and the word completion task.

Results and discussion

It was expected that listening to prosocial (relative to neutral) music would 16 decrease the accessibility of aggressive thoughts. In fact, a 2 (music condition: prosocial vs. neutral) × 2 (participant sex) ANOVA revealed the predicted significant main effect for music condition, $F(1,55) = 5.68$, $p < .05$, $\eta_p^2 = .09$. Participants who had listened to the prosocial songs ($M = 0.07$, $SD = 0.09$) had lower aggression word completion scores than those who had listened to the neutral songs ($M = 0.12$, $SD = 0.09$). The effect for participant sex, $F(1,55) = 0.56$, $p = .46$, $\eta_p^2 = .01$, and the interaction were not significant, $F(1,55) = 2.35$, $p = .13$, $\eta_p^2 = .04$. Thus, the hypothesis that exposure to prosocial (relative to neutral) music reduces aggressive cognition received initial support from the data.

STUDY 2

Study 2 was similar to Study 1, with the following modifications. First, 17 aggressive cognition was assessed in a different way, namely, participant's attitudes toward war and violence. Second, to test generality, different songs by different artists were utilized. Third, participants were from the United Kingdom (rather than from Germany). Fourth, and finally, to control for the arousal route of the GLM, participant's arousal and positive and negative mood were measured. It was expected that listening to prosocial (relative to neutral) music would lead to less positive attitudes toward war and violence.

Method

Participants and design

Participants were 38 students (33 women and 5 men) at the University of 18 Sussex. There were 22 participants (20 women and 2 men) in the prosocial condition and 16 participants (13 women and 3 men) in the neutral condition.

Procedure and materials

At the outset, participants learned that they would participate in two unrelated 19 studies. Participants were told that in the interest of experimental economy, both studies would be carried out within a single experimental session. The first study was described as dealing with their musical preferences, whereas the second study involved answering questions about their feelings and attitudes. As in Greitemeyer (2009b), participants in the prosocial condition listened to: "Love generation" (Bob Sinclair) and "Feed the world" (U2 with Band Aid), whereas participants in the neutral condition listened to: "Rock this party" (Bob Sinclair) and "Vertigo" (U2). Pilot testing, reported in Greitemeyer (2009b), revealed that the lyrics of the prosocial songs were perceived as being more prosocial than the lyrics of the neutral songs. In addition, the songs were matched on mood and arousal dimensions, and liking and perceived aggressive content of the songs were relatively similar.

As in Study 1, participants learned that a short delay was necessary 20 before they could evaluate the songs and thus in the meantime they would participate in the second study. First, participant's perceived arousal and mood were assessed. Arousal was assessed by employing the Perceived Arousal Scale (Anderson, Deuser, & DeNeve, 1995), which contains 31 adjectives describing feelings of arousal (e.g., *aroused*) or lack of arousal (e.g., *drowsy*). Lack of arousal items was reverse-scored. Positive and negative emotions were assessed by employing the PANAS (Watson, Clark, & Tellegen, 1988). Participants then completed the Revised Attitudes Toward

Violence Scale (RATVS; Anderson, Benjamin, Wood, & Bonacci, 2006). The RATVS contains 39 statements, which measure the favorability of attitudes toward four forms of war and violence. The four subscales are attitudes toward war (12 items; $\alpha = .91$; e.g., "Killing of civilians should be accepted as an unavoidable part of war"), penal code violence (7 items; $\alpha = .85$; e.g., "Violent crimes should be punished violently"), corporal punishment of children (8 items; $\alpha = .87$; e.g., "A parent hitting a child when he/she does something bad on purpose teaches the child a good lesson"), and intimate violence (12 items; $\alpha = .60$; e.g., "It is all right for a partner to shoot the other if they are unfaithful"). Participants were asked to indicate the extent to which they agree or disagree with these statements, assessed on a 5-point Likert-type scale (1 = *strongly disagree*, 5 = *strongly agree*). This scale successfully predicted self-reported violent behavior (Anderson et al., 2006) and self-reported trait aggression, anger, and hostility (Carnagey & Anderson, 2007).

Results and discussion

Because there were only five men in the sample, participant sex was not 21 included in the main analyses. Mean and standard deviations of the main dependent measures as a function of type of music as well as test statistics are reported in Table 1.

TABLE 1
Means and standard deviations for responses to the dependent measures as a function of type of music (Study 2).

	Music condition			
Dependent measures	*Prosocial*	*Neutral*	*t(36)*	*d*
Attitudes toward violence				
War	2.03 (0.68)	2.60 (0.61)	2.66*	0.88
Penal code violence	2.13 (0.76)	2.96 (0.80)	3.24**	1.06
Corporal punishment of children	1.63 (0.62)	1.66 (0.56)	0.13	0.05
Intimate violence	1.16 (0.19)	1.11 (0.19)	0.76	0.26
Positive mood	2.36 (0.75)	2.02 (0.84)	1.31	0.43
Negative mood	1.40 (0.38)	1.44 (0.42)	0.32	0.10
Perceived arousal	2.88 (0.74)	2.68 (0.85)	0.78	0.25

Standard deviations are in parentheses.
*$p < .05$.
**$p < .01$.

Attitudes toward violence

Music condition had significant effects on two of the RATVS subscales: par- 22
ticipants who had listened to the prosocial (relative to the neutral) music had
more negative war attitudes and were less accepting of penal code violence.
In contrast, attitudes toward corporal punishment of children and attitudes
toward intimate violence were not significantly affected by music exposure
(see Table 1).[1]

Mood and arousal

There were no significant effects of music condition on participants' mood, 23
neither on the positive affect scale nor on the negative affect scale. In addition,
there were no significant effects on perceived arousal (see Table 1). Finally,
when controlling for positive and negative mood and perceived arousal,
the effects of type of music on attitudes toward war, $\beta = 0.40$, $t(33) = 2.56$,
$p < .05$, and penal code violence, $\beta = 0.40$, $t(33) = 2.72$, $p = .01$, were still
evident. Thus, different mood and arousal states are unlikely to account for
the effect of listening to prosocial music on attitudes toward violence.

In sum, as in Study 1, exposure to prosocial music reduced aggressive cog- 24
nition. Study 2 further showed that this effect remained reliable when controlling for the mood and arousal properties of the songs used. Study 3 will
address the effects of prosocial music exposure on aggressive affect as well as
aggressive cognition.

STUDY 3

Study 3 once again tested the effect of prosocial music exposure on aggressive 25
cognition, but a different measure of aggressive cognition was employed. In
addition, Study 3 addressed the effects of exposure to prosocial (relative to
neutral) music on aggressive affect. Anderson et al. (2003) have shown that
participants who were exposed to antisocial songs reported higher levels of
state hostility than did participants who were exposed to neutral songs. Likewise, it was expected that listening to prosocial (relative to neutral) music
would reduce reported state hostility. Finally, the potential moderating effects
of trait aggression were examined. According to the GLM, person (such as
trait aggression) and situation (such as media exposure) variables may interact
in influencing aggressive behavior. For instance, Bushman (1995) found that
media violence was more likely to evoke aggressive affect and behavior in high
trait aggressive individuals than in low trait aggressive individuals. However,

---

[1] The absence of significant effects of music condition on attitudes towards corporal punishment and particularly intimate violence may have been due to a floor effect; that is, the low
means indicate that there was little room for exposure to prosocial music to further reduce
endorsements of these attitudes.

another research (Anderson et al., 2003) failed to find significant interactive effects between music exposure and trait aggression. Thus, there were no clear predictions whether people high or low in trait aggression would be more susceptible to prosocial music exposure.

Method

Participants and design

Participants were 80 students (42 women, 38 men) at the University of Sussex. 26 There were 40 participants (20 women, 20 men) in the prosocial condition and 40 participants (22 women, 18 men) in the neutral condition. All participants were tested individually.

Procedure and materials

After participants were welcomed by the experimenter, they filled in the Buss 27 and Perry (1992) aggression questionnaire, which consists of four subtraits. The physical aggression subtrait consists of 9 items (e.g., "If someone punches me, I punch back."); verbal aggression consists of 5 items (e.g., "I can't help getting into arguments when people disagree with me."); anger consists of 7 items (e.g., "I have trouble controlling my temper."); and hostility consists of 8 items (e.g., "I sometimes feel that people are laughing at me behind my back."). All items were rated on a Likert scale ranging from 1 (*extremely uncharacteristic of me*) to 5 (*extremely characteristic of me*). Internal consistencies were very good: physical aggression, $\alpha = .93$; verbal aggression, $\alpha = .93$; anger, $\alpha = .89$; hostility, $\alpha = .87$. Participants then listened to either the prosocial or the neutral songs (the same songs were used as in Study 2), which was followed by measures of aggressive affect and cognition.

Aggressive affect

To assess aggressive affect, participants completed the State Hostility Scale 28 (Anderson et al., 1995). This scale consists of 35 mood statements (e.g., "I feel furious" and "I feel irritated"), and participants are asked to indicate the extent to which they agree or disagree, assessed on a 5-point Likert-type scale (1 = *strongly disagree*, 5 = *strongly agree*). Scale reliability was very good ($\alpha = .94$).

Aggressive cognition

To assess aggressive cognition, participants completed a word pair task 29 (adapted from Anderson et al., 2003; Bushman, 1996). Participants were presented with pairs of words. There were 20 words in total: 10 words that are clearly aggressive in meaning (e.g., *fight, gun, kill*) and 10 words that are ambiguous in meaning, having both aggressive and nonaggressive meanings (e.g., *alley, police, rock*). Using these words, Bushman (1996) found that participants who scored highly on trait hostility perceived greater similarity of meaning between pairs of aggressive and ambiguous words than did participants who scored lowly on trait hostility. As in Anderson et al. (2003), participants received all possible pairs of these 20 words and rated how similar, associated, or related they find each word pair, ranging from 1 (*not at all similar, associated, or related*) to 7 (*extremely similar, associated, or related*). Based on these responses, three average similarity scores were calculated for each participant: aggressive–aggressive word pairs, aggressive–ambiguous word pairs, and ambiguous–ambiguous word pairs. Anderson et al. found that participants who had listened to violent (relative to neutral) songs gave larger similarity ratings of aggressive–ambiguous word pairs relative to their ratings of ambiguous–ambiguous and aggressive–aggressive word pairs. Likewise, it was expected that listening to prosocial (relative to neutral) songs would lead to smaller ratings of similarity of aggressive– ambiguous word pairs relative to ratings of ambiguous–ambiguous and aggressive–aggressive word pairs.

Results and discussion

Aggressive affect (state hostility)

As predicted, when state hostility was regressed on music condition, trait 30 aggression, and participant sex, music condition received a significant regression weight, $\beta = .27$, $t(76) = 2.90$, $p < .01$. Participants in the prosocial condition ($M = 1.82$, $SD = 0.47$) reported lower levels of state hostility than did participants in the neutral condition ($M = 2.14$, $SD = 0.62$).[2] There was also a significant effect of trait aggression, $\beta = .45$, $t(76) = 4.58$, $p < .001$. Those participants who scored high on trait aggression tended to score high on state hostility. Sex of participants did not significantly predict state hostility, $\beta = .13$, $t(76) = 1.32$, $p = .19$.

Aggressive cognition (word pair ratings)

Trait aggression and participant sex did not significantly interact with music 31 condition.

---

2 Anderson and Carnagey (2009) broke the state hostility into several subscales, namely, feeling unsociable, feeling mean, lack of positive feelings, and aggravation. They found that antisocial video game effects were stronger for the subscales feeling mean and aggravation than for the subscales feeling unsociable and lack of positive feelings. Interestingly, in the present study, feeling mean, $t(78) = 2.42$, $p < .05$, $d = 0.56$, and aggravation, $t(78) = 3.96$, $p < .001$, $d = 0.89$, were significantly affected by music condition, whereas lack of positive feelings was not, $t(78) = 0.99$, $p = .32$, $d = 0.22$. Note, however, that in Study 5 of the present paper, there was a significant effect of music condition on all three subscales and effect sizes were comparable in its size. Nevertheless, this is an important avenue for future research. The items of the subscale feeling unsociable were not significantly correlated and thus due to low reliability they were not combined.

TABLE 2

Effects of type of music on perceived similarity of aggressive–aggressive (AgAg), aggressive–ambiguous (AgAm), and ambiguous–ambiguous (AmAm) word pairs (Study 3).

Music condition	*Word pair type*				
	AgAg	AmAm	*Control average: AgAg and AmAm*	AgAm	*Contrast: control AgAm*
Prosocial	4.13 (0.79)	1.84 (0.61)	2.98 (0.64)	2.24 (0.78)	0.75 (0.34)
Neutral	4.81 (0.66)	2.45 (0.62)	3.63 (0.56)	3.17 (0.65)	0.46 (0.29)

Standard deviations are in parentheses.

Table 2 presents the mean similarity ratings (and standard deviations) as a 32
function of music condition and word type. Following Anderson et al. (2003),
a contrast score was computed. First, each participant's aggressive–aggressive
and ambiguous–ambiguous scores were averaged. From this control rating,
each participant's aggressive–ambiguous score was then subtracted. A small
contrast score indicates that the aggressive–ambiguous pairs were perceived
as relatively more similar than the control word pairs, whereas a large contrast
score indicates that the aggressive–ambiguous pairs were perceived as relatively more dissimilar than the control word pairs.

As expected, participants in the prosocial condition ($M = 0.75$, $SD = 0.34$) 33
had larger contrast scores than did participants in the neutral condition
($M = 0.46$, $SD = 0.29$), $\beta = .39$, $t(76) = 4.09$, $p < .001$.[3] There was also a significant effect of trait aggression, $\beta = -.28$, $t(76) = 2.87$, $p < .01$. Those participants who scored high on trait aggression tended to have small contrast
scores. Sex of participant also significantly predicted word pair ratings, $\beta =
.33$, $t(76) = 3.34$, $p < .01$: female participants ($M = 0.52$, $SD = 0.31$) had smaller
contrast scores than did male participants ($M = 0.70$, $SD = 0.36$). Trait aggression and participant sex did not significantly interact with music condition.

As in Studies 1–2, exposure to prosocial music reduced aggressive 34
cognition: participants who had listened to prosocial music rated aggressive

---

3 As can be seen in Table 2, participants in the prosocial (relative to the neutral) condition
rated not only the aggressive–ambiguous words as less similar, $t(78) = 5.81$, $p < .001$,
$d = 1.30$, but also the control words, $t(78) = 4.77$, $p < .001$, $d = 1.08$. However, inasmuch as
the latter effect was less pronounced than the first effect, there were larger ratings of similarity of aggressive–ambiguous word pairs relative to ratings of ambiguous–ambiguous and
aggressive–aggressive word pairs in the prosocial, relative to the neutral, condition.

and ambiguous words as less similar than participants who had listened to neutral music. Study 3 also provided a first test of the idea that prosocial music exposure is associated with aggressive affect. In fact, listening to prosocial music decreased state hostility. Finally, Study 3 extended Studies 1–2 by including a measure of trait aggression into the analysis. It is noteworthy that both the personal (trait aggression) and the situational (music condition) variable independently predicted aggressive cognition and affect. Moreover, there was no significant interaction between music condition and trait aggression for both aggressive cognition and affect. Thus, the effects of prosocial music exposure on aggressive cognition and affect materialize even when accounting for trait aggression and are reliable for both people high and low in trait aggression.

STUDY 4

After Studies 1–3 have shown that listening to prosocial (relative to neutral) 35 music decreases aggressive cognition and affect that, as outlined by GLM, may reduce aggressive behavior, Study 4 examines whether listening to prosocial music indeed affects antisocial action. Concretely, it was examined whether listening to prosocial (relative to neutral) music would decrease relational aggressive behavior.

As an additional refinement, a manipulation check was included. This was 36 done to (a) make sure that the songs differ in the extent to which they are perceived as being prosocial and (b) to test whether perceived content mediates the effect of type of music on aggression. If prosocial content indeed is what distinguishes the songs used, this is exactly what should occur (Bushman & Anderson, 2002).

Method

Participants and design

Participants were 90 students (78 women and 12 men) at the University of 37 Sussex. There were 45 participants (40 women and 5 men) in the prosocial condition and 45 participants (38 women and 7 men) in the neutral condition. All participants were tested in small groups of three to four people.

Procedure and materials

The procedure was similar to the previous studies, with the following modi- 38 fications. After listening to each song (the same songs were used as in Studies 2–3), participants rated to what extent the song lyrics were about helping and cooperation, respectively. These ratings were highly correlated (Bob Sinclair: $\alpha = .78$; U2: $\alpha = .94$) and all four ratings were thus combined to a prosocial index ($\alpha = .83$). Then, participants responded to some unrelated filler items (e.g., the New Ecological Paradigm, Dunlap, Van Liere, Mertig, & Emmet-Jones, 2000). Finally, to measure aggression, participants were asked to make an evaluation of a doctoral student who had allegedly created the question-naire and who had applied to be a research assistant in the Department of Psychology at the University of Sussex. Participants learned that this position was very competitive so the Psychology Department was trying to get several evaluations of each candidate and that their judgment would influence the decision whether the candidate would get the position or not. Participants judged the candidate by answering the following three questions: "Would you recommend hiring the doctoral student?", "How competent do you think is the doctoral student?", and "How likeable do you think is the doctoral student?". All items were assessed on a 7-point Likert-type scale (1 = *not at all*, 7 = *definitely*). Scale reliability was very good (α = .88). Many previous investi-gations have relied on similar job-relevant evaluations to measure aggression (e.g., Coyne et al., 2008; Stucke & Baumeister, 2006; for a review, Bushman & Anderson, 1998). Finally, participants were thoroughly debriefed about the real aim of the study. Special attention was given to inform participants that the doctoral student was nonexistent and thus that they did not harm any-body.

Results and discussion

Because there were only 12 men in the sample, participant sex was not 39 included in the main analyses. The manipulation check was successful: The perceived content of the prosocial songs received a higher score on the proso-cial index (M = 4.05, SD = 0.50) than the perceived content of the neutral songs (M = 2.28, SD = 0.69), $t(88)$ = 13.97, p < .001, d = 2.94.

Aggressive behavior

As predicted, participants in the prosocial condition (M = 3.73, SD = 0.73) 40 judged the doctoral student more positively than participants in the neutral condition (M = 3.40, SD = 0.69), $t(88)$ = 2.18, p < .05, d = 0.46.

To test whether indeed the extent to which the songs are prosocial in 41 content (and not any other song features) accounts for the effect of type of music on aggression, judgment of the doctoral student was regressed onto music condition and the prosocial index. In fact, the effect of music condition was no longer significant, β = 0.14, $t(87)$ = 0.75, p = .46, whereas the prosocial index received a significant regression weight, β = 0.44, $t(87)$ = 2.40, p < .05. Thus, one can have confidence that indeed the extent to which the songs are prosocial in content (and not any other song features) accounts for the effect of music exposure on aggression. On the other hand, it should be noted that the manipulation check itself may have affected the dependent measure.

It may be that the manipulation check has primed the concept of helping, and such a prime could reduce aggressive responses. To avoid this possible confound, in Study 5, no manipulation check was assessed between manipulation and main dependent measures.

STUDY 5

So far, the results show that prosocial music exposure decreased aggressive 42 cognition and affect (Studies 1–3) and aggressive behavior (Study 4). However, inasmuch as aggressive behavior and the possible mediators were assessed in different studies, it remains unclear what variable constitutes the mediating path from music exposure to action. Thus, in Study 5, aggressive cognition, affect, and behavior were all assessed. In addition, the third route (arousal) proposed by the GLM on how media exposure influences social behavior was also incorporated. Finally, the measurement of aggressive behavior differs from Study 4 in two important ways. Study 4 assessed the effects of prosocial music exposure on indirect, relational aggression (Crick & Grotpeter, 1995) toward a target person who did not provoke the participant. Study 5 examines the effects of prosocial music exposure on direct, physical aggression toward a target person (administering hot chili sauce) who had insulted the participant.

Method

Participants and design

Participants were 50 adults (24 women and 26 men) of a community sample 43 in Brighton, UK. Two participants (2 men) were excluded from the following analyses. One participant suspected correctly that there was no other individual participating in the study; one participant gave an extreme response on the chili sauce task (more than 5 SD above the mean). Meanage was 29.9 years ($SD = 11.0$). There were 24 participants (12 women and 12 men) in the prosocial condition and 24 participants (11 women and 13 men) in the neutral condition. All participants were tested individually.

Procedure and materials

At the outset, participants learned that the aims of the experiment were to 44 examine (a) their musical preferences and (b) human communication patterns and thus they would be later interacting with another participant of the same sex. As a starting point for this coming interaction, both participants had to write a personal essay. After completion, the participant's essay was taken away to be shown to the other participant (who was, actually, nonexistent) for evaluation. Meanwhile, the participant received the partner's essay (which was, actually, written by the experimenter). A short time later, the experimenter returned the participant's own essay with comments allegedly made by the other participant. All participants received bad evaluations and a concluding comment stating "This is a rather boring essay." This method has been used in several studies to evoke aggression (e.g., Bushman & Baumeister, 1998; Twenge, Baumeister, Tice, & Stucke, 2001).

Participants then listened to either the prosocial or the neutral music (the same songs were used as in Studies 2–4), which they should allegedly later evaluate. Afterwards, measures of aggressive affect, aggressive cognition, and arousal were taken. Concretely, participants responded to the State Hostility Scale, the RATVS, and the Perceived Arousal Scale. 45

Participants were then informed that hot and sweet sauces would be tested in context of another marketing study. Because the experimenter had to be blind for the experimental condition (i.e., whether hot or sweet chili sauce was administered), the participant was asked to administer the chili sauce. The participant learned that the other participant does not like hot spices at all, but that because of good payment would be willing to participate in the marketing study. It was stressed that it was completely up to the participants to decide how much chili sauce they would administer, that the other participant would have to consume all of it, and that the other participant would not learn who administered the sauce. The participant was then shown a bottle of hot chili sauce, a spoon, and a plastic cup. Participants were asked to use the plastic spoon to test the taste of the chili sauce and then to pour the chili sauce into the plastic cup. Actually, participants always got the hot chili sauce to taste and to administer. The administered amount of chili sauce was measured in grams and utilized as a behavioral measure of aggression (Fischer, Kastenmüller, & Greitemeyer, 2010; Lieberman, Solomon, Greenberg, & McGregor, 1999). 46

Finally, participants were thanked and fully debriefed. They were told that their essay had not actually been evaluated and learned that the other participant did not actually exist and thus that no one had to taste the chili sauce. 47

Results and discussion

Responses in the chili sauce task considerably violated the normal distribution so these data were log-transformed. Mean and standard deviations of the main dependent measures as a function of type of music as well as test statistics are reported in Table 3. 48

Aggressive affect (state hostility)

A 2 (music condition: prosocial vs. neutral) × 2 (participant sex) ANOVA revealed the predicted significant main effect for music condition, 49

$F(1,44) = 9.68, p < .01, \eta_p^2 = .18$. Participants in the prosocial music condition reported lower levels of state hostility than did participants in the neutral music condition (see Table 3). The effects for participant sex, $F(1,44) = 1.15$, $p = .29, \eta_p^2 = .03$, and the interaction, $F(1,44) = 0.05, p = .83, \eta_p^2 = .00$, were not significant.

Aggressive cognition (attitudes toward violence)

With regard to attitudes toward war, an ANOVA revealed a significant 50 main effect for music condition, $F(1,44) = 7.50, p < .01, \eta_p^2 = .15$. Participants in the prosocial music condition had more negative war attitudes than did participants in the neutral music condition (see Table 3). The effect for participant sex was marginally significant, $F(1,44) = 3.58$, $p = .07, \eta_p^2 = .08$. In addition, the interaction was significant, $F(1,44) = 5.78, p < .05, \eta_p^2 = .12$. Male participants in the prosocial music condition ($M = 2.26, SD = 0.64$) had more negative war attitudes than did male participants in the neutral music condition ($M = 3.24, SD = 0.69$). In contrast, female participants' attitudes toward war in the prosocial music condition ($M = 2.36, SD = 0.61$) and the neutral music condition ($M = 2.42, SD = 0.68$) did not differ. With regard to attitudes toward penal code violence, participants in the prosocial music condition were less accepting of penal code violence than participants in the neutral music condition, $F(1,44) = 10.31, p < .01, \eta_p^2 = .19$. The effect for participant sex was not significant, $F(1,44) = 0.01, p = .93, \eta_p^2 = .00$. The interaction was marginally significant, $F(1,44) = 3.07, p = .09, \eta_p^2 = .07$. (The effect of music condition on attitudes toward penal code violence was stronger for male participants than for female participants.) With regard to attitudes toward corporal punishment of children, participants in the prosocial music condition were less accepting of corporal punishment of children than participants in the neutral music condition, $F(1,44) = 7.35, p = .01$, $\eta_p^2 = .14$. The effect for participant sex was not significant, $F(1,44) = 0.00$, $p = 1.00, \eta_p^2 = .00$. However, the interaction was significant, $F(1,44) = 4.50, p < .05, \eta_p^2 = .09$. Male participants in the prosocial music condition ($M = 1.25, SD = 0.25$) were less accepting of corporal punishment of children than were male participants in the neutral music condition ($M = 2.22, SD = 0.82$). In contrast, female participants' attitudes toward corporal punishment of children in the prosocial music condition ($M = 1.68, SD = 0.83$) and the neutral music condition ($M = 1.80, SD = 0.65$) did not differ. With regard to attitudes toward intimate violence, the effect for music condition was not significant, $F(1,44) = 0.65, p < .43, \eta_p^2 = .01$. Likewise, the effect for participant sex, $F(1,44) = 0.08, p = .78, \eta_p^2 = .00$, and the interaction, $F(1,44) = 2.81, p = .10, \eta_p^2 = .06$, were not significant.

TABLE 3
Means and standard deviations for responses to the dependent measures as a function of type of music (Study 5).

Dependent measures	Music condition		t(46)	d
	Prosocial	Neutral		
State hostility				
Attitudes toward violence	1.66 (0.27)	2.07 (0.60)	3.09**	0.88
War	2.31 (0.61)	2.86 (0.78)	2.71**	0.79
Penal code violence	2.21 (0.92)	3.07 (0.90)	3.25**	0.95
Corporal punishment of children	2.03 (0.76)	1.46 (0.66)	2.73**	0.80
Intimate violence	1.16 (0.23)	1.23 (0.33)	0.88	0.25
Perceived arousal	3.60 (0.59)	3.81 (0.60)	1.25	0.35
Administered chili sauce	0.38 (0.73)	0.82 (0.53)	2.43*	0.69

Note: Standard deviations are in parentheses.
*$p < .05$.
**$p < .01$.

Arousal

Participants' reported arousal in the prosocial and the neutral music condi- 51 tion did not differ, $F(1,44) = 1.47$, $p = .23$, $\eta_p^2 = .03$ (see Table 3). In addition, the effect for participant sex, $F(1,44) = 0.27$, $p = .60$, $\eta_p^2 = .01$, and the interaction, $F(1,44) = 0.03$, $p = .87$, $\eta_p^2 = .00$, were not significant.

Aggressive behavior (chili sauce)

Participants in the prosocial music condition administered less hot chili sauce 52 than did participants in the neutral music condition, $F(1,44) = 6.57$, $p < .05$, $\eta_p^2 = .13$ (see Table 3). The effect for participant sex was not significant, $F(1,44) = 2.78$, $p = .10$, $\eta_p^2 = .06$. The interaction was marginally significant, $F(1,44) = 3.90$, $p = .06$, $\eta_p^2 = .08$. (The effect of music condition on attitudes toward penal code violence was stronger for female participants than for male participants.)

Mediational analysis

Bivariate correlations between the main dependent measures are reported in 53 Table 4. As can be seen, administered chili sauce only significantly correlated with state hostility.[4] Thus, I tested whether state hostility would mediate the

---

4 To further test whether aggressive cognition might (partially) mediate the effect of song condition on aggressive behavior, those attitude subscales that were highly correlated were combined. However, neither a combination of attitudes towards war and penal code violence nor a combination of attitudes towards war, penal code violence, and corporal punishment was significantly correlated with aggressive behavior (albeit in the predicted direction).

TABLE 4
Intercorrelations among variables (Study 5).

Variable	1	2	3	4	5	6	7
1. State hostility	–						
2. Attitudes toward war	.24	–					
3. Attitudes toward penal code violence	.29*	.73**	–				
4. Attitudes toward corporal punishment	.31*	.68**	.68**	–			
5. Attitudes toward intimate violence	.05	.35*	.39**	.63**	–		
6. Arousal	.26	.27	.26	.26	–.12	–	
7. Administered chili sauce	.37	.25	.19	.12	–.08	.17	–

$^*p < .05.$
$^{**}p < .01.$

effect of music condition on administered chili sauce. To test this potential mediation effect, a bootstrapping analysis based on 1000 bootstraps was run (Preacher & Hayes, 2004). Results showed a significant direct effect of music condition on administered chili sauce, $t = 2.43$, $p < .05$, which was reduced to non-significance, $t = 1.50$, $p = .14$, when controlling for state hostility. Moreover, the indirect effect was significantly different from zero ($p < .05$, 95% confidence interval = −0.47, −0.02). In sum, it appears that the effect of listening to prosocial music on aggressive behavior is mediated by differences in the reported aggressive affect.[5]

GENERAL DISCUSSION

Previous research has provided abundant evidence that exposure to antisocial 54 media increases aggression and aggression-related variables (e.g., Anderson et al., 2010; Bushman & Huesmann, 2006). In contrast, research concerning whether media exposure may also decrease aggressive outcomes has been very limited. Based on the GLM as a theoretical framework, the present research aimed to fill this gap. In fact, the present five studies showed that listening to prosocial (relative to neutral) music decreased aggression and

---

5 Inasmuch as the effect of music condition on aggressive cognition was stronger for male than for female participants, it may be that aggressive cognition mediates the effect of music condition on aggressive behavior for male participants only. However, including male participants only, the bivariate correlations between measures of aggressive cognition and behavior were not significant, all r values (25) <.18, all p values >.41.

aggression-related variables. Study 1 revealed that exposure to prosocial music reduced the accessibility of aggressive thoughts. Study 2 replicated and extended this finding by using a different measure for aggressive cognition and by controlling for mood and arousal. Study 3 showed that prosocial music exposure did not only decrease aggressive cognition but also aggressive affect. Study 4 then provided a first test of the idea that prosocial music exposure decreases aggressive behavior. In fact, participants who had listened to prosocial music were less aggressive than participants who had listened to neutral music. Because measurement of the possible mediators (aggressive cognition and affect) may change subsequent measures of aggressive behavior (e.g., Lindsay & Anderson, 2000), behavior and the possible mediators were assessed in different studies. Thus, it remained unclear what variable constituted the mediating path from music exposure to action. Study 5 provided some initial evidence about the causal mechanism: it appears that prosocial music exposure decreases state hostility, which in turn reduces aggressive behavior. Taken together, these studies provide supportive evidence of the predictive validity of the GLM for the effects of listening to prosocial music on antisocial outcomes. On a more general level, by documenting (a) media effects on aggressive behavior and (b) the mediating path from media exposure to action, the present research offers the first comprehensive test of the effects of prosocial media exposure on aggression and aggression-related variables.

IMPLICATIONS, LIMITATIONS, AND FUTURE DIRECTIONS

The present set of studies lends further credence to GLMs assumption that 55 media content significantly influences the consequences of media exposure. Whereas listening to antisocial music increases aggressive cognition, affect (Anderson et al., 2003), and behavior (Fischer & Greitemeyer, 2006), listening to prosocial music decreases it. Moreover, the present research addressed why listening to prosocial (relative to neutral) music decreases aggressive behavior. Based on the GLM, it was examined whether prosocial music would activate two of the main routes (cognition and affect) proposed to mediate the effects of media exposure on behavior (while measuring and controlling for the arousal route of the model). In fact, listening to prosocial music decreased aggressive cognitions and affect. However, only the latter significantly instigated aggressive behavior. Thus, it appears that the effect of prosocial music on aggressive behavior operates through the affective (rather than the cognitive) route of the model.

However, it is important to note that, in Study 5 of the present research, 56 there was a positive (although not significant) association between (the combination of the four measures of) aggressive cognition and aggressive behavior ($r = .18$). If sample size were bigger (and thus statistical power improved), aggressive cognition might have (partially) accounted for the effect of music condition on aggressive behavior. In addition, other measures of aggressive cognition may show stronger associations with aggressive behavior. Finally, only one behavioral measure was employed (i.e., participant's direct, physical aggressive behavior as a response to a provocation, which might be a behavioral response that is especially prone to be influenced by affective measures). Thus, future research may well find that, under certain circumstances, prosocial music does decrease (e.g., nonprovoked) aggressive behavior not only because of reduced aggressive affect but also because of reduced aggressive cognition.

Interestingly, however, the effect of prosocial music on prosocial behavior 57 also appears to be mediated by affective rather than cognitive variables (Greitemeyer, 2009b). Although listening to prosocial music increases both the accessibility of prosocial thoughts and empathy, only empathy instigated helping behavior. In contrast, the effects of playing video games on social behavior are mediated by cognitive rather than affective variables. Playing antisocial video games increases both aggressive cognition and affect, but only cognition instigates aggressive behavior (e.g., Anderson & Dill, 2000). Likewise, playing prosocial video games increases the accessibility of prosocial thoughts (Greitemeyer & Osswald, 2010) and empathy (Greitemeyer et al., in press), but only accessibility of prosocial thoughts elicits helping behavior (Greitemeyer & Osswald, 2010). Finally, cognitive variables also account for the effects of racing game exposure on risk taking: playing a racing game alters self-perceptions of being a reckless driver, which in turn increases risk taking behavior (Fischer et al., 2009).

Combined, these findings appear to suggest that the effects of music expo- 58 sure on social behavior work through the affective route, whereas the effects of playing video games work through the cognitive route of the GLM. It seems fair to conclude that the GLM provides a useful framework for explaining the effects of media exposure on interpersonal behavior, but more research is needed to further refine the model. For instance, Anderson et al. (2003) found that listening to antisocial music increased aggressive cognition and affect, but no aggressive behavior was measured. Fischer and Greitemeyer (2006) found that antisocial music increased aggressive behavior, but they did not test for mediation. Thus, future research investigating the underlying mechanisms by which exposure to antisocial music instigates aggressive behavior would be fruitful. Likewise, future research should examine whether and why exposure to prosocial video games decreases aggressive behavior. Greitemeyer and Osswald (2009) showed that playing prosocial video games reduced aggressive cognition, but no aggressive behavior was measured. Perhaps listening to antisocial music increases aggressive behavior via increased aggressive affect, whereas playing prosocial video games decreases aggressive behavior via decreased aggressive cognition. Such findings would further suggest that the effects of music and video game exposure on social behavior are similar (both antisocial music and antisocial video games increase aggressive outcomes and decrease prosocial outcomes, whereas both prosocial music and prosocial video games decrease aggressive outcomes and increase prosocial outcomes), but the underlying mechanisms are different (music effects operate through affective variables, whereas video game effects operate through cognitive variables).

It is noteworthy that prosocial music decreased aggression and aggression- 59 related variables although participants were exposed to only a few songs. If people repeatedly listen to prosocial music, aggressive tendencies might be even more reduced. To test this claim, longitudinal studies on the effects of exposure to prosocial music on aggression and aggression-related variables are clearly needed. Such a study should be also interesting in terms of how prosocial music exposure decreases aggressive behavior. As pointed out by the GLM, repeated encounters with prosocial media may affect long-term behavior through the development and construction of knowledge structures (see also Huesmann & Miller, 1994). Thus, it may be that long-term effects of prosocial music on aggressive behavior are mediated by aggressive cognition (and/or by aggressive affect).

Finally, one may wonder to what extent both the music and the song 60 lyrics contribute to the observed effects of music exposure on aggression and aggression-related variables. Would the music alone in absence of the lyrics produce similar effects? Would the prosocial song lyrics exclusively reduce antisocial responses? Or, is the interplay between music and song lyrics obligatory to produce a unique set of effects of music exposure? Note that the music characteristics of the prosocial and neutral songs were controlled by matching genre and mood and arousal properties. Note also that Study 4 provides some evidence that the song lyrics account for the observed effects in that the effect of music condition on aggressive behavior was mediated by differences in the perceived content of the song lyrics. Thus, it appears that the effects of prosocial music on aggression are (in part) a result of the prosocial content of the lyrics. Nevertheless, future research that separately examines the effects of prosocial music (without the lyrics), prosocial song lyrics (without the music), and the combination of prosocial music and song lyrics would be informative in this regard.

CONCLUSION

Music exposure is omnipresent in our daily life. For instance, the average 61 American college-age student listens to music for over 4 hours a day (Rubin et al., 2001). Given this amount, there is considerable interest in the effects of listening to music. Previous research has almost exclusively focused on negative effects of exposure to music with antisocial lyrics. However, it is important to note that individuals do not only listen to antisocial music, but to other music as well. In fact, some of the prosocial songs used in the present research have been very popular. "We are the world" has been named the biggest-selling single of all time; "Love generation" was the most popular song in Germany in 2006; "Ein bißchen Frieden" won the Eurovision Song Contest and sold more than 3 million copies (the English version "A little peace" topped the charts in the United Kingdom). Thus, the present findings are not only of theoretical significance, but have important practical implications as well in suggesting that depending on the content of the song lyrics music exposure may reduce aggressive encounters.

REFERENCES

Anderson, C. A., Benjamin, A. J., Wood, P. K., & Bonacci, A. M. (2006). Development and testing of the Velicer Attitudes Toward Violence Scale: Evidence for a four-factor model. *Aggressive Behavior, 32,* 122–136.

Anderson, C. A., & Carnagey, N. L. (2009). Causal effects of violent sports video games on aggression: Is it competitiveness or violent content? *Journal of Experimental Social Psychology, 45,* 731–739.

Anderson, C. A., Carnagey, N. L., & Eubanks, J. (2003). Exposure to violent media: The effects of songs with violent lyrics on aggressive thoughts and feelings. *Journal of Personality and Social Psychology, 84,* 960–971.

Anderson, C. A., Deuser, W. E., & DeNeve, K. (1995). Hot temperatures, hostile affect, hostile cognition, and arousal: Tests of a general model of affective aggression. *Personality and Social Psychology Bulletin, 21,* 434–448.

Anderson, C. A., & Dill, K. E. (2000). Video games and aggressive thoughts, feelings, and behavior in the laboratory and in life. *Journal of Personality and Social Psychology, 78,* 772–790.

Anderson, C. A., Gentile, D. A., & Buckley, K. E. (2007). *Violent video game effect on children and adolescents. Theory, research and public policy.* New York: Oxford University Press.

Anderson, C. A., Shibuya, A., Ihori, N., Swing, E. L., Bushman, B. J., Sakamoto, A., et al. (2010). Violent video game effects on aggression, empathy, and prosocial behavior in Eastern and Western countries. *Psychological Bulletin, 136,* 151–173.

Arnett, J. (1991). Heavy metal music and reckless behavior among adolescents. *Journal of Youth and Adolescence, 20,* 573–592.

Arnett, J. (1992). The soundtrack of recklessness: Musical preferences and reckless behavior among adolescents. *Journal of Adolescent Research, 7,* 313–331.

Berkowitz, L. (1989). The frustration–aggression hypothesis: Examination and reformulation. *Psychological Bulletin, 106,* 59–73.

Buckley, K. E., & Anderson, C. A. (2006). A theoretical model of the effects and consequences of playing video games. In P. Vorderer, & J. Bryant (Eds.), *Playing video games: Motives, responses, and consequences* (pp. 363–378). Mahwah, NJ: Lawrence Erlbaum Associates.

Bushman, B. J. (1995). Moderating role of trait aggressiveness in the effects of violent media on aggression. *Journal of Personality and Social Psychology, 69,* 950–960.

Bushman, B. J. (1996). Individual differences in the extent and development of aggressive cognitive–associative networks. *Personality and Social Psychology Bulletin, 22,* 811–819.

Bushman, B. J., & Anderson, C. A. (1998). Methodology in the study of aggression: Integrating experimental and nonexperimental findings. In R. G. Geen, & E. Donnerstein (Eds.), *Human aggression: Theories, research, and implications for social policy* (pp. 167–202). San Diego, CA: Academic Press.

Bushman, B. J., & Anderson, C. A. (2002). Violent video games and hostile expectations: A test of the general aggression model. *Personality and Social Psychology Bulletin, 28*, 1679–1686.

Bushman, B. J., & Baumeister, R. F. (1998). Threatened egotism, narcissism, self-esteem, and direct and displaced aggression: Does self-love or self-hate lead to violence? *Journal of Personality and Social Psychology, 75*, 219–229.

Bushman, B. J., & Huesmann, L. R. (2006). Short-term and long-term effects of violent media on aggression in children and adults. *Archives of Pediatrics & Adolescent Medicine, 160*, 348–352.

Buss, A. H., & Perry, M. (1992). The aggression questionnaire. *Journal of Personality and Social Psychology, 63*, 452–459.

Carnagey, N. L., & Anderson, C. A. (2007). Changes in attitudes towards war and violence after September 11, 2001. *Aggressive Behavior, 33*, 118–129.

Cialdini, R. B., Baumann, D. J., & Kenrick, D. T. (1981). Insights from sadness: A three-step model of the development of altruism as hedonism. *Developmental Review, 1*, 207–223.

Coyne, S. M., Nelson, D. A., Lawton, F., Haslam, S., Rooney, L., Titterington, L., et al. (2008). The effects of viewing physical and relational aggression in the media: Evidence for a cross-over effect. *Journal of Experimental Social Psychology, 44*, 1551–1554.

Crick, N. R., & Grotpeter, J. K. (1995). Relational aggression, gender, and social–psychological adjustment. *Child Development, 66*, 710–722.

Dunlap, R. E., Van Liere, K. D., Mertig, A. G., & Emmet-Jones, R. (2000). Measuring endorsement of the new ecological paradigm: A revised NEP scale. *Journal of Social Issues, 56*, 425–442.

Fischer, P., & Greitemeyer, T. (2006). Music and aggression. The impact of sexual–aggressive song lyrics on aggression-related thoughts, emotions and behavior toward the same and the opposite sex. *Personality and Social Psychology Bulletin, 32*, 1165–1176.

Fischer, P., Greitemeyer, T., Morton, T., Kastenmüller, A., Postmes, T., Frey, D., et al. (2009). The racing-game-effect: Why do video racing games increase risk-taking inclinations? *Personality and Social Psychology Bulletin, 35*, 1395–1409.

Fischer, P., Kastenmüller, A., & Greitemeyer, T. (2010). Media violence and the self: The impact of personalized gaming characters in aggressive video games on aggressive behavior. *Journal of Experimental Social Psychology, 46*, 192–195.

Gan, S., Zillman, D., & Mitrook, M. (1997). Stereotyping effect of Black women's sexual rap on White audiences. *Basic and Applied Social Psychology, 19*, 381–399.

Gentile, D. A., Anderson, C. A., Yukawa, S., Ihori, N., Saleem, M., Ming, L. K., et al. (2009). The effects of prosocial video games on prosocial behaviors: International evidence from correlational, longitudinal, and experimental studies. *Personality and Social Psychology Bulletin, 35*, 752–763.

Gentile, D. A., Lynch, P. J., Linder, J. R., & Walsh, D. A. (2004). The effects of violent video game habits on adolescent hostility, aggressive behaviors, and school performance. *Journal of Adolescence, 27*, 5–22.

Greitemeyer, T. (2009a). Effects of songs with prosocial lyrics on prosocial thoughts, affect, and behavior. *Journal of Experimental Social Psychology, 45*, 186–190.

Greitemeyer, T. (2009b). Effects of songs with prosocial lyrics on prosocial behavior: Further evidence and a mediating mechanism. *Personality and Social Psychology Bulletin, 35*, 1500–1511.

Greitemeyer, T., & Osswald, S. (2009). Prosocial video games reduce aggressive cognitions. *Journal of Experimental Social Psychology, 45*, 896–900.

Greitemeyer, T., & Osswald, S. (2010). Effects of prosocial video games on prosocial behavior. *Journal of Personality and Social Psychology, 98*, 211–221.

Greitemeyer, T., Osswald, S., & Brauer, M. (in press). Playing prosocial video games increases empathy and decreases schadenfreude. Emotion. doi:10.1037/a0020194.

Hearold, S. (1986). A synthesis of 1043 effects of television on social behavior. In G. Comstock (Ed.), *Public communication of behavior* (pp. 65–133). San Diego, CA: Academic Press.

Huesmann, L. R., & Miller, L. S. (1994). Long-term effects of repeated exposure to media violence in childhood. In L. R. Huesmann (Ed.), *Aggressive behavior: Current perspectives* (pp. 153–186). New York: Plenum Press.

Lieberman, J. D., Solomon, S., Greenberg, J., & McGregor, H. A. (1999). A hot new way to measure aggression: Hot sauce allocation. *Aggressive Behavior, 25*, 331–348.

Lindsay, J. L., & Anderson, C. A. (2000). From antecedent conditions to violent actions: A general affective aggression model. *Personality and Social Psychology Bulletin, 26*, 533–547.

Mares, M. L., & Woodard, E. (2005). Positive effects of television on children's social interactions: A meta-analysis. *Media Psychology, 7*, 301–322.

North, A. C., Desborough, L., & Skarstein, L. (2005). Musical preference, deviance, and attitudes towards music celebrities. *Personality and Individual Differences, 38*, 1903–1914.

Preacher, K. J., & Hayes, A. F. (2004). SPSS and SAS procedures for estimating indirect effects in simple mediation models. *Behavior Research Methods, Instruments, & Computers, 36*, 717–731.

Rubin, A. M., West, D. V., & Mitchell, W. S. (2001). Differences in aggression, attitudes toward women, and distrust as reflected in popular music preferences. *Media Psychology, 3*, 25–42.

Stucke, T. S., & Baumeister, R. F. (2006). Ego depletion and aggressive behavior: Is the inhibition of aggression a limited resource? *European Journal of Social Psychology, 36*, 1–13.

Twenge, J. M., Baumeister, R. F., Tice, D. M., & Stucke, T. S. (2001). If you can't join them, beat them: Effects of social exclusion on aggressive behavior. *Journal of Personality and Social Psychology, 81*, 1058–1069.

Watson, D., Clark, L. A., & Tellegen, A. (1988). Development and validation of brief measures of positive and negative affect: The PANAS scales. *Journal of Personality and Social Psychology, 54*, 1063–1070.

QUESTIONS

1. How does the study reported on in this article differ from related earlier studies?
2. What is the hypothesis of this study?
3. What are some of the effects of exposure to antisocial media?
4. What is the most significant result of each of the five studies described in this article?
5. What, according to the author, are the limitations of the studies reported on in this article?
6. What related studies does the author recommend be undertaken in the future?
7. Select any one of the five studies described in this article. Write a brief (one to three paragraphs) analysis and synthesis of this study, as it might appear in your college or university newspaper.

8. Do the results of the research presented here conform to your own experience? Do you think you are more mellow after you listen to prosocial music? Do you think your friends are?

9. In the play *The Mourning Bride*, produced in 1697 and written by William Congreve, one of the characters famously says that "Music hath charms to soothe a savage breast, to soften rocks, or bend a knotted oak." Relate this quote to the article.

10. The author states, "If people repeatedly listen to prosocial music, aggressive tendencies might be even more reduced." Do you agree?

11. Will this study have any effect on your own choice of the music you listen to?

12. If you were the parent of a 14-year-old, would you monitor your child's music to make certain he or she is not listening to too much antisocial music?

This article was published in *Lit: Literature Interpretation Theory*, volume 22, issue 2, 2011, pages 79–95.

Evil Children in Film and Literature: Notes Toward a Genealogy[†]

Karen J. Renner*

When I sent out a call for essays on evil children in film and literature, never 1 in my wildest nightmares did I imagine that I would end up encountering—to quote Obi Wan Kenobi—such a " "wretched hive of scum and villainy." " I had feared that the topic would be too outré to be taken seriously. I was dead wrong. In fact, the number and range of submissions that arrived were so impressive that the editors of *LIT: Literature Interpretation Theory* generously allowed me to compile a two part issue: the second collection of essays will comprise the journal's subsequent issue. A number of scholars have examined the role of children in literature and film, some even focusing upon evil children in particular, but this pervasive plot convention has not been given adequate attention.[1] I hope that these special issues of *LIT* are one step in that direction.

EVIL CHILDREN IN FILM AND LITERATURE: A BRIEF HISTORY

In 2010, Meredith O'Hayre published a book entitled *The Scream Queen's* 2 *Survival Guide*, which promised to teach us how, if suddenly plunged into a horror movie, we could conquer its clichés and emerge if not unscathed, then at least alive. The subtitle of the book offers three brief directives: to *Avoid Machetes, Defeat Evil Children, and Steer Clear of Bloody Dismemberment.* That evil children—and I will discuss that problematic term in a moment— are mentioned alongside machetes and dismemberment speaks to the serious and pervasive threat they have come to represent within the horror genre. But this threat seems largely a contemporary one: we would be hard-pressed, I think, to discover many instances of wicked youngsters in earlier literature, even though plenty of examples existed in the real world.[2] However, during the second half of the twentieth century, such figures began to possess the

---

[†] Karen J. Renner, "Evil Children in Film and Literature: Notes Toward a Genealogy," in *Lit: Literature Interpretation Theory*, 22(2), June 2011, pages 79–95. Reprinted by permission of Taylor & Francis Ltd, http://www.tandf.co.uk/journals.

* Karen J. Renner is a Visiting Instructor of American Literature at Northern Arizona University. An excerpted version of her dissertation, *Perverse Subjects: Drunks, Gamblers, Prostitutes, and Murderers,* recently appeared in *Nineteenth-Century Literature,* and she is revising *Perverse Subjects* for publication. In addition, she is working on a second book tentatively titled *Bad Seeds and Injured Innocents: The Evil Child in the Contemporary Imagination.*

imaginations of writers and filmmakers alike. Regrettably, due to space restrictions, I am unable to offer a comprehensive survey, so the brief history I will provide will focus primarily on British and American contributions.

Around the 1950s, the subgenre of evil children really hit its stride. What is noteworthy about these early texts is their tendency to claim that evil children are born bad. In Ray Bradbury's "The Small Assassin" (1946), a newborn emerges with an innate desire (and ability) to kill; while no motive or reason is confirmed, the baby's father, David, surmises that since "[i]nsects are born self-sufficient" and "most mammal and birds adjust" in a few weeks, perhaps "a few babies out of all the millions born are instantaneously able to move, see, hear, think" (383). Resenting its removal from the womb where it was "at rest, fed, comforted, unbothered," such a child, David muses, would have the capacity to avenge all these perceived wrongs (384). Bradbury's "The Veldt" (originally published as "The World the Children Made" in 1950) picks up similar themes in a futuristic world in which technology can transform playrooms into virtual reality spaces that catch "the telepathic emanations" of whoever's in the room and "and create life to fill their every desire" (268). When the world the children make takes on a menacing air, their father decides to disengage the room, but the children beg for one last round of play, and he acquiesces. The children then conjure virtual lions to take vengeance on their parents. Richard Matheson's very short story "Born of Man and Woman" (1950) is narrated by a monstrously deformed child who never clearly details its own appearance, but the fact that it describes its blood as an "ugly green" and refers at one point to "all my legs" suggests it is a human-sized, spider-like creature (514, 515). The child is kept locked away in a basement and is beaten regularly and thus is initially an object of some pity. At the end of the story, however, the child alludes to prior acts of aggression and hints that more are soon to come: "I have a bad anger with mother and father. I will show them. I will do what I did that once. I will screech and laugh loud. I will run on the walls. Last I will hang head down by all my legs and laugh and drip green all over until they are sorry" (515). While the creature is incensed by its parents' abuse, it seems to have been quite violent to begin with.

The tendency to see evil children as inherently so continued to dominate later works from the 1950s, such as Jerome Bixby's short story "It's a Good Life" (1953), William Golding's *The Lord of the Flies* (1954), John Wyndham's *The Midwich Cuckoos* (1957), and one of the most famous stories about an evil child, William March's *The Bad Seed* (1954), all of which quickly were adapted for the screen.[3] Anthony, the three-year-old terror in Bixby's short story, can read the minds of the adults around him, and if they or anything else displeases him, he punishes the transgression in whatever way he sees fit simply by thinking it so (though on the suggestion of his father, he kindly

3

4

teleports his dead victims out to a cornfield, so that the sight of them will not upset the townspeople). In the opening scene of the story, Anthony is controlling a rat with his mind, "making it do tricks" (523); by the end of the scene, the rat has "devoured half its belly, and... died from pain" (525). Anthony's abilities and tendency to act out in rage is inborn: "when Anthony had crept from the womb and old Doc Bates... had screamed and dropped him and tried to kill him,... Anthony had whined and done the thing" (541). Similarly, Golding himself has claimed the boys in *Lord of the Flies* descend into savagery because they "are suffering from the terrible disease of being human" (89), and Wyndham's beastly blond children are at least half extra-terrestrial, born with no natural attachments to their human caretakers and, like Anthony, able to punish whomever stands in their way just by willing it. In titling his novel *The Bad Seed*, March also implies that evil is a congenital condition, and the book confirms this claim, for Rhoda Penmark, the child at the center of the novel, seems to have inherited her penchant for murder from her grandmother, the accomplished serial killer Bessie Denker.

This interest in evil children continued into the 1960s, though with some-   5
what less ferocity. These texts were less interested in children who were born bad but rather in those who had been made so. Jack Clayton's adaptation of Henry James's 1898 novel *The Turn of the Screw, The Innocents* (1961), adds details to emphasize the evil tendencies of little Miles and Flora. In one scene of Clayton's film, for example, the governess observes Flora watching with fascination as a butterfly slowly dies in a spider's web, and in another the governess discovers a dove with a broken neck under Miles's pillow; soon after, Miles bestows upon her a far-too-lengthy kiss, then leans back on his pillow and gazes at her with dreamy eyes that bespeak romantic if not erotic desire. While these details make the children more suspect, Clayton also makes it clear that their abnormal behavior is due to their "possession" by the ghosts of former caretakers who corrupted them. During the 1960s, Shirley Jackson, Flannery O'Connor, and Joyce Carol Oates also turned their Gothic eyes upon the subject of children. In Jackson's novel *We Have Always Lived in the Castle* (1962)—the last she was to publish before her death in 1965—the eighteen-year-old narrator confesses to having murdered her parents, aunt, and younger brother six years before by lacing the sugar bowl with arsenic. O'Connor's short story "The Lame Shall Enter First" (1965) features a street urchin named Rufus who convinces the son of the man who kindly takes him in to hang himself, and Oates's *Expensive People* (1968) opens with the pro-vocative line "I was a child murderer" (3), and the narrator, Richard Everett, goes on to reveal that the act that earned him this designation was com-mitted at the tender age of eleven. The decade then concluded with Ira Levin's *Rosemary's Baby* (1967), one of the most famous stories about the most evil

child of them all: the son of Satan himself. Roman Polanski adapted the novel into a film the following year, and both received popular and critical acclaim. While many narratives in the 1960s had scrutinized the psychological forces and familial dynamics that might produce an evil child, *Rosemary's Baby* took the approach more popular in the previous decade, presenting the evil child as simply born that way.

Influenced by and perhaps hoping to capitalize upon the success of *Rosemary's Baby,* authors in the 1970s and early 1980s produced an enormous number of texts about evil kids, many of which were instantly seared into cultural memory, and directors were quick to offer their cinematic renditions. In fact, the 1970s produced a number of fictional evil children, so many, in fact, that one *Newsweek* editorial worried that the era was one of "growing anti-child sentiment," pointing to a recent poll of 10,000 mothers, 70% of whom said that if given the choice again, they would opt not to have children (Maynard 11). Although *Rosemary's Baby* steered many in the direction of the demonic, both types of evil child—the satanic and the psychologically deviant—were explored. The most successful venture into the first category was *The Exorcist.*[4] Indeed, William Friedkin's 1973 adaptation of William Peter Blatty's 1971 novel caused such a stir that, according to Nick Cull, many audience members fainted and one even "charged the screen in an attempt to kill the demon" (46). Friedkin's film even prompted a scene-by-scene Turkish remake entitled *Seytan* (1974).[5] Richard Donner's 1976 movie *The Omen* gave birth to yet another demonic threat, Damien, whose name has become shorthand for monstrous youngsters of all kinds. Thomas Tryon's bestselling novel *The Other* (1971), however, offered psychological rather than metaphysical explanations for his evil child. In the book, eleven-year-old Niles commits a series of disturbing and violent acts, which he attributes to his twin, Holland, whom we later discover is dead. *The Other* received a cinematic tribute in 1972, and though neither are well known today, Tryon's focus on insanity rather than demonic possession helped set the stage for later texts that would increasingly examine childhood manifestations of dangerous derangements.

It was also during this decade that several writers who would become our virtuosos of horror launched their careers with stories centering around evil children. Dean Koontz started early, publishing *Demon Child* in 1971 under the pseudonym Deanna Dwyer.[6] However, his first big success in the subgenre came with *Demon Seed* (1973), which tells the story of a woman impregnated by the computer that controls her house, Proteus, so that it can better understand human nature; the book was made into a 1977 film starring Julie Christie.[7] In 1976, Anne Rice published the first and most popular of her *Vampire Chronicles, Interview with the Vampire,* a considerable portion of which is devoted to a child vampire, Claudia. The relish with which Claudia feeds—"I want some more," Claudia says in a petulant voice after feeding on her first human (93)—while all the while exuding the charms of young girl-hood is one of the most horrifying aspects of the novel. Stephen King, too, first received serious attention after publishing his novel *Carrie,* and Brian De Palma's 1976 cinematic adaptation only bolstered his reputation. King promptly went on to write several other stories about evil children, including "Children of the Corn" (1977), *The Shining* (1977), *Firestarter* (1980), and *Pet Sematary* (1983), all of which were eventually made into movies. Indeed, the 1984 adaptation of *Children of the Corn* has prompted an unrivalled franchise of evil children, with six sequels and a recent remake in 2009.

These early horror texts, Gary Hoppenstand has argued, were largely responsible for moving horror from a peripheral genre to a mainstream concern, making room for other lesser-known writers who, at least momentarily, made a career out of books about evil children, including John Saul, Andrew Neiderman, and Ruby Jean Jensen.[8] As a result, the covers of novels from the late 1970s to the early 1990s began to feature a veritable bevy of creepy kids, as Will Errickson has shown in his blog *Too Much Horror Fiction.*[9] Even canonical authors called upon the trope of the evil child, such as Toni Morrison with *Beloved* (1987) and Doris Lessing with *The Fifth Child* (1988), the latter of which Daniel Sullivan and Jeff Greenberg will examine in detail in their essay in this volume. Even television proved eager to get in on the action. Bart Simpson made his debut on the *Tracey Ullman Show* in 1987, and though Bart is more errant than evil, he paved the way for one of the most despicable cartoon children ever to make an appearance: Eric Cartman of *South Park* (1997–).[10] Soon after, the creators of *Family Guy* (1999) would offer their own animated evil child in Stewie Griffin. 8

Nowadays, the evil child is almost a trite plot device. The Internet Movie Database, imdb.com, lets you to search for films using the keyword of "evil child," and Netflix allows you to cater your "Storylines" taste preferences to announce that you "often" watch movies that feature "evil kids," thus ensuring that Netflix will make relevant recommendations for you in the future.[11] The contributions of this century's filmmakers—William Wandless will introduce us to several noteworthy examples in his insightful essay—promise to quickly eclipse those of the prior century: of the over two hundred films I have identified that portray some kind of evil child, over one hundred, or almost half, have been produced since the year 2000. Television has succumbed to the same phenomenon: it seems that every season of *Law and Order: Special Victims Unit* offers at least one episode that centers upon a wicked adolescent of some kind,[12] and even reality television has ventured into the genre in the United States and the UK with *Nanny 911* (2004–) and *Supernanny* 9

(2005–), both of which display a series of badly behaved though ultimately redeemable youngsters. A common element of video games,[13] evil children have even crept into children's literature, most prominently in the form of Tom Riddle in the *Harry Potter* series (a figure Holly Blackford investigates in her article) and in the children who fight to the death in Suzanne Collins's popular trilogy, *The Hunger Games*.[14]

A DISCLAIMER ABOUT TERMINOLOGY

By now, it has probably become obvious that the term "evil children" is far 10 too simplistic to account for the range and complexity of characters to whom I have applied it. To be sure, both parts of the term are problematic. Defining the term "child" poses difficulty since the laws that govern certain rights— voting, drinking alcohol, consenting to sex—vary, each suggesting that a different age marks the boundary between adult and child. And these laws differ again by nation and, within this country, sometimes even by state. For the sake of simplicity, I will rely on markers of citizenship and define a "child" as anyone under the age of 18. Even far more fraught is the word "evil." Hard enough to apply to adults, the term becomes even more difficult to apply to children who often lack the maturity and forethought necessary for moral decision-making. Who, out of the crowd of children I've discussed, constitutes a truly *evil* child? Is it *The Bad Seed's* Rhoda Penmark, who at the age of eight bludgeons a classmate to death with her shoes because he wins the penmanship medal she covets and who burns alive a man she fears has evidence of the murder she committed?[15] Is it Damien from *The Omen,* the son of Satan, who, among other evil deeds, wills his nanny to hang herself, pushes his adopted mother over a high balcony, and at the end of the film smiles coyly into the camera to show us just how much he's enjoying himself? Is it Jack and Emily Poe from the 2008 film *Home Movie* who slaughter all of their pets—progressing from goldfish to frog to the family cat and dog—and then butcher their parents? Certainly, these children seem to fit the bill of "evil child" pretty straightforwardly.

But applying that label becomes harder when we consider less clear-cut 11 examples. What do we do, for example, with Regan in *The Exorcist*? When demon-possessed, Regan hurls obscenities, violent blows, and pea-green vomit at her mother and the priests who come to help her, but once exorcised, she turns back into the innocent adolescent she was before her possession. Isn't it more accurate to say that Regan is temporarily corrupted rather than evil? Scalpel-wielding Gage of *Pet Sematary* is similarly problematic, for he has returned from the dead and thus is more zombie than boy. The children in *Village of the Damned,* as I've noted, are at least half extraterrestrial, the triad of ten-year-old killers in *Bloody Birthday* (1981) have been affected in some way by the solar eclipse during which they were born, and the homicidal adolescents in both the 2006 film *The Plague* and the 2008 film *The Children* appear to have been infected by some mysterious disease; all of these children are more possessed than inherently evil. And what about the carnivorous newborns featured in such films as *It's Alive* (1974) and the 2008 film *Grace*? These babies emerge from their mother's womb with a thirst for human blood, but we can't really say that their intentions are "evil" or even malicious. Like any other born predator, they are just doing what they need to do to survive.

While "evil children" is admittedly an inadequate catch-all phrase, these 12 figures, I would argue, play a similar role: they force us to consider the age-old question about the nature of humankind. Is the evil child the result of an imperfect environment and thus redeemable, or a sign of inherent corruption? Our explanation for the evil child mirrors the way we view ourselves: is there evil in the world because we have gone astray, or because we have a natural propensity for wickedness and cruelty? Because the answers to these questions are culturally determined and shift throughout time, different categories of evil child have emerged, each offering a response to suit the *zeitgeist*. Even when the dominant type of evil children during a particular epoch cannot easily be labeled "evil," this fact alone tells us much about the predominant ideologies and presumptions that prevent a more straightforward type of evil child from forming in the cultural imagination. Casting my net wide allows me to determine what sorts of "evil" children prevailed during different eras and why their particular brand of evil was so compelling. It is these categories I will be concerned with in my introduction to the second issue of "Evil Children in Film and Literature."

MONSTROUS INFANTS, UNCANNY THROWBACKS, YOUNG SOCIOPATHS, AND THE RIDDLE OF *HARRY POTTER*

The essays included in this issue certainly have cast their net wide. In "My 13 Baby Ate the Dingo: The Visual Construction of the Monstrous Infant in Horror Film," Steffen Hantke explores a technique he terms *visual reticence*—a director's refusal, for at least most of the film, to provide viewers with a clear visual image of the creature (a technique used to its fullest potential in *The Blair Witch Project* [1999]). Hantke argues against the common perception that visual reticence is a more sophisticated and effective means of creating terror and instead examines other factors that influence its deployment, using *Rosemary's Baby* and *It's Alive* to illustrate his points. *Rosemary's Baby,* Hantke argues, is more interested in exploring the pressures of motherhood and the delusions it may cause the isolated and possibly hysterical Rosemary than it is in the physical being of the antichrist, and this partly explains Polanski's decision to withhold a final visual disclosure of the eponymous child. By contrast, Cohen's *It's Alive,* which features a lethal newborn, is more of a "sociological meditation," as Hantke puts it, "on parental responsibility, the ambiguous allegiances between family and community, and the hardships that occur when children alienate parents from the larger community" (103). As a result, Cohen chooses to construct his movie so that the baby arrives early in the film, and characters and viewers immediately are given bloody proof of its existence in the ravaged bodies of the murdered hospital staff that attended its birth. Because Cohen's film is interested not in psychological monsters but rather in the way that society responds to monsters that actually exist, "the materiality" of Cohen's creature, Hantke concludes, "is its very point" (107) and thus must be displayed and confirmed.

And yet as Hantke notes, Cohen still relies somewhat on visual reticence 14 in that he allows very few clear or sustained shots of the monstrous baby. Hantke argues that Cohen's choice here is less a thematic concern and more a practical one: the special effects technology available in the early 1970s would not have allowed Cohen to construct a very convincing monster. Although Cohen acknowledges the absurdity of the film's premise and the inadequacy of his special effects in several campy moments of self-effacing humor, he refrains from sliding too much into comedy because, Hantke insists, "*It's Alive* is at the core a deeply serious film" (107). Computer Generated Imagery (CGI) has become refined and inexpensive enough today to be used within even relatively low-budget films, and Hantke concludes his essay by considering the developments that may occur within the monstrous infant subgenre as result. To do so, he analyzes two recent films, a 2008 remake of *It's Alive* by Joseph Rusnak and Vincenzo Natali's *Splice* (2009), which centers around Dren, a creature concocted by parents Elsa and Clive whose DNA is an engineered mix of human and animal genes. Hantke explores the reasons that would make Rusnak almost entirely reject and Natali fully embrace the potential of CGI. Hantke concludes that Rusnak's decision is merely the (failed) attempt of a would-be auteurist to make his end product more respectable by choosing the putatively more sophisticated style of visual reticence. Natali's converse preference is not motivated simply by a vain desire to show off the technological prowess of himself and his crew, argues Hantke, but rather, as with Cohen's film, the monster's physicality is crucial to the movie's thematic concerns. As Hantke explains, *Splice* reveals that even *this* family displays all the "darkest enactments of [the] Freudian family romance," and, in order for us to view Dren as a victim of "the social forces of family and the apparatus of technoscience," her material body must be writ large (110).

If Hantke is interested in the factors that affect how (and if) a monstrous 15 infant is displayed in film, in "Monstrous Children as Harbingers of Mortality:

A Psychological Analysis of Doris Lessing's *The Fifth Child*," Daniel Sullivan and Jeff Greenberg are more concerned with why certain infants are perceived as monstrous in the first place. Even when in the womb, Ben, the fifth child of Harriet and David Lovatt, announces his monstrosity: the pregnancy is terribly taxing on Harriet, sapping her of strength and leading her to wonder what exactly is growing inside her. Once born, Ben confirms that he is indeed an abomination, more animal than human, not only in his appearance and eating habits, but also in his tendency to inflict harm on those around him: as an infant, Ben kills a household pet and consistently poses a serious threat to his siblings. To understand why Ben's particular characteristics prove especially disturbing, both to readers and to his family, Sullivan and Greenberg take an approach informed by their backgrounds in psychology: terror management theory (TMT). A theory that has been validated empirically by experiments, TMT holds that humans are motivated by a "non-conscious desire to transcend... mortal limitations" through various types of "immortality striving" (119); the two most pertinent to *The Fifth Child*, Sullivan and Greenberg claim, are the biological mode—a drive to produce offspring who will preserve not only their parents' genes but, more importantly, their "cherished values" (129)—and the cultural mode, a desire to achieve "symbolic mortality" through culturally-validated accomplishments, such as a legacy of artistic achievements or philanthropic deeds. The Lovatts' need to produce a large family—they had aimed to have six children until Ben arrived—in spite of their inability to financially and emotionally handle such a horde and in the face of family disapproval, demonstrates their rejection of the cultural mode of immortality striving in favor of the biological. Since the former is the more culturally acceptable to the society in which the Lovatts exist, the Lovatts find themselves slowly estranged from family and friends.

According to Sullivan and Greenberg, Ben is monstrous because he points 16 out that the Lovatts' immortality striving is ultimately a doomed venture. Ben's "creatureliness" reminds the Lovatts and readers that, like all animals, we all will one day die. Furthermore, as Sullivan and Greenberg make clear, Ben also demolishes his parents' hopes to achieve symbolic immortality through the biological mode. Not only does Ben break up their immediate family—the rest of the children find ways to flee the house so as to avoid associating with their monstrous brother—but he also disrupts their ties with their extended family as well, who no longer choose to spend their holidays in the Lovatt home. Furthermore, Sullivan and Greenberg point out, Ben refuses to function as a vehicle through which the Lovatts could transmit their moral values and beliefs into the future, for Ben finds a more suitable set of companions in a local biker gang, whose members embody all the aspects of the larger world that the Lovatts find so distasteful. Thus, Sullivan and Greenberg conclude,

Ben is monstrous because, in these various ways, he is a "symbol of punishment for doomed immortality striving" (130).

Sullivan and Greenberg offer a psychological explanation for why a savage 17
and inassimilable child like Ben could prove monstrous. By contrast, the
evil children that William Wandless studies in "Spoil the Child: Unsettling
Ethics and the Representation of Evil" are far different in nature. Strange,
certainly, but hardly sub-human, the children in the films Wandless scrutinizes—Rob Zombie's 2007 adaptation of John Carpenter's *Halloween* (1978),
Joshua (2007), *Home Movie* (2008), and *Orphan* (2009)—are psychological
and moral abominations whose brand of "evil" frustrates facile psychological
explanations. Wandless begins with the premise that viewers are reluctant to
view evil children as ethical agents with "their own methods and motives"
(135). Instead, viewers likely search for environmental factors that would
maintain their belief that evil children are produced by deviant upbringings or other "atypical" factors. The four movies Wandless considers all offer
potential explanations that help viewers dismiss the distressing possibility
that evil child could emerge from "normal" and "healthy" situations, but those
provided by *Joshua* and *Home Movie* offer only a modicum of comfort.

Zombie's decision, as Wandless puts it, to "retrofit the original narrative [of 18
Halloween] with a prefatory arc designed to illuminate the characterological
consequence" of Michael's dysfunctional childhood *seems* to suggest that the
seemingly random acts of violence we know he will later commit as an adult are
legible psychological responses to his early experiences. Not only is Zombie's
Michael abused in various ways, but the film hints that an Oedipal complex is
at play as well: his beloved mother, Deborah, is a stripper, and Michael's decision to slaughter all members of his family except for her (and the baby sister
he adores) could suggest a desire to eliminate all competitors for his mother's
affection. Not all of the murders Michael commits as an adult, though, can
be explained as resulting from Michael's childhood experiences: as Wandless
points out, Michael kills people whom—according to the film's psychological
logic—he should have no desire to murder. However, the brutalities Michael
commits as a child are extenuated to a large degree, thus making Zombie's
film perhaps "the second most comforting film of the new millennium,"
according to Wandless (138). The movie *Joshua* initially *seems* to establish
family dynamics that, while different from that of Michael Myers, still promise
to account for the title character's bizarre and malicious behavior. A cold, distant, and yet uncannily mature child, nine-year-old Joshua appears to get pleasure (or at least satisfaction) from the fact that his new baby sister, Lily—once
the apple of her parents' eyes—has become a cantankerous infant, much as he
was as a child; there is even evidence that Joshua is inciting Lily's discontent.
Even though Joshua proves abnormally devious and cruel—responsible for his

mother's descent into madness, his grandmother's death, and his father's false imprisonment for child abuse—viewers initially assume that Joshua's behavior is an extreme response to the "boy's understandable fear of displacement" (141). And yet the end of film reveals that from the very beginning, Joshua has been arranging matters so that he can end up with his beloved uncle, and the "deep premeditation... [and] perfect understanding of domestic and societal dynamics" that Joshua's plan requires is, Wandless asserts, a "discomfiting disclosure" that "expos[es] the motives and machinations of the young and remind[s] adults of their vulnerability" (144, 145).

As my earlier description of the children in *Home Movie* made clear, Jack 19 and Emily Poe are much more disturbing figures, killing numerous animals and ultimately murdering and likely cannibalizing their parents. In stark contrast to their ebullient parents, the twins are, even from the beginning, almost entirely devoid of affect and affection except for a brief interlude during which they seem miraculously healed and freely gambol with their parents, behavior that is later revealed to be a ruse. But while we could diagnose the Poe children as sociopaths and thus attribute their alarming aberrations to psychological disorder, Wandless shows that the film provides reason to believe that their appetite for human flesh may have been inspired by various stimuli to which they were exposed by their parents, especially a bedtime story featuring a dragon who earns the trust of children only to devour them. (Of course, in doing so, the viewer must assume that the story inspired their cannibalistic tendencies, not that it appealed because it reflected their already deepest desires and instincts.) Even if we decide to attribute their penchant for human fare to misinterpreted cues, we ultimately cannot forget the "performative self-awareness" that the children demonstrate, Wandless concludes, and thus the viewer is left with "provocative yet partial explanations of pathology and fresh sources of distress" (149). Wandless concludes his essay with discussion of *Orphan,* which, he claims, incites none of this anxiety: though we first think adopted Esther is simply a "different" little girl, she is revealed to be a 33-year-old homicidal woman named Lena, a fact that explains away her strange behavior, her advances toward her father, and her hostility toward her mother. In addition, since she is an adult, Lena is entirely accountable for her actions, and thus we can cheer for her death at the end of the film without any reservation. For these reasons, *Orphan* is the most reassuring of the four films and perhaps even, as Wandless declares, "the most comforting film of the new millennium" (150).

We might expect evil children to appear in horror films such as those 20 that Wandless studies, but they have also encroached upon the realm of children's literature, as Holly Blackford makes clear in her essay entitled "Private Lessons from Dumbledore's 'Chamber of Secrets': The Riddle of the Evil Child in *Harry Potter and the Half-Blood Prince.*" Blackford focuses on

Tom Riddle, who, as the child precursor of the evil Lord Voldemort, is defined by many of the wizard adults as innately evil. However, Blackford demonstrates that in many ways Tom is merely a reflection of a "hidden curriculum" that Hogwarts School of Witchcraft and Wizardry refuses to acknowledge. While Tom's desire to hoard objects is treated as an indicator of his naturally nefarious character, Blackford argues that "the child who covets trophies and the prestige they convey" is merely a reflection of the "general atmosphere of the capitalistic display pervasive in the school's culture" (158). Furthermore, while Tom is derided for his ability to assemble about him a questionable group of peers, Blackford points out that this capacity is "explicitly encouraged by the division of students into houses and classes that define their primary friendships" (160). Likewise, Tom's skill at manipulation is identified as yet another marker of his evil nature, but again Blackford demonstrates that "all the characters in the wizarding world are masters of these skills" (160). Perhaps the most damning proof of Tom's innately malevolent character is his desire to make Horcruxes, objects into which wizards "can embed their souls and thereby earn immortality" but only through murdering another person in the process (161). But even this overtly abominable act, Blackford claims, has a motive distinguishable from simply a penchant for wickedness: "Tom's need to turn founder objects into his Horcruxes is an attempt at adoption by not one but four families, a 'magpie' desire to hoard family and its special heirlooms" (162). Tom is the embodiment of unacknowledged lessons at Hogwarts that its officials wish to deny; in labeling Tom as evil, teachers and administrators can avoid culpability for the demonic figure he became.

Blackford also calls upon queer theory to further explain Tom's development. Noting that Harry displays many of the same characteristics as Tom, she asks why Harry's story is one of success and Tom's that of moral failure. Blackford concludes that the best way to approach *Half-Blood Prince* is to connect "Harry's 'coming out' as a wizard to the queer child's experience" and to view Tom's narrative, in turn, as "a coming-out story that fails and creates a very closeted monster" (157, 170). Drawing parallels between the shame that Tom feels due to his upbringing and uncertain lineage and the history of gay shame, Blackford concludes that he "exemplifies the dangers of refusing children support for all their issues" (171). That the "evil" child might be "a synecdoche for cultural conditioning" is a possibility "too complicated for the analyst or courts to handle; thus he is treated as an individual with pathological tendencies and 'instincts'" (172), much as Tom is.

CONCLUSION: A NEW TURN TO THE GENRE?

Blackford's suggestion that the "evil child" might be a construction to ease the facilitation of the legal system is a concept that deserves further thought.

The texts about evil children that have appeared so far this century are too numerous and varied to be treated as a single, coherent body, but one characteristic does seem unique to our era. The title of a 1976 film about a pack of homicidal youngsters asked a provocative question, *Who Can Kill A Child?* The question at first seemed rhetorical: by interweaving opening credits accompanied by the eerie sound of children singing with shocking footage documenting the atrocities done to children during such horrific events as the Holocaust, the Civil War between India and Pakistan, and the Korean War, the movie supplies an obvious answer—well, apparently *lots* of adults can. However, the movie also shows that outside of the world of war, killing a child, regardless of how evil and dangerous he or she may be, is no easy undertaking. In one scene of *Who Can Kill a Child?*, for example, a father allows his tearful daughter to lead him off by the hand toward the horde of her savage compatriots—even though he is well aware that they have killed all the adults on the island on which they live and that he will certainly face the same fate—because he ultimately cannot resist the tug of paternal protectiveness. Violence against children is difficult for both the fictional characters who face this prospect and the audience members who witness the consequences of their decision, and certainly one of the most dangerous weapons that evil children wield are our presumptions of their innocence and our reluctance thus to deal them a fatal blow.[16]

But the protagonists of *Who Can Kill a Child?*—Tom and his pregnant 23 wife, Evelyn—learn from the father's mistake: when a young child threatens to kill Evelyn, Tom shoots him without hesitation. Although both husband and wife are appalled by what he has done, the gang of children threatening them temporarily disbands. "Nobody dared to attack a child, to kill one of them," Tom says. "That's why they weren't afraid, but now they are." Other protagonists also kill off the evil children who plague them. In *It Lives Again* (1978), Cohen's sequel to *It's Alive,* parents decide that they must shoot their monstrous newborn when they see him slaughter another person. In *The Good Son* (1993), a mother has the choice to save either the nephew she knows to be good or the son she knows to be evil and opts to save her nephew. And in *Pet Sematary,* the father gives his son Gage a lethal injection, even though it was his overwhelming grief over Gage's death that led him to bury the child in the supernatural cemetery in the first place, thereby enabling his unnatural resurrection.

But contemporary films express far greater hesitation about punishing 24 even the vilest child with death. The subtitle of O'Hayre's book, after all, tells us to "*defeat* evil children," a word carefully swabbed clean of all bloody implications. And yet directors have found ways to have their cake and eat it, too. As Wandless's essay demonstrates, *Orphan* sanctions the pleasure viewers get from watching adopted mother Kate kick Esther in the face and send her to her death by reassuring them that Esther is, in fact, a woman. But Isabelle Fuhrman, the actress who played Esther, was just twelve when the movie *premiered,* and regardless of how hard the film tries to convince us that she's a grown woman, what we witness is an adult attacking a child.

Other more recent films have found similar ways for us to savor the fatal 25 punishments inflicted on children without any pangs of conscience. In *Case 39* (2010), the main character, Emily kills her villainous foster daughter, Lilith, but her actions are endorsed because Lilith is not really a little girl at all but some sort of demon. Throughout most of the film, however, the demon cloaks itself in Lilith's body, and it is a little girl we see Emily try to kill, and we root her on. *The New Daughter* (2009) unfolds according to a similar logic, but in this film, the daughter, Louisa, is not a demon but rather has been selected to become the queen of a hive of all male, human-sized creatures. Unable to help, all her father, John, can do is watch her descend into stranger and more hostile behavior. In the middle of the film, John encounters another man, Roger Wayne, whose granddaughter suffered a similar fate. Rather than stand idly by, Roger killed the child, he says, because "[s]he wasn't my grand-daughter anymore. I had to do it. So will you…. A father will do anything for his daughter, even the worst thing." Roger's prediction comes true: John causes an explosion that destroys the hive, Louisa, and himself. Although a very brief moment of CGI confirms that Louisa indeed has become one of the creatures, what we actually *see* for the bulk of the film is a young girl who becomes so evil that the only choice left is to kill her.

Films like *Case 39* and *The New Daughter* operate according to the logic 26 that even though it looks like a child, talks like a child, and acts like a child, it really isn't a child at all, and thus violence is warranted. What strikes me as further noteworthy about *Case 39* and *The New Daughter* is that both feature very familiar faces: Renee Zellweger takes on the role of Emily, and Kevin Costner plays the part of John James. Both actors have a history of playing relatively likeable and trustworthy characters and their squeaky clean appearances lend a special authority to the executions they carry out.

Interestingly, these films mirror a conflict embedded in our justice system. 27 Recent Supreme Court decisions that ruled death penalties and life sentences for minors unconstitutional suggest that United States policy toward juvenile criminals, at least at the most official levels, is moving away from punishment and toward rehabilitation.[17] While these decisions may indicate a shift toward leniency, one cannot assume that they reflect public opinion or the attitudes of judges and juries. Jeffrey Fagan, for example, has shown that the number of juveniles serving time in adult jails between 1990 and 2004 rose 208 percent even though juvenile crime decreased dramatically during that time (95). That more minors ended up in jail though fewer were committing crimes can only indicate an increased tendency to punish minors with stricter sentences than juvenile courts allow. Likewise, recent films about evil children have found ways to dispatch them without any qualms. Lilith and Louisa may be unwitting vessels for external sources of evil, but nevertheless these films imply that once the child is corrupted (or has committed a crime), she cannot be redeemed. Death, not rehabilitation, *is* the only option, and the fictional contrivances of the films allow us to act out this belief with an entirely clean conscience.

NOTES

A special thanks to Tara Harney-Mahajan both for helping me to compile and edit this special issue and for offering her feedback on this introduction.

1. Numerous articles have been written about the major works in the genre, but I've not yet discovered a book-length study on specifically *evil* children. Some noteworthy single-author studies that contain important discussions include Sabine Büssing's *Aliens in the Home: The Child in Horror Fiction* (1987), Ellen Pifer's *Demon or Doll: Images of the Child in Contemporary Writing and Culture* (2000), and Lynn Schofield Clark's *From Angels to Aliens: Teenagers, the Media, and the Supernatural* (2003), but as their titles suggest, these authors examine child as both demon and doll, angel and alien. Barbara Creed's *The Monstrous-Feminine: Film, Feminism, Psychoanalysis* (1993) also focuses on other matters than evil children, as the title suggests, but her book does examine several important films in the genre, including *Alien* (a film about monstrous births if there ever was one), *The Exorcist* (1973), *The Brood* (1979), and *Carrie* (1974). Evil children also are discussed at some length throughout the introduction of David J. Hogan's *Dark Romance: Sexuality in the Horror Film* (1986) and within his chapter entitled "Turgid Teens" (pp. 122–37); in a chapter entitled "It's Alive, I'm Afraid" in David J. Skal's *The Monster Show: A Cultural History of Horror* (1993) (pp. 287–306); and in William Paul's *Laughing Screaming: Modern Hollywood Horror and Comedy* (1994) (pp. 255–380). Various edited collections, such as Gary Westfahl and George Slusser's *Nursery Realms: Children in the Worlds of Science Fiction, Fantasy, and Horror* (1999) and Steven Bruhm and Natasha Hurley's *Curiouser: On the Queerness of Children* (2004), contain relevant work as well.

2. In 1874, for example, Jesse Pomeroy was convicted of killing a ten-year-old girl and four-year-old boy; he was 14 at the time of the murders. For discussion of British child murderers, see Loretta Loach's *The Devil's Children*.

3. Bixby's short story became a 1961 episode of *The Twilight Zone*; Golding's novel led to a 1963 movie; John Wyndham's *The Midwich Cuckoos* inspired the 1960 film *Village of the Damned* and a 1963 sequel *Children of the Damned*; and stage and screen versions of *The Bad Seed* appeared in 1954 and 1956, respectively, and the latter was nominated for four Academy Awards. All of these would be revisited again in later years as well: "It's a Good Life" resurfaced in *Twilight Zone: The Movie* (1983) and a sequel entitled "It's Still a Good Life" was included in the first season of a new *Twilight Zone* series (2002–2003); a made-for-television version of *The Bad Seed* starring Lynn Redgrave and David Carradine aired in 1985; and a second rendition of *Village of the Damned*, starring Christopher Reeve and Kristie Alley, hit theaters in 1995. That all of these texts have seen multiple film adaptations suggests that these narratives—and the evil children they involve—struck a resounding chord that has reverberated across time.

4. While *Rosemary's Baby* was nominated for Best Adapted Screenplay and Ruth Gordon received an Oscar for her supporting role as Minnie Castevet, *The Exorcist* easily surpassed that success with eight nominations and two Academy Awards.

5. I have yet to view it for myself, but the description on Netflix, which remarks that *Seytan's* "highlights include the green-vomit scene, which has been transformed to a mustard-spitting sequence, and a demonic voice that sounds more like a drunken pirate than Satan," suggests that this film was hardly a flattering homage.

6. The book is out of print and hard to find, but the cover proclaims that the story is about "a child accursed" who summons the protagonist to "a house of terror—and an appointment with death!"

7. In the 1980s, Koontz penned *Twilight* (1984), later re-released as *The Servants of Twilight* (1990) and made into a film the next year. The novel and film portray a child suspected of being the antichrist, a suspicion that is never fully allayed.

8. Hoppenstand specifically credits *Rosemary's Baby, The Other,* and *The Exorcist* for this shift. Featuring children who are both victims of and portals for evil, Saul's almost annual contributions during this period include *Suffer the Children* (1977), *Punish the Sinners* (1978), *Cry for the Strangers* (1979), *Comes the Blind Fury* (1980), *When the Wind Blows* (1981), *The God Project* (1982), *Nathaniel* (1984), *Brainchild* (1985), *The Unwanted* (1987), and *Second Child* (1990). The titles of Neiderman's novels—*Brainchild* (1981), *Imp* (1985), *Teacher's Pet* (1986), *Surrogate Child* (1988), *Blood Child* (1990), and *Child's Play* (1990)—proclaim his similar interests. Though Ruby Jean Jensen began her prolific writing career in the 1970s, her most notable works in this genre are *Hear the Children Cry* (1981), *Such a Good Baby* (1982), *Best Friends* (1985), *Jump Rope* (1988), *Vampire Child* (1990), *Lost and Found* (1990), *The Reckoning* (1992), and *The Living Evil* (1993). Jensen is also responsible for contributions to the "evil doll" genre, which also became popular during this time and which bears an obvious connection to evil children. Jensen's *Mama* (1983), *Annabelle* (1987), *Victoria* (1990), and *Baby Dolly* (1991) likely inspired such films as *Dolly Dearest* (1992), *Demonic Toys* (1992), and, of course, a series of films featuring the most famous evil doll of all—Chucky. Since *Child's Play* appearance in 1988, four sequels have been produced, and a remake is scheduled to appear this year.

9. See, for example, Errickson's entries entitled "*Pin* by Andrew Neiderman (1981): The Kids Want Something to Do," "*Tricycle* by Russell Rhodes (1983): Out of His Way, Mister, You Best Keep," "William W. Johnstone: The Paperback Covers," "Ruby Jean Jensen: The Paperback Covers," and "*The Next* by Bob Randall (1981): Mommy, Can I Go Out and Kill Tonight?" The URL for Errickson's blog is http://toomuchhorrorfiction.blogspot.com/.

10. In one particularly memorable episode, "Scott Tenorman Must Die" (Season 5, Episode 4, 11 July 2001), Cartman takes revenge on the title character, who throughout the episode has humiliated him in various ways. Cartman ultimately wins the duel between them by killing Scott's parents and mixing their corpses in with a vat of chili, a portion of which he offers to Scott. When Scott begins to eat, Cartman asks, "Do you like it? Do you like it, Scott? I call it, 'Mr. and Mrs. Tenorman Chili.'" Scott paws through the bowl, only to find a finger with his mother's wedding ring still on it. Realizing what Cartman has done, Scott breaks down into hysterical tears, and Cartman begins licking the tears from Scott's face, exclaiming, "Oh, let me taste your tears, Scott. Mmm. Your tears are so yummy and sweet."

11. Thanks to "Mister" Greg Semenza for pointing this out.

12. See, for example, "Prodigy" (Season 3, Episode 13, 8 Jan. 2002), "Juvenile" (Season 4, Episode 9, 22 Nov. 2002), "Damaged" (Season 4, Episode 11, 10 Jan. 2003), "Soulless" (Season 4, Episode 25, 16 May 2003), "Mean" (Season 5, Episode 17, 24 Feb. 2004), "Sick" (Season 5, Episode 19, 30 Mar. 2004), "Conscience" (Season 6, Episode 6, 9 Nov. 2004), "Game" (Season 6, Episode 14, 8 Feb. 2005), "Web" (Season 7, Episode 21, 9 May 2006), and "Unorthodox" (Season 9, Episode 13, 15 Jan. 2008).

13. The examples are endless. The first of the six *Silent Hill* games, which appeared in 1999, features "grey children," child-like monsters who carry small knives and attack the player's avatar,

and one possible ending to the game involves a monstrous, demonic birth. *American McGee's Alice* transforms Lewis Carroll's character into a young girl wielding a butcher knife, whose apron is splattered with blood. The covers of *F.E.A.R.* (2005) and *F.E.A.R. 2: Project Origin* (2009) display a creepy little girl with dark hair hanging in her face; this character, Alma, menaces players throughout the game. (*F.E.A.R. 3* is scheduled to be released shortly.) In *Bioshock* (2007) and *Bioshock II* (2010), players must decide whether to "harvest" or rescue the Little Sisters they encounter, genetically altered little girls who have been trained to extract a valuable substance called ADAM from corpses and who are guarded by destructive Big Daddies, humans in armored diving suits. A third video game in the series is scheduled for 2012. A society of girls named the Red Crayon Aristocrats terrorizes players in *Rule of Rose* (2006), and in *Limbo* (2010), small shadowy children take inventive measures to try to kill the main character as he navigates through a series of dangerous and puzzling obstacles.

14. Collins's trilogy consists of *The Hunger Games* (2008), *Catching Fire* (2009), and *Mockingjay* (2010). See also, for example, Lynn Reid Banks's *Angela and Diabola* (1997) and Nancy Farmer's *The House of the Scorpion* (2002).

15. Later in the novel, we discover that this is not the first example of Rhoda's capacity for murder. Not only did she push a puppy out her window when caring for it interfered with playtime, but she also shoved an elderly woman down the stairs in order to claim the opal pendant that the woman has promised her in her will.

16. In *The Omen,* Damien's adopted father, Robert Thorn, is just about to kill his son, whom he knows to be the antichrist, but the sight of the boy squirming and begging for his life causes him to hesitate long enough for the police to shoot him before he can complete his mission to save the world. As a result, Damien continues his reign of terror for two more sequels, whereupon his daughter Delia takes over in *Omen IV: The Awakening,* and in 2006, Damien was resurrected for a remake and started all over again. One can only wish that Robert would have been more decisive. And at the end of the French film *Them* (2006), the female protagonist refuses to smash a boy's head with a rock, even though his gang has been terrorizing her and her husband for an entire night; in fact, she just witnessed this particular boy cause her husband's death. However, when the boy covers his face with his hands and exclaims, "Don't hit me! I didn't do anything! We just want to play," she drops the rock and instead tries to escape. She fails.

17. *Roper v. Simmons* (2005) banned death sentences and *Graham v. Florida* (2010) life sentences for crimes committed by juveniles.

WORKS CITED

Bixby, Jerome. "It's a Good Life." 1953. *Science Fiction Hall of Fame: The Greatest Science Fiction Stories of all Time.* Ed. Robert Silverberg. New York: Avon, 1970. 523–42. Print.

Bradbury, Ray. "The Small Assassin." 1946. *The Stories of Ray Bradbury.* New York: Knopf, 1980. 372–86. Print.

___. "The Veldt." 1950. *American Gothic Tales.* Ed. Joyce Carol Oates. New York: Plume, 1996. 264–77. Print.

Bruhm, Steven, and Natasha Hurley, eds. *Curiouser: On the Queerness of Children.* Minneapolis: U of Minnesota P, 2004. Print.

Büssing, Sabine. *Aliens in the Home: The Child in Horror Fiction.* Contributions to the Study of Childhood and Youth. Vol. 4. New York: Greenwood P, 1987. Print.

Case 39. Dir. Christian Alvert. 2010. Paramount, 2011. DVD.

Clark, Lynn Schofield. *From Angels to Aliens: Teenagers, the Media, and the Supernatural.* New York: Oxford UP, 2003.

Creed, Barbara. *The Monstrous-Feminine: Film, Feminism, Psychoanalysis.* New York: Routledge, 1993.

Cull, Nick. "*The Exorcist.*" *History Today* 50.5 (May 2000): 46–51. PDF File.

Errickson, Will. "*The Next* by Bob Randall (1981): Mommy, Can I Got Out and Kill Tonight?" *Too Much Horror Fiction.* 7 June 2010. Web. 7 Mar. 2011.

____. "*Pin* by Andrew Neiderman (1981): The Kids Want Something to Do." *Too Much Horror Fiction.* 18 Nov. 2010. Web. 7 Mar. 2011.

____. "Ruby Jean Jensen: The Paperback Covers." *Too Much Horror Fiction.* 16 Aug. 2010. Web. 7 Mar. 2011.

____. "*Tricycle* by Russell Rhodes (1983): Out of His Way, Mister, You Best Keep." *Too Much Horror Fiction.* 26 Oct. 2010. Web. 7 Mar. 2011.

____. "William W. Johnstone: The Paperback Covers." *Too Much Horror Fiction.* 23 Sept. 2010 Web. 7 Mar. 2011.

Fagan, Jeffrey. "Juvenile Crime and Criminal Justice: Resolving Border Disputes." *The Future of Children* 18 (Fall 2008): 81–118. *JSTOR.* Web. 31 Dec. 2010.

Golding, William. "Fable." *The Hot Gates and Other Occasional Pieces.* New York: Harcourt, 1966. 85–101. Print.

The Innocents. Dir. Jack Clayon. 1961. Twentieth Century Fox, 2005. DVD.

Hogan, David J. *Dark Romance: Sexuality in the Horror Film.* Jefferson, NC: McFarland, 1986.

Hoppenstand, Gary. "Exorcising the Devil Babies: Images of Children and Adolescents in the Best-Selling Horror Novel." *Images of the Child.* Ed. Harry Edwin Eiss. Bowling Green, OH: Bowling Green U Popular P, 1994. 35–58. Print.

Loach, Loretta. *The Devil's Children: A History of Childhood and Murder.* London: Icon, 2009. Print.

Matheson, Richard. "Of Man and Woman Born." *The Dark Descent.* Ed. David G. Hartwell. New York: Tor, 1987. 513–15. Print.

Maynard, Joyce. "The Monster Children." *Newsweek* 26 (July 1976): 10–11. PDF File.

Oates, Joyce Carol. *Expensive People.* 1968. New York: Modern Library, 2006. Print.

O'Hayre, Meredith. *The Scream Queen's Survival Guide: Avoid Machetes, Defeat Evil Children, Steer Clear of Bloody Dismemberment, and Conquer Other Horror Movie Clichés.* Avon, MA: F + W Media, 2010. Print.

Paul, William. *Laughing Screaming: Modern Hollywood Horror and Comedy.* New York: Columbia UP, 1994. Print.

Pifer, Ellen. *Demon or Doll: Images of the Child in Contemporary Writing and Culture.* Charlottesville: UP of Virginia, 2000. Print.

Rice, Anne. *Interview with the Vampire.* 1976. New York: Ballantine, 1997. Print.

"Scott Tenorman Must Die." *South Park.* Comedy Central. 11 July 2001. Television.

Seytan. Netflix. Web. 8 Mar. 2011.

Them. Dir. David Moreau and Xavier Palud. 2006. Dark Sky Films, 2008. DVD.

Skal, David J. *The Monster Show: A Cultural History of Horror.* New York: Norton, 1993. Print.

The New Daughter. Dir. Luis Berdejo. 2009. Anchor Bay, 2010. DVD.

Westfahl, Gary, and George Slusser, Eds. *Nursery Realms: Children in the Worlds of Science Fiction, Fantasy, and Horror.* Athens: U of Georgia P, 1999. Print.

Who Can Kill a Child? Dir. Narciso Ibáñez Serrador. 1976. Dark Sky Films, 2007. DVD.

QUESTIONS

1. What is the thesis of this article?
2. Is this an expository or persuasive essay or a combination of both? Explain.
3. Compare the voice (see page 132) of this humanities article with the voice of the social science articles in Part Three and assess the differences.
4. What are the problems the author has in defining her key term, "evil children?" How does she resolve the challenge?

5. Reviewing a range of books and films and some television programs which feature evil children, the author offers a wide-ranging explanation for the reasons why a child might be or become evil. What are these reasons? Which reason makes the most sense to you?
6. The evil child might be featured in a comedy or in a horror story. Describe an example of each from your own reading or viewing experiences.
7. How, if at all, has the evil child as a fictitious character evolved since the 1950s?
8. Why can the figure of the evil child be so disturbing to readers and viewers?
9. How does the author account for our fascination with the character of the evil child?
10. Watch or re-watch *Harry Potter and the Half-Blood Prince*. What do you think of Holly Blackford's analysis of the character of Tom Riddle?
11. Consider *Twilight* and *The Hunger Games* books and films in the context of this article. To what extent are these "evil children" books and films and what are the causes of the evil, if any, that the children in these books and films enact?

This article was published in the *Journal of Sport and Social Issues*, volume 20, 2012, pages 1–7.

The Morality of Fighting in Ice Hockey: Should It Be Banned?*

Ryan T. Lewinson[1, †] and Oscar E. Palma[2, ‡]

¹University of Calgary
²York University

ABSTRACT

Ice hockey is a popular sport throughout North America and most of Europe; however, all too often, a midgame fistfight between two players will occur. Although this behavior is not allowed at any level of play in the game rules, the fights are typically allowed to proceed to completion—especially at the professional level. Knowing that the behavior is illegal in the sport, can fighting in hockey be a moral act? Does player safety outweigh the pleasures that fans and teammates experience when they witness a fight? Should fighting in hockey be abolished? This article aims to address these ethical questions and more, using virtue, utilitarian and deontological theoretical approaches supplemented with real-life on-ice examples that have occurred.

KEYWORDS

code of ethics, moral ethics, sport philosophy

INTRODUCTION

Countless injuries have occurred as a result of hockey fights and senseless violence, and as such, ethicists are beginning to take their positions in regards to whether a legitimate hockey fight is morally acceptable. Fights have occurred where even the fans of the game were mortified by the players' behaviors; thus, 1

* Ryan T. Lewinson and Oscar E. Palma, "The Morality of Fighting in Ice Hockey: Should It Be Banned?", *Journal of Sport and Social Issues*, 36(1), February 2012, pages 106–112. Copyright © 2012 by SAGE Publications. Reprinted by Permission of SAGE Publications.

† **Corresponding Author:** Ryan T. Lewinson, Human Performance Laboratory, University of Calgary 2500 University Drive N.W., Calgary, AB T2N IN4, Canada
Email: lewinson@ucalgary.ca

Ryan T. Lewinson is currently a PhD student in Biomedical Engineering at the University of Calgary's Human Performance Laboratory. His research focuses on the identification of mechanical risk factors for sport injuries, and the development of mechanical interventions for the treatment and prevention of sport injuries.

‡ **Oscar E. Palma** is currently a JD student at Osgoode Hall Law School of York University. He holds a MA in Philosophy from the University of Ottawa.

the inevitable question arises of whether fighting in hockey is truly a core feature of being named a *moral hockey athlete*. How does fighting fit in with the expectations of a hockey athlete by professional, international, and community standards? Is fighting something a hockey player is really supposed to do, both morally, and legally, within a hockey players' code of ethics? Should fighting in hockey be abolished from all levels of play? Using moral theory, this article aims to address these questions. In what follows, it will be identified how fighting violates what it means to be a morally correct hockey athlete and, in turn, why fighting should be abolished from all levels of hockey. First, a universal hockey player code of ethics will be constructed in order to base all arguments on existing conceptions of the ideal hockey athlete.

Since this article is addressing fighting in hockey at all levels, a combined   2 code of ethics will be synthesized using previously established codes from sports bodies such as the National Hockey League (NHL), International Olympic Committee (IOC), and a community league in Ottawa, Canada, the Nepean Minor Hockey Association (NMHA), to ensure the list is complete on a professional, international, and community scale.

The NHL has recently partnered with the U.S. Army to create themes and   3 values for professional game play (NHL, 2009a). Adapted from the U.S. Army code, they are as follows: (a) *Loyalty:* Bear faith and allegiance to your team; (b) *Duty:* Do what you are required to do by obligation; (c) *Respect:* Treat others as you expect to be treated; (d) *Selfless Service:* Put the welfare of your team before your own; (e) *Integrity:* Do what is right, legally, and morally; and (f) *Courage:* Face fear, danger, or adversity even if it compromises your own safety. From the IOC's code of ethics (IOC, 2007) we can include international expectations of a hockey athlete, (g) *Dignity:* The safeguarding of each player's safety. Aspects from the community level may be drawn upon using the NMHA (2009) code of conduct. It is important to include the community level so that players of all ages and skill level may be included in the discussion. The following features will be added to the list: (h) *Play for fun, not for victory,* and (i) *Practice teamwork, sportsmanship, and discipline.*

The global ideal for a morally correct hockey athlete can be summarized   4 as one who is committed to the team's glory yet respects and abides by the rules of the game with the ultimate reason in playing for fun. Enforcement of the code of ethics will be done by the game officials, coaches, family, and management by way of the official rulebook of hockey. With a code of ethics established, we may now draw upon theory to guide our argument.

VIRTUE ETHICS IN FIGHTING

Virtues and vices are traits of character that are manifested through habitual   5 action (Rachels & Rachels, 2007). The former are desirable, but the latter are not. A virtue can be defined as a mean along a continuum of opposing character traits and vices as the polar-opposing traits in themselves. For example, the virtue of courage may be found between the vices of foolhardiness and cowardice (Rachels & Rachels, 2007). Edmund Pincoffs (1986) has suggested that it is these virtues and vices that we refer to when deciding whether a person is to be sought or to be avoided, or better yet, whether an action is morally correct or incorrect.

In regards to fighting in hockey, what virtue is being broken? Let us start 6 by considering discipline. Discipline will be defined as the ability to behave in a controlled and calm fashion even under a difficult or stressful situation. Therefore, any player who fights because (a) his team is losing, (b) a wrong was committed against him by an opposing player, or (c) it is his duty on the team shows no discipline. Fighting for these causes is not in sync with the definition of a morally correct hockey athlete, as defined in the previous section.

Next, consider integrity. By virtue, integrity is a combination of justice and 7 fairness, so the question becomes "Is a hockey player acting fairly, morally, and legally while fighting?" Although both players usually do consent to the fight, this does not mean all hockey fights are fair. For example, imagine the fight that occurred on January 31, 2004, between Zdeno Chara (6'10, 260 lbs) and Bryan McCabe (6'1, 215 lbs) (Leafclub, 2009). Fighting someone almost a foot higher, and close to 50 lbs heavier, does not seem too fair. As another piece of anecdotal evidence, consider the Jonathan Roy saga, where he brutally attacked the other team's goalie without his consent (CTV, 2008). In both cases, fighting seems less fair and more immoral. What about legally? Hockey fights are against the rules in the game since a major penalty is issued to any player who fights (NHL, 2009b), and fighting in general is not allowed in society, so why should fighting continue? Hockey fights seem unjust and, at times, unfair. Furthermore, the player who chooses to engage in fighting is at disciplinary fault. Therefore, allowing players to fight defies the established code of ethics by demonstrating a lack of virtue.

Many virtues and facets of the previously proposed hockey code of ethics 8 are defied when one chooses to fight. However, certain aspects of the code and certain virtues are still being practiced. For example, Don Cherry (2008) has argued that a player could be acting out of courage to protect another teammate; this also shows selfless service and loyalty to the team. However, such an argument neglects two crucial points: (1) Not all fights are acts of courage and loyalty for the sake of protecting the team; some are for revenge, to instigate or to strike fear into the opposing team. What at times gets interpreted as a courageous or loyal decision to engage in a fight could very well be motivated by intentions grounded in vice and, as such, could not be considered virtuous at all. Thus, on the whole, they are very wicked acts and should not happen. (2) There would be no need to act courageously in regards to fighting if there were no fight in the first place. To have this, fighting must be abolished.

In the case of a fight out of evil intent, it seems clear that this violates what it means to be a moral athlete in all regards. But in the case of a fair fight, with no evil intent, it seems that when a player is faced with the decision of engaging in a fair fight there are two conflicting sides of virtue he must attune to. On the one hand, he will be displaying self-discipline, justice, and integrity by not fighting, and on the other, he will be viewed as courageous, loyal, and selfless when he chooses to fight. So, which is he to follow? Which are most important? These questions cannot be answered by virtue ethics alone, and, therefore, we will turn to utilitarianism to help guide our action.

UTILITARIAN CONSIDERATIONS

Utilitarianism is based primarily on the principle of utility, which holds that morally correct decisions are those whose consequences bring about the most happiness to the most people, with each person's happiness counting the same (Rachels & Rachels, 2007). So, with hockey fighting in question, what makes the most people happy? Does being courageous, loyal, selfless, and fighting yield the most happiness, or does being disciplined, just, and avoiding fighting yield the most happiness? Before this can be answered, it must be established who "everyone" is. Usually, fights are a one-on-one scenario, and so we will use this for our discussion.

Based on the principle of utility, in any fighting situation in hockey, no one is considered more valuable—even in a fight between Wayne Gretzky and "John Smith." Let us consider two scenarios. In the first, Player X and Player Y mutually agree to fight each other. The fight results in Player X getting his jaw broken and in Player Y receiving praise by his team and fans for having done it. We can assume that Player X is unhappy, given that having one's jaw broken tends to be a painful experience, and that Player Y is happy, in virtue of the fact that he is being praised for having broken Player X's jaw. In the next scenario, imagine Players X and Y mutually agree not to fight. No one gets hurt, and no praise is given. Thus, in this situation, no one is happy and no one is unhappy. So then, what do we choose—a state of affairs where one person is happy and another person unhappy, or a state of mutual complacency where neither is happy or unhappy? As the father of Utilitariansim, Jeremy Bentham states, the value of happiness is measured by intensity multiplied by duration (in Rachels & Rachels, 2007). So in the scenario where Player X gets his jaw broken, the intensity of unhappiness and duration will be quite high, whereas Player Y will be very happy but probably for a much shorter duration. Thus, in terms of magnitude, Player X's unhappiness outweighs Player Y's happiness, and therefore, it is better to choose the "no fighting" option. However, such a conclusion does not help us resolve the dilemma of deciding which virtues to follow, and when; as it stands, not fighting still seems to require the abandonment of virtue in some way. We will continue our attempts to solve this problem in the section on deontology.

Those in favor of fighting may counter that in order to consider what out- 12 come produces the most happiness, one must include everyone—specifically the fans. It has been shown through research that the fans really do like to watch fighting for their own enjoyment (Paul, 2003). Surely there are more fans than there are players, and so one may argue in favor of keeping fighting in hockey because more happiness is produced in total for the fans. However, cases have occurred where fans (and players) have put their own enjoyment second to something more important: the players' safety. On March 8 2004, Todd Bertuzzi of the Vancouver Canucks "sucker-punched" Steve Moore of the Colorado Avalanche, causing Moore to break three vertebrae and suffer a concussion (CBC, 2005). Fans and players alike were completely outraged with Bertuzzi's behavior. Clearly then, there is a fine line between how much violence causes entertainment and how much violence causes social disgust. When it comes to episodes of violence where the violence itself is kept to a minimum and no one really gets hurt, fighting is entertaining, and even encouraged. However, as soon as someone is greatly injured, the same sort of fighting is suddenly categorized as *immoral* even though the executed behaviors remain the same and the level of violence does not change. Ultimately, such a reaction suggests that fans and players care most for each other's safety: therefore, if injury makes the most people upset, then avoiding injury should make the most people happy. In order to do this, fighting in hockey must be abolished.

When it comes to determining the total happiness that is derived from a 13 situation where two players have chosen to engage in a fight, the most crucial notion to consider is player safety. Moreover, in a simple one-on-one scenario, it is best to avoid fighting completely if one truly wishes to maximize happiness and minimize unhappiness. However, utilitarianism has not helped solve the dilemma presented in the previous section because virtue will be abandoned, in one way or another, regardless of the player's choice to fight or not. Consequently, the question that remains is as follows: In terms of choosing to abolish fighting from hockey, which decision will yield the most happiness for everyone, while still abiding by the code of ethics and fulfilling all virtues? The following section on deontology aims to answer this question.

DEONTOLOGICAL APPROACH

Deontology is based on the concept that the right thing to do is obligatory 14 without regard for consequences (Rachels & Rachels, 2007). This idea, central to Immanuel Kant, further states that there are two things to consider when deciding whether any action is morally correct. First, for an action to be morally correct, the principle of universalizability must hold. This principle argues that we must accept the action being done in all circumstances and by all people, or in other words, making that action a universal law. The second pillar of deontology is that we must always show respect for persons. Specifically, this means we must never treat people as means to our own ends and only as ends in themselves.

It is now worth considering what the possible consequences would be if 15 one applies these two Kantian principles to the case of fighting within hockey. If one were to universalize fighting within hockey, can you imagine the possible outcomes that would derive? Undoubtedly, chaos would occur. For example, could "each time an opposing player harms one of your own, upsets you, or gets in your way, whether intentionally or unintentionally, you should fight him" be made universal? The arena would turn into a wrestling ring if this were the case and destroy the game of hockey completely. Looking back on utilitarianism, this would probably cause a lot of unhappiness for hockey fans and players alike; a vicious, never-ending cycle of violence and injury would occur, and so perhaps it is best to leave this type of behavior to other disciplines of sport, such as boxing or ultimate fighting. On the other hand, what if we were to say, "Each time an opposing player harms one of your own, upsets you, or gets in your way, whether intentionally or unintentionally, you should let the game officials handle the situation." Could this be universalized? Yes it could. The game would still continue; the player who caused the harm would be penalized, just as the rulebook outlines; and injury would be minimized. Furthermore, if the team scores a power-play goal because of the other player's punishment, then this will make the fans and the players happy—perhaps even more so than they would be from watching a fight—because it could result in their team winning the game. Thus, making fighting a universal law does not work, yet making no fighting a universal law does work. Therefore, fighting should be banned.

The second argument stems from Kant's respect for persons and is quite 16 simple. Sometimes, a team will acquire a player for the sole purpose of being the team fighter. Because his actual hockey playing skills are subpar, his use will be to injure or intimidate other skilled players, and as such, the suspension he may or may not receive from this is acceptable because it benefits the team as a whole. This violates Kant's law that no one must use another human as means to their own individual ends. This should never occur, and the easiest way to prevent it is by abolishing fighting from hockey. This would eliminate the need for teams to select unvirtuous goons to their team who are destined to no real purpose.

Making no fighting a universal law would force players to ignore parts of 17 virtue and the code of ethics, for example, loyalty. How is a player being loyal to his team when he chooses not to defend one of his teammates? The answer to this question is simply that the player will represent loyalty, and other virtues, in other ways. As discussed, by choosing not to fight, the other team will get a penalty, and your team's probability of scoring will increase for the next two minutes. Therefore, you are being loyal to your team by putting the greater good of the outcome of the game before retribution.

Deontology is known to support retributive or "eye for an eye" punish- 18 ment. So then how can we say that deontology proves that fighting should not be allowed? Using retributive theory, if someone hurts one of our own, aren't we obliged to harm them back? In theory, yes, this would be the case; however, if deontology were truly being applied and practiced, then the initial harm should not be occurring in the first place, thus eliminating the need for retributive punishment.

Deontology shows that fighting should not be allowed because no uni- 19 versal law concerning it can be made and because teams must not treat their players as means to their own ends. Furthermore, deontology allows us to answer the question based on virtue ethics, that is, which virtues to follow, by stating that no virtue is broken by electing not to fight.

CONCLUSION

Based on the viewpoints of classical moral theory, it is suggested that the abol- 20 ishment of fighting from hockey be considered. All theories advise toward the notion that it is best not to fight to respect the code of ethics of a moral hockey athlete. By removing fighting, this will increase the number of moral hockey athletes and hopefully improve the quality of the game. Although this article supplies positive and negative outcomes grounded in ethical theory associated with the banishment of fighting from hockey, the arguments of other ethicists and individuals strongly involved in hockey should be considered before any final decision is made. Specifically, the coaches, management staff, family, and fans should all be areas of concern in future ethical discussions on this topic.

DECLARATION OF CONFLICTING INTERESTS

The author(s) declared no potential conflicts of interest with respect to the research, authorship, and/or publication of this article.

FUNDING

The author(s) received no financial support for the research, authorship, and/or publication of this article.

REFERENCES

CBC. (2005). *A star player goes offside*. Retrieved March 20, 2009, from www.cbc.ca

Cherry, D. (2008). *NHL HNC's Don Cherry in defense of hockey fighting*. Retrieved March 20, 2009, from http://www.youtube.com/watch?v=qkr1yHOpoeg

CTV. (2008). *Roy's son admits to acting in "unacceptable way."* Retrieved March 20, 2009, from http://www.ctv.ca

International Olympic Committee. (2007). *Code of ethics*. Retrieved March 20, 2009, from http://www.olympic.org

Leafclub. (2009). *McCabe: Last days*. Retrieved March 20, 2009, from http://leafclub.blogspot.com/

National Hockey League. (2009a). *Hockey's finest presented by Army*. Retrieved March 20, 2009, from http://www.nhl.com

National Hockey League. (2009b). *Official NHL rulebook*. Retrieved March 20, 2009, from http://www.nhl.com

Nepean Minor Hockey Association. (2009). *Code of conduct*. Retrieved March 20, 2009, from www.nepeanhockey.on.ca

Paul, R. J. (2003). Variations in NHL attendance: The impact of violence, scoring, and regional rivalries. *American Journal of Economics and Sociology, 62*, 345–364.

Pincoffs, E. L. (1986). *Quandaries and virtues: Against reductivism in ethics*. Lawrence: University of Kansas Press.

Rachels, J., & Rachels, S. (2007). *The elements of moral philosophy* (5th ed.). New York, NY: McGraw-Hill.

QUESTIONS

1. What is the thesis of this article?
2. The authors construct a nine-point code of conduct to provide context for their thesis. What is your opinion of this code of conduct?
3. Provide an example wherein the authors acknowledge and refute the opposing point of view.
4. Do you think the authors' argument based upon utilitarian theory is effective? Explain your answer.
5. In your own words, define "deontology."
6. Why, according to the authors, is it wrong for a team to use a player whose primary role is as a fighter?
7. Watch the YouTube video of one of the fights referenced in this article. Are you more or less likely to agree with the authors' thesis, having seen the video?
8. What is the strongest argument the authors use in support of their thesis? The weakest?
9. What is the best feature of the style of this article? Can you recommend ways in which the writing style might be improved?
10. Do you think this article will effect any rule changes in professional hockey?

This article was published in the *Review of European Community & International Environmental Law*, volume 20, issue 1, 2011, pages 29–38.

Reconciliation, Indigenous Rights and Offshore Oil and Gas Development in the Canadian Arctic[†]

Kirsten Manley-Casimir*

In this article, the author addresses the potential impacts of Arctic offshore oil and gas development on Indigenous communities who reside in northern Canada. She argues that the potential environmental, social and cultural harms of such development may disproportionately affect such Indigenous communities. Relying on Canadian jurisprudence, she suggests that the principle of reconciliation may help mitigate the negative impacts of the development of Arctic offshore oil and gas resources. A fulsome conception of reconciliation supports meaningful consultation, efforts to substantially address Indigenous concerns, and ongoing collaborative negotiations in the context of offshore oil and gas development in the Arctic.

INTRODUCTION

Interest in the expansion of offshore[1] oil and gas development in the Arctic 1 continues to gain momentum as the global demand for oil and gas resources increases, more accessible petroleum resources are depleted and climate change in the Arctic makes such resources more accessible.[2] In the Canadian context, the Indigenous Peoples who inhabit the Arctic regions – the Inuit, Inuvialuit, Athabaskans and Dene[3] – have a strong political voice in raising awareness on the differential impacts of development and reliance on fossil fuels on northern Indigenous communities.[4] The impact of increased offshore oil and gas development in the Arctic would have a disproportionate impact upon these Indigenous communities due to their close relationship with their traditional territories, reliance on subsistence hunting, fishing and gathering, and historical occupation of more remote territories within Canada. As interest in the development of offshore oil and gas exploration

---

[†] Kirsten Manley-Casimir, "Reconciliation, Indigenous Rights and Offshore Oil and Gas Development in the Canadian Arctic," in the *Review of European Community & International Environmental Law*, 20(1), April 2011, pages 29–38. Copyright © 2011 by John Wiley & Sons, Inc.
* Kirsten Manley-Casimir, BA (Hon.), LL.B, LL.M, is a PhD candidate at the University of British Columbia Faculty of Law. Her dissertation deals with Aboriginal title claims to offshore water spaces. She is also acting as Co-director of the Intensive Program in Aboriginal Lands, Resources and Governments, an internationally-recognized clinical education programme at Osgoode Hall Law School. She is currently a research lawyer at the Law Commission of Ontario, working on projects relating to disability law, family law and the rights of vulnerable workers in precarious employment situations. It is important to note that none of the views in this article are a reflection of the views of the Law Commission of Ontario.

and extraction increases in the Arctic, the principle of reconciliation may be useful in mitigating the negative environmental, cultural and political impacts of such development on Indigenous communities in Canada's north.

HISTORY OF OFFSHORE OIL AND GAS DRILLING IN THE CANADIAN ARCTIC

Indigenous peoples have known about and used hydrocarbons for oil in the Arctic for centuries and likely used tar for, among other things, sealing the seams of boats.[5] The first oil and gas exploration drilling occurred in 1919 in the Norman Wells area of the Northwest Territories.[6] In the 1950s and 1960s, approximately 350 wells were drilled in the southern Northwest Territories,[7] and several wells were drilled in the Yukon.[8] Interest and exploratory activity in the Beaufort Sea and Mackenzie Delta areas increased during the 1970s with some significant oil and gas discoveries being made at Bent Horn and the Panarctic, respectively.[9]

In 1977, Mr Justice Thomas R. Berger released his report entitled *Northern Frontier, Northern Homeland: The Report of the Mackenzie Valley Pipeline Inquiry* (the 'Berger Inquiry')[10] in which he investigated the social, environmental and economic impact of a proposed gas pipeline that would run through the Yukon and the Mackenzie River Valley of the Northwest Territories. After hearing testimony from numerous stakeholders, including Aboriginal leaders and community members, Justice Berger recommended that no pipeline be built through northern Yukon and that the building of a pipeline through the Mackenzie Valley should be delayed for ten years in order to allow for the settlement of Aboriginal land claims.[11]

In response to the report, a ten-year moratorium was put into place on the construction of a pipeline along the Mackenzie to southern markets. This moratorium slowed down exploration in the Arctic region because it also froze the issuance of new exploration rights,[12] but it did not halt exploratory activity altogether. In the late 1970s, exploratory activity continued and was focused in the Arctic offshore areas of the Beaufort-Mackenzie region,[13] which is credited with 53 oil and gas discoveries, with 44 of those in the offshore.[14] Exploration has increased since the late 1990s due to rising gas prices.[15]

Presently, several large companies hold exploratory licences for offshore Arctic drilling. In the past several years, successful bidders have included Chevron (US$103,300,000) in 2009–2010, BP (US$1.18 million) in 2008 and Imperial Oil (US$585,000,000) in 2007.[16] Many smaller companies also hold valid licences.[17] Since interest in developing the offshore area remains high, increased exploration activities may continue, although the activity level may depend on decisions about where a pipeline might be installed;[18] if a pipeline were installed through Alaska, development on the American side of the Beaufort Sea may be given priority over that in the Canadian Arctic.[19] Canada's Natural Energy Board is presently undertaking a review of general requirements concerning the safety and environmental risks of Canadian off-shore drilling with recommendations expected by the end of 2011.

With respect to areas of interest in the Canadian Arctic, the Beaufort 6 Sea and Mackenzie Delta are likely the areas that would be developed more quickly than areas in the Eastern Arctic. Although the Eastern Arctic has high potential for exploitable stores of oil and gas, the transportation costs,[20] geographic remoteness and the fact that some of the basins that potentially hold oil and gas lie beneath the shifting Arctic Ocean ice pack may limit, or at the very least delay, the development of offshore oil and gas in that region.[21]

Development of Arctic offshore oil and gas would take place within the 7 traditional territorial waters of Indigenous peoples within the Canadian Arctic as well as in waters further out. The Inuvialuit Final Agreement[22] (IFA) covers the land bordering the Beaufort Sea as do the lands covered by Treaty 11.[23] It is important to note that the IFA gives the Inuvialuit the right to participate in decision making related to conservation and economic development in the Beaufort Sea since the sea is within the settlement region.[24] Maps of the areas where exploration licences have been issued in the Beaufort Sea show that many of the exploration areas are within close proximity to the Inuvialuit Settlement Lands and to Treaty 11 lands.[25] In the Eastern part of the Arctic, the Nunavut Land Claims Agreement[26] covers much of the land bordering the Arctic Ocean.

Regardless of the exact location of the wells, however, offshore oil and gas 8 development has the potential to negatively affect the reliance of Indigenous peoples on the subsistence harvesting of ocean resources in all the Arctic regions. The Inuvialuit, for example, rely on the subsistence hunting of belugas and bowhead whales in the Beaufort Sea, which migrate to waters within the Inuvialuit Settlement Region.[27] As discussed below, the potential for environmental harm from offshore oil and gas development would likely disproportionately affect Indigenous communities within the Canadian Arctic.

ENVIRONMENTAL IMPACTS OF ARCTIC OIL AND GAS DEVELOPMENT

The development of Arctic offshore oil and gas has the potential to create 9 generations of damage to the ecosystem and environment upon which Indigenous communities within Canada rely. The potential for environmental harm in the context of Arctic oil and gas development is intensified due to the climactic and logistical challenges of drilling and extraction in the Arctic region and due to the particular reliance of Indigenous communities on the resources within their traditional territories.

Challenges of offshore oil and gas development in the arctic

The Arctic environment creates particular challenges for the development of 10
offshore oil and gas. Challenges that increase the risk of environmental harm
in the context of Arctic oil and gas development include:

- the increased risks associated with the use of equipment and installations that have been developed for warmer climates;[28]
- the difficulty of ensuring same season relief well (SSRW) capacity for Arctic rigs;
- the logistical challenges associated with well-drilling as water depth, well depth and pressure transition increase;[29]
- the high reliance on additional vessels, which may increase the chances of vessel collisions leading to a blowout;[30]
- severe weather and ice conditions, along with increased extreme weather events due to climate change;[31]
- low visibility due to fog and darkness, which can last for months;[32]
- the need to drill wells over a number of warm seasons (open water seasons), which would likely require multiple well suspension and re-entries, causing increased risks due to either leaving well structures on the sea floor over the winter months or suspensions occurring during difficult conditions as winter approaches;[33] and
- the increased risk due to disconnecting while drilling as a result of rapid changes in weather or ice conditions in the Arctic.[34]

It is important to note that this list is not exhaustive given that extensive 11
offshore oil and gas development has not yet taken place in the Arctic, particularly at significant depths, so there may be many more risks particular to
such development that have yet to be identified. But also, some of the above-noted risks may not result in harm.

Challenges of containment in the arctic

Once a major oil spill occurs, the issue of containment becomes paramount. 12
Many of the factors that increase the risks of an oil and gas spill also would
impede efforts to effectively deal with such a spill. The World Wildlife Fund
(WWF) notes that: 'The same environmental conditions that contribute to oil
spill risks—lack of natural light, extreme cold, moving ice floes, high winds
and low visibility—can also make spill response operations extremely difficult
or totally ineffective.'[35] Furthermore, oil spills can occur during any stage of
oil and gas exploration, extraction or transport.[36]

In offshore areas, negative environmental impacts can occur through long- 13
range transport of contaminants by wind and sea currents, and rivers as well

as sediment transport in sea ice.[37] In the Arctic, the winter freeze could make access impossible for purposes of responding to and containing spillage.[38] Oil persists longer in Arctic conditions because it evaporates more slowly due to colder temperatures and may get trapped under ice, making it less susceptible to degradation.[39] In addition, remoteness, lack of infrastructure, transportation challenges and the small population in the Arctic would likely impede an effective response to an oil and gas spill such as the drilling of a SSRW.[40]

These environmental and logistical challenges combine to increase the 14 probability that if an oil spill were to occur, the timeliness of containment efforts would be impeded.[41] Any time-lapse makes spilled oil more difficult to track, recover and treat.[42] To date, no comprehensive 'response gap' analysis has been conducted for the Arctic, but the National Commission on the BP Deepwater Horizon Oil Spill and Offshore Drilling estimates that Arctic temperatures alone would prevent containment responses up to 50–64% of the time in the winter months.[43]

Environmental impacts of contaminants in the arctic

The environmental impacts of a blowout of an offshore oil and gas facility are a 15 cause for great concern,[44] as are the detrimental impacts of smaller leakages of petroleum products in the daily operations of such facilities and during the transport of such products.[45] Oil and gas spills have detrimental effects on the marine environment, including harm to the food chain and to marine organisms.[46] These detrimental effects also include death, the disruption of mating behaviour, coating of animals with oil, the ingestion of oil and the alteration of habitat.[47]

There are also risks of environmental harm as a result of the activities associ- 16 ated with oil and gas extraction. These activities include use of power generation equipment, supply activities and shuttle transportation, which can contribute to air pollution.[48] As well, the installation of equipment on the sea floor can negatively impact flora and fauna in the immediate vicinity and negatively affect fish and other water-dwelling species in those areas.[49] These risks are particularly threatening in the Arctic environment due to the fact that it is currently undergoing accelerated climate change and supports a fragile ecosystem.[50]

Effects of environmental harm for indigenous peoples

The risk of environmental harm is higher for Indigenous communities than 17 non-Indigenous people within Canada. Indigenous Peoples inhabit more remote areas in Canada's Arctic region than non-Indigenous people and Indigenous traditional territories often extend up into the sea ice in the Arctic. Indigenous communities have a close spiritual relationship with their traditional territories and rely more heavily on resources drawn directly from their lands and waters than non-Indigenous communities.[51] Indigenous communities also bear increased risks of environmental harm that are indirect, such as lack of access to traditional subsistence resources due to climate change[52] and air and water pollution that travels into their territories from more remote developments.[53] As a result, environmental harm and degradation disproportionately affect Indigenous communities and have the potential to threaten the traditional subsistence livelihood of the Indigenous Peoples within northern Canada.

Along with increased risk of suffering from environmental harms, 18 Indigenous communities often do not benefit financially from resource development activities that take place within their traditional territories.[54] In the case of offshore oil and gas development, for example, people who are brought in who already have the specialized skill sets largely staff such development projects. Indigenous communities may benefit from subsidiary service provision such as in the hospitality or restaurant industry or in the low-paying, unskilled jobs associated with oil and gas development; however, non- Indigenous people staff most of the high paying jobs. Unless there are particular benefits agreements negotiated, therefore, Indigenous peoples may not benefit economically to a large extent from such developments.

Indigenous communities also live with the consequences of environ- 19 mental harm from such developments for their lifetimes. Most offshore oil and gas development operations last for 20–50 years.[55] Once the petroleum resources are depleted, most of the non-Indigenous people that came to work on the development leave. However, local Indigenous communities remain and live within their traditional territories. This leaves Indigenous communities with the burden of dealing with environmental and social harms that were created as a result of resource development.[56] Furthermore, the influx of non-Indigenous people into previously isolated Indigenous communities can create social problems within such communities. Once petroleum resources are extracted, many of the towns that are set up to support the development are abandoned, leaving Indigenous populations with few economic options and increased social problems.[57]

RECONCILIATION AS A GUIDING PRINCIPLE

Given the increased risks of environmental, social and cultural harm in the 20 context of offshore oil and gas development for northern Indigenous communities, the principle of reconciliation may provide a starting point for respecting the rights of Indigenous Peoples in conflicts between Indigenous and non-Indigenous interests. The Supreme Court of Canada has increasingly elaborated upon reconciliation as a guiding principle to resolve disputes between Indigenous and non-Indigenous people. Similarly, theorists in dispute resolution have also considered reconciliation as a guiding principle in crafting strategies to resolve disputes. The following discussion provides a starting point on the evolving thinking in the Canadian context about reconciliation and how this principle might be applied to offshore oil and gas development in the Arctic.

Reconciliation has been enunciated as a guiding principle in the context of Aboriginal[58] rights litigation within Canadian jurisprudence. In *R. v. Van der Peet*,[59] the Supreme Court of Canada recognized that 'one of the fundamental purposes of s. 35(1) [which constitutionally affirms existing Aboriginal and treaty rights within Canada] is the reconciliation of the pre-existence of distinctive aboriginal societies with the assertion of Crown sovereignty'.[60] Moreover, the court has enunciated that the principle of reconciliation requires both Aboriginal and common law perspectives be taken into account and that '[t]rue reconciliation will, equally, place weight on each'.[61] Here, the court formulates reconciliation as a bridging concept that equally values pre-existing Indigenous cultures and non-Indigenous societies.[62]

In the following sections, I explore two aspects of reconciliation that the courts have identified as central to the resolution of Aboriginal rights claims in Canada: the duty to consult and accommodate, and the duty to negotiate.

Duty to consult and accommodate

Recent case law establishes that the principle of reconciliation manifests in the procedural requirements of the duty to consult and accommodate Aboriginal interests. In *Haida Nation v. British Columbia (Minister of Forests)*,[63] the Supreme Court of Canada held that the duty to consult and accommodate flows out of the principle of reconciliation,[64] and requires the federal and provincial governments to consult and potentially accommodate Aboriginal interests in the case of proven and not-yet-proven claims by Aboriginal communities.[65] The court held that: 'The foundation of the duty in the Crown's honour and the goal of reconciliation suggest that the duty [to consult] arises when the Crown has knowledge, real or constructive, of the potential existence of the Aboriginal right or title and contemplates conduct that might adversely affect it'.[66] In *Haida Nation,* the court also clarified that the principle of reconciliation requires balancing and compromise[67] and good faith effort on the part of government to substantially address the concerns of Aboriginal communities.[68]

In the context of Arctic offshore oil and gas development, preliminary exploration could result in environmental harm that may adversely affect Indigenous interests in the area. The decision regarding whether or not to issue exploration licenses, which would happen through the Canadian National Energy Board, therefore could potentially infringe Aboriginal rights. In *Standing Buffalo Dakota First Nation v. Enbridge Pipelines Inc.,*[69] the Canadian Federal Court of Appeal held that the NEB was not required to determine whether the government had met its duty to consult prior to approving project proposals from private companies related to three pipelines. It is likely, therefore, that the NEB would not be required to ensure that the government had consulted sufficiently in relation to issuing exploration licences regarding Arctic offshore oil and gas development.

With respect to historic treaties, in *Mikisew Cree First Nation v. Canada (Minister of Canadian Heritage),*[70] the Supreme Court of Canada clarified that the government has an ongoing duty to consult and accommodate in the context of such treaties.[71] The federal government would therefore have a duty to consult with the signatories to the Treaty 11 First Nations with respect to any development that might affect their interests. **25**

In the context of the opening up of Arctic offshore oil and gas in relation to the IFA and Nunavut Agreement, case law clearly establishes that where a modern land claims agreement is in effect, the government has a duty to consult and accommodate.[72] Similarly, case law supports the conclusion that the existence of a final agreement does not abrogate the common law duty to consult with Aboriginal communities. In *Little Salmon/ Carmacks First Nations v. Yukon (Minister of Energy, Mines and Resources),*[73] the Yukon Territorial Court of Appeal found that 'there can be no doubt that the duty to consult is recognized as a constitutional duty.'[74] Although in this case, the Court of Appeal held that the government had met its duty to consult, the court clearly established that the duty to consult continues to exist and may require further consultation with the relevant Indigenous communities beyond those obligations set out in a modern land claims agreement.[75] **26**

Although a legal duty to consult and accommodate exists on the part of the Canadian government where decisions have the potential to affect Indigenous interests,[76] the form and content of that duty remain relatively undefined. This is because the sufficiency of consultation and accommodation is assessed on a case-by-case basis and is highly context specific. However, the Supreme Court of Canada's articulation of the duty to consult has been critiqued by some academics as constituting a limiting vision of constitutionally protected Aboriginal rights. Gordon Christie, for example, argues that the duty to consult only requires the Canadian government to consult Aboriginal nations about the visions that the government has for the uses of Aboriginal lands but does not require that lands be used in a way that corresponds to Aboriginal nations' visions of their lands.[77] The duty to consult as currently formulated does not therefore leave room for Aboriginal peoples within Canada to promote their visions of how they want to relate to their traditional lands and waters. **27**

To create authentic social change in the form of a new relationship based on reconciliation, Indigenous peoples' voices need to be heard in a forum that encourages meaningful dialogue with the effect that their input can make a **28** difference in the outcome of decision making.[78] In the context of offshore oil and gas development, meaningful consultation should take place prior to the exploratory licensing process in order to identify any concerns that Indigenous communities may have with regard to opening up the Arctic for such development. Early consultations may reveal areas that need further research and may also highlight areas where traditional knowledge can inform decision making in relation to resource extraction. Further, processes need to be designed in a way that respects the cultural values and protocols of Indigenous communities. For example, timelines for consultation need to be reasonable to enable Indigenous leaders to consult appropriately with community members and explain relevant technical information.[79]

The duty to consult and accommodate lies on a spectrum depending on 29 the strength of the Indigenous communities' Aboriginal rights or treaty claims. The Supreme Court of Canada in *Haida Nation* elucidated how to determine the extent of consultation and accommodation in each particular case:

> At one end of the spectrum lie cases where the claim to title is weak, the Aboriginal right limited, or the potential for infringement minor. In such cases, the only duty on the Crown may be to give notice, disclose information, and discuss any issues raised in response to the notice…. At the other end of the spectrum lie cases where a strong prima facie case for the claim is established, the right and potential infringement is of high significance to the Aboriginal peoples, and the risk of non-compensable damage is high. In such cases deep consultation, aimed at finding a satisfactory interim solution, may be required. While precise requirements will vary with the circumstances, the consultation required at this stage may entail the opportunity to make submissions for consideration, formal participation in the decision-making process, and provision of written reasons to show that Aboriginal concerns were considered and to reveal the impact they had on the decision.[80]

In the context of Arctic offshore oil and gas development, the risks of envi- 30 ronmental harm to Indigenous communities within the Canadian Arctic are high as are the risks of non-compensable damage. Indigenous communities in the Canadian Arctic arguably have a strong claim for constitutional protection of their Aboriginal fishing, harvesting and hunting rights, and that such rights could be significantly infringed by the development of offshore oil and gas resources. It is arguable therefore that within this context the Canadian government has a significant duty to consult and accommodate the interests and concerns of the affected Indigenous communities.

The duty to accommodate flows from the concerns raised during mean- 31 ingful consultations. In *Haida Nation*, the Supreme Court of Canada elucidated on the duty to accommodate:

Balance and compromise are inherent in the notion of reconciliation. Where accommodation is required in making decisions that may adversely affect as yet unproven Aboriginal rights and title claims, the Crown must balance Aboriginal concerns reasonably with the potential impact of the decision on the asserted right or title and with other societal interests.[81]

In *Wii'litswx v. British Columbia (Minister of Forests)*,[82] the British 32 Columbia Supreme Court held that the duty to accommodate requires the Crown to demonstrate that it has listened to the First Nations concerns 'with an open mind', made a 'good faith effort to understand and address' such concerns, with a view to minimize the 'adverse effect of the decision' on the First Nation's interests and provide 'reasonable interim accommodation'.[83] In *Gitanyow First Nation v. British Columbia (Minister of Forests)*,[84] the British Columbia Supreme Court held that to fulfill the duty to accommodate, the Crown 'must be willing to make reasonable concessions based on the strength of the Aboriginal claim and the potentially adverse effect of the infringement in question'.[85] Case law therefore supports that accommodation must be reasonable and that the government must be willing to make concessions or change its decisions to appropriately address the concerns of Aboriginal communities whose interests may be adversely affected by such decisions.

In the context of offshore oil and gas development in the Arctic, the 33 British Columbia Supreme Court's decision in *West Moberly First Nations v. British Columbia*[86] may be relevant. In this case, exploration activity related to the development of a coal mine was stayed for ninety days in order to allow for appropriate consultation to put a plan into place to protect the habitat for the Burnt Pine herd of caribou, upon which the West Moberly First Nations relied. The court held that of the four measures the provincial government had taken to accommodate the West Moberly First Nations' concerns, two had been taken prior to consultation occurring and a third was taken for economic reasons. The fourth measure—a Caribou Mitigation and Monitoring Plan—was found by a government forest ecologist as insufficient to curb the destruction of 'substantial amounts of core winter and summer habitat' for the herd.[87] Further, the court held that it was not a reasonable accommodation for the government to say 'hunt elsewhere'.[88] In the context of Arctic offshore oil and gas development, *West Moberly* supports the need for the federal government to meaningfully consult, develop a mutually agreeable and appropriate plan to mitigate environmental harms and accommodate Aboriginal interests by potentially changing plans to develop oil and gas in the offshore.

Given the high risks of environmental harm and non-compensable 34 damage to the ecosystem and resources upon which the Indigenous peoples inhabiting the Canadian Arctic region, the government's duty to accommodate would likely be high in this context. Appropriate accommodations may range from ensuring that sacred cultural sites and significant fishing and harvesting areas are protected should development proceed to imposing a complete moratorium on development pending more scientific and environmental assessments of the risks of opening up the Arctic for offshore oil and gas development.

The duty to negotiate

Negotiation with Aboriginal communities is another key process flowing out of the principle of reconciliation. In *Rio Tinto Alcan Inc. v. Carrier Sekani Tribal Council*,[89] the Supreme Court of Canada recognized that the principle of reconciliation is aimed at promoting ongoing negotiations.[90] In *Mikisew Cree*, the court confirmed that the negotiation of a binding treaty does not end the government's duties of consultation and accommodation that flow out of the principle of reconciliation.[91] Instead, reconciliation requires ongoing dialogue as decisions are made that may negatively impact Aboriginal communities[92] whether or not they are signatories to a Treaty.[93]

The principle of reconciliation supports the ongoing negotiation and settlement of Indigenous land and self-determination claims over traditional territories, including water spaces. Although Canada is well known internationally for its comprehensive land claims agreements,[94] there remains a large number of Indigenous Peoples with which no settlement agreement has been concluded. Reconciliation supports the Canadian government's duty to negotiate fair and equitable settlement agreements, particularly in advance of decision making in relation to opening up the Arctic for increased offshore oil and gas development, which may have detrimental impacts on the constitutional rights of northern Indigenous communities.

Where resource development takes place within or in close proximity to traditional Indigenous territories, it is becoming increasingly common for development companies to negotiate Impact and Benefit Agreements (IBAs) with Indigenous communities whose rights will be affected by resource extraction.[95] Such IBAs may include compensation and other benefits for Indigenous groups such as employment practices and targets, business opportunities, training, scholarships and community projects.[96] Such agreements compensate Indigenous communities for increased risks to their territories and traditional livelihoods. In some cases, Indigenous communities have benefited from such agreements. However, oil and gas development companies may not believe that it is necessary to negotiate benefits agreements with those Indigenous communities without formal settlement agreements concluded with the Canadian government. This may put such communities at a distinct disadvantage and serve to foster ill will among Indigenous communities themselves.

Not only does the duty to negotiate flow out of the principle of recon- 38
ciliation, but also the duty to create ongoing collaborative processes in which
negotiations can continue to take place throughout development is central to
reconciliation. John Paul Lederach asserts that to create mutual respect and
provide the basis for redefining the relationship between Indigenous and non-
Indigenous people, it is necessary to create a 'context-based, permanent, and
dynamic platform'[97] that encourages 'ongoing genuine engagement between
opposing sides'.[98] This engagement is central to reconciliation since, in his
view, 'conflict is embedded in relational spaces, networks and connections'
and solutions need to 'emerge from relational resources, connections and
obligations'.[99] Through the creation of respectful spaces for negotiation, constructive dialogue can take place that has the potential to change the quality
and future of the relationship between Indigenous and non-Indigenous communities within Canada.

Shin Imai argues that Indigenous communities and the Canadian govern- 39
ment have a deep, ongoing and complex relationship and negotiations need
to foster collaboration.[100] He advocates culturally appropriate negotiation
which involves both parties in the design of the negotiation.[101] He also argues
that narrowing the scope of negotiation is counterproductive since it removes
the fundamental issues from the dialogue, such as whether or not resource
extraction should even take place.[102]

A key aspect of respectful negotiations is allowing appropriate time for 40
negotiations to take place, for Indigenous leaders to consult with their community members, and for Indigenous parties to the negotiations to access
experts to explain technical details before making any final decisions. There
is an inherent conflict between the need for legal certainty in the context of
resource extraction and the call for moral justice for Indigenous communities
whose lands have been taken, exploited and degraded without permission.[103]
The imperative of moral justice cannot be rushed: 'People working with reconciliation need to rethink healing as a process paced by its own inner timing,
which cannot be programmed or pushed to fit a project. People and communities have their own clocks.'[104] The principle of reconciliation therefore
is not merely procedural, but also can be applied to create ongoing, dynamic
processes to foster collaboration and respect between Indigenous communities, the Canadian government and industry.

TOWARDS A WORKING DEFINITION OF THE PRINCIPLE
OF RECONCILIATION

The principle of reconciliation holds promise to support the formulation of 41
a new respectful relationship between the Canadian government and Indigenous peoples within Canada. However, the way in which the Supreme Court

of Canada has conceptualized reconciliation is limiting as it constrains Indigenous peoples to adjust their visions of their relationships to their territorial lands and waters to comply with the plans that the Canadian government has for those lands. As Mark Walters argues, this type of 'one-sided reconciliation' requires Indigenous peoples to resign themselves to the reality that they must live according to the Canadian government's vision of how their territories should be used and adjust their expectations accordingly.[105] Although the court's pronouncements on the principle of reconciliation are helpful as a starting point, reconciliation needs to be developed more fully to provide substantive justice to Indigenous peoples within Canada.

The principle of reconciliation embodies a promise that the interests of Indigenous communities within Canada will be respected and their rights will be constitutionally protected. Reconciliation is an idealistic principle that involves moral, ethical and legal obligations on the part of government to ensure that Indigenous rights are respected, Indigenous voices and concerns are heard, and a new respectful relationship is created between Indigenous peoples and the Canadian State.

A central aspect of reconciliation, as the Supreme Court's conceptualiza- 42 tion illustrates, is the creation of a new relationship. This new relationship has at its foundation the creation of respectful spaces that encourage dialogue between Indigenous peoples and non-Indigenous governments and corporate actors. Consultation, accommodation and negotiation are all based on the creation of respectful dialogue where Indigenous peoples can share their concerns and have those concerns taken seriously in decision-making processes. Reconciliation is an approach that attempts to give proper recognition to the interests of parties to the greatest degree possible.[106] As Mark Walters argues, a fulsome conceptualization of reconciliation involves the idea of 'mutual reconciliation' which 'implies a process of mutual adjustment and adaptation by both aboriginal and non-aboriginal legal traditions' creating 'the articulation of a constitutional middle ground upon which a truly intersocietal law may emerge'.[107] The goal of reconciliation is to restore and rebuild the relationship[108] between Indigenous communities and the Canadian government based on mutual respect, collaborative dialogue and meaningful communication.

CONCLUSION

The opening up of offshore oil and gas development in the Arctic is fraught 43 with uncertainty. At this point, what is certain is that Arctic conditions, both environmental and logistical, create high risks of environmental harm and high risks of such harm disproportionately impacting Indigenous communities within Canada's northern territories. The principle of reconciliation supports meaningful consultation with Indigenous communities, efforts to substantially address Indigenous concerns and ongoing collaborative nego-tiations in the context of such development. Infused with ethical and moral imperatives, reconciliation may even result in a halt on offshore oil and gas development in the Arctic until more information on the risks becomes avail-able and Indigenous Peoples are satisfied that such development does not threaten their livelihoods, cultural communities and traditional territories. Finally, this fulsome and robust conception of reconciliation may also lead to the final decision that developing offshore oil and gas resources in the Arctic is not a reasonable way to achieve the goal of a new respectful relationship between the Canadian governments and northern Indigenous communities within Canada.

NOTES

1 The term 'offshore' in this article captures all oil and gas development in sea spaces, and includes all drilling and exploration at sea.

2 R.S. Fjellheim, 'Arctic Oil and Gas: Corporate Social Responsibility', 4 *Gáldu Cala: Journal of Indigenous Peoples Rights* (2006), 8, at 9, found at <http://www.galdu.org/govat/doc/oilengelsk2 .pdf>; WWF, *Oil Spill: Response Challenges in Arctic Waters* (WWF International Arctic Pro-gramme, 2007), at 7, found at <http://assets.panda.org/ downloads/nuka_oil_spill_response_ report_final_jan_08.pdf>.

3 See Arctic Transform, 'Policy Options for Arctic Environmental Governance' (Indigenous Peoples Working Group, 5 March 2009), at 1, found at <http://arctic-transform.org/download/ IndPeEX.pdf>. Arctic Transform identifies Inuit, Inuvialuit, Athabaskans and Dene as the Indigenous Peoples of the Canadian Arctic. It is these four Indigenous communities that I refer to throughout this article, although the implications for opening up offshore oil and gas development in the Arctic may be similar for other Indigenous communities in States bordering Arctic waters other than Canada.

4 This is demonstrated by the Inuit Circumpolar Conference's international legal challenge in rela-tion to the United States' inaction to reduce fossil fuel consumption and its contribution to climate change that disproportionately affects Inuit communities in the Arctic. See S. Watt-Cloutier et al., *Petition to the Inter American Commission on Human Rights Seeking Relief from Violations Result-ing from Global Warming Caused by Acts and Omissions of the United States* (2 December 2007), found at <http://www.ciel.org/Publications/ ICC_Petition_7Dec05.pdf>.

5 'History of Oil and Gas in the NWT' (Government of Northwest Territories, Industry, Tourism and Investment, undated), 1, at 1, found at <http://www.iti.gov.nt.ca/mineralsoilgas/historyoilgas.shtml>.

6 Ibid., at 2.

7 Ibid., at 3.

8 'Oil and Gas Resource Assessments' (Government of Yukon, Energy, Mines and Resources, undated), 1, found at <http://www.emr.gov.yk.ca/oilandgas/oilgas_resource_assessments.html>.

9 See 'History of Oil and Gas in the NWT', n. 5 above, at 4.

10 Mr Justice Thomas R. Berger, *Northern Frontier, Northern Homeland: The Report of the Mac-kenzie Valley Pipeline Inquiry* (Douglas & McIntyre, 1988). This investigation was commissioned by the federal government.

11 Ibid., at ix.

12 Northern Oil and Gas Directorate, *Petroleum Exploration in Northern Canada: A Guide to Oil and Gas Exploration and Potential,* Catalogue No. R72-239/1995E, Indian and Northern Affairs Canada (Minister of Public Works, 1995), at Preface, found at <http://www.collectionscanada .gc.ca/webarchives/20071122052027/http://www.ainc-inac.gc.ca/oil/bkgd/prospectus/index_ e.html>.

13 See 'Oil and Gas Resource Assessments', n. 8 above, at 13; and ibid., at 3.

14 See Northern Oil and Gas Directorate, n. 12 above, at 65.

15 Ibid., at 5.

16 For information on which companies hold exploration licences in the Beaufort Sea and Mackenzie Delta, see the Government of Canada, Indian and Northern Affairs website [INAC website], found at <http://www.ainc-inac.gc.ca/nth/og/rm/ri/bsm/index-eng.asp>.

17 Ibid.

18 See 'History of Oil and Gas in the NWT', n. 5 above, at 5.

19 Ibid.

20 See Northern Oil and Gas Directorate, n. 12 above, at 80.

21 Ibid., at 96.

22 Canada, *The Western Arctic Claim: The Inuvialuit Final Agreement* (Ministry of Indian Affairs and Northern Development, 1984), found at <http://www.collectionscanada.gc.ca/ webarchives/20071115155259/http://www.ainc-inac.gc.ca/pr/agr/inu/wesar_e.html>.

23 *Treaty No. 11 (June 27, 1921) and Adhesion (July 17, 1922) with Reports, etc.* Reprinted from the 1926 edition by Edmond Cloutier, c.m.g., o.a., d.s.p., (Queen's Printer and Controller of Stationery, 1957), found at <http://www.ainc-inac.gc.ca/al/hts/tgu/pubs/t11/trty11-eng.asp>.

24 W. Spicer and T. Bath, 'The Canadian Arctic: The Changing Seascape of Offshore Oil and Gas Exploration Issues', 48 *Alta. L. Rev.* (2010), 255 at para. 83.

25 See INAC website, n. 16 above.

26 *Agreement Between the Inuit of the Nunavut Settlement Area and Her Majesty the Queen in Right of Canada* (25 May 1993), found at <http://www.tunngavik.com/documents/publications/ 1993-00-00-Nunavut-Land-Claims-Agreement-English.pdf>. For settlement legislation, see the *Nunavut Land Claims Agreement Act,* SC 1993, c. 29. It is important to note that Spicer and Bath (n. 24 above, at paras. 89–93) highlight the importance of the North Baffin Regional Land Use Plan, which was prepared by the Nunavut Planning Commission, and took effect in June 2000. The Plan provides for the duty to consult in Article 3.7 in the context of oil and gas exploration in the Arctic region.

27 L.A. Harwood and T.G. Smith, 'Whales of the Inuvialuit Settlement Region in Canada's Western Arctic: An Overview and Outlook', 55 (Supp. 1) *Arctic* (2002), 77 (translated by Nesida Loyer), at 77.

28 See R.S. Fjellheim, n. 2 above, at 10.

29 Ecojustice, *Suggested Studies and Preliminary Response to CFI #1 and #2* (Ecojustice, 2010), at 10, found at <https://neb-one.gc.ca/ll-eng/livelink.exe?func=ll&objd=654255&objAction= browse>.

30 Ibid., at 11.

31 Ibid.

32 See WWF, n. 2 above, at 3 and 15.

33 See Ecojustice, n. 29 above, at 12.

34 Ibid., at 13.

35 See WWF, n. 2 above, at 3. It is important to note, however, that WWF recognizes (at 15) that some Arctic conditions may in fact help containment in certain circumstances (i.e., sea ice may trap spilled oil or provide a platform from which to respond to spillage). However, studies of other oil spills in harsh weather conditions support the conclusion that logistical challenges, remote locations and harsh weather complicate oil spill responses (Ibid., at 22).

36 Ibid., at 7.

37 *Arctic Council, Arctic Offshore Oil and Gas Guidelines,* Protection of the Marine Environment Working Group (Arctic Council, 29 April 2009), at 7.

38 National Commission on the BP Deepwater Horizon Oil Spill and Offshore Drilling, 'The Challenges of Oil Spill Response in the Arctic', Staff Working Paper No. 5 (October 2010), at 2, found at <https://www.neb-one.gc.ca/ll-eng/livelink.exe/fetch/2000/90463/621169/649241/654255/A1W4D1_-_Attachment_11 National_Commission_Staff_Working_Paper_on_Oil_Spill_Response_in_ the_Arctic,_Oct_2010.pdf?nodeid=654370&vernum=0>.

39 See WWF, n. 2 above, at 7.

40 See Ecojustice, n. 29 above, at 30.

41 Ibid., at 30.

42 Ibid., at 31, citing Nuka Research and Planning Group and US Arctic Program, Pew Environment Group, *Oil Spill Prevention and Response in the US Arctic Ocean: Unexamined Risks, Unacceptable Consequences* (November 2010), at 64, found at <https://www.neb-one.gc.ca/ll-eng/livelink.exe/fetch/2000/90463/621169/649241/654255/A1W4S1_-_Attachment_15_-_PEW_Arctic_Oil_Spill_Prevention_and_Response_Report,_Nov_2010.pdf?nodeid=654792&vernum=0>.

43 See National Commission on the BP Deepwater Horizon Oil Spill and Offshore Drilling, n. 38 above, at 11, citing Shell, 'Chukchi Sea Regional Exploration Oil Discharge Prevention and Contingency Plan' (March 2010), at 3-20, found at <http://alaska.boemre.gov/fo/ ODPCPs/2010_Chukch_cPlan.pdf>.

44 Although recognizing there is a wide range of estimates for the probability of a blowout in the Arctic, Ecojustice, on behalf of WWF, estimates one blowout every 16 years if ten wells per year were drilled in the Canadian Beaufort Sea. See Ecojustice, n. 29 above, at 10. Many people world-wide are particularly concerned about the negative environmental impacts of a blowout due to the recent BP oil spill in the Gulf of Mexico.

45 In M.W. McPhee, *Offshore Oil and Gas in Canada: West Coast Environmental, Social and Economic Issues* (Westwater Research Centre (UBC), 1982), at 4. McPhee notes that routine spillage can occur whenever oil and gas products are transported.

46 WWF (n. 2 above, at 1) notes that in the Arctic, the polar bear, which stands at the top of the food chain, is particularly susceptible to any changes in the ecosystem. Furthermore, endangered dolphins, whales and porpoises rely on Arctic food sources and are susceptible to noise from seismic exploration for oil.

47 See M.W. McPhee, n. 45 above, at 64.

48 See Arctic Council, n. 37 above, at 8.

49 Ibid.

50 Ibid.

51 B.J. Richardson, 'The Ties that Bind: Indigenous Peoples and Environmental Governance', in B.J. Richardson, S. Imai and K. McNeil (eds), *Indigenous Peoples and the Law: Comparative and Critical Perspectives* (Hart, 2009), 337, at 348.

52 See S. Watt-Cloutier et al., n. 4 above, at 39.

53 See, e.g., Ecojustice, 'Mercury Threat Rising in Ontario: Northern Mining May Compromise Health of Ontario Fish-eaters', Media Release (6 March 2008), found at Ecojustice <http://www .ecojustice.ca/media-centre/press-releases/mercury-threat-rising-in-ontario>; see also Ecojustice's Charter challenge under ss. 7 and 15 for violations against the Aamjiwnaang First Nation stemming from toxic air pollution in Sarnia, Ontario, described in K. Mitchell, 'Human Rights and Pollution in Sarnia's Chemical Valley', Ontario Bar Association – Environews (6 December 2010), found at <http://www.ecojustice.ca/ media-centre/press-clips/human-rights-and-pollution-in-sarnias- chemical-valley>.

54 See R.S. Fjellheim, n. 2 above, at 13.

55 Ibid., at 12.

56 Ibid., at 13.

57 Ibid.

58 I use the term 'Aboriginal' to denote the particular legal meaning within the *Constitution Acts 1982,* being Schedule B to the *Canada Act 1982* (UK), c. 11, which defines this term to include 'Indian, Inuit and Métis peoples of Canada' (s. 35(2)).

59 *R. v. Van der Peet* (1996) 2 SCR 507 *(Van der Peet).*

60 Ibid., at para. 49. Justice McLachlin's dissent in *Van der Peet* illustrates that there exist divergent views within the court itself on the practical implications of the principle of reconciliation in resolving Aboriginal rights disputes. In her dissent at paragraphs 310-315, Justice McLachlin argues that the majority's interpretation of reconciliation under s. 35 elevates the interests of non-Indigenous people within Canada and may have the effect of transferring the rights of Aboriginal peoples to non-Aboriginal in certain circumstances (for example in regards to fishing). Instead, she advocates negotiated settlements as the way to promote reconciliation of the interests of Aboriginal and non-Aboriginal peoples.

61 Ibid., at para. 50.

62 It is important to note that despite the promise of reconciliation in s. 35 of the *Constitution Acts 1982* for Indigenous peoples within Canada, the Supreme Court of Canada has not always found the principle of reconciliation to be supportive of Indigenous rights. In *R. v. Gladstone,* (1996) 2 SCR 723 *(Gladstone),* the court held that limits placed on Aboriginal rights can be justified on the basis of the principle of reconciliation 'where the objectives furthered by those limits are of sufficient importance to the broader community as a whole' (at para. 73). In *Gladstone,* the court gives as examples conservation as well as the pursuit of economic and regional fairness as potential limits that might be justified on the basis of reconciliation (at paras. 74–5). It is important to note that in mentioning economic and regional fairness, the court was clear that it was not making a definitive statement on whether those might justify the infringement of Aboriginal rights. Further, in *Delgamuukw v. British Columbia,* (1997) 3 SCR 1010 *(Delgamuukw),* the court enumerated a long list of limits that might be justified in infringing Aboriginal rights in keeping with the principle of reconciliation (at para. 165). As well, in *Mitchell v. Canada (MNR),* (2001) 1 SCR. 911 *(Mitchell),* at para. 164, the court held that the principle of reconciliation should be interpreted to affirm the collective sovereignty of Canadians with the result being the denial of Mohawk sovereignty in crossing the United States–Canada border with goods to gift to members of their community who lived on the opposite side of the international border. As the next section illustrates, more recent

cases have interpreted the principle of reconciliation to impose particular obligations on the federal and provincial governments to consult, accommodate and negotiate. However, the previously mentioned cases are still good law and it remains to be seen whether the more recent case law will provide a turning point in the way in which reconciliation is both interpreted and applied in the context of Aboriginal claims.

63 *Haida Nation v. British Columbia (Minister of Forests)* (2004) 3 SCR 511 *(Haida Nation).*

64 Ibid., at para. 32.

65 Ibid., at para. 27.

66 Ibid., at para. 35.

67 Ibid., at para. 50. See also *Taku River Tlingit First Nation v. British Columbia (Project Assessment Director),* (2004) 3 SCR 550 (Taku River).

68 See *Haida Nation,* n. 63 above, at para. 49.

69 *Standing Buffalo Dakota First Nation v. Enbridge Pipelines, Inc.* (2009), 313 DLR (4th) 217 (FCA).

70 *Mikisew Cree First Nation v. Canada (Minister of Canadian Heritage) (2005) 3 SCR 388.* In *Mikisew Cree,* the Supreme Court of Canada rejected the government's position that it could make unilateral decisions regarding lands subject to historic treaties on the basis that the land had been surrendered: 'There is in the Minister's argument a strong advocacy of unilateral Crown action (a sort of "this is surrendered land and we can do with it what we like" approach) which not only ignores the mutual promises of the treaty, both written and oral, but also is the antithesis of reconciliation and mutual respect' (at para. 49).

71 Ibid., at para. 55.

72 See *Quebec (Attorney General) v. Moses,* [2010] SCJ 17; see also *Qiliqtani Inuit Assn. v. Canada (Minister of Natural Resources),* [2010] NUCJ 12.

73 *Little Salmon/Carmacks First Nations v. Yukon (Minister of Energy, Mines and Resources)* (2008) YJ No. 55 *(Little Salmon).* This case was heard by the Supreme Court of Canada in 2009, but the decision has not yet been released.

74 Ibid., at para. 88.

75 See W. Spicer and T. Bath, n. 24 at para. 106.

76 In D. Reid and S. Hickman, 'Aboriginal Rights and the Atlantic Canada Petroleum Industry', 30 *Dalhousie L.J.* (2007), 383, at 421-2, the authors opine that there would likely be no duty to consult with Aboriginal communities in connection with offshore oil and gas development but that onshore developments, such as storage facilities may affect Aboriginal rights and as a result could potentially attract a duty to consult and accommodate.

77 G. Christie, 'A Colonial Reading of Recent Jurisprudence: Sparrow, Delgamuukw and Haida Nation', 23 *Windsor Y.B. Access Just.* (2005), 17, at para. 56.

78 J.P. Lederach, *The Moral Imagination: The Art and Soul of Building Peace* (Oxford University Press, 2005), at 56.

79 First Nations of Quebec and Labrador Sustainable Development Institute, 'Consultations Protocol of First Nations of Quebec and Labrador' (Assembly of First Nations of Quebec and Labrador, 2005), at 8.

80 See *Haida Nation,* n. 63 above, at paras. 43–4.

81 Ibid., at para. 50.

82 Wii'litswx v. British Columbia (Minister of Forests) (2008) BCJ No. 1159 (BCSC).

83 Ibid., at para. 220. In this case, the British Columbia Supreme Court held that the Crown had breached its duty consult and accommodate.

84 *Gitanyow First Nation v. British Columbia (Minister of Forests)* (2004) 38 BCLR (4th) 57 (BCSC). In this case, the Crown was held to have honoured its duty to consult, but the court ordered the parties to continue to negotiate and find accommodation.

85 Ibid., at para. 50.

86 *West Moberly First Nations v. British Columbia* (2010), 6 BCLR (5th) 94 (BCSC) *[West Moberly]*.

87 Ibid., at para. 57.

88 Ibid., at para. 62. Another case in which the British Columbia Supreme Court held that the government had not met its duty to accommodate is *Huu-Ay-Aht First Nation v. British Columbia (Minister of Forests),* (2005), 3 CNLR 74 (BCSC). For detailed summaries of Canadian case law relating to Aboriginal rights, including the duty to consult, see S. Imai, *The 2011 Annotated Indian Act and Aboriginal Constitutional Provisions* (Carswell, 2011).

89 *Rio Tinto Alcan Inc. v. Carrier Sekani Tribal Council* (2010) 4 CNLR 250.

90 Ibid., at para. 38.

91 See *Mikisew Cree,* n. 70 above, at para. 54.

92 Ibid.

93 Ibid. See also *Beckman v. Little Salmon/Carmacks First Nation,* [2010] SCJ No. 53, at para. 91. Further, the principle of reconciliation has been used as an interpretive tool for the court to determine the meaning of various treaty provisions (see, e.g., *R. v. Morris,* [2006] 2 SCR 915, at para. 38).

94 See, e.g., G. Nettheim, G.D. Meyers and D. Craig, *Indigenous Peoples and Governance Structures: A Comparative Analysis of Land and Resource Management Rights* (Aboriginal Studies Press, Australian Institute of Aboriginal and Torres Strait Islander Studies, 2002), at 475.

95 IBAs are also known as 'Participation Agreements'. For a discussion of the practical considerations in the negotiation of IBAs, see S. Gogal, R. Riegert and J. Jamieson, 'Aboriginal Impact and Benefit Agreements: Practical Considerations', 43 *Alta. L. Rev.* (2005), 129.

96 Canadian Institute of Resources Law, *Independent Review of the BHP Diamond Mine Process* (Canadian Institute of Resources Law, 30 June 1997), at 28. IBAs are confidential documents usually containing a non-disclosure clause that serves to reinforce the power of development companies in negotiating agreements and limit the access of other Indigenous communities to precedents in negotiating their own IBAs.

97 See J.P. Lederach, n. 78 above, at 47.

98 Ibid., at 58.

99 Ibid., at 76–7.

100 S. Imai, 'Sound Science, Careful Policy Analysis and Ongoing Relationships: Integrating Litigation and Negotiation in Aboriginal Lands and Resources Disputes', 41 *Osgoode Hall L.J.* (2003), 587, at paras. 57 and 105.

101 Ibid., at paras. 107–8.

102 Ibid., at para. 112.

103 P. Regan, *Unsettling the Settler Within: Indian Residential Schools, Truth Telling and Reconciliation in Canada* (UBC Press, 2010), at 17.

104 See J.P. Lederach, n. 78 above, at 160.

105 M. Walters, 'The Morality of Aboriginal Law', 31 *Queen's L.J.* (2006), 470, at para. 56.

106 The Honourable Justice Frank Iacobucci, '"Reconciling Rights": The Supreme Court of Canada's Approach to Competing Charter Rights', (2003) SCLR (2d), 137, at 162 and 167.

107 See M. Walters, n. 105 at para. 56.

108 J.P. Lederach, *Building Peace: Sustainable Reconciliation in Divided Societies* (United States Institute of Peace, 1997), at 24.

QUESTIONS

1. What is the thesis of this article?
2. What negative impact on the Arctic Indigenous communities might oil and gas exploration have?
3. What positive impact on the Arctic Indigenous communities might oil and gas exploration have?
4. The Berger Report did not encourage exploration, yet several oil companies petitioned for exploratory licenses. How do you explain this apparent contradiction?
5. Provide an example wherein the author acknowledges an opposing point of view.
6. Why is the threat of an oil spill especially significant in the Arctic?
7. Why are the economic benefits to Indigenous communities resulting from oil and gas exploration not as significant as they might be?
8. Summarize and synthesize the author's arguments in opposition to oil and gas exploration in the Arctic.
9. What is the "principle of reconciliation"?
10. Select a paragraph the topic sentence of which is developed effectively by the use of examples.
11. Select a paragraph the topic sentence of which is developed effectively by definition of key term or terms.
12. Under what circumstances might the government impose a complete moratorium on oil and gas exploration and development in the Arctic?
13. The author of this article tends to avoid emotional appeals in support of her arguments. Write a paragraph, related to the topic of this article, which contains an emotional appeal.
14. Define the term "culturally appropriate negotiation."
15. What, according to the author, are the limitations of the principle of reconciliation as it is presently constructed?

This article was published in the *Journal of Sex Research*, volume 49, issue 2–3, 2012, pages 274–281.

Young Adults and Casual Sex: The Relevance of College Drinking Settings[†]

Melina M. Bersamin[a, *], Mallie J. Paschall[b], Robert F. Saltz[b] & Byron L. Zamboanga[c]

[a]*Department of Child Development, California State University, Sacramento*
[b]*Prevention Research Center*
[c]*Department of Psychology, Smith College*

Version of record first published: 24 May 2011

This study investigated the relevance of college drinking settings on the likelihood of students having sexual intercourse with a stranger. A random sample of 7,414 undergraduates at 14 public California universities responded to questions regarding frequency of attendance at six different setting types since the beginning of the semester (e.g., Greek, residence-hall parties, and bars or restaurants), drinking behavior, and sexual activity. Multi-level modeling examined the association between each setting type and the occurrence of alcohol-related sexual intercourse with a stranger. Findings indicated strong, positive associations between frequency of attendance at Greek parties, residence-hall parties, off-campus parties, and the occurrence of alcohol-related sex with a stranger. Frequency of attending the six settings and proportion of times drunk at the settings were also positively associated with alcohol-related sex with a stranger. Efforts aimed at preventing outcomes associated with casual sex (e.g., pregnancy, sexually transmitted infections, or mental health) should target specific drinking settings where students might be at high risk for risky alcohol use and unsafe sex behaviors.

Several studies have found that casual sex is not an unusual event among college students. For example, a random sample of undergraduate students found that 30% had engaged in sexual intercourse with a stranger or brief acquaintance in college, and 48% had some physical interaction (but no sexual intercourse) with a stranger in college (Paul, McManus, & Allison, 2000). A study of Canadian university students found that 33% of college males reported having had sex with someone they had met that day or evening compared to 16% of females (Herold, Maticka-Tyndale, & Mewhinney, 1998). Young adults who have engaged in sexual intercourse with a relative stranger are

[†] Melina M. Bersamin, Mallie J. Paschall, Robert F. Saltz, and Byron L. Zamboanga, "Young Adults and Casual Sex: The Relevance of College Drinking Settings," in the *Journal of Sex Research*, Volume 49, Issue 2-3, 2012, pages 274–281. Reprinted by permission of Taylor & Francis Ltd, http://www.tandf.co.uk/journals.

* Correspondence should be addressed to Melina M. Bersamin, Department of Child Development, California State University, Sacramento, 6000 J St., Sacramento, CA 95819-6139. Email: bersamin@csus.edu

NEL

significantly more likely to report a sexually transmitted infection (STI) than those who have not (Tanfer, Cubbins, & Billy, 1995). It may be that the risk for STIs is potentially higher with partners whose sexual history is unknown. Sexual experiences outside of a romantic context have also been linked to negative socio-emotional outcomes, such as depression (Grello, Welsh, & Harper, 2006). Given that adolescents and young adults acquire half of all new STIs (Centers for Disease Control, 2010), continued research on college students' risky sexual behavior can help inform appropriate and effective STI prevention strategies for this population.

Research with college students has documented a relationship between heavy alcohol use and risky sexual behaviors (Cooper, 2002). For example, a recent study examined the relationship between condom use, alcohol use, and partner type and found that alcohol use decreased condom use in casual sex partnerships (LaBrie, Earleywine, Schiffman, Pedersen, & Marriot, 2005). In addition, several studies have found a positive association between drinking and having a more casual sexual relationship, as measured by partner intimacy (e.g., from someone you just met to your fiancée; Cooper, Peirce, & Huselid, 1994; Cooper, Skinner, & George, 1990; Graves & Leigh, 1995; Testa & Collins, 1997), whereas others have found a positive association between heavy drinking and having multiple sexual partners (Poulin & Graham, 2001; Santelli, Robin, Brener, & Lowry, 2001; Thompson, Kao, & Thomas, 2005; Wechsler, Dowdall, Davenport, & Castillo, 1995). Research has explored psychological and cognitive mechanisms that may explain the relationship between drinking and risky sexual behavior (e.g., alcohol-related sexual expectancies, alcohol myopia theory, or propensity for sensation-seeking), and psychosocial risk factors that contribute to alcohol-related sexual behavior. This study examined the relevance of drinking context on young adult sexual behaviors. This is an important avenue of research for both students and college administrators as it contributes to better understanding environmental factors associated with unwanted pregnancy, STI, and poor mental health outcomes in a college population.

A majority of studies that examine the relationship between alcohol use and sexual behavior utilize global associations—that is, simply assessing the correlation between the key variables of interest (e.g., frequency of binge drinking and frequency of casual sex). This methodology is limited because it does not take into account the co-occurrence of the two behaviors. The relationship between alcohol use and risky sexual behavior might be an artifact of a third variable, such as sensation-seeking; thus, drinking and risky sex may be occurring on separate occasions (see Cooper, 2002). Event analyses studies are a methodological improvement on previous work in that these studies focus on a specific sexual incident (e.g., most recent sexual experience) and explore the use of alcohol and/or risky sexual behavior during that event. This study is an improvement to previous research in that there is a shift away from global associations between drinking and sexual behaviors and toward event analysis; specifically, measures of location/drinking context, alcohol use, and sexual behavior are linked to one occasion.

To date, few studies have taken an ecological approach to examine how drinking contexts or settings may relate to the co-occurrence of alcohol use and risky sexual behaviors. This is surprising, as a significant body of literature has focused on the role of settings on alcohol expectancies (e.g., Wall, McKee, & Hinson, 2000; Wall, McKee, Hinson, & Goldstein, 2001; Wigmore & Hinson, 1991; Zamboanga, 2005; Zamboanga & Ham, 2008) and drinking behaviors (Clapp, Shillington, & Segars, 2000; Demers et al., 2002; Paschall & Saltz, 2007). The situational-specificity hypothesis suggests that drinking behaviors and patterns are a function of environmental cues (see Wall et al., 2001). Cues unique to each environment influence alcohol expectancies (Wall et al., 2001), as well as memory associations (Lau-Barraco & Dunn, 2009), which, in turn, may influence alcohol use patterns. As such, different environments or contexts engender different cues leading to unique patterns of drinking behaviors. Similarly, it can be argued that alcohol-related risky sexual behavior differs based on contextual factors associated with specific drinking locations.

To complement research focusing on individual risk factors for alcohol-related risky sexual behavior, research should also consider drinking settings. Focusing on specific localities provides public health practitioner researchers with additional tools to utilize in their efforts to effectively provide health-related information and resources (e.g., condoms, attending events with a group of friends that can provide support, knowing and trusting the local bartender or party host, or using environmental strategies to create a low-risk drinking setting, such as responsible beverage service training and low alcohol content beverages). For example, the social context of a bar may be more (or less) strongly associated with the likelihood of risky alcohol-related sexual behavior among college students compared to the context of a party in a residence hall or an off-campus apartment. Unique setting characteristics may exist that increase students' risk for alcohol-related sexual behavior, regardless of drinking behavior or other individual characteristics. Arguably, it would follow to direct resources, intended to support healthy behaviors, to this venue. This study focused on how college-specific drinking settings (fraternity or sorority [Greek] parties, residence-hall parties, off-campus parties, campus events, bars or restaurants, and outdoor settings) are associated with having sexual intercourse with a stranger as a result of drinking, controlling for individual- and population-level factors.

4

5

DRINKING SETTINGS, DRINKING BEHAVIOR, AND DRINKING-RELATED CONSEQUENCES

Several studies have found associations between specific drinking settings and   6
alcohol consumption. For example, a recent survey of students at a California
public university found that alcohol consumption among students, both under
and of the legal drinking age, was higher if they were drinking in public bars
in Mexico versus private parties in the United States. In addition, a hierarchical
regression model predicting alcohol consumption found that the addition of
a location variable (public bars or private parties) significantly increased the
model's predictive power (Clapp, Reed, Holmes, Lange, & Voas, 2006). A study
based on the Canadian Campus Survey, a random sample of 8,864 students from
18 universities in Canada, also examined the relationship between drinking setting and alcohol consumption per drinking occasion. A multi-level analysis
found that while individual-level characteristics (e.g., gender) were associated
with alcohol intake per occasion, so were situational characteristics (e.g., private
settings or bars). Specifically, college students who drank off campus and at
bars or discos were at greater risk for higher levels of alcohol consumption than
those who drank on campus or at home (Demers et al., 2002).

Studies have also examined how drinking settings are associated with   7
negative drinking outcomes. For example, a study based on data from the
National Alcohol and Drug Survey of Canadian households found an association between drinking at bars or taverns and self-reported drinking problems.
Specifically, respondents who identified themselves as current drinkers were
asked if their alcohol use in the past year had caused any problems (e.g., social,
physical, or financial). Multivariate analyses that controlled for demographic
variables and drinking behaviors found that the proportion of total drinking
done at bars or taverns and parties or weddings were positively related to the
total number of alcohol-related problems. Conversely, the proportion of total
drinking conducted at home, restaurants, or during recreational activities was
not associated with alcohol-related problems (Single & Wortley, 1993).

STUDY AIMS AND HYPOTHESES

This study extends previous research by examining how six different types of   8
drinking settings—Greek fraternity or sorority parties, residence-hall parties,
campus events (e.g., concert or sporting event), parties at off-campus houses
or apartments, restaurants or bars, and outdoor settings (e.g., park or beach)—
might impact sex with a relative stranger after drinking at those settings in a
large sample of college students. Given previous research suggesting a relationship between having sex with a relative stranger and STIs, it is important to
examine how individual characteristics are associated with this sexual behavior
and examine how unique contexts may impact this behavior. Findings from this
research can be used to identify physical locations where prevention efforts can

be targeted precisely at the point when risk is present, and reach students who may be at risk, simply as a result of attending a particular venue. In addition, we can train wellness educators to discuss risks that may emerge at specific venues, as well as educate individuals who work at high-risk venues.

Unlike prior studies, we used within-student, setting-level data to examine   9
relationships between drinking settings and the incidence of having sex with a stranger, controlling for student- and college-level factors that may account for those relationships. We also accounted for potential confounding factors, including frequency of attendance and drinking behavior at each setting, to ensure that effects were a result of setting characteristics and not a simple function of exposure (e.g., young people having a location to congregate, consume alcohol, and meet strangers). We hypothesized that sex with a stranger would be most likely to occur at drinking venues with the lowest level of social controls (e.g., absence of law enforcement, security, or residence-hall monitors), such as Greek and off-campus parties, and that these differences would remain even after adjusting for student- and college-level characteristics that could influence opportunities for risky alcohol-related sexual behavior.

METHOD
Procedure

In the Fall of 2003, a random sample of 14,280 undergraduates at 14 public   10
California universities (eight from the University of California system and six from the California State University system) participated in a Web-based or mailed confidential survey. Institutional review boards from all participating universities and research institutions approved the human subject protocol. The survey data were collected at baseline as part of a multi-campus intervention study. A simple random sample of 2,000 undergraduate students per college campus was targeted for data collection, for a total of 28,000. A "pre-notification" letter informed students of the study. An email invitation followed with a URL that the student could click on to go to a Web site that hosted the survey. Additional follow-up attempts included two email reminders and a hard copy of the questionnaire sent to their home address. This was followed by a postcard and final duplicate questionnaire. On average, the questionnaire took approximately 30 min to complete. The electronic and paper versions included identical items, although skip instructions had to be followed on paper, whereas the skip logic was built into the Web version. Students completed surveys beginning in November and ending in December of 2003. The overall response rate was 51%, for a final sample size of 14,280. Students received a $10 incentive for completing the questionnaire. For the analyses reported here, students were selected if they were between the ages of 18 and 25, non-married, heterosexual, past-year drinkers, and did not have any missing data for the selected variables at the individual level ($N = 7,414$).

MEASURES

Settings. A series of questions specific to six drinking settings were presented 11 to respondents. The settings were (a) fraternity or sorority parties (Greek parties), (b) residence-hall parties, (c) campus events (e.g., concert or sporting event), (d) parties at off-campus houses or apartments, (e) restaurants or bars, and (f) outdoor settings (e.g., park or beach). Students were asked whether and how often they went to each setting since the beginning of the semester, how often they consumed any alcohol, how often they drank enough to get drunk, and possible consequences of drinking for each setting. Thus, each student could provide information for up to six different settings, which created an opportunity to conduct analyses at three levels: setting level (within-student), student level, and college level. Dummy-coded variables were created to represent the settings. Outdoor setting was selected as the reference group as prevalence of the behavior was lowest at this setting.

SETTING-LEVEL VARIABLES

Alcohol-related sex with a relative stranger. For each setting, college students 12 were asked to indicate how many times since the beginning of the semester or quarter they had had sex with someone they had just met as a result of drinking. This allowed us to specifically assess how specific drinking settings (e.g., bars or dorm parties) and casual sex behavior might be associated with one another. Six response options ranged from "never" to "10 or more times." However, as a result of a skewed distribution and infrequent occurrence of this behavior, a dichotomous measure was created to represent the occurrence of sex with a relative stranger versus non-occurrence.

Frequency of attendance—drinking settings. Students were asked to indi- 13 cate how many times since the beginning of the semester or quarter they had gone to each of the six settings. The response option was open-ended.

Proportion of times drunk at settings. Students were also asked to indicate 14 the number of times they had attended each setting and how many times they had drank enough to be drunk. This value was then transformed into a proportion based on the total number of times drunk at all settings divided by the total number of times they went to all the settings.

STUDENT-LEVEL VARIABLES

Sexual experience. Students were asked how many people they had sexual 15 intercourse with since the beginning of the school year. Responses ranged from "none" to "10 or more." A dichotomous measure was created to represent college students with current sexual experience and those without current sexual experience.

Heavy drinking. Respondents were asked, "Since the beginning of the 16 semester/quarter, how often would you say you drank enough to have been drunk?" Students were given seven possible ascending response options including "never," "less than once a month," "one to three times a month," and "almost every day." Due to overlap among some of the response categories, some response categories were collapsed, yielding a five-level ordinal heavy-drinking measure.

Background variables. Respondents were asked to provide their age, gender, 17 and race or ethnicity. Given that a positive association exists between White college students and heavy alcohol use (Bersamin, Paschall, & Flewelling, 2005), a dummy variable for being White was created. Students were also asked to indicate their living arrangement. Research shows that Greek residence and living in a co-ed dormitory are correlates of binge drinking (Wechsler et al., 1995). Therefore, two dummy variables were created to represent students who lived in Greek housing and students who lived in a residence hall (other places of residence; e.g., off-campus apartment or house, at home with parents was the referent category).

In addition, a variable was created to control for issues associated with 18 "time at risk." For example, one student may have completed the survey in October and, therefore, only be at risk for 30 days, whereas another may have completed the survey in December and, therefore, be at risk for 60 days. The timing variable represents the number of days since participants were asked to participate in the survey and the date the survey was completed.

COLLEGE-LEVEL VARIABLES

College population-level characteristics considered for this study included 19 student population size, percentage of students that live on campus, percentage of students who were White, and percentage of students who were members of a Greek organization. Fall 2003 data for these variables were typically available online, but in some instances were requested from the university's institutional research office.

DATA ANALYTIC STRATEGY

A multi-level modeling approach was used to examine the unique effects 20 of drinking setting or venue on alcohol-related sexual intercourse with a stranger, controlling for individual and college population-level effects. A three-level model allowed us to concurrently model and examine the effects of drinking at specific settings (Level 1); individual-level effects, such as gender or overall drinking (Level 2); and college population-level variables (percentage of college students who live on campus [Level 3]) on alcohol-related sexual behavior with a stranger. Data were analyzed using HLM 6.0 (Scientific Software International, Lincolnwood, IL) with a logit link to account for the binary outcome. Three datasets were created for each level of the analysis. The first dataset (setting level) was created by restructuring the dataset from variables into cases. Thus, each drinking location was converted into a case and individual responses to behavior at each drinking setting were associated with that case. The second dataset was based on individual student character-istics, and the third dataset (college population level) was based on archival data available for each college. A final model was specified that included all of the setting variables: Greek, residence-hall, and off-campus parties; bars or restaurants; and campus events. Two additional setting-level characteristics were also added—frequency of attending events at that setting and proportion of times one was drunk at the location—to control for exposure to events and exposure to events while being drunk. We anticipated that the likelihood of meeting a stranger increases as individuals increase their exposure to various settings. Likewise, we expected that risk was higher with increasing frequency of drunkenness at a given setting. By controlling for both these exposure vari-ables, there is greater confidence that a setting is having a unique influence and not just increasing the likelihood of intoxication.

Individual and college-level predictors. Age, White ethnicity, gender, sexual 21 experience, drinking behavior, timing, and percentage of students who live on campus were also incorporated into the final model. Note, however, that initial models included the college-level variables: student population, per-centage of White students, and percentage of students that are members of a Greek organization; and the individual-level variables: dorm and Greek residence. However, preliminary analyses found that these items did not contribute to the model in any significant manner and, therefore, they were deleted from the final model.

The full model is a result of three regression equations being simultane- 22 ously modeled—that is, setting-level events or episodes nested within indi-vidual student-level variables nested within colleges or

Level 1 : $log[P/(1 - P)]$

$= P0 + P1 \times (GREEK) + P2$

$\times (RESIDENCE\ HALL) + P3 \times (CAMPUS)$

$+ P4 \times (OFF\ CAMPUS) + P5 \times (BAR)$

$+ P6 \times (FREQUENCY\ OF\ ATTENDANCE)$

$+ P7 \times (PROPORTION\ DRUNK\ AT\ SETTING)$

$+ R$

Level 2 : $P0$

$= B00 + B01 \times (AGE) + B02 \times (WHITE)$

$+ B03 \times (MALE) + B04 \times (SEX\ EVER)$

$+ B05 \times (DRUNK) + B06\ (TIME\ AT\ RISK)$

$+ R0$

Level 3 : $B00 = G000 + G001\ (ON\ CAMPUS) + U00$

RESULTS

Attrition Analyses

Based on data provided by the university, we were able to determine whether 23 students who participated in the survey differed from those who did not participate with regards to year in college and gender. No differences emerged with regards to grade level; however, a significantly higher number of women participated in the survey than men. As indicated earlier, the response rate was 51%; however, the response rate varied by institution, with a high of 64.6% and a low of 37%.

PRELIMINARY FINDINGS

Table 1 provides an overview of individual-level characteristics of the study 24 population. The sample was 54.4% men, 48.7% White, and 38.1% age 21 and over. A little less than one half (43.9%) of the students reported not getting drunk since the beginning of the quarter or semester. Conversely, 10.3% reported being drunk once per week or more since the beginning of the quarter or semester. A total of 46.8% of the population reported being sexually active since the beginning of the quarter or semester, and 2.2% reported sexual intercourse with a stranger.

TABLE 1
Descriptive Statistics, Student Level.

Variable	M (SD) or %
Male (%)	54.4
White (%)	48.7
Age 21 and over (%)	38.1
Prior sexual experience (%)	46.8
Times drunk since beginning of semester/quarter	0.90 (1.00)
Never (%)	43.9
1–5 days this semester/quarter (%)	32.3
6–10 days this semester/quarter (%)	13.5
Once a week or more (%)	9.9
Almost every day (%)	0.4
Reported sexual intercourse with a stranger (%)	2.2
Days to complete survey	64.21 (16.60)

Note. N = 7,414.

Of the six college drinking settings polled, students were most likely to fre- 25 quent bars or restaurants ($M = 5.81$) since the beginning of the semester (see Table 2). This was followed by off-campus parties ($M = 5.56$) and Greek parties ($M = 5.20$). Results also indicate that heavy drinking occurred at higher percentages of off-campus and Greek parties (36% and 34%, respectively). This was followed by dorm parties, bars or restaurants, and outdoor settings. Heavy drinking occurred least frequently at campus events (20%). Alcohol-related sexual intercourse with a stranger occurred at a greater percentage of Greek party events (4%), followed by off-campus (3%) and residence-hall parties (3%).

MULTI-LEVEL ANALYSES

Setting level. Results from the HLM 6.0 analyses indicated that relative to out- 26 door settings, all settings (with the exception of campus events and bars or restaurants) were positively and significantly associated with the occurrence of alcohol-related sexual intercourse with a stranger (see Table 3). Specifically, alcohol-related sexual intercourse with a stranger was 10 times more likely to occur after a Greek party relative to an outdoor setting (odds ratio [OR] $= 10.09$, $p < .01$). Alcohol-related sexual intercourse with a stranger was four times more likely to occur at or after a residence-hall party (OR $= 4.96$, $p < .01$) or an off-campus party (OR $= 4.92$, $p < .01$) relative to an outdoor setting. Frequency of attending the six settings and proportion of times drunk at the settings were also positively associated with alcohol-related sex with a stranger.

TABLE 2
Frequency of Setting Attendance and Risky Behavior by Students.

Setting	Attendance		Drunk		Sex with a Relative Stranger	
	M	SD	M	SD	M	SD
Sorority/fraternity parties	5.20	8.61	0.34	0.40	0.04	0.27
Residence-hall parties	4.28	7.04	0.31	0.40	0.03	0.37
Off-campus parties	5.56	7.77	0.36	0.39	0.03	0.32
Campus events	2.74	3.40	0.20	0.37	0.00	0.08
Bars/restaurants	5.81	8.03	0.30	0.38	0.01	0.14
Outdoor settings	3.62	7.62	0.24	0.40	0.00	0.10

TABLE 3
Results of Multi-Level Analysis Predicting Likelihood of Sex with a Stranger.

Fixed Parameters	Odds Ratio	95% Confidence Interval
Intercept	0.00	0.00, 0.00
Level 1: Setting event level ($N = 18,623$)[a]		
Greek	10.09	4.54, 22.40
Residence hall	4.96	2.10, 11.67
Campus events	0.88	0.22, 3.49
Off campus	4.92	2.23, 10.86
Restaurant/bar	2.04	0.85, 4.89
Frequency of attendance—all settings	1.03	1.02, 1.04
Proportion of times drunk—all settings	2.93	1.89, 4.55
Level 2: Individual level ($N = 7,414$)		
Age (over 21)	0.91	0.64, 1.30
White	0.70	0.50, 0.98
Gender (male)	1.62	1.20, 2.20
Sexual experience	23.77	10.43, 54.18
Drunk	1.61	1.34, 1.94
Days to complete survey	0.99	0.97, 1.02
Level 3: College level ($N = 14$)		
Percentage living on campus	0.98	0.96, 0.99

[a]The reference group for all Level 1 variables is outdoor settings.

Individual level. Gender, ethnicity, heavy drinking behavior, and previous 27 sexual behavior were significantly associated with alcohol-related sexual intercourse with a stranger. Specifically, males (OR = 1.62), students who reported being drunk in the past semester or quarter (OR = 1.61, $p < .01$), and those who reported having sexual intercourse in the past semester or quarter (OR = 23.77, $p < .01$) were more likely to report having alcohol-related sexual intercourse with a stranger than others. Ethnicity was moderately associated with alcohol-related sexual intercourse with a stranger (OR = 0.70, $p = .03$).

College level. The percentage of students living on campus was inversely, 28 although modestly, related to the occurrence of alcohol-related sexual intercourse with a stranger such that campuses with a greater number of students living on campus were less likely to report instances of this risky behavior (OR = 0.98, $p = .02$).

DISCUSSION

A key finding of this study is that drinking settings have a unique influence on 29 alcohol-related risky sexual behavior apart from student-level factors that may predispose individuals to engage in this risky behavior. Specifically, the results indicated that Greek parties, followed by residence-hall and off-campus parties, are high-risk settings for having alcohol-related sexual intercourse with a stranger relative to other locations. Just as important, this effect persisted even after controlling for several exposure variables: frequency of attending settings and proportion of getting drunk at settings, as well as individual and population-level characteristics. These findings are in line with the situation-specificity hypothesis and highlight the impact that environmental cues may have on drinking patterns and behaviors.

The lack of an association between bars or restaurants and alcohol-related 30 sexual behavior was unexpected given previous research, which found that these venues are significantly associated with high levels of drinking and negative alcohol-related outcomes (Clapp et al., 2006; Demers et al., 2002; Single & Wortley, 1993; Stockwell, Lang, & Rydon, 1993). It is difficult to ascertain whether this apparent discrepancy may be unique to college student drinking, where licensed establishments are "competing" with other venues that may not be so easily available to non-college populations, or perhaps related to the fact that most students are minors (and not legally permitted to drink in bars). Our results may also differ because we were able to separate the exposure variables and drinking within those same settings, which is not common in most other studies.

Finally, although we were not focused on student-level effects here, we 31 note the unsurprising results that gender, sexual experience, and frequency of being drunk increased the odds of sex with a stranger. More interesting, however, we found no significant risk of living in a Greek house (once setting-level variables were included). This suggests that the "risk" of being a member of a Greek organization may not be related to the kind of people attracted to such organizations, but rather to the nature of the parties they host. Many Greek parties are not limited to members of a Greek organization. Indeed, more than one half our sample who reported attending such parties were not members themselves. A parallel phenomenon appears for residence-hall parties versus living in those halls.

Additional research is necessary to understand why specific drinking set- 32 tings may influence drinking behaviors, as well as negative alcohol-related outcomes. For example, settings may attract individuals with specific shared beliefs and expectations. Individuals with a high level of motivation to participate in sexual intercourse may select one drinking venue over another. These locations may then become known for their "sexual" atmosphere and, therefore, draw like-minded patrons, resulting in social contexts where drinking and sexual behavior with strangers are more likely to occur. On a related note, it may be that some drinking venues have low levels of social control (e.g., lack of oversight by responsible adults or monitoring by law enforcement agents), which contribute to alcohol misuse and risky sexual behavior. Perceived peer attitudes and behaviors (i.e., normative beliefs) may also be setting-specific and, thus, contribute to venue effects on behavior through maintenance or promotion of risky alcohol-related sexual behaviors. If so, it is not surprising that Greek, residence-hall, and off-campus parties are associated with this risky sexual behavior, as these venues are likely to be "invitation-only" or private parties drawing like-minded people, and with little or no security and safety monitoring other than that provided by the hosts. In addition, these locations are all tied to a residence that increases the likelihood of finding or accessing a semi-private "setting" or, more candidly, a "bed" or bedroom where sexual intercourse can occur. Note, however, that risk is significantly higher at Greek parties in comparison to parties off campus or at residence halls. Campus events and outdoor settings (e.g., park or beach) are public locations with greater degrees of social control, which may explain the lower likelihood of alcohol-related sex with a stranger relative to other high-risk settings. Additional research is necessary to test these hypotheses and further explore how setting influences drinking-related sexual behavior.

This study specifically focused on one alcohol-related sexual behavior: having sex with a stranger. Although recent research suggests that settings are associated with pre-loading behavior (Paschall & Saltz, 2007), it is unknown whether drinking venues have similar effects on other risky sexual behaviors. It may be that bars or restaurants are positively associated with condom use, as bars are located near retail outlets, thereby increasing condom availability. Future research should also investigate how different drinking venues impact a range of high-risk sexual behaviors. 33

This study had a number of limitations. First, the low response rate raises issues of selection bias and generalizability to the overall college student population. However, a review of survey research by Krosnick (1999) indicates that, among probability samples, low response rates do not necessarily translate into an inability to generalize results of a research study or, alternatively, that high response rates are needed for sample representativeness. Second, all items were based on self-report, and the sensitivity of those items relating to sexual behavior and alcohol use may have led to underreporting. Likewise, our dependent measure was based on students' attribution of alcohol use to the occurrence of sex with a stranger. Some students may have engaged in the same risky behavior after drinking, but did not attribute the behavior to drinking. 34

Third, the degree of risk each individual student experienced is unknown. 35 Due to the wording on the questionnaire, we were unable to determine whether students interpreted "sexual intercourse" to signify oral, vaginal, or anal intercourse, each with different degrees of risk. Similarly, we did not capture condom use. The risk of sexually transmitted disease is significantly decreased when condoms are used. Future studies may want to focus on identifying the degree of risk, both social and emotional, associated with drinking-related casual sex by focusing on specific sexual behaviors, as well as prophylactic use. Finally, there may have been an issue with accuracy of recall, particularly as the behavior was associated with alcohol consumption. Our hope was that the relaively recent timeframe (since the start of the semester or quarter) would minimize the likelihood of recall bias.

Despite these weaknesses, a major strength of the study is the research 36 design that allows for event-specific analysis—specifically, measuring the occurrence of drinking-related casual sex linked to specific venues. In moving away from global correlations between sex, alcohol use, and setting, a more comprehensive understanding of the role of location and context on drinking-related sexual behavior can be developed.

Taken together, these findings may lead to a broader understanding of 37 the nature of "risk" associated with drinking and, from that, greater appreciation of the value of a more comprehensive set of prevention strategies. As we move from assuming that risk of unsafe sex is limited to the attributes of individuals to specific settings or venues as well, we can give more attention to intervention and prevention strategies that directly impact those settings. For example, the high level of risk associated with Greek parties, independent of individual characteristics, may help universities recognize the need to reduce the occurrence of such parties, take steps to improve safety precautions (e.g., provide condoms, reduce access to private rooms, or create social networks to provide support), work with campus and local police to enforce policies that are often violated at these parties (e.g., serving alcohol to underage students or violation of public nuisance ordinance), and educate individuals who work at high-risk venues, as well as those who attend these locations.

This research was supported by Grant #R01 AA012516-08 from the National Institute on Alcohol Abuse and Alcoholism. We thank Jamie Sullivan for her editorial assistance with this manuscript.

REFERENCES

Bersamin, M., Paschall, M. J., & Flewelling, R. L. (2005). Ethnic differences in relationships between risk factors and adolescent binge drinking: A national study. *Prevention Science, 6*(2), 127–137. doi:10.1007/s11121-005-3411-6

Centers for Disease Control and Prevention. (2010). *Sexually transmitted disease surveillance 2009.* Atlanta, GA: U.S. Department of Health and Human Services.

Clapp, J. D., Reed, M. B., Holmes, M. R., Lange, J. E., & Voas, R. B. (2006). Drunk in public, drunk in private: The relationship between college students, drinking environments, and alcohol consumption. *American Journal of Drug and Alcohol Abuse, 32,* 275–285. doi:10.1080/00952990500481205

Clapp, J. D., Shillington, A. M., & Segars, L. (2000). Deconstructing contexts of binge drinking among college students. *American Journal of Drug and Alcohol Abuse, 26,* 139–154. doi: 10.1081/ ADA-100100596

Cooper, M. L. (2002). Alcohol use and risky sexual behavior among college students and youth: Evaluating the evidence. *Journal of Studies on Alcohol, 14,* 101–117. Retrieved from http://www.collegedrinkingprevention.gov/media/Journal/101-Cooper.pdf

Cooper, M. L., Peirce, R. S., & Huselid, R. F. (1994). Substance use and sexual risk taking among Black adolescents and White adolescents. *Health Psychology, 13,* 251–262. doi:10.1037/02786133.13.3.251

Cooper, M. L., Skinner, J. B., & George, W. H. (1990). Alcohol use and sexual risk-taking among adolescents: Methodological approaches for addressing causal issues. In D. Seminara, R. R. Watson, & A. Pawlowski (Eds.), *Alcohol, immunomodulation, and AIDS* (pp. 11–19). New York, NY: Liss.

Demers, A., Kairouz, S., Adlaf, E. M., Gliksman, L., Newton-Taylor, B., & Marchand, A. (2002). Multi-level analyses of situational drinking among Canadian undergraduates. *Social Science & Medicine, 55,* 415–424. doi:10.1016/S0277-9536(01)00258-1

Graves, K. L., & Leigh, B. C. (1995). The relationship of substance use to sexual activity among young adults in the United States. *Family Planning Perspectives, 27,* 18–22, 33. Retrieved from http://www. alanguttmacher.org/pubs/journals/2701895.pdf

Grello, C. M., Welsh, D. P., & Harper, M. S. (2006). No strings attached: The nature of casual sex in college students. *Journal of Sex Research, 43,* 255–267. doi:10.1080/00224490609552324

Herold, E. S., Maticka-Tyndale, E., & Mewhinney, D. (1998). Predicting intentions to engage in casual sex. *Journal of Social and Personal Relationships, 15,* 502–516. doi:10.1177/0265407598154004

Krosnick, J. A. (1999). Survey research. *Annual Reviews of Psychology, 50,* 537–567. doi:10.1146/annurev.psych.50.1.537

LaBrie, J., Earleywine, M., Schiffman, J., Pedersen, E., & Marriot, C. (2005). Effects of alcohol, expectancies, and partner type on condom use in college males: Event-level analyses. *Journal of Sex Research, 42,* 259–266. doi:10.1080/00224490509552280

Lau-Barraco, C., & Dunn, M. (2009). Environmental context effects on alcohol cognitions and immediate alcohol consumption. *Addiction Research & Theory, 17,* 306–314. doi:10.1080/16066350802346201

Paschall, M. J., & Saltz, R. F. (2007). Relationships between college settings and student alcohol use before, during, and after events: A multi-level study. *Drug and Alcohol Review, 26,* 635–644. doi:10.1080/09595230701613601

Paul, E. L., McManus, B., & Allison, H. (2000). Hookups: Characteristics and correlates of college students' spontaneous and anonymous sexual experiences. *Journal of Sex Research, 37,* 76–89. doi:10.1080/00224490009552023

Poulin, C., & Graham, L. (2001). The association between substance use, unplanned sexual intercourse and other sexual behaviors among adolescent students. *Addiction, 96,* 607–621. doi:10.1046/ j.1360-0443.2001.9646079.x

Santelli, J. S., Robin, L., Brener, N. D., & Lowry, R. (2001). Timing of alcohol and other drug use and sexual risk behaviors among unmarried adolescents and young adults. *Family Planning Perspective, 33,* 200–205. Retrieved from http://www.guttmacher. org/pubs/journals/3320001.pdf

Single, E., & Wortley, S. (1993). Drinking in various settings as it relates to demographic variables and level of consumption: Findings from a national survey in Canada. *Journal of Studies on*

Alcohol and Drugs, 54, 590–599. Retrieved from http://www.jsad. com/jsad/article/Drinking_in_Various_Settings_As_It_Relates_to_ Demographic_Variables_and_Lev/1949.html

Stockwell, T., Lang, E., & Rydon, P. (1993). High risk drinking settings: The association of serving and promotional practices with harmful drinking. *Addiction, 88,* 1519–1526. doi:10.1111/j.1360-0443.1993.tb03137.x

Tanfer, K., Cubbins, L. A., & Billy, J. O. G. (1995). Gender, race, class and self-reported sexually transmitted disease incidence. *Family Planning Perspectives, 27,* 196–202. Retrieved from http://www. guttmacher.org/pubs/journals/2719695.pdf

Testa, M., & Collins, R. L. (1997). Alcohol and risky sexual behavior: Event-based analyses among a sample of high-risk women. *Psychology of Addictive Behaviors, 11,* 190–201. doi:10.1037/0893-164X.11.3.190

Thompson, J. C., Kao, T., & Thomas, R. J. (2005). The relationship between alcohol use and risk-taking sexual behaviors in a large behavioral study. *Preventative Medicine, 41,* 247–252. doi:10.1016/j.ypmed.2004.11.008

Wall, A., McKee, S. A., & Hinson, R. E. (2000). Assessing variation in alcohol outcome expectancies across environmental context: An examination of the situational-specificity hypothesis. *Psychology of Addictive Behaviors, 14,* 367–375. doi:10.1037/0893-164X.14.4.367

Wall, A., McKee, S. A., Hinson, R. E., & Goldstein, A. (2001). Examining alcohol outcome expectancies in laboratory and naturalistic bar settings: A within-subject experimental analysis. *Psychology of Addictive Behavior, 15,* 219–226. doi:10.1037/0893-164X.15.3.219

Wechsler, H., Dowdall, G. W., Davenport, A., & Castillo, S. (1995). Correlates of college student binge drinking. *American Journal of Public Health, 85,* 921–926. http://www.ncbi.nlm.nih.gov/ pmc/articles/PMC1615519/pdf/amjph0045-0027.pdf

Wigmore, S. W., & Hinson, R. E. (1991). The influence of setting on the consumption in the balanced placebo design. *British Journal of Addiction, 86,* 205–215. Retrieved from Academic Search Premier database.

Zamboanga, B. L. (2005). Alcohol expectancies and drinking related behaviors in Mexican American college students. *Addictive Behaviors, 30,* 673–684. doi:10.1016/j.addbeh.2004.08.013

Zamboanga, B. L., & Ham, L. S. (2008). Alcohol expectancies and context-specific drinking behaviors among female college athletes. *Behavior Therapy, 39,* 162–170. doi:10.1016/j.beth.2007.06.002

QUESTIONS

1. How does the study reported on in this article differ from previous studies on the same topic?
2. What are the hypotheses of this study?
3. A report on a social science study is expository, (see page 55), but it may have a persuasive undertone. What is the persuasive undertone in this article?
4. What, in the context of this study, is the difference between "student-related variables" and "college-related variables"?
5. Is there a gender difference in the frequency of casual sex, and, if so, how do you explain this?
6. In your opinion, what is the most surprising result of this study?
7. In your opinion, what is the least surprising result of this study?
8. Will reading this study impact your own behaviour in any way?

9. What further research do the authors recommend?
10. What, do the authors admit, are the limitations of this study?
11. This study seems to establish a connection between the hosts and the location of a party and the frequency of casual sex. How can this connection be explained?
12. Based upon the results of this study, should college/university administrators take any action, and, if so, what action should they take?

This article was published in *Performance Research: A Journal of the Performing Arts,* volume 16, issue 2, 2011, pages 145–153.

If Ya Liked It, Then You Shoulda Made a Video: Beyoncé Knowles, YouTube and the Public Sphere of Images*
Kirsten Pullen

On 8 October 2008, Beyoncé Knowles released the first two singles from 1
I Am … Sasha Fierce: 'If I Were a Boy' and 'Single Ladies (Put a ring on it)'. The videos for both premiered on MTV's *Total Request Live* a few days later. 'Single Ladies' quickly became the more successful of the two, undoubtedly in part because of its arresting video: Beyoncé and two back-up dancers perform pelvic thrusts and hip shakes, run up a wall, and flash their ring fingers in time to a thumping bass line. The video quickly became ubiquitous: it played in heavy rotation on MTV and BET and was available on YouTube as a promotion for the album. It just as quickly spawned a series of imitations that premiered in a variety of media forms, including TV, film and YouTube. A large cross-section of North Americans and Europeans have seen the dance,[1] whether as the original Beyoncé video, the *Glee* episode when Kurt teaches the football team to dance and comes out to his father, Beyoncé's self-parody on *Saturday Night Live,* Liza Minnelli covering the song in *Sex and the City II* or the YouTube mash-up that combines Minnelli's vocals with the visuals from *Cabaret's* 'Mein Herr'. Many have also attempted the choreography themselves; there are hundreds of amateur versions available on YouTube, including a version from the PSi#16 conference (PSingle Ladies).

While many versions of 'Single Ladies' are amateur videos produced 2
in basements, living rooms and parking lots, many others are corporate-sponsored and professionally produced. 'Single Ladies' (the song, the original video, the amateur recreations and the citations in other films, videos and television programmes) can be understood as a negotiation between official

---

[1]Beyoncé's video has been viewed on YouTube nearly 100 million times (though of course many of those may be repeat views) and was in heavy rotation on MTV in 2008 and 2009. It was named video of the year at the 2009 MTV Video Awards, the BET Awards and the MTV Europe Music Awards. The song itself won Grammies for Song of the Year, Best R&B Song and Best Female R&B Performance. At the PSi#16 conference in Toronto in June 2010, all but one of the twenty-six attendees at the panel where I presented this paper had seen at least one version of the choreography.

public culture, exemplified by Beyoncé's performances as well as other commercial versions, and potential counterpublics created by amateur recreations[2] of the choreography, especially those available on YouTube. In important ways, 'Single Ladies" proliferation across a number of platforms and featuring a wide variety of dancing bodies suggests how even corporate-produced and distributed media products belong to a public sphere of images.

Jürgen Habermas defines the public sphere as 'the world of letters (1989: 30–1) enabling 'private people' to 'come together as a public [... and to engage in] debate over the general rules governing relations in the basically privatized but publicly relevant sphere of commodity exchange and social labour' (27). For Habermas, then, the public sphere both depends on a print culture able to produce and distribute 'news' to a literate public as well as an understanding of commerciality and consumerism as important and newsworthy. Furthermore, the public sphere is characterized by words, both those printed and read by the public and those verbally expressed through debate. Here, I rearticulate Habermas's public sphere to account for the ways in which digital media is supplanting print culture. Public debate now relies heavily on visual images rather than verbal discourse, as traditional news outlets as well as new media news traffic in images as much as words. (For example, US television election coverage uses enormous interactive maps that shade into blue and red to indicate voting results rather than newscasters reading reports.) As cell phone cameras, surveillance videos and self-made digital recordings proliferate, literacy increasingly includes the ability to produce and read images as well as words.

As the ubiquity of 'Single Ladies' videos demonstrates, this public sphere of images offers similar opportunities for citizens to engage in public debate, as well as similar limits (especially those around questions of access, in this case access to digital recording equipment, broadband and technological savvy) as Habermas's original articulation. At the same time, it is equally marked by tensions between commercialism and democratic exchange; these tensions, however, do facilitate counterpublics. Following Michael Warner's formulation in *Publics and Counterpublics,* I argue that counterpublics are groups who are aware of their subordinate status but claim public space and enter public debate through the same mechanisms as those groups generally

---

[2]Though the 'Single Ladies' dances might also be termed imitations or interpretations, and the thousands of versions address different audiences and different aesthetic aims, I'm specifically using 'recreation' to describe them all. First, many of the YouTube dancers at least attempt to authentically reproduce the choreography and *mise-en-scène* in homage to the original. More important, recreation connotes a level of agency and activity that parallels Michael Warner's articulation of counterpublic, a crucial distinction as the argument develops.

recognized to be part of 'the public'. In particular, counterpublics attempt to transform public space and public life by bringing forward concerns (especially about gender and sexuality) that were previously understood to be private (see especially Warner 2002: 63ff and 114–19). The multiple dancing bodies (differently marked by gender, class, dance technique, and technological savvy) visible in the 'Single Ladies' recreations constitute a counterpublic, one that challenges the slickness and commercial sexuality of Beyoncé's original. In this paper, I trace the creation, production and distribution of several versions of 'Single Ladies', suggesting how dancing bodies intersect with traditional notions of dance performance, the archive and artistic value, enabling counterpublics based on commercial but also joyful images.

By now, most performance scholars recognize that YouTube offers digital   5 space to millions of performers.[3] YouTube's visual archive is generally understood to be potentially more open than traditional archives, though also potentially more difficult to categorize and navigate. Tara McPherson, writing in *Cinema Journal*, explains that 'the videos collected there may often be amateurish or even silly, but the videos themselves are not the most interesting thing about the space. The practices facilitated via YouTube … encourage a networked, public mode of visual expression' (McPherson 2009: 123). Thousands of YouTube users post videos of themselves dancing original compositions and recreating other performances. Amateurs dance next to Martha Graham and Beyoncé Knowles and are as available and often more popular than historically important or aesthetically nuanced videos. Of course, in some cases popularity reflects how badly or comically the dancers are dancing. Regardless, this digital archive concentrates on bodies and images rather than text, inviting debate over dance technique, aesthetics and history that visually reference real-world examples of how people dance.

Beyoncé Knowles's original video for 'Single Ladies' wouldn't exist without   6 YouTube; it's important to note that similar images began circulating on television and YouTube long before Beyoncé put on her leotard.[4] Elements of its *mise-en-scène* and choreography are taken from 'Mexican Breakfast', a Bob Fosse dance created for his wife Gwen Verdon and first broadcast on *The Ed Sullivan Show* in 1969. Though Beyoncé frequently quotes Fosse, 'Single Ladies' 'is also generically and technologically linked to 'Walk it Out, Fosse!!', a 2008 mash-up available only on YouTube (it has since been removed for copyright violation). Diamond Creative, an LA design company, replaced 'Mexican Breakfast's' original soundtrack with Unk's 2006 hip-hop hit 'Walk it Out'. This version generated over 2.5 million views and *USA Today* and NPR discussed the video. Introducing 'Single Ladies' on BET's *106 and Park*,

---

[3]For more on YouTube as archive, see Carroll, Cermatori et al., Gehl, Gracy, McPherson and Salvato.

[4]I take my summary of the evolution of the videos from Priscilla Peña Ovalle's discussion.

Beyoncé cited both versions as the source for her own video. She describes seeing 'Walk it Out' on YouTube but stresses that she was drawn to Verdon's virtuosity. Music videos often rely on editing, special effects, and tricky camera angles for their impact; Beyoncé wanted to create something 'simple' and 'classic' in order to highlight her dancing body (Beyoncé 2008).

Beyoncé uses her physical body and choreography to incorporate and   7 challenge the previous versions of Fosse's dance. In all, three women dance in a straight line or circle. They often take tiny steps with their feet close together (both forward and to the side) while thrusting their pelvises. This small, jerky movement is frequently contrasted with static lower bodies and large, fluid arm movements. Fosse's version has several high kicks in rapid succession. Beyoncé emphasizes hip shakes, complicated arm and leg patterns and vogues, such as the 'If ya liked it then ya shoulda put a ring on it' chorus, when the women stand with one hand on their hip and flash their left hands back and forth. This is both the strongest break from Fosse's choreography and the most easily imitated segment of the video (even President Obama can do it).

In important ways, Beyoncé's citation of Fosse as well as Diamond Creative   8 legitimates and encourages amateur dancers uploading their own versions: she models appropriation from YouTube as an archival source. Though it's nearly impossible to determine what creates a viral phenomenon such as 'Single Ladies', I suggest that Beyoncé's own appropriation of an appropriation facilitated the amateur recreations of this dance. Beyoncé was open about the sources for her video, offering fans tacit permission to recreate her dance moves and methods. In fact, once the recreations began to multiply, the practice overtook its source material such that many of the amateur dancers may not have heard of Gwen Verdon nor seen 'Walk it Out, Fosse!!'. These multiple and varied citations demonstrate the ways in which dance circulates, concretizing what constitutes contemporary vernacular dance and how those dances are spread.[5]

These three videos (Beyoncé's 'Single Ladies', 'Walk it Out, Fosse' and   9 'Mexican Breakfast') illustrate one of the values of YouTube as an archive: it's relatively easy to compare dancers and dance styles.[6] These comparisons may reveal how dancing bodies are racialized and classed, facilitating historically grounded, nuanced critique. On the one hand, 'Single Ladies' reverses the pattern of cultural appropriation most familiar to dance and popular music

---

[5]Dance circulates in clubs, dance studios and aerobics classes as well as on YouTube. For a more historical discussion of the dissemination of vernacular dance, see Anthea Kraut's '"Stealing Steps" and Signature Moves: Embodied theories of dance as intellectual property'.
[6]These videos illustrate one of the significant problems with the YouTube archive as well. Neither 'Walk it Out, Fosse!!' nor 'Mexican Breakfast' is currently available on YouTube because of copyright claims.

scholars[7]: Beyoncé is an African American artist using the movements of a white choreographer and white dancers most associated with white audiences. Second, Diamond Creative's mash-up suggests how particular choreographers and audiences can elide whiteness. The interest of 'Walk it Out, Fosse!!' depends on the dissonance between the white, polyester-clad, middle-aged women and the throbbing hip-hop. This dissonance invites viewers to reconsider Fosse, Verdon and even *The Ed Sullivan Show,* suggesting how women's bodies are and are not sexualized through dance choreography. In particular, Verdon's and Fosse's whiteness is highlighted: movements that seem relatively innocuous when set to trippy 1960s pop music seem more parodically sexual when underscored by 'black' music. Using the YouTube dance archive to compare different dancing bodies allows users to recognize and highlight how racial, classed or sexual counterpublics mobilize dance. Following from Warner, when dancers from traditionally marginalized groups appropriate dance styles from recognized publics, they insert their bodies and aesthetics into public debate. Scholars using the YouTube archive can investigate not only historical dance steps but also how different groups negotiate dance at different historical moments.

Scholarly intervention is crucial for enabling the YouTube archive to facilitate counterpublics. While professional (and especially amateur) recreations of famous choreography do allow new and different images to circulate through the archive, they are most easily read in stereotypical ways. As Priscilla Peña Ovalle points out, the videos illustrate a sonic color line: 'Though the movements do not change from 'Mexican Breakfast' to 'Walk It Out, Fosse', the choreography's pelvic tilts, leg shakes and head rolls read very differently when accompanied by Unk's track' (Peña Ovalle 2009). Furthermore, when Beyoncé performs Fosse's choreography and Verdon's steps in her black leotard, snapping her hips and flipping her hair, the video reads as especially sexual, not only because of the music and costume. Her body signifies youthful sexuality, and her sassy attitude demonstrates just what her lover will be missing because he didn't put a ring on it. Also, the fact that Beyoncé is a black woman with an especially curvy figure allows viewers to activate racist fantasies of hypersexual black femininity. The liberatory potential of a counterpublic enabled by digital media must always be tempered with the recognition of not only its consumerism but also its potentially regressive representations of race, class and gender. 10

---

[7]See for example Kraut, Brenda Dixon Gottschild's *The Black Dancing Body: A geography from coon to cool,* Julie Malnig's *Ballroom, Boogie, Shimmy Sham, Shake: A social and popular dance reader* and Eric Lott's seminal *Love and Theft: Blackface minstrelsy and the American working class.*

As anyone who has spent time looking for teaching clips, browsing 11
popular videos or watching what's posted by friends and family can attest,
YouTube performers seem to come from a broad range of racial, cultural and
economic backgrounds. The site expands daily: according to YouTube's self-
congratulatory 'Fact Sheet', 'every minute, 24 hours of video is uploaded to
YouTube'. Further, they claim that the 'user base is broad in age range 18–55,
evenly divided between males and females and spanning all geographies',
though over 70 per cent of its users are North Americans and Europeans;
Africans account for less than one percent of total users (Anand 2010). In
general, YouTube videos reflect the demographics of US race, class and
gender: though its audience is multi-racial and geographically diverse, there
appear to be more visibly white, middle-class users than those belonging to
other groups.

Beyoncé's 'Single Ladies' has been viewed on YouTube over ninety mil- 12
lion times, and inspired thousands of recreations. The videos as well as their
comments challenge and recite norms of blackness, femininity and masculinity, heterosexuality and dance technique, indicating the ambivalences built
into dancing bodies. These amateur recreations seem to be more racially and
economically diverse than YouTube videos as a whole. Though some of the
dancers are white, the majority are African American. Virtually all are either
women or men who announce their homosexuality or mark themselves as
queer; in the scores of videos I've viewed, none of the amateur male dancers
specifically represents himself as heterosexual. Inserting themselves into this
dance archive, then, 'Single Ladies' performers challenge traditional hierar-
chies of artistic value, insisting that anyone can and should dance. On the
other hand, Nick Salvato argues that YouTube users 'regularly and consistently affirm the professional, produced and defined in tandem with and at
the ultimate expense of the amateur' (2009: 69) because they ape the editing,
costuming and lighting conventions of the videos they recreate. Though
amateurs aspiring to the 'slickness' of the music industry are not especially
liberating examples, their physical bodies may challenge traditional dance
discourses of technique, tradition and aesthetics.

Some dancers use 'Single Ladies' to bridge the high/low art and amateur/ 13
professional divide. Miami Ballet dancers Alex Wong and Jeremy Cox recreate the dance in their dressing room while costumed as Don Quixote and
Sancho Panza. They highlight their Classical expertise by completing several
additional arabesques, sending up the codes of contemporary ballet as well
as musical video (juice1881). Wong is familiar to many YouTube viewers, in
part because of his appearances on *So You Think You Can Dance*. In 2009, he
auditioned but was unable to compete because of his Miami Ballet contract.
In 2010, he joined the show as a strong favorite, but withdrew due to injury.

His dances for the television competition, clips of his work at the Miami Ballet and recreations of popular dances (he and Cox have at least two available versions of 'Single Ladies', and he has uploaded a 'Dancers Gone Haywire' series that parodies cheerleading, earnest contemporary dance, and Latin competition choreography) are available on his YouTube channel, which reaches over 850,000 subscribers (alexdwong's Channel). Wong demonstrates how professional dancers use digital media to crossover to other dance styles and other dance audiences.

Queer dancers especially mark how digital recreations circulate vernac- 14 ular dance styles, constructing counterpublics by reversing traditional patterns of appropriation. Just as Beyoncé reappropriates Fosse for many of her R&B videos, she cribs 'Single Ladies' voguing from the same urban, queer club scene that Madonna made famous twenty years ago. When queer black bodies re-reappropriate the moves, they may highlight the athleticism of the dance and their own extreme musculature. For example, Darius Crenshaw, Grasan Kingsberry and Brian Brooks from the national touring company of *The Color Purple* call themselves Purple Haze and perform the moves in their costumes from the musical.[8] In their smart 1930s vests, ties and hats, they present a version of African American masculinity and history that traditionally silenced queer expressions of desire. Terrifically performed and precisely executed, they finish by dramatically removing the pocket squares from their vests, mop their sweating faces, return them with a flourish and 'sashay' to the back of the stage. This finale marks the performers as at least effeminate if not gay. But because their actual bodies (especially as costumed) are not traditionally read as queer, they implicitly challenge African American constructions of masculinity. Others, such as Angel Pariz, explicitly perform their queerness. Pariz is relatively androgynous. His video, performed in what appears to be his living room, faithfully recreates the choreography: he's good. It also includes several pop-ups announcing 'I'm a boy! A boy!' (111288CBaby). There are dozens of other queer recreations of 'Single Ladies' on YouTube. Some viewers seem to have stumbled upon them and react with hostility. All include homophobic comments: Pariz is referred to as a 'faggot' several times, and even the comments about Purple Haze on the gay website Towleroad include the sentiment: 'Could have been more masculine' (Joe.My.God). Even so, these multiple queer dances expand the dance archive in order to offer non-traditional dancing bodies, especially in contrast to the hyper-masculinity and heterosexuality of much R&B music, 'Single Ladies' included.

---

[8]Though I don't know for certain that these men are gay, they are heralded on several blogs written by gay men. See, for example, http://joemygod.blogspot.com/2008/12/purple-haze-takes-on-single-ladies.html.

Young black women, however, dance the majority of the 'Single Ladies' 15 recreations. Most of these recreations are three women dancing together, though there are individual and larger group versions. These include Ebony, Desiree and LaTerra, who note in the 'more info' section that they 'just learned this in like 40 minutes.lol so bare with us.lol' (desireetwyman). Their dance isn't especially polished, but they largely get a pass on the choreography. YouTube users posted comments focusing on their dancing bodies rather than the dance itself. As one 'poster' remarks, 'Sorry can't dance, but that one in the center is fine!' Viewers can also watch Secret Trois, three very obese African American women, perform about a minute of the choreography: nearly seven million users have viewed this 'Big Girls Remix'. The performers are praised for completing the challenging choreography and celebrating their bodies but are also mercilessly mocked. As these examples suggest, dancers' material bodies are interesting to viewers, often for what they seem to express about the dancers' personalities and values as well as their ability to recreate Beyoncé's choreography.

Many of these videos are notably amateur, especially in terms of filming, 16 lighting and editing. For example, Tayla and Pierrea offer a very polished version of the choreography (dancebaby530), but it appears that they've simply pressed record and begun dancing. At times, one or the other moves too far to the right and is cut out of the camera frame. One representative comment notes, 'U guys were great! But it was really annoying to hear the taps from your shoes.' What this viewer finds annoying, I find compelling. Tayla and Pierrea's high heels click and slide across the floor, sometimes drowning out the lyrics and often at odds with the song's insistent bass line. Though probably unintentional, the sound of the shoes asserts the authenticity of the performance. This version bears evidence of the labour involved in dance, highlighting how amateur dancers struggle to accurately and authentically represent professional choreography.

Furthermore, amateur recreations expand the dance archive in terms of 17 dance space as well as dance bodies. Videos are filmed in parking lots, living rooms, empty dance studios, and college dorms. As Samantha Carroll points out,

> [p]erhaps the most interesting use of online hosting, dissemination and accessing of audio visual material by … dancers is the increase in footage of ordinary people in their everyday dance environments… [I]ncreased access to digital audio visual media has given individual dancers more opportunities to participate in mediated dance discourse and for creative self-expression. As a result, we see more contributions to this discourse, from a wider variety of people. (2008: 194)

This variety of people suggests that dance can be legitimated outside of 18 dance class and the concert stage.

Dancers also take up public space in order to disrupt the meanings of 19 those spaces, often by 'flashdancing'. Flashdance, like its antecedent the flash mob[9], is a brief performance presented by groups who anonymously gather and then rapidly disperse. There are several 'Single Ladies' flashdances available for viewing on YouTube, both amateur (see for example 'Peter and Matt's Wedding: Flash Mob "Single Ladies"') and professional. In April 2009, Trident Unwrapped promoted its gum and a contest to win free Beyoncé tickets with 100 'single ladies' throwing off their trench coats and dancing in London's Piccadilly Circus; YouTube videos of the event have been viewed over ten million times.

As the Trident 'Single Ladies' video demonstrates, corporate flashdances 20 are readily available (and often very popular) on YouTube. Of course, because they are designed as advertising opportunities, it's unsurprising that their sponsors want them to reach the widest possible audience. They are also pleasurable to watch, combining a spontaneous, DIY aesthetic with expertly shot footage, tightly executed choreography and professionally mixed sound. The first flashdance may be T-Mobile's January 2009 'Life's for Sharing' commercial. Over 400 professional dancers dressed in street clothes and transit uniforms danced to a medley of pop, hip hop and classical music at the Liverpool Street Tube Station. T-Mobile aired the commercial on the BBC, and passersby filmed the dance on mobile phones, uploaded it to YouTube, and spread it virally as well (lifesforsharing). Several similar flash dances followed. In April 2009, commuters, school children and transit workers danced to 'Do-Re-Mi' in an Antwerp train station to advertise the reality TV show *A Problem Like Maria,* a nationwide talent search to find an actress to play Maria in a new version of *The Sound of Music* (music04777). Alex Leo, writing for *The Huffington Post,* remarks, 'it's a publicity stunt for a reality show, but that doesn't seem to bother anyone, they just like it for what it is: a really cool, well shot video, that lets average people express their joy and talent and make those around them happy for a brief period.' Though carefully rehearsed, flashdances seem spontaneous, and that spontaneity invites the audience to join in; many do, or at least clap and bop along.

Although these flashdances are marketing techniques, they illuminate how 21 performance creates counterpublics. Recordings of the dances are uploaded to

---

[9] In May 2003, Bill Wasik invented the flash mob to test the relationship between hipster culture and mega-corporations, theorizing that those who considered themselves 'hip', 'urban' and 'edgy' would quickly spread flash mobs via the internet and other mobile communication devices. Marketing companies, he theorized, would harness flash mobs to create 'buzz' for their products (2006: 57).

YouTube, and literally millions of people view them; in fact, they are designed primarily as viral marketing, intended for digital consumption by millions of viewers rather than the few hundred who might witness the live performance. Both passersby and YouTube audiences are usually enchanted, and the meanings they take from the performances are not necessarily those that corporate producers intended. Furthermore, I insist that their commercial message is overshadowed by the pleasure of the dancing bodies.[10] The 'Do-Re- Mi' video reached hundreds of thousands of people who may never know it's supporting a Belgian television programme that they can't watch even if they want to. Also, corporate flashdancing bodies are notably diverse. 'Life's for Sharing' and 'Do-Re-Mi' include elementary-age children and senior citizens, bespoke-suited businesswomen and homeless men, and black, Asian and white dancers. The London women who perform 'Single Ladies' are relatively homogenous, but even this homogeneity opens the song and dance to new readings: if white British women can get down to hip-hop music, then what barriers between nations, races or classes remain? Of course, as part of a marketing campaign that targets a broad audience (as well as plays on viewer fantasies of technologically mediated, post-racial utopias), this diversity can certainly be viewed cynically. I argue, however, that these bodies join a growing image archive that challenges traditional notions of who can dance, where and for whom.

Like Beyoncé videos, corporate flashdances inspire amateur recreations. 22 At Texas A&M University, where I teach, students formed FlashDance, an organization 'who dance[s] publicly and sporadically across the Texas A&M campus with the goal of bringing people joy through the performing arts and encouraging them to join in' (Texas A&M FlashDance). TAMU flashdancers promote the idea that everyone can and should dance, an idea that's not particularly radical on most campuses but challenges understandings of TAMU as a football and engineering school that's too conservative to support the arts. These young women and men performed 'Single Ladies' in November 2009, not only because they liked it but also to comment on TAMU's reputation as the campus where everyone (male and female) expects to be engaged

---

[10] In *Performing Consumers: Global capital and its theatrical seductions*, Maurya Wickstrom explains how pleasure can be co-opted by commercial forces: we 'desir[e] the pleasure of materializing the brand's transformative promise as if it were our own' (2006: 3). Wickstrom argues that commercial experiences are theatricalized in order to intensify the embodied event and somatic pleasure of buying and believing the brand. She further asserts that part of that pleasure is acknowledging the capitalist frameworks of our pleasure—recognizing that we are interpolated into the marketplace—alongside the kinesthetic and aesthetic experience of embodying a fictional self that is better than our own. Though Wickstrom develops a provocative thesis, I want to suggest that the pleasure we may take in our own and others' dancing bodies does escape (perhaps only briefly) the fetters of consumer culture.

before they graduate. By dancing, these students disrupted expectations of what it means to be an Aggie, demonstrating with their bodies that there are multiple ways to perform Aggie identity and community in addition to traditional events like Muster, Yell Practice, Bonfire and Hullabaloo. In important ways, this and other similar 'Single Ladies' flashdances rearticulate the meanings of Beyoncé's song, offering visible evidence of counterpublics.

Performance studies scholars can help facilitate YouTube as a counter-   23 public archive by critically engaging and contributing to it ourselves. First, we must acknowledge its limits and develop strategies for augmenting its usefulness. The YouTube archive is always partial. As the students and faculty involved with Yale University's *Project O* (a reimagining of the Orpheus myth) discovered, at some point 'our kinesthetic imagination fail[s]'. The project's choreographers based the production's dances on vernacular social dance from the 1950s. Teaching the dancers, they 'conveyed the outer shell of movement that in historical context carried an entirely different weight' (Cermatori et al. 2009: 9). YouTube is a terrific resource for learning the basic steps and gestures, but it is inadequate for providing context, nuance, meaning. Instead, the dances must be performed in new contexts, noting how bodies respond to and even change unfamiliar choreography. Moving beyond watching dance videos to critiquing them and creating our own, we might intervene in YouTube's archival practices in order to create a more democratic, reflexive and critical repository. The transformative value of the public sphere of images on discourses on race, class, gender and sexuality requires active engagement on the part of scholars who recognize YouTube's archival value but also its political promise.

As a preliminary strategy, we might upload our own and our students   24 (messy, partial, even failed) performance work to the archive. At the PSi panel where I delivered this paper, I asked participants to join the 'Single Ladies' viral phenomenon. We didn't have much time: our version isn't especially polished, and we completed only one verse and chorus. Our dance may not have radically changed us, or the conference, or the world. But dancing creates community and allows participants to take pleasure in their bodies. That happened. Some audience members were quite practiced at the dance and helped teach others. Some were reluctant to participate, and others insisted on the value of performing and recording the dance. We laughed at ourselves and one another, sharing a moment at the end of a long day of travel, panels and networking. More important, our dance intervenes in the academic tradition that often privileges critique and analysis over practice. Though our shaking hips and flashing ring fingers are only a single (and as yet unpopular) addition to the 'Single Ladies' archive, we contributed to its counterpublic of dancing bodies: neither the setting nor the dancers are typical YouTube recreations of Beyoncé's choreography. As young, middle-aged, and aging dancers with a variety of body types and dance skill who represent an international community of scholars, we are unique among the 'Single Ladies'. Our recreation inserts bodies that challenge not only traditional but also YouTube dance aesthetics. I hope that this experiment demonstrates why and how performance scholars who use the YouTube archive must also become performers who produce it.

REFERENCES

111288CBaby (2008) 'Beyonce Single Ladies', 19 October, www.youtube.com/watch?v=7rknRJVdpOo, accessed 12 October 2009.

alexdwong's Channel, www.youtube.com/user/ alexdwong?blend=2&ob=1, accessed 5 October 2010.

Anand (2010) 'Popularity of YouTube Videos by Geography', 26 February, http://gorumors.com/crunchies/popularity-of-youtube-videos-by-geography, accessed 2 October 2010.

Beyoncé, interview with Rocsi and Terrence J (2008) *106 and Park,* Black Entertainment Television (BET), New York, accessed 6 June 2010.

Carroll, Samantha (2008) 'The Practical Politics of Step-Stealing and Textual Poaching: YouTube, audio-visual media and contemporary swing dancers online', *Convergence* 14(2): 183–204.

Cermatori, Joseph, Coates, Emily, Krier, Kathryn, MacArthur, Bronwen, Randle, Angelica and Roach, Joseph (2009) 'Teaching African-American dance/ history to a 'post-racial' class: Yale's *Project O' Theatre Topics* 19(1): 1–14.

conanbelletty (2009) 'Beyoncé 100 Single Ladies Flash-Dance Piccadilly Circus, London for Trident Unwrapped', 21 April, www.youtube.com/ watch?v=de8oaegzb_0, accessed 11 October 2009.

d$_3$mentedangel (2007) 'Walk it Out, Fosse!!', 21 August, www.youtube.com/watch?v=KU3N5c2Kxnw, accessed 12 October 2009 (no longer available).

dancebaby530 (2008) 'The REAL Single Ladies Remake', 13 November, www.youtube.com/watch?v=Dk0_fhPZLf8, accessed 9 October 2009.

Desireetwyman (2008) 'Single ladies (Ebony, Desiree and LaTerra) dance', 21 November, www.youtube.com/ watch?v=nXgad35WzHc, accessed 12 October 2009.

Gehl, Robert (2009) 'YouTube as Archive: Who will curate this digital Wunderkammer?' *International Journal of Cultural Studies* 12(1): 43–60.

Gottschild, Brenda Dixon (2005). *The Black Dancing Body: A geography from coon to cool,* London: Palgrave Macmillan.

Gracy, Karen (2007) 'Moving Image Preservation and Cultural Capital', *Library Trends* 56(1): 183–97.

Habermas, Jürgen (1989) *The Structural Transformation of the Public Sphere: An inquiry into the category of bourgeois society,* trans. Thomas Burger with the assistance of Frederick Lawrence, Cambridge, Massachusetts: MIT Press.

Joe.My.God (2008) http://joemygod.blogspot.com/2008/12/purple-haze-takes-on-single-ladies.htm, accessed l 7 June 2010.

juice1881 (2009) 'Single Ladies Beyoncé, Alex Wong and Jeremy Cox', www.youtube.com/watch?v=cndFGDygwSw, accessed 17 June 2010.

Kraut, Anthea (2010). '"Stealing Steps" and Signature Moves: Embodied theories of dance as intellectual property', *Theatre Journal* 62(2): 163–79.

Leo, Alex (2009) 'Sound of Music train station dance: Why is it so popular?', *The Huffington Post,* 17 April, www.huffingtonpost.com/2009/04/12/sound-of-music- train-stat_n_186016.html, accessed 17 June 2010.

lifesforsharing (2009) 'The T-Mobile Dance', 16 January, www.youtube.com/
watch?v=VQ3d3KigPQM, accessed 26 September 2010.

Lott, Eric (1995) *Love and Theft: Blackface minstrelsy and the American working class,* New York: Oxford University Press.

Malnig, Julie (ed.) (2008) *Ballroom, Boogie, Shimmy Sham, Shake: A social and popular dance reader,* Champaign: University of Illinois Press.

McPherson, Tara (2009) 'In Focus: Digital scholarship and pedagogy', *Cinema Journal* 48(2): 119–23.

music04777 (2009) 'Dance Train Station Belgium do-re-mi The Sound of Music - Julie Andrews', 13 April, www.youtube.com/watch?v=WkBepgH00GM, accessed 15 April 2009.

Peña Ovalle, Priscilla (2009) 'Aurally, Visually, Virally: Choreographing race from Fosse to Beyoncé', Flow TV, http://flowtv.org/?p=3308, accessed 6 June 2009.

'Peter and Matt's Wedding: Flash mob "Single Ladies"' (2009) www.youtube.com/watch?v=HejQ3XJkdc. 1 December, accessed 4 October 2010.

Salvato, Nick (2009) 'Out of hand: YouTube amateurs and professionals', *TDR* 53(3): 67–83.

SecretTrois (2008) 'Single Ladies (Big girl remix)', 26 October, www.youtube.com/watch?v=7uuxQFEOzcc, accessed 11 October 2009.

Texas A&M FlashDance (2009) www.facebook.com/#!/ group.php?gid=145191873716&ref=ts, accessed 2 June 2010.

Warner, Michael (2002) *Publics and Counterpublics,* New York: Zone Books.

Wasik, Bill (2006) 'My crowd: Or, phase 5: A report from the inventor of the flash mob', *Harper's Magazine* (March): 56–66.

Wickstrom, Maurya (2006) *Performing Consumers: Global capital and its theatrical seductions,* New York: Routledge.

'YouTube Fact Sheet', www.youtube.com/t/fact_sheet, accessed 2 October 10.

QUESTIONS

1. What is the thesis of this article?
2. How does the author account for the success of Beyoncé's "Single Ladies" video? Why has it so often been imitated, mocked, re-enacted, recreated?
3. What connections does the author draw between the Beyoncé video and race relations?
4. What connections does the author draw between the Beyoncé video and homophobia?
5. How have advertisers appropriated YouTube? Provide an example other than the ones referenced in the article.
6. Why do so many people post, on YouTube, videos of themselves performing?
7. Using this article as your model, analyse a YouTube video that you have seen recently.
8. The author focuses more on the dance that accompanies "Single Ladies" than on its lyrics. To what extent do the song's lyrics account for its popularity?

Index